Michele Schweisi...

Education for All: Is the world on track?

Education for All
IS THE WORLD ON TRACK?

UNESCO Publishing

The designations employed and the presentation of the material in this publication do not imply the expression of any opinion whatsoever on the part of UNESCO concerning the legal status of any country, territory, city or area, or of its authorities, or concerning the delimitation of its frontiers or boundaries.

Published in 2002 by the United Nations Educational,
Scientific and Cultural Organization
7, Place de Fontenoy, 75352 Paris 07 SP

Graphic design by Sylvaine Baeyens
Graphics by Visit-Graph
Printed by Graphoprint, Paris
ISBN 92-3-103880-X

Printed in France

Foreword

The aim of extending a basic level of education to all children, young people and adults around the world has captured the imagination of all nations. It was a major outcome of the World Conference on Education for All, held in Jomtien in 1990, and was reconfirmed in a series of summits throughout the following decade. The aim was re-specified as six major goals at the World Education Forum, held in Dakar in April 2000, two of which were adopted as Millennium Development Goals in the same year. Provision of basic education was thereby properly recognized as being a central part of the world's strategy to halve the incidence of global poverty within less than a generation.

At the Dakar Forum, a new resolution made plain that all parties should be accountable for their record in meeting the commitments they had made. National governments agreed to dedicate themselves to securing the goals, while international agencies pledged that no country thus committed would be prevented from achieving them by a lack of resources. One of the instruments for securing greater accountability for the implementation of these pledges was the establishment of the EFA Global Monitoring Report.

This Report has been produced by an independent international team based in UNESCO. Work began to be commissioned in July 2002, but the team was not fully in place until the beginning of September. Preparation of this report was thus extremely time-constrained. Longer preparation cycles of 12–18 months will become established in annual editions over the next few years. The Report charts progress against the six Dakar goals and targets, highlights effective policies and strategies, and alerts the global community to emerging challenges for action and cooperation. Drawing upon the latest available data, it sets out a challenging framework for reform.

The goals of EFA are of enormous significance. Without constant and steady progress towards them, development cannot be judged to be happening. The Report shows that the challenge faced by the nations of the world remains substantial. Although planning is under way, it needs to be strengthened. National commitment by both governments and civil society is the key to securing the goals, but costs and resources are crucial considerations, too. Although most countries will be able to meet these costs and find the necessary resources, the report shows that a significant minority will not if existing trends persist. In response, as yet, the international community has not adequately demonstrated its own commitment. In spite of grand promises, the aid record (both overall and for education) over the 1990s was both disappointing and worrying. Since Dakar, the question of education, especially basic education, has risen higher on the international agenda, but much remains to be done to ensure that aid flows are adequate, timely and well-targeted. Future practice has to be different from the past if our joint responsibilities are to be met and if the EFA goals are to be achieved. This Report is the first in a new tradition of reporting that will, I am confident, help us to secure those ends.

Koïchiro Matsuura
Director-General of UNESCO

Contents

List of figures, tables and text boxes

Figures

Tables

Text boxes

Acknowledgements

This Report was prepared in a very short period of time, and without the help and cooperation of a very large number of individuals and institutions it could not have been completed.

Special thanks are due to John Daniel, UNESCO's Assistant Director-General for Education, and to Abhimanyu Singh, Lead Manager in UNESCO'S Dakar Follow-up Unit and his colleagues.

The shape of the 2002 Report benefited from the advice of the international Editorial Board and its chairperson, Anil Bordia.

Denise Lievesley, Director of the UNESCO Institute for Statistics (UIS), provided excellent support through the EFA Observatory group in UIS. They worked very closely with the Report Team in the development of the statistical tables and provided some material for Chapter 2.

Particular thanks are due to all those who prepared background papers for the Report on extremely short notice. These were Sabina Alkire, Samer Al-Samarrai, Dipa Bagai, Aaron Benavot, Paul Bennell, Lene Buchert, Edward Fiske, R. Govinda, Ingemar Gustafsson, Esme Kadzamira, Michael Kelly, Kin Bing Wu, Helen Ladd, Keith Lewin, Angela Little, Alain Mingat, Karen Mundy, Lynn Murphy, Margaret Sinclair, Marc Sommers, Juan Carlos Tedesco and Katarina Tomasevski.

The Report has benefited considerably from the advice and support of individuals, Divisions and Units within UNESCO's Education Sector. The International Institute of Educational Planning (IIEP) and the International Bureau of Education (IBE) both responded to requests for assistance quickly and helpfully. UNESCO's Regional Offices provided information on EFA plans, as did some EFA National Coordinators.

A number of individuals also contributed advice and comments, including Aya Aoki, John Bennett, Alan Blancheton, Peter Buckland, Francoise Caillods, Vittoria Cavicchioni, Gwan Chol Chang, Ashgar Mir Husain, Cynthia Guttman, Anne Jellema, Gareth Jones, Ruth Kagia, Maria Lourdes-Khan, Lesley Limage, Greg Loos, Colette Faure-Ligou, Mamadou Ndoye, Mary Jo Pigozzi, Roberty Prouty, Mohamed Radi, Michel Ribaud, Clinton Robinson, Kenneth Ross, Paulo Santiago, Susanne Schnuttgen, Christopher Talbot, Patrick Watt and Carolyn Winter.

The production of the Report depended heavily on the editorial expertise of Judith Crews and Wenda McNevin, and on the assistance of Sonia Fernandez-Lauro in UNESCO's Education Documentation Centre.

The EFA Global Monitoring Report Team

Director
Christopher Colclough

Steve Packer (Deputy Director), Simon Ellis (Head, EFA Observatory, UIS), Jan Van Ravens, Ulrika Peppler Barry, Nicole Bella, Valerie Djioze, Hilaire Mputu, Carlos Aggio, Mariana Cifuentes-Montoya, Pascale Pinceau, Delphine Nsengimana

Summary

This Report is about opportunities to learn. Its primary purpose is to assess the extent to which the benefits associated with education are being extended to all children, youths and adults around the world and whether the commitments made two years ago in April 2000 at the World Education Forum in Dakar are being met. It offers an interim answer to the question as to whether the world is on track to achieve Education for All (EFA) in 2015.

The World Education Forum (2000) agreed on six EFA goals, which were considered to be essential, attainable and affordable given strong international commitment and resolve. The Dakar Framework for Action declared that by 2015, *all* children of primary-school age would participate in free schooling of acceptable quality and that gender disparities in schooling would be eliminated. Levels of adult illiteracy would be halved, early childhood care and education and learning opportunities for youth and adults would be greatly increased, and all aspects of education quality would be improved. In the same year, the Millennium Development Goals were agreed, two of which – universal primary education (UPE) and the elimination of gender disparities in primary and secondary education – were defined as critical to the elimination of extreme poverty.

The Report is presented in six parts. Chapter 1 reaffirms why Education for All is of such overriding importance. Chapter 2 updates our understanding of progress towards, and prospects for, achieving the six EFA goals. Chapter 3 examines the international response to the call for EFA National Action Plans, the engagement of civil society in planning, and whether the distinctive challenges of HIV/AIDS, and conflict and emergency are being confronted. Chapter 4 assesses the costs of achieving the EFA goals and the availability of the resources to secure them. Chapter 5 explores whether the international commitments made in Dakar, and subsequently, are being met and, if so, by what means. Finally, Chapter 6 pulls some of these threads together as a basis for looking forward and identifying opportunities for sustaining the momentum generated by the World Education Forum.

The Report draws on data from the statistical annex and from a wide range of other sources.[1] These data are essential to assessing whether progress is being made, in identifying serious gaps in our knowledge, and in calculating past trends and future prospects. However, the preparation of this Report has highlighted major gaps in our knowledge. For example, primary-school net enrolment data for 1999 are not available for well over seventy countries. Comparative analysis on education policies and plans is limited. Country-level information on the financing of education is weak. And the database on aid to education is still bedevilled by conceptual problems and reporting inadequacies. While it is still possible to arrive at informed judgements, better monitoring will require additional investment in the collection and analysis of data, and in policy-related research and evaluation.

The six Dakar goals

7. We hereby collectively commit ourselves to the attainment of the following goals:

- expanding and improving comprehensive early childhood care and education, especially for the most vulnerable and disadvantaged children;
- ensuring that by 2015 all children, particularly girls, children in difficult circumstances and those belonging to ethnic minorities, have access to and complete free and compulsory primary education of good quality;
- ensuring that the learning needs of all young people and adults are met through equitable access to appropriate learning and life skills programmes;
- achieving a 50% improvement in levels of adult literacy by 2015, especially for women, and equitable access to basic and continuing education for all adults;
- eliminating gender disparities in primary and secondary education by 2005, and achieving gender equality in education by 2015, with a focus on ensuring girls' full and equal access to and achievement in basic education of good quality;
- improving all aspects of the quality of education and ensuring excellence of all so that recognized and measurable learning outcomes are achieved by all, especially in literacy, numeracy and essential life skills.

Source: The Dakar Framework for Action, Education for All: Meeting our Collective Commitments, adopted by the World Education Forum (Dakar, Senegal, 26–28 April 2000), Paris, UNESCO, 2000, para 7.

Millennium Development Goals (MDGs) relating to education

Goal 2. Achieve universal primary education

Target 3. Ensure that, by 2015, children everywhere, boys and girls alike, will be able to complete a full course of primary schooling

Goal 3. Promote gender equality and empower women

Target 4. Eliminate gender disparity in primary and secondary education, preferably by 2005, and to all levels of education no later than 2015

Source: United Nations General Assembly, Resolution A/56/326, 6 September 2001.

1. The Annex provides the latest annual administrative data collected by the UNESCO Institute for Statistics, namely for the school year starting in 1999.

Chapter 1. 'Education for All' is development

For those who work for, and benefit from education, its intrinsic worth is clear to see. For those who are confronted with making difficult choices about priorities, reforms and the allocation of resources, in national and state governments, and in international funding agencies, making the case for education explicit remains important. Are the six EFA goals, individually and collectively, genuinely of over-riding importance? There are three important answers to this question.

Where the right to education is guaranteed, people's access to and enjoyment of other rights is enhanced.

Education as a human right

The right to education is articulated clearly in Article 26 of the Universal Declaration of Human Rights (1948). This recognizes the intrinsic human value of education, underpinned by strong moral and legal foundations. Seen in this light, education is also an indispensable means of unlocking and protecting other human rights by providing the scaffolding that is required to secure good health, liberty, security, economic well-being, and participation in social and political activity. Where the right to education is guaranteed, people's access to and enjoyment of other rights is enhanced.

A rights based approach to education has gathered pace in recent years, providing the basis for comparative assessments of national progress against international commitments, including those made in Dakar. Providing the right to education is an obligation of governments and requires that they translate their international commitments into legislation against which their citizens have legal recourse. Without legislation it is difficult to monitor and enforce obligations, so mobilizing governments to develop and modernize national legislation is a critical element of implementing the Dakar Framework for Action.

Education and human capabilities

A significant shift in thinking about human development has taken place in the past 20 years, with Amartya Sen as one its leading advocates. To redress the narrow focus on growth in per capita incomes as the central indicator of successful development policies, a new framework has emerged which emphasizes the extent to which people's capabilities have been enhanced and their choices widened in order to enjoy the freedoms that make life meaningful and worthwhile. These freedoms encompass the rights of access to resources that allow people to avoid illness, have self-respect, be well nourished, sustain livelihoods and enjoy peaceful relationships.

In this framework, education is important for at least three reasons. First, the skills provided by basic education, such as being able to read and write, are valuable in their own right, as a fundamental outcome of development. Second, education can help to displace other more negative features of life. For example, free and compulsory primary education will reduce child labour. Third, education has a powerful role in empowering those who suffer from multiple disadvantages. Thus women who have benefited from education may simply survive better and longer than they would otherwise. Defined in this way, education that is universal, attained by all, regardless of class or caste or gender, has a powerful impact in addressing social and economic barriers within a society and is central to realizing human freedoms.

Education and other development goals

If all people have a right to education, and if the impact upon people's capabilities is intrinsically part of our understanding of development, it follows that the provision of a basic level of education for all people must be made universal. The case is clear and uncompromising. But this conclusion does not in itself answer the question how much education should be universally available. Here, there are neither easy nor universal answers. Country specific contexts are important. Nevertheless, understanding the relationship between education and other development goals is helpful, especially in relation to whether education is defined as productive.

Despite a range of methodological problems, there is a compelling body of international evidence that demonstrates that schooling improves productivity in rural and urban self-employment. Many of these benefits stem from literacy, which requires a minimum of five to six years of full time primary education of good quality. Good primary education also has a positive impact on lower fertility rates, better diets and the earlier and more effective diagnosis of illness. The link between literacy and life expectancy is strong. Parents – particularly women – with greater amounts of schooling have healthier, longer-living children. This micro-level evidence reveals the interconnections between the constituent parts of human development and makes a compelling contribution to the case for investing in education. In addition, a new generation of economic growth models gives human resources a central position in increasing development returns.

A compelling triumvirate of arguments

Rights, freedoms and development benefits constitute a powerful triumvirate of arguments for Education for All. Together, they demonstrate that there is a fundamental identity between EFA and development and that each of the EFA goals brings separate opportunities for securing other gains. The challenge for individual countries is to recognize the validity of these arguments, define their own distinctive policy priorities and map their own routes to achieving all of the EFA and MDG education-related goals.

Chapter 2. Progress towards the goals

Is the world on track?

Progress towards EFA can be monitored in two main ways. The priority is to record and interpret progress at national level against each of the EFA goals and, if possible, for the set of six goals as a whole. However, it is also important to monitor the means to these ends, including legislation, policies, plans, resources, programmes and levels of international assistance, in line with the commitments of Dakar and other major agreements.

This Report re-confirms the diagnosis of the World Education Forum that almost one-third of the world's population live in countries where achieving the EFA goals remains a dream rather than a realistic proposition, unless a strong and concerted effort is made. High-risk countries are found primarily in South and West Asia, sub-Saharan Africa and the Arab States and North Africa. The populous countries of East Asia and the Pacific are making some progress but will not achieve EFA without an intensified effort, while a number of countries in Central and Eastern Europe, with a rich education tradition, are in jeopardy of falling back from goals that had been attained.

If a combination of the three quantitative indices of primary net enrolment,[2] levels of adult literacy, and gender parity in primary school gross enrolment[3] is analysed on the basis of distance from each of the goals using the latest available data, in concert with an assessment of trends and levels of progress over the 1990s, the following conclusions can be drawn for 154 countries for which data are available:

- 83 countries have already achieved the three goals or have a good chance of doing so by 2015.
- 43 countries have made progress in the 1990s but at least one goal is likely to be missed by 2015.
- 28 countries are in serious risk of not achieving any of the three goals.

Almost one-third of the world's population live in countries where achieving the EFA goals will remain a dream unless a strong and concerted effort is made.

2. The net enrolment ratio (NER) is the number of pupils in the official school-age group expressed as a percentage of the total population of that age group.

3. The gross enrolment ratio (GER) expresses the total enrolment of pupils in a grade or cycle or level of education, regardless of age, expressed as a percentage of the corresponding eligible age group population in a given school year.

The first of these categories represents 32.4% of the world's population, including all of the countries in North America, Western Europe and Central Asia, 87% of countries in Central and Eastern Europe, 81% in East Asia and the Pacific and 69% in Latin America and the Caribbean. Four E-9[4] countries are in the second group – Bangladesh, China, Egypt, and Indonesia – which in total represents 35.8% of the world's population. The third, high-risk group consists primarily of countries in sub-Saharan Africa but also includes India and Pakistan. It covers just over 25% of the world's population. This is where the overall challenge of EFA is greatest.

A high-risk group consists primarily of countries in sub-Saharan Africa but also includes India and Pakistan. It covers just over 25% of the world's population. This is where the overall challenge of EFA is greatest.

Universal primary education (UPE)

The UPE goal can be interpreted and monitored in more than one way. The most demanding interpretation would be that by 2015, all children in the relevant age-cohort should be enrolled in, and complete, the final year of primary school. This would require universal Grade 1 enrolment in 2009, for a six-year cycle, with neither drop out nor repetition in subsequent years. The least challenging interpretation would be that from 2015, all children should be able to join, and subsequently complete, primary schooling. The requirement that primary education should be free, compulsory and of good quality also deserves monitoring. The indicators selected for monitoring the Millennium Development Goal for UPE are the achievement of NER *and* Grade 4 completion rates of 99%, which is close to the first interpretation given above.

Based on 1999 data, the latest year for which statistics are available, an estimated 115.4 million school-age children were out of school, of which 56% were girls. Thus, there is little or no change to the figure of 113 million, cited in Dakar, for 1998. Some 94% of these children were living in developing countries. Least developed countries accounted for one-third of the total, while 49% were in the E-9 countries. Just over one-third of the children were in sub-Saharan Africa, a further third in South and West Asia, and 13% in East Asia and the Pacific.

In the 1990s, rapid enrolment growth resumed in South and West Asia, the Arab States and North Africa, and Latin America and the Caribbean, remained slow in sub-Saharan Africa and Central Asia, while levels fell in some Central and East European countries. By the end of the decade, countries with GERs below 70% were concentrated in sub-Saharan Africa. Angola, Burkina Faso, Burundi, Eritrea, Guinea, Niger, Sierra Leone, Sudan and the United Republic of Tanzania reported particulary low enrolments. But for 85 countries worldwide, GERs were in excess of 100%, indicating late enrolment and high rates of repetition.

Net enrolment ratios (NERs) exclude children older and younger than a country's official school-age group. In Central and Eastern Europe where economic decline and the erosion of social capital have hit some countries hard, the NER is only slightly higher than that of developing countries. But the most serious enrolment problems occur in some Arab States and in sub-Saharan Africa. Of the 25 countries that have recorded NERs below 70%, 18 are in sub-Saharan Africa.

One of the key criteria for UPE is the achievement of NERs close to 100. Only countries with high intake levels of children of official school age will achieve the goal in these terms. Systems that have high over-age intake tend to have high rates of drop out before Grade 5. Countries, such as Uganda and Equatorial Guinea, with survival rates[5] of 45% and 16% respectively, illustrate how education systems with large numbers of over-age entrants have difficulty in keeping children enrolled. This is particular true of girls. In reverse, countries, such as Djibouti, Burkina Faso and Niger have high survival rates but serve only a small proportion of the primary school age children.

What are the prospects for achieving UPE? Analysis of net enrolment data for 128 countries[6] shows that 50 have NERs of 95% and over and can be said to have achieved UPE. Of the balance of 78 countries, four scenarios can be developed. For those with NERs of 80% or more and able to sustain the progress they were making in the 1990s, there is a good chance of achieving UPE.

4. Nine of the world's high-population countries: Bangladesh, Brazil, China, Egypt, India, Indonesia, Mexico, Nigeria and Pakistan. Together these countries account for more than 50% of the world's population.

5. Survival rate is the percentage of a pupil cohort that enters together in the first grade of primary education and that reaches a given grade (e.g. Grade 5) or the final grade of an education cycle with or without repeating a grade.

6. This survey used annual administrative data collected by the UNESCO Institute for Statistics for the school year starting in 1999 and the data from the EFA 2000 Assessment.

However, 16 countries where there was progress in the 1990s but where NERs are below 80%, have a low chance of achieving the goal. For 20 countries that moved away from the goal in the 1990s despite having NERs of over 80% there will have to be renewed efforts. Twenty-one countries face the greatest challenge with NERs below 80% and moving in a direction that takes them further away from UPE.

Gender equality

Worldwide, girl's enrolment in primary school improved in the 1990s. Girls' GERs increased by 3 percentage points, from 93.1% in 1990 to 96.5% in 1999 while over the same period, GERs for boys fell from 105.5% to 104%. The Gender Parity Index (GPI)[7] improved in all regions and in nearly two-thirds of the 92 countries for which data are available. But overall the GPI remained below 0.9 and in favour of boys in South and West Asia, the Arab States and sub-Saharan Africa.

If a Gender Parity Index of between 0.97 and 1.03 is taken to represent the elimination of gender disparities, 86 countries out of 153 for which disaggregated gross primary enrolment data are available have achieved the goal. Of the remaining 67, only 18 have a good chance of attaining the goal by 2015 (but not 2005) based on their level of progress in the 1990s and their relative distance from the target GPI in 2000. Of the remaining 49, just fewer than 50% are in sub-Saharan Africa. There are also a number of countries in Latin America and the Caribbean where the GPI is in favour of girls.

Gender-disaggregated data on secondary education is less readily available. The participation rates for girls are increasing but it remains true that where there are major gender disparities in primary education, this is amplified at the secondary level; hence some of the lowest levels of secondary enrolment for girls are in Central and West Africa.

The goal for 2005 is particularly challenging. However, policies are available that can have significant impact on the enrolment and retention of girls in school over the short term. These are issues that will be a central theme for the 2003 Global Monitoring Report.

Adult literacy

The meaning of literacy has developed radically since the World Conference on Education for All in Jomtien in 1990. Conceived now in the plural as 'literacies', and embedded in a range of life and livelihood situations, literacy differs according to purpose, context, use, script and institutional framework. But its conceptual advancement has not been matched by the priority accorded to it in policy and resource allocation, in part because many governments perceive the expansion of primary education as the main driver for the eradication of illiteracy.

Nevertheless, progress towards higher proportions of literate men and women over the age of 15 is taking place, albeit slowly. From roughly 70% adult literacy in 1980, the figure increased to 80% in 2000. In absolute numbers, the gains are modest, from 870 million people defined as illiterate in 1980, to 862 million in 2000, reflecting high rates of population growth over the last 20 years. The gender gap is wide and narrowing only slowly. Two-thirds of the illiterate population are women.

Of the estimated 862 million illiterate people in 2000, over one-third live in India. China, Pakistan and Bangladesh combined, accounted for a further 27%, so that 61% of people who lack literacy live in four of the world's high-population countries. Based on current trends it is estimated that these four countries will have an almost identical share of the 800 million people that it is projected will remain illiterate in the year 2015, assuming that policies and contexts don't change.

If the analysis is restricted to youth literacy (15–24 years olds) and even assuming expansion in primary education, it is projected that there will be 107 million young people who will be illiterate in 2015 (of which 67 million will be female) compared with 140 million in 2000 (86 million female).

Based on an analysis of 97 countries with adult literacy rates of below 95% in 2000, 18 have a high chance of meeting the Dakar goal based on the rate of progress achieved in the 1990s. Of the remaining 79, 40 have literacy rates below 70%

The meaning of literacy has developed radically since the World Conference on Education for All in Jomtien in 1990.

Of the estimated 862 million illiterate people in 2000, over one-third live in India.

7. The gender parity index (GPI) is the ratio between boys' and girls' enrolment ratios. Parity = 1.

The forthcoming United Nations Literacy Decade (2003–2012) is an important opportunity to focus on literacy and to improve assessment and monitoring.

and on recent rates of progress will not achieve the Dakar goal. Twenty-two of these countries are in sub-Saharan Africa, eight in the Arab States and North Africa and four in South and West Asia.

The forthcoming United Nations Literacy Decade (2003–2012) is an important opportunity to focus on literacy and to improve its assessment and monitoring. Work on a common international approach would represent an important advance in mapping progress against the objective agreed in Dakar.

Early childhood care and education

Early childhood care and education is a highly diverse area of learning which lacks good comparative data and widely accepted indicators.

The extent of early childhood care and education (ECCE) is still relatively uncharted territory. This is a highly diverse area of learning which lacks good comparative data and widely accepted indicators. It includes learning opportunities that range from formal pre-schools in the national education system, via kindergartens and other centres, where care, play and education go hand in hand, to more informal, often home based activities. Most national ECCE policies focus on expanding and improving access to pre-primary care and education for children aged three and over, based on the knowledge that the learning outcomes of primary education are improved when learning during the early years of life precedes regular schooling.

While ECCE continues to be strongly identified with those with full time employment in urban areas, increasingly it is being seen as a process of social inclusion for disadvantaged children and their mothers. Where resources are scarce the more likely it is that provision is home or community based.

From a limited database, which is primarily descriptive of government-administered programmes, it is clear that some countries do accord ECCE high priority in their education strategies. An analysis of enrolment in undifferentiated ECCE programmes in 124 countries in 1999/2000 shows 25 states with GERs of over 50%, 36 countries under 20%, and a further 20 below 5%, three quarters of which were in sub-Saharan Africa.

While there is some evidence to point to an increase in ECCE in both developed and developing countries, a major and worrying trend during the 1990s was the decline in enrolments in Eastern Europe and Central Asia. Kazakhstan had a GER of 72.3% in 1990 but 11.4% in 1999; Bulgaria fell to 67.2% from 91.6% and Georgia from 59% to 37%.

Learning needs of all young people and adults

The Dakar goal covers a kaleidoscopic area of learning, with close links to the goal on literacy and continuing education for adults. A comprehensive picture of what is happening worldwide is not yet possible, in part because there are unresolved conceptual issues. While the nature of lifelong learning has been elucidated for many years, the meaning of life skills remains the subject of much debate. In addition, typologies of programmes, levels of participation and assessments of learning outcomes are limited and, understandably, are usually specific to individual countries.

However, there is a growing body of knowledge on learning for sustainable livelihoods, and on the importance of generic skills including communication and problem-solving. There is also a much clearer recognition that it is essential that adult learning and life-skills programmes draw their *raison d'être* from a well defined demand that reflects people's wishes to lead more fulfilling and productive lives.

Monitoring this area of the Dakar Framework requires work to analyse the results of topic, target group and country-specific studies of the sort to which this Report makes very brief reference.

Education quality

This composite goal is designed to ensure that the quality of education receives the attention that many feel that it failed to receive during the 1990s. Encompassing all of the Dakar goals, it is intended to give new impetus and weight to the promotion of quality in education. However, at present the ability to monitor the quality of education is limited and there is a heavy reliance on proxies as distinct from a true assessment of learning outcomes. In this context, this Report restricts itself to a very preliminary look at the quality of primary schooling.

Levels of investment in primary education give a partial insight into the attention which quality is receiving. A comparison of levels of current expenditure and primary enrolments over the period 1975–1999 suggest that additional investment in sub-Saharan Africa and South and West Asia has been devoted primarily to expanding enrolments whereas in Latin America and the Caribbean, East Asia and the Pacific, and the Arab States and North Africa, additional resources have been spent on higher levels of spending per student. In this second group, pupil teacher ratios have dropped and stabilized at around 25. In South and West Asia there has been a downward trend from approximately 45, while in sub-Saharan Africa a downward trend has been reversed, rising towards 40 students per teacher. These figures hide enormous variations across and within countries.

Well-trained teachers are critical for good quality primary education and more are needed. Estimates of the number of additional teachers that will be needed worldwide to achieve UPE by 2015 range from 15 to 35 million. A minimum of 3 million is needed in sub-Saharan Africa. But the number of teachers that it is possible to employ depends in part on cost, which is mediated by salary levels. If salaries are too high this will constrain capacity and if they are too low then access, equity and quality all suffer.

High levels of grade repetition and drop out point to low levels of system efficiency and quality of learning. In more than 50% of countries in sub-Saharan Africa, more than one student in ten repeats at least one grade in primary school. And many studies show that repeaters do not learn from duplication and either keep on repeating or drop out.

These and other input and process indicators are important, but of growing significance is comparative evidence of learning outcomes, expressed in terms of standards, attainment and what students really learn. It is surveys[8] of the last of these that offer the most promising source of policy-relevant information, particularly when they are fine-tuned to the particular policy challenges of the countries involved. This type of evidence will be critical to the future monitoring of quality, not only in formal systems but also across the full spectrum of EFA.

Chapter 3.
Planning for EFA

EFA national action plans

If the expectation from the World Education Forum was that there would be a set of finely honed, comprehensive national EFA action plans by the end of 2002, that would provide the basis for an early dialogue with international agencies for enhanced levels of funding, then that target has not been met. Based on evidence that should be treated with the utmost caution, 22 countries, 50% in sub-Saharan Africa, are reported to be completing national EFA action plans by the end of this year, although these are not necessarily plans that have been adopted by governments as the basis for budgetary allocations to the education sector, nor are they necessarily comprehensive in nature.

If a broader interpretation of planning for EFA is used, whereby countries are revisiting their goals and targets for EFA, building on existing plans and strategies, and promoting EFA in other planning processes, including Poverty Reductive Strategy Papers (PRSPs), then there is a stronger story to be told in a much larger group of countries.

In some instances, separate EFA planning that draws its legitimacy from the World Education Forum appears to run the risk of duplicating or running parallel with existing education planning processes. Conversely, in some cases, Dakar has given impetus to EFA being given greater priority in national development debate and policy development.

An analysis of sixteen full PRSPs indicates that UPE is clearly delineated in all but one case but that only seven countries retained the EFA/MDG

Separate EFA planning that draws its legitimacy from the World Education Forum appears to run the risk of duplicating or running parallel with existing education planning processes.

8. For example; TIMSS: Third International Mathematics and Science Study; PIRLS: Progress in Reading Literacy Study; SACMEQ: Southern Africa Consortium for Monitoring Educational Quality; PASEC: Programme d'Analyse des Systemes Educatifs des pays de la CONFEMEN; MLA: Monitoring Learning Achievement; PISA: Programme for International Student Achievement.

goal for eliminating gender disparities in primary and secondary education. Learning opportunities for youth and adults was ranked second in importance. A separate analysis of recent education EFA and sector plans for thirty-one countries comes to a similar pattern of conclusions.

Whether in EFA plans, sector plans or PRSPs, there is often a weak link between the diagnosis of education and poverty on the one hand and the education outcomes and actions that are proposed on the other. This is particularly noticeable in relation to gender. It is also true that detailed costing for education is relatively rare in PRSPs and in EFA and/or sector plans.

At least 73 countries are undergoing an internal crisis or are engaged in post-crisis reconstruction.

The World Education Forum was clear that governments should engage with a much wider constellation of people in shaping policy and planning for EFA. Work is under way by inter national NGOs to assess whether this is happening. It is certainly not easy to make judgements from government documentation alone. While there is some evidence to suggest that there has been an increase in formal set-piece consultation, including through the establishment of EFA Forums, it is much less clear whether this technical engagement with civil society is extending to a much more open and ongoing political process. Where this is occuring there are valuable lessons to be learned.

Planning for HIV/AIDS

There is increasing evidence that planning to achieve the EFA goals must take account of HIV/AIDS and that the spread and intensification of the pandemic will not be prevented in the absence of progress towards EFA. This is an extremely important message in a world where 40 million adults and children live with AIDS, and where the number of orphans will continue to grow from the estimated level of 14 million children in 2001.

There is an important and expanding international resource to facilitate new ways of planning including the work of the UNAIDS Inter-Agency Task Team on Education, new planning tools and resource units in sub-Saharan Africa and innovative non-governmental alliances.

Planning to combat conflict, disaster and instability

At least 73 countries are undergoing an internal crisis or are engaged in post-crisis reconstruction. Planning workable strategies for EFA in these circumstances is demanding and highly context-specific. It includes not merely the sustenance of damaged school systems, but also the development of skills for conflict resolution and peace, and preparing for reconstruction and social and economic development.

The experiences of Afghanistan, Argentina, Kosovo, the Palestinian Autonomous Territories and East Timor indicate the need for well-designed emergency planning and programming to meet immediate and short-term needs, as well as strategies to prepare the ground for longer-term reconstruction and development. As yet, international agencies have not found it easy to bring together these two interrelated strands of education planning and practice, nor to embed this work in the wider processes of conflict resolution.

Nevertheless, there is an important and growing body of work designed to support planning for education in crisis situations. The Inter-Agency Network for Education in Emergencies (INEE) and the work of UNICEF and UNHCR on the ground are important in this regard.

Credible planning, credible plans

At the World Education Forum it was agreed that no country seriously committed to education for all will be thwarted by a lack of resources. The existence of a credible plan was posited as one indicator of commitment, and a prerequisite for external funding.

Six significant aspects of credibility are gaining ground, partly as a result of the World Education Forum. The first is that if planning is conceived as a purely technical and apolitical process it is unlikely to serve poor and disadvantaged people well. Second, planning should not be circumscribed by age, the differential income of learners or by a particular cycle of education. Third, gender responsive planning is essential. Fourth, planning must be inclusive and responsive to demand and to diversity. Fifth, priorities should be set and strategies fully-costed. Finally, dialogue with funding agencies increasingly focuses upon outcomes (rather than activities), requiring well-defined indicators that can be monitored and evaluated jointly.

Different agencies have different priorities and approaches to planning. UNESCO promotes the EFA national action plan. The World Bank prioritizes UPE and is focusing on strategies for its attainment. Some bilateral agencies prioritize the MDGs, using projects or budget support. This lack of international consensus is a handicap for the effective dialogue needed at country level.

Chapter 4. Resource requirements for reaching EFA

The costs of achieving the EFA goals and the availability of resources to secure them are likely to have a decisive influence upon whether the goals are reached. To understand the level and the nature of these costs requires careful country-by-country analysis, but the available resource requirement projections are inadequate as even a rough guide to assess overall public expenditure needs and the levels of external aid that will be required. For some of the EFA goals the data are very weak or simply not available.

For UPE and the elimination of gender disparities

However, studies to estimate the resource requirements of achieving the UPE goal in developing countries have been completed in the last two or three years by UNESCO, UNICEF and the World Bank. Each of them utilized country-level data but their assumptions and approaches to estimating required public expenditures on primary schooling differed. For 46 developing countries included in each study, the World Bank's projected additional required expenditures are some 70%–95% higher than the other two studies and amount to some US$8.4 billion.

The Bank study is the only one of the three to provide estimates of levels of external funding required to achieve UPE by 2015. It projects that the requirement will run at an average level of US$2.5 billion over the fifteen-year period (although it will peak at US$4.5 billion in 2015). Sub-Saharan Africa will require 85% of this assistance. Five countries[9] are estimated to have financing gaps of more than US$100 million per annum which represents 42% of the external funding requirement. Another seven[10] are projected to require, on average, US$50–$100 million per annum. These calculations are based in large measure on the ability of developing countries to generate resources through economic growth and fiscal reform. Some of these assumptions appear to be optimistic. If this proves to be the case the resource gap in 2015 could be at least double the Bank's estimate.

Each of the studies focuses upon the supply side. However, the removal of gender inequalities requires a strong demand-side response, especially for the poorest households in low-income countries. Effective incentive programmes for girls – or more generally, children from poorer households – might add at least 5% to the average unit costs of primary schooling which, if applied to the World Bank's analysis, would translate into US$1.3 billion extra public spending by 2015, adding about US$0.4–$0.6 billion to the average annual expenditures required.

For HIV/AIDS

The HIV/AIDS pandemic also has implications for the level of resources needed for education and for household costs. HIV/AIDS is likely to reduce the overall resource envelope for education and affect the allocation of available resources within the sector. It has cost implications for learners, for educators and for the development of new education programmes responsive to HIV/AIDS. Additional costs are likely to be incurred from the training and the salaries of additional teachers, the provision of death benefits, introducing HIV/AIDS throughout the school curriculum, managing systemic change, increasing counselling services and providing incentives to attend school.

Lack of international consensus is a handicap for the effective dialogue needed at country level.

The resource gap in 2015 could be at least double the World Bank's estimate.

9. Democratic Republic of the Congo, Ethiopia, Nigeria, Pakistan and Sudan.

10. Cameroon, Côte d'Ivoire, Mali, Niger, Senegal, Uganda, United Republic of Tanzania.

The cost implications of HIV/AIDS are so extensive and so pervasive that they may serve better than anything else to demonstrate the urgency of using the potential of education to extend greater protection to society.

The World Bank's UPE analysis does demonstrate that HIV/AIDS adds substantially to overall education costs. It suggests that in countries such as Rwanda, Malawi and Zambia the incremental costs due to HIV/AIDS will increase recurrent budgets by more than 45%. However, it is probable that the budgetary impact of AIDS is even more dramatic. This Report estimates that the total additional annual costs of the epidemic for the achievement of universal primary education as US$975 million per year, compared to US$560 million estimated in the Bank's simulations. The cost implications of HIV/AIDS are so extensive and so pervasive that they may serve better than anything else to demonstrate the urgency of protecting the education sector against the ravages of the epidemic and of using the potential of education to extend greater protection to society.

For conflict, disaster and instability

Recent history would suggest that at least four or five countries are likely to face major complex humanitarian emergencies during the course of the next decade, with many more experiencing disaster, conflict and other types of instability. In all of these countries the costs of achieving the EFA goals will be greater than what is currently predicted, as infrastructure, supplies and human resources would be diminished. Moreover, the means of meeting these costs will be reduced by declining income flows, by human death and displacement, and by the reallocation of potentially available resources from education to other, equally pressing, demands.

If the impact of such events were to increase the additional annual costs of reaching UPE by 25% in four or five countries, between US$0.4–US$0.5 billion would be added to the average annual costs of UPE across all countries. This would increase the projected total costs by 2% to 3%, but if the affected countries were among those that are expected to face financing gaps, it would represent an increase in the Bank's projected funding requirement by around one-fifth.

The impact of introducing a less demanding agenda for domestic revenue growth and fiscal reform in recipient countries increases the annual average external financing gap projected by the World Bank study from US$2.5 billion to US$4.2 billion. The inclusion of the further resource requirements for enhancing girls' enrolments, and the costs of HIV/AIDS and of support to education in countries experiencing conflict and emergency increase the magnitude of the external resources required by an additional US$1.4 billion, to a total of US$5.6 billion per year. This estimate is for only one – albeit the most costly – part of the EFA agenda and is based on an analysis of 47 countries. Although these included almost all of the most educationally disadvantaged states, some others are likely to require assistance in order to achieve the EFA goals.

Chapter 5. Meeting international commitments: the response to Dakar

The Dakar Framework for Action is a collective commitment. Partners to this commitment comprise governments and civil society institutions, working with regional and international agencies. The latter are expected to mobilize additional resources underpinned by a new global initiative and to work in a coordinated way with other partners in support of EFA plans. The challenge is judged to be greatest in sub-Saharan Africa, in South Asia and in the least developed countries. Countries in transition and those affected by conflict and crisis are deserving of strong support.

UNESCO has a strong mandate to continue to coordinate EFA partners and maintain their collective momentum, including through the work of an annual, small and flexible High-Level Group, and to facilitate the preparation of an annual report to monitor progress on the EFA goals.

Aid flows for EFA

The mobilization of aid flows to basic education should be set within the wider context of aid to developing countries. Between 1991 and 2000, the real value of all grants and concessional loans to developing countries had fallen by one-sixth, from US$60 billion per annum to US$50 billion per year. In 2000, 70% of total aid was from bilateral agencies, while the World Bank and the European Community provided 64% of all multilateral assistance. Over the whole decade, approximately two-thirds of total development assistance went to sub-Saharan Africa, South and Central Asia and the Far East.

The trend of bilateral flows to education was also downwards, from around US$5 billion at the start of the decade to US$4 billion at its end. The most dramatic decline occurred in 2000, when commitments fell to US$3.5 billion, representing a 30% decline in real terms from 1990 and accounting for 7% of total bilateral aid.

Reliable information on the composition of aid to education is difficult to obtain because of under-reporting and because a significant proportion of education aid straddles each of the subsectors and therefore cannot be allocated to just one of them. However, estimates based upon direct surveys of funding and technical assistance agencies suggest that by the mid-1990s, 20% of bilateral aid was committed for basic education, which is consistent with OECD DAC data.

Sub-Saharan Africa received 47% of all education aid commitments in 2000 compared with 37% of its share of total development assistance. In South and Far East Asia the figures were 23% and 34%. Some 50% of all new bilateral aid commitments to sub-Saharan Africa in 2000 were to basic education.

Multilateral aid to education also declined sharply over the period 1991 to 2001. World Bank IDA loans appear to have been roughly halved since the mid-1990s, falling to US$0.4 billion in 2001. However, the proportion allocated to basic education was higher than bilateral commitments and was maintained over the decade at about 40%. The European Union allocated some two-thirds of its education assistance to basic education.

The external funding to basic education of US$1.45 billion in 2000 is approximately equivalent to one quarter of the additional external assistance that is likely to be needed each year to 2015, to achieve the two Millennium Development/EFA goals. Aid to primary schooling would need to be quintupled, with much of it concentrated in sub-Saharan Africa.

Aid to primary schooling needs to be quintupled, with much of it concentrated in sub-Saharan Africa.

New levels of support for EFA?

A number of new international commitments and initiatives have been announced in support of education since the World Education Forum. Education was an important part of the debate at the World Summit on Children and at the World Summit on Sustainable Development. It has been a significant item on the agenda of G8 countries, most recently at Kananaskis (Canada) where a series of recommendations were adopted to assist developing countries to achieve UPE and equal access to education for girls, with a special emphasis on sub-Saharan Africa.

Education also received attention in the context of a new global approach to financing development put together at the United Nations International Conference on Financing for Development at Monterrey, 2002, through the work of the New Partnership for Africa's Development (NEPAD), and in the redesign of the European Union's strategies for education for all.

However, it is not easy to assess the extent to which the commitments that have been set out at recent international conferences and in individual and bilateral agency statements measure up to the financial challenge facing developing countries. If the Monterrey commitment of US$12 billion by 2006 were to be spent in the same pattern as the current average across all sectors, US$1 billion would be made available to the education sector, of which US$0.3 billion would be allocated to basic education. A further US$1.2 billion additional annual assistance was pledged during 2002 by the World Bank, Japan and non-EU bilaterals. Thus the G8 pledges would need to meet around US$4.4 billion of the US$5.6 billion anticipated in this Report as the external aid requirement to achieve the UPE and gender goals by 2015.

The G8 pledges need to meet around US$4.4 billion of the US$5.6 billion anticipated in this Report as the external aid requirement to achieve the UPE and gender goals by 2015.

The Fast-Track Initiative (FTI) was launched at the meeting of the Development Committee of the World Bank in April 2002.

This provides an indication of the extent to which the US$0.3 billion sum mentioned above would need to increase.

Heavily Indebted Poor Countries (HIPC) debt relief was an important source of additional finance for education in 26 countries in 2002. It seems that around US$400 million should be available for education over the period 2001–2005. But it is not clear what proportion of these funds represent genuine new resources to the nations concerned, if not to their education sectors.

Thus, very considerable increases in aid finance to basic education will be needed for the achievement of EFA. G8 pledges are currently insufficient to meet the likely shortfalls. Some redirection of aid from other education sectors will be needed (since basic education currently receives only 30% of the support to the sector as a whole). Nevertheless, overall, additional aid will be required.

The Fast-Track Initiative

The Fast-Track Initiative (FTI) was launched at the meeting of the Development Committee of the World Bank in April 2002. A first group of 18 low-income and low-enrolment countries, each having a Poverty Reduction Strategy Paper, were selected as recipients for early external assistance in achieving the education MDGs. This initiative is reflected in the recommendations of the G8 education task force and the new European Union draft policy statement on education. It has three main goals: deeper commitment to education policy reform and the efficient use of resources in developing countries; increased and better coordinated aid from industrialized countries, to be provided within the framework of PRSPs; and improved assessment based on better data.

FTI has been welcomed and supported by UNESCO and UNICEF, by bilateral agencies, by regional organizations such as the European Union and by the Global Campaign for Education. It has injected some necessary urgency into international dialogue and action. Nevertheless concern has been expressed at the speed and the extent of domestic policy reform required to improve efficiency and raise revenues; the danger of ignoring countries that do not fulfil the criteria; and its exclusive focus on the MDGs. Of the 28 countries identified in this Report as being at greatest risk of not achieving any of the three quantifiable EFA goals, only six are on the Fast-Track list. It has also been questioned as to whether the FTI lives up to the Dakar commitment to a Global Initiative. Without a medium- to longer-term perspective the Initiative may limit governments in their ability to plan with flexibility. It also runs the risk of being dominated by the concerns of a minority of core partners rather than necessarily reflecting the broader consistency, coordination and coherence sought by Dakar.

International coordination

The World Education Forum gave UNESCO a major technical and political challenge in sustaining international commitment and support for EFA. It provided the organization with an opportunity to demonstrate international leadership at a critical point in the global effort to realize the right to education and eliminate poverty.

UNESCO is pro-active in promoting the importance of good data for effective policy through the UNESCO Institute for Statistics, in arguing for EFA plans and in establishing and contributing to thematic Flagship programmes. The implications of EFA are being integrated throughout its regular programmes and in UNESCO's specialized institutes. Some 41% of UNESCO's regular programme budget for education is now assigned for basic education.

However, it is finding other aspects of its international role more challenging. This is partly because the objectives of exercising major influence on the world's political leaders and of mobilizing significant international resources are intrinsically difficult to achieve. Nevertheless, over the period 2000–2002, UNESCO's interpretation of its mandate has been conservative with an emphasis on facilitating dialogue and promoting partnerships rather than attempting to provide strong international leadership. Partnerships and alliances are important, but in the context of recent international events, UNESCO has had the opportunity to be more openly proactive in analysing and arguing the case for global action in support of EFA.

It is doubtful whether UNESCO can play this type of international role unless it is better resourced, in ways that harness strong technical capability and authoritative policy analysis as the basis for exerting influence. Well-coordinated, in-house capacity is needed to analyse international developments, changing aid modalities and requirements, and comparative experience of education reforms. Their implications need debate in forums having a real opportunity to make things change. The High-Level Group is potentially important in this respect.

Overall, while recent international commitments, initiatives and programmes demonstrate that a cooperative spirit exists across the international community, translating these into real resources directed towards priority ends, and turning the language of coordination into practice remains some distance away. It remains doubtful whether the international partners are yet working according to a commonly interpreted agenda as opposed to the separate mandates and strengths of their individual organizations.

Chapter 6. Prospects and opportunities

Progress, planning, costs and resources

Progress towards the goals is insufficient: the world is not on track to achieve EFA by 2015. Twenty-eight countries are at serious risk of not achieving any of the three quantifiable goals by 2015. The absence of Education for All both infringes the human rights of the excluded and prevents their capabilities being enhanced in ways they value. In cases where the absolute number of people excluded is rising, it is difficult to judge whether development is occurring.

Planning for EFA takes diverse forms and not necessarily in ways that respond directly to the call for national EFA plans made in Dakar. It is constrained by the lack of good data, particularly financial and demand-side information. Alternative reform strategies need exploration. The engagement of civil society remains characterized by token consultation in too many countries. The demands placed on governments by international agencies to prepare plans for different purposes can be dysfunctional. Potential overlaps and conflicts need to be resolved both generically and in national dialogue.

The *costs* of achieving EFA are large, but not beyond the means of most states, but the level of aid *resources* has been underestimated, partly because the costs associated with addressing demand-side issues – especially gender – and those of HIV/AIDS and of supporting education in circumstances of conflict and emergency have been omitted or underplayed. Country-level financial analysis using nationally verified data is essential for a sound assessment of funding requirements.

Progress towards the goals is insufficient: the world is not on track to achieve EFA by 2015.

International cooperation

There was a startling decline in the real values of both total and education aid in the years 1991–2000, which was particularly heavily felt in sub-Saharan Africa. However, in the new millennium there are indications that the climate for policy reform is better than during the 1990s, with governments being more willing to initiate policy dialogue. New aid instruments, especially where these are designed to support long-term education sector development, have the potential to have real impact on the achievement of the EFA goals. The most critical ingredient in national plans for EFA, whether in the Fast-Track Initiative, or in the context of broader agency support, is the extent to which governments genuinely embrace a process of national reform. There remains a concern that national governments may agree to reform proposals based on financial appraisals with neither the political nor the technical capacity to implement them. It will be critically important to take planning processes well beyond the level of a costing exercise, if the past gaps between plans and implementation are not to recur.

It would be entirely counterproductive if the EFA goals and the MDGs were perceived to be in any way in conflict with one an other.

Improving the availability and quality of data

The limitation of the coverage and reliability of data is a significant problem. Major efforts are needed to improve the coverage of internationally gathered information on public spending on education. There is also an acute need to improve the availability and quality of much national data, and their comparability with the pre-1997 UNESCO database needs to be secured. In addition, the information available to monitor aid flows to education remains open to considerable improvements in quality and coverage. If donor commitments and disbursements in support of EFA goals are to be monitored effectively, more efforts in reporting complete and consistent information are urgently required.

EFA and the Millennium Development Goals

It would be entirely counterproductive if the EFA goals and the MDGs were perceived to be in any way in conflict with one an other. The overall MDG framework provides an opportunity to argue the case for EFA in the collective endeavour to eliminate poverty. UPE and the elimination of gender disparities are major priorities, but a broader EFA case can be made for the contribution of basic education to sustainable livelihoods, the reduction of child mortality, improvements in maternal health, the fight against HIV/AIDS, and a sustainable environment. In this context the development of the Fast-Track Initiative affords a chance to promote the broader objectives of EFA rather than interpreting the specificity of the MDG targets as a constraint.

Future monitoring challenges

This Report has sought to initiate a sense of accountability towards commitments made at the World Education Forum. It will be important in future years to map – much more clearly than has been possible here – the extent to which a significant shift in policy and practice in support of EFA is taking place. In particular, more weight will need to be given to the achievements and the progress of individual countries, policies and strategies that are making a difference, and the evidence of national monitoring processes as well international analyses. Shifts in the policy and practice of development agencies will also deserve attention.

Since the World Education Forum, there has been some ambiguity as to whether EFA underpins a global movement or whether it is primarily a vehicle for focusing on developing countries, to help the excluded and most disadvantaged to benefit from a basic education. The balance has been more towards the latter than the former, and this emphasis is reflected in this Report. However, many of the challenges of EFA extend well beyond developing countries. The needs of those living in poverty in industrialized societies, issues of quality and relevance, of gender equality, of literacies responsive to the revolution in communications technology, and the challenge for education posed by drug dependency, are all issues deserving of international attention. If EFA is treated as an issue specific to a particular group of countries, it runs the risk of being separate or partial. Future Global Reports will begin to redress this imbalance.

EFA Global Monitoring Report 2002

©UNESCO/Jean Mohr

Chapter 1

'Education for All' is development

This Report assesses the extent to which the benefits associated with having had a basic level of education are being extended to all children, young people and adults around the world. This objective was strongly articulated at the first World Conference on Education for All in Jomtien in 1990. It was reaffirmed by the World Education Forum, meeting in Dakar in 2000. Delegates at the latter meeting declared that by 2015, all children of primary-school age would participate in free schooling of acceptable quality and that gender disparities in schooling would be eliminated. Adult illiteracy was to be halved, early-childhood education and programmes for out-of-school youth would be greatly increased, and all aspects of education quality would be improved. The first two of the above objectives were adopted – with wording that is different in detail, but not in intent – as two of the eight Millennium Development Goals (MDGs), to which all countries are committed. Thus, the notion of education for all was made concrete, and placed centrally within the international development agenda. This Report examines whether due progress towards achieving it is being made and, where that is not so, what changes in policy may be needed.

The right to education straddles the division between civil and political rights on the one hand, and economic, social and cultural rights on the other.

The extent of progress – for individual countries and regions – is summarized and discussed in Chapter 2. Although not all the Dakar goals can be monitored with the same ease, a mixed picture emerges, with many successes, but also with a substantial number of countries at risk of not achieving the goals. The third chapter, which assesses the state of planning for education for all (EFA), shows that, while there may be fewer completed National Action Plans than expected, the World Education Forum has created a widespread sense of urgency and commitment to EFA objectives. Chapter 4 examines the costs of achieving the goals. Their associated external funding requirements are expected to be higher than other recent estimates have suggested. Furthermore, as shown in the fifth chapter, aid to education has fallen sharply over the past decade, and recent commitments – though substantial – seem unlikely to be able to fill the funding gaps presently anticipated. The final chapter draws together the arguments of the Report, and concludes with some challenges for national and international policy.

In this opening chapter, however, it is worth examining why such attention to the goals is necessary. Is their achievement genuinely of over-riding importance not only for national policy, but also as a focus for international assistance? Three types of argument and evidence have led, in recent years, to this being widely agreed. The first derives from ideas of human rights. The second is a framework informed by notions of individual capacity and capability. The third perspective concerns the ways in which education helps people and societies to achieve other desired development goals. Each of these will be briefly discussed.

Education as a human right

The right to education is well established.[1] Article 26 of the Universal Declaration of Human Rights (1948) declared that 'elementary' education shall be free and compulsory, and that the higher levels will be equally available to all on the basis of merit. That these conditions were not fully achieved half a century later testified to the need for special efforts. Accordingly, a rights-based approach to improving access to education of acceptable quality gathered pace, providing a basis for a comparative assessment of national progress, including against international commitments such as those made in Dakar.[2]

The intrinsic human value of education – its ability to add meaning and value to everyone's lives without discrimination – is at the core of its status as a human right. But education is also an indispensable means to unlock and protect other human rights. It provides some of the scaffolding necessary for the achievement of the rights to good health, liberty, security, economic well-being and participation in social and political activity. Where the right to education is guaranteed, people's access to and enjoyment of other rights is enhanced and the imbalances in life chances are lessened.[3]

The right to education straddles the division between civil and political rights on the one hand, and economic, social and cultural rights on the other. It embodies them all. For example, it is of central importance for implementing the rights of girls and women, and the rights of the child. Patterns of exclusion from school are usually not gender-neutral. The commitment to increase girls' access to education has focused on the identification and elimination of obstacles. In turn, this has revealed that discrimination is often complex, with ethnicity, religion, poverty and gender being intertwined. Under these circumstances, merely providing opportunities to attend school will not suffice to eliminate discrimination or to universalize participation. This implies that all human rights *within* education also need *to* be addressed if the right to education is to be achieved.

1. See for example, UNESCO (2000*i*).

2. UNESCO (2002c).

3. Tomasevski (2002).

Children and young people cannot secure their right to education by themselves, although in many developing countries they constitute the majority of the population. They rely on their parents and their teachers. But few of their parents directly provide the tax revenues from which education is financed, and their votes may have only a weak impact upon budgetary allocations. Many teachers are preoccupied with having to battle for their own rights. Therefore, the recognition of children's right to education needs to transcend national borders, although its realization requires governments to commit themselves to universal obligations.

Since education is a universal human right, those denied access to it have their rights violated. Attribution of responsibility for human rights violations is a powerful lever for change. As with other human rights, providing for people's right to education is an obligation of governments, because markets, or charity, are insufficient to secure their implementation. Accordingly, this approach places major responsibility for ensuring service delivery and monitoring on governments,[4] underpinned by accountability to the national and international instruments of human rights. Such an approach in turn assumes that governments have translated international obligations into national legislation against which citizens have recourse. This is often not the case. Without legislation it is difficult to enforce obligations and lessen the incidence of their violation. In the industrialized world, especially in Western Europe, there is now a substantial body of case law on the right to education, but other parts of the world are less comprehensively served.

The human rights approach to achieving EFA has much in common – both conceptually and operationally – with human development and poverty reduction paradigms. It is holistic, it highlights performance targets and accountability, and facilitates international partnerships around agreed universal objectives. It provides a strong platform for advocacy, stressing that the denial of education is morally unacceptable.

However, translating into practice the principle of human rights as a basis for education policy is more problematic. Firstly, securing a shift in budgetary priorities and planning practices at the national level so as to give first call to EFA goals is not an easy process. Until recently this has been more common among international agencies[5] than at the level of individual governments. Secondly, progress within a human rights framework for education depends upon careful monitoring, upon the commitment of individual governments and the ability of international bodies such as the United Nations to seek compliance to human rights treaties, conventions and agreements. These conditions, however, are not widespread. Nevertheless, the human rights dimension is an essential component of the national and international processes needed to deliver EFA. It provides a strong moral and legal basis without which the Dakar agenda will not be achieved.

Providing for people's right to education is an obligation of governments, because markets, or charity, are insufficient to secure their implementation.

Education and human capabilities

The second half of the twentieth century was a fertile period for theories of economic development. Economists and other social theorists shifted away from their earlier preoccupations with the short run, to consider questions of long-run growth and development – rather in the way the classical economists had done a century or more earlier. The context, however, was different. The new interest in growth and development was focused not upon Europe, but upon post-colonial societies where poverty was ubiquitous. Naturally enough, in those circumstances, income growth was seen as an overwhelming priority, and successful development policies were those which generated a sustained growth in per capita incomes. Economic growth, measured in this way, became the criterion for achieving development and, in some writings, increasingly appeared to define it.

Throughout this period there were, of course, criticisms of the tendency to reduce complex social outcomes to a single, economistic indicator.[6]

4. It is also clear that both the Universal Declaration of Human Rights (United Nations, 1948 and 1950) and subsequent reaffirmations up to and including the Dakar Framework for Action (United Nations, 1979, Articles 13–14; UNESCO, 2000a) have committed governments to the free provision of primary schooling. Fees and charges are still levied in some countries – until recently with international agency support. As indicated later in this Report, this practice has contributed to maintaining low enrolments in some countries.

5. Perhaps most notably illustrated by UNICEF's strategy on the Convention on the Rights of the Child; see Pigozzi (1997).

6. This was particularly so among Latin American sociologists and economists in the 'structuralist' and 'dependency' traditions during the 1970s; see also Seers (1969).

However, the most trenchant critic of such reductionism, and the most creative advocate of alternative criteria for judging development success has been Amartya Sen. The fundamental insight of his 'capability approach' is that development occurs when people are more able to achieve what makes their lives valuable. Accordingly, the objective of development should be to promote and expand the freedom that people have to enjoy 'valuable beings and doings.'[7] The 'beings and doings' that people value will vary. They may include such things as avoiding illness, being well-nourished and literate, having self-respect, or enjoying relationships and work that matters.

Amartya Sen argues that development occurs when people are able to achieve what makes their lives valuable.

Thus, the capability approach fundamentally shifts the objective of development from income or economic growth as ends in themselves, to people. Markets and income are tremendously important of course, but only because they are means by which people live healthier and more fulfilling lives. The 'good life' is partly a life of genuine choice, and not one in which the person is forced into a particular life – however rich it might be in other respects.[8] Essentially, this implies that development can be seen as a process of expanding the real freedoms that people enjoy.[9]

As with the earlier frameworks of Aristotle and Marx, among others, Sen's capability approach holds that freedom has intrinsic as well as instrumental value. However, freedom here is used in a different and broader sense than is usually the case in western political philosophy. In particular, freedom entails not only negative liberties – for example the rights not to be arbitrarily imprisoned or harmed – but also rights of access to the particular resources that differently-placed individuals would need. For example, a disabled person, a manual labourer, and an elderly grandparent would all require different resources in order to enjoy basic health.

The capability approach thus gives rise to a distinct framework for evaluating development policies and processes. Policies are judged to be successful if they have enhanced people's capabilities – whether or not they have also affected income, growth, and other important means to this end. From this capability perspective, then, education is important for a number of reasons.[10]

First and most fundamentally, having the skills provided by basic education, such as being able to read and write, is valuable in and of itself (Box 1.1). As Sen puts it,

> it is often asked whether certain political or social freedoms, such as the liberty of political participation and dissent, or opportunities to receive basic education, are or are not 'conducive to development'. In the light of the more foundational view of development as freedom, this way of posing the question tends to miss the important understanding that these substantive freedoms (that is, the liberty of political participation or the opportunity to receive basic education or health care) are among the *constituent components* of development. Their relevance for development does not have to be freshly established through their indirect contribution to the growth of GNP or to the promotion of industrialization.[11]

Hence, education counts as a 'valuable being or doing', as an 'end' of development.

Box 1.1. Valuing literacy

A Freire-style phonetic literacy course for women was held in the peri-urban slums of Lahore, Pakistan. The course gathered women who wished to attend a literacy course as a means to generating income. As it turned out, their income did not increase – which was significant as they were very poor. And yet graduates could clearly articulate a set of additional reasons why literacy had been valuable to them. When she was asked what the literacy class had taught her, eloquent Shabnam said that literacy enabled her to trust her own judgement: 'Women think they are like a flower bud – that they do not understand with their own eyes. But we are not buds, we are mountains. We can do anything with our lives. So I tried to open my eyes, and my eyes were opened.'

Nargis spoke about her knowledge: 'We studied the word "food" in class. We knew that we are poor, we can not drink milk, eat many foods; we eat little meat. We learned that it was not necessary . . . Chick peas are 4 rupees a pound, and they have many vitamins. Apples are expensive; carrots are not. But carrots are good for health – as good as expensive things. . . .'

Source: Alkire (2002*b*).

7. Sen (1999), p. 75.

8. Sen (1996), p. 59.

9. Sen (1996), p. 1.

10. See Dreze and Sen (1995), Chap. 2; Alkire (2002*a*).

11. Sen (1996), p. 5.

Second, the process of education may be instrumental to displacing other negative processes. For example, compulsory primary education, if it is both provided and enforced, will reduce child labour. Integrating different castes or races of children in the classroom may likewise be valuable as a way of bridging social barriers.

Third, empirical studies have regularly indicated that education has a particularly important role in empowerment of disadvantaged groups, including women. An educated person is more able to understand and invoke her or his own legal rights. By lacking education, conversely, the deprived may not even be able to access the public support that is available to them. Women who are educated, or who have employment may, quite simply, survive better and longer than they would otherwise.[12] Furthermore, persons who are able to access information and formulate positions may join together to achieve collective goals and participate in political change. For example, people may demand financial accountability, or pressure their government to provide resources to avert a famine in a neighbouring district. In contrast, illiteracy can 'muffle the political voice of the underdog'.[13] In this way, education that is *universal* – attained by all persons regardless of their class or caste or gender – has a further impact in addressing social and economic barriers within a society.

The human capabilities approach to education then, like that of human rights, recognizes that education is intrinsically valuable as an end in itself. While the human rights approach specifies the moral obligation upon others to fulfil this right, the capability approach goes further, clarifying the diverse reasons for education's importance. Although many of the traditional instrumental arguments for education (see below) are accepted, the distinctive feature of the human capability approach is its assessment of policies not on the basis of their impact on incomes, but on whether or not they expand the real freedoms that people value. Education is central to this process.

Education and other development goals

If all people have a right to education, and if its impact upon people's capabilities is intrinsically part of our notion of development, it follows that the provision of a basic level of education for all people must be made universal. The case is clear and uncompromising: countries' development strategies cannot be judged successful without EFA.

Nevertheless, these arguments do not resolve the question as to how much education should be universally available. The Universal Declaration of Human Rights and each of its successors – including the Dakar Framework – deliberately left the definition of the primary span of education unspecified. At present the length of primary systems around the world varies between four and seven years of schooling. Thus, the attainment of universal primary education (UPE) would seem to represent the provision of almost twice as much schooling in some countries as in others. Should, then, minimum levels of provision be four years, six years – or perhaps even longer? Further, how should different vehicles and types of education be compared? Are pre-school arrangements to take precedence over literacy schemes, and how should both of these, in terms of national expenditure priorities, compare with primary schooling?

There are neither easy nor universal answers to these questions, if only because their resolution must depend partly upon the particular country-context in which they are raised. Priorities for new educational provision surely depend both upon what is already available and upon the level of a country's development. Nevertheless, some insights can be gained from consulting the large body of literature that has examined the relationship between education and the attainment of other development goals. Much of this is in the 'human capital' tradition. It has used economic research techniques to investigate whether education is productive,[14] and how the benefits and costs of its provision compare across different levels and types of education.

The 'good life' implies genuine choice, not being forced into a particular life – however rich it might be in other respects.

12. Sen (1990, 1992).

13. Sen (2002).

14. Most of this literature has investigated the impact of formal education, although work on the costs and impact of non-formal approaches is beginning to emerge.

Compulsory primary education, if it is both provided and enforced, will reduce child labour.

The returns to formal education

It has long been accepted that schooling has productive value. However, the extent to which its productivity compares well with other investments, and the contrasts between the private and social benefits associated with each level of education, have been areas of much greater controversy. Available estimates of rates of return[15] for developing countries consistently show that both private and social returns to primary schooling are higher than at secondary and tertiary levels. Their magnitudes are generally greater than typical returns to capital in other economic sectors. The most recent comparison of such rates for forty-two countries indicates that average returns to a further year of education across all countries are about 10%.[16] However, returns are sharply higher in developing countries than in the OECD countries. For example estimated 'social' returns to primary schooling range from around 16% in Asia, Middle East, North Africa and Latin America, to about 25% in sub-Saharan Africa.

The interpretation of these results is hampered by a range of methodological problems. First, estimates of social rates of return to education assume that market wages reflect productivity differences. Yet labour markets do not work perfectly, and earnings are a particularly fallible indicator of productivity where – as in many developing countries – large proportions of the wage-employed are in the public sector, on administered pay scales. Second, most estimates do not allow for differences in ability, parental background, or the quality of the schools attended by workers included in the samples.

Third, the full costs to households of sending children to school are often underestimated. For example, families may lose the value of their children working in the house or on the family farm, which can represent a substantial cost to poorer households. The frequent omission of these 'opportunity costs' from calculations of the net benefits of schooling may cause some upward bias in the estimated returns at primary, relative to higher levels of schooling.

Finally, in many countries labour shortages have shifted upwards towards those with secondary and tertiary education. Wage differentials increasingly reflect this, and some evidence from Africa suggests that private returns to education may now be rising at secondary and tertiary levels relative to primary level.[17] This work is, as yet, suggestive, and further work for other countries would be valuable.

Non-market effects and externalities

Many of the important benefits of education cannot be measured by market wages. A great deal of evidence as to their significance exists. No attempt to summarize details will be made here. However, the following generalizations are broadly supported.

Many studies have shown that schooling improves productivity in rural and urban self-employment. Early evidence suggested that four years schooling was a critical period.[18] More recent work has suggested that additional years continue to make a difference.[19] Many of these benefits stem from literacy which requires schooling of five to six years to be permanently acquired.[20] Surveys of the urban informal sector in a range of countries have indicated that primary schooling improves participation in urban informal sector work, and that more education brings an earnings pay-off for such workers. Years spent in both primary and secondary schooling appear to encourage – or facilitate – entrepreneurship.[21] Thus, schooling appears to have a positive impact on both rural and urban informal production.

In addition to its direct impact on productivity, schooling has a range of other effects upon population control, health and nutrition, with benefits for development. For example, it is well established that primary and secondary schooling significantly facilitates the demographic transition from high to moderate rates of population growth.[22] Schooling not only increases the ability of women to regulate their fertility through contraception, but it is also associated with a rise in the age of marriage and an increase in the perceived cost of child-bearing – arising partly from the economic returns to schooling already discussed. The World Fertility Survey shows that, in Africa, Asia and Latin America, women with seven or more years of schooling have lower fertility rates (by between

15. These calculations usually compare the estimated an difference in lifetime earnings resulting from an additional year of education with the costs of its provision to individuals, in the case of private rates, or to society, in the case of social rates of return.

16. Psacharopoulos and Patrinos (2002).

17. See Knight and Sabot (1989) for Kenya; Schultz (1995) for Côte d'Ivoire and Ghana; and the useful review given in Appleton (1999). See also Bennel (1996).

18. Lockheed et. al. (1980).

19. See, for example, Weir (1998).

20. See the evidence in World Bank (2002a), p. 8.

21. World Bank (1991), Figure 3.3.

22. Cochrane (1988); Schultz (1995).

two to three children) than women with only up to three years schooling.[23]

The effects of schooling on health are also consequential. Education is associated with improved nutritional content of diets, and earlier and more effective diagnosis of illness. A study in Ghana, for example, showed that an increase in the education of the household head from none to complete primary schooling was associated with a reduction in the household's daily calorie gap by an amount equal to one-fifth of an adult's typical daily caloric requirement.[24]

There is a strong relationship across countries between life expectancy and literacy. Moreover, infant and child mortality decreases as the mother's level of schooling rises.[25] The proportionate reduction in child mortality associated with an additional year of mother's schooling is between 5% and 10% in both rural and urban areas of low income countries.[26] Children of more educated mothers tend to be better nourished, and there is evidence that they suffer illness less frequently and less severely than other children.[27] Thus, there is well-documented evidence that parents – and particularly women – with more schooling have healthier, more vigorous children.

The evidence given above is only a part of what is relevant in determining the productive value of investment in human resources. Many cross-national correlation studies have examined the relationships between per capita income growth and human development indices of various kinds. Most of the recent studies find a positive association.[28] A new generation of growth models has given a central place to human resources, and often attributes to them the characteristic of 'increasing returns'.[29] However, the studies discussed above[30] comprise the most compelling contributions to the debate; it is the micro evidence revealing the interconnections between the constituent parts of human development, to provide an instrumental case for investments in education which is extremely difficult to dismiss. In that context it is – though not proven – hard to believe that existing social rate-of-return estimates significantly over-value the social productivity of the schooling process, particularly at the primary and secondary levels.

Conclusion

This chapter has argued that there is a fundamental identity between securing EFA and achieving development. Both on the grounds of human rights, and of human capabilities, the latter requires that the former be attained.

There is substantial evidence of the benefits from formal education with respect to a wide range of development goals. Most of these benefits begin to appear after five or six years of primary schooling. Countries that can afford to universalize a primary school system of only just six years duration could still expect to gain substantial benefits from doing so. Primary systems of shorter duration, however, would be less likely to deliver those benefits.

A primary school system of only six years duration can still bring substantial benefits to countries.

The achievement of permanent literacy and of basic numeracy are important ends-in-themselves for many people. They also have a substantial development pay-off. School systems of less than five or six years in duration are unlikely to deliver permanent literacy and, for that reason alone, it appears that a minimum primary cycle length can be defined. Focused literacy campaigns for those beyond school-going age are also capable of bringing substantial benefit to those whose literacies are supported.

As indicated, each of the EFA goals brings separate opportunities for securing other development objectives. Every country will need to define policy priorities in its move towards the individual EFA goals where these have not yet been achieved. Nevertheless, there is an agreed commitment for each country to achieve them by 2015. The next chapter assesses the progress made so far, and the magnitude of the tasks that remain.

23. United Nations (1987), Tables 112/115.

24. Kyereme and Thorbecke (1991).

25. O'Hara (1979); World Bank (1991), p. 55.

26. Mensch et. al. (1986).

27. Schultz (1995).

28. Barro (1999); de la Fuente and Domenech (2000).

29. Lucas (1988); Romer (1990, 1994); McMahon (1999).

30. Only a small part of the evidence has been mentioned here. See the references in World Bank (2002) for other recent contributions.

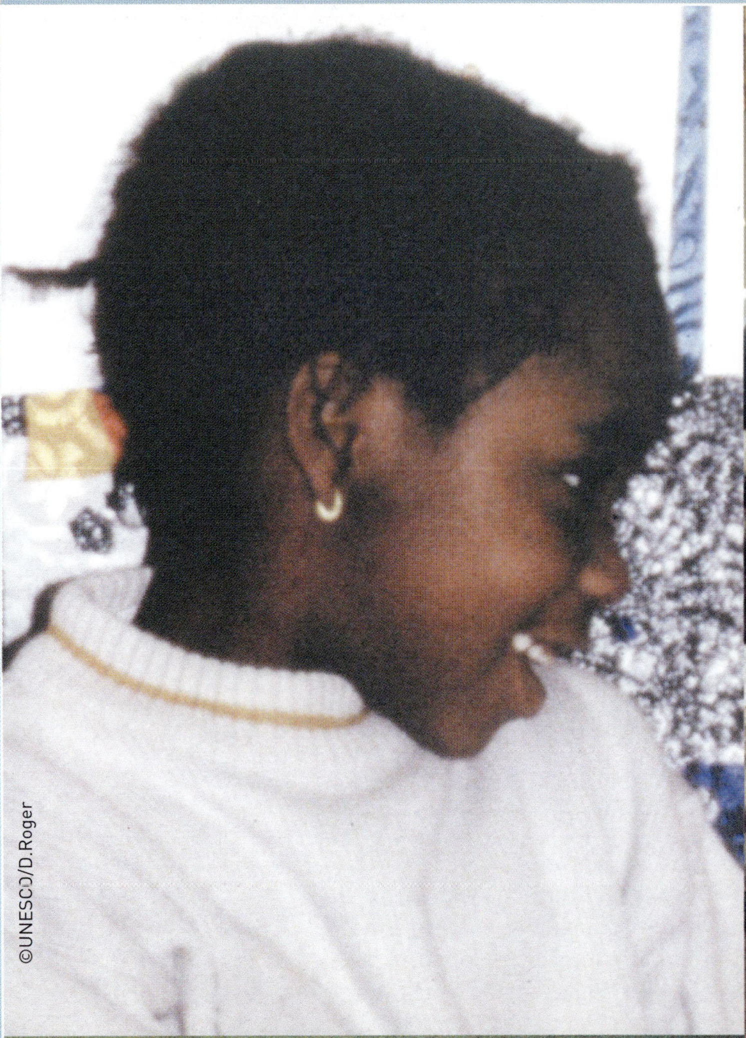
©UNESCO/D.Roger

©UNESCO/Vidal

©UNESCO/Vidal

Chapter 2

Progress towards the goals

This chapter takes stock of progress towards the Dakar goals: to what extent are countries, regions and the world on track to achieve the goals set at the World Education Forum in Dakar? The first six sections of this chapter will address the six goals separately, while the final section attempts to assess progress in a more general sense.

It is not possible to report on detailed progress made *since* the Dakar Forum in 2000, because the most recent year for which data are available is the school year starting in 1999.[1] Moreover, few quantitative indicators are available regarding early childhood care and education (Goal 1); none can be used to assess developments regarding life skills (Goal 3); and indicators to monitor education quality (Goal 6) are often proxies of quality, or are available for only limited groups of countries. Accordingly, the analysis presented on the three latter goals will be predominantly qualitative in nature.

A more quantitative assessment of developments is possible for the goals of universal primary education (Goal 2), literacy (Goal 4) and gender (Goal 5). It is on the basis of indicators regarding these goals that the final section of this chapter will develop a methodology to assess overall progress.[2]

Goal 1

Early childhood care and education

. . . expanding and improving comprehensive early childhood care and education, especially for the most vulnerable and disadvantaged children . . .

Both the World Declaration on Education for All (Jomtien, 1990) and the Dakar Framework for Action (2000) have underscored the importance of early childhood care and education (ECCE) as part of a comprehensive approach to achieving EFA.

Early learning has strong and positive impact on further learning in primary education and beyond.

Learning begins at birth. Throughout the world there is growing understanding that the period from birth to the start of primary education is a critical formative stage for the growth and development of children. The learning outcomes – norms and values, knowledge, skills – of primary education are stronger when learning occurs in the years preceding precedes regular schooling. There is also evidence that early learning improves the child's chances of enjoying good health, of finding work later in life, of social inclusion and of being less likely to commit crime.

The benefits of early childhood care and education

ECCE has a strong and positive impact on further learning, in primary education and beyond. In the Brazilian PROAPE project, it was found that the total costs of schooling – including the early learning programme itself, for pupils up to Grade 2 of primary education, was 11% lower for those who participated in ECCE than for those children who did not. In this and other programmes, drop-out and grade repetition in primary education turned out to be lower as well (Myers, 1992). Similar outcomes were found for the Integrated Child Development Service in India, a project serving 32 million children (Young, 2002).

The benefits of ECCE and of the more successful learning experiences that flow from it contribute to higher income, less dependency on welfare, and better health and hence lower health-care costs. Projects that are well known for their monitoring of these externalities are the Perry Preschool, Head Start and Early Head Start programmes in the United States of America. The Perry Preschool, targeting low-income Afro-American families, revealed a sevenfold return on the initial investment in the programme (Myers, 1992). Researchers found that an annual public investment of 18 million Swiss francs in a project in Zurich, Switzerland, is offset by at least 29 million Swiss Francs in terms of additional tax revenues alone (Bennett, forthcoming).

In addition to this evidence, there is a growing body of knowledge resulting from recent developments in brain research that supports ECCE policies. The notion of 'sensitive periods', in which certain things are best learned, has been sharpened. It appears that there are very specific and sometimes brief periods in which the developing brain is particularly fit to learn certain tasks. These tasks themselves have also been broken down (for example, language acquisition consists of a multitude of sub-tasks with differing sensitive periods) (OECD, 2002). After, or before, these periods, it is not impossible to learn the same tasks (Bruer, 1999), but it would require greater efforts and more resources. In general, these research outcomes point towards intensifying structured learning experiences during ages earlier than those that have usually been the subject of most education policies.

A diverse area of learning

ECCE is a highly diverse area of learning (UNESCO, 2000*d*). In very broad terms, early childhood learning opportunities range from formal pre-school, integrated in the national education system, via kindergartens and other centres where care, play and education go hand in hand, to include more informal, often home-based activities.

1. We refer here to the annual administrative data collected by the UNESCO Institute for Statistics. Other information is available to monitor progress for particular countries and goals, but it is very partial in nature.

2. It should be noted that the quality – availability, coverage and reliability – of some data is less than satisfactory. When particular caution should be exercised in interpreting data used in this chapter, the reader's attention will be drawn to this fact.

The diversity in ECCE provision can be understood through its historical development. The pattern of ECCE development in industrialized countries shows that it was expanded after universal primary schooling had been achieved. This is not to say that ECCE was perceived to be less important from an educational point of view, but that priority in terms of resource allocation was given first to primary schooling. However, some regions and countries have a long-standing tradition in ECCE. In Eastern Europe and Latin America, relatively high proportions of young children attend various forms of pre-school or other care.

For a long time, ECCE was a privilege enjoyed by those living and holding jobs in urban areas, who were able to have their young children cared for and educated, and this pattern remains strong. Private provision dominates in this respect. But increasingly, ECCE is also identified as a potentially effective strategy for the social inclusion of children – and often their mothers, too – in disadvantaged areas or situations. Where the resources to address the needs of these groups are scarce, these strategies often result in informal ECCE activities. In developing countries, these activities, which are often home-based, may be rooted in indigenous traditions of child raising. More institutionalized forms of provision can be found in a number of countries that have made a conscious choice to facilitate universal access to ECCE, the most institutionalized form being a pre-school that is an integral part of the regular education system.

However, for most countries around the world, this field is a relatively new and uncharted area of learning. The challenge is to develop strategies – formal and informal – that respond to specific socio-cultural and economic contexts, in countries where governments are constrained in their ability to find resources for ECCE.

Data and indicators

Data about ECCE are in their infancy at both national and international level. This hinders policy development and the assessment of global progress. Data collection and monitoring are rendered more complex by the diversity of ECCE provision; it is much easier to collect data on attendance in government pre-schools than on participation in community-run or family-based arrangements. Five Asian countries – Cambodia, Kazakhstan, Kyrgyzstan, Tajikistan and Viet Nam – are cooperating with international organizations and the Consultative Group on ECCE to identify and describe types of ECCE and develop common indicators. Figure 2.1 features the various main categories of this type of education by age group, and illustrates how data collection could spread from the 'easy' fields (government-provided ECCE for ages 3–6) to the more difficult ones. Box 2.1 describes in more detail a programme in Brazil to establish the facts before developing education policy.

At both national and international level, indicators and data are lacking.

Figure 2.1. Early childhood care and education

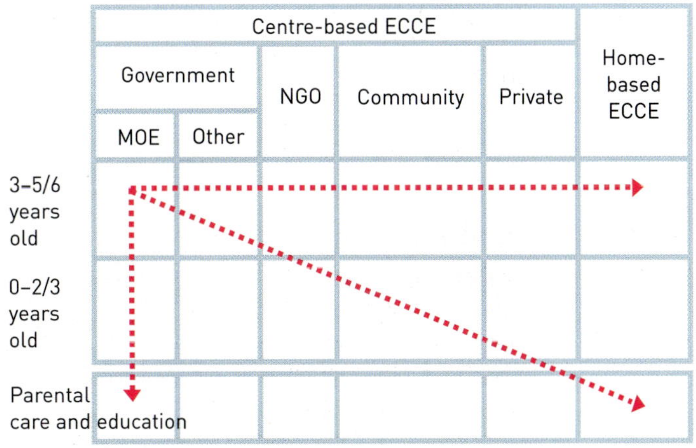

Relative indications of difficulty in monitoring numbers and quality, by age group and type of provision. Ease decreases from top left (oldest children, in state-supported structures) to bottom right (youngest children, at home).

Source: Adapted from UNESCO, ISCED (1997).

Box 2.1. Putting the data system before policy development in Brazil

Most ECCE policies focus on expanding and improving access to pre-primary care and education for children aged 3 and older. Many education ministries are, however, aware of the difficulties of reaching even this age group through the formal system and are exploring non-formal alternatives. Some are also developing plans to include children under age 3 as well.

The experience of the Ministry of Education in Brazil suggests that the problem in developing a more comprehensive ECCE policy may reside not so much in a lack of willingness but, in large part, in the limited data systems of education ministries.

In 1996, day-care centres (ages 0–3) and pre-schools (ages 4–6) in Brazil were integrated under the Ministry of Education. One of the first steps in implementing this broader mandate was to collect data on these services. In 1997, the ministry's annual school census included data on day-care centres linked to schools. In 2000, the ministry conducted a nationwide survey to collect baseline data on early childhood education, the first of its kind carried out by the ministry. Significantly, the survey covered day-care centres as well as pre-schools.

The data on day-care centres were incomplete, because the survey could not map all centres across the country. However, even this partial baseline data helped the ministry embrace the entire 0–6 age range within its policy planning. The ministry acknowledged that the data played an important role in this process. Before carrying out the survey, the ministry revised legal guidelines for early childhood institutions, which helped register and accredit day-care centres as well as other services that had been outside the orbit of government administration. Thanks to this exercise, day-care centres could be surveyed and eventually included in the Ministry's national policy purview of Early Childhood.

The Brazilian experience may not be unique, but it illustrates two important points. First, the Ministry sought to develop a comprehensive data set covering the 0–6 age group before embarking on policy development. Notably, it was among the first tasks it undertook upon being given its expanded mandate. Second, it paid attention to the system development for identifying and recognizing the day-care centres before proceeding to collect data on them.

This policy prioritization is noteworthy because, more often than not, early childhood policies are developed without the support of sound data. Whether or not such an improved data system will eventually lead to a comprehensive policy plan on access in the case of Brazil remains to be seen. But, already, the approach seems to have worked to the extent that the Ministry sought to include early childhood beyond pre-primary education, and thereby brought this earlier age group and related services into the policy discussion.

Source: UNESCO (2002*d*).

Patterns of provision

Using the rough typology of formal, centre- and home-based provision, it is clear that the first type, generally administered by government at national or local level, usually provides the best participation statistics. The information on participation in centre-based ECCE varies widely, and the home-based activities are almost a 'black box' (see also the Goal 3 section of this chapter, below, on learning programmes for youth and adults, where a similar problem exists). This fact should be kept in mind when interpreting Table 2.1, which provides figures on participation in early learning for a number of developing countries, with, for most countries, an indication of the number of hours per week. Bahrein, Lesotho, Mongolia, the Republic of Moldova, Suriname, and Trinidad and Tobago all have participation rates higher than 20% for the age group (36–59 months), and programme duration of 20 hours or more per week.

Table 4 in the Annex provides data on ECCE participation – also by sex – for a much larger number of countries, but with no indication of the duration of programmes. The figures could refer to programmes of just a few hours per week, and just a few weeks per year, so it should therefore be treated with the utmost caution. Table 2.2, derived from Annex Table 4, features countries in developing regions that stand out for their relatively high levels of participation in ECCE.

Table 2.1.
Children aged 36-59 months attending some form of organized early childhood education programme (2000)

Country	Total (%)	Median number of hours per week	36–47 mos. (%)	48–59 mos. (%)	Sample size
Lebanon	85.5	na	72.2	92.8	
Trinidad and Tobago	71.5	25.0	58.6	81.2	433
Dominican Republic	49.5	16.0	38.5	61.6	793
Tunisia	46.7	na	–	–	2824
Equatorial Guinea	45.4	12.0	34.0	58.9	979
Viet Nam	42.3	na	–	–	2218
Bahrain	38.3	20.0	26.3	49.7	278
India	37.7	na	–	–	
Guyana	35.1	na	18.1	54.4	
Yugoslavia	31.4	na	24.2	38.1	674
Suriname	36.9	20.0	14.1	61.4	684
Georgia	30.9	na	27.2	34.4	1596
Moldova	30.4	35.0	32.4	28.5	709
Bangladesh	25.6	na	–	–	
Lesotho	22.5	20.0	16.7	28.6	1376
Mongolia	21.0	40.0	16.2	25.4	
Sudan	20.2	8.0	16.2	24.8	93
Uzbekistan	20.0	10.0	19.4	20.6	1412
Sao Tome and Principe	18.2	20.0	14.4	22.7	830
Albania	17.3	7.0	16.6	18.5	632
Bolivia	17.3	15.0	7.7	25.8	1211
Gambia	16.3	20.0	11.2	22.3	1171
Cameroon	15.4	25.0	9.7	21.3	1292
Swaziland	14.7	15.0	8.5	16.3	1048
Botswana	14.5	2.0	10.5	19.1	1134
Comoros	14.3	12.0	9.9	19.3	2004
Kenya	12.8	25.0	5.3	21.5	3100
Philippines	12.5	10.0	–	–	3852
Sierra Leone	11.7	5.0	7.7	16.9	1091
Azerbaijan	11.4	35.0	8.7	13.9	856
Bosnia and Herzegovina	11.4	na	6.9	10.9	1189
Myanmar	9.4	na	7.1	12.3	5570
Togo	9.4	na	6.5	11.0	1156
Senegal	8.1	16.0	7.5	8.8	3412
Lao PDR	7.5	na	5.0	10.8	1796
Angola	6.6	na	5.0	8.6	2100
Guinea-Bissau	6.5	4.0	5.1	7.9	2280
Egypt	6.4	na	2.6	10.7	4179
Côte d'Ivoire	6.2	20.0	4.2	8.8	2834
Madagascar	5.5	23.0	3.0	8.3	2326
Burundi	4.6	2.0	3.6	5.9	1230
Tajikistan	4.0	36.0	3.5	4.5	1262
Dem. Rep. of Congo	3.0	15.0	1.5	4.4	3467
Central African Republic	2.7	12.0	1.8	3.8	5075
Rwanda	2.6	na	1.4	3.9	1214
Niger	2.5	25.0	1.6	3.5	2010
Somalia	1.9	11.0	1.1	2.6	1617
Chad	0.8	4.0	0.6	1.0	2221

Source: Hansen and Loaiza (2002).

ECCE is a potentially effective strategy for the social inclusion of children and their mothers in disadvantaged areas or situations.

Table 2.2.
Participation in ECCE, selected countries in developing regions (1999/2000)

Country	Gross enrolment ratio (GER) Total	Male	Female	Gender parity index (F/M)
Barbados	79.1	77.5	80.7	1.04
Brazil	59.7	59.7	59.7	1.00
Chile	76.7	77.0	76.4	0.99
Costa Rica	81.9	82.1	81.6	0.99
Cuba	104.4	103.0	105.9	1.03
Ecuador	65.6	64.7	66.5	1.03
Israel	78.4	78.7	78.2	0.99
Jamaica	88.1	86.6	89.7	1.04
Lebanon	66.8	67.6	65.9	0.97
Liberia	69.5	73.7	65.3	0.89
Malaysia	51.8	50.9	52.8	1.04
Mauritius	96.1	95.2	97.0	1.02
Mexico	76.3	75.3	77.4	1.03
Morocco	58.0	74.4	41.0	0.55
Namibia	64.7	60.2	69.3	1.15
Netherlands Antilles	98.0	97.5	98.5	1.01
Paraguay	83.0	81.9	84.1	1.03
Peru	59.0	58.3	59.7	1.02
Saint Lucia	63.6	60.9	66.5	1.09
Thailand	83.5	84.0	83.0	0.99
Trinidad and Tobago	60.2	60.4	60.0	0.99
United Arab Emirates	78.4	78.8	78.1	0.99
Uruguay	59.2	58.5	59.8	1.02
Vanuatu	73.1	69.9	76.5	1.09

Source: Annex, Table 4.

Fewer than half of all children in the world participate in early childhood programmes.

Figure 2.2. GER for ECCE, worldwide, by number of countries (1999/2000)

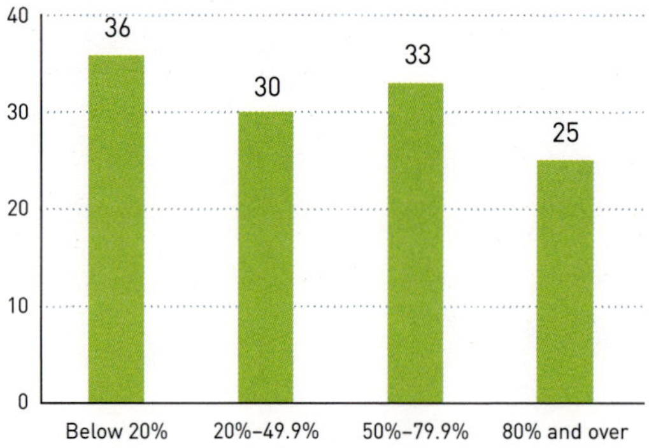

Source: Annex, Table 4.

Developing countries with particularly high levels of attendance, notably 75% or higher, are Barbados, Cuba, Jamaica, Mauritius, Mexico, Paraguay and Thailand. Of these countries, Cuba is the benchmark; it has achieved universal early childhood education.

However, in twenty countries – three quarters of which are found in sub-Saharan Africa – ECCE gross enrolment rates are under 5%. And many other countries are not doing much better; more than half of the countries are below GER level of 50%, as Figure 2.2 indicates.

Access to early childhood services is unequal for various social groups. As already indicated, the chances of enrolling in early childhood activities are greater for children living in urban areas with parents who hold jobs. The educational attainment of the mother also makes a difference. Three countries, however – Albania,

Table 2.3. Countries showing marked growth in ECCE participation (1990–1999)

Country	GER 1990	GER 1999	Variation 1990–1999	Gross enrolment ratio (GER)		
				Male	Female	Gender parity index (F/M)
Croatia	28.3	53.4	25.1	54.3	52.5	0.97
India	3.4	30.0	26.6	30.1	29.9	0.99
Japan	48.1	83.5	35.4	83.5	83.6	1.00
Latvia	45.3	73.3	28.0	75.1	71.4	0.95
Luxembourg	91.7	117.1	25.3	132.1	101.2	0.77
Mauritius	56.1	96.1	40.0	95.2	97.0	1.02
Namibia	14.4	64.7	50.3	60.2	69.3	1.15
Paraguay	27.1	83.0	55.9	81.9	84.1	1.03
Peru	29.9	59.0	29.1	58.3	59.7	1.02
Switzerland	59.7	94.6	34.9	95.2	94.0	0.99
Thailand	43.3	83.5	40.2	84.0	83.0	0.99
Trinidad and Tobago	8.8	60.2	51.4	60.4	60.0	0.99
United Arab Emirates	51.9	78.4	26.6	78.8	78.1	0.99
United Kingdom	52.4	79.1	26.6	79.1	79.0	1.00

Source: Annex, Table 4.

Bolivia and Suriname – managed to attract more children from the poorest homes than from the richest households.

With regard to gender, there does not seem to be the level of disparities associated with primary and secondary education. As Tables 2.2 (and Table 4 in the Annex) illustrate, as many girls attend ECCE as boys in many countries. In Western and Central Africa, boys attend slightly more, whereas girls are in the majority, and perhaps more markedly, in Asian, and Eastern and Southern African countries.

Trends in participation in ECCE

To assess progress in ECCE since the World Education Forum in Dakar (2000) is not yet possible. Data at macro-level are no more recent than 1999. It is, however, possible to compare these with the data for 1990. Annex Table 4 reveals that marked changes are taking place in a number of countries, for the better and for the worse. Table 2.3 contains a selection from Annex Table 4, this time highlighting countries with growth in enrolment of 25% or more.

Once again, these figures must be treated with caution. Nevertheless, three general observations can be made on the basis of Table 2.3 and Annex Table 2.1. First, the table suggests that developing and developed countries alike are expanding ECCE provision. In both parts of the world there are countries with a rich tradition in ECCE, and others that are catching up. Secondly, in a number of countries in Eastern Europe and Asia, enrolment in ECCE is falling. Thirdly, a number of countries, mostly in sub-Saharan Africa, combine low enrolment rates with a lack of progress. This is the case for Burkina Faso, Congo, Djibouti, Ethiopia, Niger, Senegal and Togo.

It is not yet possible to assess progress in ECCE since the World Education Forum in Dakar (2000).

Goal 2

Universal primary education

. . . ensuring that by 2015 all children, particularly girls, children in difficult circumstances and those belonging to ethnic minorities, have access to and complete, free and compulsory primary education of good quality . . .

More than 100 million children in the world are still deprived of access to primary education.

In the half-century that has passed since the Universal Declaration of Human Rights established education as a fundamental right for all, many countries have achieved the goal of universal primary education (UPE), or have made substantial progress towards doing so. Some countries have proven that this is possible despite difficult economic circumstances, natural disaster or a history of conflict. Yet more than 100 million children in the world are still deprived of access to primary education, while a number of countries are clearly not on track to achieve its universal provision. Some have actually been moving away from it. Nearly all out-of-school children live in developing countries, and a majority of them are girls.

Enrolment in primary education

Enrolment rates are key indicators of the extent to which the education system manages to serve all children. The gross enrolment ratio (GER) expresses the number of pupils at a given level of schooling – regardless of their age – as a proportion of the number of children in the relevant age group. The GER can be higher than 100% if children begin their first grade when they are older (or younger) than the official starting age, or if there is grade repetition. Both of these phenomena lead to over-age enrolment, particularly in the higher grades.

Figure 2.3 compares GERs across major world regions, over the decade 1990–1999. During the economic difficulties of the 1980s, the rate of expansion of school systems had slowed as compared with the previous two decades. This was particularly so for primary schooling, and especially in Africa, where primary enrolment growth fell below the rate of growth of population, and where, in a number of countries, enrolments actually declined in absolute terms. Figure 2.3 indicates mixed progress during the 1990s, although in some parts of the world, rapid enrolment growth appears to have resumed. GERs have expanded strongly in South and West Asia, the Arab States and North Africa, and in Latin America and the Caribbean. In the latter region, GERs were already greater than 100 in

Figure 2.3. Gross enrolment ratios by region (1990–1999)

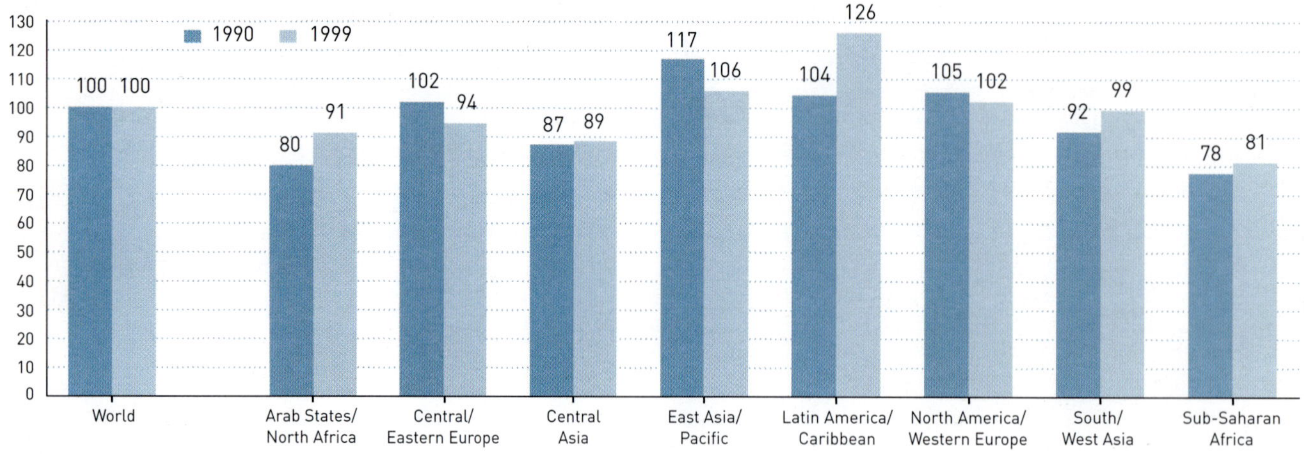

Source: Annex, Table 6.

Figure 2.4. Variation in gross enrolment ratios, by region (1999)

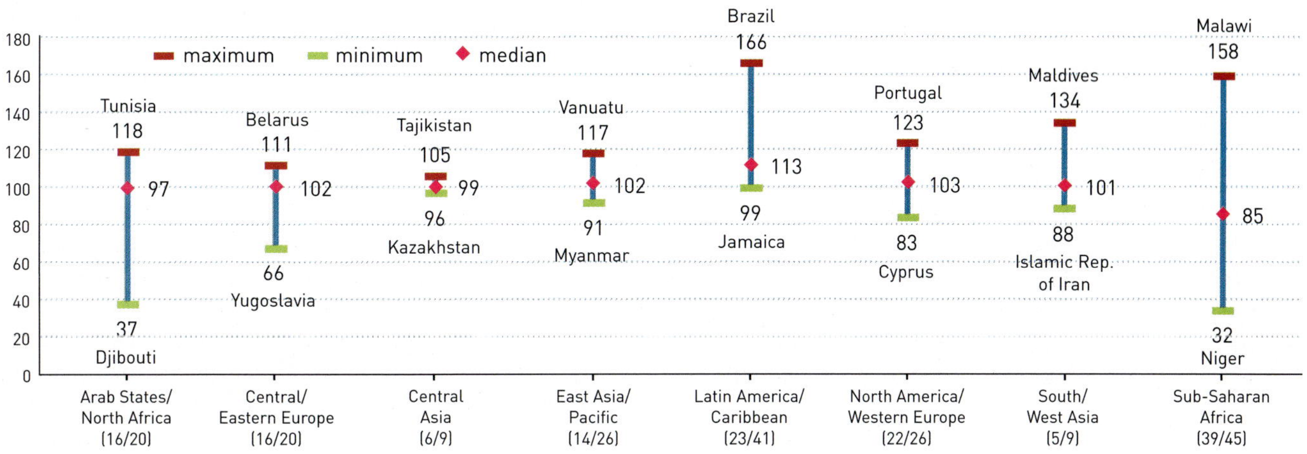

Source: Annex, Table 6.

1990 and rose to a mean level of 126 by the end of the decade. On the other hand progress in sub-Saharan Africa and Central Asia remained slow, while total enrolments fell in some of the countries of Central and Eastern Europe. The declines in GERs for East Asia and the Pacific, and for North America and Western Europe suggest a reduction in the number of pupils who are beyond the official school age in those regions, although without reliable data on net ratios for the earlier period, this cannot yet be demonstrated. As regards developing countries, although their average GER is now close to 100, the regional variations can be starkly seen, with Latin America and the Caribbean having a 50% higher GER than sub-Saharan Africa.

Nevertheless, the population-weighted means shown in Figure 2.3 hide very considerable disparities in enrolment rates between countries. Figure 2.4 shows that the range of variation is particularly wide in sub-Saharan Africa, in the Arab States and in Latin America. The median values in the figure show that, in most cases, the GER of the country in the middle of the range is close to 100. However, there is a four- to five-fold difference between the GERs in the top and bottom ranking countries of sub-Saharan Africa, and of the Arab States and North Africa, where a number of countries with extremely low enrolment ratios are to be found.

Nearly all out-of-school children live in developing countries, and the majority of them are girls.

Figure 2.5. Net enrolment ratios by region and development status (1999)

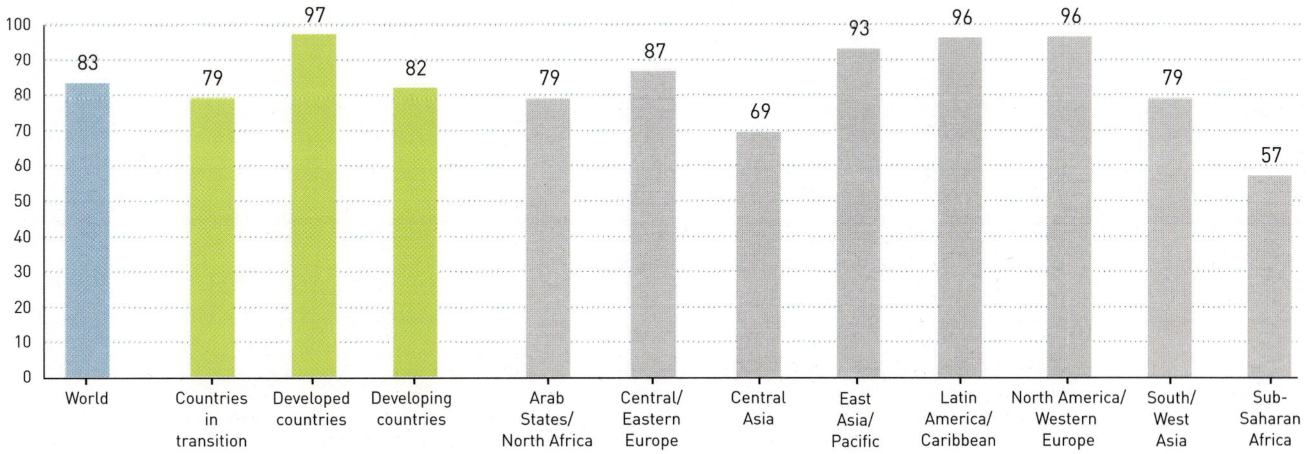

Source: Annex, Table 6.

Table 2.4. Classification of countries/territories according to the level of their gross enrolment ratios (1999)

	GER < 70%	70% >= GER < 100%	GER > 100%	Data not available
Arab States/ North Africa (20)	Djibouti, Saudi Arabia, Sudan (3)	Egypt, Kuwait, Lebanon, Mauritania, Morocco, Oman, United Arab Emirates (7)	Algeria, Bahrain, Iraq, Jordan, Palestinian A.T., Tunisia (6)	Libyan Arab Jamahiriya, Qatar, Syrian Arab Republic, Yemen (4)
Central/Eastern Europe (20)	Yugoslavia (1)	Croatia, Russian Federation, The former Yugoslav Rep. of Macedonia (3)	Albania, Belarus, Bulgaria, Czech Republic, Estonia, Hungary, Latvia, Lithuania, Poland, Romania, Slovakia, Turkey (12)	Bosnia and Herzegovina, Republic of Moldova, Slovenia, Ukraine (4)
Central Asia (9)		Azerbaijan, Georgia, Kazakhstan, Mongolia (4)	Kyrgyzstan, Tajikistan (2)	Armenia, Turkmenistan, Uzbekistan (3)
East Asia/Pacific (26)		Myanmar, Republic of Korea, Thailand (3)	Australia, Cambodia, China, Indonesia, Japan, Lao PDR, Malaysia, New Zealand, Vanuatu, Samoa, Viet Nam (11)	Cook Islands, DPR Korea, Fiji, Kiribati, Marshall Islands, Nauru, Niue, Papua New Guinea, Philippines, Solomon Islands, Tonga, Tuvalu (12)
Latin America/ Caribbean (41)		Guatemala, Jamaica (2)	Argentina, Barbados, Belize, Bolivia, Brazil, Chile, Colombia, Costa Rica, Cuba, Dominican Republic, Ecuador, Mexico, Netherlands Antilles, Nicaragua, Panama, Paraguay, Peru, St Lucia, Trinidad and Tobago, Uruguay, Venezuela (21)	Anguilla, Antigua and Barbuda, Aruba, Bahamas, Bermuda, British Virgin Is., Cayman Is., Dominica, El Salvador, Grenada, Guyana, Haiti, Honduras, Montserrat, St Kitts and Nevis, St Vincent and the Grenadines, Suriname, Turks and Caicos Is. (18)
North America/ Western Europe (26)		Canada, Cyprus, Greece, Luxembourg, United Kingdom, United States (6)	Austria, Belgium, Denmark, Finland, France, Germany, Iceland, Ireland, Israel, Italy, Netherlands, Norway, Portugal, Spain, Switzerland, Sweden (16)	Andorra, Malta, Monaco, San Marino (4)
South/West Asia (9)		Islamic Republic of Iran, Pakistan (2)	India, Maldives, Nepal (3)	Afghanistan, Bangladesh, Bhutan, Sri Lanka (4)
Sub-Saharan Africa (45)	Angola, Burkina Faso, Burundi, Eritrea, Guinea, Niger, Sierra Leone, United Republic of Tanzania (8)	Benin, Cameroon, Chad, Comoros, Congo, Côte d'Ivoire, Ethiopia, Gambia, Guinea-Bissau, Mozambique, Senegal, Zambia, Zimbabwe (13)	Botswana, Equatorial Guinea, Gabon, Lesotho, Liberia, Madagascar, Malawi, Mauritius, Namibia, Rwanda, South Africa, Swaziland, Togo, Uganda (14)	Cape Verde, Central African Republic, Democratic Rep. of the Congo, Ghana, Kenya, Mali, Nigeria, Sao Tome and Principe, Seychelles, Somalia (10)

Figures in brackets indicate the number of countries/territories.
Source: Annex, Table 6.

A high number of children repeating grades represents a serious drain on education system capacity.

Table 2.4 provides an overview of the distribution of GERs at country level. The concentration of enrolment ratios less than 70 in sub-Saharan Africa stands out. However, many countries from all regions have GERs greater than 100. As indicated earlier, their frequency indicates the presence of over-age children in school arising partly from late enrolment, but particularly from high rates of grade repetition. In some countries, grade repetition is absent by regulation, while in others it occurs only to a moderate extent. However, in some cases the number of children repeating grades represents a serious drain on the capacity of the system. In such cases, repeaters are often occupying places that could otherwise be taken by children at present out-of-school.

The net enrolment ratio (NER) takes account of the age structure of those enrolled by excluding all those children who are older or younger than the officially school-eligible age group from the numerator of the ratio. Thus, by definition, it cannot exceed 100%. Figure 2.5 shows NERs in 1999/2000, by development status and region.

Figure 2.6. Variation in net enrolment ratios by region (1999)

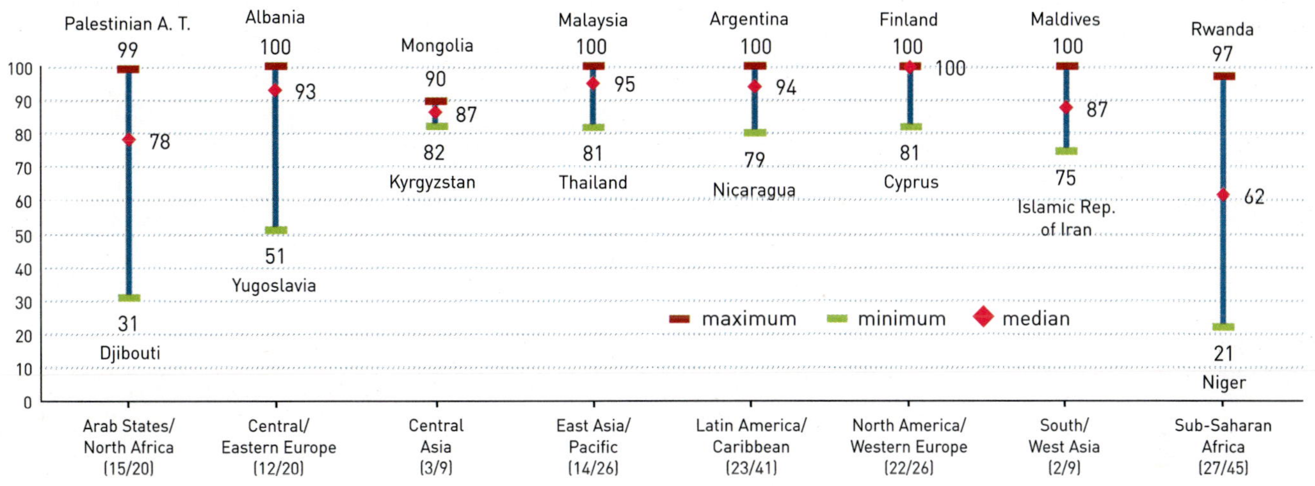

Source: Annex, Table 6.

It should be noted that no major region, not even those that include the more industrialized countries, achieves average net ratios of 100. In Latin America and the Caribbean, in North America and Western Europe, and to a lesser extent in East Asia and the Pacific, the NER is close to, but still less than 100. The gaps in these regions are attributed partly to forms of exclusion from education that are difficult to avoid, such as illness or incapacity, partly to some children being educated by their parents, and partly to some primary-age children being enrolled in pre-primary and secondary programmes. Nevertheless, in some regions there are also increasing problems related to social exclusion.

The latter seems true for some parts of Central and Eastern Europe, where a rich tradition of education has been threatened by economic decline and erosion of social capital. On average, the NER in Central and Eastern Europe is only slightly higher than the NER of developing countries as a group, while the NER for countries in transition – encompassing a larger area than Central and Eastern Europe – is even lower. Within the developing world, the Arab States and the countries of South and West Asia have NERs close to 80%, although both regions have serious gender gaps (see discussion under Goal 5).

Very serious enrolment problems occur in the Arab States and, in particular, in sub-Saharan Africa (where NERs are, on average, less than 60%). Although there have been reporting problems for these data, in these regions net enrolments appear to have either faltered or scarcely increased during the 1990s. Where average enrolment rates are low – given that they are often much lower in the most problematic sub-regions – going to school can become an exception rather than the norm. Figure 2.6 shows the variation of NERs, which is wide, particularly in the above two regions. Table 2.5 also indicates the heavy concentration of countries with NERs less than 70 in sub-Saharan Africa (18 of the 25 cases) and, to a lesser extent, in the Arab States. In some of these countries only a minority of children attend school, and of those who do, many live in a home environment where support for learning is lacking, and in communities which have great difficulty in sustaining their schools in quantitative and qualitative respects.

Where average enrolment rates are low, going to school can become an exception rather than the norm.

Goal 2. Universal primary education

Table 2.5. Classification of countries/territories according to NER level (1999)

	NER < 50%	50% >= NER < 70%	70% >= NER < 90%	90% >= NER < 100%	Data not available
Arab States/ North Africa (20)	Djibouti, Sudan (2)	Kuwait, Lebanon, Saudi Arabia, Oman (4)	Morocco, United Arab Emirates (2)	Algeria, Bahrain, Egypt, Iraq, Jordan, Palestinian A.T., Tunisia (7)	Libyan Arab Jamahiriya, Mauritania, Qatar, Syrian Arab Republic, Yemen (5)
Central/Eastern Europe (20)		Yugoslavia (1)	Croatia, Hungary (2)	Albania, Bulgaria, Czech Republic, Estonia, Latvia, Lithuania, Poland, Romania, The former Yugoslav Rep. of Macedonia (9)	Belarus, Bosnia and Herzegovina, Republic of Moldova, Russian Federation, Slovakia, Slovenia, Turkey, Ukraine (8)
Central Asia (9)			Mongolia, Kyrgyzstan, Tajikistan (3)		Armenia, Azerbaijan, Georgia, Kazakhstan, Turkmenistan, Uzbekistan (6)
East Asia/Pacific (26)			Cambodia, Lao PDR, Myanmar, Thailand (4)	Australia, China, Indonesia, Japan, Malaysia, New Zealand, Rep. of Korea, Samoa, Vanuatu, Viet Nam (10)	Cook Is., Dem. People's Rep. Korea, Fiji, Kiribati, Marshall Is., Nauru, Niue, Papua New Guinea, Philippines, Solomon Islands, Tonga, Tuvalu (12)
Latin America/ Caribbean (41)			Barbados, Chile, Colombia, Guatemala, Nicaragua, Venezuela (6)	Argentina, Belize, Bolivia, Brazil, Costa Rica, Cuba, Dominican Republic, Ecuador, Jamaica, Netherlands Antilles, Mexico, Paraguay, Peru, Panama, St.Lucia, Trinidad and Tobago, Uruguay (17)	Anguilla, Antigua and Barbuda, Aruba, Bahamas, Bermuda, British Virgin Is., Cayman Is., Dominica, El Salvador, Grenada, Guyana, Haiti, Honduras, Montserrat, St. Kitts and Nevis, St. Vincent and the Grenadines, Suriname, Turks and Caicos Is. (18)
North America/ Western Europe (26)			Cyprus, Germany (2)	Austria, Belgium, Canada, Denmark, France, Greece, Finland, Iceland, Ireland, Israel, Italy, Luxembourg, Netherlands, Norway, Portugal, Spain, Sweden, Switzerland, United Kingdom, United States (20)	Andorra, Malta, Monaco, San Marino (4)
South/West Asia (9)			Islamic Republic of Iran (1)	Maldives (1)	Afghanistan, Bangladesh, Bhutan, India, Nepal, Pakistan, Sri Lanka (7)
Sub-Saharan Africa (45)	Angola, Burkina Faso, Burundi, Eritrea, Guinea, Niger, United Republic of Tanzania (7)	Chad, Comoros, Côte d'Ivoire, Gambia, Guinea-Bissau, Lesotho, Madagascar, Mozambique, Senegal, Sierra Leone, Zambia (11)	Benin, Botswana, Equatorial Guinea, Namibia, Zimbabwe (5)	Mauritius, Rwanda, Togo, Swaziland (4)	Cape Verde, Central African Republic, Congo, Cameroon, Dem. Rep. of the Congo, Ethiopia, Gabon, Ghana, Kenya, Liberia, Mali, Malawi, Nigeria, Sao Tome and Principe, Seychelles, Somalia, South Africa, Uganda (18)

Figures in brackets indicate the number of countries/territories.

Source: Annex, Table 6.

Table 2.6. Estimates of primary school enrolment and attendance (1998–2001)

Country	Survey data source	Date of survey (fieldwork)	Survey estimate (NAR)	EFA estimate (NER) 1999/2000	Difference survey – EFA estimate
Algeria	MICS report	May 2000	97.0	97.2	-0.2
Angola	MICS microdata	2000	64.2	27.3	36.9
Benin	DHS microdata	2001	53.5	70.3	-16.8
Botswana	MICS microdata	May–July 2000	83.7	83.6	0.1
Burkina Faso	DHS microdata	Nov. 1998/99–March 1999/2000	27.4	34.6	-7.2
Burundi	MICS microdata	April–May 2000	46.5	44.5	2.1
Cameroon	MICS microdata	July–Aug. 2000	73.7		
Central African Republic	MICS microdata	April–Dec. 2000	42.9		
Chad	MICS microdata	May–Sep. 2000	39.2	56.6	-17.4
Comoros	MICS microdata	Sep.–Nov. 2000	33.7	54.8	-21.1
Côte d'Ivoire	MICS microdata	June–Aug. 2000	57.3	58.4	-1.1
Dem. Rep. Congo	MICS microdata	2000	51.4		
Egypt	DHS microdata	Feb.–April 2000	85.1	92.3	-7.2
Equatorial Guinea	MICS microdata	2000	49.0	79.0	-30.0
Ethiopia	DHS microdata	Feb.–May 2000	30.2		
Gabon	DHS report	July 2000–Jan. 2001	93.2		
Gambia	MICS microdata	May–June 2000	46.3	69.8	-23.5
Ghana	DHS microdata	Nov. 1998/99–Feb. 1999/2000	74.3		
Guinea	DHS microdata	April 1999/2000	39.3	49.0	-9.7
Guinea-Bissau	MICS microdata	April–May 2000	41.1	53.5	-12.4
Kenya	MICS microdata	Sep.–Oct. 2000	73.8		
Lesotho	MICS microdata	March–May 2000	65.0	58.5	6.5
Madagascar	MICS microdata	Aug.–Oct. 2000	51.8	65.2	-13.4
Malawi	DHS report	July–Nov. 2000	78.2		
Niger	MICS microdata	April–Aug. 2000	30.2	21.2	8.8
Nigeria	DHS microdata	March–May 1999/2000	55.6		
Rwanda	MICS microdata	July–Oct. 2000	67.8		
Sao Tome and Principe	MICS microdata	Aug.–Sep. 2000	73.6		
Senegal	MICS microdata	May–July 2000	47.3	61.7	-14.4
Sierra Leone	MICS microdata	March–May 2000	36.6		
Somalia	MICS microdata	1999/2000	11.6		
South Africa	DHS microdata	1998	88.6		
Sudan	MICS microdata	2000	55.2	44.7	10.5
Swaziland	MICS microdata	July–Sep. 2000	70.7	92.8	-22.1
Togo	MICS microdata	2000	63.0	91.4	-28.4
Tunisia	MICS report	March–April 2000	94.4	98.2	-4.2
Uganda	DHS EdData report	April–July 2001	87.1		
U.R. Tanzania	DHS microdata	Sep.–Nov. 1999/2000	48.9	46.7	2.2
Zambia	MICS microdata	Oct. 1999/2000	61.5	66.4	-4.9
Zimbabwe	DHS microdata	Aug.–Nov. 1999/2000	84.9	80.2	4.7

Explanatory notes. Net Attendance Rate (NAR): Multiple Indicator Cluster Survey (MICS) by UNICEF; and Demographic and Health Survey (DHS) by USAID, 1998–2001. Net Enrolment Rate (NER): UIS data for 1999/2000; see Annex, Table 6.

Age groups for MICS and DHS: Gabon and South Africa data for ages 6–10 (official primary age 6–11 and 6–12), Tunisia 6–12 (official primary age 6–11). Sub-Saharan Africa includes all countries above except Algeria, Egypt, Sudan and Tunisia. Sudan includes only northern Sudan. Averages are weighted by the total population of each country.

Source: UNICEF and UIS.

Enrolment vs. attendance

One problem in assessing participation in primary education is that official statistics (the basis for calculating GER and NER) include only the numbers of children who are formally registered as pupils, even though it is not certain that they actually attend school. Information on attendance rates is needed to analyse this issue. However, most information available on these indicators is gathered through household surveys, and not on a regular basis (Huebler and Loaizia, 2002). Table 2.6 shows such results for 40 African countries, and compares these data with the NERs for 25 of them. It indicates that the estimates of attendance are usually lower – and in some cases much lower – than the NER statistics, based upon enrolment data supplied by governments. Seventeen of the 25 household survey attendance rate estimates shown in the table are lower than the corresponding NER

Figure 2.7. Variation in gross intake rate by region (1999)

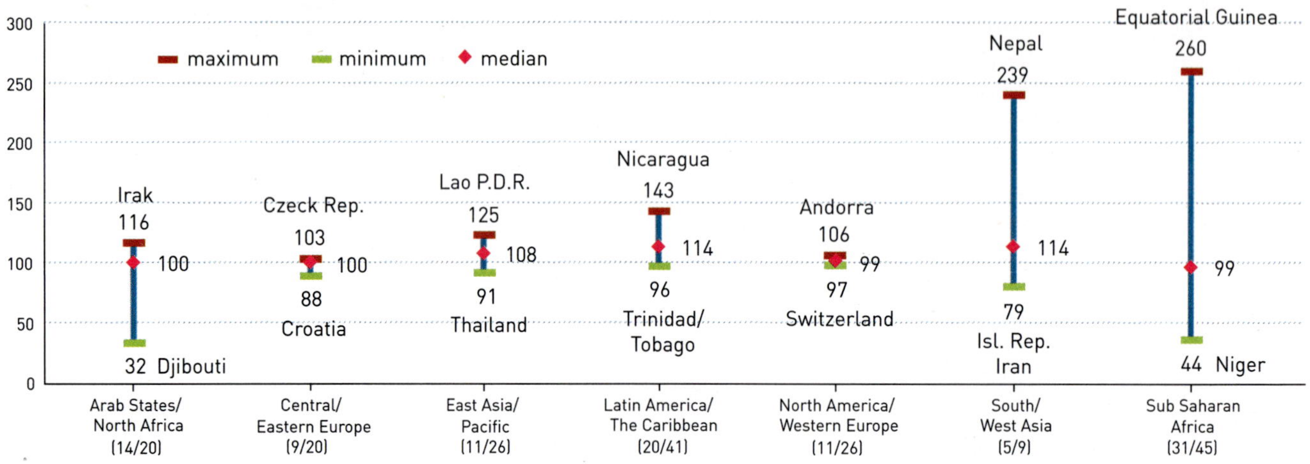

Source: Annex, Table 5.

estimates – on average by 14%. Clearly this questions the reality of enrolment statistics in a good number of countries, where many pupils may register at the beginning of the year, but do not subsequently attend on a regular basis.

Access to primary schooling

It will be clear from the foregoing that the characteristics of children who enter the first grade of primary schooling have a very important influence upon the size of the system and upon its age characteristics. They also provide one important influence upon the differences that emerge between GERs and NERs. If children enrol in school late, and do not drop out of school, they will emerge as being over-age in the higher grades.

In a good number of countries, many pupils may register at the beginning of the year but not subsequently attend on a regular basis.

Figure 2.7 shows the gross intake rate (GIR) for 101 countries in 1999. The GIR expresses the total number of children entering school in a certain year regardless of their age, as a proportion of the total number of children in the country who are at the official entry age. The GIR can be higher than 100% if older children enter (in theory, but predominantly not in practice, this is also true of younger children). In 1999, some 59 countries had a GIR greater than 100%.

A comparison between Figure 2.7, which shows the variation in GIR, and Figure 2.4, which shows the variation in GER, points to two distinct phenomena. In Central and Eastern Europe and in North America and Western Europe, GIRs fall within a narrow band. This means that schools in these regions take in children at the proper age. However, the variation in GERs shown in Figure 2.4 for these regions is wider, because grade repetition and drops out are influencing enrolment to different degrees in the various countries. Latin America and the Caribbean also have greater variation in GERs than in GIRs, while the reverse is the case for South and West Asia.

The net intake rate (NIR) adjusts for the age of children entering school. The NIR is defined as the number of children entering school at the official entry age as a proportion of the total number of children of that age in the population. Figure 2.8 shows that countries where a high proportion of entrants are admitted at the official school entry age also tend to have high NERs, and vice versa. The ways in which over-age entry and repetition interact to produce large gaps between the GER and the NER are indicated in Table 2.7. Of those countries with more than a thirty-point GER-NER gap, most had a high intake of children who were outside the official entrance age (GIR-NIR gap), a large proportion of over-age children enrolled, and a relatively high proportion of repeaters. Clearly, if one of the criteria for UPE is that of achieving NERs at or close to 100, only those countries with high net intake rates will be able to achieve the goal.

Figure 2.8. The relationship between net intake rates and net enrolment ratios (1999)

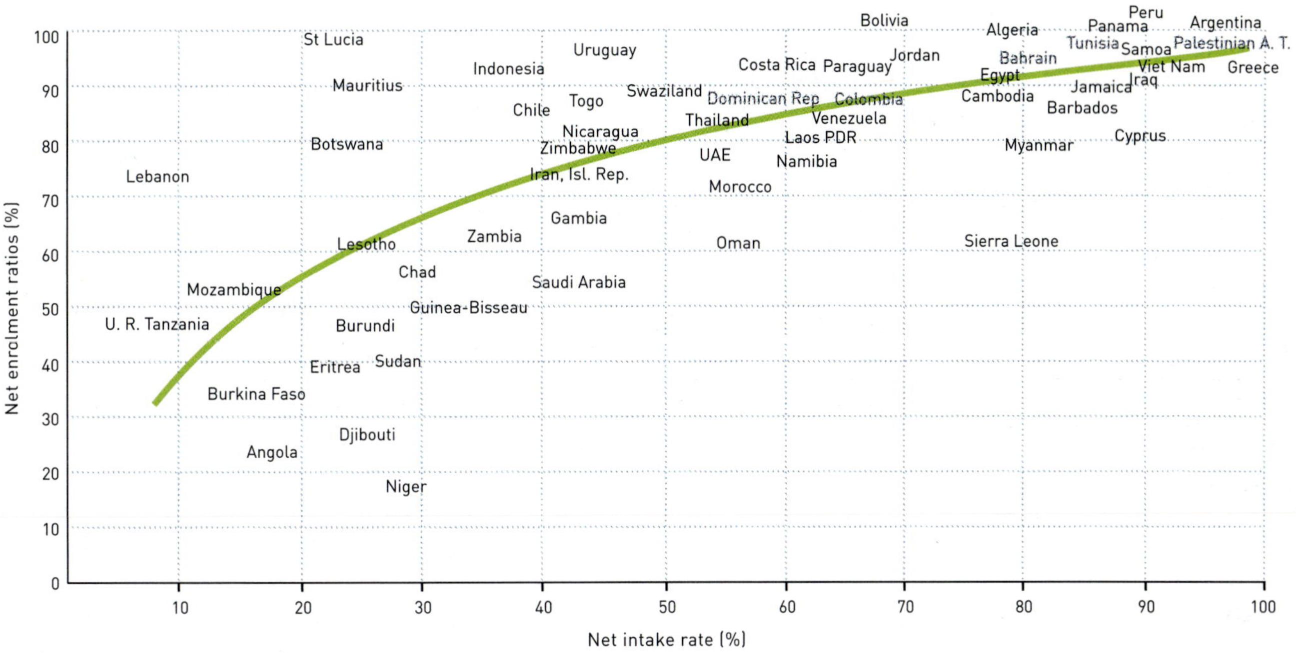

Source: Annex, Tables 5 and 6.

Survival in school

The school survival rate is the proportion of a cohort of pupils enrolling in Grade 1 who stay in school up to a given higher grade. The survival rate to Grade 5 is particularly relevant, since the successful completion of at least four years of primary education is considered an important threshold. The indicator measures early drop-out. It tells us about children who leave school before reaching Grade 5, and who may subsequently relapse into illiteracy.

Figure 2.9 shows the relationship between GIR and survival to Grade 5. It indicates that those countries with very high rates of over-age enrolment in Grade 1 tend to have high rates of drop-out before Grade 5. Some countries, such as Uganda and Equatorial Guinea, having survival rates of 45% and 16%, respectively, illustrate how education systems with large numbers of over-age entrants have difficulty in keeping children enrolled. Problematic in a different way are systems which have high survival rates, but which – like those in Djibouti, Burkina Faso and Niger – serve only a small proportion of the age group. There is, however, a strong concentration of countries with GIRs between 80% and 120% having survival rates of between 75 and 100%. Again, it seems that the age of entry is influential in helping to secure some of the important intended outcomes from the schooling process.

Table 2.7.
Primary education: GER-NER gap, GIR-NIR gap, over-age pupils and grade repetition, selected countries (1999/2000)

Country	Gap GER-NER (percentage point)	Gap GIR-NIR (percentage point)	Percentage of over-age students in primary (%)	Total percentage of repeaters in primary (%)
Angola	37	47	53.3	29.4
Brazil	69	–	39.2	23.0
Comoros	29	–	33.3	26.0
Eritrea	21	47	32.0	19.4
Guinea-Bissau	29	78	31.8	24.0
Lao PDR	34	65	29.1	19.7
Lesotho	45	71	42.9	20.4
Madagascar	35	–	33.2	27.9
Mozambique	35	84	38.9	23.7
Rwanda	25	–	18.3	29.1
Swaziland	32	68	24.4	17.1

Source: Annex, Tables 5 and 6.

Goal 2. Universal primary education

Figure 2.9. GIR and survival rate to Grade 5, selected countries (1999/2000)

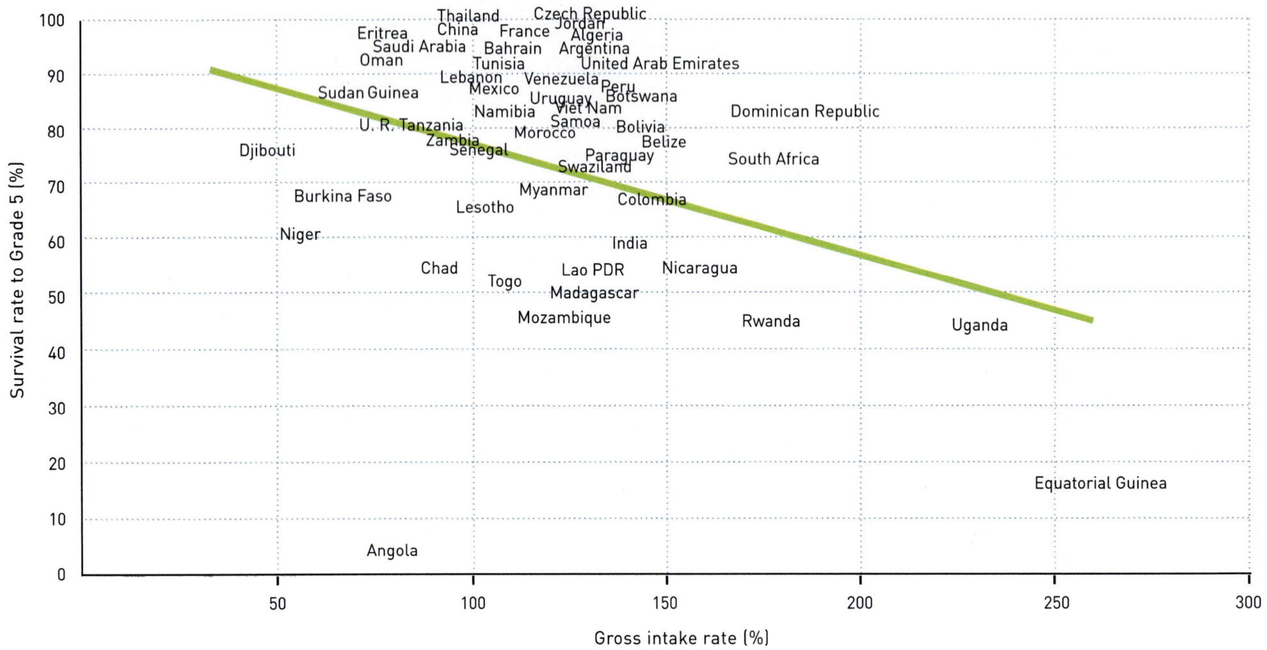

Source: Annex, Tables 5 and 10.

Out-of-school children

The number of out-of-school children, as well as the trend towards it, depend both on the level of the NER and the size of the school-age population. Thus, regions like South and West Asia and sub-Saharan Africa still see their numbers of out-school-children growing, even where NERs are rising, because of the continued impact of high rates of population growth. There were 115.4 million children out of school worldwide in 1999 (a slight increase on the previous year's estimate of 113.6 million).[3] An estimated 56% of them, in both years, were girls; 94% of these children were living in developing countries. Least developed countries alone accounted for over one-third of this share, while 47% of out-of-school children were concentrated in the 9 high population (E-9) countries. Figure 2.10 shows their distribution across regions, which indicates that just over one-third of the children were in sub-Saharan Africa, with a further third being in South and West Asia.

3. These estimates are based on school enrolments as reported by countries, together with the United Nations 2000 revised population estimates for the relevant national age groups.

Figure 2.10. Out-of-school children: distribution by region (1999/2000)

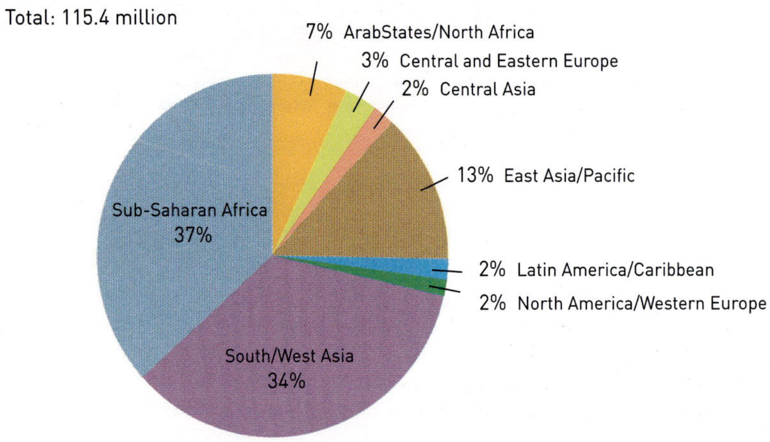

Source: Annex, Table 13.

Compulsory schooling

As the wording of the goal suggests, it seems straightforward to expect that a government that genuinely expected to provide sufficient school places for all, and intended that these should be fully utilized, would introduce legislation to make schooling compulsory for the relevant age group. In fact, such legislation is widespread, typically stipulating both the minimum duration of school attendance in years and the ages during which it should occur. Table 2.8 shows that, during recent decades its incidence has substantially increased. In 1965, 80% of all independent

Table 2.8. Extension of compulsory schooling, by region (1965–2000). Percentage of countries in each region that have passed compulsory schooling legislation (number of cases in parentheses).

Region	Year				
	1965	1975	1985	1995	2000
Latin America/Caribbean	100.0 (22)	100.0 (26)	100.0 (33)	97.1 (34)	100.0 (34)
Sub-Saharan Africa	54.2 (24)	65.1 (43)	73.3 (45)	89.6 (48)	89.6 (48)
Asia/Pacific	71.4 (21)	66.7 (27)	72.7 (33)	76.5 (34)	79.4 (34)
Middle East/North Africa	71.4 (14)	77.8 (18)	73.7 (19)	80.0 (20)	85.0 (20)
Central Europe/former USSR	100.0 (5)	100.0 (5)	100.0 (5)	100.0 (21)	92.3 (26)
North America/Western Europe	100.0 (21)	100.0 (23)	100.0 (23)	100.0 (25)	100.0 (27)
World totals	80.4 (107)	80.3 (142)	83.5 (158)	91.1 (182)	91.0 (189)

Notes: Only countries that were politically independent at the dates shown have been included. Final column includes data for 2000, or for the most recent year available. Composition of world regions is different from that in other tables and figures in this *Report*.

Source: Benavot (2002).

Table 2.9. Mean duration of compulsory schooling in years, by region (1965–2000)

Region	Year				
	1965	1975	1985	1995	2000
Latin America/Caribbean	6.09 (22)	7.38 (26)	7.94 (33)	8.30 (33)	8.35 (34)
Sub-Saharan Africa	7.85 (13)	7.50 (28)	7.33 (33)	7.21 (43)	7.16 (43)
Asia/Pacific	6.93 (15)	7.44 (18)	7.17 (24)	7.88 (26)	7.70 (27)
Middle East/North Africa	6.70 (10)	7.29 (14)	7.57 (14)	7.75 (16)	8.00 (17)
Central Europe/former USSR	8.40 (5)	8.40 (5)	8.80 (5)	9.00 (21)	9.08 (24)
North America/Western Europe	8.29 (21)	9.04 (23)	8.74 (23)	9.44 (25)	9.71 (24)
World totals	7.24 (86)	7.79 (114)	7.78 (132)	8.16 (164)	8.21 (169)
Standard deviation	1.28	1.61	1.71	1.93	1.85

Notes: Only countries that were politically independent at the dates shown have been included. Final column includes data for 2000, or for the most recent year available. Composition of world regions is different from that in other tables and figures in this *Report*.

Source: Benavot (2002).

countries had passed such legislation; by the year 2000, even though the number of independent nation-states had increased sharply, fully 91% of all independent countries had passed compulsory school legislation. One region – Central Europe and the former Soviet Union – fell back from complete coverage in the last few years of the century. This was a reflection of the number of new states that were established during the 1990s, and the volume of new legislation that this required. The region is expected to move back towards 100% over the next few years.

Goal 2. Universal primary education

Table 2.10. Comparison of enrolment rates in countries with and without compulsory schooling legislation

Region	Number of countries with compulsory schooling	Number of countries without compulsory schooling	Average duration of compulsory schooling (years)	Average primary NER in countries with compulsory schooling	Average primary NER in countries withou compulsory schooling
Arab States/North Africa (20)	14	6	7.71	81.03	75.00
Central Asia (9)	7	2	9.86	90.36	87.80
Central/Eastern Europe (19)	18	1	8.50	88.40	93.12
East Asia/Pacific (25)	21	4	7.81	91.94	98.99
Latin America/Caribbean (40)	40	0	8.43	92.83	
North America/Western Europe (26)	25	1	9.80	97.51	
South/West Asia (9)	6	3	6.67	79.16	76.34
Sub-Saharan Africa (45)	40	5	7.21	60.50	72.92
Total	171	22	8.22	84.32	79.19

Source: Calculations based on Annex, Table 6; EFA 2000 Assessment (CD-ROM); and UIS (2001).

The impressive expansion of compulsory schooling in sub-Saharan Africa is especially noteworthy.

Elsewhere, progress was steady and strong. In Latin America and the Caribbean, and in Western Europe and North America, all countries have had compulsory schooling laws in effect throughout the period under consideration, including newly independent ones. In the Middle East and North African region, and in Asia, the percentage of countries with such legislation increased from 70% to 80%–85%. Especially noteworthy is the impressive expansion of compulsory schooling in sub-Saharan Africa. While in 1965 just over half (54%) of the 24 independent countries had laws compelling school attendance, by 2000 some 90% of the 48 independent countries had instituted such legislation.

Among those countries having passed compulsory attendance laws considerable national differences are apparent in the number of years children are required to attend school. In some countries this is as few as 4 or 5 years, while in others the legislation mandates as many as 12 to 13 years. Table 2.9 shows that the global mean duration of compulsory education has, over the past 35 years, increased by 1 year: from 7.2 in 1965 (n = 86) to 8.2 in 2000 (n = 169). Increases are reflected in all world regions except sub-Saharan Africa. The latter may reflect the changing composition of countries from which the regional mean was calculated, or an inability of some countries in this region to mobilize the necessary financial resources.

It will be noted that both the incidence of legislation and the length of attendance required are less in Africa and Asia than in Latin America. Moreover, its average duration in the industrialized countries, which all have compulsory schooling, is almost 10 years – much higher than elsewhere. The question arises therefore as to whether there is any relationship between the non-enactment of legislation and the incidence of low enrolment ratios caused by low demand for schooling. If so, the act of legislating could be expected to bring a pay-off in terms of increased enrolments.

This question raises complicated issues about the interaction of the supply of and the demand for school places, which will not be fully explored here. However, what can be said is that a surprisingly large number of countries with low net enrolments have laws making primary-school attendance compulsory. For example, there are 31 countries with primary NERs less than 75% having such legislation.[4] Twenty-one of these countries are in sub-Saharan Africa, and they include 6 countries where fewer than 40% of children in the primary-school age group were enrolled in 1999. Furthermore, Table 2.10 reveals the rather surprising fact that in sub-Saharan Africa and the East Asia/Pacific region, the 9 countries without compulsory schooling legislation have significantly higher net enrolments than those with it. Clearly, a number of countries have found that legislation was not decisive in achieving universal participation in schooling. Where large numbers of children do not attend school because there are insufficient places available, it is difficult for the law to insist that attendance should be compulsory for those who do not seek it. The evidence from industrialized countries suggests that compulsory schooling legislation does promote continued high levels of enrolment, once sufficient numbers of places are genuinely available. Where the coverage of school systems remains partial, such regulations may often be of little help.

4. The thirty-one countries are as follows: Angola, Benin, Burkina Faso, Burundi, Central African Republic, Chad, Comoros, Côte d'Ivoire, Croatia, Djibouti, Eritrea, Ethiopia, , Guinea, Guinea-Bissau, Haiti, India, Islamic Republic of Iran, Kiribati, Kuwait, Lesotho, Madagascar, Mali, Morocco, Mozambique, Niger, Nigeria, Senegal, Sudan, United Republic of Tanzania, Yugoslavia and Zambia.

Box 2.2. Measuring and monitoring UPE

The wording of some of the Dakar Framework goals can be interpreted in different ways, raising questions as to how progress should be monitored, and what should count as successful achievement. It is perhaps most marked in the case of the goal for universal primary schooling (UPE): 'Ensuring that by 2015 all children, particularly girls, children in difficult circumstances and those belonging to ethnic minorities, have access to and complete, free and compulsory primary educatio of good quality'. The wording of the Millennium Development Goal for primary schooling is consistent with this, but more direct: 'Ensure that, by 2015, children everywhere, boys and girls alike, will be able to complete a full course of primary schooling.'

The most demanding interpretation of both of these formulations – implied by their reference to completion – would be that, by 2015, all children in the relevant age-cohort should be enrolled in, and complete, the final year of primary schooling. This would require universal Grade 1 enrolment in 2009 (for six-year cycles), with neither drop-out nor repetition occurring as the cohort progressed up the primary system. It would also seem to require that in each subsequent year from 2009, the same enrolment parameters should apply. Otherwise, it would not be possible for all children to be enrolled in the year 2015 and to be able (in due course) to complete primary school. By 2015, under these circumstances, net (age-adjusted) completion rates, GERs and NERs would each be 100.

A second interpretation would be that all eligible children should be enrolled by 2015, and that they should all eventually complete – but not necessarily within the six-year period implied by the duration of the primary cycle. This would require NERs of 100, but it would allow the possibility of repetition (though not of drop-out). Thus, GERs could be greater than 100, and completion rates need not be 100, in net (age-specific) terms by 2015: it might, for example, take children seven or eight years to complete a six-year cycle, if repetition rates were high. On the other hand, if repetition rates were fairly evenly spread throughout the system, gross completion rates could be expected to be close to 100.

A third, and less demanding, interpretation of the goal would be that primary GERs should be at least 100 by 2015. This criterion has frequently been used in the past to indicate the attainment of UPE. It would indicate that a school system had the capacity to enrol all eligible children, and to allow them to complete, even if some school places were occupied by older children who had either enrolled late, or who were repeating a year. Thus, the capacity of the primary-school system to secure NERs and completion rates of 100% would be in place, but specific values for these parameters would not be not implied.

Finally, the least challenging interpretation would be that, from the year 2015, all children should be able to join and (subsequently) complete primary schooling. This would require universal Grade 1 enrolment in that year, with negligible drop out thereafter. It would carry no implications for the levels of either the GER or the NER in 2015. It would, however, mean that in each successive year the cohort with universal enrolment would increase by one grade. Six years later, the NER would be 100 and it would be equal to the completion rate at that time.

The indicators selected by the international community for the purpose of monitoring progress towards the Millennium Development Goal for primary education are the achievement of NERs of 99%, and Grade 4 completion rates of 99% by 2015. These conditions are closest to the second interpretation of the meaning of the goal, although they are not exactly consistent with it. The modal length of primary systems is six years, not four. So universal completion of four years by 2015 imposes the first or second interpretation of the goal (depending upon whether completion is measured in gross or net terms) for the first four years, but not for the last two. However, the requirement that NERs for the whole of primary schooling should be 99% in that year effectively means that completion rates in the final two years would also need to be at similar levels. It has recently been agreed that the UNESCO Institute for Statistics (UIS) will amend the existing indicator on cohort survival to Grade 5. Instead of expressing the number of children entering Grade 5 as a proportion of those who started four years earlier, they will be shown as a percentage of the population of Grade 5 age. It is intended to use this as a proxy indicator for gross completion rates. Thus, the indicators selected for the purpose of monitoring the goal effectively (albeit not quite literally) adopt the second interpretation of its meaning.

It is clear that no single statistic is adequate for monitoring the achievement of UPE. The completion rate focuses upon only one year of the primary school system. Thus variations in enrolment over the previous five years (of a six-year system) are ignored, and the statistic would fail to give warnings of enrolment decline in times of adversity. Equally, where expansion had been very rapid, both the capacity of the system and current enrolments in grades below the final year would be much higher than the completion rate could suggest. In such circumstances, therefore, the completion rate would provide a very conservative estimate of the coverage of the system. Although in one sense, time series information on the completion rate would provide a picture of the development of the primary system, it would do so with a five-year lag. Thus, it needs to be supplemented both by the GER, which indicates the capacity of the system and includes those pupils who are outside the primary school age-group, and by the NER, which is the only statistic which indicates the extent to which the target population is actually enrolled in school.

There are three other conditions associated with this goal, in its Dakar formulation. These are that primary schooling should be free, compulsory and of good quality. Interpretations of the last two of these are discussed under Goals 2 and 6. The interpretation of 'free' schooling is less straightforward than it might at first seem. Schooling costs often include fees, other direct costs, such as books and uniforms, and indirect costs, such as the loss of child-labour time, which are particularly important for many poorer families. Thus, while fees are only part of the schooling costs faced by households, removing them is usually taken to be a sufficient condition to make schooling free.

Goal 3

Learning needs of all young people and adults

. . . ensuring that the learning needs of all young people and adults are met through equitable access to appropriate learning and life skills programmes . . .

The monitoring of this Dakar goal presents major conceptual and methodological challenges which this Report is in no position to address. Nevertheless, it is important to identify some of the issues to which future reports will need to respond.

Learning should not be restricted to school age, nor to any other age.

By its very name education for all is not age specific. The World Education Forum was very clear that all young people and adults must be given the opportunity to gain the knowledge and develop the values, attitudes and skills that will enable them to develop their capacities to work, to participate fully in their societies, to take control of their own lives and to continue learning. This is Dakar's interpretation of learning needs and life skills and defines a vast territory of educational activity.

It is a domain that is rarely encompassed by a single policy or managed by a unitary authority. It has numerous providers, many of them small and locally based, and it is characterized by a mix of formal, non-formal and informal provision. The new communication technologies are proving instrumental in expanding learning and opportunities and diversifying ways of learning. It is an area too where there is a rich conceptual debate, including on the meaning of life skills and in the search for meaningful indicators. And there is major overlap with the Dakar goal on literacy.

This Report takes a very preliminary look at the diversity of provision, and at the problems of measurement. It makes no attempt to resolve the conceptual challenges beyond noting that the meaning of life skills is open to a variety of interpretations (see for example Box 2.3). One approach is to define skills that should enable to people to live safer, healthier, and more economically and socially productive lives. The next section offers some examples in this regard.

In many industrialized countries, life skills refer to more generic cross cutting skills, such as communication, problem-solving and team working. Whereas these skills may be seen as universal, their elucidation and application in different societies is not as straightforward as some models may suggest.

A more powerful approach may be to build on the human capabilities argument set out in the previous chapter, conceiving the development of life skills (be they technical or generic) as the means of gaining access to resources that enhance the choices and freedoms which lead to a better life. In turn this implies a focus on people to whom learning opportunities are frequently denied: particularly the growing number of young people and adolescents for whom life chances are restricted by the lack or limited nature of their school education.

Box 2.3. Visions of life skills, South and North

The Ministry of Education in Zimbabwe issued the following statement regarding the education for skills with which people should be provided: '[This is] an education which is holistic in nature, which equips an individual to live constructively and wholesomely in the community. The survival kit includes the development of interpersonal and social skills such as those related to health and civic education; functional literacy and numeracy skills; basic physical, technical, scientific, information and communication skills that will enable an individual to manage his/her social and physical environment and also co-exist in a global and competitive world.'

The Organisation for Economic Co-operation and Development (OECD) developed the following definition of 'generic skills' under the DeSeCo project:

- acting autonomously and reflectively (self-motivation, creativity and problem solving);
- using tools interactively (communication, physical dexterity and IT); and
- joining and functioning in socially heterogeneous groups.

Learning programmes for youth and adults: a world of diversity

Learning programmes for young people and adults are characterized by diversity in the nature of their provision, organization and governance, by their terminology, and by their approach to monitoring and evaluation (Oxenham, 2000). Effective programmes are likely to respond to both the intellectual curiosity of the learner and to the demand for a better life.

A comparative study of Senegal, Guinea, Uganda and Kenya, found that adult education programmes are more likely to succeed if the acquisition of literacy is an integral part of activities designed to improve livelihoods, rather than the other way around (Oxenham et al, 2001) (see also Box 2.3). The participants, all poor, and most of them women from rural areas, needed clear, concrete and immediate reasons to enrol and persevere. Learning about credit and small-business management was more successful when access to credit was part of the programme. The lasting acquisition of newly won skills was demonstrated by the confidence of the participants and their willingness to take new initiatives to develop their cooperatives and their own livelihoods. In projects run by Pact in Nepal training for more sustainable livelihoods is also combined with social and political activity (World Bank, 2002e).

In a similar way, some programmes for the integration of immigrants into OECD countries, aim at bringing people quickly to the minimum literacy level required for a certain job, instead of beginning with extensive language training. Through frequent contacts with others and the immersion in work and society, the further acquisition of language skills is facilitated.

Better health is a significant trigger for learning. UNICEF has found that programmes designed to prevent and combat HIV/AIDS will be more effective when they are embedded in broad based programmes of personal and social development encompassing generic skills such as communication, negotiation and other interpersonal skills; information gathering, critical thinking and decision making; self-awareness, coping, assertiveness and handling emotions.

Box 2.4. Farmers' schools in Asia

The Farmers' Schools were first established in the 1980s as a way to disseminate good agricultural practices and correct use of pesticides. However, since that time their role has expanded to cover almost all of the domains covered by the term 'life skills' and, in some places, they have now been designated Farmer Life Schools.

It was discovered that many of the life problems encountered by rural families could be explained in agricultural terms. For example, the use of pesticides to eliminate plant disease became a model for discussion of health awareness and the elimination of human diseases such as HIV/AIDS. The need for labour on the farm could be related to family planning issues.

In Cambodia, such an approach has been formalized as Human Eco-System Analysis (HESA). With this tool, farmers assess threats to their livelihood, and sort related influences into six categories: economy, health, education, social relations, culture and environment.

World Education, an NGO which has sponsored many of these farmers' schools, has linked their curriculum to generic skills including literacy, oral fluency, self-confidence, leadership, critical thinking and problem-solving. Thus the Farmers' schools demonstrate a clear strategy linking generic skills with a more operational application, all in a life skills framework.

Source: C. Shrestha, Sustainable and Transferable Learning Abilities: Building Experience from the Field, paper presented at Policy Dialogue on Adult and Lifelong Learning, Hyderabad, April 2002.

Care for the environment is another avenue into learning, and here synergy with local knowledge is an important theme. Many communities possess valuable expertise and mechanisms for coping with local environments. Similarly, learners experience the changing environment first-hand, and build on knowledge that has accumulated for centuries.

In Fiji, an association of traditional healers, nurses, environmentalists and community educators are promoting the use of safe and effective traditional medicines and the conservation of medicinal plants. The goal is to preserve important knowledge and assets and develop new ways to generate income from old traditions. A Philippines project to develop sustainable fishing techniques is an example of how scientific knowledge merges with local know-how.

Gender and family life are themes where the learning of practical and generic skills goes hand in hand with the acquisition of literacy. A project in India (see Box 2.5) illustrates how raising women's awareness of their disadvantages, educating them about their rights and helping them shape their own lives provides skills as

Life skills are the skills that people need to build a sustainable livelihood and to fully participate in society.

Learning about small-business management is more likely to succeed if learners actually have access to credit.

Box 2.5. Empowering women in India

Mahila Samakhya aims to help poor rural women become more active in shaping their lives and environments. The programme is run by women activists and mechanics, and it combines literacy teaching with practical skills and training such as water pump maintenance.

Training women as hand-pump mechanics has helped them build confidence, increase mobility and break stereotypes. It has also increased their capacity to deal with authorities, demand basic necessities and information from authorities, and lobby government for change.

The programme has a community participation approach that starts with women's experiences in their own communities and then gradually introduces them to basic education and literacy teaching. Thus instead of offering education and literacy as a cure for their problems, it begins by affirming women's existing knowledge and skills; initiating a process of critical questioning and analysing with regard to issues such as survival or discrimination within the family; and promoting a new and active role for women in their communities.

The project is guided by the understanding that adult learning is not just about transferring skills, but also enabling women to use their skills and negotiate more effectively.

Monitoring non-formal education has not been well developed.

practical as operating and maintaining water pumps, with a generic skill such as interacting with authorities, and with literacy.

There is an important secondary function to programmes responding to the learning needs of women. Their level of education is a critical influence on the learning achievement of their children (see Goal 6 of this chapter, below, on education quality). Furthermore, programmes that address mothers and young children simultaneously have a positive impact on both, as is shown in Box 2.6 (below) and also under Goal 1, on early childhood care and education.

Programmes on family life typically address family planning, child care, adolescence, disease (especially HIV/AIDS) and death. Not unlike the Indian case, a programme in The Gambia targeting both women and girls sets these family issues in the wider context of the ability to make decisions independently (UNDP, 1998).

Box 2.6. Mother-child training programme in Turkey

This programme, which is being implemented in fifty provinces in Turkey, is intended to create a more literate family environment for both parents and children. Training for the mother consists in two different activities: one is designed to foster cognitive development of the child, and the other gives support to the mother in fostering the socio-emotional and personality development of the child.

The programme has been extended to include reproductive and family health, aiming not only to upgrade the pre-literacy and numeracy skills of the child, but also to increase the literacy of the mother. These goals, in turn, support a more functionally literate society.

The programme shows that there are effective ways besides formal education to shape individuals' level of literacy and life skills. It also raises questions about the role of literacy environments and family literacy.

Monitoring progress

The monitoring of the Dakar goal at the national and international levels presents a a major set of methodological problems which are akin to those described in the section on early childhood care and education. First, there is a need to get a better of understanding of exactly what is taking place in terms of programme provision. A comprehensive picture of who is doing what in support of the learning needs of adults and young people requires well developed typologies that include coverage of programme theme, objectives, duration, frequency and delivery methods.

Second, data on participation is particularly important if access and opportunity is to be assessed. Household surveys are a potentially important source of information in this regard. Third, and much more challenging, are assessments of how learning outcomes impact on people's lives and livelihoods. This requires an understanding of the knowledge that has been gained and the skills that have been learned. A study from Cambodia provides an interesting insight (see Box 2.7).

The Cambodian survey is one example of international interest in the direct assessment of literacies and human competencies. In the industrialized world there are a growing number of international surveys designed to draw cross national comparisons, for example, the International Adult Literacy Study (IALS, data collection 1994-1998) and the Adult Literacy and Life Skills Study (ALLs, data collection in progress). A number of Latin American and Caribbean countries participate in ALLs. The first study addresses (functional) literacy among adults, whereas the latter also examines some generic skills. The IALS has proved to be very relevant for policy purposes. Since background characteristics of respondents are known, it is possible to trace the impact on competence of factors such as gender, social-economic status, work experience and, not least, education and training.

The application of skills assessments in countries where large numbers of people are working in the subsistence and informal sectors is a challenging task, given the highly contextual nature of most programmes. Cooperation on a regional basis, between countries with sufficient similarities, is one way forward.

There is also a need to monitor the provision and management of programmes. With the support of UNESCO, and in collaboration with partner agencies, a number of pilot projects aimed at developing a non-formal education management information system (NFE-MIS) and the corresponding monitoring methodology are taking place in some countries (see Box 2.8, below). The strategy is to spread the basic NFE-MIS system to a growing number of countries and local districts, while building operational capacities and gathering feedback to improve methodology and tools. The UNESCO Institute for Statistics (UIS) will gather core NFE data from countries and disseminate NFE indicators for use in policy-making at both international and national levels.

Box 2.7. Assessing life skills in Cambodia

In 1999, the Government of Cambodia, UNDP and UNESCO Cambodia conducted a comprehensive literacy assessment of the country's population aged 15 and over. One element of the assessment evaluated life skills, using three levels of achievement:

- basic: the ability to tell the time from a clock face;
- medium: the ability to understand the address on a letter, a bus schedule with prices, a television schedule, arrangements for a meeting, and identifying their province on a map;
- self-learning: awareness of how to prevent HIV/AIDS, and filling in a civil request for marriage.

Overall, 37% of respondents were classified as literate. Of those who were literate, 11% attained basic level, 64% reached medium level and 25% were considered self-learners. Separate results were not reported for the life skills element of the tests.

Source: Kingdom of Cambodia (2000).

Box 2.8. NFE-MIS Pilot Projects

UNESCO and local partners in Cambodia, India and the United Republic of Tanzania are developing and field-testing a set of international methodologies and software for establishing a Non-Formal Education Management Information System (NFE-MIS). The system is designed to collect, process and analyse data, produce and disseminate directories, and manage information at the national and sub-national levels. The system will be used to develop policies, plan and coordinate programmes, and inform and motivate potential learners.

A basic NFE-MIS technical package is being field-tested in the pilot countries. It includes: a general manual on NFE monitoring concepts and methodologies; a handbook for developing district-level monitoring; and a database demonstration software for use in advocacy and training, which can be eventually adapted and used in processing NFE monitoring information.

This innovative programme balances two related demands: the need for a practical, internationally applicable approach to NFE monitoring that generates meaningful and reliable information for use at the international and national levels; and the need for flexible methods and tools for managing information on NFE activities at the local level. By involving governmental agencies and NGOs in building a common NFE monitoring system and database, this programme helps build partnerships and civil society involvement that are the key principles of the Dakar Framework for Action.

Programmes that address mothers and young children have a great positive impact on both.

The International Adult Literacy Study has proved to be very relevant for policy purposes.

Goal 4

Adult literacy

. . . achieving a 50% improvement in levels of adult literacy by 2015, especially for women, and equitable access to basic and continuing education for all adults . . .

Both the World Conference on Education for All in Jomtien in 1990, and the World Education Forum in Dakar in 2000 firmly underlined the importance of literacy for the development of the individual and society. To be able to read, write and calculate has been acknowledged as a human right. These basic skills are needed to build and sustain a livelihood and to participate in society, and are a stimulus for further learning. However, in the decade following Jomtien, international attention and action focused heavily on getting children into school, and there is evidence that there has been a similar trend since Dakar. At a conceptual level over the same period, there has been considerable progress in the understanding of and attitudes towards adult literacy. Literacy is now understood as a structural phenomenon and a social practice (see Box 2.9). Similarly, where literacy used to be viewed only as an individual skill, it is now seen in the context of broader educational and socio-economic interventions. The task can be seen less as eradicating illiteracy and more as creating increasingly literate environments and learning societies.

To be able to read, write and calculate has been acknowledged as a human right.

Box 2.9. Literacy and 'literacies'

Literacy is no longer seen as a singular concept, but rather as plural 'literacies'. These literacies differ according to purpose, context, use, script, language and institutional framework. As individuals we all use multiple literacies – for example, for work, for personal matters, in different languages, and so on. Within any community there will be a range of literacies – understanding what these are and how they are structured is important for negotiating whether and how literacy might be acquired.

Literacy, as communication involving the use of text, is now understood as one of a number of communication practices which societies adopt to meet their needs. As such, it functions alongside orality, mass media, electronic forms of communication and so on. Both in the industrialized and developing world literacy as a communication practice also serves the purposes of livelihood; in fact literacy is almost always embedded in other purposes – social, cultural, economic, religious. Thus literacy is frequently acquired alongside other life skills, as was noted in the previous section, and enhances them.

Situations vary greatly in the proportion of the use of literacy as a communication practice from one context to another – which is why the old hard and fast distinction between literate and illiterate is breaking down. The focus today is on the spectrum of literacy practices in the broader context of communication, on how far people participate in such practices and on what opportunities they do and do not obtain through such participation. This understanding affects the use of terms. In this section 'illiterate' and 'illiteracy' are used in the technical sense of a low use of literacy, often expressed as a percentage of the population not able to interact adequately with their wider society through literacy. These terms say nothing about communities' or individuals' ability to engage in other kinds of communication practice, nor do they imply the pejorative connotations with which those terms have often been associated in the past.

This section will look primarily at the development of adult literacy at the macro-level: global, regional and national. It will address literacy as an outcome of learning, rather than focus on literacy programmes. Some examples of current literacy work will be given, and the section will end with a consideration of literacy assessment.

Development of adult literacy

Although there are no widely available data on literacy that are more recent than 1999/2000, it is possible for a fair number of indicators to assess progress from 1990–1999. This permits rudimentary projections – not forecasts – of the situation in 2015, under the artificial assumption that policies and contexts do not change. Differences in the ways in which countries gather data on literacy mean that caution is needed in the interpretation of the indicators.

The macro-level assessment will show principally that promoting literacy against the backdrop of population growth is like rowing against the current: possible but challenging. In all regions, the literate population is projected to grow in relative terms, even though the pace of growth is not yet sufficient to meet the goal of a 50% improvement by 2015. In the least developed countries, absolute numbers of illiterates might even rise, which urges immediate action. However, a significant number of countries demonstrates that meeting this Dakar goal is feasible.

Global level

Figure 2.11 charts the development of the proportion of literate men and women (over age 15) of the adult world population. It shows that progress is undeniable but slow.

Past decades saw steady growth of the literate share of the adult world population from roughly 70% in 1980, 75% in 1990 to 80% in 2000. But a closer look tells us that there is a slightly slackening pace, so acceleration is needed to meet the Dakar goal. Halving the illiteracy problem at global level by 2015 would mean a further growth to 90%, where the actual result would be 85%, assuming that policies and contexts do not change.

In absolute numbers, the gains appear even more modest. In 1980 the world numbered approximately 870 million illiterates. This number grew to 880 million in 1990, as the reduction of illiteracy did not keep pace with population growth. Around 2000 it was down to roughly 860 million. At this pace, the figure for 2015 would be around 800 million, which would be far above the target.

Figure 2.11. Adult literacy rates worldwide (1980–2015)

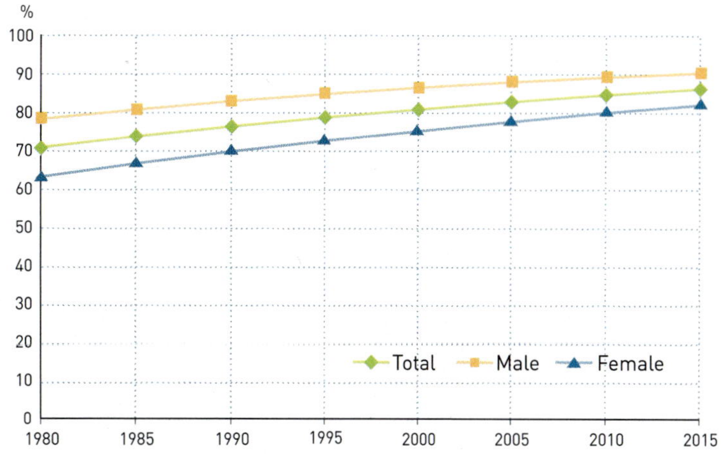

Source: Annex, Table 2.

Figure 2.12. Literates and illiterates worldwide by gender (1980–2015)

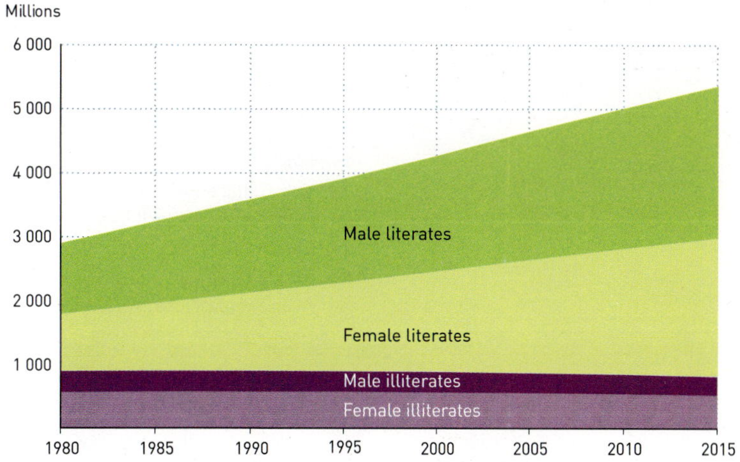

Source: Annex, Table 2.

Figure 2.12 illustrates how population growth (broken down by sex) and the promotion of literacy interact.

Finally, figures 2.11 and 2.12 both show that illiteracy at world level is much more widespread among women than among men. In 2000, close to two-thirds of all illiterates were female, and the gap is closing exasperatingly slowly.

In the least developed countries, the absolute numbers of illiterates may in fact rise.

Regional level

In Figure 2.13 the world trend in the adult literacy rate is broken down for developing regions and shows that sub-Saharan Africa, the Arab States and North Africa, and South and West Asia have come a long way, starting from an adult literacy rate of 40% in 1980. These regions made immense progress, all the more so in light their high rate of population growth.

Figure 2.13. Adult literacy rates by region (1980–2015)

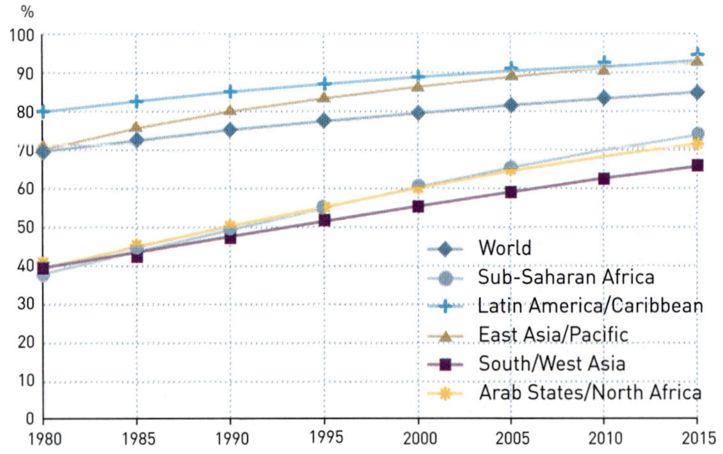

Source: Annex, Table 2.

Figure 2.14. Gender gap in literacy rates, by region (2000 and 2015)

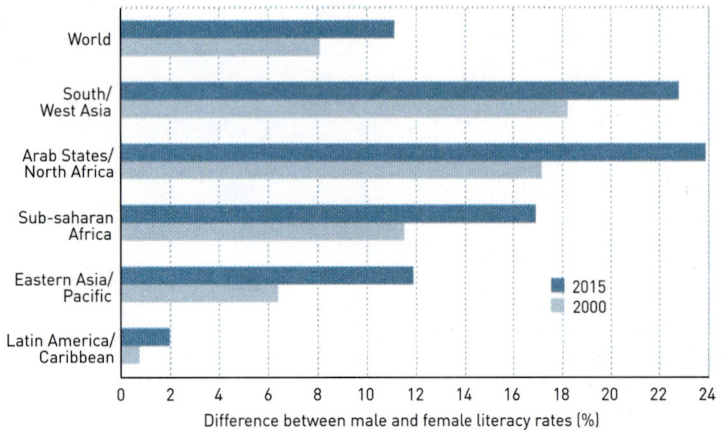

Source: Annex, Table 2.

In absolute numbers, illiteracy increased in all three regions during the 1990s. And together they accounted for 65% of the world's illiterate population in 1990. That figure increased to 70% in 2000, and it will move towards 80% in 2015. Adult literacy rates in these regions now hardly reach 60%. An acceleration will be needed to avoid a level of only 65%–75% literacy in 2015 – the target is 75%–80%.

The curves for East Asia and Pacific, and especially for Latin America and the Caribbean, reveal another problem: the closer countries approach the goal of universal literacy, the more difficult it is to reach and educate the final groups of marginalized people. And the resources needed to include them in literacy programmes tend to rise accordingly. So in these regions, too, we observe a slackening pace.

Within all regions, literacy rates are higher among men than among women, although the gap is tending to close in all cases, as is shown in Figure 2.14.

Literacy by development status

Figure 2.15 once again shows the world trend in adult literacy broken down for development status in this case: least developed, developing, and developed countries and countries in transition. The data are also separated by gender.

Not surprisingly, the problems appear to be most pronounced in the least developed countries, where there is also high population growth. It is here in particular that the relative numbers of illiterates are decreasing, and even at a fairly steep rate, but this decrease is combined with increasing absolute numbers of illiterates. The absolute numbers of illiterates in least developed countries rose from 165 million in 1990 to 185 million in 2000, and are heading towards a level of 207 million in 2015, if trends in adult literacy acquisition and population growth do not change.

Figure 2.15. Total and female adult literacy rates by development level of country (1980–2015)

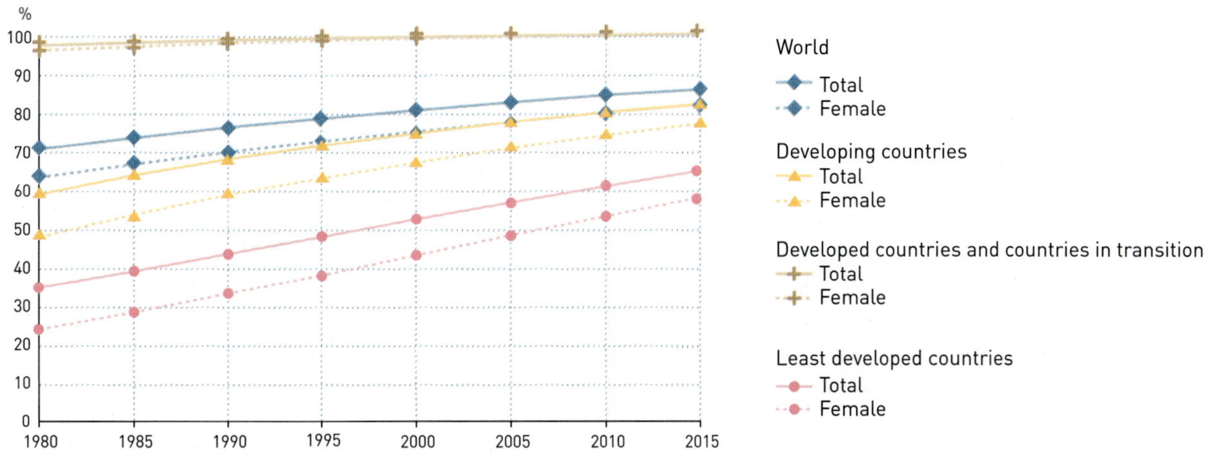

Source: Annex, Table 2

Box 2.10. Regional collaboration moves literacy forward in Caribbean

Cuba's Literacy and Mass Communication Media project received an honourable mention for the King Sejong Literacy Prize – a UNESCO literacy award – in 2002 for cooperation with neighbouring country Haiti. The project was the joint collaboration of Cuba's Ministries of Education, and Youth and Sports, together with Haiti's Ministry of National Education. At Haiti's request Cuba signed an agreement to help tackle the huge literacy challenge in that country. Only an estimated 8% of girls and boys complete secondary school. This South-South collaboration builds on Cuba's own experience in increasing literacy rates.

Radio – a way to reach many

Radio has been used in many countries to bring literacy and development information to places where more formal face-to-face teaching methods are not possible. However, this project did not take use of radio for granted. Surveys were carried out to find out where the radios were located, who listened to them and at what times, as well as establishing literacy and schooling rates. The key issue of power supply was also investigated. Owing to the lack of full national coverage, some areas of Haiti could not use a radio-based approach – here monitors used cassette recordings.

Once the feasibility was established, a small pilot project was carried out to test the materials. These consisted principally of a learners' guide and a monitors' handbook, using Creole, the local language.

Training – the key

In order to be sustainable, literacy work requires a heavy investment in training. Trainers of trainers must be available, as well as adequately trained administrators and managerial staff.

Cuba's main contribution was organizing training in all aspects of the project. This included not only monitors in communes and neighbourhoods, but also survey researchers, coordinators and supervisors. Radio was used in the training of monitors, along with written materials.

Outputs

The goals of this project were nothing less than raising the literacy rate across the whole country, with a clear emphasis on bringing literacy provision to where the people are, whatever their socio-cultural or physical environment. Since the start of the collaborative project in 2000, the outputs by December 2001 were as follows:

- 6,250 people reached with literacy provision;
- publication of 300,000 copies the of learners' guide *Apraun*;
- publication of 10,000 copies of the monitors' guide *Anseye*;
- recording of 52 radio classes for reading, writing and numeracy;
- training of more than 10,000 monitors;
- design of 62 radio classes for teaching French as a second language; and
- preparation of learners' and monitors' handbooks for French as a second language.

Source: UNESCO (2002*d*).

The closer countries approach the goal of universal literacy, the more difficult it is to reach and educate the final groups of marginalized people.

Everywhere, literacy rates are higher among men than among women.

National level

A systematic overview of the state of affairs and developments in individual countries requires some form of categorization. In Table 2.11, countries are grouped in terms of their adult literacy rate: <50%, 50-70%, 70-90% and 90-100%. The groupings show the results for both 2000 and for the projected score in 2015, assuming once again that policy and context does not change for the country.

It can be observed from Table 2.11 that a substantial proportion of the countries is projected to 'graduate' to a higher category in the efforts towards the Dakar deadline. This concerns the countries in the cells headed by Benin, Algeria and Albania. The situation is worrisome for the Comoros, Egypt, Eritrea, India and Liberia, and in particular for Burkina Faso, Mali, Mauritania and Niger. In these countries, no major improvement is expected while literacy levels are at present below 70% or even 50%. In fact, the phenomenon of rising absolute numbers of illiterates is likely to persist in these – and some other – countries.

According to the Dakar goal, countries should achieve a 50% improvement in levels of adult literacy by 2015. In other words, the literacy gap that existed in 2000 should be halved. The final section of this chapter examines which countries have been making the progress needed to do so in the past decade.

Table 2.11. Progress towards literacy, by country/territory (2000–2015)

LITERACY RATE IN 2000	LITERACY RATE IN 2015			
	<50%	50–70%	70–90%	>=90%
<50%	Burkina Faso, Mali, Mauritania, Niger	Benin, Burundi, Central African Republic, Chad, Côte D'ivoire, Ethiopia, Gambia, Guinea-Bissau, Haiti, Morocco, Mozambique, Nepal, Pakistan, Senegal, Yemen		
50–70%		Comoros, Egypt, Eritrea, India, Liberia	Algeria, Cambodia, Democratic Rep. of the Congo, Djibouti, Guatemala, Lao People's Dem. Republic, Madagascar, Malawi, Nicaragua, Nigeria, Papua New Guinea, Rwanda, Sudan, Togo, Uganda	
70–90%			Botswana, Cameroon, Cape Verde, Dominican Republic, El Salvador, Ghana, Honduras, Islamic Rep. of Iran, Kuwait, Lesotho, Libyan Arab Jamahiriya, Mauritius, Myanmar, Oman, Qatar, Saudi Arabia, Swaziland, Syrian Arab Republic, Tunisia, United Arab Emirates, United Republic of Tanzania, Zambia	Albania, Bahrain, Bolivia, Brazil, China, Congo, Equatorial Guinea, Indonesia, Jamaica, Jordan, Kenya, Lebanon, Malaysia, Namibia, Peru, Reunion, South Africa, Turkey, Zimbabwe
>=90%				Argentina, Armenia, Bahamas, Barbados, Belarus, Belize, Brunei Darussalam, Bulgaria, Chile, Colombia, Costa Rica, Cuba, Cyprus, Ecuador, Estonia, Fiji, Guyana, Kazakhstan, Latvia, Lithuania, Macau, Maldives, Malta, Martinique, Mexico, Mongolia, Panama, Paraguay, Philippines, Puerto Rico, Republic of Korea, Republic of Moldova, Slovenia, Sri Lanka, Tajikistan, Thailand, Trinidad and Tobago, Ukraine, Uruguay, Uzbekistan, Venezuela, Viet Nam

Source: Annex, Table 2.

Figure 2.16. Adult illiterate population (2000 and 2015)

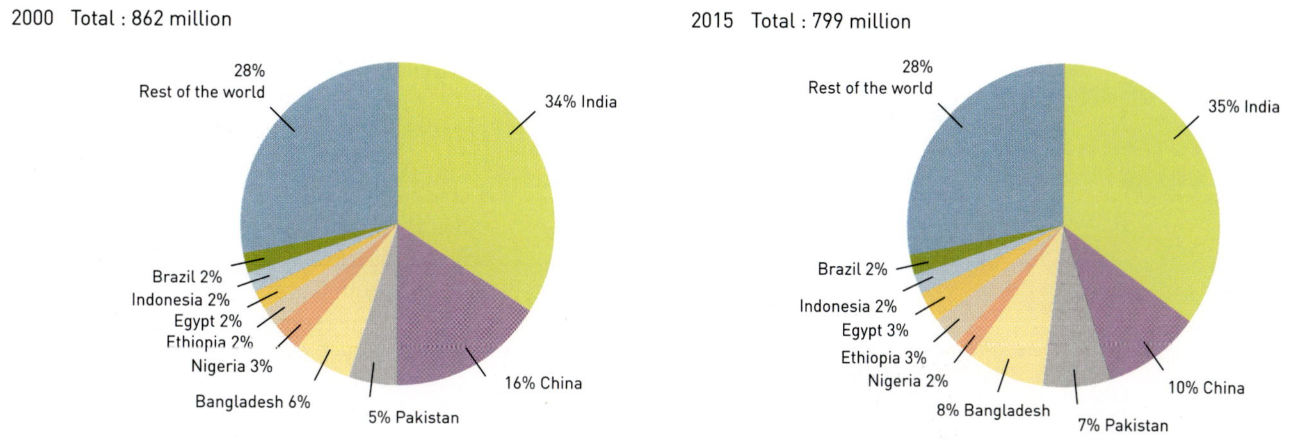

Source: Annex, Table 2.

Another indication of country problems is to determine which countries have the largest absolute numbers of illiterates (although this is of course mediated by the size of the population). Figure 2.16 shows the shares in the world illiterate population of the nine countries with the highest numbers of illiterates. All but one (Ethiopia) belong to the E-9 group of high population countries.

It can be noted that the expected changes in the percentages between 2000 and 2015 are limited, except for China. Of the nine countries, China and Indonesia are projected to meet the Dakar goal and approach universal literacy; the latter also holds for Brazil.

Box 2.11. Literacy for women and girls in Pakistan

With a female literacy rate of only 28%, Pakistan faces a huge challenge in providing education for all. The Bunyad Literacy Community Council (BLCC), an NGO based in Lahore, has been adapted by the Pakistan Literacy Commission for the promotion of non-formal education in Pakistan. In 2002 BLCC won one of the two King Sejong Literacy Prizes (given by UNESCO) in recognition for its pioneering efforts and innovative approaches. Over the nine years since BLCC started, in 1993, it has developed 2,808 non-formal education centres in 1,886 villages. Partnership is one of its fundamental principles, putting decision-making power into the hands of local village and family committees.

The programme focuses especially on girls and young women who are excluded from education. Many of them work in the carpet and football-stitching industries as child labour. The programme has had significant success in bringing children, boys as well as girls, out of child labour into education.

BLCC works with the community from the outset, well before the start of any teaching. Staff work with existing NGOs, undertake consciousness-raising and motivation work and stimulate interest at village level in starting a non-formal education centre. Only after a local woman has been selected as teacher, local village and family committees have been formed and thirty children have been selected does the teaching begin. Materials are prepared which focus on health and hygiene, reproductive health issues and environmental issues.

BLCC's three general objectives are:

- to utilize non-formal channels to increase women's participation and reduce drop-out rates at the primary level;
- to provide social protection to working children and rehabilitate them; and
- to be the springboard for social development activities in the rural communities.

A programme of such size requires careful management. At village level, the teacher and committees are responsible, but at higher levels a system of centres and groups of centres has been devised. A total of 78,776 learners have participated in the programme, about 75% of them girls and women.

Source: UNESCO (2002*i*).

Figure 2.17. Adult and youth literacy rates (1980–2015)

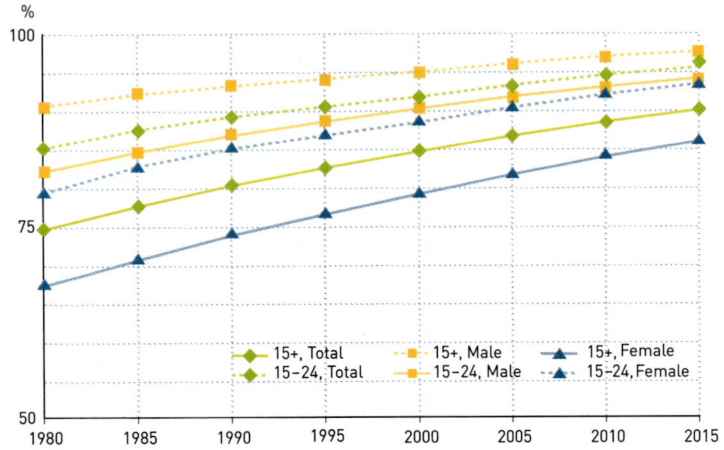

Source: Annex, Table 3.

Youth literacy

One of the most powerful drivers for the eradication of illiteracy is, of course, the expansion of primary education. As Figure 2.17 illustrates, youth literacy rates are well above adult literacy rates, and it is just a matter of time before the two finally converge.

One of the most powerful drivers for the eradication of illiteracy is the expansion of primary education.

In the light of this figure there are, however, three important reasons not to assume that adult literacy will simply fade away as schooling expands.

- First, as the figure shows, even youth literacy is not projected to become universal by 2015, because there is no guarantee that the goal of universal primary education will be achieved in the upcoming years. Too many children miss out on school, and too many who do attend school do not become literate. Furthermore, the gender gap for youth literacy will close only slowly. In fact, there were 140 million illiterate young people in the world in 2000 (86 million of these were female), whereas this figure only drops to 107 million by 2015 (67 million female) at the current rate of growth in access to basic education.
- Second, the gains in the quality of education for which the Dakar goal is aiming will need to be fully realized if the numbers of adult illiterates are not to be swollen by school-leavers and school drop-outs, for whom the system has failed to provide an adequate level of literacy.
- Third, if policies do not address youth and adult literacy simultaneously, many school children will grow up in a home situation where illiteracy is still the norm. Policies will be ineffective – and indeed cynical – if they do not address adult literacy. Even if huge strides are made in child and youth literacy, it would not be right to consider the present adult illiterates as a problem that will simply fade away in time.

Literacy assessment

There is broad agreement that improving the assessment of literacy – both indicators and methods – is a priority in the implementation of the Dakar goals, and in the forthcoming United Nations Literacy Decade (2003–2012), which will be an integral part of EFA efforts. As the Dakar Framework directs, assessment should track not only the increase in numbers and percentage of literate people, but also the graduation of literate people into higher levels and additional practices of literacy (e.g. languages, life skills, health and nutrition, technologies, science, etc.).

With the spread of interest in conducting literacy surveys that actually test and measure the literacy level of the population, UNESCO, in collaboration with the World Bank and other partner agencies and expert networks, is currently exploring how best to support such literacy measurement initiatives. At the national and international levels, this implies the identification of typical literacy scales, practices and criteria, and ways and means to apply them in national contexts and local environments so that the resulting literacy indicators can be meaningfully understood by stakeholders ranging from policy makers to the general public. Today most countries use a 'functional definition' of literacy in national assessments – one that captures the ability of people to use literacy to carry out everyday tasks. However, these common tasks vary according to local context, culture and requirements, which may not make the results strictly comparable between one place and another.

It has been proposed that work to improve literacy assessment should draw upon the latest advances in measurement theories, practices

Box 2.12. Improving literacy assessment in developing countries

The Literacy Assessment Practices (LAP) project examined how literacy rates are determined in countries with the world's largest illiterate populations (India, China, Nigeria and Mexico).

The goal was to come up with a set of assessment guidelines to help developing countries improve data collection and analysis in practical, cost-effective ways to help decision-makers both in the field and at the national level. Currently, they lack essential information about whether or not participants in literacy and non-formal education programmes are learning what is taught, and about how well they are learning to apply new knowledge and skills to their life goals and to solving problems of daily life.

Most countries, industrialized and developing, have been accustomed to relying on surrogate or proxy measures for literacy, such as the assumption that any person with five or eight or more years of schooling can be considered literate. This practice has possibly given inaccurate and misleading results.

The LAP approach holds that learning achievement is a critical and often missing component in measuring, monitoring and developing literacy initiatives. LAP suggests that by combining actual learning achievement data with other forms of data, much stronger and more credible statements can be made about 'what works' in literacy learning, instruction and impact.

The most typical method of gathering national data on literacy is through the national census. Other methods include household surveys, post-census sample enumeration, special literacy surveys and programme evaluation. LAP focuses on household surveys because they are cost-effective while providing a number of advantages. They gather adequate information, make direct measures of literacy skills, permit greater focus on local culture and context, are accessible to the non-expert user, and provide baseline data on learner skills and the learner's community.

The LAP study described three major components to survey design: assessment instruments for literacy skills; a separate instrument to measure attitudes, values and life skills; and collection of background variables that allow analysis of, for example, literacy skills by gender, as well as information about literacy determinants.

A major lesson learned from the LAP country case studies is that literacy assessment practices have a great deal in common at the national level in each country. However, the LAP study also found that there are few, if any, commonplace assessment practices that would stand up today to expert scrutiny.

Source: University of Pennsylvania, International Literacy Institute, 2002.

and experiences, such as those of the IALS, and should at the same time take full account of diverse cultural and linguistic contexts in making literacy assessments meaningful and cost-effective for implementation in developing countries. Projects such as the Literacy Assessment Practices project (see Box 2.12) suggest that, while the individual indicators used in national literacy assessments (see Box 2.13) may be culturally sensitive, it might be possible to find a common framework for indicators, or at least a common international approach to literacy assessment.

Box 2.13. The first national literacy survey in the Lao People's Democratic Republic

When the EFA 2000 Assessment showed that the Lao People's Democratic Republic had weak information and insufficient data on literacy, the government set out to conduct its first nation-wide literacy survey. Lao National Literacy Survey (LNLS) developed by the Ministry of Education got underway in November 2000, with technical assistance from UNESCO and funding from UNICEF. Its objectives were to:

- attain reliable estimates of literacy rates by gender, age group, major ethnic group, region and urban-rural population;
- test and estimate functional literacy rates;
- build capacity of the education ministry through on-the-job training to set up, use, maintain and monitor databases for literacy, and conduct future surveys; and
- provide in-depth analysis of the results and findings for future literacy programmes and interventions, and for EFA national plan preparation.

The survey measured both the reported literacy rate and the tested literacy rate. A literate person was defined as one who can read and write simple sentences in Lao and perform simple arithmetic calculation.

The first part of the survey consisted of interviews with 8,100 respondents, mostly heads of households. The reported literacy rate was assessed by asking whether each household member aged 6 and above could read, write and perform simple calculations.

The second part of the survey was a functional literacy test given to randomly selected household members aged 15–59 who were reported as literate, and had a maximum education level of incomplete lower secondary. The in-depth interview conducted separate tests for reading, writing, numeracy and visual literacy. Each test had five questions, ranging from simple to difficult. If a question could not be answered, the test was ended.

The results of the survey have not yet been published. But it is already apparent that the initial design of a literacy survey, especially costing and scheduling, should be carefully considered. Also, consensus among users regarding the objectives, expected outcomes and limitations of the survey is essential at the design stage.

Source: UNESCO-Bangkok (2002).

Goal 5

Gender equality

. . . eliminating gender disparities in primary and secondary education by 2005, and achieving gender equality in education by 2015, with a focus on ensuring girls' full and equal access to and achievement in basic education of good quality . . .

Gender equality, including in education, is a condition for development.

Education is a fundamental right for all, including for girls and women. Yet, despite significant progress, they are still less educated and more likely to be illiterate than men in many countries. Poverty is, of course, a significant factor in this situation. However, this inequality must also be explained in the light of the status of women in a number of societies.

Gender equality, including in education, is a condition for development, and awareness of the gender dimension and action to promote gender equality have grown at the international level. Indeed, after decades of intense debate, the world has reached consensus that no country's development can be judged satisfactory if women do not fully participate in community life, in society and in work. This consensus was reaffirmed at several global conferences such as the Fourth World Conference on Women in Beijing (1995), the World Summit for Children (1990), and in education, the World Conference on Education for All in Jomtien (1990) and the World Education Forum in Dakar (2002). Gender equality became one of the eight United Nations Millennium Development Goals at the Millennium Summit of world heads of state in New York in 2000.

Growing awareness of the importance of gender equality is also visible at the country level. Thus, throughout the 1990s, following the Jomtien Conference, innovative programmes were launched by many governments in collaboration with international organizations and NGOs, and incentives were put in place to encourage girls' participation in education. Scholarships or free access for girls, improved school environments, and incentives to increase the share of female teachers are among the most frequent initiatives.

This section will examine progress on this Dakar goal throughout the past decade and will focus on gender parity in primary and secondary education, with a concluding discussion about the gender balance among teachers.

Box 2.14. National actions to narrow the gender gap

Pakistan. All primary schools will be co-educational, and all new primary schools are required to have ratios of 60 girls to 40 boys, and proportions of 70% women teachers to 30% men teachers. Where the number of women teachers is inadequate, age and qualification requirements for them will be relaxed. Special incentives, e.g. monetary incentives, will be used to attract and retain female teachers in rural areas and under-served regions of the country.

Benin. School fees for girls will be eliminated in public primary schools in rural areas. A campaign to sensitize parents on gender issues in education will be conducted through the media.

Mauritania. An overall strategy with an integrated socio-economic, cultural and institutional approach has been developed to improve girls' participation in education. Incentives include reducing the distance children have to travel to school, increasing the number of women teachers, establishing scholarships for girls, and increasing the number of school canteens.

Niger. The 1998 orientation law stipulates: 'The State is committed to identify and remove sociocultural barriers, pedagogical hurdles and other obstacles which hinder the full development of girls and women in the learning process.'

Sources: Benin, Mauritania and Pakistan, see EFA 2000 Assessment country reports; Niger, see Abdelkader (2001).

Enrolment in primary education

Disparities between girls and boys start with access to primary school. In fact, prior to this level of education, in early childhood care and education (ECCE) programmes, there are few gender disparities in most countries as revealed by data on ECCE programmes under Goal 1 of this chapter. Poverty is an important element that contributes to this situation. In the poorer countries that are most affected, opportunity costs increase as children get older and become a source of income and labour for their parents. In social and cultural contexts not favourable to women, girls are more affected by this phenomenon than boys, because they are most often required to help families with household and agricultural chores and to care for younger siblings, or for elderly or sick family members. Further research will be needed to elucidate questions about the links between ECCE and the primary level. Could ECCE be an important phase in which to address gender issues? Do girls who participate in ECCE have a better chance of going on to primary school?

Caution is needed when comparing GER data from 1990/91 and 1999/2000, both because of the adoption of the revised International Standard Classification of Education (ISCED 1997) by the UNESCO Institute of Statistics, and because of the use of different sets of the United Nations population estimates (1998 for 1990 indicators and 2000 for the 1999 indicators). Nevertheless, certain trends over the 1990s can be identified.

Global level

At the global level, the slowing in primary enrolment during the 1990s affected boys more than girls. Girls' GER increased by more than 3 percentage points, from 93.1% in 1990 to 96.5% in 1999, while the boys' rate fell slightly from 105.5% to 104% (Table 2.12). Improvement in girls' enrolment worldwide is due mainly to trends in developing countries where the gender parity enrolment index (GPI: ratio between girls' and boys' rates) went from 0.86 to 0.92 while the situation has hardly changed in industrialized countries, where both sexes enjoy the same learning opportunities.

All developing regions but one (Latin America and the Caribbean, where gender parity is almost a reality, GPI = 0.98) experienced improvement in girls' enrolment. Despite this trend, disparities in favour of boys are still a general rule in South and West Asia, the Arab States and sub-Saharan Africa with GPIs of 0.84, 0.88 and 0.89 respectively in 1999.

Country level

Progress towards gender parity in enrolment was widespread during the 1990s. In nearly two-thirds of the ninety-two countries for which data were available, girls improved their situation in enrolment. Disparities eased in Guinea, Benin, Chad, the Gambia and Mali – these were among the countries with the highest disparities in 1990. Among the Arab States, substantial progress was registered in Mauritania, Morocco and the Sudan.

Table 2.12. Trends in primary GER, by sex and region (1990 and 1999)*

	Girls	Boys	GPI (F/M)
World	93.1	105.5	0.88
	96.5	104.0	0.93
Industrialized countries	104.6	104.6	1.00
	101.5	102.5	0.99
Developed countries	91.8	106.6	0.86
	96.2	104.7	0.92
Countries in transition	91.6	91.8	1.00
	90.1	91.4	0.99
Arab States	70.8	89.7	0.79
	85.0	97.0	0.88
Central Asia	87.8	86.4	1.02
	88.0	89.0	0.99
Central/Eastern Europe	99.6	103.9	0.96
	92.6	96.1	0.96
East Asia/Pacific	113.5	119.9	0.95
	105.9	105.5	1.00
Latin America/Caribbean	103.1	105.4	0.98
	124.5	127.5	0.98
North America/Western Europe	105.3	105.4	1.00
	101.6	102.7	0.99
South/West Asia	78.4	104.2	0.75
	90.0	107.8	0.84
Sub-Saharan Africa	68.3	86.7	0.79
	76.3	86.0	0.89

* Shaded rows indicate GER for 1990; unshaded rows, for 1999.

Among countries of South and West Asia, Pakistan and Nepal experienced marked improvement (Figure 2.18).

Eleven countries experienced a decline in their GPI, but in some of these countries girls were in a favourable position compared with boys, and the GPI moved closer to the parity line. These countries are mostly in Latin American and the Caribbean (Colombia and Nicaragua), and in Southern Africa (Botswana, Namibia and Lesotho), or in the Pacific (Samoa).

In twenty-five countries, the GPI remained unchanged over the period. Most of them are in Latin America and the Caribbean and in Southern and Eastern Africa, where the gender parity index was already close to 1, with the exception of Ethiopia, Mozambique and Cameroon, where this indicator is still quite low (0.67, 0.75 and 0.85 respectively).

Progress towards gender parity in enrolment was widespread during the 1990s.

Goal 5. Gender equality

Figure 2.18. Trends in gender disparities in GER in primary-school education (1990–1999)

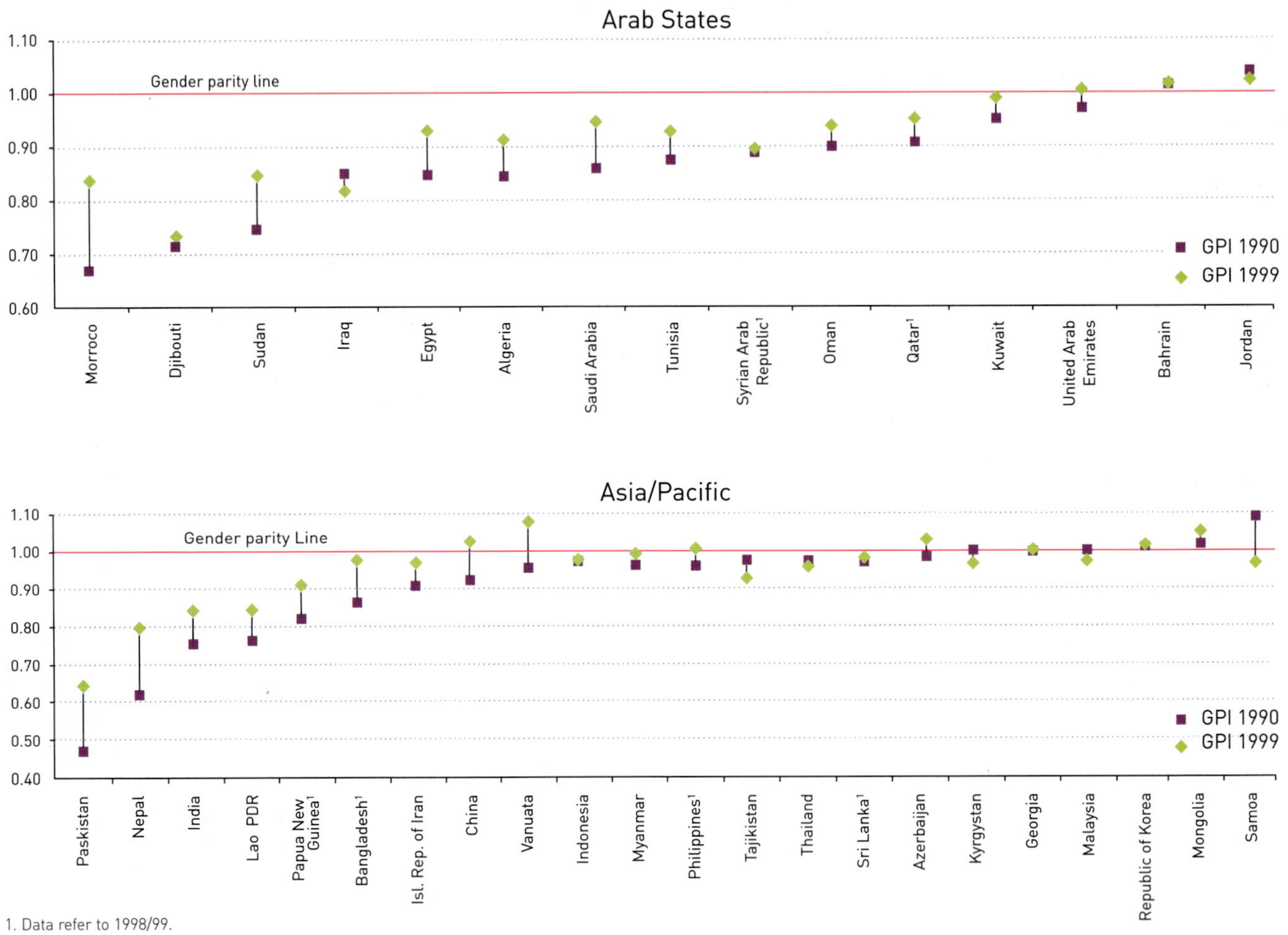

1. Data refer to 1998/99.

Source: Annex, Table 6

Some countries are not on track to achieve the 2005 gender goal.

Despite the general trends towards gender parity, in many countries there remain strong disparities in favour of boys. This is the case in some countries in Central and West Africa and, to a lesser extent, in the Arab States. It is also the case in some Asian countries, especially in South and West Asia. Disparities are particularly high in Yemen, Chad, Central African Republic, Ethiopia, Guinea-Bissau, Niger, Benin, and Pakistan, where enrolment ratios for girls are two-thirds or less than those registered for boys. In most of these countries, the absolute gender gap (male minus female GER) exceeds 30 percentage points, and is as high as 43 points in Yemen and Pakistan. Quite obviously, these countries are not on track, and will probably not achieve the Dakar goal for gender in 2005, nor even in 2015, unless highly focused strategies in favour of girls are implemented.

Net enrolment and gender parity

Disparities between girls' and boys' enrolment in school are usually lower when only children of regular school age are taken into account (net enrolment ratios). The differences are slightly more significant in sub-Saharan African countries and the Arab States than in Latin America and the Caribbean, and in Asia. Thus it appears that although more boys are enrolled overall, they also make up the majority of the over-age pupils, mostly because they repeat grades more frequently than girls (see below).

Figure 2.18. (continued)

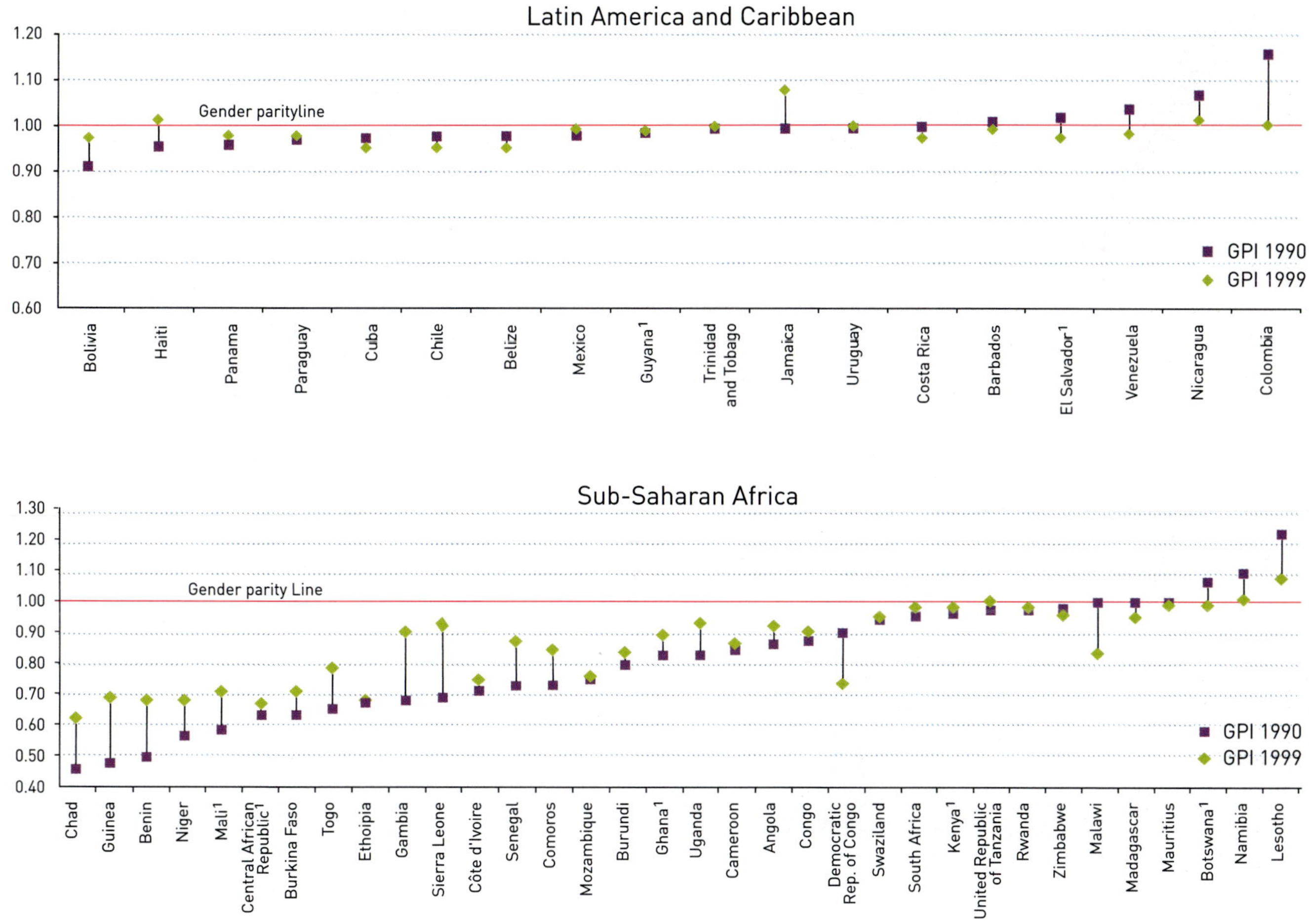

Access issues

As regards disparities in access to school between girls and boys, the latest available data for gross intake rates for school year 1999/2000, revealed three scenarios.

- *Disparities in access favour boys.* Many countries fall into this category (see Figure 2.19 below). In some countries of Central and West Africa, as well as Ethiopia and Yemen, the gross intake rate for girls was less than three-quarters of the rate for boys.
- *Gender parity.* This pattern is found in many countries of Latin America and the Caribbean, in some Arab States and in the Asia and Pacific region.
- *Disparities in access favour girls.* In the Southern and Eastern Africa region, slight disparities in favour of girls are noted in Namibia, Lesotho, Malawi, Mauritius and Zambia. In the first two countries, this is explained mostly by the traditional role of boys in minding livestock. Gender imbalances in favour of girls are also observed in some Asian, Latin American and Caribbean countries, although this is not so pronounced as in other levels of education.

Disparities between girls and boys start with access to primary school.

In the majority of countries studied, boys repeat grades more than girls.

Figure 2.19. Countries with gender parity index below 0.95: gross intake rates in primary-school education, by sex (1999/2000)

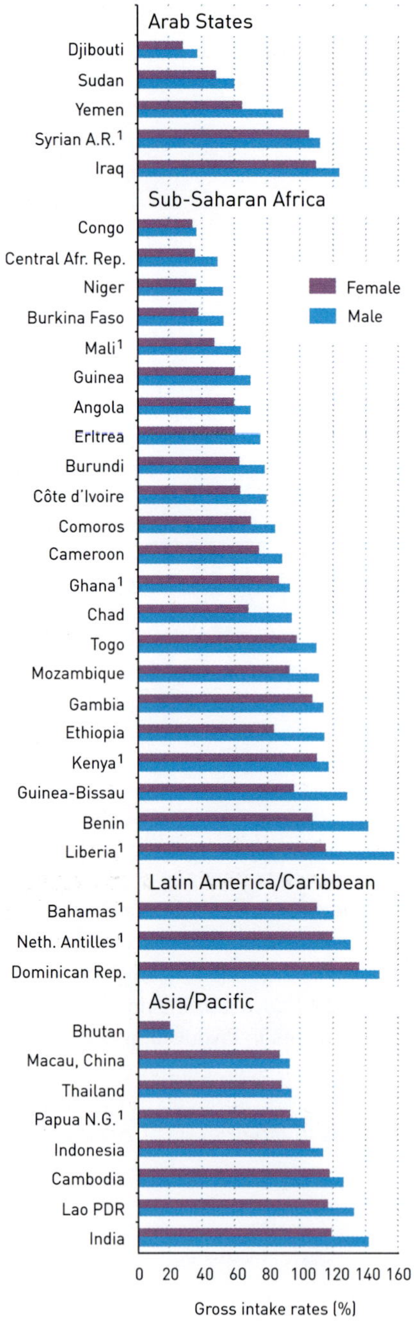

1. Data refer to 1998/99.

Source: Annex, Table 5.

Learning process

Gender disparities, where they exist, concern not only access to school, but also differential progress with the learning process, including rates of primary school completion. The extent to which gender equality is maintained throughout the school cycle may be seen as part of the internal efficiency of the school system. Internal efficiency is measured here through percentage of repeaters and the proportion of pupils that reach Grade 5.

Repetition

In the majority of countries studied, boys repeat grades more than girls (Figure 2.20). The countries where girls repeat more than boys are almost all in sub-Saharan Africa, where overall repetition levels above 15% are not uncommon. Countries with higher girls' repetition rates also tend to have the greatest disparities in favour of boys' access and enrolment. Thus, here, girls not only have less access to school, but are also faced with more difficulties in the learning process. The need for girls to attend to domestic and other chores, the low expectations of girls' performance in school on the part of parents and society, curriculum and pedagogical biases may be cited among possible factors determining this particular pattern in these countries.

Figure 2.20. Percentage of repeaters in primary-school education, by sex (1999/2000)

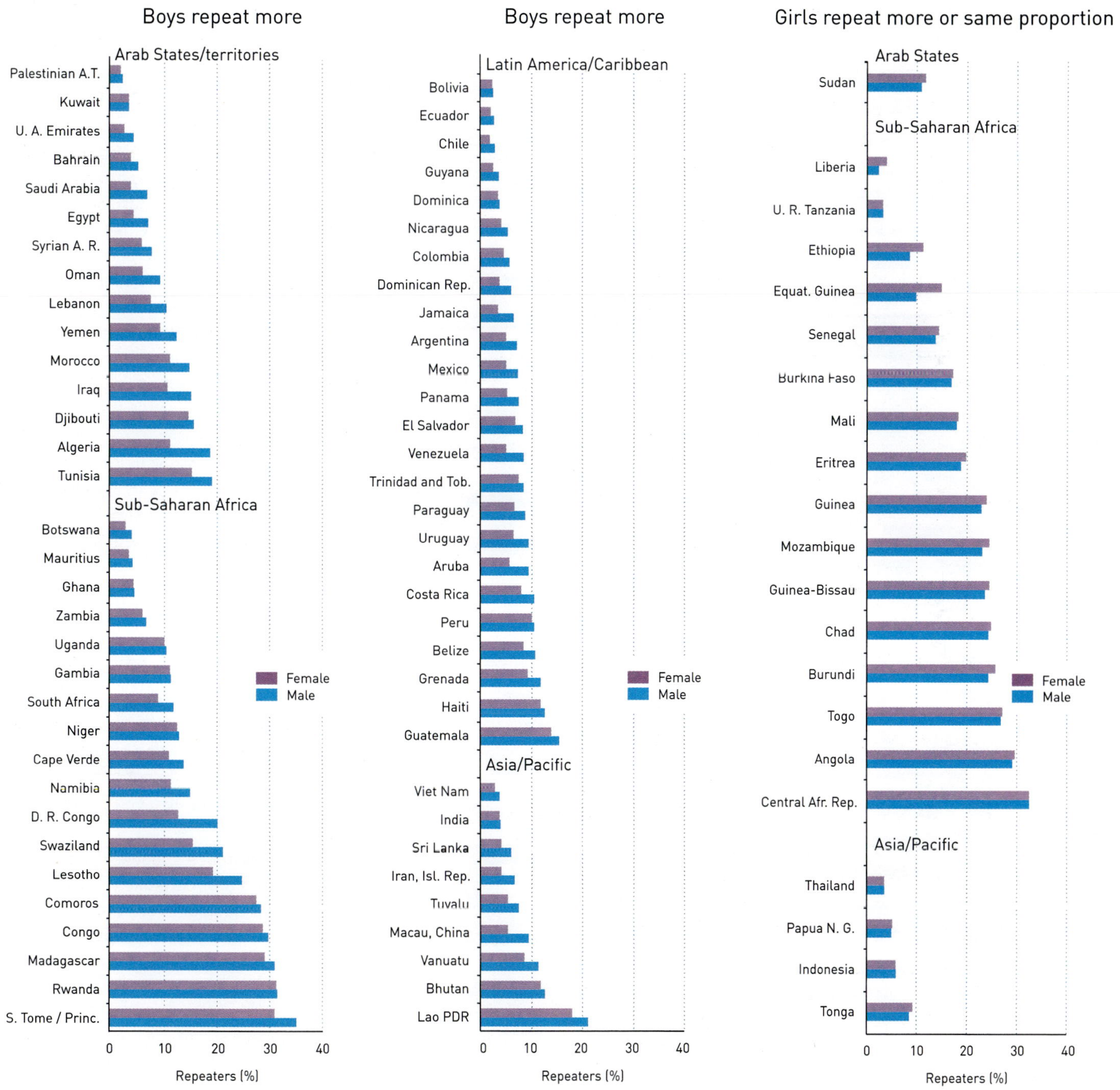

Source: Annex, Table 9.

Goal 5. Gender equality

Figure 2.21. Survival rate to Grade 5, by sex (1999/2000)

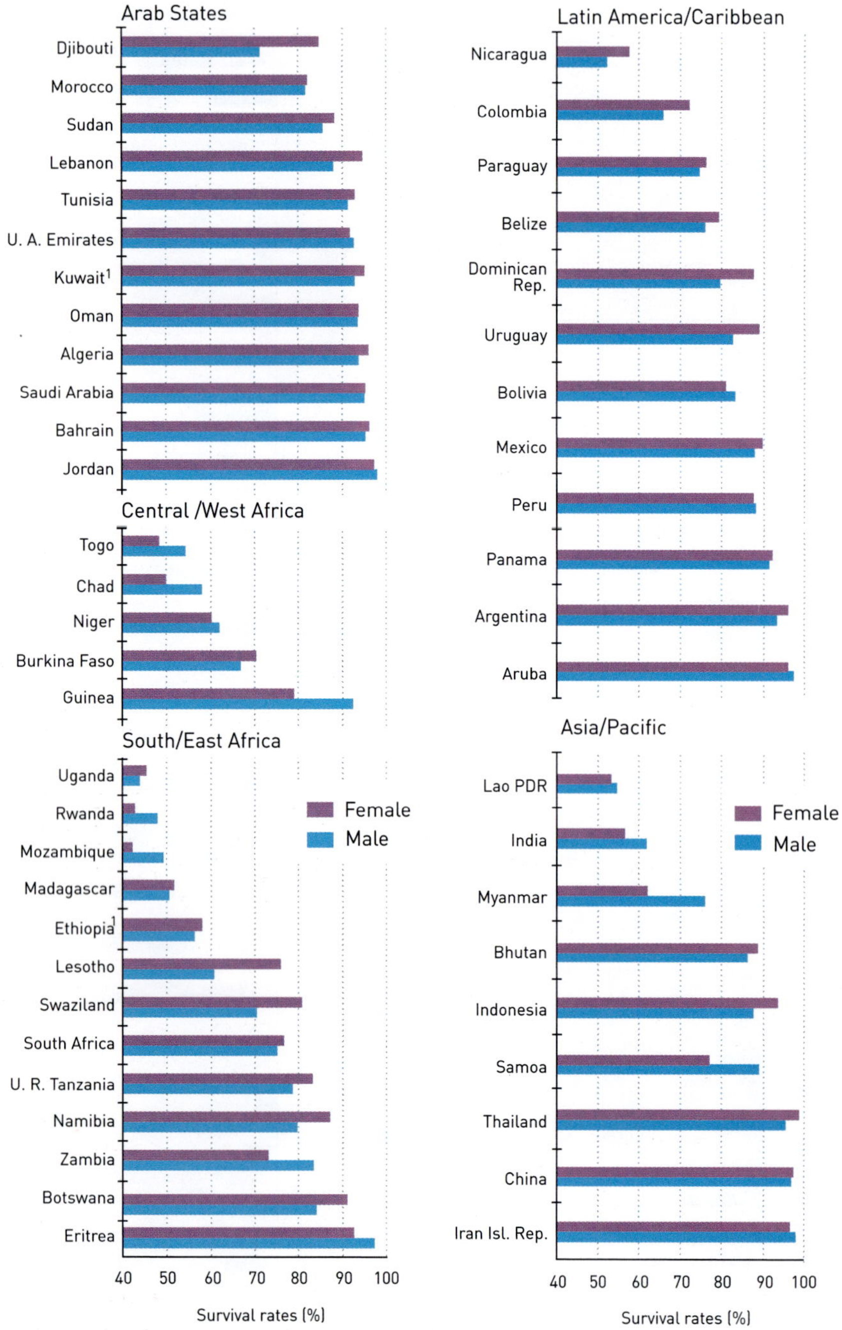

1. Data refer to survival to Grade 4 (last year of primary education).

Source: Annex, Table 10.

Survival to Grade 5

As stated in the section on universal primary education (Goal 2, above), the survival rate to Grade 5 is an indicator of early drop-out, which is caused both by external and school-related factors such as high repetition rates.

In some countries girls suffer from a double inequity: they not only have less access to schooling in comparison with boys, but they are also more likely to drop out before they reach Grade 5. On the other hand, where gender disparities are less or do not exist in terms of access, they are also less or non-existent in terms of survival to Grade 5. Evidence from countries where data were available for the school year 1999/00 indicates the following facts (see Figure 2.21):

- In a number of countries in Latin America and the Caribbean, Southern Africa, Asia and the Arab States, boys are more likely to drop out of school than girls. Most of these countries are also those where access to schooling is in favour of girls.
- There is still, however, a significant number of countries where girls drop out more than boys, particularly so in countries where overall survival rates are low and gender disparities high. In most of these countries, girls not only have low access, but they also complete school less than boys.
- The overall evidence suggests that although boys are more likely to be enrolled in school, girls are more likely to stay there until Grade 5. This means that once girls are in school they tend to progress as well as, or better than boys.

Secondary education

There has been a significant increase in participation rates at secondary level since 1990. Figure 2.22 indicates that this was beneficial to girls, with a reduction in gender disparities being evident in most of the countries shown. In general, the following two observations can be made.

- Progress towards gender parity has been substantial in the Arab States, and in some sub-Saharan African countries, particularly in Comoros, the Gambia, Kenya, Niger and Rwanda. Disparities have narrowed substantially in South Asian countries.
- In countries where the gender gap favoured girls at the beginning of the decade, there has been a move to near-parity, with the exception of Mongolia, where the disparity in favour of girls has become more pronounced. In South Africa the positive balance in favour of girls dipped below the parity line; in view of the socio-political changes of the 1990s, this is a matter for concern, and will require close attention as the school system continues to undergo reform.

Once girls are in school they tend to progress as well as, or better than boys.

Figure 2.22. Trends in gender disparities in GER in secondary education (1990–1999)

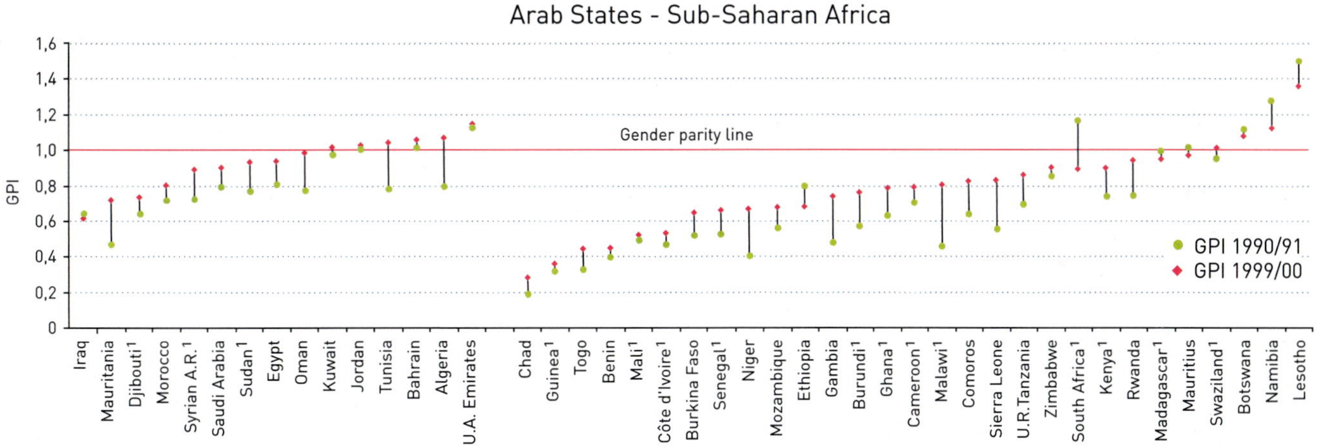

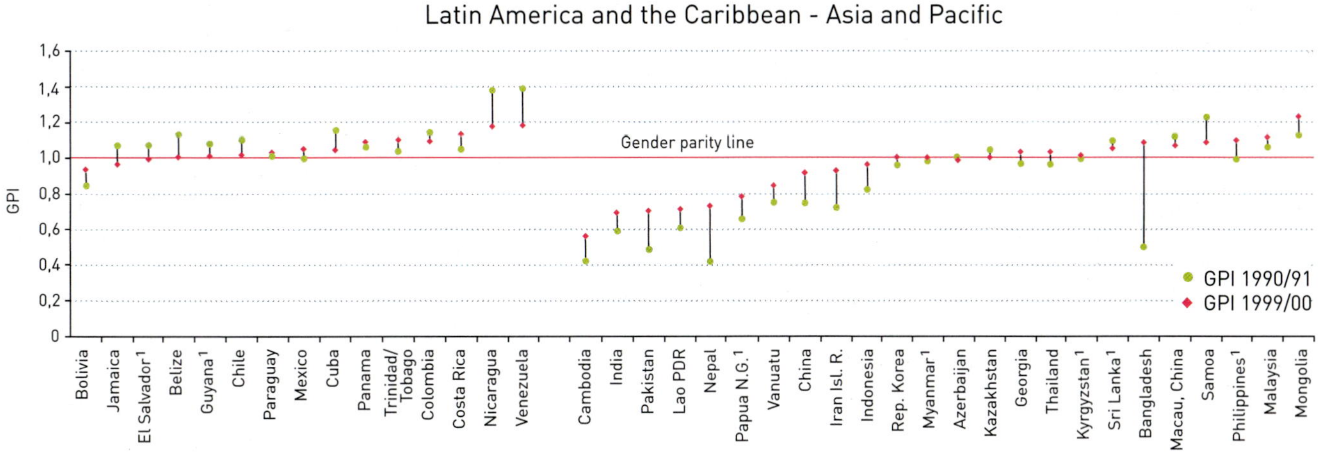

1. Data for the latest year refer to 1998/99.
Source: Annex, Table 7.

Goal 5. Gender equality

Table 2.13. GER in secondary-school education by sex, GPI and gender gap, by region (1999/2000 or 1998/99)

	Countries with gender parity or disparities in favour of girls					Countries with disparities in favour of boys									
	GPI=0.99 and over					Moderate disparities (0.99 > GPI > 0.80)					High disparities (GPI=0.80 and below)				
Region	Country	Male GER	Female GER	GPI (F/M)	Gender gap (M/F)	Country	Male GER	Female GER	GPI (F/M)	Gender gap (M/F)	Country	Male GER	Female GER	GPI (F/M)	Gender gap (M/F)
Arab States/ North Africa	U. A. Emirates	70	80	1.15	-10	Oman	68	67	0.98	1	Morocco	44	35	0.80	9
	Libyan A.J.[1]	75*	83*	1.11	-8	Sudan[1]	31	29	0.96	1	Mauritania	21	15	0.72	6
	Lebanon	75	82	1.09	-7	Egypt	86*	80*	0.94	6	Djibouti1	19	14	0.72	6
	Algeria	65	69	1.07	-5	Saudi Arabia	72	65	0.90	7	Iraq	47	29	0.62	18
	Bahrain	99	105	1.06	-6	Syrian A. R.[1]	44	39	0.89	5	Yemen[1]	69	25	0.37	43
	Palestinian A.T.	78	83	1.06	-5										
	Tunisia	73	76	1.04	-3										
	Jordan	86*	89*	1.03	-3										
	Kuwait	55	56	1.02	-1										
Central/ West Africa						Gabon[1]	58	51	0.87	8	Cameroon[1]	22*	17*	0.78	5
						Sierra Leone	26	22	0.82	5	Ghana[1]	42	33	0.78	9
											Burundi[1]	8*	6*	0.75	2
											Gambia	31	23	0.74	8
											Liberia	27	18	0.69	8
											Niger	8*	5*	0.65	3
											Senegal[1]	24	15	0.64	8
											Burkina Faso	12	8	0.64	4
											Guinea-Biss.	26	14	0.54	12
											Côte d'Ivoire[1]	28*	15*	0.53	13
											D.R. Congo[1]	24*	13*	0.52	12
											Mali[1]	20	10	0.52	9
											Benin	30	14	0.45	17
											Equat. Guinea	43*	19*	0.44	24
											Togo	50*	22*	0.44	28
											Guinea[1]	20*	7*	0.36	13
											Chad	18	5	0.28	13
South/ East Africa	Lesotho	24	32	1.37	-9	Mauritius	108	106	0.98	2	Malawi[1]	50*	40*	0.80	10
	Namibia	56	63	1.12	-7	Madagascar[1]	15*	14*	0.96	1	Zambia[1]	29	22	0.77	7
	South Africa[1]	86*	97*	1.12	-11	Rwanda	12	12	0.95	1	Angola	18*	13*	0.77	4
	Botswana	78	85	1.09	-7	Kenya[1]	31*	28*	0.90	3	Eritrea	33	23	0.70	10
	Swaziland[1]	60*	60*	1.01	0	Zimbabwe	48	43	0.88	6	Ethiopia	6	4	0.68	2
						U.R. Tanzania	6	5	0.86	1	Mozambique	17	11	0.68	5
						Comoros	2*	18	0.82	4					
Caribbean	St Lucia	85*	104*	1.22	-19	Jamaica	85	82	0.96	3					
	Neth. Antilles	79	88	1.12	-9										
	Trinidad/Tob.	75	82	1.09	-7										
	Barbados	99	103	1.04	-4										
	Guyana[1]	80	82	1.02	-1										
	Belize	72	72	1.00	0										
Latin America	Dominic. Rep.	60*	73*	1.22	-13	Peru[1]	83	78	0.94	5					
	Venezuela	54*	65*	1.19	-10	Bolivia	81*	76*	0.93	5					
	Nicaragua	55*	65*	1.19	-10	Guatemala	35	30	0.87	5					
	Uruguay	84	99	1.17	-15										
	Costa Rica	48	54	1.12	-6										
	Brazil	98	109	1.11	-11										
	Colombia	67	75	1.11	-7										
	Argentina	91	97	1.07	-6										
	Panama	67	71	1.07	-4										
	Cuba	80	84	1.04	-4										
	Mexico	72	75	1.04	-3										
	Paraguay	56	58	1.04	-2										
	Chile	87	88	1.02	-2										
	Ecuador	56	57	1.02	-1										
	El Salvador[1]	50	50	0.99	0										
Central Asia	Mongolia	58	71	1.23	-13	Tajikistan	82	70	0.86	12					
	Kyrgyzstan[1]	82	84	1.03	-2										
	Georgia	77	78	1.02	-1										
	Kazakhstan	87	87	1.01	0										
	Azerbaijan	80	80	1.00	0										
South/ West Asia	Bangladesh	52	56	1.08	-4	Iran Isl. R.	83	77	0.92	6	Nepal	62	45	0.72	17
	Maldives	41	44	1.07	-3	Bhutan	12	9	0.82	2	Pakistan	46	32	0.70	14
	Sri Lanka[1]	70*	74*	1.07	-5						India	59	40	0.68	19
East Asia	Brunei Daruss.	105	116	1.10	-11	Indonesia	56*	54*	0.95	3	Lao PDR	42	29	0.70	12
	Malaysia	94	104	1.10	-10	Viet Nam	68	61	0.91	6	Cambodia	22	12	0.55	10
	Philippines[1]	73	79	1.09	-7	China	66*	60*	0.90	6					
	Macau	90	97	1.08	-7										
	Thailand	78	80	1.02	-2										
	Japan	101	103	1.01	-1										
	Myanmar[1]	35*	35*	1.00	0										
	Rep.of Korea	98	97	1.00	0										
Pacific	Samoa	73	80	1.09	-7	Vanuatu	31	26	0.83	5	Papua N.G.[1]	24	18	0.78	5

* Data are from the UNESCO Institute for Statistics.
1. Data refer to school year 1998/99.

Disparities in primary education tend to be further amplified in secondary education: if the GPI for enrolment in primary education is below the parity line, the GPI for secondary is usually further below it; and if primary GPI is around or above the parity line, secondary GPI is often further above it.

GER data for 1999/2000 show that the lowest levels of secondary enrolment, especially for girls, are found in Central and West Africa – as is the case for primary education. The enrolment situation is more favourable to young women in countries of Southern and Eastern Africa, again as it is for other levels and aspects of education. In this sub-region, South Africa, Botswana and Mauritius have gross secondary enrolment ratios higher than 70%, similar to rates in regions where the development of secondary education is among the most advanced. On the other hand, the secondary GER for girls was less than 10% in Ethiopia, Burkina Faso, Chad, Niger and the United Republic of Tanzania (Table 2.13).

Teachers in primary education

Increasing the proportion of women teachers is itself a measure of gender equality, an integral part of improving women's participation in all economic and social sectors. It is also a strategy used by many countries to facilitate girls' access to education and to help improve their learning process. Therefore, it is important to analyse the percentage of female teachers by country, as well as the percentage of those who are trained in comparison with their male counterparts.

Figure 2.23 shows that, in most countries for which data are available, the proportion of women teachers increased over the period 1990/91 to 1999/00. Bahrain, Mauritania, Chad, Ethiopia, India, Nepal and Pakistan, where the proportion of female teachers was among the lowest in 1990, experienced the highest increases (30% and more) in relative terms. By contrast, substantial decreases (over 20%) seem to have occurred in Togo, Djibouti, the Gambia, Eritrea and Tuvalu, even though women represent far fewer than 50% of the total in some of these cases. On the other hand, moderate decreases or stability are observed in Latin America and the Caribbean, the region with the highest proportion of women teachers – three-quarters or more of teaching staff.

The figure also shows that the proportion of women among the teaching staff varied considerably from one world region to another in 1999.

- Sub-Saharan Africa has the highest number of countries where women represent less than half of the teaching staff – and the lowest shares of women teachers. All countries where fewer than one teacher in four is a women are in Central and West Africa, with the exception of Mozambique. The proportion of women teachers is as low as 10% in Chad and 13% in Togo. The highest values – women representing two out of three teachers or more – are found in Southern Africa.
- Primary teachers are predominantly women in Latin America and the Caribbean, with the exception of Haiti, where women represent only one-third of the total number of teachers.
- In the Arab States, women represent one-half or more of the teachers in two-thirds of the countries for which data are available, ranging from 20% in Yemen to 75% in Qatar.
- In Asia and the Pacific, there are wide variations with the lowest values in South Asian countries, higher values in East Asia and the Pacific, and the highest, almost 100%, in Central Asian countries.

Finally, as regards gender disparities in teacher training, the available data (Figure 2.24) show that in most cases there are more trained women than men teachers in primary education. However, there are notable exceptions from all regions in countries such as, Eritrea, Ethiopia, Malawi, Sierra Leone, Sudan, Trinidad and Tobago and in United Arab Emirates. In some of these countries, the percentage of all trained teachers (both men and women)is generally very low (Malawi, Sudan).

Disparities in primary education tend to be further amplified in secondary education.

Sub-Saharan Africa has the lowest numbers of women teachers.

Figure 2.23. Trend in the percentage of women teachers, by region (1990–1999)

1. Data for 1990/91 include pre-primary-school teachers.
2. Data for the latest year refer to 1998/99.
Source: Annex, Table 8.

Examining education through a gender lens reveals not only the pervasiveness and the depth of gender disparity in schooling, but also how gender-orientated initiatives can become effective in a relatively short span of time. Most countries, thanks both to their own and to international efforts, have made progress in closing the gender gap in education in the decade between Jomtien and Dakar. The analysis of gender in education shows that gender equality is a broad societal issue, and it is plain that promoting gender equality in education is part of, and must be accompanied by measures to promote gender equality throughout society.

Paying attention to the plight of girls in terms of gender disparity also helps reveal areas and levels of education, regions and countries, where boys are at a disadvantage. In other words, a gender lens allows decision-makers at all levels – politicians, officials and parents – to see the circumstances, needs and potential of both girls and boys more clearly. The path to the Dakar goal of gender equality in education may be

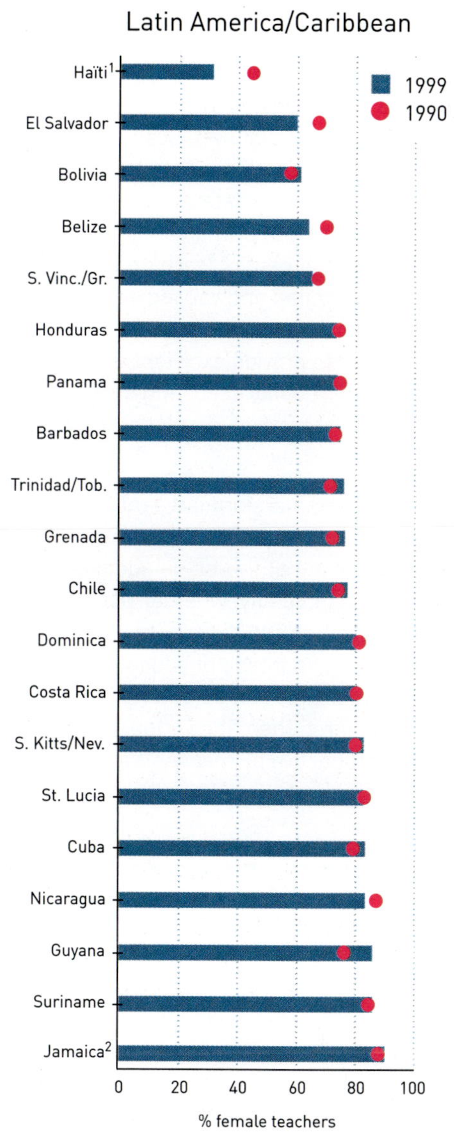

better built, not with gender-neutral approaches that flatten the learning environment, but with gender-fair measures that recognize and respond appropriately to the differences between girls and boys (and indeed among other subsectors of the population such as ethnic minorities and persons with disabilities). In this way, a gendered approach to education can bring benefits for all students.

Figure 2.24. Percentage of trained teachers, in primary-school education, by sex (1999/2000)

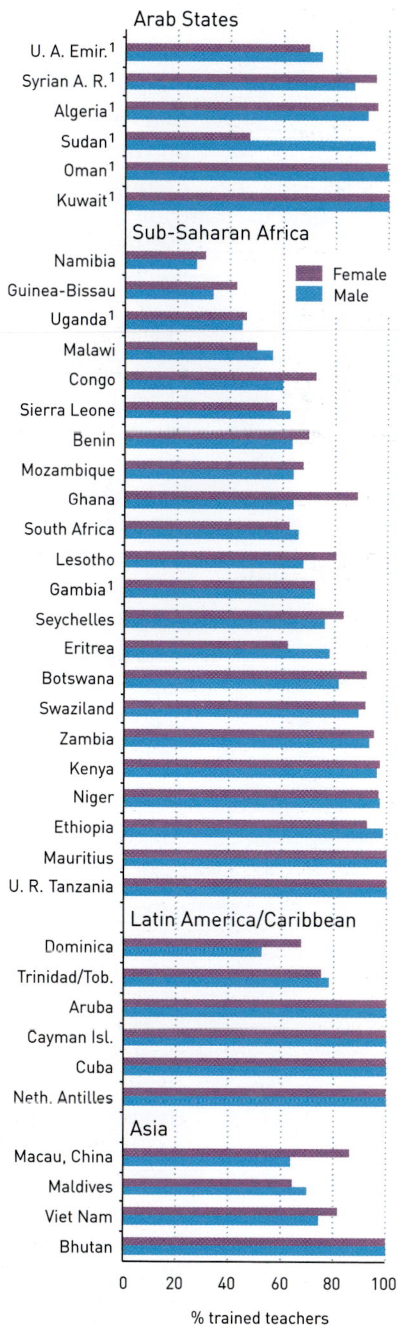

1. Data refer to 1998/99.

Source: Annex, Table 8.

Goal 6

Education quality

. . . improving all aspects of the quality of education and ensuring excellence of all so that recognized and measurable learning outcomes are achieved by all, especially in literacy, numeracy and essential life skills.

The Dakar Framework for Action gave new impetus to the promotion of quality in education.

The Dakar Framework for Action gave new impetus to the promotion of quality in education, based on the consensus that expanding access to education will have a beneficial impact on individuals and on society only if the education is of good quality. Quality is a multi-faceted concept. It encompasses how learning is organized and managed, what the content of learning is, what level of learning is achieved, what it leads to in terms of outcomes, and what goes on in the learning environment. For example, if parents do not believe that what their children learn is relevant to life, they will not send their children to school even if the opportunity exists. This is all the more true if opportunity costs are high, if the school is far away, and if going or being there is not safe. Where the modes of delivery of adult learning are inappropriate or demotivating, or where adult educators are untrained or poorly trained, it is unlikely that adults will avail themselves of the educational offer.

It has frequently been thought that quality could be achieved only at the expense of increased access. It is clear that both quality and access must receive attention, and the one must not be sacrificed in a 'trade-off' against the other. Hence, it is as important to keep track of education quality as it is to monitor the expansion of education systems. At present, such monitoring is possible only to a limited extent. Systematic reporting on world progress in education quality since the Dakar forum is possible at present only by using two proxies of quality for which statistics are available: educational expenditure and the pupil-teacher ratio. These two indicators apply above all to primary education; indicators of quality for early childhood, life-skills learning programmes or adult literacy have not yet been adequately developed, as was indicated in the relevant sections of this chapter (above). Scarcity of data also means that this section will address only formal education, and only at primary level. Other proxy indicators in primary education, as well as direct assessment of learning outcomes, are available for limited and varying sets of countries. The objective of the process envisaged at Dakar was not to provide excellent education for some and poor quality schooling for the others, a situation that even developed countries avoid only with difficulty.

This Report cannot, therefore, present worldwide progress on education quality, nor is the information sufficient at this stage adequately to monitor changes in quality, whether positive or negative. However, on the basis of the data and material available, an image of education quality in developing countries can be outlined from various angles. First, then, the various indicators are put into perspective by means of a simple conceptual framework.

What is education quality?

Defining the quality of education is not easy. However, one framework which can help is shown in Table 2.14. In this input-process-output framework, the various stakeholders in education (learners, parents, teachers, communities, government) and the various levels (classroom, school, national policy) find their places. The framework can guide a step by step assessment of educational quality, which will follow after some general comments on Figure 2.14.[5]

The arrows in the table indicate the directions in which input influences process, and in which process influences outcome. The body of knowledge regarding education has not yet reached the stage at which solid generalizations can be made about the strengths of these causal relations; this is due partly to contextual factors.

5. This approach is used as an organizing framework for the discussion, and not as a definitive model of school quality. Other approaches exist which are equally valid.

Table 2.14. An input-process-outcome framework for assessing education quality

INPUTS

School
- curriculum content
- textbooks and learning materials
- teacher qualifications, training, morale and commitment
- adequate facilities
- parent/community support

Student characteristics
- aptitude, ability perseverance/commitment
- nutrition and health
- school readiness
- attended ECCE
- gender

Household/community characteristics
- parental attitudes
- household income
- community economic and labour market conditions
- cultural/religious factors

PROCESS

School climate
- high expectations
- strong leadership
- positive teacher attitudes
- safe and gender-sensitive environment
- incentives for good results
- flexibility/autonomy

Teaching/learning
- sufficient learning time
- active teaching methods
- integrated systems for
- assessment and feedback
- appropriate class size
- appropriate use of language

OUTCOMES

Achievement
cognitive development
- literacy, generic skills
- good citizenship
- personal development
- positive attitudes towards learning
- healthy behaviour

Attainment
- formal completion
- diplomas/qualifications

Standards
- official learning objectives (desired outcomes)

Contextual factors
- Macro-economic and fiscal policies, political stability, decentralization and governance, civil service quality
- National goals and standards for education, curricular guidelines, sources of funding and allocation, teacher recruitment/deployment
- Education system management
- Participation, progression, completion and transition
- Engagement and use of time
- Peer effects, parental support, promotion policies

Source: derived from Heneveld and Graig (1995), OECD/INES (2001), Scheerens (2002).

In the light of this framework, significant differences have been noted between industrialized and developing countries. Everywhere, external factors such as parental income and educational background are important in learner achievement. Other factors, such as school materials and facilities, make little difference in industrialized countries, but are significant in developing countries. In the former, the variation in provision is much less than in the latter countries. Likewise, in developing countries, large in-country disparities occur as regards the pupil-teacher ratio, trained teachers, the availability of textbooks, and so on.

Input and context are the most 'visible' elements in this framework; process is the 'black box'. In developing and industrialized countries alike, it is difficult to collect reliable and comparable information on what goes on in the classroom. Proxies, such as grade repetition, are often taken to reflect process quality, and the preparedness of teachers, both in terms of content and didactics, is of importance. As far as curriculum is concerned, we shall see that the intended parameters by which national policy steers the learning process do not always reflect reality.

Everywhere, external factors such as parental income and educational background are important in learner achievement.

Goal 6. Education quality

Figure 2.25. Current expenditure and primary enrolments (1975–1997)

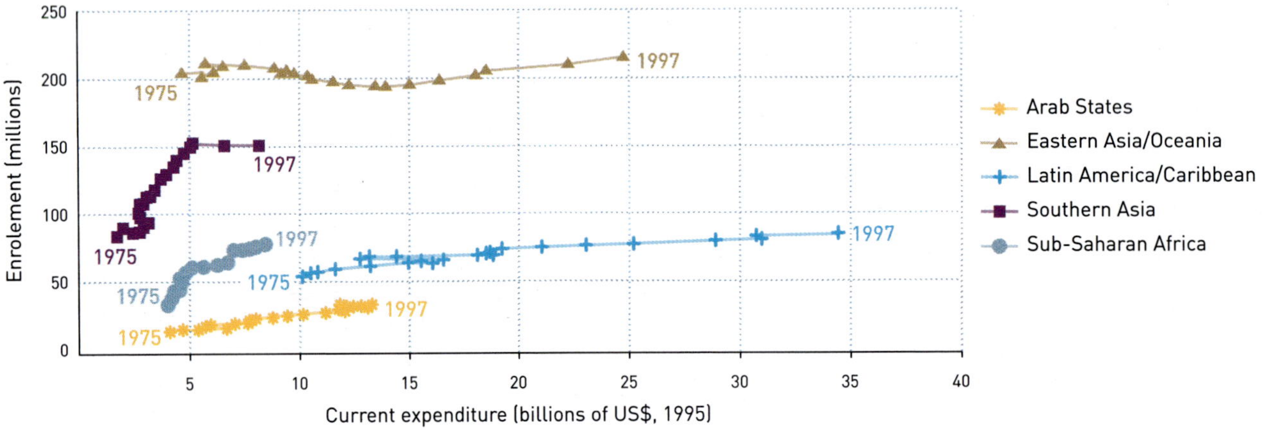

Source: UIS database, Brossard (2000).

Figure 2.26. Current expenditure and the pupil-teacher ratio (1975–1997)

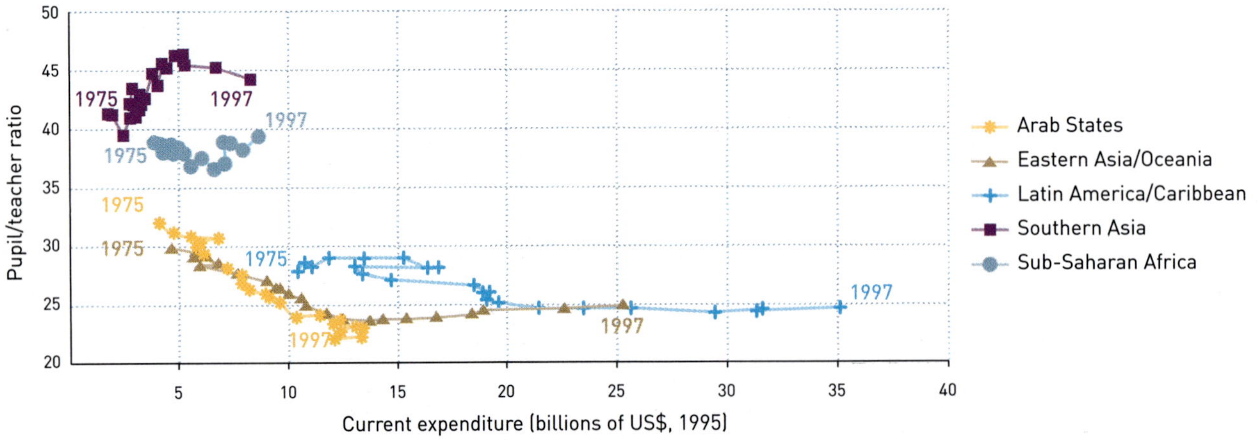

Source: UIS database, Brossard (2000).

It is important to distinguish three aspects of the outcomes:

- *achievement*: what students really learn;
- *attainment*: the number of students that actually meet the standards, by passing the exams and acquiring formal qualifications; and
- *standards*: the outcomes sought by society.

More easily measured, attainment data tend to dominate over achievement. It is important to note that in countries where attainment is high, achievement can actually be low and vice versa.

Inputs: financial and human resources

Of all possible input indicators, finance and human resources are the more readily available on a global scale, and they allow comparison by region. Figure 2.25 shows the evolution since 1975 of enrolment and public investment in primary education for five developing regions.

In South and West Asia, as well as in sub-Saharan Africa, the number of enrolled pupils almost doubled over the period in question, while the level of current expenditure, expressed in constant US$ for 1995, increased modestly. In contrast, enrolments remained fairly stable in Latin America and the Caribbean and in East Asia, whereas current expenditure increased at a much more rapid rate than in the other two regions. In fact, expenditure in East Asia grew as much, in absolute terms, in the period 1995—1997, as expenditure in sub-Saharan Africa did over the past 25 years.

The 'diagonal' patterns for sub-Saharan Africa and South and West Asia suggest that countries in these regions have been investing in quantity (the expansion of enrolment), while the 'horizontal' patterns of the other regions – where enrolment rates were higher to begin with – indicate the allocation of additional resources to reach higher levels of spending per pupil.

In sub-Saharan Africa and South and West Asia, expenditure has not kept pace with the growth of population and of the enrolment rate. In consequence, spending per pupil has declined in these regions.

In education, a relatively large proportion of expenditure is spent on human resources. Increases in expenditure thus tend to translate into higher numbers of teachers, although this increase can be offset by changes in the level of teacher salaries, which will be addressed below. Figure 2.26 shows, again for the five regions and for the period 1975–1997, the development of the pupil/teacher ratio against the backdrop of changes in expenditure.

In the Arab States, Eastern Asia and Oceania, and in Latin America and the Caribbean, the ratio has dropped from about 30 to 25 and stabilized at that level. In South Asia, there is recent indication of a downward trend for the pupil/teacher ratio, after rising from 40 to 45 in the years before. The reverse is the case for sub-Saharan Africa: a downward trend has recently been reversed into a rise towards approximately 40.

For a variety of reasons, the data in Figure 2.26 do not directly demonstrate developments in education quality. First of all, the pupil-teacher ratio varies widely among countries in the same region. For example, in Central and West Africa, the ratio varies from 30 in Sierra Leone to 94 in Mali, and in South and East Africa, from 15 in Seychelles to 63 in Malawi. Secondly, the pupil/teacher ratio is not the same as class size. Classes can be bigger than the ratio indicates, since not all of available teacher-time is spent on teaching. Classes can also be smaller, namely when one teacher has a workload of several classes which he or she teaches either consecutively or simultaneously. The latter practice – also referred to as multigrade teaching – can have a positive impact on learning outcomes; the former does not. Thirdly, there is no consensus about the relation between class size and the quality of teaching. There is a fair amount of agreement that reduction of class size has a positive impact on learning outcomes when the number of children per class is already very low, e.g. twenty or less. There is, however, conflicting evidence on whether the reduction has a significant and worthwhile impact on classes of between twenty and forty pupils. In fact, some Asian countries have had excellent results with classes of fifty children. But these outcomes are hardly relevant for countries where classes can be much larger still (Box 2.15).

Classes can be bigger than the ratio indicates, since not all of available teacher-time is spent on teaching.

As has already been mentioned, the relation between expenditure and absolute numbers of teachers is mediated by the salary of teachers, which is therefore an important policy lever. The general rule is that salaries that are too high bring costs for capacity, and salaries that are too low bring costs for quality. Recent research shows that the former tendency is very strong.

Box 2.15. **Not enough primary school teachers**

EFA represents a broad range of goals, within which primary school teachers play a vital role. In 1999/2000 there were 25.5 million primary teachers worldwide, with widely varying qualifications and training. Estimates of the number of additional teachers required by 2015 vary from 15 to 35 million. In sub-Saharan Africa, without factoring in any improvements in efficiency or education quality, the number of additional primary teachers exceeds 3 million, including more than one million in Nigeria alone.

The issue here is not just a matter of numbers. The quality of teaching significantly affects pupil achievement, particularly in terms of teaching methods, subject-specific expertise, motivation and attitudes. In Brazil, only 3% of primary teachers in the states of Bahia or Para have tertiary-level training, compared to 42% in the state of São Paulo. In the United States, data suggest that in high-poverty areas, as many as half of all new teachers leave the profession in the first five years. In many countries attrition due to health reasons, such as HIV/AIDS, has an immediate and often dramatic impact. For example, in Zambia the estimated number of primary-school teachers who died from AIDS in 2000 was equal to 45% of all teachers trained that year.

For many countries, pupil-teacher ratios are already at very high levels. In the least developed countries (LDCs), the ratio is three times higher than in developed countries, while classes with 100 pupils are no exception. This suggests that further demand on teachers could be detrimental to teacher capacity and morale, resulting in diminished learning outcomes among pupils.

Source: Motivans (2002); UNESCO/ILO (2002).

Figure 2.27 shows that the salary of primary teachers for a number of African countries varies widely: from 1.6 times GDP per capita, to 9.6 times, and that this affects gross enrolment. A marginal increase in teachers' salary by one unit of per capita GDP implies, on average, a reduction of almost 5 percentage points in the gross enrolment ratio.

Figure 2.27. Relationship between GER and teacher salary

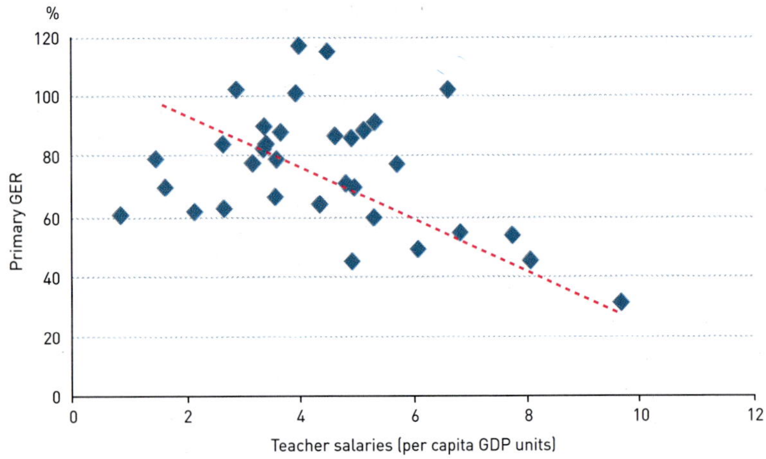

Source: Mingat (2002).

Higher teacher salaries – if it results in teachers – also affect equity. Disadvantaged groups suffer the most from lack of capacity. For example, where salaries reach the level of approximately twice per capita GDP, the gender ratio – gross enrolment of girls over boys – averages about 10 percentage points less than when it is seven times per capita GDP.

Data on other inputs are not yet available on a cross-country basis to allow adequate monitoring of progress. Systematic data collection is needed, particularly for developing countries where school infrastructure and the school environment affect enrolment, gender equity and quality. Indicators could include the following:

- school infrastructure: distance to school,; student/classroom ratios, school libraries and other learning resources;
- health: availability of girls' and boys' toilet facilities, safe drinking water, status of student nutrition.

Process: indicators of system efficiency and curriculum

Grade repetition and drop-out are generally seen as signs of inefficiency in an education system. Where there is already limited capacity in an education system, a repeater is taking the place of another child that could otherwise have been enrolled.

In over half of the countries of sub-Saharan Africa, more than one pupil in ten repeats at least one grade in primary school. To a lesser extent this occurs is the Arab States, Latin America and the Caribbean. Grade repetition is rather low in Central Asia.

Interpretation of the phenomena of grade repetition and drop-out requires caution. High levels of repetition usually indicate system inefficiency, but they can also be a sign of severe testing and graduation practices. Likewise, high drop-out rates are sometimes the accepted consequence of a selective education system. By contrast, some countries have chosen automatic graduation and completion, partly on pedagogical grounds. What remains beyond doubt is that grade repetition is a problem for education systems with insufficient capacity.

Figure 2.28 focuses on the pattern of grade repetition through the school career in countries with particularly high levels of repetition. Covering only a few countries from different regions, the figure does not permit generalization. It serves merely to illustrate the point that grade repetition may remain high or be concentrated in the early grades, as is the case for the three countries to the right. Here, however, it may be at the expense of retention, since drop-out rates are known to be rather high in these three countries.

Another critical ingredient of process is the curriculum. A predominantly qualitative item, curriculum is difficult to compare over countries and regions. One can, however, single out some quantitative aspects, such as the number of teaching hours. Figure 2.29 shows, for a number of developing countries, the official number of teaching hours according to national standards, as well as the observed numbers of teaching

Figure 2.28.
Repetition rates, Grades 1 and 5, in selected countries (1999/2000)

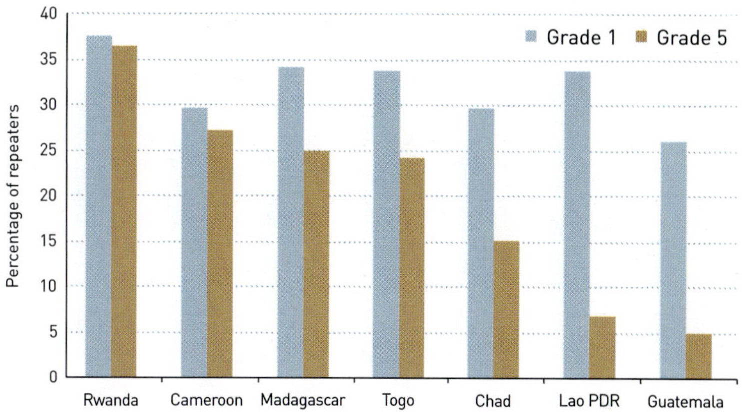

Source: Annex, Table 9.

hours. Again, the selection of countries allows no generalization, but Figure 2.29 does illustrate the wide variation in the expected number of hours between countries. Actual hours taught were always less, although differences were often not great. that exists in three areas: the official numbers of hours, the actual numbers of hours, and the discrepancies between the two.

Recent research has addressed the relationship between instructional time and other variables, such as economic indicators. Table 2.15 shows that in richer countries, pupils tend to receive more class teaching in primary schooling than pupils in lower-income countries, particularly in the lower grades. Taking all grades together, high-income countries allocate 400 more hours teaching time than those in the lowest income group.

Further systematic data for monitoring purposes might include:

- curriculum and pedagogy: textbook provision; use of languages and multilingual approaches; place of local knowledge; use of information technology; and
- training and research: teacher training statistics; numbers and output of educational research institutes.

Taking all grades together, high-income countries allocate 400 more hours teaching time than those in the lowest income group.

Figure 2.29. Expected and actual number of hours in the first year of primary school (1994/95)

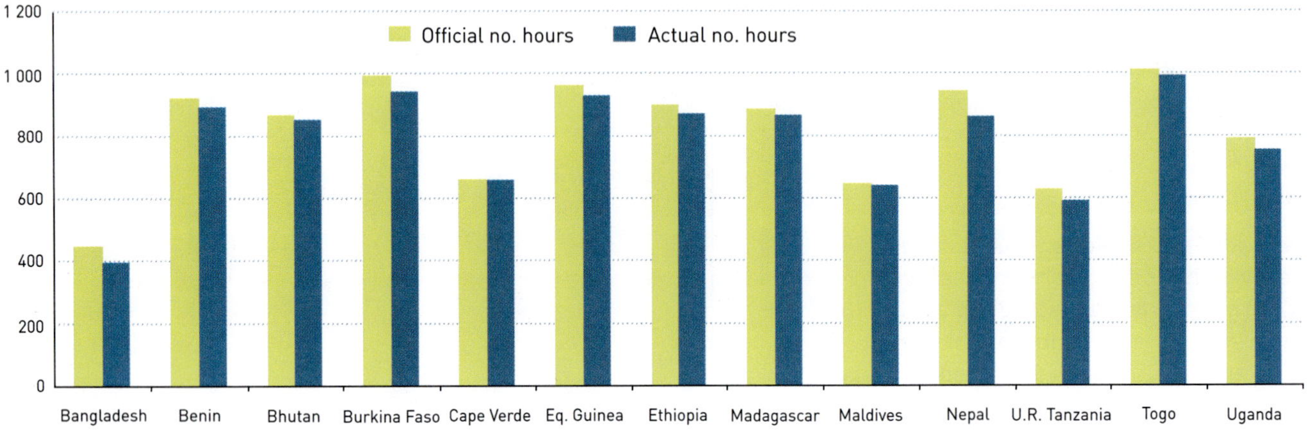

Source: Postlewaite, Schleicher and Sinalsco (1995).

Surveys of student achievement are informative, but they are complex, expensive and scarce.

Outcomes: assessment of student achievement

Three dimensions of education outcomes were distinguished in Table 2.14.

- standards: the desired outcomes;
- attainment: the numbers of students who formally meet the standards;
- achievement: what students really learn.

Clearly, there is a trade-off between the usefulness of these indicators. Standards may be easy to identify, but not very informative. Attainment tells us more, but is harder to measure. Most informative are surveys of student achievement, but they are complex, expensive and scarce.

In essence, surveys test reading, mathematics, science and generic skills (see the section on Goal 3 in this chapter, on life skills)

Since the background characteristic of the students, the schools and the environment are usually also reported, the measured differences in performance can be traced back to their probable causes.

The International Association for the Evaluation of Educational Achievement (IEA) has pioneered achievement surveys. Projects such as the Third International Mathematics and Science Study (TIMSS) and Progress in Reading Literacy Study (PIRLS) became very influential. IEA's example has been followed both in developing countries where the Southern Africa Consortium for Monitoring Educational Quality (Sacmeq), Programme d'Analyse des Systemes Educatifs des pays de la CONFEMEN (Pasec), Monitoring Learning Achievement (MLA) and Laboratorio studies were conducted, and in developed countries where the OECD initiated the Programme for International Student Achievement (PISA) study.

Comparable studies regarding adult literacy have also been developed. Finally, a project is being conducted under the aegis of the European Union, in which regular school tests – in this case English as a second language – are made comparable over a number of countries. Taking a lower level of accuracy for granted, this procedure reduces the costs of data collection, and could be a promising model for developing regions.

Table 2.15. Mean intended instructional time in annual hours for Grades 1 to 6, by per capita income levels (1997)

	Mean intended instructional time in each grade (in annual hours)						
	Grade 1	Grade 2	Grade 3	Grade 4	Grade 5	Grade 6	Grades 1-6
Low income: < $1,500 per cap. (15)	667.3	668.7	702.7	759.7	810.2	827.8	4 436.4
$1,501–$3,100 per capita (20)	686.5	705.0	722.4	740.7	788.9	813.0	4 456.5
$3,101–$5,200 per capita (22)	667.4	705.7	737.4	757.8	811.0	832.3	4 511.7
$5,201–$12,100 per capita (24)	739.4	750.0	778.8	798.8	811.6	825.2	4 703.8
High income: > $12,100 per cap. (28)	752.9	763.3	800.4	818.5	842.8	845.3	4 823.0
World totals (109)	708.7	725.0	755.2	779.5	815.2	829.9	4 613.5
Standard deviation	145.9	132.8	127.9	124.5	107.9	103.5	679.4

Number of cases in brackets.
Source: Benavot, 2002.

The Sacmeq, Pasec, MLA and Laboratorio studies are not strictly comparable. They might never be so, because it is essential that achievement surveys correspond to the needs and characteristics of the country in question.

Thus, surveys are most relevant when fine-tuned to the specific policy questions and policy levers of participating countries (Ross et al., 1999). It follows that they do not provide an overall picture of progress regarding student achievement.

Within each region, however, surveys do provide crucial feedback to countries about their standing, about which countries are leading in certain respects, and about how they can learn from one another's experience. Some general lessons appear to be the following.

- Some countries or sub-regions prove that good performance and excellence is possible, even with modest means.
- The tendency for girls to perform better than boys seems increasingly widely spread (Sacmeq, MLA, TIMSS, PISA).
- Student characteristics such as parental income and parental education level have a strong impact on learning outcomes (Figures 2.30 and 2.31). This is true for both developed and developing countries. In the latter, differences between urban and rural schools emerge strongly as well.
- In developing countries, school characteristics are still important. Some of these are illustrated in Figure 2.31. Shift-teaching needs to be used carefully if achievement is not to be impaired. Full availability of textbooks and other learning material, the possibility of extra instruction, and experienced teachers are far from omnipresent, and therefore make a difference to learning outcomes.

Parental income and parental education level have a strong impact on learning outcomes.

Goal 6. Education quality

Figure 2.30. Percentage of pupils meeting minimum reading mastery levels, by highest and lowest wealth asset score (1995/96)

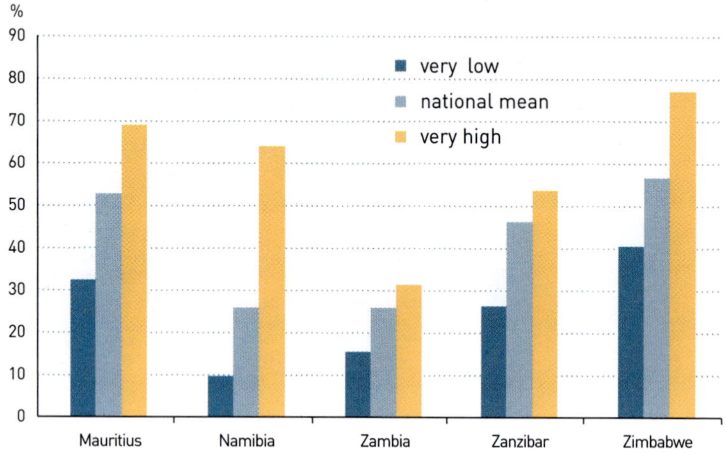

Compared to overall national mean score.
Source: From Sacmeq country reports (1998).

Figure 2.31. Impact of school organization and pupil characteristics on achievement scores in five Francophone African countries, mid-1990s

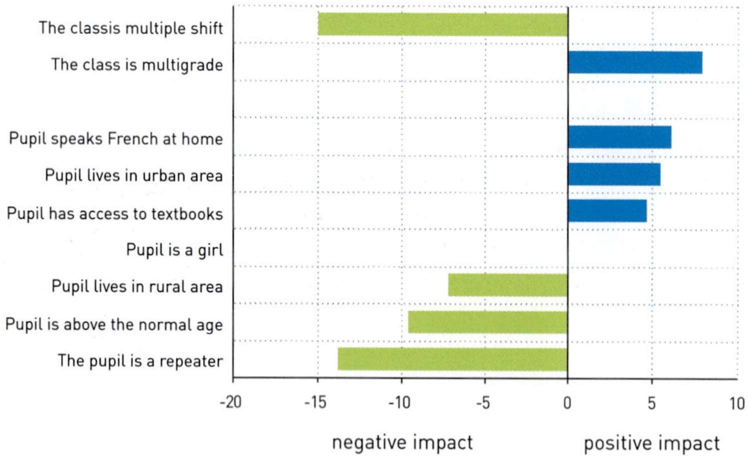

Source: From Pasec (2002).

Is the world on track?

The preceding six sections of this chapter took stock of progress towards each of the six Dakar goals individually. For some goals, the indicators are sufficiently reliable to indicate which regions – and sometimes which countries – are on track in meeting the goal in question, and which regions or countries are at risk of failing to do so. However, this approach has not addressed the more general question that needs to be raised. To what extent is the world – all regions and countries combined – on track for achieving the six goals of the Dakar Framework for Action taken *as a whole*?

In an ideal statistical world a well-balanced composite indicator, or 'Dakar-index', would provide the answer. This index would incorporate numerous indicators, which would together cover all six goals, ranking regions and countries both in static (Are they close to or far way from the goal?) and in dynamic terms (Are they moving towards or away from the goal, and how quickly?). At present, however, it is not possible to construct such an index because the necessary range of statistics is not yet available from a sufficient number of countries. Nonetheless, this final section of the chapter will attempt to take the first step in measuring general progress.

After the methodology has been presented, three of the six Dakar goals, namely universal primary education (UPE), adult literacy and gender equality, will be addressed. The section will conclude with an overall assessment of the world's progress towards meeting them.

Methodology

The methodology is based essentially upon the following observations. Any country occupies a certain position in relation to each of the Dakar goals: it may have reached the goal already, or be close to it or far away; this will be called the static dimension. Any country is also located in a certain trajectory in relation to each goal, moving towards it or away from it; this is termed the dynamic dimension. The two dimensions are integrated and compared on the basis of explicit criteria, forming a matrix of four quadrants (see Figure 2.32). Countries that have already achieved the goal are not included in the matrix.

Some countries will – in relation to a certain goal – find themselves in Quadrant II: 'Countries close to the goal(s) and moving closer'. This quadrant is labelled: 'High chance of achieving the goal(s)'. Other countries are far from the goal and moving away from it. They have been placed in Quadrant IV, labelled 'Serious risk of not achieving the goal(s)'. Quandrant I comprises countries that are at risk of not achieving the goal(s) (close to the goal but moving away from it). Finally, Quandrant III consists of those with low chance of achieving the goal(s) (far from the goal but moving towards it).

Finally, the separate matrices are consolidated into one. This allows generalizations concerning the progress still to be made towards the goals in a more general sense. Observations and calculations can be made – at global and regional level – about the total numbers of countries (and their populations) where chances are high for achieving the goals (or countries that have already done so); those that show insufficient progress; and those seriously at risk of not achieving the goals.

To what extent is the world on track for achieving the six goals of the Dakar Framework for Action taken *as a whole*?

At present, it is not possible to construct a 'Dakar index' because the necessary range of statistics is not yet available from a sufficient number of countries.

Conclusion. Is the world on track?

Figure 2.32. Analytical framework

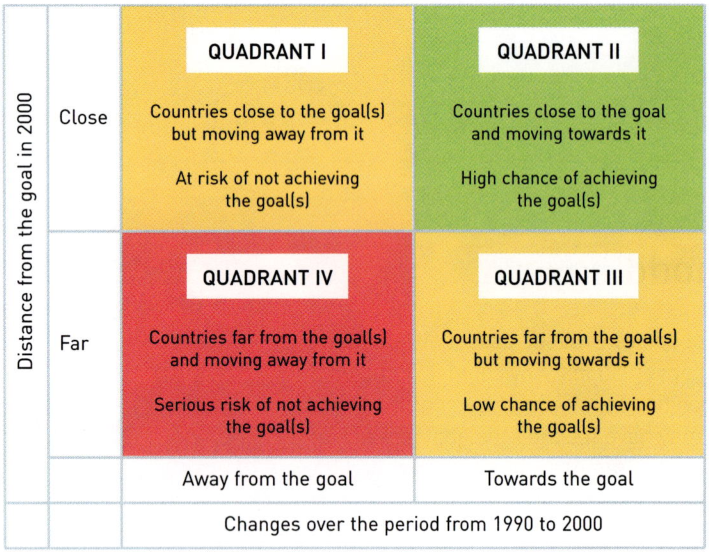

At present, three of the goals – universal primary education (UPE), adult literacy and gender parity – have indicators making it possible to compare country progress. In principle, comparisons would also be possible for early childhood care and education (ECCE). However, the data are at present only partial and are insufficiently meaningful to be useful, since attendance on a weekly basis varies – between countries – from just a few hours to a full school week. For the goal of life skills, no quantitative indicator whatsoever is available; and for education quality indicators are either proxies of quality (funding; pupil/teacher ratio) or available for only small sets of countries (surveys of student achievement).

Data for the years 1990 and 1999 are used whenever possible.[6] Additionally, data from the EFA 2000 Assessment have been used to increase the number of countries available, especially for the primary NER, where coverage of countries in the Statistical Annex is too low.[7] By consequence, 176 countries are included in the analysis, representing 90% of all countries worldwide and 98% of world population. It should, however, be noted that information for some of these countries is not available for all three indicators.

Table 2.16. Countries that have achieved UPE,[1] by region (1999)

Region	Countries	A: number of countries that have achieved UPE	B: number of countries in region	A/B (as %)
Arab States/ North Africa	Algeria, Libyan Arab Jamahiriya, Tunisia	3	16	18.8
Central Asia	Kazakhstan	1	7	14.3
Central/Eastern Europe	Bosnia and Herzegovina, Bulgaria, Hungary, Poland	4	10	40.0
East Asia/Pacific	Fiji, Japan, Malaysia, New Zealand, Niue, Philippines, Republic of Korea, Samoa, Vanuatu, Viet Nam, Australia	11	16	68.7
Latin America/ Caribbean	Antigua and Barbuda, Argentina, Bahamas, Belize, Bolivia, Brazil, Cayman Islands, Cuba, Ecuador, Grenada, Mexico, Netherlands Antilles, Panama, Peru	14	29	48.3
North America/ Western Europe	Belgium, Canada, Denmark, France, Greece, Ireland, Netherlands, Norway, Portugal, Spain, Sweden, Switzerland, United Kingdom, United States	14	15	100.0
South/West Asia	Maldives	1	5	20.0
Sub-Saharan Africa	Rwanda, Seychelles	2	30	6.7
Total		50	128	39.0

1. Defined for these purposes as NERs of 95% or more.

Source: Calculations are based on Annex, Table 6; supplemented by EFA 2000 Assessment (CD-ROM).

6. Data for these two years are not strictly comparable. Those for 1990 have yet to be revised using United Nations 2000 population data, and there are also issues related to the International Standard Classification of Education (ISCED) used in each case. The comparability problem is particularly important in those countries where the variation between both years has been small. In these cases, most of the variation results from the different population projections used, rather than from differences in the variables.

7. Those countries where data were taken from the EFA 2000 Assessment are for the earliest and latest year available in the 1990s.

Figure 2.33. Primary education net enrolment ratio: countries in each quadrant

Distance from 100% NER in 1999				
Close NER 80%–95%		**QUADRANT I** At risk of not achieving the goal(s) Bahrain, Barbados, Botswana, China, Cyprus, Gabon, Georgia, Guyana, Indonesia, Jamaica, Kyrgyzstan, Mauritius, Paraguay, St Kitts and Nevis, St Vincent and the Grenadines, Syrian Arab Republic, The former Yugoslav Republic of Macedonia, Turkey, Uzbekistan, Venezuela **20** countries	**QUADRANT II** High chance of achieving the goal(s) Azerbaijan, Bangladesh, Chile, Costa Rica, Dominica, Guatemala, Honduras, Iraq, Jordan, Lao P.D.R., Latvia, Mongolia, Qatar, Romania, Sri Lanka, Swaziland, Tajikistan, Thailand, Togo, Trinidad and Tobago, Uganda **21** countries	**41**
Far NER <80%		**QUADRANT IV** Serious risk of not achieving the goal(s) Burundi, Central African Republic, Comoros, Croatia, Djibouti, Equatorial Guinea, Yugoslavia, Iran, Kiribati, Kuwait, Lebanon, Lesotho, Madagascar, Namibia, Niger, Nigeria, Oman, Saudi Arabia, United Arab Emirates, United Republic of Tanzania, Zambia **21** countries	**QUADRANT III** Low chance of achieving the goal(s) Benin, Bhutan, Burkina Faso, Chad, Côte d'Ivoire, Dem. Rep. of the Congo, Eritrea, Ethiopia, Gambia, Haiti, Malawi, Mali, Mauritania, Morocco, Mozambique, Nicaragua **16** countries	**37**
Total		**41** countries	**37** countries	**78**
		Away from the goal	Towards the goal	
		Changes over the period from 1990 to 2000		

Source: Calculations Based on Statistical Annex, Table 6; EFA 2000 Assessment (CD ROM).

Universal primary education

The exercise to analyse progress towards the goal of universal primary education (UPE) has been based on country net enrolment ratios (NER). First, the criteria according to which countries are considered as having achieved the goal, being close to the goal, or being far from it, must be determined. For the purpose of this comparison, countries with NERs higher than 95% are considered to have achieved the goal. As indicated above, few countries achieve NERs of 100%, and caution must be used as regards reporting errors. Table 2.16 shows the countries that have reached the goal according to this criterion.

The NER value of 80% was utilized to divide countries into two groups: close to the goal and farther away. Figure 2.33 shows the position in the matrix of the seventy-eight countries (for which data were available) whose NERs fell below 95%.

It can be seen from Figure 2.33 that forty-one countries are close to the goal. Including the fifty that have already achieved it (Table 2.16), this group comprises a total of ninety-one countries, or 70% of all the countries included in this exercise. However, twenty of the countries close to the goal are moving away from it. Although it should be emphasized that even a small move in the wrong direction places a country in this category, the fact remains that this group of countries has not made progress over the past decade. Thus, only seventy-one countries – just over half of the total – have either achieved the goal or stand a strong chance of doing so.

From Figure 2.33 it can also be seen that the countries far from the goal are mainly in the Arab States and North Africa, but especially in sub-Saharan Africa. The sample contains thirty sub-Saharan countries; twenty-two are still far from the goal, and for eleven of them, the distance from the goal has risen in recent years. Latin America as a whole is much nearer to the goal than other developing regions.

There are unfortunately no data for four of the E-9 countries. For the other five, two have achieved the goal – Brazil and Mexico – and two more are close to the goal – China and Bangladesh. Nigeria is far from the goal, and some data suggest that it has moved even further away from it during the 1990s.

The countries far from the goal are mainly in the Arab States and North Africa, but especially in sub-Saharan Africa.

Adult literacy

The *rate* of progress has been used as the criterion for dynamic dimension in achieving adult literacy.

For the present analysis, countries with an adult literacy rate of 95% or higher are considered as having reached the goal. The demarcation line between 'close to the goal' and 'far from the goal' was set as adult literacy rate of 70%. The countries that had achieved the goal of adult literacy by 2000 are listed in Table 2.17; it will be observed that fewer than 30% of the countries included in this exercise are on the list. There are no countries from sub-Saharan or North Africa and the Arab States. By contrast, a fairly high percentage of countries in East Asia and the Pacific, as well as all the Central and Eastern European countries, have reached the goal. Unfortunately, only a few countries in Western European and North America were included in this exercise.[8]

To determine the dynamic dimension in adult literacy comparisons, a slightly different methodology was necessary. Almost all countries reduced their illiteracy rates from 1990–2000 to some degree, so there would be no point in distinguishing between movement towards or away from the goal. Neither can the target for 2015 – halving the literacy gap by that date – provide the line of demarcation. This means that, for a country with a literacy rate of 60%, the target for 2015 would be a rate of 80%, while for a country with a rate of 80%, the target would be 90%. In other words, the target rate varies from country to country. The *rate* of progress has thus been used as the criterion for dynamic dimension in this exercise. It can been seen that all countries have progressed, but some countries are progressing rapidly enough to reach the target in 2015. These countries are labelled 'fast performers'. Countries that will not reach their targets at their current pace are labelled 'slow performers'. Figure 2.34 shows the results of the exercise for adult literacy.

Fifty-seven countries are close to the goal; with the thirty-eight countries that have achieved the goal (Table 2.17) they compose a group of ninety-

Table 2.17. Countries that have achieved the goal of adult literacy,[1] by region

Region	Countries	A: number of countries that have achieved adult literacy	B: number of countries in the sample	A/B (as %)
Arab States/ North Africa	none	0	19	0.0%
Central Asia	Armenia, Azerbaijan, Georgia, Kazakhstan, Mongolia, Tajikistan, Uzbekistan	7	7	100.0%
Central/Eastern Europe	Belarus, Bulgaria, Croatia, Estonia, Hungary, Latvia, Lithuania, Moldova, Poland, Romania, Russian Federation, Slovenia, Ukraine	13	16	81.3%
East Asia/Pacific	Rep. of Korea, Samoa, Thailand	3	12	25.0%
Latin America/ Caribbean	Argentina, Bahamas, Barbados, Chile, Costa Rica, Cuba, Guyana, Netherlands Antilles, Trinidad and Tobago, Uruguay	10	29	34.5%
North America/ Western Europe	Cyprus, Greece, Italy, Spain	4	7	57.1%
South/West Asia	Maldives	1	7	14.3%
Sub-Saharan Africa	None	0	38	0.0%
Total		38	135	28.1%

* Defined for these purposes as an adult literacy rate of 95% or more.
Source: Calculations are based on Statistical Annex, Table 2; supplemented by EFA 2000 Assessment (CD-ROM).

8. Table 6 in the Statistical Annex has no data for most of the OECD Member States; nor is there data in the EFA 2000 Assessment for these countries.

Figure 2.34. Adult literacy rate: countries in each quadrant

Level of adult literacy rate in 2000		Changes over the period from 1990 to 2000: Slow performer	Changes over the period from 1990 to 2000: Fast performer	
High literacy: >70% and <95%		QUADRANT I At risk of not achieving the goal(s) Antigua and Barbuda, Bahrain, Botswana, Brazil, Cameroon, Cape Verde, China, Colombia, Dominica, Dominican Republic, Ecuador, El Salvador, Ghana, Honduras, Jamaica, Kuwait, Lebanon, Lesotho, Malta, Mauritius, Mexico, Myanmar, Namibia, Panama, Paraguay, Peru, Qatar, Saudi Arabia, South Africa, Sri Lanka, Swaziland, Syrian Arab Republic, Tunisia, Turkey, United Arab Emirates, United Republic of Tanzania, Venezuela, Viet Nam, Zambia **39** countries	QUADRANT II High chance of achieving the goal(s) Albania, Belize, Bolivia, Bosnia and Herzegovina, Congo, Equatorial Guinea, Fiji, Indonesia, Iran, Israel, Jordan, Kenya, Libyan Arab Jamahiriya, Malaysia, Palestinian A.T., Philippines, Portugal, Zimbabwe **18** countries	**57**
Low literacy: <70%		QUADRANT IV Serious risk of not achieving the goal(s) Algeria, Bangladesh, Benin, Burkina Faso, Burundi, Cambodia, Central African Republic, Chad, Comoros, Dem. Rep. of the Congo, Djibouti, Egypt, Eritrea, Ethiopia, Gambia, Guatemala, Guinea, Guinea-Bissau, Haiti, India, Iraq, Liberia, Madagascar, Malawi, Mali, Mauritania, Morocco, Mozambique, Nepal, Nicaragua, Niger, Nigeria, Pakistan, Papua New Guinea, Rwanda, Senegal, Sudan, Togo, Uganda, Yemen **40** countries	QUADRANT III Low chance of achieving the goal(s) **0** countries	**40**
Total		**79** countries	**18** countries	**97**

Source: Calculations based on Statistical Annex, Table 2; EFA 2000 Assessment (CD-ROM).

five countries, i.e. 70% of all countries included in the exercise. However, there is noticeable imbalance between fast- and slow-performing countries. Among countries close to the goal, thirty-nine are slow performers against eighteen fast performers, while among countries far from the goal, there are no fast performers at all. This indicates serious stagnation, and the regions most in trouble are, once again, sub-Saharan Africa (twenty-three countries in Quadrant IV), the Arab States and North Africa (eight) and South Asia (four). Five of the E-9 countries are in this group: India, Pakistan, Bangladesh, Egypt and Nigeria. The high number of illiterates in these countries as a percentage of the world total has been emphasized earlier in this Report.

In Quadrant I – close to the goal but performing slowly – there are three E-9 countries: Brazil, Mexico and China. The other countries are mostly from sub-Saharan Africa and the Arab States and North Africa. It is, however, encouraging that there are some sub-Saharan and North African countries to be found in Quadrant II, with a high chance of achieving the goal.[9]

Gender equality

The gender equality goal explicitly targets both primary and secondary education, but insufficient data are at present available for the latter. For primary education, countries are considered to have achieved the goal if their gender parity index (GPI) is between 0.97 and 1.03. Table 2.18 lists these countries. More than half of the countries in this exercise have achieved the goal of gender parity, while the disparities between the regions are less marked than for the two other goals examined in this section. Sub-Saharan Africa and the Arab States and North Africa nevertheless lag somewhat behind.

The dividing line for determining proximity or distance from the goal has been set at GPI of 90%. Figure 2.35 presents the dynamic dimension of results for gender parity.

As has already been indicated in the section in this chapter on Goal 5, significant gender gaps occur in the Arab States and North Africa and in South and West Asia. In sub-Saharan Africa, half of the countries remain far from the goal and one quarter are moving away from it.

9. The imbalance between fast and slow performers – 18 versus 79 – could be explained here by the relatively 'severe' criterion of sufficient/insufficient progress in cutting the literacy gap in half. In order to test the sensitivity of the results with respect to the choice of the criterion, the exercise has been repeated using a less severe cut-off point, namely 75% of the progress needed for halving the literacy gap. The two figures below show the differences in outcomes.

Sufficient/insufficient progress needed to halve the gap (as in Figure 2.34):

39	18
40	0

More/less than 75% of the progress needed to halve the gap (alternative calculation):

13	44
36	4

It readily appears that the outcomes for the countries close to the goal are sensitive to the choice of criterion. But the outcomes for the countries far from the goal are hardly sensitive. The conclusion remains that these countries are in serious trouble.

Table 2.18. Countries that have achieved gender parity in primary education GERs

Region	Countries	A: number of countries that have achieved gender parity	B: number of countries in the sample	A/B (as %)
Arab States/ North Africa	Bahrain, Jordan, Kuwait, Palestinian A.T., United Arab Emirates	5	16	31.3%
Central Asia	Azerbaijan, Georgia, Kazakhstan, Kyrgyzstan, Uzbekistan	5	7	71.4%
Central/Eastern Europe	Albania, Belarus, Bosnia and Herzegovina, Bulgaria, Croatia, Czech Republic, Hungary, Lithuania, Latvia, Poland, Romania, Russian Federation, Slovakia, The former Yugoslav Rep. of Macedonia, Yugoslavia	15	17	88.2%
East Asia/Pacific	Australia, China, Fiji, Japan, Malaysia, Myanmar, Niue, New Zealand, Philippines, Rep. of Korea, Viet Nam	11	16	68.8%
Latin America/ Caribbean	Argentina, Bahamas, Barbados, Bolivia, Cayman Islands, Colombia, Costa Rica, Dominican Republic, Ecuador, Honduras, Nicaragua, Mexico, Panama, Peru, Trinidad and Tobago, Turks and Caicos Islands, Uruguay, Venezuela	18	30	60.0%
North America/ Western Europe	Austria, Belgium, Canada, Cyprus, Denmark, Finland, France, Germany, Greece, Iceland, Ireland, Israel, Italy, Luxembourg, Netherlands, Norway, Spain, Sweden, Switzerland, United Kingdom, United States	21	22	95.5%
South/West Asia	Maldives	1	7	14.3%
Sub-Saharan Africa	Botswana, Gabon, Kenya, Malawi, Mauritius, Namibia, Rwanda, Seychelles, U.R. Tanzania, Zimbabwe	10	38	26.3%
Total		86	153	56.2%

Source: Calculations are based on Statistical Annex, Table 2; supplemented by EFA 2000 Assessment (CD-ROM).

Figure 2.35. Primary gross enrolment rate gender parity index: countries in each quadrant

Distance from the goal (GPI = 1) in 2000				
Close 0.90 <GPI< 0.97 or 1.03 <GPI< 1.10	QUADRANT I At risk of not achieving the goal(s) Belize, Chile, Cuba, Estonia, Indonesia, Jamaica, Madagascar, Mongolia, Paraguay, Samoa, South Africa, St Kitts and Nevis, St Vincent and the Grenadines, Swaziland, Tajikistan, Thailand, Turkey, Vanuatu **18** countries	QUADRANT II High chance of achieving the goal Algeria, Bangladesh, Cape Verde, Congo, Egypt, Gambia, Haiti, Iran, Lesotho, Mauritania, Oman, Portugal, Qatar, Sierra Leone, Syrian Arab Republic, Tunisia, Saudi Arabia, Uganda **18** countries	**36**
Far (GPI< 0.90 or GPI > 1.10	QUADRANT IV Serious risk of not achieving the goal Angola, Burundi, Cameroon, Equatorial Guinea, Ethiopia, Grenada, Iraq, Mozambique **8** countries	QUADRANT III Low chance of achieving the goal(s) Benin, Bhutan, Burkina Faso, Central African Republic, Comoros, Côte d'Ivoire, Chad, Djibouti, Dominica, Ghana, Guatemala, Guinea, Guinea-Bissau, India, Lao P.D.R., Mali, Morocco, Nepal, Niger, Pakistan, Senegal, Sudan, Togo **23** countries	**31**
Total	**26** countries	**41** countries	**67**
	Away from the goal	Towards the goal	
	Changes over the period from 1990 to 2000		

Source: Calculations are based on Statistical Annex, Table 2; supplemented by EFA 2000 Assessment (CD-ROM).

Table 2.19. Dakar goal achievement by region

Region	1. High chance of achieving or having achieved all three goals	2. At least one goal likely to be missed	3. Serious risk of not achieving any of the three goals	Total
Arab States/ North Africa	Jordan, Libyan Arab Jamahiriya, Palestinian A.T., Tunisia 4	Algeria, Bahrain, **Egypt,** Kuwait, Mauritania, Oman, Qatar, Saudi Arabia, Syrian Arab Republic, U.A. Emirates 10	Djibouti, Iraq, Lebanon, Morocco, Sudan 5	19
Central Asia	Azerbaijan, Georgia, Kazakhstan, Kyrgyzstan, Mongolia, Tajikistan, Uzbekistan 7			7
Central/ Eastern Europe	Albania, Belarus, Bosnia and Herzegovina, Bulgaria, Croatia, Estonia, Hungary, Latvia, Lithuania, Poland, Romania, Russian Federation, The former Yugoslav Rep. of Macedonia 13	Turkey, Yugoslavia 2		15
East Asia/ Pacific	Australia, Fiji, Japan, Malaysia, Myanmar, New Zealand, Niue, Philippines, Rep. of Korea, Samoa, Thailand, Vanuatu, Viet Nam 13	**China, Indonesia,** Lao P.D.R. 3		16
Latin America/ Caribbean	Antigua and Barbuda, Argentina, Bahamas, Barbados, Belize, Bolivia, **Brazil,** Cayman Islands, Chile, Colombia, Costa Rica, Cuba, Dominican Republic, Ecuador, Guyana, Honduras, **Mexico,** Netherlands Antilles, Panama, Peru, Trinidad and Tobago, Uruguay 22	Dominica, Grenada, Guatemala, Haiti, Jamaica, Nicaragua, Paraguay, St. Kitts and Nevis, St. Vincent and the Grenadines, Venezuela 10		32
North America/ Western Europe	Belgium, Canada, Cyprus, Denmark, France, Greece, Ireland, Israel, Italy, Netherlands, Norway, Portugal, Spain, Sweden, Switzerland, United Kingdom, United States 17			17
South/ West Asia	Maldives 1	**Bangladesh,** Bhutan, Iran, Sri Lanka 4	**India,** Nepal, **Pakistan** 3	8
Sub-Saharan Africa	Congo, Gabon, Kenya, Rwanda, Seychelles, Zimbabwe 6	Botswana, Cape Verde, Côte d'Ivoire, Gambia, Ghana, Lesotho, Malawi, Mauritius, Namibia, South Africa, Swaziland, Togo, Uganda, U.R. Tanzania 14	Benin, Burkina Faso, Burundi, Cameroon, Central African Republic, Chad, Comoros, Democratic Rep. of Congo, Equatorial Guinea, Eritrea, Ethiopia, Guinea, Guinea-Bissau, Madagascar, Mali, Mozambique, Niger, **Nigeria,** Senegal, Zambia 20	40
Overall total	83	43	28	154
Percentage of world population	32.4%	35.8%	26.8%	95.0%

Note: **Boldface** indicates E-9 countries.

Source: Calculations are based on Figures 2.33–2.35, above. Population estimates are from the Tables in the Annex.

In sub-Saharan Africa, half of the countries remain far from the gender goal and one quarter are moving away from it.

Some conclusions about overall progress worldwide

The consolidation of the calculations concerning the three goals was carried out using the following 'credit-point' system.

Score	Points
Goal achieved	3
Score in quadrant 2	2
Score in quadrant 1 or 3	1
Score in quadrant 4	0
missing value	Average of both other values

Sixty-six countries have values for only two of the three goals. Excluding these countries from the exercise would have seriously narrowed the basis for the calculation in the final analysis, and they were thus included on the assumption that their missing values were equal to the averages of the other two values.[10]

The highest attainable score would be 9 (all goals achieved); a score of 0 indicates that all three scores fall into Quadrant III. Countries can be categorized as follows:

- 6–9 points: has achieved all three goals, or has a high chance of doing so;
- 3–5 points: at least one goal is likely to be missed;
- 0-2 points: there is serious risk that none of the three goals will be achieved.

Table 2.19 presents the results of calculating Dakar goal achievement by region, based on this method.

Finally, progress across regions was analysed. Figure 2.36 presents – by region and for the world – the numbers of countries with a high chance of achieving the goal or having already done so (green bars); the numbers of countries with insufficient progress (yellow bars); and the numbers of countries seriously at risk of not achieving the goals (red bars).

10. Because of the linkages between the three goals, this is a plausible assumption: high NER values will imply high GPIs and, if sustained over time, higher values for adult literacy.

There are many countries proving to the world that it is really possible to bring education systems to maturity within a relatively short time span.

Figure 2.37 indicates the population distribution – by region and worldwide – on the same basis.

The results of this analysis indicate that the world is *not* yet on track.

In terms of numbers of countries (Figure 2.36), more than half have either reached the goal or will probably do so (83 out of 154 countries). But in terms of numbers of people (Figure 2.37), a quite different picture emerges. Of the E-9 countries, only Mexico is very close to the goals (two achieved), while Brazil has a high chance of achieving them. For Bangladesh, China, Egypt and Indonesia, at least one goal is likely to be missed, and India and Pakistan run a high risk of not achieving the goals.

> Almost one-third of world population lives in countries where achieving the goals set out in the Dakar Framework for Action will remain a dream unless strong and concerted effort is made to reverse the observed trends. Countries in the regions of South and West Asia, sub-Saharan Africa and the Arab States and North Africa are hardly even moving in the right direction at present, and there is a high risk that they will not be able to achieve the goals by 2015. The populous countries in East Asia and Pacific are making some progress, but will not achieve the goal without intensified effort.

Countries in North America and Western Europe have all reached the goals or are close to them. By contrast, in Central and Eastern Europe, a rich educational tradition is being threatened. For Latin America and the Caribbean, finally, the Dakar goals seem within reach.

There are many countries proving to the world that it is really possible to bring education systems to maturity within a relatively short time span. These successful cases – and they are to be found in all regions worldwide – can serve as sources of inspiration for other developing countries and for the world community. Chapter 4 will attempt to quantify the efforts needed for this leap forward to be made.

Figure 2.36. Assessment of Dakar goal achievement, by region

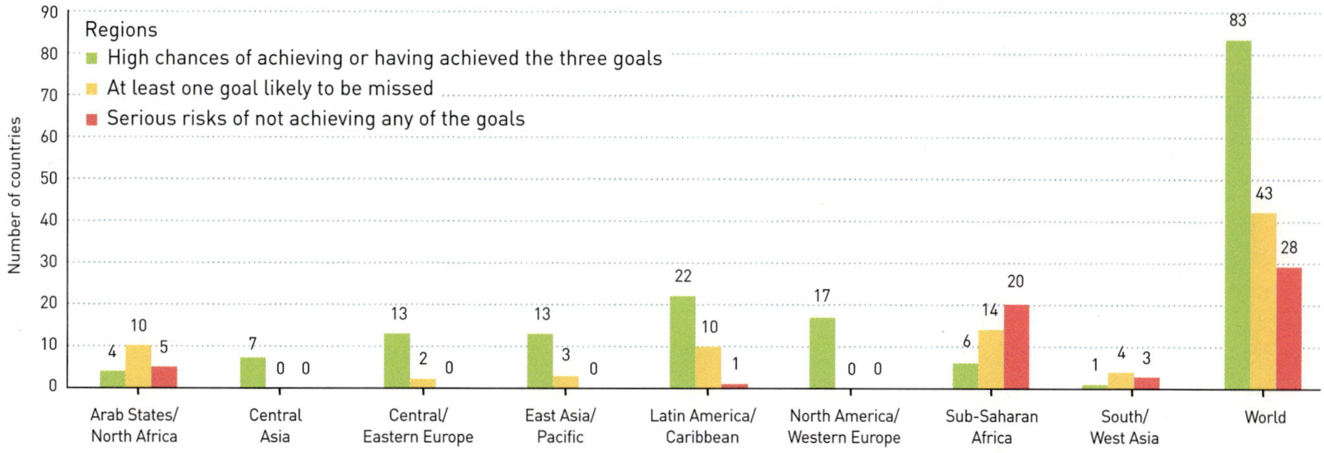

Source: Table 7.19.

Figure 2.37. Assessment of Dakar goal achievement, by population

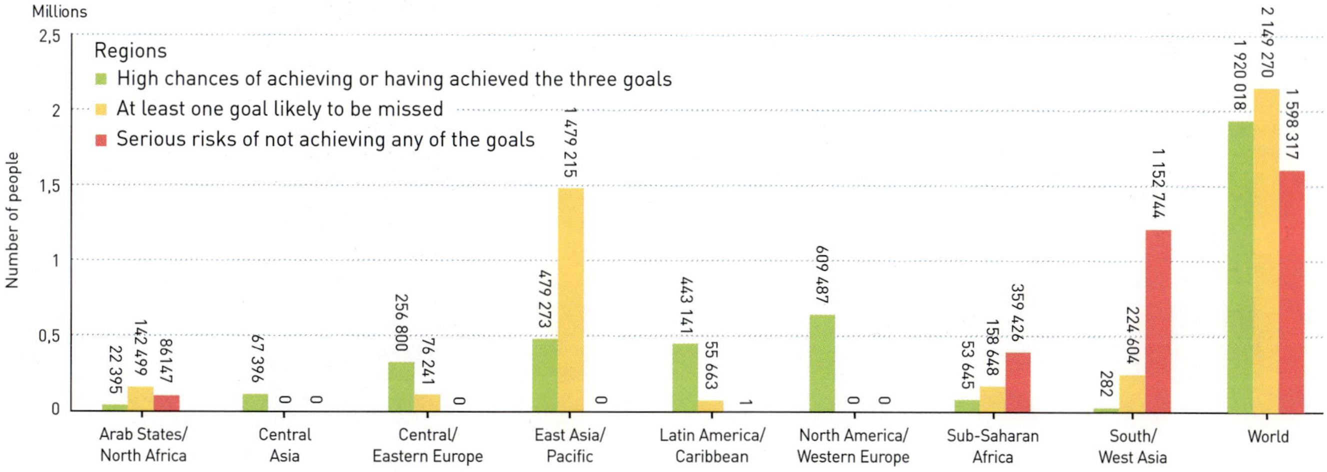

Source: Table 2.19.

อ.แม่สาย

Chapter 3

Planning for education for all

If the end of 2002 was expected to bring a set of finely honed, comprehensive National EFA Action Plans that would provide a basis for dialogue with international agencies for enhanced levels of funding then this target has not been met. If, on the other hand, Dakar is assessed in terms of injecting some urgency and some EFA focus into education and development planning, then there is evidence that this is taking place. Plans that are gender sensitive, inclusive and, where appropriate, responsive to the circumstances of HIV/AIDS and conflict, will be truly supportive of EFA. Plans that lack the financial credibility *and* human resource capability required to make them effective will not work. The urgency implicit in the 2002 planning target and the 2005 and 2015 EFA goals must be sustained.

Dakar's planning challenge

The Dakar Framework for Action (UNESCO, 2000) is subtitled *Meeting Our Collective Commitments*. Since the World Education Forum in 2000, the Dakar commitments have been quoted, interpreted and promoted by many governments, supported strongly by civil society bodies, and endorsed by United Nations agencies, the World Bank and significant and influential groups of countries such as the G8.

The Dakar Framework for Action specifies a set of actions that are designed to instil a sense of urgency and create a climate of accountability.

Broad commitments can be made relatively easily. Following them through is more problematic, as the experience of the decade following the World Education Conference at Jomtien in 1990 demonstrates (Little and Miller, 2000; Torres, 1999). However, unlike Jomtien, the Dakar Framework for Action specifies a set of actions that are designed to instil a sense of urgency and create a climate of accountability. Some of these key actions are time-bound. All of them are based on the need for strong political commitment and for well-conceived, well-managed, and securely funded strategies, twelve of which are elaborated in the Framework for Action (Box 3.1). Effective planning receives a particular emphasis.

The Framework elaborates a set of policy development and planning challenges that are addressed primarily but not exclusively to governments. It requires that countries should prepare or strengthen comprehensive National EFA Action Plans by 2002 at the latest. It makes clear that planning for EFA should be integrated into wider education sector, poverty reduction and development frameworks to ensure that EFA receives the attention and the priority that it requires, as well as the budgetary allocations that are needed if national EFA goals are to be secured. The Framework is clear too, that the demands and the needs of those who are excluded from educational opportunities must be met. Finally, it argues strongly that civil society should be closely engaged in the formulation, implementation and monitoring of strategies designed to achieve EFA.[1]

These challenges are neither new nor straightforward but must be addressed if EFA is to become a reality. The first part of this chapter – 'Is the planning challenge being met?' – includes an interim assessment of the extent of the substantive response to the challenges of planning for EFA. How have governments interpreted their own commitment to the Framework for Action? Are they giving more weight and importance to basic education? Is there evidence of planning for the inclusion of those who are marginalized and disadvantaged? Is planning gender responsive? The extent to which there is a comprehensive approach to planning for EFA is also examined, including an assessment of whether the Dakar 2002 target has been or will be met. The weight that is given to the achievement of EFA goals in Poverty Reduction Strategy Papers (PRSPs) is analysed, and a preliminary assessment is provided on the scope and the nature of the engagement of civil society in planning, given its importance as an indicator of national commitment to EFA.

The World Education Forum underscored the urgency of developing ways of mitigating the impact of HIV/AIDS on education and developing education strategies to combat the pandemic. It also recognized that countries in conflict or facing reconstruction require special attention. The second part of the chapter – 'Planning for HIV/AIDS' – will examine the development of planning that is responsive to the circumstances of people who live with HIV/AIDS, and to those who survive in the face of crisis, conflict and emergency.

The final section – 'Credible planning, credible plans' – examines the concept of a *credible plan*. This is a term used at Dakar to define a prerequisite for funding agencies and other partners in the process of assisting countries implement and sustain their EFA programmes. Since Dakar, the concept of a credible plan has been closely associated with the commitment in the Framework for Action (para. 10), 'that no countries seriously committed to education for all will be thwarted in their achievement of this goal by a lack of resources'.

1. Many of these requirements are explored further in the EFA Regional and E-9 Frameworks that are an integral part of the Dakar Framework for Action (UNESCO, 2000*a*, pp. 23–72).

Is the planning challenge being met?

The underlying principles and goals of EFA were set in Jomtien. They were reaffirmed and expanded in Dakar where there was the opportunity to draw on a broad spectrum of comparative educational knowledge and experience. Children excluded from school, girls' education and the participation of disabled learners were among the issues discussed. Community partnerships in education and the role of non-governmental organizations, school health and nutrition, literacy and education, early childhood care and development and the application of new technologies for education also received attention (UNESCO, 2001 *a,c–f,h,j,l,o–q*). Internationally, there is an enormous fund of knowledge and comparative experience on how to provide good quality education for young children, how to promote gender equality, and how to reach the poor and the excluded. This knowledge is not always shared or well communicated but it exists (e.g. UNICEF, 1999*b*, 2002*a*; Scheerens, 2000; Save the Children, 2001; UNGEI website).

However, in many respects, Dakar is of political rather than technical and professional significance. It will be judged less by the soundness of its technical debates, and much more by the extent to which it promotes commitment and mobilizes human and financial resources in support of the strategies agreed at the World Education Forum (Box 3.1). The realization of Education For All requires sustained political support, realistic choices about the allocation of scarce resources, and an environment that enables people to engage in an inclusive process of making plans and taking decisions. It is also about developing a global understanding of EFA that underpins support for international investment in education.

Box 3.1. Twelve strategies for achieving EFA

To achieve these goals, we the governments, organizations, agencies, groups and associations represented at the World Education Forum pledge ourselves to:

(i) mobilize strong national and international political commitment for education for all, develop national action plans and enhance significantly investment in basic education;

(ii) promote EFA policies within a sustainable and well-integrated sector framework clearly linked to poverty elimination and development strategies;

(iii) ensure the engagement and participation of civil society in the formulation, implementation and monitoring of strategies for educational development;

(iv) develop responsive, participatory and accountable systems of educational governance and management;

(v) meet the needs of education systems affected by conflict, national calamities and instability and conduct educational programmes in ways that promote mutual understanding, peace and tolerance, and help to prevent violence and conflict;

(vi) implement integrated strategies for gender equality in education which recognize the need for changes in attitudes, values and practices;

(vii) implement as a matter of urgency education programmes and actions to combat the HIV/AIDS pandemic;

(viii) create safe, healthy, inclusive and equitably resourced educational environments conducive to excellence in learning with clearly defined levels of achievement for all;

(ix) enhance the status, morale and professionalism of teachers;

(x) harness new information and communication technologies to help achieve EFA goals;

(xi) systematically monitor progress towards EFA goals and strategies at the national, regional and international levels; and

(xii) build on existing mechanisms to accelerate progress towards education for all.

Source: UNESCO (2000a), para. 8.

EFA National Action Plans

If the Dakar commitment that *countries will prepare comprehensive National EFA Plans by 2002 at the latest* is interpreted as meaning any new plan should encompass all of the Dakar goals and result from a strong and politically credible process, then the target has been met in only a relatively small group of countries. Based on the evidence of UNESCO surveys and summary reports from its Regional Bureaux, in the middle of 2002, the twenty-two countries listed in Table 3.1 below have either indicated their completion of, or intention to finalize a National Plan of Action for EFA by the end of 2002.

The list in Table 3.1 should be treated with the greatest possible caution as it is based on incomplete data and reports that are not easily comparable. In some cases it may overstate progress and the degree to which a plan is comprehensive. On the other hand, it may exclude countries such as Pakistan that have undertaken a considerable amount of work on an EFA plan that is awaiting finalization and approval.[2]

In many respects, Dakar is of political, rather than technical or professional, significance.

2. A recent return of work done in Pacific island states indicates that all countries are preparing EFA plans. In Latin America and the Caribbean, 15 countries are working on EFA plans (based on the coutcomes of a UNESCO regional Meeting in Santo Domingo, August 2002).

Table 3.1. National EFA plans, completed or expected to be finalized by the end of 2002

Arab States	Djibouti, Mauritania
Asia	Bangladesh, Cambodia, India, Kazakhstan, Kyrgyzstan, Nepal
Latin America/Caribbean	Cuba, Dominican Republic, Ecuador
Sub-Saharan Africa	Angola, Cameroon, Central African Republic, Chad, Ethiopia, Guinea, Guinea-Bissau, Namibia, Niger, Senegal and Zimbabwe.

Source: Interpretation of formal reports to UNESCO (mid-2002) from UNESCO Regional Bureaux; surveys conducted by UNESCO's Division of Educational Policies and Strategies (EPS), 2002.

The extent is to which there engagement with civil society that goes beyond set-piece consultation has not always been well defined.

A completed plan is not necessarily one that has been adopted by Government and approved as the basis for budgetary allocations in the mainstream of sector and development policy. In some countries, the plans are a restatement or reformulation of existing plans. And the extent is to which there engagement with civil society that goes beyond set-piece consultation has not always been well defined.

If a broader and wider interpretation of planning for EFA is used, wherein countries are revisiting their goals and targets for EFA, building on existing sector strategies and plans, and promoting EFA in other planning processes such as PRSPs, then there is a much stronger case to be made for a larger group of countries.

A diversity of response

UNESCO has been the leader in promoting the Dakar commitment to develop EFA National Action Plans and it is the main repository of progress reports, through its Paris headquarters and Regional Bureaux. But as yet, there is no authoritative global analysis that draws on detailed country studies. As a consequence, it is difficult to assess with any degree of confidence, how national governments have interpreted the Dakar planning commitment. Data that are available at the international level are limited, uneven and sometimes difficult to interpret. Nevertheless, reports from UNESCO's Regional Bureaux highlight a range of education sector planning activities and a considerable variety of interpretations regarding the call for a comprehensive EFA National Action Plan by 2002 (UNESCO, 2002*e*, 2002*j*; Global March website).

One preliminary conclusion that can be drawn, illustrated by the twenty-two countries presented in Table 3.1, is that the Dakar planning commitment is perceived primarily as an exercise for developing countries. There are some exceptions to this, however, as the creation of sub-regional forums for the Nordic and Baltic countries and for three Caucasus states demonstrates. Spain is developing an EFA plan and there is similar work underway in Eastern European countries such as Estonia and Republic of Moldova (Virtosu, 2002). However, it is broadly true that industrialized countries do not see the goals of EFA as providing the parameters for national education planning. Indeed, this perception is not restricted to planning and can be applied to EFA in more general terms. This has important implications for EFA as a global commitment.

Based on a questionnaire survey carried out in June 2002, UNESCO headquarters has collected data on EFA-related planning activities in fifty-four countries (ten from sub-Saharan Africa, eleven Arab States, thirteen from Asia and the Pacific, fourteen from Latin America and six from Europe). These data suggest that 70% of the countries have set up EFA Forums. They also suggest that 75% of the sample countries are engaged in planning processes that encompass some or all of the Dakar goals, whether in the form of a separate and distinct National EFA Plan or within broader planning frameworks such as education sector plans and national development strategies.

The survey records some of the difficulties that confront education sector planners: the lack of reliable data, inadequate technical skills for policy formulation and planning, the absence of robust analyses on costs and the financing of EFA, and the associated difficulty of developing reliable budget projections. These are issues to which further attention is paid in Chapter 4.

UNESCO's Regional Bureaux have conducted their own surveys of planning for EFA. These provide headline information on the status of plan development, difficulties that are being experienced and the existence of related planning documents and frameworks. From this information it is possible to draw some additional but tentative conclusions. Five EFA regions are examined briefly below.[3]

In the nineteen Arab States, all but one country is recorded as having set up a national EFA team or committee. Five countries (Iraq, Libyan Arab Jamahiriya, Palestinian Autonomous Territories, Syrian Arab Republic and Tunisia) have prepared the first draft of an EFA plan. Mauritania is reported as having finalized its plan.

In East Asia, most of the twelve countries in the region have indicated that their national objectives will derive from existing policy documents and education sector plans and that additional objectives will be defined for EFA components not covered under existing policy documents and plans.[4] Each country is interpreting the Dakar commitment in a context-specific way. Malaysia has already addressed the EFA goals within its existing national education sector development plans, but along with six other countries, it is reported as having established an EFA Forum or a national EFA committee (Cambodia, Democratic People's Republic of Korea, Indonesia, Lao People's Democratic Republic, Malaysia, Mongolia and Myanmar). Cambodia is a country that has chosen to develop an EFA plan that encompasses goals and strategies already embedded in existing plans (Box 3.2). China and the Democratic People's Republic of Korea are both reported to have prepared the first version of an EFA Plan.

Of the nine countries of South and West Asia, Bangladesh and Pakistan have developed draft plans. Pakistan has prepared a national EFA Plan for the period 2000–2015 (Pakistan, 2001*a*), defined as an integral part of Pakistan's Education Sector Reforms: 2001–2004 (Pakistan, 2001*b*). In the draft EFA Plan, it is estimated that the Government can fund 40% of an enlarged budget but that external funding will be required to fill the financing gap. The EFA Plan makes specific reference to the Dakar commitment that no countries seriously committed to Education for All will be thwarted in their achievement by a lack of resources.

Box 3.2. Planning for EFA in Cambodia

The Government of the Kingdom of Cambodia created the National Education for All Committee in October 2001. It has 150 members and is chaired by the Prime Minister with cross-ministry representation. The Committee has a secretariat in the Ministry of Education. EFA committees are being established at province, municipality, district and community levels.

Six working groups have been established to work on each of the Dakar Goals. These groups are working with NGOs and international agencies. The key task is to develop an EFA National Plan of Action that integrates existing education plans, since, as is explained in the report, 'The challenge has been to link the existing Education Strategy Plan (ESP) and the Education Sector Support Programme (ESSP) with the Education for All Plan of Action.'

Since the ESSP focuses mainly on formal education, there is a need to develop programmes to reach the unreached – street children, minority groups, indigenous groups, communities in remote rural areas and girls – by promoting programmes in the area of non-formal education and literacy.

Source: Kingdom of Cambodia (2002).

India's Plan of Action will be finalized by the end of 2002. It will reflect and complement the Sarva Shiksa Abhiyan programme for Universal Elementary Education (UEE) that is designed to ensure that all children aged 6 to 14 will receive eight years of quality education by 2010, as well as India's 10th Five-year Plan 2002–2007 (India, 2002), which includes literacy strategies as well as UEE.

Both Bangladesh and Nepal are scheduled to have finalized EFA planning documents by the end of 2002. An assessment of Sri Lanka's interpretation of the Dakar commitment, arguing that Sri Lanka has a portfolio of plans, is presented in Box 3.3.

In the Latin America and the Caribbean region there are forty-one countries. Here too, existing policies and plans are being revised to take a more comprehensive approach to EFA. For example, the Government of Brazil has worked to ensure that the Dakar goals are addressed in its national education plan for 2001–2010 (Box 3.4). In Bolivia, the existing 20-year plan for basic education and the country's PRSP provide the main frameworks for addressing the goals of EFA. Nicaragua's National Education Plan

The government of Brazil has worked to ensure that the Dakar goals are addressed in its national education plan for 2001–2010.

3. Information was also made available to the Global Report on Europe (see Chapter 5) and the countries of the Pacific.

4. Information provided by UNESCO Office in Bangkok and Regional Bureau for Education (Thailand), 2002.

Box 3.3. EFA in Sri Lanka: a portfolio of plans

Policy development

Jomtien and Dakar emphasize the importance of National EFA Plans. Yet both frameworks pay limited attention to the development of national policies and to the scope for policies and goals that differ from EFA. In Sri Lanka, EFA-related goals have underpinned educational policies for many years and the process that underpins the formulation of policy has been vital to the development and implementation of plans.

In the 1990s, the main responsibility for formulating education policy rested with the National Education Commission (NEC) which was established to advise the President on continuity in educational policy and to ensure responsiveness to changing needs.

In 1995, the President stressed the importance of improvements in education within the overall development policy. Resources for education had declined (from around 4% of GDP or 15% of government expenditure in the 1960s, to 3% of GDP or 10% of government expenditure in the 1990s). This accentuated inequities and the quality of education declined. The government's medium-term investment strategy envisaged an increase in public resources to education, and initiatives to reduce or remove inequities, upgrade the quality of education, expand opportunities for vocational training and restructure the tertiary system.

Later that year, the National Education Policy appeared in two parts: 'Towards a National Education Policy', and 'An Action Oriented Strategy'.

On primary education, NEC emphasized investment in quality across the system, the need to democratize access for the 5–14 age group, and for regulations on compulsory education for that age group. These directives became the key reference point for the Presidential Task Force on Education, the Education Reforms Implementation Unit in the Ministry of Education, and for specialist planning groups such as the group that developed the Five-year Plan for Primary Education (FYPE).

Sri Lanka's approach to planning

Planning responds to these evolving policy frameworks. With respect to the six EFA Goals, the following approaches appear to have been adopted.

Early Childhood Care and Development (ECCD) is the responsibility of the Children's Secretariat in the Ministry of Social Welfare. In 2002, after a change of government, an Inter-Ministerial Advisory Committee on ECCD was established. Work on legislative provision is ongoing.

Life skills and learning opportunities for youth and adults are addressed through secondary education programmes, under the National Commission on Vocational and Technical Training, and through the work of NGOs and the Youth Services Council. There is no co-ordinated plan of action.

The **elimination of gender disparities** is not elevated to the level of national educational policy in Sri Lanka. Access to, and the quality of, basic education is remarkably even for males and females, and has been for much of the 1990s. Where specific disparities have been manifest, for example among girls in the plantations, these have been addressed within programmes targeted on the plantation schools.

UPE and the **quality of education** are reflected in the work of numerous policy and planning groups. Most recently, the Primary Education Planning Project (PEPP) in the Ministry of Education published eight Provincial Plans for Primary Education (1999–2004) and the Five-year Plan for Primary Education (FYPPE 2000–2004).

The National Plan of Action – post-Dakar

The National Plan of Action (2002–2004) draws on an array of plans and initiatives, many of which predate Dakar. This is a portfolio plan, developed by groups comprising senior staff from agencies, including the Ministry of Education, the National Institute of Education, the Presidential Secretariat, the Open University, the Child Protection Authority, UNICEF, and representatives of NGOs. Much of the technical work was contributed by Technical Support Groups from the Ministry, the National Institute of Education, the Children's Secretariat and Sri Lankan consultants. A national EFA coordinator, supported by eight provincial coordinators, drew the plan together.

The Sri Lankan National Action Plan is derived from plans developed for each of the EFA Goals and from a mix of planning structures and policies. The plans for primary education have not been created or re-created to respond to Dakar. They were developed prior to Dakar and have been edited and re-presented alongside plans that meet the other Dakar Goals. While some countries may need to create plans de novo others may simply require a translation of existing material into a slightly different format, highlighting those aspects that reflect the Dakar criteria. And since it is unlikely that a single Ministry can develop all plans to meet all the EFA Goals, the National Action Plan is better thought of as a portfolio of complementary plans.

The Plan for primary education and Dakar criteria for EFA plans

FYPPE 2000–2004 resonates with several of the criteria for National EFA plans suggested at Dakar:

- Plans should be developed with government leadership in direct and systematic consultation with civil society. FYPPE was derived from the National Policy on Education developed in consultation with members of national civil society.
- Plans should attract coordinated support of all development partners. The plans of all current development partners (Ministry of Education, Provinces, NIE, foreign-funded projects, etc.) have been incorporated within the structure of FYPPE.
- Plans should specify reforms addressing all EFA goals. FYPPE addresses two of the goals.
- Plans should set in place a sustainable financial framework. FYPPE presents a costed plan over five years, identifies resource gaps and ways of meeting those gaps from both domestic and foreign sources.
- Plans should be time-bound and action-oriented. FYPPE presents an implementation schedule over five years, and is activity-based. Annual implementation plans are expected at the school, zone, province and national levels.
- Plans should include mid-term performance indicators. FYPPE presents a detailed framework for the monitoring of goals from school to national level.
- Plans should achieve a synergy of all human development efforts, through its inclusion in the national development planning framework and process. FYPPE is consistent with the National six-year multi-sector development plan.

Source: See Little (forthcoming).

2001–2015 indicates that all the goals and strategies of the Framework for Action are included within its structure, an operational framework for 2002–2008 already having been finalized.

In Cuba, it is expected that an EFA Plan will be completed in 2002 to complement the existing 15-year national plan of action. The Dominican Republic and Ecuador both indicate that new EFA plans should be ready by the end of 2002. In the Caribbean, all countries report existing policies and plans that address EFA goals. Dominica reports that its 1999 Education Development Plan, revised in 2002, addresses EFA objectives. Only Trinidad and Tobago is reported as preparing a separate EFA Plan.

For the forty-six countries that comprise the sub-Saharan Africa region, detailed analysis is limited (UNESCO-BREDA, 2002). As can be seen in Table 3.1, eleven countries are recorded as having EFA plans due for completion by the end of 2002. Other countries are developing their existing sector plans. For example, The Gambia is developing an Action Plan that builds on its current Education Master Plan, 1998–2006 and its updated Public Expenditure Review (2001). Thirteen countries are included in the first tranche of nations identified under the World Bank's Fast-Track Initiative for UPE, which includes a requirement that a country have both a PRSP and an education sector plan. These countries are Burkina Faso, Democratic Republic of the Congo, Ethiopia, The Gambia, Ghana, Guinea, Mauritania, Mozambique, Niger, Nigeria, Uganda, the United Republic of Tanzania and Zambia.

These summary regional reports suggest that there are many more than the twenty-two countries listed in Table 3.1 working on existing policies and plans to embrace some or all of the EFA goals agreed in Jomtien and under The Dakar Framework for Action. The *International Strategy to Put the Dakar Framework for Action on Education for All into Operation* (UNESCO, 2002*h*) states that by March 2002, around seventy countries had developed plans for Education for All, although the evidence base for this assertion is not provided. Clearly there is currently some rethinking and modification taking place regarding education plans and strategies tailored to reflect the strengths of existing policies and plans as well as the relevance of the EFA goals to national circumstance. For example, the government of Democratic People's Republic of Korea is focusing on life skills and the quality of education in the belief that it has met the other goals. There is evidence too of the establishment of EFA Forums and committees even if a new and/or formal EFA plan is not being constructed, although data on the roles, composition and work of these forums are not readily available.

For the future, if there is to be an effective monitoring process at the regional and international level, there is a clear need for a comprehensive database on country-level legislation, policies and plans. This is a matter that UNESCO, its specialized institutes, and other international organizations should address. It is a development with which the Global Report is well placed to assist.

In advance of the availability of such a resource, the EFA Global Monitoring Report undertook two exercises. A rapid survey of readily accessible national policy and planning documents developed over the last five years was undertaken for forty countries. The results are indicative, not comprehensive. There were five broad objectives:

Box 3.4. Brazil's National Education Action Plan, 2001–2010

In January 2001, the President of the Republic, Fernando Henrique Cardoso, approved the new national education plan. Formulated through a participatory process involving civil society, government and the legislature, the Plan sets guidelines, goals and priorities to be implemented by the end of this decade. Its premises and proposals are in tune with the EFA Goals of the World Education Forum.

According to the plan, the three levels of government – federal, state and municipal – are committed to adopting measures to raise the population's level of schooling, improve the quality of instruction, reduce social and regional inequalities and democratize the management of public education by the end of the decade. Plans are being developed at municipal and state levels to guarantee that the commitments and the goals of the national education plan can be achieved.

In a country the size of a continent, with 27 States and 5,561 municipalities, 170 million inhabitants and over 55 million students, including 36 million in basic education – this commitment is a major challenge.

Sources: Taken from Guimaraes de Castro (2002).

1. establish whether there has been recent legislative change to strengthen the right to education and provide a strong basis for EFA planning and programme development;
2. identify the primary policy and planning instruments and frameworks for EFA;
3. see whether clear timelines for the achievement of EFA goals and targets are in place;
4. see whether there are commitments to increase or reallocate budgets for EFA; and
5. assess whether the engagement of civil society in planning for EFA is a reality.

Legislation that introduces or strengthens the provision of free and compulsory primary education is most significant .

The forty countries/territories are listed in Table 3.2. They were selected in order to include a relatively large sample of countries each of which possesses one or more of the following characteristics: low levels of primary school net enrolment, substantial numbers of school age children out of school, low levels of adult literacy, high recent or current prevalence rates of HIV/AIDS among adults, and the incidence of conflict. Countries with large and small total populations were included.

Together, these countries comprise 40% of the global school-age population in 1999/2000. The twenty-three countries from sub-Saharan Africa account for 73% of the sub-continent's school-age population while the six countries from South and West Asia account for 94%. Only four countries in the sample have adult literacy levels of over 80%. Fourteen countries have HIV prevalence rates of over 5%. At least twelve of the sample countries are living with conflict or emergency.

In addition to this survey, work was commissioned on the extent to which EFA and MDG goals are reflected in Poverty Reduction Strategy Papers (PRSPs), in both the process of their development and their product (Bagai, 2002). Work by ActionAid is also instructive in this regard (ActionAid, 2002).

Legislative change

In the 1990s nearly 55% of the countries listed in Table 3.2, enacted legislation for education. Most significant is legislation for introducing or strengthening the provision of free and compulsory primary education. This is true of Cambodia, Lao People's Democratic Republic, Thailand, Argentina, Guinea, Madagascar, Niger, Nigeria and Uganda. Since Dakar, India has passed its 93rd Constitutional Amendment Bill (November 2001), which states that education for children in the age group 6–14 years is a fundamental right. Legislation is currently being prepared to delineate responsibilities between the central government, state governments and local bodies, define the parameters of an acceptable quality of education and institute mechanisms for redress when the right is violated. In Nigeria, a bill to Provide Compulsory, Free Universal Basic Education is designed to underpin and strengthen Nigeria's Universal Basic Education Programme. Amendments to Nepal's Education Act (2002) have clarified the concept of free primary education and the role of communities in education.

These enactments set an essential basis for strengthening the right to education and creating a platform on which EFA planning can build, placing sound policies in a legal framework. South Africa provides a strong example in this regard (Box 3.5). Monitoring the legislative basis for the right to education deserves more detailed attention internationally, including support for the work of the United Nations Special Rapporteur on the Right to Education.

Planning frameworks

Education for All goals and objectives appear across a range of national-, state- and province-level policies and plans. They appear in overall development frameworks including Poverty Reduction Strategy Papers (PRSPs), within education sector, subsector and EFA plans, across the strategies of different ministries, and in separate plans and programmes to meet the needs of particular groups of people. The experience of India demonstrates some of these complexities and relationships (Box 3.6).

Based on policy papers and education plans from thirty-six of the forty countries listed in Table 3.2, eighteen or 50% have education sector plans that provide the basis for implementing strategies to achieve EFA goals. All but four of the eighteen had sector plans in place prior to Dakar. A further twelve countries have elaborated detailed subsector plans and programmes either within or outside of a wider sector framework. These may reflect particular levels of education such as early childhood care and development or primary education, specific goals or themes such as literacy, or particular groups such as girls, HIV/AIDS orphans or nomads. For example, in Yemen there is a national strategy for literacy, a strategy for girls' education and a population plan of action that includes education.

Some countries are in the process of developing an overarching poverty strategy, a long-term education sector investment framework and an EFA plan, all at the same time. Malawi is a case in point. The pressures to develop these three different levels of policy analysis and planning are often external. They flow directly from requirements established by The World Bank, bilateral agencies working on sector programmes, and indirectly from the wish to respond to, and report on, the international commitments made in Dakar and elsewhere. Articulating a productive relationship between the three is challenging, particularly in systems with limited planning capacity. The different demands of agencies can result in planning exhaustion. This comes at a time in Malawi when there is an urgent need to improve the quality of education following substantial enrolment gains with the introduction of Free Primary Education in 1994 (Kadzamira, 2002).

Where countries are developing separate EFA plans, it is clearly important that they are doing so not just to meet an international commitment but in order to respond to national EFA challenges in a manner which strengthens existing planning processes. Towards the end of 2002, it is extremely difficult to judge the extent to which new and separate EFA plans will have a well-defined place in the pantheon of national planning instruments. This judgement may be further complicated by the new proposals and planning submissions for the World Bank Fast-Track Initiative which may form another instrument in the ledger of planning requirements (see Chapter 5).

Box 3.5. The right to education in South Africa

In 1994 Nelson Mandela took office as the first president of a new democratic South Africa, and shortly afterwards South Africa was invited to participate in the EFA process. The task facing the 'government of national unity' that Mandela led was not the typical challenge for developing countries of enhancing access and quality in an existing state education system. Rather the need was to dismantle an existing system and replace it with new structures oriented around radically different values.

Consistent with the principles of EFA, the country's new constitution, adopted in final form in 1996, refers to nine years of compulsory schooling, thereby making education for black Africans compulsory for the first time. Significantly, under the Constitution a person's right to a basic education is unqualified and, in contrast to that of other public services such as health care and social security, is not limited by phrases referring to the availability of funds.

Consistent with the country's new democratic values, an important objective of the new government was to equalize the distribution of state funds among the nine new provinces, whose assets vary widely. Provinces such as Gauteng and Western Cape, home to the major cities of Johannesburg and Cape Town respectively, have substantial economic and other resources at their disposal, while others, such as Eastern Cape, crafted largely out of two former African black 'homelands', begin with few economic resources and little functioning infrastructure.

Despite the constraint of no additional funding resources, consistent with a conservative macro-economic policy, South African policy-makers were largely successful in equalizing the distribution of state funds among the nine provinces. Pupil spending in the Eastern Cape rose from 78% to 87% of the overall average between 1991 and 2001, while spending in the Western Cape decreased from 180% to 119% of the average.

Sources: Drawn from Fiske and Ladd (2002).

PRSPs are taking on increasing importance for overall national development policy and planning in the world's poorest countries. Globally, forty-eight countries are in the process of developing interim or full PRSPs. These are designed to describe a country's economic and social policies over a 3-year or longer time horizon and to be the operational vehicle for translating a poverty reduction strategy into an action plan – an action plan underpinned by sector strategies. Given the growing dominance of PRSPs, and of their objective of achieving the MDGs, it follows that education and the attainment of the EFA goals should hold a prominent place in their development and implementation.

For interim and full PRSPs in twenty-five countries, ActionAid notes that most strategies identify universal primary education (UPE) as a key goal and define it invariably in terms of gross

Some countries are in the process of developing an overarching poverty strategy, a long-term education sector investment framework and an EFA plan, all at the same time.

Table 3.2. Selected background indicators for 40 countries/territories*

	PRIMARY EDUCATION					
	Net enrolment ratios (NER)		Gross enrolment ratios (GER)		Survival to Grade 5	
	Both sexes	Gender parity index (F/M)	Both sexes	Gender parity index (F/M)	Both sexes	Gender parity index (F/M)
Arab States						
Mauritania[3]	63.0	0.95	84.3	0.94	...	...
Palestinian Aut. Terr.	99.1	1.00	108.6	1.01	...	...
Yemen	...	...	...	...	...	...
Asia/Pacific						
Afghanistan	...	...	...	...	...	...
Bangladesh[3]	81.4	1.04	...	...	...	...
Bhutan[3]	52.9	0.81	...	...	...	...
Cambodia	88.6	0.88	102.4	0.87	...	
India	...	...	100.9	0.85	59.7	0.91
Lao P.D.R.	81.8	0.92	115.3	0.85	54.2	0.98
Nepal	...	...	126.4	0.80	...	...
Pakistan	...	...	96.0	0.63	...	...
Thailand	81.4	0.96	93.5	0.95	97.1	1.03
Vanuatu	96.1	0.92	117.1	1.08	...	...
Latin America/Caribbean						
Argentina	106.4	1.00	118.9	1.00	94.7	1.03
Haiti[3]	66.3	1.00	126.0	0.96	40.8	1.07
Sub-Saharan Africa						
Benin	70.3	0.69	85.9	0.67	...	
Botswana	83.6	...	108.4		87.6	1.08
Burkina Faso	34.6	0.69	42.9	0.70	68.3	1.05
Dem. Rep. of the Congo	...	...	...	...	...	...
Equatorial Guinea	79.0	0.8	124.8	0.82	16.3	1.3
Eritrea	40.3	0.86	61.2	0.82	95.3	0.95
Ethiopia	...	...	70.8	0.67	...	...
Gambia	69.8	0.87	75.1	0.90	...	...
Guinea	49.0	0.73	62.8	0.68	86.9	0.86
Guinea-Bissau	53.5	0.71	82.7	0.67	...	...
Kenya	...	...	...	...	...	...
Lesotho	58.5	1.14	103.5	1.09	68.4	1.25
Madagascar	66.4	1.01	101.8	0.96	51.1	1.02
Malawi	...	...	158.1	1.00	...	...
Mali[3]	39.9	0.69	50.0	0.67	78.1	...
Mozambique	50.1	0.83	85.4	0.75	46.2	0.85
Niger	21.2	1.06	32.4	0.67	61.3	0.97
Nigeria	...	...	...	...	...	...
Rwanda	97.3	1.00	122.4	0.98	45.4	0.89
Sierra Leone	65.2	0.93	65.2	0.92	...	...
Sudan	44.7	0.84	55.0	0.85	86.8	1.03
U.R. Tanzania	46.7	1.04	63.0	1.00	80.9	1.06
Togo	91.4	0.81	123.8	0.78	51.6	0.89
Uganda	...	...	140.9	0.93	44.7	1.04
Zambia	66.4	0.98	78.7	0.94	78.2	0.87

1. World Bank data (2002a). These data are not a substitute for the sustained collection of standardized international education statistics through UIS. They were produced to help update the global picture of progress to date.

2. Trend rate is the average annual percentage point change in primary completion rate from 1990 to the most recent year. Data for the most recent year are generally for 1999.

3. Data on enrolment and survival rates are from EFA 2000 country reports.

PRIMARY EDUCATION				LITERACY		EDUCATION FINANCE				HIV/AIDS
Primary completion rate in[1]			*Estimated number of out-of-school children (000)*	Adult literacy rate (15+)		Education spending as %[1]		Primary education spending as %[1]		*Incidence of HIV/AIDS among 15-49 year olds*
1990	Most recent year[2]	Trend rate from 1990 to most recent year[2]		Both sexes	Gender parity index (F/M)	Govt spending	GDP	Education spending	GDP	
34	46	1.47	...	40.2	0.59	13.7	3.6	49.0	1.8	...
...	...	...	3	...	...	...	...	...	...	...
n/a	40	n/a	...	46.4	0.37	13.0	5.1	54.2	2.7	0.1
22	8	-1.39	...	...	...	...	...	...	...	...
	70		...	40.0	0.61	9.6	1.9	49.9	0.9	<0.1
7	23	2.69	...	...	...	...	...	...	...	<0.1
52	60	0.67	251	68.0	0.71	15.0	1.7	51.0	0.9	2.7
66	67	0.21	...	57.2	0.66	17.4	2.6	38.5	1.0	0.8
44	64	2.53	132	64.8	0.70	3.1	0.5	58.6	0.3	<0.1
49	57	0.82	...	41.7	0.40	11.1	1.9	63.8	1.2	0.5
n/a	n/a	n/a	...	43.2	0.49	8.3	1.7	62.2	1.1	0.1
93	84	-1.34	1214	95.5	0.97	...	...	...	...	1.8
90	86	-1.25	...	...	...	...	...	...	...	...
			...	96.8	1.00					0.7
28	70	5.28	...	49.8	0.92	17.0	1.9	38.7	0.7	6.1
23	39	1.94	323	37.4	0.45	16.5	2.5	62.6	1.6	3.6
...	...	...	49	77.2	1.07	...	...	...	...	38.8
19	25	0.75	1298	23.9	0.42	17.1	2.5	64.0	1.6	6.5
48	40	-0.82	...	61.4	0.69	3.2	0.3	65.1	0.2	4.9
...	...	...	46.6	83.2	0.80	...	...	...	...	3.4
19	35	2.05	288	55.7	0.66	8.0	2.8	53.6	1.5	2.8
22	24	0.24	...	39.1	0.66	15.0	2.7	46.2	1.2	6.4
40	70	3.33	56	36.6	0.68	16.6	3.1	51.7	1.6	1.6
16	35	1.90	642	...	...	18.1	2.0	37.2	0.8	...
16	31	1.24	84	38.4	0.43	9.8	1.9	35.0	0.7	2.8
63	58	-1.00	...	82.4	0.86	26.2	6.3	44.2	2.8	15.0
64	69	0.83	146	83.4	1.29	22.2	8.0	40.2	3.2	31.0
34	27	-0.93	729	66.5	0.81	18.8	2.0	54.7	1.1	0.3
30	50	4.00	...	60.1	0.62	19.8	3.6	49.2	1.8	15.0
11	23	1.56	...	25.6	0.45	13.7	2.3	42.1	1.0	1.7
30	36	0.76	1232	44.0	0.48	18.1	2.0	46.4	1.0	13.0
18	20	0.29	1408	16.0	0.36	31.5	2.9	62.0	1.8	...
72	67	-0.53	...	64.0	0.78	9.9	4.6	41.0	1.9	5.8
n/a	n/a	n/a	32	66.8	0.82	32.6	3.2	44.7	1.4	8.9
n/a	37	n/a	236	...	...	30.4	3.5	51.3	1.8	7.0
35	n/a	n/a	2576	57.7	0.67	16.2	1.8	50.5	0.9	2.6
46	59	1.63	3543	75.0	0.79	16.4	1.8	63.0	1.1	7.8
41	63	2.50	64	57.1	0.59	25.6	3.8	48.3	1.8	6.0
39	61	2.21	...	67.0	0.73	30.1	3.2	53.2	1.7	5.0
97	80	-3.4	664	78.2	0.84	12.3	2.3	43.2	1.0	21.5

* Five criteria were used in selecting the countries: 1. low primary education enrolment/completion rates; 2. Large numbers of out-of-school children (>1 million); 3. low levels of adult literacy; 4. high prevalence of HIV/AIDS (> 5%); and 5) crises/conflicts (or post-conflict situations) and emergency. Besides these criteria, an attempt was made to cover all the developing regions and to include some small countries.

Box 3.6. Planning for EFA in India

India began its journey towards the goal of creating a system of mass education freely accessible to all children of the country more than fifty years ago. Considerable progress has been made, but the goal of universal education for all as enshrined in the Indian Constitution has still eluded the country.

Education for All: some figures for India (1951 and 2002)

	1951	2002
Literacy rate	18%	65.38%
Female literacy	8.9%	54.16%
Children in school		
Lower primary school GERs, Grades 1–5	42.60%	95%
Girls	24.8%	85%
Upper primary school GERs, Grades 6–8	12.70%	59%
Girls	4.6%	50%
Of 100 children in school		
Boys	86	56
Girls	14	44

With more than thirty constituent states and union territories, India has traditionally had a national government focuses only on broad policy issues. However, the National Policy on Education (1986) gave national government a more proactive role in promoting adult literacy and primary education. Significant improvements were registered during the 1990s. The literacy rate improved from 52.2% to 65.4%. The absolute number of illiterates fell by 32 million. The number of lower primary schools increased by 14% and the upper primary schools by 36%. Altogether, 24.3 million more children entered school, 130,000 new schools opened and 530,000 additional teachers were appointed. The share of girls in total enrolment went from 41% to 44% in primary and from 38% to 40% in upper primary. Expenditure on education in the Government sector went up from 3.84% to 4.11% of GDP.

Interfacing national action with Dakar goals

India has been implementing a number of specially designed programmes to move towards universal primary education and eradicating adult illiteracy. For the first time, an attempt has been made to link national and global targets on EFA:

- Early Childhood Care and Education: integrated Child Development Services scheme is being universalized. Estimated cost, US$3.3 billion 2002–2007.
- Sarva Shiksha Abhiyan (Movement for Education for All) aims to provide eight years of quality education to all children in age group 6–14 by 2010. Estimated cost, US$20 billion.
- A comprehensive plan for adolescents, especially for girls, in the Tenth Five-year Plan.
- National Literacy Mission to provide functional literacy to illiterate adults in the age group 15–35. Achieve sustainable threshold level of 75% literacy by 2005. Estimated cost US$1.3 billion over 5 years.
- Special schemes targeted at girls, apart from focus on girls in general schemes. Removal of all disparities, including gender, in primary (class I–V) by 2007 and elementary (I–VIII) by 2010.

These targets surpass the international expectations articulated in the Dakar Framework. An urgent requirement is to re-establish public faith in the state-sponsored primary schools and adult literacy programmes by demonstrating effectively functioning institutions that meet the aspirations of society.

Current EFA strategies

Strategies for achieving total literacy and universal elementary education focus on several interrelated strategies.

Decentralization. The government of India encourages state governments to generate contextualized action plans and supports them through the centrally sponsored programmes of SSA and NLM. The focus is on reaching the unreached through innovative modes of schooling.

Child labour. The employment of children in work is viewed as a direct denial of their fundamental right to education. Action from the State has been slow but it has become a major plank of action in several parts of the country due to the significant role played by NGOs. But much greater support from parents and employers will be critical.

The right to education. Action has been taken to remove legal hurdles in accessing basic education as a fundamental right. The Indian Constitution has been amended, making basic education a justiceable right in line with the Convention on the Rights of the Child.

Social mobilization. Social mobilization and eradicating adult illiteracy through mass literacy campaigns, largely as a national programme but planned and implemented at the district level are being complemented by state governments action such as *jan sampark abhiyan* (people's contact campaign) of Madhya Pradesh and by civil society organizations such as *prjayatna* (people's effort) in Karnataka.

Role of the media. There is greater coverage of basic education in the media, particularly TV, thereby helping to articulate public perceptions and mobilizing pressure groups, coupled with a move in many states towards 'right to information' which has helped place facts related to basic education in public sphere. Many state governments are attempting to use ICT capabilities for this purpose.

Civil society participation. NAFFRE (National Alliance for Fundamental Right to Education) has emerged as a coalition to articulate the voice of the civil society in favour of education for all as a fundamental right.

EFA planning and monitoring in India

In such a vast country it is not easy to prepare a national plan of action for EFA. Different states are in different situations with respect to the goals of EFA. A genuine national plan will have to take inter-state variations into consideration. The Plan will also have to reflect the perspectives of the civil society organizations which are involved in educational activities on a large scale across the country. Four regional consultations have been conducted to elicit the perspectives of official leadership and NGOs in different states. The states are preparing basic inputs for the EFA plan with concrete reference to the six Dakar EFA goals. It has been proposed that a national consultation should be held involving NGO representatives and professional educators and planners.

An Action Plan prepared only at the behest of the international community could remain a mere statement of intention. Making the plan a credible one and translating it into reality hinge on two factors. First, the international commitments have to converge with national proposals. Second, the political commitment of the national leadership as well as the genuine support of civil society are needed.

Though there has been a heightened level of political and social mobilization in favour of elementary education and literacy activities, are they adequate to reach the goals and targets set by the country? At a formal level, the political leadership has shown its willingness to commit itself to the goal of EFA by placing elementary education as a fundamental right of every citizen of the country. The question remains, however, of when education will rise to the top of the political agenda of the country. India cannot work in a micro-incremental way in its efforts to reach basic education for all, as has been the case during the past fifty years. Change has to be substantial and progress much faster if the aspirations of the people as well as the newly made commitment of pursuing quality basic education as a fundamental right of all citizens are to be met. This will demand a massive movement through political and social mobilization to create a common platform with the sole agenda 'Quality Education For All' as envisaged by Sarva Shikha Abhiyan as well as the Dakar EFA Framework for Action.

Source: Govinda (2002), EFA in India.

enrolment rates (rather than net enrolment rates or completion rates, which are less ambiguous indicators of progress). Only four countries, The Gambia, Guinea-Bissau, Malawi and Viet Nam, adopt part or all of the gender-related education Millennium Development Goal. Improving levels of adult literacy appears as a goal in ten PRSPs and as key policy action in Ghana, Guyana, Malawi, Mozambique, Rwanda, Uganda and Zambia. Non-formal education features strongly in the PRSPs of Ethiopia and Guinea. Only Rwanda states its intention to operationalize its policies through an EFA Action Plan.

ActionAid finds that there is a strong focus on the quantitative aspects of UPE and a heavy emphasis on inputs. It also finds clear evidence of World Bank policy prescriptions including decentralization, the role of the private sector post-primary education, targeted public subsidies and an emphasis on cost-efficiency. ActionAid (2002) concludes

> Unless the optimistic growth and revenue projections in PRSPs are met . . . the education goals will be difficult to finance. The few progress reports that have been produced point to these potential difficulties (for example Uganda's progress report shows several of the education goals to be unrealistic within the original timeframe and budget plans (p. 3).

The Global Monitoring Report survey of sixteen full PRSPs completed up to July 2002 concludes that while education is recognized as a significant dimension of policies to reduce poverty in PRSPs, the absence of standardized, comparable education indicators leads to considerable variation in the depth to which education is reflected. Most of the PRSPs present a mix of access, completion, quality and financial indicators and in some cases disaggregate these by gender, income, and urban and rural dimensions. Mozambique illustrates a clear effort to disaggregate data in this way (see Table 3.3).

Most countries refer to the Millennium Development Goals (MDGs) relating to education and/or to the EFA goals in the education strategies within the PRSPs, but they do not necessarily use the EFA goals as the basis for selecting key education outcomes.

Most countries do not necessarily use the EFA goals as the basis for selecting key education outcomes.

Table 3.3. Mozambique: primary-school completion and enrolment, by rural/urban, sex and poverty status

Education indicators		Rural				Urban				All Mozambique			
		Very poor	Poor	Non-poor	All	Very poor	Poor	Non-poor	All	Very poor	Poor	Non-poor	All
Head of household who completed primary education or higher (%)		9.8	11.1	17.0	13.4	25.4	28.7	58.4	41.9	12.6	14.1	25.3	18.6
Children enrolled, aged 7–11 (%)	M	48.2	50.1	55.9	51.5	52.7	57.9	77.6	65.6	49.1	63.0	75.2	54.5
	F	29.1	32.9	34.4	62.3	47.2	51.8	75.1	61.4	32.3	50.5	66.3	403

Source: Mozambique Poverty Reduction Strategy Paper (PRSP), 10 January 2001.

The matrix set out in Table 3.4 presents an overview for the sixteen countries on the level of convergence between key education outcomes and MDGs and EFA goals.

Universal Primary Education is clearly delineated in fifteen of the sixteen PRSPs, but only seven countries have retained the EFA goal and the MDG for eliminating gender disparities in primary and secondary education. Learning opportunities for youth and adults is ranked second. In a similar exercise for thirty-one of the forty countries listed in Table 3.2, a comparable pattern emerged. Only Malawi, Nepal, Niger, and the Palestinian Autonomous Territories had clear coverage of all six EFA goals. Paradoxically, Niger is the one country that is not listed under UPE in the PRSP survey.

Table 3.4. EFA and MDG education goals in PRSPs

Education for All Goals	Millennium Development Goals	Albania	Bolivia	Burkina Faso	Gambia	Guinea	Guyana	Honduras	Mauritania	Mozambique	Nicaragua	Niger	U.R. Tanzania	Uganda	Viet Nam	Yemen	Zambia	Total
Expanding and improving comprehensive early childhood care and education, especially for the most vulnerable and disadvantaged children				√		√	√	√			√	√			√		√	8
Ensuring that by 2015 all children, particularly girls, children in difficult circumstances and those belonging to ethnic minorities, have access to and complete free and compulsory primary education of good quality	Ensure that, by 2015, children everywhere, boys and girls alike, will be able to complete a full course of primary schooling	√	√	√	√	√	√	√	√	√	√		√	√	√	√	√	15
Ensuring that the learning needs of all young people and adults are met through equitable access to appropriate learning and life skills programs		√	√	√	√	√	√			√		√		√	√	√	√	12
Achieving a 50% improvement in levels of adult literacy by 2015, especially for women, and equitable access to basic and continuing education for all adults				√					√	√	√		√	√	√			7
Eliminating gender disparities in primary and secondary education by 2005, and achieving gender equality in education by 2015, with a focus on ensuring girls' full and equal access to and achievement in basic education of good quality	Eliminate gender disparity in primary and secondary education preferably by 2005 and to all levels of education no later than 2015				√	√				√		√	√			√	√	7
Improving all aspects of the quality of education and ensuring excellence of all so that recognized and measurable learning outcomes are achieved by all, especially in literacy, numeracy and essential life skills		√	√	√	√	√	√				√		√		√			9
	Total (average)	3	3	5	4	5	4	2	2	4	4	3	4	3	5	3	4	

In most cases, education goals are set out in very general terms rather than as specific outcomes that can be assessed or measured. The eighteen core EFA indicators that provided the basis for the 2000 EFA Assessment are not widely used and most PRSPs do not have clear timelines to match proposed key education outcomes.

PRSPs map policy actions in key sectors such as education in different ways, usually at a subsector level, but in some cases against broad objectives or themes. Yemen is an example of the former and Nicaragua of the latter (Table 3.5).

There is an enormous array of proposed policy actions, which revolve primarily around increased coverage, improved financing, better governance and management, better quality, increased literacy and improvement in higher education. It is extremely difficult to assess the financial feasibility of education strategies in PRSPs, which in most cases set out a broad global sector or social sector budget. Burkina Faso is unusual in providing detailed costing of its policy actions for education for the first four years of the programme.

Three broad conclusions emerge from these surveys.

- Whether in PRSPs, or EFA sector plans, there is often a failure to develop a clear relationship between the diagnosis of education and poverty on the one hand, and the education outcomes and actions that are proposed in the plans and strategies on the other. A World Bank study of PRSPs and girls' education also suggests a weak linkage between identification of the need and priority actions (Burnett and Winter, 2002).
- There are not enough clearly set intermediate targets.
- While there are broad indications of intentions to increase expenditure on education and improve internal efficiency, there is rarely detailed costing.

Setting EFA goals and targets

Based on an analysis of the education plans of thirty countries[5] (out of the forty countries in the Global Monitoring Report survey shown in Table 3.2), it is possible to chart the extent to which governments are setting time-bound EFA targets. As for PRSPs, UPE expressed in terms of enrolment, and, less frequently, completion, receive the most attention. In addition to broad unqualified statements about achieving UPE, all but four of the countries have set specific targets, including intermediate targets. Thus, Mali, intends to achieve 75% primary gross enrolment rates by 2008. Rwanda will increase primary school net enrolment rates from 73% in 2001 to 80% in 2005, to 90% in 2010. Burkina Faso plans to increase the proportion of Grade 1 pupils who will reach the last year of the primary cycle from 60% to 75% by 2010. While in Pakistan, it is forecast that the participation rate of 5- to 9-year-olds should grow from 66% in 2000 to 79% in 2005 to 90% in 2010. A characteristic of these targets is that they predict quite substantial percentage increases over relatively short periods of time. Eritrea projects an annual increase of 10% in primary enrolment rates, Benin plans an increase of 15% points, from 55% to 70%, in the rate of pupils finishing primary school by 2004/05. The assumptions that underpin these projections are rarely provided.

Targets for the elimination of gender disparities are expressed almost entirely in terms of enrolment, with the occasional reference to time-bound targets for increasing the numbers of female teachers, for example, in Ethiopia and Guinea-Bissau. Cambodia, Guinea, United Republic of Tanzania and Yemen have 2005 targets for lessening gender disparities but there is little direct reference to the MDG for eliminating gender disparities or to the gender-related EFA goal. Targets for adult literacy are set primarily in terms of overall literacy rates. There is rarely reference to female literacy although Mali is an exception. The target annual rates of growth are usually much more modest than those set for primary education.

Assessing goals for the achievement of ECCE and for increasing learning opportunities for youth and adults is more difficult. The evaluation of strategies to improve all aspects of educational quality is also far from straightforward. However, in broad terms the survey of national planning documents confirms the pattern of goal coverage set out in the

In most cases, education goals are set out in very general terms, rather than as specific outcomes that can be assessed or measured.

5. Benin, Bhutan, Botswana, Burkina Faso, Cambodia, Eritrea, Ethiopia, The Gambia, Guinea, Guinea-Bissau, Haiti, Lao People's Democratic Republic, Lesotho, Madagascar, Malawi, Mali, Mauritania, Mozambique, Nepal, Niger, Nigeria, Pakistan, Palestinian Autonomous Territories, Rwanda, Sierra Leone, Sudan, United Republic of Tanzania, Uganda, Yemen and Zambia.

Table 3.5. Contrasting approaches to education in the PRSPs of Nicaragua and Yemen

Nicaragua: Policy actions in education (PRSP)		Yemen: Policy actions in education (PRSP)	
Areas of Intervention	**Objectives/Targets**	**Subsectors**	**Objectives/Targets**
▪ Increase coverage	▪ Increase net primary enrolment to 83.4%, from 75% in 1999 ▪ Reduce illiteracy rate to 18% in 2004, from 19% in 1998	▪ Basic education	▪ Raise enrolment to 69% by 2005 ▪ Reduce gender gap; promote enrolment of girls
▪ Improve the quality of education	▪ Improve the quality of education by improving relevance of teaching	▪ Vocational training and technical education	▪ Raise the percentage of those enrolled in vocational training and technical education ▪ Try to meet the current and future needs of the labour market quantitatively ▪ Encourage girls and boys as well as children from poor families and remote areas to enrol in vocational and technical fields
▪ School decentralization	▪ Improve participation of families and communities ▪ Improve financial efficiency and transparency management	▪ Higher education	▪ Develop university education to keep pace with advances in science and technology ▪ Increase percentage of girls to 27% of total students ▪ Increase specialized science and practical field graduates to 16%
▪ Improve social protection for school children	▪ Design and implement interventions for social protection based on specific vulnerability characteristics		

Source: IDA/IMF, Review of the Poverty Reduction Strategy Paper (PRSP) Approach: Early Experiences with Interim PRSPs and Full PRSPs, March 2002.

It is not possible in the present Report to assess the financial allocations being given to all six Dakar goals.

analysis of PRSPs (Table 3.4). Even though targets may be set, the extent to which they determine strategy content is less clear.

Budgetary allocations for EFA

The Dakar Framework for Action states that national plans:

> will address problems associated with the chronic under-financing of basic education by establishing budget priorities that reflect a commitment to achieving EFA goals and targets at the earliest possible date, and no later than 2015 (para 9).

It is not possible in the present Report to assess financial allocations to all six Dakar goals. the annex tables show, international data on education finance is weak. Furthermore, the absence of data to enable assessment of the education components of the health budgets and of those allocated to ministries such as population and women's affairs, is also limiting.

However, it is possible to gain some insight into the extent to which countries intend to increase the share of their education budgets relative to total public spending or GDP. For thirteen of the forty countries, Table 3.6 suggests that planning horizons are lengthening – perhaps reflecting the timescale required to achieve many of the educational goals. No very clear pattern can be discerned from this small sample. However, countries working within relatively short time horizons, with severe financing constraints are not well placed to achieve long-term EFA goals.

As regards the proportion of the budget allocated to education, there is marked variation among the thirty-one countries (from the forty) presenting the data. This gives some broad sense of the priority that is accorded to education but says little about key policy reforms.

A better indicator of a government's commitment to EFA is the proportion of the education budget allocated to primary education. As Table 3.8 shows, there are again very considerable variations. It is possible to have a relatively small percentage of the budget for education but accord high priority to primary education within it. For example in Lao PDR, Nepal, Congo DR and Pakistan, education receives a small percentage of the government budget but primary education is clearly a priority.

Table 3.6.
Time horizons and stated intentions to increase budgetary allocations

Time from 1999 to target date	Increase in percentage points: Increase the share of education in the government budget by more than 4 points	Increase in percentage points: Increase the share of education in the government budget by less than 4 points
More than five years	Yemen (2005)* Mali (2008)* Malawi (2012) Burkina Faso (2010) Cambodia (2005)* Lao PDR (2020)* Bangladesh (2015)*	Niger (no date)* Mauritania (2015) Guinea (2005)*
Less than five years	Zambia (2002)* Madagascar (2002/03) Guinea-Bissau (2004)	Pakistan (2003/4) Nepal (2004)

* Countries that have set clear targets within their policies and plans for the achievement of UPE.
Source: Table 3.2 in this chapter and EFA Monitoring Report 2002 survey.

Civil society and planning for EFA

One of the strongest messages to emanate from Dakar is the importance of civil society to the achievement of EFA:

> Learners, teachers, parents, communities, non-governmental organizations and other bodies representing civil society must be granted new and expanded political and social scope, at all levels of society, in order to engage governments in dialogue, decision-making and innovation around the goals for basic education.

The Dakar Framework for Action contends that governments need to engage with a much broader constellation of people in shaping policy and planning. Creating and sustaining new learning opportunities is dependent upon individual citizens, civil society and non-governmental organizations having a strong role in their design (UNESCO-IBE, 2001). While governments have the primary responsibility for ensuring that people's right to education is honoured, civil society organizations need to be accepted as policy partners.

To what extent is this happening? Has Dakar been instrumental in forging new partnerships? While there is a broad body of evidence on the service provider role of NGOs, the evidence is much more limited as regards the engagement of civil society in policy dialogue and planning. However, important work is underway by international and regional coalitions and networks such as CCNGO, ASPBEA and the Global March for the Elimination of Child Labour in charting progress and identifying innovative and productive ways of working, as well as the barriers to genuine participation. Evidence for changes in relationships between government and civil society actors is difficult to assess from official documents. So, the results from the survey of plans conducted by the Global Monitoring Report are supplemented by reference to both the work of funding agencies and the research literature.[6]

Participatory planning is a political, institutional and social process. Two issues should be kept in mind. First, it is important to know where the entry points are for an individual citizen to become involved in the process of setting of education priorities. Constitutional and legal rights to education represent an important indicator of what may be possible for civil society engagement. Second, there are ways in which 'spaces' to participate are available or have been created. These may be the 'traditional' spaces afforded by governments and the less formal, more autonomous 'spaces' created outside of government (Brock, Cornwall and Gaventa, 2001).

In some countries, broader governance and development reforms have established new policy processes in which civil society can participate. Much has been written about the influence that decentralization has had in participatory processes. One analysis (Schonwalder, 1997) highlights a pragmatic approach whereby decentralization is a policy tool, an approach that relies on organizations and intermediaries that operate between the state and local communities. In other words decentralization is a *technical* and administrative process. Whereas, a *political* approach to decentralization has a much broader meaning. It has the potential to open up new channels for participation in the political system and offers new avenues for direct participation. It is to both approaches that The Dakar Framework for Action refers, but the spirit and intention of EFA is directed towards the latter.

6. Evidence on the participatory processes in the development of PRSPs suggests that considerable caution should be exercised in drawing substantive conclusions on the basis of the process described in government documents (McGee and Norton, 2000). Donelly-Roark et al., (2001).

Table 3.7. Share of government budgets allocated to education

Education receives more than 20% of the government budget	Education receives between 10% and 20% of the government budget	Education receives less than 10% of the government budget
Kenya, Lesotho, Niger, Rwanda, Sierra Leone, Togo, Uganda	Benin, Burkina Faso, Cambodia, Ethiopia, Gambia, Guinea, Haiti, Madagascar, Malawi, Mali, Mauritania, Mozambique, Sudan, United Republic of Tanzania, Yemen, Zambia	Bangladesh, Democratic Republic of the Congo, Eritrea, Guinea-Bissau, Lao Peoples Democratic Republic, Nepal, Nigeria, Pakistan

Source: Table 3.2 in this chapter.

Table 3.8. Allocations to primary education

> 55%	45%–55%	< 45%
Benin, Burkina Faso, Dem. Rep. of Congo, Lao PDR, Nepal, Niger, Pakistan, U. R. Tanzania	Bangladesh, Cambodia, Eritrea, Ethiopia, Gambia, Madagascar, Malawi, Mauritania, Mozambique, Sierra Leone, Sudan, Togo, Uganda, Yemen	Guinea, Guinea-Bissau, Haiti, Kenya, Lesotho, Mali, Nigeria, Rwanda, Zambia

Source: Table 3.2 in this chapter.

In Mali, the decentralization process in the education sector includes wide consultation and dialogue at community level.

There is a range of examples of opportunities provided by government to enable formal consultation to take place. In Mali, the decentralization process in the education sector has included wide consultation and dialogue at community level. This has provided opportunities to clarify roles and responsibilities. In The Gambia, regional consultations on the outcomes of the EFA 2000 assessment and the World Education Forum have taken place. Key documents have been translated into local languages. Consultations have been held across the country including meetings with young people. The Cambodian Government has created a broad-based National EFA Committee that involves NGOs on a consultative basis.

Less common are examples – at least from the evidence of government documents – where more autonomous dialogue and engagement of civil society is an integral element of educational planning in a regular and sustainable way. In Ghana, a national coalition of NGOs and civil society groups campaigns for basic education of good quality for Ghanaian children, irrespective of gender, ethnicity and geographical location. The campaign acts as a pressure group on the government, urging the Ministry of Education and the Ghana Education Service to keep their promise for education reform, free and compulsory universal basic education and Education for All. It is involved in policy dialogue at the national level and carries out research and advocacy activities (UNESCO-IBE, 2001). Burkina Faso offers another example of where a move is taking place in the direction of regular and ongoing engagement (Box 3.7).

In Bhutan, community participation encompasses not only the building and maintenance of school facilities (especially in rural areas), but extends to the development of non-formal education programmes built around community-learning centres. School head-teachers and elders from the community are responsible for the planning and management of the literacy programmes. There are possibilities for government to incorporate this type of 'autonomous space' activity in a formal and sustainable process of decentralization.

The evidence so far available suggests that the Dakar challenge has been met with a mixed response and that the 'technical' approach is more prevalent than the 'political'. The extent to which these different forms of dialogue are connected in the processes of policy development and planning is difficult to track. For civil society engagement to expand, a strong sense of what constitutes a *good planning process* is needed (McGee and Norton, 2001). In addition, more 'spaces' are needed to allow review as a matter of course, rather than as part of the occasional consultation.

Furthermore, in many countries, international partner agencies are increasingly seeking to provide development assistance through central and sector budget support where domestic policies are judged to reflect a 'credible' national consensus resulting the engagement of civil society.

The balance sheet two years on from Dakar

So, what is the balance sheet two years after Dakar? The answer is that the full account has not yet been compiled. However, if the expected outcome was a set of finely honed National EFA Plans, providing the basis for an early dialogue with international agencies for enhanced levels of funding, then this expectation has not been met. If, on the other hand Dakar is assessed in terms of injecting some urgency and some EFA focus into the education and development planning process, then there is some evidence to suggest that this is happening. The available database does not support a clearer or stronger conclusion.

In some cases, EFA planning appears to run the risk of duplicating or running parallel with existing planning processes. It is important to ensure that systems with scarce technical capacity do not follow this path. It is also necessary for EFA to be argued strongly and energetically across national planning processes. As Chapter 1 has demonstrated, the case for EFA is a strong one, but EFA must not create a fence around itself. It is a national priority that cuts across many dimensions of social and economic development.

Planning for HIV/AIDS

> The extent to which schools and other education institutions are able to continue functioning as part of the essential infrastructure of societies and communities will influence how well societies eventually recover from the epidemic (UNAIDS, 2002*d*).

The scale of the HIV/AIDS pandemic is set out in stark terms in the *Report on the Global HIV/AIDS Epidemic*: 40 million adults and children live with HIV/AIDS, 28.5 million in sub-Saharan Africa. Some 14 million children up to and including the age of 14 have lost one or both of their parents; 508 thousand children died from AIDS in 2001. It follows then that for countries where the impact of HIV/AIDS is high, there are major challenges in planning for, and sustaining progress towards, the attainment of EFA goals.

In 14 of the 29 countries shown in Table 3.2 for which there is HIV/AIDS data, over 5% of 15—49-year-olds live with HIV/AIDS. The impact is highest in Southern Africa. In Botswana, the figure is 38.8%, in Zambia, 21.5% and in Lesotho, 30%. In the 29 countries together, nearly 22 million children and adults live with HIV/AIDS: 3.9 million in India, 3.5 million in Nigeria and 2.1 million in Ethiopia. This is more than 50% of the global total.

The most visible demographic impact of the HIV/AIDS epidemic is the growth in the number of orphans (Kelly, 2000). In the Democratic Republic of the Congo it is estimated that nearly 1 million children (aged 0–14) are AIDS orphans. In Uganda, the figure is 810,000 and in Zambia, it is well over half a million. Based on a study of 34 countries (26 in Africa), one estimate suggests that by 2010 there will be 44 million orphans. Of these, 70% of those who have lost their mother or both parents will be orphans of the impact of HIV/AIDS (Hunter and Williamson, 2000). A global estimate predicts that the number of orphans will continue to rise for at least the next decade. Today's prevalence rates will largely determine the geography of orphans for the next ten years

Box 3.7. Improving civil society engagement in planning for EFA: Burkina Faso

Burkina Faso has a long history of including its local-level institutions in governance. In the early 1980s, a policy of participatory development was launched to promote the systematic involvement of all communities in planning processes across sectors. However, the relationship between civil society and the military was not conducive to a genuine process of participation (Bangura, 1999). Then, the new democracy of the 1990s opened the door for more plural politics. In 1995, a Dialogue Framework in Basic Education (*Cadre de concertation en education de base au Burkina Faso*, CCEB/BF) began a process for civil society engagement in educational planning. To start with, the NGOs that operated in the education sector were identified to facilitate better coordination of their activities. This process evolved into a 'space' where NGOs and other bodies had the opportunity to become more involved in planning for EFA. However, while structures have been developed, the quality of civil society involvement in the planning process has not been totally productive.

Neither citizens nor government have found it easy to reflect fully the views of citizens in major forums and meetings (GREFCO, 2001). But in April 2000, the Ministry of Education (MEBA) established committees that included CSOs and NGOs as part of a nationwide consultation process. Committees at the national, regional and provincial level, comprising a broad spectrum of civil society and public institutions, worked to develop the Ten-Year Plan for the Development of Basic Education (*Plan décennal de développement de l'éducation de base*, PDDEB). This Plan now sits within the wider objectives of the United Nations Development Assistance Framework (UNDAF) and the PRSP (GREFCO, 2001). With inter-agency cooperation these development frameworks are being integrated and EFA goals included within them.

Education reforms that encourage plurality are still taking root, slowly modifying the forms of engagement between civil society and the state at lower levels of authority. This process is foreseen as a basis for sustainable and community-driven education planning (Donnelly-Roark et al., 2001).

Sources: Bangura (1999), GREFCO (2001), and NSSD, Burkina Faso: Planning Framework, http://www.nssd.net/country/burkina/bfo2.htm

(UNICEF/UNAIDS/USAID, 2002). While the numbers say something about the scale of the pandemic, they cannot convey the real story of being an orphan and the poverty of the life which young children are forced to live (Box 3.8).

So, in systems that in many cases already require radical sector reforms and significantly increased levels of resources for education, the challenge of planning to achieve EFA is complicated and compounded by HIV/AIDS.

Ministries and institutions are losing skilled and experienced staff who are difficult – sometimes even impossible – to replace, due to HIV/AIDS.

The HIV/AIDS pandemic impacts on learning opportunities and education systems in a myriad of ways. Enrolments fall. Orphans become children out-of-school. The gender gap widens. Schools are unable to function effectively so the quality of learning deteriorates. Resources are diverted from education to meet the demands being placed on the health and welfare services. Ministries and institutions lose skilled and experienced staff that are difficult and sometimes impossible to replace.

The impact on teachers deserves particular attention. An estimated 860,000 children lost their teachers to AIDS in sub-Saharan Africa in 1999. The World Bank refers to recent research that suggests that teachers are affected in the same proportion as adults in general, sickness evolves over ten years and, on average, during that period, teachers are absent for 260 days (World Bank, 2002*a*). However some evidence emerging from Southern Africa suggests that mortality rates among teachers may be lower than that of the general adult population and that within the profession, rates vary according to gender, qualifications, marital status and location (Bennell et al., 2002).

What then is needed to plan and implement strategies that can sustain and strengthen education in the face of the pandemic and prevent the further spread of HIV/AIDS? What are the dimensions of the task and how should they be addressed?

Hyde suggests that an understanding of the complex relationships between HIV/AIDS and education has developed quite rapidly in the last few years but that the number of detailed local and country studies on HIV/AIDS and education still remains small (Hyde et al, 2002). For nearly two decades, the response of the education sector to HIV/AIDS has been muted and fragmented. Now, there is a clearer understanding that for a growing number of countries, HIV/AIDS is not just an additional factor that needs to be accommodated in educational planning and practice (e.g. Bennell et al., 2002; Coombe, 2000; ID21 website; Kelly, 2000; UNICEF, 2002*c*; Whiteside, 2000; World Bank, 2002*b*). It is now a fact of life that requires that every policy, procedure and activity should be re-worked and rethought within an AIDS-centred policy framework. This in turn requires a major shift in the mindset and the process of educational planning. Kelly identifies nine policy development and planning imperatives:

- mainstream HIV/AIDS across the education sector;
- keep the education system functioning;
- adopt prevention, care and support as basic principles to guide system and institution interventions and programmes;
- keep the curriculum under constant review to ensure that it is relevant in a world with HIV/AIDS;
- ensure that the needs of the poorest and those in difficult circumstances are met;
- address the gender inequalities that fuel HIV/AIDS;
- build capacity for the management and control of the epidemic;
- promote community participation and support; and
- work multi-sectorally and with a wide range of partners.

This list embraces quite fundamental processes, many of which lie at the heart of education reform but take on added significance within a framework of education and HIV/AIDS. Strategic planning which integrates all relevant government structures is needed to protect and sustain systems and to develop measures for achieving EFA within the framework of AIDS (Kelly, 2002; Bennell et al., 2002).

Two years after Dakar there are good examples of efforts that are being made to plan for education in the context of HIV/AIDS, although the 40-country survey does not suggest that planning for EFA within a national AIDS framework is a reality in most countries with high prevalence rates. But Botswana, Thailand and Uganda provide examples of countries that are taking the task seriously.

Box 3.8. The characteristics of orphanhood: Zomba, Malawi

Zomba, Malawi[1]

There are three cycles of deprivation associated with orphanhood. The poor give birth to children who are likely to become poor, orphans procreate children likely to become orphans, and HIV-positive parents produce children likely to become HIV-positive. The poverty and exclusion associated with girl orphans is a significant feature of this deprivation. Orphans have little food, few clothes, no bedding and no soap. The hunger and social exclusion that result undermine school attendance and lead to further social exclusion. Many orphans are socially excluded and feel disillusioned and desperate.

Some elements of community provision that work well include distribution of food and clothing, and support. Less successful are fund-raising or provision of education (chiefly vocational), school fees and food. As a whole, community care is overwhelmed by the numbers, and is breaking down. Vocational education is in great demand by both orphans and those who care for them.

AIDS orphans[2]

The increase in numbers of AIDS orphans is stretching the capacity of families and societies at large. In many cases, the extended family is finding it extremely difficult to cope economically and psychologically with the numbers that is required to absorb. Few orphans are able to pay their school and training fees. Many have to care for others in the home where they live. Many have to work to support themselves or younger siblings dependent on them. Many carry responsibilities well beyond their capabilities as children. Some are so traumatized by what they have experienced when their family member died of AIDS that they cannot learn. A significant number are at risk of contracting HIV/AIDS through virtually inescapable income-generating prostitution.

Most of these orphans are excluded from the joy and gaiety of a normal childhood. Economically and psychologically, they have needs that differ from those of other children in school, needs to which the school must necessarily respond.

Source: 1. McBride (2002), reported in *ID21*, http://www.id21.org/, (August 2002); 2. Kelly (2000).

Botswana has one of the highest HIV/AIDS prevalence rates in the world. In the past three years there has been a discernible change in the approach of the Botswana government to the HIV/AIDS pandemic stimulated in part by the launch of the Botswana Human Development Report for 2000, which demonstrates very clearly the decline in human development performance and in the rates of increase in the level of GDP as a result of HIV/AIDS (UNDP, 2000). The report is the product of a strong upstream research partnership between the Government and UNDP.

HIV/AIDS has been declared a national crisis, resulting in the creation of a National Aids Coordinating Agency (NACA). This is the secretariat for the National AIDS Council that is chaired by the President of Botswana. NACA is charged with responsibility for mobilizing and coordinating a multi-sectoral approach to HIV/AIDS. One result of this approach is that a full education sector review has been instituted, backed by research and assisted by external agencies. One study has assessed the impact of HIV/AIDS on primary and secondary schooling (Bennell et al., 2001) and its summary findings are set out in Box 3.9. These findings have policy implications for sex and health education in the curriculum, school and community welfare services, and teacher support and management.

In **Thailand** the situation is different. There has been research on HIV/AIDS stretching over nearly twenty years. After experiencing escalating infection rates in the 1980s, Thailand initiated a comprehensive prevention programme. This included the 100% condom programme targeted at brothels; broad-based awareness activities, which involved many sectors of society; and strong human rights protection measures. By the end of the 1990s, the number of new infections had fallen by 80% from the levels prevalent prior to the national prevention programme (Global Action Group Prevention website).

Adult prevalence rates are now below 2% although 670,000 adults and children continue to live with HIV/AIDS and there are 290,000 orphans. So while prevalence rates have fallen there remains concern for localized epidemics and children and young adults (World Bank, 2002*b*). Interventions are needed to strengthen and, where necessary, re-orient education and training programmes. This requires strong partnerships across government ministries, NGOs, community organizations, and the business sector, to ensure good programme coverage and a sufficiency of resources to reduce risks among the young.

Schools provide a strong base for teaching sex education but significant education challenges remain, which are being assessed and planned for by a number of ministries. The Department of Health is promoting wider public acceptance of sex education as a necessary part of life. Together with the Department of Mental Health,

Botswana has one of the highest HIV/AIDS prevalence rates in the world.

Box 3.9. Research on HIV/AIDS and education in Botswana

Research findings

- A sharp drop in teenage pregnancy and sexually transmitted diseases since the mid-1990s, but the HIV prevalence rate among pregnant girls aged 15–19 remains high – 28.6% in 1998 and 25.3% in 2000.
- Sexual relationships are reported to be common in secondary schools. The 'integration and infusion' of HIV/AIDS topics into the primary and secondary school curriculum has not produced the desired changes in sexual behaviour.
- Double orphans account for 10% of children in Botswana, a figure projected to reach 35% to 40% by 2010. Orphans from the poorest households generally have the most problems with their education, although the overall attendance of orphans at school is surprisingly good.
- Mortality rates among teaching and other Ministry of Education staff are currently at least one-half the overall adult mortality rate. Teacher mortality currently accounts for one-third of all attrition, and is highest among male primary teachers.
- Teacher absenteeism is not generally perceived to be a serious problem at most schools, but at least one teacher was reported to be 'persistently' ill at each of the survey schools.
- Detailed demographic projections show that the school-age population will be 30% smaller in 2010 than it would have been without AIDS.

Source: Excerpt from *ID21* (2002), summary; Bennell et al. (2002).

guidelines are being prepared for a sex-education curriculum across the formal education system. These include human development, sexual health, sexual behaviour, personal skills, and social, cultural and gender issues. This framework enables the Ministry of Education to develop the detailed school curriculum. Additionally, government agencies and NGOs that provide counselling services are encouraged to network and coordinate their work, share their knowledge and experiences and strengthen the referral system. Box 3.10 provides an interesting example of a response by Buddhist monks.

HIV/AIDS was first recognized in **Uganda** in 1982. By 1993, the country had the highest prevalence rates in the world. Now, it is one of very few countries to have succeeded in reversing the epidemic. President Museveni announced recently that prevalence rates were down to 6.1% from 30% in 1990, with the most noticeable decline being in the 15–29 age group.

The Uganda AIDS Commission was established in 1992 under the Office of the President to coordinate national strategies. Its work has been characterized by a multi-sectoral approach involving a wide range of stakeholders backed by open political commitment at the highest level of the Government (UNFPA, 2001). HIV/AIDS programmes are integrated within the country's revised Poverty Eradication Action Plan and HIV/AIDS has a special vote in the national budget (UNDP, 2001).

Under the national poverty reduction strategy, civil society is engaged in the development of the Education Sector Investment Plan (ESIP) that together with support for the networks of People Living with HIV/AIDS has promoted a strong coalition of involvement with HIV prevention programmes. New alliances and coalitions, often with NGOs at their centre, have opened up opportunities for people living with HIV/AIDS to influence policy debate and reduce discrimination and stigma. There is now a public voice able to influence policy frameworks and legal systems in order to eliminate practices that discriminate against those living with HIV/AIDS.

Within the context of Uganda's National Strategic Framework and Action Plan for HIV/AIDS and its own sector planning, the Ministry of Education and Sports has set out nine major objectives for combating HIV/AIDS over a five year period:

- develop and implement effective policies for the sector;
- intensify advocacy efforts for children's rights and needs in the context of AIDS;
- incorporate HIV/AIDS into the curriculum, across all education institutions and non-formal venues;
- promote skills-based teacher training in colleges;
- promote AIDS education, counselling and health services support at educational institutions at all levels;
- foster the welfare of AIDS orphans;
- build partnerships with community and non-governmental organizations, and undertake joint activities and
- encourage research on various aspects of HIV/AIDS and its impact on education and related sectors; and
- promote joint planning, coordination, monitoring and evaluation of HIV/AIDS activities in the education sector (Malinga, 2000).

These broad objectives have been translated into a set of quantifiable goals. For example, by 2005–06, at least 90% of teacher-training collectives will have introduced skills-based modules on HIV/AIDS into their programmes. By the same year, at least 50% of educational institutions will have introduced welfare and support schemes for HIV/AIDS orphans, 80% of the institutions will have started HIV/AIDS counselling and health services, and at least five major research studies on education and HIV/AIDS will be underway.

The action plan utilizes a wide variety of communication strategies. These include workshops, training kits and modules, competitions for best article or performance, the use of radio, video and television, lobbying and outreach activities, T-shirts and trophies, curriculum redesign, press campaigns, national debates, parental involvement and joint projects with community organizations.

These three countries demonstrate the value and importance of education policies and plans for HIV/AIDS that are clearly part of a wider and well-integrated national effort that is designed to create and build close relationships across groups, communities, associations and faiths. This national effort has to deal with the impact of the disease on key national institutions including strategies for personnel and human resource support, re-training and replacement. It needs good research and the means to use and communicate the findings. It is also critical that strategies are gender sensitive. All of these needs and plans have their costs, an issue which is explored in Chapter 4.

There is a growing international resource, on which those charged with policy development and planning responsibilities can draw: the newly established UNAIDS Inter-Agency Task Team on Education. This now involves eight agencies including UNDP, UNDCP, UNESCO, UNFPA, UNICEF and WHO. The Team is developing a strategic framework which takes as its starting point the UNGASS Declaration of Commitment on HIV/AIDS which sets the target of reducing HIV infection among 15–24-year-olds by 25% in the most affected countries by 2005 and globally by 2010. It calls on governments to develop by 2003 and implement by 2005, national strategies to provide a supportive environment for orphans and children infected and affected by HIV/AIDS (UNAIDS, 2002*a*).

A new World Bank strategy document (World Bank, 2002*b*) concludes that providing a basic education to children and especially equal opportunity for girls, is among the most promising directions in responding to HIV/AIDS. Long-term strategic planning, school-based prevention programmes, peer education and a focus on youth, support for orphans and out of school youth, multi-media campaigns and strong partnerships, national and international, are all seen as essential.

Box 3.10. The Sangha Metta project in Thailand

The Sangha Metta Project engages Buddhist monks in HIV/AIDS prevention and care. It was initiated by the monks themselves who wished to take a more active role in HIV/AIDS prevention and care. Taking the Buddha's teachings as their inspiration, the monks concluded that a core aspect of HIV/AIDS was ignorance about the condition among both the sufferers and the general public.

Home visits

In line with their traditional role as teachers, the monks decided they could teach both groups about the realities of HIV/AIDS. The project teaches monks, nuns and novices about HIV/AIDS. It equips them with modern participatory social management skills and tools so that they can work effectively in their communities to prevent further HIV transmission and to help families living with HIV/AIDS. A crucial part of training is close contact between monks and sufferers, which includes monks having to accept and eat alms food prepared by people with HIV/AIDS. Sensitized in such basic ways they are soon able to work freely with affected people.

Young novices

In strong contrast with their formal roles, project-trained monks have become active in community work. Using Buddhist ethics as their guideline, they now teach villagers how to avoid high-risk behaviour, help to set up support groups, train people with HIV/AIDS in handicrafts, donate their alms and take care of AIDS orphans. Because local people are accustomed to telling monks their troubles, the latter have become a conduit for identifying many secret HIV+ people who, once identified, can be referred to support groups and public assistance programmes. 'HIV-friendly' temples encourage these people to participate in community activities. They also provide training in meditation as well as grow and dispense herbal medicines in collaboration with local hospitals. This more active role among monks is strengthening trust between them and the people. It is also developing community potential and encouraging greater grass roots participation in solving problems at the local level. Because the project has given monks a way to become actively involved in their communities, something they have always wanted, it is spreading rapidly into other regions of Thailand, as well as neighbouring countries such as Lao People's Democratic Republic, Myanmar, Cambodia, Southern China, Viet Nam, Mongolia and Bhutan.

Source: Taken from Buddha Dharma Education Association website. http://www.buddhanet.net/sangha-metta/project.html

Box 3.11. Alliance of mayors and municipal leaders on HIV/ AIDS in Africa

In 1997, during the Tenth International Conference on STD/AIDS (Abidjan, Côte d'Ivoire), an Alliance of Mayors Initiative for Community Action on AIDS at the Local Level (AMICAALL) was established to promote an expanded, multisectoral response to the HIV/AIDS epidemic. It was designed to provide concrete examples of how local governments, working in partnership with civil society and local communities, could translate principles and goals into actions. The Alliance strategy is inclusive (involving a broad range of stakeholders), responsive (reacting to locally articulated needs and brokering dialogue among local people, municipalities, policy-makers and decision-makers), gender sensitive (responding to the different experiences of men and women in terms of vulnerability, response and impact), and dynamic (local action informs national policy which in turn supports a more enabling environment for sustained responses; strengthened management and financial systems at the local level provide the foundations for scaling up responses to the epidemic). It develops mechanisms to facilitate rapid disbursement of funds to communities in need and to help countries diversify their sources of funding to address the epidemic. Additionally, action-oriented monitoring and reporting tools are also being developed to promote understanding of what is working, and what is not, and to make the necessary adjustments.

This Alliance is part of a broader International Partnership against AIDS in Africa, where actors who have chosen to work together to achieve a shared vision for scaling up efforts in Africa to curtail the spread of HIV, reduce its impact and halt the further reversal of human, social and economic development.

Source: From Alliance of Mayors and Municipal Leaders on HIV/AIDS in Africa's Website (2002); UNAIDS (2002*b*); UNAIDS Policy Notes.

UNESCO's International Institute for Educational Planning (IIEP) has created the Global HIV/AIDS Impact on Education Clearing House that provides access to comparative information on formal and non-formal systems and experience of measures to cope with, as well as curb, the pandemic. UNICEF too has been active in this field, in addressing the needs of young people (UNICEF, 2002c) and orphans (UNICEF/UNAIDS/USAID, 2002).

The HIV/AIDS pandemic will not be addressed in the absence of progress towards the EFA goals.

A growing number of international partnerships can assist with planning and programming. In partnership with DFID, IIEP and Partnership for Child Development, the World Bank is working with educational planners in Africa on the new Ed-SIDA/AIDS planning tool, designed to quantify the impact of HIV/AIDS on education supply and demand. Mapping this relationship makes it possible to estimate the number of teachers needed to meet the EFA goals in the context of HIV/AIDS. UNESCO, UNICEF, WHO, the World Bank and Education International are also working with other agencies in support of school-based prevention programmes using the FRESH framework (Focusing Resources on Effective School Health).

Funded by USAID, and founded by the University of Natal in 2000, The Southern Africa Mobile Task Team on HIV/AIDS in Education (MTT) assists ministries of education to develop strategic planning responses to mitigate the impact of HIV/AIDS on education. A rather different example of an international partnership is the Alliance of Mayors and Municipal Leaders on HIV/AIDS in Africa (Box 3.11).

All of this suggests a growing understanding that planning to achieve the EFA goals must take account of HIV/AIDS and that the HIV/AIDS pandemic will not be addressed in the absence of progress towards the EFA goals. Nevertheless, for most countries, while the importance of HIV/AIDS is acknowledged, it is still treated as one problem requiring stand-alone educational activities rather than recognizing its place at the heart of educational planning.

Planning to combat conflict, disaster and instability

> Education is probably the best tool for defusing many of the problems exacerbating and perpetuating crisis situations (Vargas-Baron, 2001).

The Dakar Framework for Action is clear:

> Conflicts, instability and natural disasters take their toll on education and are a major barrier towards attaining Education for All. The capacity of governments and civil society should be enhanced to rapidly assess educational needs in contexts of crisis and post conflict situations for children and adults, to restore learning opportunities in secure and friendly environments, and to reconstruct destroyed or damaged education systems.

As with HIV/AIDS, many countries are grappling with crisis and emergency (see also Chapter 4, section entitled 'Education in Emergencies'). One estimate suggests that seventy-three countries have an internal crisis or are engaged in post-crisis reconstruction. At the beginning of the new millennium, there were armed conflicts in fifty countries, at least thirty countries have large refugee populations from neighbouring states, and another fifteen countries were afflicted by natural disasters (Talbot, 2002*a*; Vargas-Baron, 2001).

The challenge is complex: in the midst of conflict, insecurity and instability, how can education be kept alive and contribute to the realization of sustainable peace? In countries with severe humanitarian emergencies there are major internal displacements of people. How can the educational needs of people living in camps and settlements be met? Many refugees move to neighbouring countries – some 500,000 in 2001 alone. How can host nations, many of whom are confronted with major educational challenges of their own, act as hospitable and effective educational hosts? And what are the most effective ways of rebuilding education systems after conflict and disaster? Nearly half a million people returned to their home countries in 2001.

Planning and developing workable strategies for EFA in these contexts is very demanding (Box 3.12). But it is essential to help:

- meet the psychosocial needs of crisis-affected populations;
- provide a channel for disseminating survival messages and developing skills for conflict resolution and peace building;
- prepare for reconstruction and social and economic development;
- provide protection from harm particularly for children; and
- promote personal development and readiness for responsible citizenship (Sinclair, forthcoming).

Afghanistan, Kosovo, Argentina, the Palestinian Autonomous Territories and East Timor are five countries and territories living with conflict or crisis, or engaged with reconstruction after years of trauma and destabilization. While their experience makes clear that conflict and its resolution is context specific, there are lessons to be learned and shared regarding approaches to planning for EFA.

Afghanistan is confronted with enormous challenges. It has some of the worst education indicators in the world. A recent needs assessment concluded:

> The Afghan education system has been undermined by twenty-three years of war, by widespread physical destruction, by restructuring under a communist regime, and by its use as a political and religious pawn by succeeding governments. The concept of secular education has been under constant attack for decades – first as a source of foreign ideas that led to the communist takeover and then by the Taliban who banned education for girls entirely, and promoted and expanded the system of religious schools at the expense of secular schools. As the school year started in March 2002, the capacity to supply education has been decimated in both quantity and quality (ADB, 2002).

The Assessment goes on to state that

> a revitalized education system can contribute significantly to resolving many of Afghanistan's daunting problems. Education is a key ingredient to rebuilding Afghanistan, igniting progress in all other development sectors. Education will build the human and social capital needed for economic development as well as serve as a key vehicle for promoting peace, stability and social cohesion. In short it will develop a sense of nationhood.

In the midst of conflict, insecurity and instability, how can education be kept alive and contribute to the realization of sustainable peace?

Box 3.12. Education in emergency: challenges to ministries of education

The onset of an emergency brings enormous challenges to an education system. Physical infrastructure is frequently destroyed or damaged, with school buildings often unavailable. Textbooks, reading materials, syllabi and teachers' guides may be destroyed or scarce. Children, parents and teachers may have witnessed terrible scenes of barbarity or may even themselves have inflicted violence on others. Even if people have not personally experienced the horrors of war and conflict, the fact of forced displacement to another country or region is profoundly destabilizing. Moreover, the education of children who are not displaced may be severely disrupted, as attention and resources are diverted to military or security purposes. Those who take up teaching in refugee or internally displaced camps may be unqualified and unable to cope with teaching in an unfamiliar, perturbing setting. A desperate need at the beginning of an emergency is to provide safe, structured activities for children, to help re-establish a routine of normality in their lives.

When an emergency occurs, national ministry of education managers and planners often find themselves unprepared to deal with the situation. These officials frequently feel demoralized and marginalized during emergencies, as bilateral, multilateral and non-governmental actors commonly take much of the initiative to meet the needs of populations affected by crises. The international agencies have far greater material and human resources. Ministry officials can find themselves lacking in confidence, capacity, skills, resources, credibility and even authority. There is also a tendency, in complex emergencies, for governments to assign provision of services to beneficiaries, often including education, to security-oriented ministries, leaving the technical staff of the line ministries in a weak position. Information and statistics about refugees and internally displaced persons are often fragmentary and inaccurate. Usually there is no coordinated system for collection of data on refugee or displaced students receiving assistance from different sources. As a population moves towards return, pressure may quite suddenly come upon the Education Ministry to plan and implement massive educational projects, after months or years of comparative neglect by the international community. This can cause reconstruction efforts to be hobbled from the start.

Source: From Talbot (2002).

Some broad key principles for initial investment have been agreed:

- rapid mobilization to reinstate basic education, with a goal of enrolling 1.5 million children in 2002 and at least 2 million children by 2003;
- equitable distribution of assistance so that resources reach the provinces as well as Kabul, and rural as well as urban areas;
- meeting recurring costs of the system, particularly teacher salaries;
- promoting girls' education to remedy past injustices;
- maintaining a balance between subsectors, based on demand, supply, and the contribution to national development;
- linking education and vocational training to practical skills that will lead to jobs; and
- capacity building of Afghan institutions.

International assistance is being provided throughout 2002 to support the development of a comprehensive sector strategy that will be the basis for an investment plan. UNESCO has been instrumental in helping to draw up a ten-point plan of action with the Ministry of Education. But translating these principles into action will require a concerted international effort.[7]

Kosovo illustrates many of the political, policy and practical problems that arise in post-conflict reconstruction of education provision (Talbot, 2002*b*). Concerns about ethnic identity and government legitimacy dominate the debate on education. The Serb minority disputes the legitimacy of the new Kosovo Government in the education sector. These tensions restrict rational planning and education reform. While there is a general commitment to a multi-ethnic system that recognizes cultural pluralism and minority rights, the detailed working out of that principle remains highly problematic. Languages pose a particular problem: the principle of mother tongue language is accepted but there are objections to a proposal that all students should learn Albanian.

Argentina is in the middle of a deep-seated economic crisis that started in 1998.

Argentina is in the middle of a deep-seated economic crisis that started in 1998. This has caused increased levels of poverty, unemployment and open violence, including in schools. Drug consumption among young people has increased. More than a hundred private schools have been closed, as middle class parents are unable to pay fees. Children from these families have emigrated to public schools where public school students have been dropping out of school altogether because of the increasing incidence of poverty. Many children look for work to supplement family income, while many families now find it impossible to buy textbooks or meet the cost of school transport.

Falling enrolment has lowered the demand for teachers, so teachers launched a campaign to try to persuade students back to school. UNICEF joined the campaign, as did Argentina's professional footballers. But for the education authorities, the necessity has been to focus on the short term and address immediate issues, as the budgetary allocation to education has become squeezed. For example, the provincial government in Buenos Aires province has cancelled all school scholarships.

Nepal is another country beset by conflict and more recently by a major economic downturn (Box 3.13).

The provisional Five-year Education Plan for the **Palestinian Autonomous Territories** for the years 2001–2005 identifies three major priorities: maintenance of enrolment levels for basic education in the face of a possible 30% increase in the population of primary school age children, expanded enrolment at the secondary level from 56% to 68%, and an improvement in the quality of education. It elaborates a framework of priorities against a backdrop of almost universal basic education, fiscal sustainability at current levels of provision and recognition of the need to involve civil society in enhancing the quality of education. An important objective is better coordinated donor support given a heavy dependence on investment funding by external agencies.

With the advent of the second Intifada, and civil strife in the West Bank and Gaza, there has been a significant loss of revenue and a consequent decline in public services. Budget shortfalls are being met in part by emergency donor support but non-salary costs are being squeezed. As a

7. The nature of this international support is elaborated further in Chapter 4.

result, education has been hit hard. Damage to schools, curfews and frequent closures reduce learning opportunities, teaching hours have been shortened, and teachers have difficulty in reporting to school. A World Bank assessment suggests that the inability to meet recurrent expenses, brought about by the current crisis, could cause the educational system to collapse and consequently risk resources that the Palestinian authority and donors have invested over the last eight years (World Bank, 2002*d*). But the cost is greatest in the lives of children and young people. All of this is taking place in an environment where it is estimated that half the population is living below the poverty line (UNRWA website).

The present imperative is to keep the formal education system operational; a point clearly made in the *Palestine Human Development Report 2002* (UNDP, 2002). One international response is the development of the Trust Fund Credit for an Emergency Services Support Project (World Bank, 2002*d*). This includes assistance for the provision of textbooks, school furniture, administrative costs such as water electricity and transport, refurbishment of damaged infrastructure, scientific and computer laboratories and teacher training.

East Timor is building its education system after achieving independence from Indonesia and the ravages inflicted on the country immediately after the referendum in August 1999. Pro-Indonesian militia burned down 95% of the schools and Indonesian teachers left with the result that the education sector collapsed completely.

Two years later in 2001, 86% of school classrooms had been rehabilitated and made useable. Nine hundred and twenty two schools were operational. There was a substantial increase in enrolment from poor households, among girls and for rural children aged 6–14. The gap in school participation rates narrowed between the richest and the poorest, boys and girls, and urban and rural areas.

A number of factors contributed to stimulating demand: national pride, the rebuilding of the nation by the East Timor Transitional Administration (ETTA) with the assistance of the United Nations and multilateral and bilateral agencies, allied to a reduction in the costs of schooling through the abolition of school fees and the need to wear school uniforms. Enrolments in primary education rose from about 167,000 in 1998/99 to about 183,000 in 2001, although enrolments in junior secondary education declined over the same period, largely due to the lack of qualified teachers and the partial rehabilitation of facilities.

These are important first steps. International support has been, and will be, an essential component of the national effort to rebuild and strengthen education. A variety of organizations are at work, among them UNICEF and the World Food Programme, which responded very quickly to immediate needs, and the World Bank, which is providing project grants for both short- and longer-term reconstruction (Box 3.14).

These brief examples highlight a few of the complex challenges of keeping education alive, being responsive to emergency needs and retaining a longer-term vision and strategy for the rebuilding and strengthening of systems, which is in itself a critical contribution to sustaining peace. Work is now emerging, stimulated in part by Dakar, that draws lessons and offers guidance to those directly engaged in planning and implementing education in situations of conflict, disaster and instability.

Box 3.13. Nepal's uncertainty

In the Government of Nepal's 10th Development Plan (2002-2007) education expenditure is planned to increase by 63% (2002/2003 to 2006/2007). In the Medium Term Expenditure Framework (MTEF 2002//03-2004/05) education expenditure is set to increase by 30%. This prognosis depends on relatively high rates of economic growth, sustained foreign assistance (in loans and grants), improvements in governance as set out in the Local Governance Act of 1999 and on an improved security situation in the face of a Maoist insurgency in the country.

However, Nepal's situation changed dramatically after the violent death of the King in mid-2002 and the spread of violence within the country. Government revenues declined and subsequent expenditure on security surged dramatically to over 15% of the annual budget. 'There is virtually no revenue surplus for development activities' (*The Kathmandu Post*, 23 August 2002).

Speaking about the Tenth Plan, an adviser at the Ministry of Finance said that 'the Plan has lost relevance as the country's conditions and political scenario has changed . . . from the scenario when its drafting was started. The current thrust is the restoration of peace and security in the country and if need be, a plan holiday should be announced to achieve this goal'

Source: The Kathmandu Post (2002).

East Timor is building its education system after achieving independence from Indonesia and the ravages inflicted on the country immediately after the referendum in August 1999.

Box 3.14. International support for education in East Timor

UNICEF: Immediate interventions revived the primary education system and brought routine back to shattered lives. It was important that some order be re-established in East Timor's devastated communities. By establishing volunteer committees in the districts, UNICEF helped organize teachers and reopen schools, even without furniture, textbooks or a curriculum. Providing basic teaching and learning materials, and supplying a financial incentive to all primary school teachers were crucial in getting more than 170,000 children into primary school by the end of the teaching year. In the next two years, the teacher-training programme will be greatly expanded through teacher resource centres and a management training programme for primary school principals, most of whom were grade teachers until last year. A range of appropriate teaching materials will be developed, and a school health and nutrition programme will aim to improve the health of all children at school, particularly those with special needs. To better understand the requirements of teachers and pupils, support will be given to the emerging East Timor education department to improve

The World Bank has provided grants for two projects; the first for an Emergency School Readiness Project (ESRP) which supported the rebuilding of classrooms to a basic operational level as well as the provision of furniture, textbooks, information and management support. Launched in July 2000, ESRP was completed in twenty-four months. The second project, the Fundamental School Quality Project (FSQP), supports follow-on educational infrastructure development. The objectives of FSQP are to maintain the existing level of primary education enrolment and possibly increase it as still more refugees return and school-age population grows; and recover quality in primary and junior secondary education by rehabilitating physical facilities, providing textbooks and other instructional materials, and supporting education research and management capacity development.

Source: UNICEF (2001*a*);
Ministry of Education Culture Youth and Sports (2002).

In general, multilateral and bilateral donors have not given policy priority to emergency and post-crisis education.

One such product is set out in Box 3.15 that draws on the experience of United Nations and NGO practitioners in the field of emergency education. The basic rubric is no different from any education plan with concerns for access, quality, good management and co-ordination, and securing sufficient resources. But the interpretation of these principles is informed by urgency, by the particular circumstances, experiences and needs of children and young people, and by the art of the possible in damaged systems.

External assistance is also of critical importance in planning and helping to deliver education services in crisis situations. But it still does not fit well into the logic of most relief and development agencies, or indeed, most governments. There are particular tensions regarding international agency support for short-term emergency work as opposed to longer-term reconstruction and development. The separation of these two components can be costly, as the example of Sudan suggests (Box 3.16). This is clearly a tension that needs more concentrated international attention.

Although, in general, multilateral and bilateral donors have not given policy priority to emergency and post-crisis education, useful work by some of the international organizations is designed to support planning for EFA (Vargas-Baron, 2001). For example, UNESCO's Section for Emergency Education and Special Operations is heading an inter-agency flagship programme entitled Education in Emergencies. This has created the Inter-Agency Network on Education in Emergencies (INEE), designed to provide information on types of intervention, good practice and learning resources. A checklist has been developed which incorporates education strategies for preventing emergencies as well as responding to conflict and crisis (Inter-Agency Network for Education in Emergencies (INEE; website: http://ineesite.org/). A website partnership between UNESCO and the University of Pittsburg – Global Information Networks in Education (GINIE) – is a major feature of this work.

UNESCO IIEP is launching a programme of guidebooks and policy studies that draws heavily on country case studies. As from 2003, IIEP will offer training programmes in emergency and reconstruction education. UNICEF has an agency-wide programme for education in crisis situations with a strong emphasis on the integration of education, health and social support for families. UNHCR's education programmes for refugees and internally displaced persons are active in many countries and many valuable lessons are being learned (UNHCR, 2001).

Among bilateral agencies Swedish International Cooperation Development Agency (SIDA) includes crisis and emergency education in its overall education strategy and the Norwegian Agency for Development Cooperation (NORAD) has a long history of providing support in emergency education. Other agencies are beginning to show interest. Both DFID and USAID have sponsored publications on education in situations of conflict (Smith and Vaux, 2002; USAID*a*, 2002).

These signs are all positive, and represent both growing awareness and expanding resources. The test will be to bring awareness and resources together so as to enable those charged with education and development in their own countries, and in countries meeting the needs of refugees, to meet the burgeoning demand for education in crisis and in reconstruction.

Credible planning, credible plans

The Dakar Framework for Action calls for comprehensive National EFA Plans by 2002 at the latest. These plans will:

- be developed by government leadership in direct and systematic consultation with national civil society;
- specify reforms addressing the six EFA goals;
- establish a sustainable financial framework;
- be time-bound and action oriented;
- include mid-term performance indicators; and
- achieve a synergy of all human development efforts, through its inclusion within the national development efforts (Dakar Framework for Action, para. 16).

This statement recognizes the need for genuine and inclusive political processes, synergy with overall government policy, and results-based plans that set clear directions for programme implementation and accountability. By implication, these are broad characteristics of a *credible plan*.

Any plan should be credible, otherwise planning is of little worth. So why has the term 'credible plan' received so much attention since Dakar? In large measure it is because the notion of a credible plan is linked in the discussion in Dakar to governments needing to be seriously committed to such plans, as a prerequisite for accessing additional external financing.

But the evidence set out in the first two sections of this chapter also points to other factors which are increasingly seen by governments, funding agencies and non-governmental organizations as critical facets of planning for EFA. Six of these factors are highlighted here.

Box 3.15. Principles of emergency education

Access

- The right of access to education, recreation and related activities must be ensured, even in crisis situations.
- Rapid access to education, recreation and related activities should be followed by steady improvement in quality and coverage, including access to all levels of education and recognition of studies.
- Education programmes should be gender-sensitive, accessible to and inclusive of all groups.
- Education should serve as a tool of child protection and prevention of harm.

Resources

- Education programmes should use a community-based participatory approach, with emphasis on capacity building.
- Education programmes should include a major component of training for teachers and youth/adult educators, and provide incentives to avoid teacher turnover.
- Crisis and recovery programmes should develop and document locally appropriate targets for resourcing standards, adequate to meet their educational and psychosocial objectives.

Activities/Curriculum

- All crisis-affected children and young people should have access to education, recreation and related activities, helping meet their psychosocial needs in the short and longer term.
- Curriculum policy should support the long-term development of individual students and of the society, and for refugee populations should be supportive of a durable solution, normally repatriation.
- Education programmes should be enriched to include life skills for health, safety, and environmental awareness.
- Education programmes should be enriched to include life skills for peace/conflict resolution, tolerance, human rights and citizenship.
- Vocational training programmes should be linked to opportunities for workplace practice of the skills being learned.

Coordination and capacity-building

- Governments and assistance agencies should promote coordination between all agencies and stakeholders.
- External assistance programmes should include capacity building to promote transparent, accountable and inclusive system management by local actors.

Source: Sinclair (forthcoming).

First, and by no means specific to education, there is a growing acknowledgement that if the development of policy and planning is conceived as a purely technical process, it is unlikely to serve poor and disadvantaged people well. Unless the processes of policy development, planning and programme delivery are part of a wider engagement with people and their representatives, education that is inclusive and meaningful will be unlikely to materialize. This is not to deny the pivotal role of government, nor of the need for well-trained and committed planners, it is rather to recognize that a credible

A plan should be credible; otherwise planning is of little worth.

Box 3.16. Tensions in supporting education in Sudan

Sudan's civil war has raged for nineteen years. It has displaced more than four and a half million citizens, four million of which have remained within Sudan's borders. Given the length of the war, many Sudanese have assumed a regional perspective, viewing problems and opportunities existing not only in different parts of Sudan but in other countries as well, including the Kakuma refugee camps in North-eastern Kenya.

As Sudanese perspectives of their identity and community expand, bureaucratic viewpoints have remained inflexible. What matters is not where Sudanese go, but the territory and population category each agency is responsible for. Accordingly, agencies such as UNHCR address Sudanese refugee issues, and rarely, if ever, venture into Sudan itself. Likewise, agencies aiding Sudanese within Sudan may never visit Sudanese refugee camps. As a result, perspectives of Sudan and Sudanese vary widely. Agencies working within Sudan tend to highlight areas of stability where they can carry out initiatives such as education. They view the refugee camps as being over-invested, including the education sector, and a magnet that draws Sudanese from stable areas within Sudan. To them, the refugee camps represent locations that undermine reconstruction and development efforts.

Agencies working with Sudanese refugees, alternately, evaluate the situation within Sudan in terms of areas of war and 'pockets' of peace. Southern Sudan, the chief war zone and area where most refugees and IDPs have come from, seems inhospitable and dangerous. As a result, the agencies have concentrated their efforts on preparing Sudanese refugees for a future regardless of where that may be. In Kenya, the refugee students study a Kenyan curriculum while hoping for scholarship and resettlement opportunities elsewhere.

Considerable tensions have arisen between agencies working on education development in stable areas of Sudan and agencies working with refugees. Many of the tensions are related to the poor coordination and information sharing among education programs for Sudanese inside Southern Sudan and in nearby refugee asylum countries. Agencies may know very little about what is going on in another part of Sudan or in refugee camps. They may use different curricula and pay teachers significantly different levels of 'incentives' (no teacher salaries are provided anywhere).

Poor coordination has also arisen from the fact that relief and development agencies approach education problems in different ways. Whereas relief agencies have invested in diverse and comparatively high-quality education programmes in refugee camps, development agencies have been involved in reconstructing an education system within Sudan that was virtually eliminated by conflict. The relief agencies have essentially created separate education systems while development agencies in some areas of Sudan work with education officials from the de facto government in Southern Sudan. In terms of quality, the education available in refugee camps in Kenya and Uganda is demonstrably better than nearly anything available inside Sudan: most investments inside Sudan are spread thinly across a broad expanse, while investments for refugee communities are directed at a much smaller and relatively finite population.

The poor coordination between relief and development actors is illuminated by the fact that USAID is supporting education programming within Southern Sudan that is explicitly termed development work while the Bureau for Population, Refugees and Migration (BPRM) in the U.S. Government's State Department is supporting the education work of UNHCR in refugee camps for Southern Sudanese in Kenya. Two agencies that are part of the same government are thus working on Sudanese education but according to different goals: USAID is working to rebuild Southern Sudan's education system while BPRM is supporting education that prepares refugees either for repatriation or prolonged exile.

Source: From Sommers (2002*a*).

plan will reflect the outcomes of ongoing dialogue and participation designed to provide qualitative as well as quantitative information and understandings. This was a major message from Dakar.

Second, there is a notion of being comprehensive: all of education as well as Education for All. Different countries will have different priorities and rightly so, but EFA recognizes a full range of learning opportunities. It views education neither as circumscribed by age nor by the cycle of the formal school system, nor indeed, by the prosperity of learners. Credibility depends upon extending learning. EFA embraces all the goals, their interconnections and their cumulative benefits.

Third, planning that does not recognize that one of the single greatest stumbling blocks to the achievement of Education for All is gender discrimination (UNICEF, 2002*b*) is not credible. But the evidence from the first part of this chapter, albeit limited, does not yet suggest that gender planning and budgeting have been central to planning for EFA thus far.

Fourth, for many millions of people, planning for traditional formal systems of education is insufficiently responsive to their learning needs. For example, as this Chapter has demonstrated for a sizeable group of countries, a comprehensive understanding of HIV/AIDS is central to planning and delivering on every aspect of education. Planning that does not recognize the diversity of learning circumstances and needs is not credible.

Fifth, too many education plans have been broad statements of intent with many objectives but lacking prioritization. In these circumstances, plans have failed the test of budgetary credibility – with or without external funding. Some of the evidence in this chapter suggests that there continues to be a failure to link EFA goals to well-costed strategies.

Finally, the nature of the engagement of funding agencies with governments is changing. Dialogue is less about projects and more about overall strategy. There is growing attention to an international dialogue across agencies and with governments, seeking a clear set of outcomes, indicators and processes. Where this is present, funding agencies are increasingly willing to commit resources for longer periods of time than in the earlier era of projects.

Against this background, it is instructive to examine the interpretation of planning for EFA and credible plans in a small sample of international organizations and agencies.

UNESCO has stated that National EFA Action Plans are the very foundations of the drive towards Education for All, and it has elaborated the characteristics of a credible EFA plan, building on the statement from the Dakar Framework for Action at the beginning of this section (UNESCO, 2001*k*; 2001*m*; 2002*h*).

UNESCO has issued guidelines for preparing EFA plans (UNESCO, 2001*n*) that are described as an 'orientation', and not a technical planning tool. They emphasize participatory planning, building political and social support for EFA, prioritizing EFA in national budgets and its integration into wider sector and national development strategies, reaching the excluded, and promoting better co-ordinated international partnerships. The Organization has also developed generic criteria for assessing the credibility of National EFA Plans in both political and technical terms, analysed by planning process and by the content of plans. The office in Bangkok prepared a detailed *EFA Planning Guide for South and East Asia*, which incorporates a projection model (UNESCO-PROAP, 2001). The guide argues that 'the EFA Plan should not be an additional plan to already existing plans. Instead, the EFA Plan should be a framework, in the form of a large programme, integrating in a coherent way all EFA aspects of all other presently valid plans and policy documents.' In this interpretation (Figure 3.1), the EFA Plan is an integrating mechanism, a coherent sector-wide framework to guide the EFA activities of all government bodies. 'The normative function of this integrated EFA plan obliges all government bodies, as well their external funding partners to adhere to it and abstain from launching separate initiatives' (UNESCO-PROAP, 2001). Other UNESCO Regional Bureaux have developed their own guidelines.

It is difficult to form a judgement concerning the extent to which this guidance and other forms of technical input from UNESCO are having an impact at the country level. The approach is characterized by a relatively strict interpretation of the centrality of a distinctive EFA plan and placing considerable weight on preparation by the 2002 target date. At its best, this work is adding value to national planning processes and helping to bring coherence through EFA plans in a highly complex area. But there is also a danger, for which there is some evidence, that a separate short-term EFA planning process to meet an international requirement creates additional or parallel planning activities to the mainstream of education sector planning. If this is happening this is not a creative use of scarce resources. This raises the question that is reflected in the title of this Chapter – EFA plans or planning for EFA? The two are not necessarily the same. There is no single model.

The international NGOs also place considerable weight on national plans for EFA. Many were to the fore in Dakar, in arguing for national plans by 2002. The Global Campaign for Education (GCE) represents this view:

> . . . any global effort must be firmly rooted in national plans for achieving education for all. These should be developed with cross-sectoral participation of key ministries and civil society groups, and should be embedded wherever possible in national strategies for poverty reduction as well as in medium term expenditure frameworks (GCE, 2002*a*).

Collectively, the NGO community stresses the importance of reaching international consensus

International NGOs also place considerable weight on national EFA plans.

Figure 3.1. Relationship between EFA plans and other plans and strategic instruments, including EFA-related activities

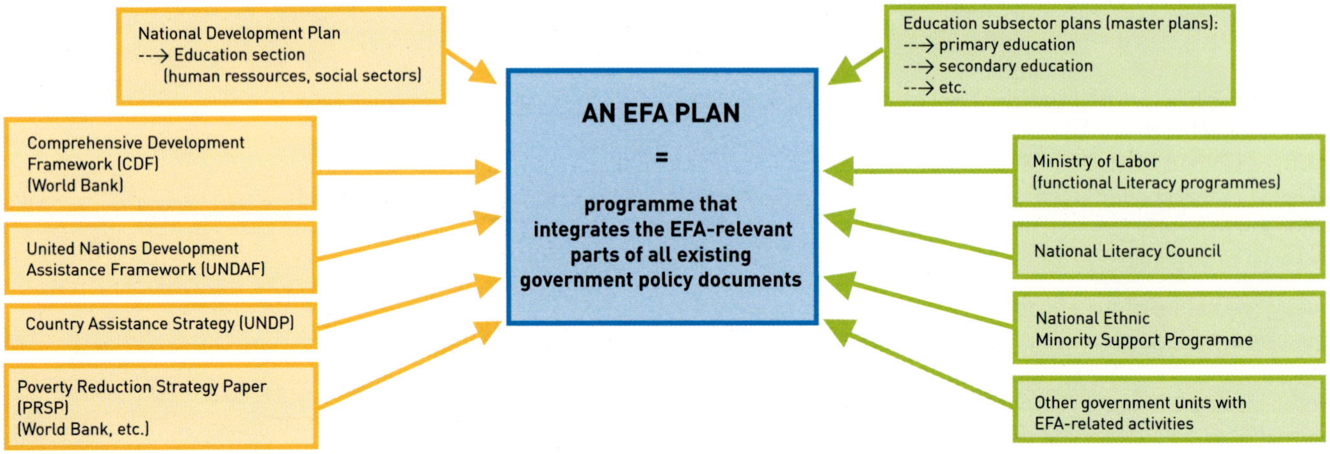

Source: UNESCO/PROAP (2001).

on criteria that define credibility and provide the basis for global and country level compacts (Box 3.17). They regard EFA plans, or plans that encompass EFA goals, as the primary basis for determining the financial gap which should be filled by external resources (see Chapter 4). As Chapter 5 outlines, international NGO campaigns have had significant political impact internationally. It is activity that is increasingly backed by strong analysis and by support for national NGOs and CSOs in their efforts to engage in planning for EFA.

The Education Task Force for G8 in 2002 emphasized that the responsibility for developing sound education plans and providing sufficient resources lies with governments of developing countries.

Since the World Education Forum in 2000, the World Bank has given priority to one of the Dakar goals in particular: universal primary education (UPE), and defined a technical framework for achieving universal primary completion, as distinct from enrolment. The Bank has not advanced a comprehensive EFA view, although it undertakes technical and project work on other EFA-related goals. Its work is informed primarily by the Millennium Development Goals (MDGs). It has certainly injected some urgency into international dialogue (see Chapter 5) on UPE, and invested in comparative analysis on the financing and management strategies that are important for achieving quality primary education for all. This analytical work (World Bank, 2002*a*) has been influential in the development of the Fast-Track Initiative (see Chapter 5).

While the Bank states the importance of context-specific, national solutions, it promotes the case for particular attention to be given to the share of the budget directed to primary education; average teacher salaries, pupil-teacher ratios, non-salary expenditure; repetition rates and unit construction costs. It builds its case on evidence from countries where progress is being made towards higher levels of primary completion.

The Bank concludes that the road to UPE will be different for different countries depending on their current and projected levels of costs and the management of their service delivery. For poorly performing countries internal sector reform is more important than incremental funding. A *credible plan* in these terms is one that establishes strategies based on a commitment to the equitable financing of primary education and is clear in its intent to deliver on major service reform. Critics hold this to be an overly narrow, technical view of planning for education. They argue that despite protestations to the contrary, the Bank is a seeking a too rigid and normative approach to planning. The fact remains that the type of comparative analysis that the Bank has conducted is significant. Its international critics need to be similarly engaged.

The Education Task Force for G8 in 2002 emphasized that the responsibility for developing sound education plans and providing sufficient resources lies with developing-country governments. Political commitment and transparent budgets are essential. National education plans should be comprehensive, and deal with access, equity, and quality issues and integrating primary education into an overall education policy. This is essentially a slight reworking of the existing Dakar Framework.

Bilateral agencies have tended to interpret Dakar according to the circumstances of the countries in which they have bilateral programmes and according to their overall development policies and strategies. They have given far less weight to the development of distinctive all-encompassing EFA Action Plans than does the United Nations system. Many place emphasis on sector-wide planning and poverty reduction strategies, and on giving priority to the goals of EFA within those planning frameworks. Some, like the United Kingdom's Department for International Development (DFID), prioritize the MDGs for education, arguing that planning for the realization of UPE and gender equality in poverty reduction is key (DFID, 2001*a*; 2001*b*). The Nordic countries emphasize the importance of planning within a human rights framework (e.g. SIDA, 2001) as does the Netherlands (Netherlands, 2000). Canadian CIDA sets planning for EFA within a broad social and human development framework (CIDA, 2002).

Box 3.17. Assessing education plans: Transparent norms

Donors and developing country governments must 'agree to agree' on a small number of flexible but specific normative criteria for transparent assessment of the strength of national education plans. These criteria should not become new conditionalities. They should be derived from the commitments made by 180 governments in Dakar, which in turn reflect growing international evidence on the prerequisites for a successful education system.

The principal benchmark of 'serious commitment' should be that the country's leaders have identified education for all (EFA) as a national priority and have put in motion a credible and participatory process for producing a cost and time-bound national plan to achieve the EFA goals. While plans must grow out of country needs and priorities, the Dakar consensus makes it evident that any serious plan would need to include:

- commitment to adequate and efficient public financing of education, the abolition of household payments for public primary education, and a net reallocation of spending in favour of educationally disadvantaged groups and schools (i.e. girls and women, working children, the rural poor, ethnic and linguistic minorities);
- a mechanism for broad, representative and sustained participation of civil society in determining education policy priorities and monitoring policy implementation;
- a sensible balance between immediate priorities, including the education MDGs; and the need for balanced education development over the longer term, with renewed commitment to the crucial role of early childhood and adult basic education in reducing poverty;
- bold reforms to improve learning outcomes (including a commitment to decent salaries and training for teachers), and increased space for local innovation within the public system; and
- steps to cope with the impact of HIV-AIDS on teachers, learners and schools.

Source: GCE (2002*a*).

Conclusions

This chapter points to some general judgements about the extent to which Dakar commitments for planning for EFA are being met, two years after the World Education Forum. Three conclusions stand out.

First, the comprehensive EFA National Action Plans prescribed by the Dakar Framework by the end of 2002 have not yet materialized widely. Government structures continue to militate against a comprehensive approach. But there is some evidence of a greater sense of urgency in planning for EFA, and of the need to be inclusive, although the evidence of gender responsive planning needs particular focus.

Second, it does seem to be the case that EFA and/or the MDGs for education are gaining higher priority in overall national government policies and plans. This is particularly so where PRSPs are being prepared and where there is a clear expression of public demand and support.

Third, there is not yet much evidence of governments being publicly held to account against their stated goals. Regional forums are potentially helpful in this regard. It would be useful to assess the role of MINEDAF and other regional forums in this respect. National monitoring reports and national education watches also have potential. *The Indian Report: A Profile of Basic Education* (Govinda et al., 2002) is interesting in this regard. The Bangladesh Education Watch Report was started in 1998; the 2001 Watch Report is entitled *Renewed Hope, Daunting Challenges: State of Primary Education in Bangladesh* (Education Watch, 2001).

It can be concluded that the jury is still out. Dakar has injected some life into a process that was flagging in the second half of the 1990s. It is absolutely critical that this momentum not be lost. Planning for EFA must remain firmly within the time-bound parameters of the EFA goals, the first of which is in 2005.

There is not yet much evidence of governments being publicly held to account against their stated goals.

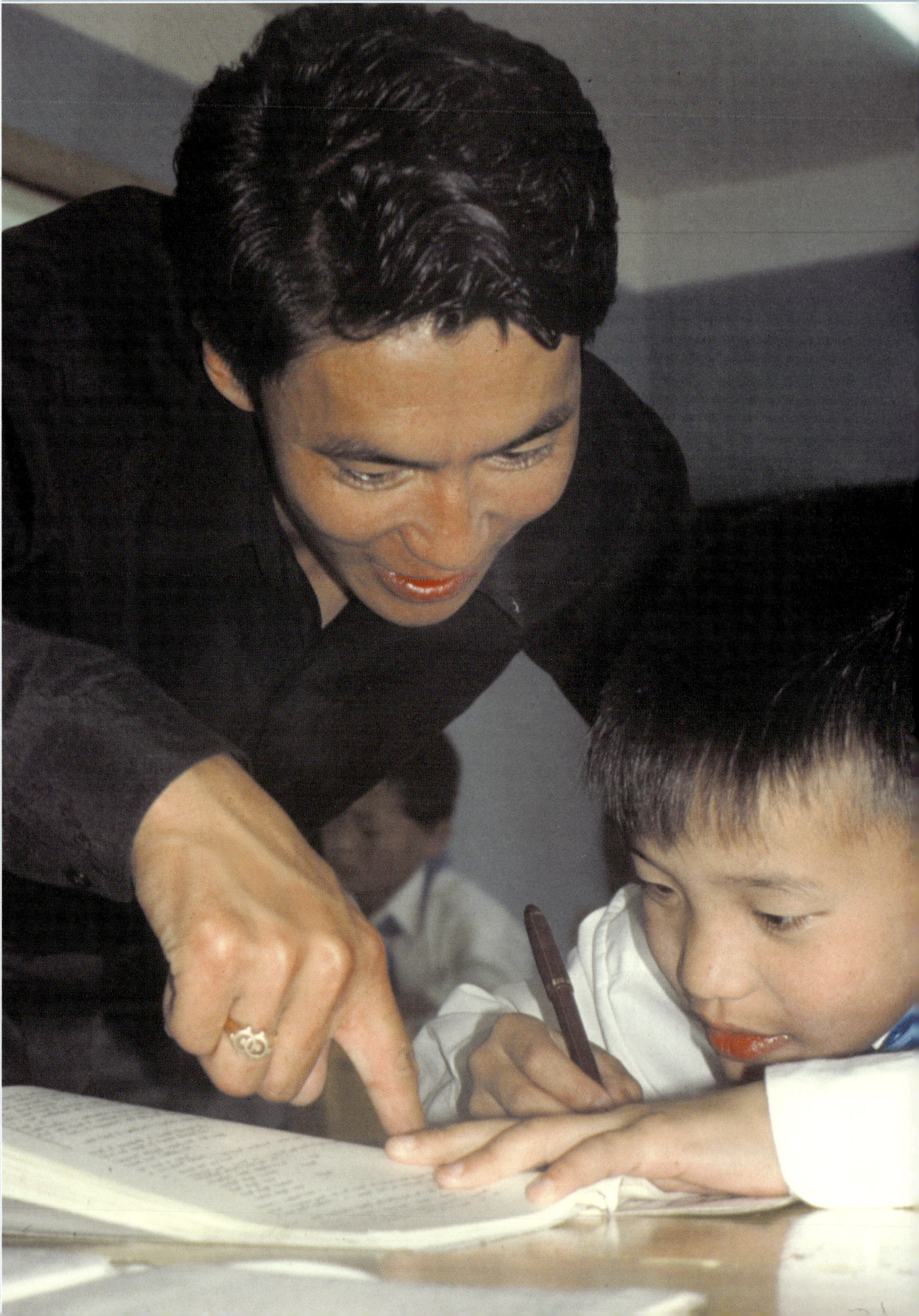

Chapter 4

Resource requirements for achieving EFA

For most countries, whether or not EFA is achieved will depend mainly upon the extent of national commitment to the goals. However, the fact that the international community has decided that these goals are to be achieved by a particular date implies that the extent of necessary policy change will be much greater for some countries than for others. Those where most change in pace will be needed are the countries which are at present at farthest from achieving the goals. They may often have lower incomes and weaker administrations than many of the others. They may also be societies where the political interests aligned against rapid reform may be at their most intense. This means that the politics, as well as the economics, of reform will have strong and separate influence upon outcomes.

Nevertheless, both the costs of achieving the goals and the availability of resources to secure them are likely to have a decisive influence upon whether or not EFA goals are reached. These two issues provide the theme for this chapter. Some of the goals cannot be addressed here, because the amount of evidence about the likely costs of their achievement is at present either very weak or very selective. Accordingly, the evidence on the costs of universalizing primary education, achieving gender equality in school participation, and improving school quality is assessed; implications for external financing requirements are drawn.

Some countries will find it particularly difficult to secure the amount of resource reallocation necessary to deliver the goals. This applies to countries strongly affected by the HIV/AIDS pandemic and to those recovering from, or still in the midst of, emergencies or conflict. This chapter will examine to what extent these circumstances affect the volume and nature of resources required.

Estimating the costs of universal primary education (UPE)

Up to now, EFA efforts have focused on children's enrolment in school, rather than on completion rates or student learning outcomes.

Several studies which estimate resource requirements for UPE in developing countries have been completed during the past two or three years by groups of researchers at UNESCO, UNICEF and the World Bank. Three of these have been selected for closer analysis here, each of which use country-level data but different approaches to estimation.[1] Their main purposes are to estimate the affordability of UPE and the extent to which external aid may be needed to supplement domestic resources. This chapter compares these estimates and assesses the extent to which the results of these studies can provide a guide for policy.

Coverage and methods

The costs of achieving UPE by a given date are determined by combining the pattern of enrolment growth over the intervening years with the resources allocated per student over the same period. Most studies focus upon public expenditures and consider whether present expenditures per student should be maintained, or adjusted over the longer run. The simplest approach has been to assume no change, whereby the cost estimation exercise is reduced to projecting the flow of pupil numbers over time, multiplied by their present unit cost. However, if school quality is judged to be too low, allowances to increase unit expenditures are usually made. Additionally, if school systems are very inefficient, the possibility of introducing reforms to reduce unit costs may be explored. Sometimes these adjustments are made by directly changing the assumed level of future unit costs. Alternatively, a more formal modelling framework can be used in order to simulate the cost impact of policy change. The UNESCO and UNICEF studies provide examples of the former approach, whereas the World Bank study is an example of the latter.

Country coverage

Coverage of the developing countries in the three studies was rather different (see Table 4.1). Although the UNESCO and UNICEF studies demonstrated similar coverage of the developing world, the former also included all of Eastern Europe and Central Asian countries, the majority of which are classified as 'developed'.

The World Bank study, on the other hand, concentrated on the 63 lowest-income countries with populations of over 1 million, 'home to 75% of all children out of school globally'. However, the actual simulation exercise covered only 47 countries, over two-thirds of which are in sub-Saharan Africa. Another 49 countries, judged 'at risk' of failing to attain UPE by 2015, were not included. Sixteen of these are eligible for low-cost IDA (International Development Association) loans and have populations of less than 1 million; 33 are richer countries eligible for normal World Bank loans, including Chile, the Islamic Republic of Iran, Malaysia, Mexico, Thailand and others.

Table 4.1. EFA cost studies: number of developing and transitional countries covered, by region

Region	UNESCO	UNICEF	World Bank
East Asia/Pacific	20	20	2
Eastern Europe/Central Asia	27	9	4
Latin America/Caribbean	29	27	3
Middle East/North Africa	16	18	1
South Asia	9	8	4
Sub-Saharan Africa	50	46	33
Total	151	128	47

Source: Brossard and Gacougnolle (2000); Delamonica et al. (2001); World Bank (2002*a*).

Assumptions and methods

Criteria for achievement of UPE. The main assumptions and methods used by the studies are summarized in Table 4.2, and some important points of difference are worth noting. First, the UNESCO and UNICEF studies each adopted the achievement of net enrolment ratios (NERs) of 100% by 2015 as the criterion for the successful implementation of UPE. The World Bank study adopted completion rates of 100% as

1. The studies are: Brossard and Gacougnolle, 2000, referred to as 'UNESCO'; Delamonica et al., 2001, referred to as 'UNICEF'; and World Bank, 2002a. At least three other studies have provided estimations, but without providing country-level data in their reports. A comparison of the different methods used in all of these studies is provided in Bennell (2002).

the criterion for success. The completion rate is defined as the total number of pupils who successfully complete the final grade of primary school, expressed as a percentage of the total population of children of school-leaving age.[2] The authors of the study have pointed out that 'to date, EFA efforts have focused heavily on getting children enrolled in school, rather than on completion rates or student learning outcomes'. Data on the number of children completing primary education are often not known. The World Bank study estimates the number of pupils completing the final grade of primary school by deducting the number of repeaters in this grade. Since this does not take into account final-year dropouts, the authors accept that their estimates are an overstatement of the true primary completion rate. Completion rates are important indicators of successful implementation of EFA. For that reason, they are alluded to in the wording of the UPE goal. However, for reasons discussed in Chapter 2 (Box 2.2) of this Report, they cannot be used as the sole criterion for its successful implementation.

Length of the primary-school cycle. The enrolment projections presented by each study are, without exception, based on the current duration of the primary-school cycle in each country. However, the World Bank study uses a standard six-year period to calculate resource requirements. This is done 'in order to avoid biasing estimates of the external financing requirements towards countries with longer primary cycles and away from countries with short ones' (World Bank, 2002, p. 18). Their cost estimates are therefore biased downwards because primary education cycles exceed six years in over one quarter of developing countries.

Data quality. As regards data quality, the World Bank study made the most concerted effort to collect accurate and up-to-date enrolment, expenditure and funding data. In particular, it utilized the global network of World Bank personnel to provide data for countries that are poorly covered by the UNESCO annual statistical surveys. The other studies relied on UNESCO data, which are compiled from questionnaires completed by Ministries of Education in each Member State.

Information about recurrent and capital expenditure on primary education by governments, donors, households, non-government organizations and other stakeholders is poor in most developing countries. What schools actually receive from government is invariably markedly less than what is indicated in official estimates of expenditure and other types of income and expenditure documentation. Unit-cost estimates are usually based upon the government's direct funding of the primary education subsector, and do not therefore include the often sizeable expenditures on administration and other key support services (including pre- and in-service teacher training, inspection and curriculum development).

Accordingly, the use of official statistics may often lead to the underestimation of public expenditures per pupil. The data, too, are patchy. For example, in the case of the UNICEF study, information on either unit costs or NERs was missing for more than one quarter of the 128 countries included. In response, the cost estimates in the study were based upon those in countries with similar income or regional characteristics, while NER estimates were based upon known gross enrolment ratios (GERs) and other data. High margins of error in the estimates for individual countries are a likely consequence of these circumstances.

Projection methods. There are important differences in the projection methods used in these studies. The UNESCO and UNICEF studies both provide simple projections of the costs of UPE based upon multiplying present public expenditures per pupil by the projected school-age population in 2015 for each country. However, all three of the studies also provide projections incorporating the impact of policy reforms that are expected to improve the quality and efficiency of school systems. To assume that present public expenditures per student will remain unchanged in the future is unnecessarily restrictive, and the assumptions made about policy reforms can considerably affect the usefulness of cost studies, because the existing pattern of expenditures is usually not optimal. In a large number of countries that achieve UPE, there are still patent needs to improve the quality

In most developing countries, information about expenditure on primary education is weak.

2. Strictly speaking, this is a measure of the 'gross completion rate'. Since it has not been adjusted for age, in systems with high levels of repetition the statistic may exceed 100%. If, from a policy perspective, we are mainly interested in the number of children who complete the primary cycle, rather than the age at which they do so, the gross rate will be preferred to the net, age-adjusted, rate.

Table 4.2. Key parameters and assumptions used in the three UPE cost studies

Parameters and assumptions	UNESCO cost study	UNICEF cost study	WORLD BANK cost study
General			
Criterion for UPE	100% NER	100% NER	100% completion rate
Number of countries studied	151	128	47
Target date	2015	2015	2015
Length of primary span	Actual	Actual	6 years
Current unit costs (US$, 2000)	188.2	42.4	32.0
Unit costs with policy measures (US$, 2000)	198.0	140.8	79.0
Projections			
Using present unit costs	yes	yes	no
Using adjusted unit costs (with reforms)	yes	yes	yes
Assumptions for private enrolments	–	–	10%
Assumptions for economic growth	–	–	not specified[1]
HIV/AIDS included	partly	partly	yes
Capital expenditures included	yes	yes	yes
Target parameters			
Quality reforms			
Pupil-teacher ratio	10% improvement	40	40
Percentage of non-salary costs in recurrent expenditures	–	15%	33%
Efficiency reforms			
Teacher salaries	70% of 1997 levels	–	3.5 times GDP per capita
Repetition	–	–	10%
Financing reforms			
Public revenues as percentage of GDP	–	–	14–18%
Education expenditures as percentage of revenues	–	–	20%
Primary expenditures as percentage of total education expenditures	–	–	50%

1. The assumptions were made, but not specified, in the text.
Source: Brossard and Gacougnolle (2000); Delamonica et al. (2001); World Bank (2002*a*).

The idea that teachers' salaries need to fall in all countries does not make sense: in some, they must rise significantly beyond present levels in order to encourage teacher morale and increase productivity.

of schooling, which will usually require increased resources per student. On the other hand, where inefficiencies are widespread, qualitative reforms may facilitate reductions that are badly needed for pedagogic reasons in repetition and drop-out rates, and which may allow costs per pupil, or per completer, to fall. Accordingly, the diagnosis of the particular resource problems faced by national systems, and of the reforms which could be introduced to tackle them, are important both for the adequacy of the cost estimates and to the encouragement of a process of national reform.

Table 4.2 summarizes the policy measures simulated in each of the studies. The UNESCO study assumed that, in each country, the number of pupils per teacher would fall by 10% by 2015 – raising unit costs – but that teachers' salaries would fall in real terms to 70% of their 1997 levels, thus reducing them. The UNICEF study also assumed a reduction in the pupil-teacher ratio – in this case to 40 in countries where higher ratios were found. In addition, the authors allowed for at least 15% of recurrent expenditure being allocated to materials and other non-wage inputs to schooling. Although most of these assumptions make sense, the idea that teachers' salaries need to fall in all countries does not: in some, pay will have to rise significantly beyond present levels in order to encourage teacher morale and increase productivity.

The World Bank study adopted a more empirical approach. Its policy simulations are based upon the specific premise that 'education systems in low-income countries that have either achieved 100% primary completion or are relatively close have some basic common features' (p. 2). The study investigates the financing characteristics of 51 countries that have provided the necessary data, distinguishing ten 'high performing countries' (defined as having GERs of over 90% and primary completion rates of over 70%) from the rest.[3] The authors found that these high performance countries:

- devote a higher share of national resources to public primary education (1.7% of GDP compared with the sample average of 1.4% of GDP);

3. The group comprised Bangladesh, Bolivia, the Gambia, India, Indonesia, Lesotho, Uganda, Viet Nam, Zambia and Zimbabwe, although the Gambia and Zambia had GERs of less than 90%.

- exhibit approximately average unit costs (spending the equivalent of 12% of per capita GDP per public primary student, compared with 13% in the full sample);
- have teacher pay levels which are similar to other groups (spending 3.6 times per capita GDP per teacher);
- spend slightly more of their recurrent budget on non-salary items than other country groups;
- have pupil-teacher ratios of about 40:1; and
- have much lower repetition rates than any of the other groups (8.2% compared with a sample average of 17%).

Using these results from the high performance countries as a guide, the World Bank adopted the set of target parameters shown in Table 4.2 as 'performance norms' for its national simulations.

The other main cost parameters that have been treated differently in the three studies include capital expenditures, private schooling, and the adjustments, if any, made for the prevalence of HIV/AIDS. As regards capital expenditures, the UNESCO study has assumed that the ratio of capital to current spending will remain the same as in the base year. The UNICEF study argues that in most of the 73 developing countries with GERs over 100%, 'enough school places exist for achieving universal coverage of primary education' (p. 13). The authors assumed therefore that additional capital expenditure requirements for these countries are zero. This assumption requires that the move to net ratios of 100% can be entirely accommodated by declines in GER, which ignores the fact that many pupils who are currently out of school live in areas where there are no school facilities at all. The UNICEF study also overlooks the impact of population growth: in many countries, the increment to the school-age population over a fifteen-year period will exceed 50%, which is substantially greater than the present gap between gross and net ratios. In such cases, even if GERs and NERs were equalized at 100% (and ignoring the problem of school location), the present number of school places would still prove to be inadequate by 2015. For the remaining 55 countries, it has been assumed that 15% of total education expenditure is being spent on capital investment. Furthermore, in the absence of adequate data, it also assumed that 'the proportion of [total education] outlays allocated to primary schooling is about the same as for recurrent expenditure' (p. 14).

The World Bank study states that country-specific data were used, when these were available. Where they are not, the authors assume that average cost of a 'fully equipped classroom' is US$8,000 in sub-Saharan Africa, and $3,500–$4,000 in South Asia. The countries where no capital expenditure data were available have not been specified. None of these studies consider the possible impact of teachers working double shifts or of multi-grade teaching on capital spending. Yet these policy options can have a major impact not only upon the number of teachers needed (and thus upon the pupil-teacher ratio), but also upon the number of classrooms required during the move towards UPE.[4]

Since these studies aim to provide estimates of the public cost of attaining UPE, the extent to which people choose to educate their children in private schools needs to be considered, because its incidence may reduce the amount of public spending required. The World Bank study – the only one to do so – assumes that 10% of a given age group will be enrolled in private schools, based on the observed average in the sample of countries for which data were available. Since this is the sample mean, for many countries it will prove to be a strong underestimate of private provision. Furthermore, it could be argued that the trend towards private schooling may well accelerate as development proceeds.

Finally, the World Bank study was the only one of the three to adjust its estimates to allow for the particular costs of the HIV/AIDS pandemic in the countries covered. The three main areas of potential impact are: lower enrolment growth rates, increased teacher morbidity and mortality, and increased numbers of orphans and of other children directly affected by the epidemic. United Nations population projections – utilized by all three studies – have been adjusted to take into account the demographic effects of the epidemic. Accordingly, even though great uncertainties remain about the impact of the

When estimating the public cost of UPE, adjustments must be made to allow for the particular costs of the HIV/AIDS pandemic.

4. An earlier set of simulations demonstrated that the introduction of double-shifting sufficient to reduce the teacher-pupil ratio by 15% was associated with a decline of classroom requirements by up to 20%, at UPE enrolment levels. See Colclough and Lewin (1993), pp. 191–7.

epidemic on fertility levels, each of the studies allows for the impact of the disease on the primary-school-aged population.

In addition, the World Bank study attempts to assess the impact of the epidemic on teachers and orphans. The authors assume that mortality rates for teachers will be similar to that of other adults, and that since teachers will be replaced at the new lower salary levels envisaged by the authors, increased mortality will actually tend to reduce teacher costs in future years. Consequently, the World Bank study concludes that the main cost burden of the HIV/AIDS epidemic with respect to the UPE target will be the additional financial support required for orphans. The authors estimate that US$50 per year (in constant 2000 price terms) will be needed to maintain each maternal and two-parent orphan in school. The combined impact of these two assumptions on the total costs of achieving UPE is significant. However, as shown later in this chapter, the assumptions appear to both understate and omit important dimensions of the likely costs involved.

Public spending in all countries taken together will need to increase significantly each year until 2015.

Results

As indicated earlier, the annual costs of UPE to a government are a product of the required enrolments by the target date and public expenditures per student at that time. Total costs are determined by how these two factors change over the intervening years. It should by now be clear that the process of estimating these apparently simple magnitudes is in fact rather complex. A significant body of assumptions is needed, each of which is capable of influencing projected outcomes. Obviously, estimates which use different assumptions cannot be expected to generate exactly the same results. However, it is reasonable to expect that they would not entirely conflict. Indeed, the process of compiling separate estimates which differ in detail, but which suggest the same type of conclusion, is an important means of providing evidence and support for desirable policy change.

Additional public expenditures required

The results from the three studies can be compared mainly by examining their conclusions concerning the extent to which public spending on primary schooling will need to increase in order to achieve UPE. Table 4.3 shows, for 46 of the countries included in the World Bank study,[5] estimates of the average additional public expenditure required annually over the period to 2015 implied in each study. These estimates have been made using different unit cost figures and the base-year figures differ substantially, with the average across all countries being much higher in the UNESCO study than the others (Table 4.2). Further variation occurs because of the different mix of quality and efficiency reforms used for of each study to estimate future unit costs, so some significant degree of variance in projected outcomes is to be expected. It is not possible, from the data provided in the documents, to compare projected expenditures with and without reforms at national level and thus to enable the separate impact of the assumptions made in each study to be identified.

The estimates suggest that public spending, in all the countries taken together, would need to increase, on average, by between $4.3 billion and $8.4 billion per year over the period. The UNICEF and UNESCO studies both produce closely similar results for these aggregate figures, while the World Bank estimate is some 70%–95% higher than the other two.

However, it can be seen from the table that many of the estimates for individual countries differ by a much larger margin. The difference between the maximum and minimum estimates is often very wide, with more than a three-fold difference occurring in 24 (52%) of the country cases. Although the UNESCO study uses higher average unit cost estimates than the others, the World Bank study estimates the highest additional costs in 32 of the countries, while the other 2 generate the highest estimates in 7 countries each. If the highest and lowest estimates are summed for each country, it can be seen from the last three columns of the table that the range of average annual additional costs increases from a minimum of $3.2 billion to a maximum of $9.4 billion over the years to 2015.

5. Since 1 of the 47 countries in the World Bank's analysis – the Republic of Moldova – was not included in the UNICEF study, it is has not been included in Table 4.3.

Table 4.3.
Average annual additional cost for achieving UPE by 2015, as estimated in three different studies, in millions of US$ (2000)

Country	UNICEF study Annual average additional cost to reach NER=100	UNESCO study Average annual extra spending Scenario 1	World Bank study Average annual extra spending	max	min	max/min
India	1 474.01	1 164.72	3 832.70	3 832.70	1 164.72	3.3
Pakistan	790.38	394.91	660.69	790.38	394.91	2.0
Nigeria	519.34	645.24	766.79	766.79	519.34	1.5
Yemen	106.86	584.86	56.70	584.86	56.70	10.3
Bangladesh	130.84	15.77	286.55	286.55	15.77	18.2
Ethiopia	253.76	93.13	201.32	253.76	93.13	2.7
Angola	68.43	250.65	207.47	250.65	68.43	3.7
Côte d'Ivoire	248.29	225.52	167.88	248.29	167.88	1.5
Sudan	94.87	30.79	194.67	194.67	30.79	6.3
Kenya	73.14	74.74	172.00	172.00	73.14	2.4
United Republic of Tanzania	86.11	59.83	171.40	171.40	59.83	2.9
Uganda	44.97	28.39	140.85	140.85	28.39	5.0
Cameroon	122.33	10.01	132.38	132.38	10.01	13.2
Democratic Republic of the Congo	29.52	76.04	125.96	125.96	29.52	4.3
Congo	117.24	7.07	50.00	117.24	7.07	16.6
Honduras	36.66	15.01	89.00	89.00	15.01	5.9
Senegal	87.13	51.24	81.82	87.13	51.24	1.7
Nepal	30.45	15.01	86.00	86.00	15.01	5.7
Mozambique	85.89	31.77	85.97	85.97	31.77	2.7
Niger	75.27	75.50	46.89	75.50	46.89	1.6
Burkina Faso	74.13	66.58	66.54	74.13	66.54	1.1
Ghana	36.94	68.65	19.68	68.65	19.68	3.5
Haiti	15.47	5.66	59.71	59.71	5.66	10.6
Guinea	40.01	21.76	58.07	58.07	21.76	2.7
Zambia	11.96	19.58	57.03	57.03	11.96	4.8
Rwanda	27.70	55.92	41.81	55.92	27.70	2.0
Mali	51.22	29.48	54.00	54.00	29.48	1.8
Cambodia	6.65	0.44	52.00	52.00	0.44	119.5
Eritrea	10.45	43.30	10.50	43.30	10.45	4.1
Georgia	0.00	0.00	42.00	42.00	0.00	42.0
Armenia	0.00	0.00	39.00	39.00	0.00	39.0
Madagascar	24.15	11.97	38.46	38.46	11.97	3.2
Malawi	22.92	10.01	34.06	34.06	10.01	3.4
Chad	17.01	11.75	33.52	33.52	11.75	2.9
Benin	26.80	11.53	32.00	32.00	11.53	2.8
Lao PDR	7.00	4.35	31.00	31.00	4.35	7.1
Burundi	10.49	25.24	20.10	25.24	10.49	2.4
Togo	16.51	6.96	21.57	21.57	6.96	3.1
Nicaragua	17.18	12.51	18.00	18.00	12.51	1.4
Central African Republic	7.52	3.92	17.45	17.45	3.92	4.5
Lesotho	8.38	15.01	16.65	16.65	8.38	2.0
Sierra Leone	11.17	2.50	14.28	14.28	2.50	5.7
Mauritania	12.28	9.57	10.80	12.28	9.57	1.3
Gambia	5.30	4.24	5.54	5.54	4.24	1.3
Guinea Bissau	2.69	2.94	5.14	5.14	2.69	1.9
Mongolia	0.00	0.76	1.00	1.00	0.00	1.0
Total	4 939.43	4 294.85	8 356.95	9 402.07	3 184.11	3.0

Cost estimates in the UNICEF and UNESCO studies have been inflated to US$ prices for the year 2000. UNICEF figures have been adjusted by the population and NER growth rates from 2000–2015 to make them comparable. Estimates shown for World Bank have been calculated by subtracting recurrent expenditures in 2000 from the average annual recurrent expenditures required for UPE.

Source: Delamonica et al. (2001), Appendix I, pp. 23–25; Brossard and Gacougnolle (2000), Table A.1, Annex 2, pp. 49–52; World Bank (2002a), Table A.6a, Technical Annex, p. 8.

External funding requirements

The World Bank study is the only one of the three to provide estimates for the extent of external funding required. This figure is derived by comparing the expected public resources available for primary education spending (derived according to the assumptions shown in Table 4.2) with the pattern of expenditures required to achieve UPE. The resulting annual gaps are summed and then averaged over the 15-year period. As indicated in Table 4.4, the authors expect an annual external funding requirement for the 47 countries of $2.5 billion under their second ('middle') scenario for domestic resource mobilization (government revenues being 14%–18% of GDP; 20% of government revenues being spent on education; and 50% of education expenditure being allocated to primary schooling).

The World Bank estimates that India will have a sizeable surplus of domestic funding for primary education, averaging nearly US$1.4 billion between 2000 and 2015.

They project that the external funding requirement for primary education will peak at US$4.5 billion per annum in 2015. Sub-Saharan Africa will require 85% of this external assistance. Five countries have annual external funding gaps of more than US$100 million per annum (Democratic Republic of the Congo, Ethiopia, Nigeria, Pakistan and the Sudan), which between them account for nearly 42% of the total external funding requirement. Another seven countries are projected to require, on average, US$50–100 million per annum in donor support (Cameroon, Côte d'Ivoire, Mali, Niger, Senegal, United Republic of Tanzania and Uganda). Aid requirements appear to be surprisingly small for countries such as Bangladesh, Malawi, Mozambique and Zambia, especially in view of current levels of donor support to their education sectors. India is projected to have a sizeable surplus of domestic funding for primary education, averaging nearly US$1.4 billion between 2000 and 2015.

How likely are these three scenarios? As will be clear from earlier commentary, the answer depends mainly upon the reasonableness of both the policy parameters set out in Table 4.2. and the revenue and expenditure assumptions discussed above.

Much could be said about the pros and cons of the values adopted for the target parameters in the World Bank study. However, they are broadly similar to those suggested by some earlier work,[6] and in other ways they are consistent both with known research results and with common sense. For example, many poor countries with high cost systems are unlikely to be able to universalize provision unless something is done to reduce unit costs. In several francophone African countries, high teacher costs are compensated by very high pupil-teacher ratios, and total costs are met by reducing enrolments relative to other countries at similar levels of income. Thus the salary bill is affordable, but it brings negative consequences for both the quantity and quality of provision.[7] As in other areas of public policy, there are clear choices to be made that are capable of affecting the possibility of services being universalized.

Nevertheless, while it may be unproblematic to advocate moving the parameters in the directions indicated by the more successful country cases, it should be recognized that the actual mechanics of doing this will often be very difficult indeed. As the World Bank study acknowledges, teachers' salaries provide a good example. Where these are very high relative to GDP per capita – as in Eritrea, Ethiopia, Haiti, Lesotho, Niger, Central African Republic, Rwanda, Mozambique, Zimbabwe and others[8] – it often reflects structural characteristics of the economy (such as a general shortage of skilled people, or a highly agrarian economy with a small formal sector), the effects of which cannot easily be disregarded. In such economies, the salary ratios – not just of teachers, but of all

Table 4.4.
World Bank estimates for average annual domestic resource mobilization and external funding requirements for 47 selected countries, in billions of US$

Region	Support for HIV/AIDS orphans	Domestic resource mobilization			External funding		
		Scenario 1	Scenario 2	Scenario 3	Scenario 1	Scenario 2	Scenario 3
47 countries	No support	4.1	4.0	4.4	1.5	1.6	1.1
	Support provided				0.6	0.6	0.6
	Sub-total				2.1	2.2	1.7
Rest of world	None required	2.3	2.3	2.1	0.3	0.3	0.3
Total		6.4	6.3	6.5	2.4	2.5	2.0

Source: World Bank (2002*a*), Table 4.13.

6. Colclough and Al-Samarrai (2000), for example, found very similar relationships between public spending and unit costs in low- and high-enrolment countries to those reported in the Bank study.

7. See Mingat (1988 and 2002); and Colclough et.al. (forthcoming).

8. In each of these countries, average teachers' salaries were more than six times as much as GNP per capita in the late 1990s, compared with an average for sub-Saharan Africa of 4.3, and for a broader sample of 56 countries of 4.4. See Colclough and Al-Samarrai (2000), Tables 3 and 5; and World Bank (2002*a*), Tables 4.1 and A11.

professional workers – tend to be higher relative to per capita income than they are in more industrialized countries, because the level of teachers' salaries is a product of the remuneration demanded by skilled and professional workers as a group, and cannot necessarily be affected in isolation. More generally, teacher salary level is also a function of the structure of the economy, which cannot easily be altered as a matter of short- or medium-term policy choice. One response, suggested by the World Bank study (pp. 41–42) is to recruit a new cadre of teachers at lower salary levels, while continuing to pay existing staff on the old scales. A number of countries, including Senegal and Mali, have adopted this approach with some success. However, the impact on average salary levels is slow, and it remains to be seen whether such a 'double' salary level for teachers can become the dominant mode of employment for the profession as a whole.

A second example is provided by average rates of repetition, where the target rate, in the World Bank study, is set at 10% for countries currently above this level, with no change envisaged for other countries. There is no doubt that high rates of repetition are dysfunctional. They are symptomatic of a discontinuity between the demands of the curriculum on the one hand, and the ability of schools and teachers to impart it, on the other. Improvements in the quality of schooling and curriculum reform provide two ways in which high rates of repetition can be tackled. In some countries, however, policies of automatic promotion have been introduced – often in the absence of reforms to improve children's learning. In these circumstances, observed repetition rates can be a poor efficiency measure. Where progression to the next grade is virtually automatic, as in many of the 'high performing' countries identified in the World Bank study, the learning outcomes of children may actually be lower than in those having end-of-year examinations which determine the possibility of progression within schools. Although repetition rates may be lower in the former group, they may be an inadequate proxy for learning outcomes. This is not to argue that repetition rates should not be reduced, but rather that the ways in which some of the 'high performing' countries have achieved these reductions may not necessarily provide the best model for policy.

The assumptions for revenue and public spending appear to be defensible in principle, but very ambitious in practice, and one way of assessing just how ambitious is to consider their implications for the extent of real expenditure growth on primary schooling over the projection period. The World Bank's simulations suggest that total expenditure on primary education in the 47 countries would need to have risen from $7.4 billion in 2000 to $23.3 billion in 2015 (World Bank, 2002*a*, p. 62) – an expenditure growth of 8% per year in real terms over the 15 years. By the final year the gap between domestic financing and total expenditures is expected to amount to $4.5 billion. This implies that domestic resources available for expenditure on primary schooling would, in 2015, amount to $18.8 billion in these countries.

In order to assess the implications for the required growth in domestic financial resources, we need to know the extent of external financing of primary schooling in these countries in 2000. This is not precisely known, but an amount of $1 billion would be consistent with the aid estimates given in the next chapter, and roughly consistent with an average funding gap of $2.5 billion over the 15 years, as reported in the Bank study.[9] In this case, the required growth of domestic resources, from $6.4 billion (i.e. $7.4 billion domestic expenditure, minus aid resources) to $18.8 billion, would amount to a growth rate of 7.5% per year over the 15 years. If domestic resource availability were less than this in the base year, its subsequent required rate of growth to 2015 would be greater than these estimates suggest.

These increased domestic resources have to be generated by economic growth, on the one hand, and/or by fiscal reform on the other. However, the recent growth record of the economies in these countries is not promising (33 of the 47 countries are in sub-Saharan Africa, where, during the 1990s, weighted real GDP growth was scarcely more than 3% per year). If this growth record were not improved, shifts in sectoral expenditure, together with more fundamental

In some countries, policies of automatic promotion are often introduced in the absence of reforms to improve children's learning.

9. Although this assumption may seem high – constituting 13.5% of public spending on primary education in these countries – aid to education in the late 1990s in nine of these countries amounted to 36% of their combined public spending on education (Colclough et al. (forthcoming), Table 7.7).

fiscal reform, would need to provide the remaining 4.5% annual real growth in resources. These expenditure shifts would represent major increases in resource requirements, and it is by no means clear that such strong and sustained changes will take place.

If resources were not secured, the gap between domestic resources and required expenditures could increase sharply. For example, if the 47 countries were able to increase real domestic resources for primary schooling by 5% per year over the 15-year period (which would be a substantial achievement), the resource gap in 2015 would amount to $9.9 billion rather than the $4.5 billion projected in the World Bank study. Furthermore, under these circumstances, the average gap to be filled by aid would rise from $2.5 billion to $4.2 billion per year over the fifteen years.[10]

Any attempt to assess the costs of achieving UPE must be done on a country-by-country basis.

UPE: Conclusion

All attempts to assess the costs of achieving UPE must be carried out on a country-by-country basis. Estimating likely resource requirement estimates at the regional or world levels underestimates global needs for three main reasons. Firstly, all estimates are extremely sensitive to the values of unit costs and these can be properly addressed only at the country level. Secondly, for cost purposes, enrolment projections conducted at world or regional levels are misleading since those countries having reductions in pupil numbers because of declining school-age populations are implicitly added to the enrolment increases required elsewhere.[11] A third, and related, point is that the financing gaps in countries unlikely to be able to finance UPE themselves should not be added to surpluses elsewhere. Thus, aggregated methods of counting either enrolments or costs will not produce helpful results. For this reason, we have included in this chapter only those recent estimates that have been based upon country-level analysis.

It has been shown, however, that these estimates differ substantially from each other. The differences illustrate the sensitivity of the cost estimates to the data used in the analysis, to the assumptions used about the extent of required or desirable policy change, and to the assumptions made about future rates of economic growth. As regards costs, there is an urgent need to improve the quality of information on public expenditures on education. There appears to have been a deterioration in the quality of these data in recent years, and without some sharp increase in coverage and quality all attempts to estimate resource requirements will be undermined. Partly as a result of this quality decrease, there are substantial differences in the unit cost information adopted in different studies, and this is one of the more important causes of their varying results.

Among the three studies analysed above, the results provided by the World Bank are the most comprehensive and dependable. Methodologically, they are superior to those in most other recent work, and the simulation framework employed allows most of the key policy variables to be integrated with the analysis. However, the Bank study almost certainly underestimates both the expenditure implications of the move to UPE and the external aid requirements quite considerably. Firstly, it covers only the countries furthest away from UPE, with populations over 1 million. Up to one quarter of children at present out of school live in countries not covered by the Bank's analysis. Secondly, its adoption of a six-year primary cycle for all countries ignores the additional costs of UPE in 25% of countries with longer systems. Both of these factors imply that the costs of reaching UPE are underestimated. The estimates made for the size of financial gaps are also reduced by the same factors. Although many of the countries omitted from the analysis should not encounter great difficulty in financing their move to UPE, some of them will undoubtedly need sustained external support.

In addition, however, it is likely that the assumptions concerning the speed of policy change and the extent of required fiscal reform envisaged in the World Bank study are too demanding. On reasonable, but still ambitious, assumptions for revenue growth and fiscal reform, it seems likely that the size of external aid requirements in the 47 countries will be up to

10. This calculation maintains the assumption that aid transfers for primary schooling in the 47 countries were roughly $1 billion in 2000. This calculation is somewhat sensitive to the division of aid resources between India and the other countries in 2000, and the division of final-year expenditures between them. However, since all countries under this lower growth scenario for domestic resources would face financing gaps, the estimate is not subject to the 'adding up' problem mentioned further in the text.

11. Projections for the 1990s showed that the simple difference between total developing country enrolments in 1990 and those that would have been required for UPE in 2000 understated gross additional enrolments – i.e. the sum of all the national increases only – by more than 25% (Colclough and Lewin (1993), p. 212).

two-thirds higher than those projected in the study. If the speed of implementing the proposed quality and efficiency reforms were to be delayed, the discrepancy would be even greater. Finally, there are some categories of policy change and resource provision that have not been covered adequately by any of these studies. These categories are of considerable importance to EFA and to a number of the goals, including those covering formal schooling. They include the treatment of gender, the impact of HIV/AIDS and the situation of countries in circumstances of emergency. These are the topics that will be discussed in the remainder of this chapter.

Figure 4.1.
Proportion of unit costs represented by public and private expenditures in seven African countries

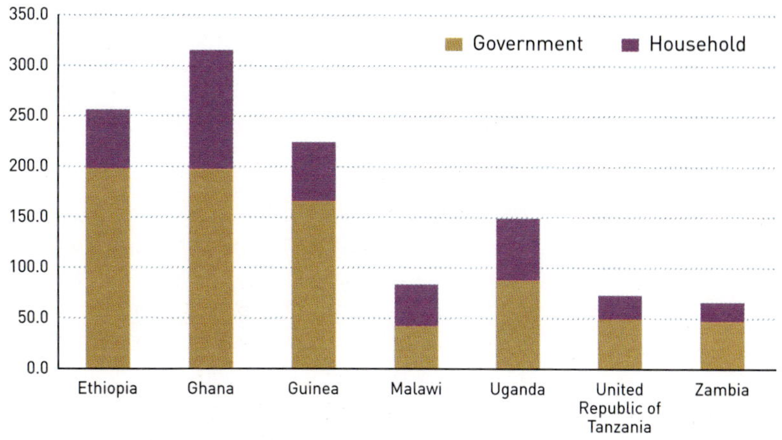

Sources:
Ethiopia: Weir and Knight (1996), education sub-sample of the Ethiopia Rural Household Survey (data include fees, stationery and clothing).
Ghana: Penrose (1998), 1995 survey (data include tuition, PTA fund, uniform, stationery, textbooks and food).
Guinea:Tembon et al. (1997).
Malawi: Rose (2001), 1998 household survey (data include school contributions, stationery, clothes and pocket money).
United Republic of Tanzania: Mason and Khandker (1996), from HRDS (data include fees and contributions, uniforms, textbooks and stationery, and other expenditure).
Uganda: Opolot (1994), 1992 survey (NB: pre-UPE) (data include uniforms, PTA fund, building fund, textbooks and stationery, extra tuition and other expenditure).
Zambia: World Bank (1996), from 1996 survey data (data includes uniform, stationery, PTA fund and general purpose fund).

Gender targets and the demand for schooling

Each of the studies assessing the costs of UPE accepts that strong supply-side, expansionary policies to support increased enrolments will be needed over the coming decade, but they do not attempt to analyse the costs of increasing the demand for schooling. Their emphasis is upon measures to improve and increase the number of schools, classes, teachers and materials. They also accept, albeit with more cursory treatment, the importance of measures to improve the quality of schooling, since low quality undermines both the value of schooling and the willingness of parents to enrol their children.

Is there demand for girls' – and boys' – schooling?

It has become clear, however, in recent years, that supply-side policies – though critically important – will be insufficient to achieve schooling for all. Research has shown that a central explanation for the continued under-enrolment of children from poorer households lies in the direct and indirect costs incurred when these families send their children to school. Such costs include, but are by no means limited to, the fees charged by some schools and countries as a condition for school attendance. Governments increasingly find that fees are not helpful to enrolment growth at primary level, and that they directly undermine the goal of achieving UPE. Even in 'fee-free' systems, however, there are many other direct costs of attendance. These include the costs of uniforms (or better clothes for children than would otherwise be needed), books, sports fees, 'voluntary' school contributions, transport and the like. These costs are often high, both absolutely and relative to public expenditures on schooling. For example, in six African least developed countries (LDCs) for which there are data (Ethiopia, Guinea, Malawi, Uganda, United Republic of Tanzania and Zambia), private household expenditures per pupil during the 1990s were, on average, slightly less than half the level of public recurrent expenditures per pupil (see Figure 4.1). In addition – and often of even greater significance for poor households – are the indirect costs of income foregone arising from the reduced availability of child labour when children go to school. These opportunity costs are strongly felt even if the children themselves do not directly generate cash income, because they often substitute for adult household labour – thereby releasing older household members for remunerative work.

The continued under-enrolment of children from poorer households can be explained by the direct and indirect costs incurred when these families send their children to school.

In many African non-pastoral households, the loss of girls' labour is more keenly felt than that of boys'.

It is likely that income-transfer schemes will be needed to provide a 'short-cut' to achieving UPE.

Gender in children's economic contribution vs. schooling

The distribution of these direct and opportunity costs is unequal by gender and by household poverty. For example, the loss of girls' labour is, in many African non-pastoral households, more keenly felt than that of boys'. Equally, the direct costs of school attendance are often greater for girls – owing to higher costs for their clothing, and for greater security for them while travelling to school. Expected future benefits to households also differ by gender. Many parents expect that the education of their sons will eventually bring them greater benefits than what they could expect from educating their daughters. All such cost and income differences are perceived more acutely, the lower the income of the households concerned. For these reasons, measures are required to reduce the private costs of educating children if UPE is to be achieved. Such cost-reduction measures are most strongly required in the case of children – and particularly girls – from the poorest households.

Some types of cost-reduction can best be achieved by 'macro' changes in policy. School fees can be abolished. Charges for books, sports and other items can also be removed. It can be argued that these types of cost-reduction policy are more efficient than compensation schemes, provided that differential cost-incidence for richer and poorer households is not an explicit aim of policy. In any case, charging differential fees to rich and poor households is not usually possible, owing to the practical difficulties of means-testing at the school level (although South Africa is an exception).

The magnitude of other elements of direct costs, such as the costs of clothing and transport, cannot be easily affected by governments or other service providers. The indirect costs are even more difficult to compensate by such means. Thus, for the very poorest households with numerous children, school enrolment in many countries will probably remain patchy. As countries develop and become richer (provided that distributional policy facilitates income growth for the poor), indirect schooling costs will become smaller relative to household incomes, and enrolments among the poorer segments of the population will, accordingly, rise. But these enrolment benefits of income growth, delivered by the development process, may take a good many years to materialize.

Educating children in extreme poverty situations: does gender play a role?

Furthermore, and more worrisome for the achievement of the international development targets, income growth that is dependent upon market processes alone risks excluding those in extreme poverty, because poor people do not participate in these processes. These groups, having neither significant incomes nor assets, find themselves ineligible for credit. For them, all available household labour may thus be needed in order merely to subsist. Thus, even where schooling is fee-free, the costs of sending children to school for these households are relatively greater than the costs for households that are relatively better off. Furthermore, such costs may be *absolutely* greater for the poorest households because they have to rely on child labour to a greater extent than the others.

As mentioned, the existing cost studies make no estimates for these kinds of 'demand-side' adjustments. Although the World Bank study explicitly states that its projections are based upon primary schooling being 'free', and although a set of policy options are mentioned which recognize the need to target the education of girls (World Bank, 2002, Box 5.1), these adjustments have not been integrated into the cost-estimation exercise. To what extent might this omission understate necessary costs?

Clearly, there is no easy answer to this question since the extent of private costs from school fees, other direct costs and opportunity costs varies significantly across countries, and there are no consistent data to assess their magnitude. Where school fees still exist, their removal implies increased costs to the state for each and every child, in a typical range of 5%–15%. Furthermore, as has been shown above, the African data suggest that the removal of both direct and indirect costs to the poor may require an increased cost to the public sector of up to 50% of current public expenditure per student for the families involved. If this is an upper bound to the extent of subsidy needed, the costs follow directly from the proportion of poor households eligible for the benefits of the scheme. For example, if the government decided to provide a subsidy equivalent to 25% of existing public spending per pupil to the poorest 10% of children in areas where attendance rates were very low, this would increase unit costs across the system by around 2.5%. Arguably this would count as a fairly modest increased cost if it were instrumental in shifting net enrolments from 90% to a level closer to 100%.

Targeted income supplementation

The main instrument available to reduce the weight of private costs (once fees and other charges have been removed) is some form of targeted income-supplementation scheme (ideally progressive, and related to the poverty of the household), conditional upon school attendance. This could be designed either in the form of scholarships, or of income transfers linked to attendance and performance of designated children in school. Such schemes are likely to be needed to provide a 'short-cut' to achieving UPE, by accelerating the enrolment changes that may eventually be delivered by the process of economic growth. There are two additional reasons for using income supplements. First, they provide not only the means for directly securing enrolment growth among the poorest families, but also an additional way to achieve the poverty-alleviation targets required by the Millennium Development Goals. By facilitating a change in time allocation, away from child labour and towards schooling, they reallocate the incomes of the poor towards investment in human capital. This is crucial to securing not only short-run school attendance targets, but also longer-run income growth for poor households. Second, by facilitating more continuous school attendance among poorer children, income transfers can be instrumental in reducing rates of repetition at primary level. Evidence from schemes in Latin America, such as Bolsa Escola in Brazil,[12] suggests that the impact of income transfers on school efficiency can be substantial. Where this is so, savings in the average cost of primary school completion for poor households can substantially reduce the net public costs of an income-transfer scheme. The implication is that such schemes could be partly self-financing through their impact in reducing repetition rates, and thus provide a useful additional means to support a rapid transition to schooling for all.

Programmes providing financial incentives for improving enrolments and gender equity in schooling have also been implemented, with donor support, in a number of African countries. These include the USAID-funded scholarship programme for girls in four pilot schools in Ghana, the GABLE fee-waiver programme for non-repeating primary- and secondary-school girls in Malawi (see Box 4.1) and the World Bank-funded scholarship programme for

12. See Lavinas (2001); and ILO/UNCTAD (2001).

Box 4.1. Gender and education policy in Malawi

During the 1990s Malawi introduced a large number of reforms aimed at increasing the participation and performance of girls in school. At primary level, most of these were associated with the Girls' Attainment of Basic Literacy and Education (GABLE) programme, launched in 1991 with the assistance of USAID. This sector reform programme aimed to promote system-wide change while also addressing gender disparities in primary schooling. Under the programme, disbursements of budgetary support were made on the condition that policy reforms would be implemented by the government.

Reforms to reduce the costs of schooling included school-fee waivers for non-repeating primary-school girls, which benefited about 1 million girls over a two-year period, and abandonment of the requirement that pupils should wear school uniforms. In 1993 a new policy on pregnancies was adopted, allowing schoolgirls to return to school after having had their baby. A social mobilization campaign was used with some success to counter negative attitudes towards girls' schooling. The curriculum and supporting textbooks were revised so as to remove gender bias. Gender training was offered to teacher trainers, primary-school advisers, and school personnel. Focus group discussions were conducted, which revealed that some parents resented that only girls were initially targeted, given that household economic constraints also strongly affected the schooling of boys. Furthermore, the new pregnancy policy was not supported by all schools, some of which continued to exclude young mothers in the belief that this served as a deterrent to others having children.

Nevertheless, the reforms did appear to stimulate the enrolment and persistence of girls in school. Over the three years 1990/91–1993/94, girls' primary enrolments increased much more quickly than those of boys (13% per year, as compared with 8%), and by the later year girls' enrolments exceeded boys' in grades 1 and 2 for the first time. Villages where the social marketing campaign had been held witnessed unprecedented increases in enrolments one year later, particularly among girls. The key to success seems to have been the way in which the various factors constraining the participation of girls in school were tackled simultaneously, in the context of a broad sectoral approach, in which other constraints to the development of the school system were also targeted.

Source: Kadzamira (2000).

secondary-school girls in the United Republic of Tanzania. This latter programme, begun in 1995, aimed to increase poor girls' participation in secondary education and to promote the effective participation of girls in secondary schools (Sumra, 1998), through selective bursaries, counselling, curriculum development and other gender-oriented improvements within the schools (Mbilinyi and Mduda, 1995). By 1998, 1,500 girls – representing approximately 1% of total female lower-secondary enrolment – had received support. The programme was successful in increasing female secondary-school participation, but less so in improving female school-achievement.

Programmes targeting girls are not always popular.

Gender considerations for policy in targeting

Programmes targeting girls are not always popular. Evidence from Malawi indicates that many parents resent girls-only benefit programmes, because boys from poor households are also often unable to attend school (Kadzamira and Chibwana, 2000; Wolf, 1995; Swainson et al., 1998). Furthermore, even with fee-waivers, it appears that very few girls from lower-income groups attended secondary school (Castro-Leal, 1996). Since the children from higher-income families were more likely to obtain better primary-school grades than were children from poorer families, more of them continued to secondary school. In these circumstances, incentives would have been better targeted at needy, primary-level children. Careful identification of eligible groups, as happened in the United Republic of Tanzania, would have been an important condition for success. Although targeting is a difficult process, communities can usefully be involved in selecting the beneficiaries, and some of the target groups requiring financial assistance are relatively easy to identify.

Table 4.5 shows the estimated impact of the introduction of an incentive programme on the base year primary unit cost in six African countries where this type of policy has recently been proposed at primary level. The base-year costs equal the total government primary education expenditure per pupil for the year of data collection. The proposed incentive programmes mainly concerned rural girls, and they provided a cost-per-beneficiary in the range of $30–$100. Strategies to provide incentives for girls were judged to be particularly important in Ethiopia, Ghana, Guinea, Mali and Senegal – countries with low enrolments and wide gender gaps. In Ethiopia, where demand for girls' education has been particularly low, for example, the proposed subsidies to cover the cost of stationery and exercise books, and of material for school clothes, would represent a substantial incentive for households to send their girls to school (Rose et al., 1997). If the subsidy were targeted at rural areas in disadvantaged parts of the country where enrolment is lowest, approximately 20% of school-aged children could benefit, thus generating a 9% increase in the base-year unit cost for Ethiopia.[13] This figure is high, but the potential benefits in terms of girls' enrolments are substantial. Proposed subsidy programmes in other countries where demand for girls' schooling has been low could be designed so as not to have a major impact upon unit costs. For example, in Ghana, Guinea, Mali and Senegal, increases in unit costs as a consequence of the proposed subsidies for rural girls would range from 0.6% in the case of Senegal, to 5% in Ghana.

13. The average primary unit cost does not increase by the total cost per beneficiary because not all enrollees would receive the subsidy.

Table 4.5.
Effect of incentive programmes on primary unit costs for six African countries

Country	Intended recipients of subsidy	School children receiving incentive (as % total enrolment)	Proposed size of subsidy per beneficiary (in $PPP)	Increase in primary unit cost (as %)
	1	2	3	4
Ethiopia	Rural girls in disadvantaged areas	20%	$100	10%
Ghana	Rural girls from disadvantaged backgrounds	15%	$61	5%
Guinea	Rural girls	13%	$31	2%
Mali	Rural girls	2%	$35	1%
Senegal	Rural children, particularly girls	2%	$44	0.6%
Zambia	Rural girls (sanitary protection)	8%	$32	4%

Column 1 describes the intended recipients of the subsidy; column 2 gives the percentage of total enrolment represented by this group in the base year (in each case, in the mid to late 1990s). Column 3 shows the proposed size of the subsidy (in purchasing power parity dollars) for each recipient, and column 4 shows the percentage increase in the base-year average weighted unit cost of the proposed incentive programme assuming the reported level of coverage (column 2) and base-year enrolment levels.

Source: Colclough et al. (forthcoming).

In general, then, the additional costs of removing gender inequalities need to be considered as a separate demand-side item which must be added to the mainly supply-side calculations of the costs of attaining UPE. This is particularly necessary for the poorest households in low-income countries. The examples given above are merely illustrative of what may be needed. But they suggest that effective incentive programmes for girls – or, more generally, children from poorer households – to attend school might add at least 5% to the average unit costs of primary schooling. In the 47 countries included in the World Bank study, this would translate into $1.3 billion extra public spending by 2015, in comparison with spending in 2000, adding about $0.4-$0.6 billion to the average annual additional expenditures required.[14] These increased costs would be likely to increase the size of the average funding gap presently projected in the World Bank study by perhaps 20% – although this would need to be calculated country-by-country to provide a reliable guide.[15]

The costs to education of HIV/AIDS

It is now seen with greater clarity than ever before that countries where HIV/AIDS prevalence is high are experiencing severe problems in maintaining progress towards the attainment of the EFA goals. This section outlines the risks that HIV/AIDS poses for the attainment of primary schooling for all, and its resultant cost implications. Some attention will also be given to the implications of HIV/AIDS for the attainment of the goals relating to the elimination of gender disparities in schools and improving educational quality, in so far as both of these are closely linked to primary schooling for all. Finally, some recent initiatives to assess the costs of HIV/AIDS to education sectors will be considered with a view to estimating the additional finances that must be raised globally for the attainment of EFA in an environment where the prevalence of HIV/AIDS is high.

Analytic framework

The HIV/AIDS pandemic has implications for both resource (supply) and cost (demand) in the achievement of the EFA goals. Resources are either mobilized domestically or come from external financing. The adverse macro-economic impacts of HIV/AIDS affect domestic resource availability in the public sector, and constrain the flow of resources from the private and household sectors. The epidemic also affects educational provision in ways that may increase or decrease the need for the financial resources that must be provided if the EFA goals are to be met by 2015.

Education systems are highly vulnerable to HIV/AIDS. The fundamental technology of one teacher with a class of ten to a hundred students has remained the same for thousands of years. Educators and education-support personnel constitute the largest proportion of public service employees worldwide. The vast numbers of students to whom they reach out constitute a significant proportion of the population. All told, an education sector may well involve a quarter or more of a country's population. Because it is so person-intensive, the sector is particularly exposed to the way HIV/AIDS can scythe its way through its personnel and operations, affecting the present adult generation in the persons of educators and support personnel, and the coming generation in the persons of learners.

An education system also comprises mainly young people. The majority of learners are in their pre-teens, teens, or early twenties, while a substantial proportion of educators are in their twenties and thirties. With the partial exclusion of those in their pre-teens, learners fall into the age groups where HIV infections most commonly occur, while educators are in the age groups where AIDS deaths are most frequent. These older age groups also encompass the parents and families of the majority of young learners, implying that for many learners participation in educational programmes occurs within the context of extensive HIV/AIDS sickness and death in their families and communities.

Adapting to these AIDS situations necessitates significant changes in school programmes. It also necessitates adjustments of management

Educators are in the age group where AIDS deaths most frequently occur.

14. For this group of countries, the impact on the financing gap would depend upon the distribution of these additional expenditures between India and the other countries.

15. It should be emphasized that a wide range of additional policy reforms will be needed to tackle gender inequalities in education effectively, beyond those discussed. These will include reforming curriculum, providing particular incentives for women teachers, organizing gender training, encouraging social marketing campaigns, and implementing a range of policies which extend beyond the limits of the education sector. A full treatment cannot be provided here. They will, however, bring additional associated costs which also need to be assessed on a country-by-country basis.

and policy frameworks at systemic level. Some of the response strategies have financial and cost implications that can be quantified. Others involve responses that impinge on costs, but in ways that are difficult to quantify. Still others have qualitative dimensions that will not affect costs until such time as specific interventions are made to respond to them.

The resource and cost implications of HIV/AIDS for the achievement of the EFA goal of good quality primary schooling for all will be examined, therefore, from the following five perspectives:[16]

- the impact of HIV/AIDS on resource availability for EFA;
- HIV/AIDS cost implications for learners;
- HIV/AIDS cost implications for educators;
- cost implications of adjusting education programmes to HIV/AIDS; and
- cost implications of the education management response to HIV/AIDS.

If, due to the HIV/AIDS epidemic, more public resources are allocated to health and other sectors, the result could be a smaller proportion for education.

The impact of HIV/AIDS on resource availability for attaining EFA

Public resources

HIV/AIDS impacts on the resources needed for the attainment of the EFA goals in two possible ways: by causing the overall resource envelope to be smaller than it would otherwise have been, and by affecting the allocation of available resources. Models that have examined the impact of HIV/AIDS on national economies generally show that the annual GDP growth rate is lower than it would have been in the absence of AIDS, but they do not show any actual decline in GDP (Barnett and Whiteside, 2002, pp. 283 ff.). The lower growth rate means fewer resources than in a no-AIDS scenario for the various categories of public spending, including education (Bonnel, 2000).

The epidemic could also potentially affect both inter- and intrasectoral resource allocations. If the epidemic leads to an increased proportion of public resources for health or other sectors, this could entail a smaller proportion for education. Thus, for some countries, achieving the target set by African leaders at the Abuja Summit in April 2001 – to allocate at least 15% of their annual national budgets to their health sectors – may limit possibilities for growth in education budgets. The World Bank has proposed that the financing measures for the attainment of the EFA goal of universal primary education of good quality include an increase in the allocation to education from the current average of 17.5% of national budgets to 20.0% (World Bank, 2002, Table A5.1). In high-prevalence HIV countries, other claims on national resources might jeopardize the possibility of securing and maintaining this increase.

Intrasectorally, HIV/AIDS is likely to augment the resource needs of other education subsectors. This is because the impacts on educators at these levels are as severe as at the primary school level, but the costs of replacements and training are considerably higher. Because much teacher specialization occurs at post-primary levels, the loss of mathematics or physics teachers, or of third-level lecturers in specialized areas, is difficult and costly to absorb.

The impacts of HIV/AIDS on human resources in society could also generate a need at secondary and tertiary levels to increase numbers, at least in certain areas, to make substantial curriculum modifications, and to introduce new areas of study and practice. AIDS increases the need for, but reduces the supply of, qualified individuals in certain skilled areas. This is very apparent in the health services, where in a climate of increasing demand, AIDS mortality is high. For instance, it is projected that in South Africa the demand for health services could be more than 11% higher in 2010 than in a no-AIDS scenario, whereas experience to date is that almost one-third of the nurses graduating from the University of Natal die within a few years of their graduation (Quattek, 2000, p. 41; Jones, 2001).

The premature death of adults in their most productive years depletes the skills base of society and calls for an accelerated production of replacements. But these replacements need to be equipped with current knowledge, understanding and skills, and with the more intangible qualities of resourcefulness and adaptability. This is because the AIDS-loss of qualified personnel makes it necessary for

16. A more detailed summary and review of available estimates is given in Kelly (2002).

others to move over sideways and take over the responsibilities of departed colleagues. In an AIDS-affected society, graduates from vocational and other third-level programmes need more than their highly compartmentalized professional skills. They must also be flexible, adaptable and innovative in response to the needs of the fast-changing and unpredictable AIDS world.

Assessing the impact of AIDS on the skill needs of the labour market, bringing about the necessary curriculum developments, increasing the output of qualified individuals with the necessary qualities, and introducing new programmes of study and skills development; all call for additional resources or for new formulas in allocating existing resources. The cost implications of responding to them could affect the resources needed to progress towards the EFA goals. Following the past pattern of allocations and concerns, the EFA areas most likely to be at risk would be adult literacy and early childhood care and education. As Chapter 2 has shown, the allocations to these areas tend to be insufficient to mark significant progress towards the agreed targets. They could become even more insufficient because of responses to HIV/AIDS needs at the secondary and tertiary levels.

Private and community resources

HIV/AIDS affects the private and industrial sector negatively by reducing productivity, increasing costs, diverting productive resources, and affecting the market for business products. These factors combine to reduce the profitability of private enterprise, leaving it less well resourced to support educational developments. At the individual and household levels, the impacts are immediate and sharp.[17] Many AIDS-affected households, which previously contributed cash and other resources for educational programmes, can no longer do so. The sickness, poverty and hunger that the epidemic has brought in its wake have left many rural communities so weakened that they cannot participate as in the past in self-help community activities for school maintenance and development. Resources, which in a no-AIDS situation would have provided for the development of the infrastructure needed for EFA, are no longer forthcoming.

The cost implications of HIV/AIDS for learners

Student numbers

HIV/AIDS affects the size of the school-age population in three principal ways: fewer births occur because of the high death rates among adults aged 20–40, their biologically most productive years; HIV-infected women have lower fertility rates; and about one-third of the children born to HIV-infected mothers are likely to acquire HIV infection perinatally, with the majority of them dying before they reach school-going age. The combination of these factors results in the population of school-going age being smaller than it would have been in a no-AIDS situation. One recent projection suggests that by 2010, the population of school-going age in Zimbabwe will be almost a quarter smaller than it would have been in a no-AIDS situation, while that in Zambia will be one-fifth smaller (Figure 4.2).

By 2010, the population of school-going age in Zimbabwe will be almost one quarter smaller than it would have been without AIDS.

Figure 4.2. Projected reduction (%) in size of primary school-age population, 2000–2010

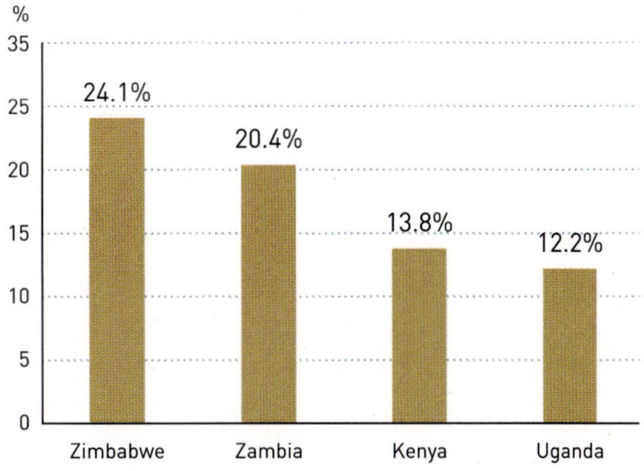

Source: World Bank, 2000, p. 3.

This implies that the financial burden for attaining universal primary education in high-prevalence HIV countries will be lower than it would otherwise have been. Fewer learners will require fewer teachers, fewer educational materials and fewer classrooms.

Projections for Botswana, South Africa and Zimbabwe suggest that HIV/AIDS will lead to actual population decline (and not just to a lower

17. See Whiteside and Sunter (2000), p. 89.

rate of growth) in the coming few years, while demographic projections for Swaziland suggest that the population of primary school students will begin to decline absolutely from 2007 (Stanecki, 2000; Swaziland, 1999). Should this occur, the costs of educational provision would in principle be lower than the current costs.[18]

Children affected by HIV/AIDS

HIV/AIDS has led to the emergence of child-headed households: there is no adult and the children must fend for themselves.

HIV/AIDS affects school participation for three different groups of children, making it difficult for them to enrol in or complete school, or to attend school on a regular daily basis. The first group – those who themselves are infected with HIV – will not be large. Projections for South Africa are that fewer than 1.2% of school-age children in any calendar year will be HIV-infected and that a much smaller proportion will be carrying the burden of AIDS illnesses (ABT Associates, 2001, p. 49). The extent to which such children will enrol in school, or continue once they come to know their HIV status, is not known. The school participation of infected children might imply some additional costs (such as for transport to facilitate their medical supervision). Their families might also need subsidies that would encourage school attendance on the part of the infected children and that would cover some of their medical costs. But given that the percentage of infected children would be small, these costs would also be relatively small.

The two other groups – orphans and HIV/AIDS-affected children – however, are much larger, and many factors prevent them from attending or completing school. Moreover, the epidemic is increasing the salience of these factors. Chief among them are:

- *Cash costs*: poor families, in rural areas and urban shanty towns, have always found it difficult to meet the cash costs associated with schooling. HIV/AIDS aggravates this difficulty by leading to losses in production, decline in family incomes, and increased medical costs.
- *Family and household responsibilities*: a significant proportion of households, particularly in rural areas, finds it difficult to do without the contribution to the household economy that comes from the labour of children, particularly girls. Because it impacts negatively on the household economy, HIV/AIDS has increased this situation.

Orphans carry an additional quota of psychological, social and material difficulties. The emotional loss they experience at the death of a parent is compounded by the dislocations they subsequently undergo. Within their new surrogate family, orphans are frequently at a disadvantage compared with the biological children. Micro-studies of small communities show that orphans frequently come last in line when food is being apportioned, carry a disproportionately large share of household chores, and do not participate in school to the same extent as children who are not orphans. They also experience greater health risks than non-orphaned children and are more likely to be stunted and malnourished (Foster and Williamson, 2000, p. S281).

HIV/AIDS has also led to the emergence of child-headed households in which there is no adult and where the children must fend for themselves. Access to school is on a very precarious footing for children in such households. There may be no way of meeting school-related costs, or nobody may be free to go to school because everybody must work to generate the resources needed for survival.

Cost implications

To ensure that the EFA goal of primary schooling for all can be met, it is necessary to ensure that every orphan or child affected by HIV/AIDS can attend school and complete the education cycle. Fees, school-related costs, the salience of their labour in the household and the additional burdens experienced by households that provide orphan care, collectively constitute the principal obstacles to the full participation of these children. The full school participation of orphans and HIV-affected children will thus depend particularly heavily on removing all compulsory cash costs associated with school attendance, and upon the provision of targeted subsidies to mitigate the direct and indirect costs for households with orphans.

The cost of any social subsidy scheme depends on two factors: the size of the target group and the amount of the subsidy. This Report takes the

18. Contraction in the numbers actually attending primary school is already manifesting itself in South Africa's most populous province, KwaZulu-Natal, which is also the area the most affected by HIV/AIDS with an antenatal HIV-prevalence rate of over 36% in 2002. School costs and a recently implemented policy on the age of Grade 1 enrolment have made their own contributions to this decline, but South African experts believe that HIV/AIDS is also having a of major impact because there are fewer young women of child-bearing age. See Badcock-Walters et al. (2002).

position that the subsidy programme should target all orphans (these will normally include those in child-headed households) and all children from poor families that have been affected by HIV/AIDS. There is no strong evidence to suggest that paternal orphans are less disadvantaged educationally than maternal or double orphans.[19] Preferably, therefore, a target group defined by orphan status should extend to all orphans.

The case for the inclusion of other vulnerable children is also strong. First, because of its impacts at the household level, HIV/AIDS is making it more difficult for children from families where there is infection to participate or continue in school. Second, targeting orphans only and excluding other vulnerable children runs the risk of putting orphans into a special class that would accentuate their sense of being different, increase their social and psychological problems and expose them to subtle forms of discrimination.

In its simulations for the costs of attaining the EFA target of universal primary education of good quality, the World Bank (2002*a*) includes provision for orphan support, but limits this to maternal and double orphans. The Bank's AIDS Campaign Team for Africa (ACTafrica) seems to have adopted the same approach in estimating the costs of scaling up HIV programme activities across Africa, defining orphans as those under 15 who have lost a mother or both parents to AIDS (World Bank, 2001, p. 16). This is in accordance with the definition given by UNAIDS in 2000 (UNAIDS, 2000*b*, p. 120), but more recently UNAIDS has defined AIDS orphans as children aged 0–14 who have lost one or both parents to AIDS (UNAIDS, 2002*d*, pp. 8 and 204).

Extending the meaning of AIDS orphans to include all who have lost one or both parents to AIDS would greatly increase the costs for orphans included in the Bank's simulations. The published costs are global estimates that include costs arising from AIDS-related teacher provision. However, it is relevant to note that orphan estimates for 34 countries in 2010 show that maternal and double orphans are likely to account for approximately 55% of the total number, and paternal orphans for 45% (Hunter and Williamson, 2000). On this basis, the increased costs of including paternal orphans in the simulation would amount to approximately $100 million per year (see Box 4.2).

In the absence of good data on the number of other vulnerable children who would need assistance, extending the estimates becomes very much more difficult. In sub-Saharan Africa, there were 42 million out-of-school children in 1998, and in South-East Asia 46 million (UNESCO, 2000). At that time, the adult HIV-prevalence rate was 8.0% in sub-Saharan-Africa and 0.7% in South and South-East Asia (UNAIDS, 1998). It is not unreasonable to assume that 8% of the out-of-school children in Africa belonged to families where there was HIV or AIDS, and 0.7% of those in South-East Asia. Application of these figures suggests that the number of out-of-school children from HIV/AIDS-affected families could be approximately 4 million. Orphans could, of course, be included in this number. Although it may be on the low side, the figure provides a starting point for estimating the number of children from AIDS-affected families who would need the incentives of subsidies to promote their school participation.

The full school participation of orphans and HIV-affected children will depend heavily on removing all compulsory cash costs for schooling.

There are considerable differences in the size of subsidy proposed for orphan support. The World Bank (2002, p. 41) applies 'a fixed rate of US$50 (in 2000 prices) per year per maternal or double orphan to the estimated population of such children in the school-age population'. The Bank's earlier ACTafrica document proposes US$9–$35 as the cost per child for community assistance with living expenses, and US$25–$33 as the costs per child for school expenses (p. 59). The latter, however, is a weighted average of primary and secondary school costs based on estimates from the United Republic of Tanzania. Moreover, while the school expenses of orphans and other vulnerable children would represent a cost to an education ministry, this cost arises in the attainment of the EFA target of free primary education and is not, in itself, determined by the HIV/AIDS situation.

A further estimate has been made by the Center for International Development at Harvard University, which proposes a community support programme for orphans costing US$250 per

19. For example, in twenty-two (out of twenty-eight) countries in Africa, Asia and Latin America, orphans had lower enrolment rates than non-orphans. In eight of these cases, only maternal orphans had lower enrolment rates. However, in four cases, only paternal orphans had lower rates, while in a further eight cases, the sex of the parent was unimportant (Ainsworth and Filmer, forthcoming).

Box 4.2. Major elements of AIDS-related incremental costs for the achievement of universal primary education

Areas for inclusion

Teacher-related: Training of replacement teachers; death benefits for deceased teachers; temporary teacher appointments to cover for extended absenteeism of teachers on sick leave.

School programmes: (1) Full curriculum implementation of HIV preventive education, including the production of learning materials and the establishment of this area as a professional subject for teacher preparation programmes in colleges and universities; (2) The provision of a cadre of qualified counsellors and the development of a counselling module for inclusion in teacher preparation programmes; (3) introducing further primary curriculum reform.

Support to orphans and vulnerable children: Providing incentives for orphans and for children from poor families with an AIDS sickness or death.

Estimates

Teachers. Death benefit payments and costs of training replacements for deceased teachers: $150 million annually

Costs of system for the training and hire of temporary teachers to cover for those who are terminally ill (estimated at half the costs of the absent teachers): $150 million annually

School programmes. Costs estimated as the mean of the low and high projected costs for the ACTafrica youth intervention programme. Programmes for secondary teachers and out-of-school youth replaced by provision of educational materials, the extension of counselling, and curriculum adjustments in primary schools: $250 million annually

Orphans and vulnerable children

- Based on World Bank estimated subsidy level of $50 for each child each year
- Maternal and double orphans (2.5 million children): $125 million
- Paternal orphans (2 million paternal orphans): $100 million
- Children from families with AIDS (4 million children: assumptions in text): $200 million

Summary: Total annual costs

Replace teachers	$150 million
Temporary teachers	$150 million
School programmes	$250 million
Maternal and double orphans	$125 million
Paternal orphans	$100 million
Children from AIDS families	$200 million
Grand Total	**$975 million**

child per year (CID, 2001). Bearing in mind the median per capita GDP of US$413 in the World Bank's sample of 33 countries (World Bank, 2002*a*, p. 29), this is almost certainly too high.

In the absence of other estimates that can be substantiated, there is merit in accepting the figure of $50 proposed by the World Bank. Applying this to the estimated number of children from HIV/AIDS-affected families, whose school participation may be contingent on the receipt of a subsidy, would add US$200 million annually to the AIDS-related EFA estimates produced by the Bank.

The cost implications of HIV/AIDS for educators

HIV/AIDS affects educators through deaths, the movement of teachers into other areas of work, sickness, absenteeism, workload effects and levels of morale.

Permanent loss of educators

There are two channels through which HIV/AIDS leads to the permanent loss of educators to an education system and teachers to classroom work, namely death and withdrawal from the teaching profession. Although some evidence seems to point to increased teacher mortality in the presence of HIV/AIDS, a more guarded view is that the rate of HIV infection among teachers is the same as in the rest of the adult population. But even in this view, the loss of teachers to AIDS may be very considerable. A model for Zambia predicts that, given the HIV prevalence in the adult population, the number of teachers would rise from 37,000 in 1999 to 50,000 in 2010, while in a no AIDS scenario the number would have risen to 59,550 (Grassly et al., 2002).

While the absence or death of non-teaching educators can seriously weaken an education system, the death of a teacher in active service brings immediate negative classroom consequences. Sometimes these are irreversible. Unless there is immediate replacement, something that seldom happens in the most severely affected countries, a whole class will be left without a teacher for a considerable length of time. This teacher loss puts at risk the very possibility of offering education to all children. Studies from West Africa report that teacher mortality due to AIDS led to 119,000 school-age children in Côte d'Ivoire receiving no education in 1997/98, and to 107 primary schools being closed in the Central African Republic (Fassa, 2000).

Absenteeism

For several years after initial infection, most HIV-infected people remain clinically healthy. But eventually the virus destroys so much of the immune system that the infected person becomes susceptible to infections that a non-infected person would normally be able to ward off. This leads to episodes of illness, followed by periods of apparent good health. The periodic bouts of illness usually increase in number and duration over time until they fuse and become almost continuous. Infected teachers are unable to teach when they experience these illnesses. This leads to frequent 'casual' absenteeism on their part, and eventually to their being placed on formal sick leave. Drawing on research at the Imperial College, London, the World Bank uses the estimate that an infected person is likely to be unable to teach for a total of 260 days prior to death from AIDS (World Bank, 2002*a*, p. 41).

AIDS also leads to considerable absenteeism on the part of healthy teachers. Two factors contribute to this: caring for sick relatives at home, and attending funerals. Since the burden of care falls mostly on women, female educators and office staff frequently find themselves pulled between the demands of their professional work and attending to sick persons who require almost round-the-clock care. In addition, de rigueur participation in funeral rites for relatives, colleagues and community members leads to teachers being frequently absent from class, sometimes for days on end.

Cost implications

Education systems that are losing teachers, whether through death or early retirement, must make good those losses through the training of additional teachers. Otherwise the education systems will not be able to provide education for all who are in need; moreover, the quality of that education will suffer. Additional training is a cost that is attributable to the impact of HIV/AIDS on teachers themselves and on the workforce in other areas. The replacement costs can be estimated, firstly, from knowing the number of teachers who are likely to leave the system permanently and prematurely because of death or taking up appointments elsewhere, and secondly, from knowing the training costs.

Account must also be taken of death benefits, payable on behalf of teachers who die while in service, to which an education system may be contractually obliged. Anecdotal evidence from Malawi and other countries is that meeting these obligations (by providing coffins, transport and cash) is crippling the operations of district education offices which find the outlays for these purposes absorbing the resources that would otherwise have supported school supplies and inspections.

Absenteeism due to AIDS-related sicknesses represents a major loss to education systems. Since no benefits accrue from the salaries paid to educators for the periods of absence, the systems lose the benefits of these resources. If they provide replacement teachers to cover for those who are absent, they will also face additional financial costs and these costs will be attributable to HIV/AIDS. In high-prevalence HIV countries that have not yet attained universal primary education, education systems seldom have the resources to provide replacements. Hence in these countries teacher absenteeism because of HIV/AIDS imposes major declines in quality and efficiency, which will further delay the achievement of the EFA goals.

When education systems lose teachers, they must make good those losses by training additional teachers.

Impact on the cost of training

For several reasons, HIV/AIDS is likely to boost the overall costs for training teachers.

- Teacher-training institutions (colleges and universities) will suffer AIDS losses among their staff in the same way as schools, but securing replacement staff will be slower and more costly than at school level.
- An enlarged and possibly accelerated training programme will be needed to make good the number of teachers and teacher trainees lost to AIDS.
- There will be need to adapt the training programme to make future teachers appropriately competent to teach understanding of and response to HIV/AIDS.
- Higher mortality of professionals in other sectors will increase the mobility of surviving teachers, further increasing the unit training costs of those who stay in the schools.

A report made to the South African National Conference on HIV/AIDS and Education in May–June 2002 indicated that while South Africa was currently training about 3,000 teachers each year, by the end of the decade, without ARV drug intervention, more than 20,000 would need to be

Education programmes should seek to empower learners to live healthy, sexually responsible lives.

trained. In the same country, more than 30% of nurses have been dying within three years of completing their studies. It may well be the same for teachers, especially women. The implications of these phenomena for teacher training are huge. Yet little thought has been given on how best to address these needs, and even less has been given to the cost implications of satisfactory and feasible responses.

One simulation for Zambia projects that teacher absenteeism due to HIV-related illness will result in the loss of 12,450 teacher years or close to 20 million teacher hours over the period 1999–2010 (Grassly et al., 2002). At a pupil-teacher ratio of 40:1, this is the equivalent of 498,000 children being left without classroom instruction for a year.

The absence of a system for the placement of temporary teachers is a problem facing many countries. More problematic is the fact that a pool of suitably qualified individuals available for temporary appointment does not at present exist. Its creation would imply costs for training and for temporary personal emoluments. Even though the salary costs of such temporary teachers would be less than for a comparable number of qualified permanent staff, their provision would represent a major additional AIDS-originated cost in ensuring that all children have access to primary education of good quality.

The cost implications for adjusting education programmes to an HIV/AIDS context

HIV prevention education

In a world where HIV/AIDS is so dominant, schools and education programmes have a cardinal responsibility to equip those for whom they have responsibility with the knowledge, skills, attitudes and values that will reduce the likelihood of their acquiring or transmitting HIV infection. This means that education programmes should seek to empower learners to live sexually responsible, healthy lives.

The first and basically correct response of education ministries to the HIV/AIDS crisis has been to strive to incorporate aspects of HIV/AIDS, sexual and reproductive health (SRH), and life skills education into the school curriculum. Studies from seventeen countries show the concern of education ministries to integrate these areas into school programmes with a view to the promotion of behaviour change (ADEA, 2001). However, for a variety of reasons, 'the school system . . . has failed to develop a coherent, comprehensive approach to HIV/AIDS and, more generally, SRH education' (Bennell et al., 2002, p. 43). The root problems arise from:

- a curriculum approach that does not acknowledge HIV/AIDS and SRH education as a professional subject area in its own right;
- curriculum design that tends to spread HIV/AIDS, SRH and life-skills education thinly across a number of carrier subjects and fails to make the all-important links with health education and health services;
- teaching methodology that places reliance on whole-class teaching in formal settings, and to some extent with examination performance in view, but with little room for peer teaching, the participation of communities, or the involvement of persons living with HIV/AIDS;
- teachers feeling inadequately prepared to teach this area, and being reluctant to deal with sensitive and, in some cases, taboo topics; and
- inadequate curriculum and teacher support, with insufficient (if any) accurate and good quality teaching and learning materials, and little provision for systems of back-up guidance, training, teacher support structures, monitoring and evaluation such as other subjects receive.

The potential of curriculum changes to empower school learners to avoid HIV infection will remain severely compromised until these issues have been adequately addressed and HIV/AIDS education has been fully professionalized. Such provision cannot be made without incurring costs.

Cost implications

UNAIDS has enumerated some of the variables affecting the costs of school and education HIV/AIDS programmes (UNAIDS, 2000*a*, *b*, pp. 16, 17). In a somewhat modified and amplified form these include:

- personnel: required for consultancies, establishing and maintaining a corps of trainers, providing backup guidance and teacher support structures;
- programme development: the amount of time and type of work invested in developing HIV/AIDS school curricula and supporting materials;
- production and distribution of educational materials: the quantity and quality of educational materials produced for each student and teacher covered by the programme;
- training school teachers: workshops and other training sessions for school staff; and
- monitoring and evaluation, conducting impact assessments, and other forms of research.

The World Bank simulations (2002*a*) make no express provision for activities of this kind. The model does, however, anticipate improvements in service delivery and envisages that one-third of total recurrent spending on primary school services will be dedicated to non-teacher salary inputs (administration, support services, textbooks and other pedagogical supplies, along with subsidies to encourage the school attendance of children in difficult circumstances). The proportion is said to be adequate to cover whatever costs may be involved in the provision of HIV/AIDS preventive education. Such an approach, however, could put high HIV-prevalence countries at the disadvantage of being left with a smaller share of their non-salary resources for other quality-enhancing inputs.

ACTafrica (World Bank, 2001) examines the costs of HIV/AIDS education programmes for those in schools and for out-of-school children and youth. For education programmes aimed at learners in primary schools, the cost per teacher trained is either US$75, for a simple programme and the provision of basic materials, or $200 per teacher for a more sophisticated programme that includes the development of training materials and the establishment of the school curriculum. The cost per secondary-school teacher is given as US$121 for a simple programme and US$241 for a more extensive programme. Finally, it is estimated that it would cost US$8.–$11.80 per person reached to provide suitable peer education for out-of-school children and youth (in the age ranges 6–11 and 12–15). The overall costs of extending coverage by 2005 so as to reach 60% of the primary-school teachers, 80% of secondary-school teachers, 15% of out-of-school children aged 6–11 and 50% of those aged 12–15 are estimated as US$211–$313 million annually for all of sub-Saharan Africa (World Bank, 2001, pp. 54, 34).

Although substantial, these costs are not sufficient to provide coverage of the entire target groups. Nor do they include provision for the production and distribution of textbooks and teaching materials, for providing the back-up support required, or for developing and establishing an appropriate curriculum at college and university levels for the preparation of college lecturers and professional pre-service training of teachers. If the ACTafrica cost estimates were apportioned equally over primary, secondary and out-of-school youth education, that estimate for primary education would be of the order of US$90 million annually, or an average of more than US$2 million per country. Education ministries might be reluctant to draw this amount – which would be far from sufficient to meet all the needs – from the resources for non-teacher salary inputs.

Responding to trauma and psychological needs

The trauma so frequently generated by HIV/AIDS has become a major care and support issue within schools. The experience of psychological distress or discrimination causes some young people to discontinue their education or to participate erratically. Others may find that they have more difficulty in learning. Prior to the advent of widespread HIV/AIDS, teachers encountered these problems less frequently. But with AIDS it is different and it is worse. The epidemic makes schools home to increasing numbers of intellectually, socially and psychologically dysfunctional learners (Coombe, 2001, p. 20).

However, not enough action has been taken, or even planned, for the establishment of the necessary psychological support systems. The work of school guidance personnel pertains

The trauma generated by HIV/AIDS has become a major care and support issue within schools.

Eleven countries stated that they had no social support programme for AIDS-infected or -affected learners.

more to providing vocational guidance than psychological support. A survey of education ministries in thirteen SADC countries, conducted in 2001, shows awareness of the problem and the inadequacy of the steps being taken to deal with it. Eleven countries stated that they had no programme of social support for infected or affected learners. Twelve also stated that neither teachers affected by AIDS, nor those who are dealing with AIDS-affected children, were being helped to cope (SADC, 2001). Such support as was available came through ad hoc, under-funded and uncoordinated NGO activities.

Adding up the costs

The principal variables that have a bearing on the additional costs that HIV/AIDS entails for the achievement of EFA goals are:

1. training additional teachers to replace those dying from AIDS;
2. providing death benefits that education ministries must pay to those who die while still in service;
3. mainstreaming HIV/AIDS within the curriculum, principally through the introduction of HIV preventive education;
4. developing, producing and disseminating textbooks and learning materials for HIV preventive education;
5. mainstreaming HIV/AIDS into programmes for teacher preparation;
6. managing functions and activities for propelling a proactive response from the system;
7. increasing capacity to provide counselling;
8. re-orienting primary education curricula; and
9. providing incentives to stimulate school participation by orphans and other children affected by HIV/AIDS.

Simulations have dealt principally with the first, second and final items on the above list. They have also given much attention to the costs that teacher absenteeism represents for education systems. But as already indicated, the absence of teachers on prolonged sick leave or for other AIDS-related reasons, will have incremental cost implications for the achievement of EFA goals only in circumstances where payments are made for temporary teachers to cover for those who are sick or absent. Severely affected countries need to make provisions to do so.

Within the context of the achievement of EFA goals, the cost implications of items 3 to 8 in the above list have not been incorporated into any model, and no attempt has been made to estimate their costs at either national or regional levels. This is not because they are not important, but because of difficulties in getting bases for the cost estimates and because there may be some misapprehension that the costs of these 'soft' items may be dwarfed by teacher and orphan costs. The ACTafrica estimates for the cost of extending the coverage of youth activities, although not cast in an EFA framework, suggest that the curriculum and various school programme costs might well exceed those involved in teacher replacements and may well be comparable with those arising from absenteeism estimates.

Ensuring the achievement of EFA goals also necessitates attention to demand factors, especially on the part of children who are in any way disadvantaged by their personal encounter with HIV/AIDS. Orphans stand out clearly as a category that should be supported, with the support extending to all orphans of school-going age. But orphans are not the only children that AIDS puts at a disadvantage in relation to living conditions and schooling. Children from poor families who have experienced AIDS are also in need of incentives that improve their living conditions and encourage their school participation.

Thus the cost implications of HIV/AIDS for the attainment of EFA goals arise from four broad areas:

1. incremental teacher costs for the training of additional teachers to replace those lost to AIDS and for the payment of death benefits;
2. the costs of training and paying temporary teachers to supply for those on extended periods of sick leave;

3. incremental school and education programme costs for mainstreaming HIV/AIDS and responses to it into the curricular and other areas of school life; and
4. orphans and vulnerable children costs for social subsidies to encourage or enable the school attendance of children from families affected by AIDS.

Estimates summarized in Box 4.2 suggest that the annual spending on these areas should be in the order of US$975 million. This figure is 74% more than the World Bank (2002*a*) estimated as the additional AIDS-related costs for 33 African countries. The increase is due principally to making allowance for education programme costs and increased coverage of orphans and other vulnerable children. The continued spread of HIV infection, even in countries where prevalence is already very high, is commentary enough on the failure to date of education programmes to make a significant impact. Widespread, almost implacable, denial, extensive discrimination, combined with potentially lethal lack of information, also indicate that education messages are not getting through. It is unlikely that they will do so until education programmes that respond in manifold ways to HIV imperatives are resolutely mainstreamed into school systems. The funding needed for this has not yet been forthcoming. The Dakar Framework for Action called on the international community to 'implement as a matter of urgency education programmes and actions to combat the HIV/AIDS pandemic'. This cannot be done without mobilizing sufficient identifiable resources for establishing and running such programmes.

Dakar also underlined the importance of ensuring that children in difficult circumstances have access to and complete primary education of good quality. HIV/AIDS has placed huge and increasing numbers of children in exceptionally difficult circumstances. Some it has orphaned. Others it has marginalized and placed at high risk of being bypassed by educational provision. The future of these children, who form a very significant proportion of the next generation, will depend heavily on resources becoming available to safeguard their schooling.

HIV/AIDS and schooling: some conclusions

The World Bank (2002*a*) estimates have properly demonstrated the potential of the AIDS pandemic to add very substantially to the overall costs that individual countries will sustain in achieving the goal of primary schooling for all (along with gender equity and improved education quality). For high-prevalence countries, such as Rwanda, Zambia and Malawi, the Bank projections show that incremental costs due to AIDS will increase the recurrent budgets by more than 45%. The analysis in this chapter indicates that the budgetary impact of AIDS is even more dramatic. But large as this provision may appear, it must be further augmented by the numerous additional hidden costs, already alluded to, that HIV/AIDS entails, and by the cost implications of the pandemic for the attainment of the other EFA goals. Recognizing that the cost implications of HIV/AIDS are this extensive and pervasive may serve, better than anything else, to demonstrate the urgency of protecting the education sector against the ravages of the pandemic and of using its potential to extend a similar protection to society.

The continued spread of HIV infection is commentary enough on the failure to date of education programmes to make a significant impact.

Education in emergencies

Defining emergency education

The Dakar Framework for Action requires countries to 'meet the needs of education systems affected by conflict, natural calamities and instability'. The theme of 'education in emergencies' became important during the 1990s, in connection with the complex humanitarian emergencies in Afghanistan, Bosnia and Herzegovina, Rwanda, Somalia, the Sudan and elsewhere (Aguilar and Retamal, 1998; Retamal and Aedo-Richmond, 1998). Such 'complex emergencies' can last for years or even decades, creating a major barrier to the achievement of EFA. For UNESCO, an educational emergency is a situation of crisis created by conflicts or disasters which have destabilized, disorganized or destroyed the education system, and which require an

It was during the 1990s that complex humanitarian emergencies began to seem commonplace.

integrated process of crisis and post-crisis support (UNESCO, 1999). This emphasis upon the need to extend support beyond the short term – when special measures are needed – is consistent with the Dakar approach. International and national responses to emergency situations can include:

- education for refugees, in camp schools or national schools;
- education for internally displaced populations (IDPs), affected by conflict or disasters;
- education in situations of armed conflict, insecurity and instability;
- education in areas of large scale repatriation of refugees and IDPs; and
- reconstruction of regional or national education systems, after conflict or disaster.

Dimensions of the problem

Emergency education classes are sometimes held in the open air, in homes and basements, or in damaged buildings of various kinds.

During the 1990s complex humanitarian emergencies began to seem commonplace. By 2000, conflicts in Afghanistan, Bosnia and Herzegovina, Burundi, Iraq, Sierra Leone, Somalia and the Sudan, had each left more than 400,000 people as refugees in other countries. Other places generating similar flows of refugees during the 1990s included Rwanda and Kosovo, while 39 other countries had been the source for over 10,000 refugees in at least one year. By 2001, there were an estimated 15 million refugees in the world, including about 7 million in populations categorized as 'assisted by UNHCR' (UNHCR, 2002), and 3.7 million Palestinian refugees, assisted by UNRWA (the United Nations Relief and Works Agency for Palestine Refugees in the Near East). Many refugees were from the developing countries of Africa (3.3 million) and Asia (5.8 million). In 2001, some 500,000 persons fled from home-country circumstances which were so dangerous that they were recognized by asylum countries as *prima facie* refugees. No comprehensive data for refugee education exist, but in the year 2000, UNHCR supported the education of some 835,000 children at primary and 63,000 young people at secondary level, often through international and national NGOs working in refugee camps and settlements.

Most of the countries at the centre of complex humanitarian emergencies also suffered massive internal population displacements, although information on the dimensions of this phenomenon is less readily available. This is partly because there has been less international access to, and assistance for, IDPs. Many internally displaced persons live in camps or settlements similar to those for refugees, but others live in the homes of, or alongside, normal populations, in ways less conspicuous and more difficult to quantify. The world total of persons internally displaced as a result of conflict and human rights violations in 2001 has been estimated as at least 25 million people (www.idpproject.org) (over 13 million in Africa, over 4 million in Asia and over 3 million in Eastern Europe). In some situations, the national education system provides well-organized education for such people, but in many other places as well, the situation is bleak (Machel, 1996, 2001).

Natural disasters – flooding, hurricanes or earthquakes – affect education systems throughout the world. Sometimes there is major damage to the education system, as with the 'millennium floods' in Mozambique. In 1998, Hurricane Mitch destroyed schools in Honduras, leaving over 250,000 children at primary and 30,000 at secondary level without access to schooling; the Ministry of Education's central offices were damaged and the bulk of the education archives were lost (UNICEF, 1999).

Conflict, insecurity and instability pose the greatest challenges to education. Educators often make gallant efforts to keep education alive during times of war or civil conflict. Classes are sometimes held in the open air, in homes and basements, or in damaged buildings of various kinds. The task of reconstruction follows. In 2000, almost 800,000 refugees in twelve major migrations returned to their homelands. Probably similar numbers of internally displaced persons returned to their places of origin. Even populations that had stayed in place throughout conflict or disaster had to work to rebuild their communities and schools. The tasks of reconstruction of education systems after conflict or disaster present major challenges to education planners and managers.

Principles of response

Every crisis is different, and there are no sure formulas for successful response. The response to acute emergencies should always be designed from the local level, using some form of participatory appraisal, in order to achieve the best results. However, there is a need to seek a national consensus on key issues such as languages of instruction, curriculum, teacher training and remuneration, and the nature of educational decentralization. United Nations and NGO practitioners in the field of emergency education have identified general principles that improve the quality of response in emergency situations (see Chapter 3, Box 3.15).

Resource requirements for emergency education

Emergency education – a necessary bridge

Education in emergencies sits uneasily between humanitarian aid and development assistance. In acute emergencies, the key institutional actors may focus on survival issues, but the refugees or other emergency-affected populations themselves give a top priority to restarting education. There is now growing recognition of education as the 'fourth pillar' of humanitarian response (Midttun, 2000). Governments such as Sweden and Norway have publicly committed themselves to supporting emergency education as a matter of policy, but there are some others for whom this step remains to be taken. Emergency education is important if the lags between ending humanitarian support and the start of funding from development assistance budgets for reconstruction are to be minimized.

Education is needed early in a crisis, for psychosocial and pedagogic reasons and to protect children. It helps to provide a sense of normalcy and hope for the future, and prevents a cohort of children from missing out on education for life. Adequate resourcing is particularly needed because children affected by crisis or conflict:

- have special needs for good teaching and learning conditions to help them build a sense of achievement and self-esteem;
- need opportunities for recreation and expressive activities to help meet their psychosocial needs;
- may not receive the normal level of emotional and developmental support from their families;
- may not have access to books or other printed materials;
- may be in schools which have had their teaching-learning resources destroyed, and where the buildings need to be repaired and re-equipped; and
- may have teachers who are undereducated and untrained, and who require additional support through training and materials to cope with difficult and unfamiliar situations.

Community participation

Crisis-affected communities provide many of the resources for emergency education. This 'bottom-up' approach is advantageous in several respects; leading assistance agencies encourage it (for examples, see Bird, 1999; Brown, 2001; Lange, 1998; Midttun, 1998; Nicolai, 2000; Sinclair, 2001; Sommers, 1999, 2002). There is a psychosocial benefit when community members are active as teachers or otherwise support the process. Moreover, where public resources have become particularly constrained it is important to educate community members about the ways in which they can support schools and other activities for young people. Good practice programmes include:

- establishment of school or community education committees;
- appointment of experienced teachers and social workers from the crisis-affected community as head teachers and youth organizers, respectively;
- use of educated persons from the crisis-affected community as the teachers and youth leaders, and providing intensive in-service training and on-the-job guidance and supervision;
- recruitment of professionals from the community as project managers and supervisors of NGO assistance projects; and
- providing training for all of the above.

Education is needed early in a crisis, for psychosocial and pedagogical reasons, and to protect the children themselves.

Fear and disruption make it difficult to maintain an atmosphere conducive to learning.

Initial roles for community education committees include organizing labour for clearing spaces for schools, erecting temporary shelter, identifying volunteer teachers and assessing the numbers of students for each year of schooling; later they can help with school management and development. The committees can also help to organize activities for pre-school children and for out-of-school adolescents and youth. UNESCO's Programme for Education in Emergencies and Reconstruction (PEER, based in Nairobi) developed the 'Teacher Emergency Package' (including educational supplies and materials) in Somalia in 1992, so that communities could initiate their own schools, despite the lack of government structures. UNESCO PEER saw school management committees as a way of bringing members of the community together as a force for peace (Retamal and Devadoss, 1998).

Human resources

In some displacement situations, experienced teachers move with their communities and can resume their teaching duties. However, in many crisis-affected communities, teachers are underqualified and untrained. Even trained teachers may have had limited exposure to modern teaching methods. Crisis may give the opportunity for a new approach to teacher training, which can help even inexperienced teachers develop the skills for effective teaching, as well as taking account of the special needs of children exposed to some form of crisis. As noted by Graca Machel (2001), 'fear and disruption make it difficult to maintain an atmosphere conducive to learning, and this can take a grievous toll on school morale. In Palestinian schools, surveys found that many teachers and students had trouble concentrating, particularly if they had witnessed or experienced violence or had family members in prison or hiding.'

Education programmes that focus on crisis-affected populations need to include a major component of carefully designed training for teachers and head teachers, for adult educators and for youth educators/youth group leaders. Such training is best provided 'in-service', through vacation and weekend courses, mobile trainers, and training of mentor teachers in the schools or school clusters, while later there can be use of open and distance learning methods.

Crisis and reconstruction often imply that it is difficult for the government to meet the costs of teacher salaries. Donors have often been unwilling to support salary costs, preferring to provide forms of assistance which carry less risk of long-term obligation. Conventional objects of support, such as educational supplies and materials, the repair or construction of schools, or in-service and pre-service teacher training, are needed. However, recurrent support for teacher salaries is often critical to restarting the system.

Resourcing levels

In high-profile emergencies, donors may be willing to give generous humanitarian support. Such assistance to displaced populations is often channelled through NGOs, which can act quickly. By contrast, assistance to national government agencies, notably for reconstruction, may face problems of absorptive capacity and effective management.

The level of resourcing for emergency education programmes is critical for achieving sustainability. For displaced populations, UNHCR suggests that shelter, equipment and materials standards be developed by reference to the general level of well-run government schools in rural areas near the national capital, rather than the dysfunctional low levels often found in neglected rural areas where refugee camps may be located (UNHCR, 1995). If a large refugee or displaced population moves into an area with weak education systems, efforts to raise standards in that area, through mobilizing national and international resources, will be required.

As regards site planning for emergency schools, UNICEF's concepts of 'child-friendly spaces' and 'child-friendly environments' are helpful. Child-friendly spaces in Albania, for Kosovar refugees, and in tent cities in Turkey after the 1999 earthquake, meant grouping together basic services for mothers and children, including basic health services, early childhood care and development, schools, recreational facilities, psychosocial support, youth activities and mother support. Emergency assistance may include imported 'kits' of educational and recreational supplies, although local procurement is preferable and brings benefits to the local economy (Sinclair, 2001). Where possible, heavy duty reproduction equipment for 'education resource centres' is commended (Aguilar and Retamal, 1998), permitting the reproduction of materials to meet urgent educational needs.

Governments facing reconstruction situations typically confront huge problems. Even the resources to formulate education needs, develop plans and make them known may be lacking. The Ministry of Education may lack furniture, typewriters, computers or even paper. Thus there is usually no lack of items upon which external resources can be quickly spent.

A major concern in post-conflict situations is to avoid replication of educational structures that may have contributed to conflict (Pigozzi, 1999; Tawil, 1997; Smith and Vaux, 2002; Isaacs, 2002). It is important that donors contribute to the 'softer' side of reconstruction, namely consensus-building on integrative approaches to education, curriculum and textbook renewal in support of peacebuilding, and investment in both in-service and pre-service teacher training. Life skills education, including education for peace, human rights and citizenship, are important in situations of protracted post-conflict displacement and reconstruction, and have resourcing implications especially for start-up (Gillespie, 2002; Baxter, 2001; Fountain, 1999; Johanessen, 2000; Talbot and Muigai, 1998). There appears to be an initial window of opportunity to initiate such changes, perhaps lasting 18 months (Vargas-Baron and McClure, 1998). The tasks of negotiating curriculum change for schools and teachers, writing and testing new textbooks, and introducing effective systems of teacher training, require commitments of five years or more.

Inter-agency cooperation is obviously needed to ensure the best use of available resources for acute emergency situations and reconstruction. However, estimating the likely annual resources required for such purposes is difficult. Most emergencies are unpredictable and the resources needed depend entirely on their nature, scale and intensity. What is 'required', furthermore, is open to different interpretations. In Afghanistan, for example, the estimates of the international community were much lower than those of the Ministry of Education (Box 4.3). Even so, the $100 million transitional requirements estimated by the international community exceeded both the commitments subsequently made and the annual average requirements for UPE in 2015 of $70 million projected by the World Bank (2002, p. 59). These estimates, in turn, were dwarfed by the Ministry's stated need for some $875 million over the two years to mid-2004.

It is difficult to draw conclusions more widely. However, recent history would suggest that at least four or five countries are likely to face major complex humanitarian emergencies during the course of the next decade, with many more experiencing disaster, conflict and instability to varying degrees. In all of these countries the costs of achieving the EFA goals would then be greater than at present predicted – because infrastructure, supplies and human

Donors must contribute to curriculum and textbook renewal in support of peacebuilding.

Box 4.3. Education reconstruction in Afghanistan

Two major needs assessments were conducted in early 2002, supported by the Asian Development Bank, World Bank and UNDP. These assessments were hampered by a lack of systematic data. The Ministries of Education and Higher Education lacked chairs, tables and paper, let alone office equipment and the capacity to collect data on country-wide needs. The best estimate was that 1.5 million children would return to school in March 2002, in response to the 'Back-to-School' campaign. Later estimates suggested that about 3 million children had been enrolled in school, including some 300,000 at secondary level. UNICEF distributed over 7,000 tons of educational supplies and materials in a few months, the largest such operation undertaken by the United Nations.

By September 2002, steps had been taken towards in-service training of teachers, renewal of teacher training systems and curriculum reform, but delays were caused, in part by a lack of basic resources within the Ministry of Education. The situation regarding payment of teachers and other staff remained fragile due to the severe constraints on government revenues, and the uncertain level of donor commitments. In July 2002, the immediate and transitional education sector requirements were estimated by the international community at $100 million, while donor commitments then totalled only $44 million. As of August 2002, the Minister of Education estimated immediate and short term requirements at $171 million, with a further $704 million needed by mid-2004. Meanwhile, planning and absorptive capacity remained limited by the delays in resourcing the Ministry itself and in training to update its staff.

Source: Sinclair (2002).

resources would be diminished. Moreover, the means of meeting these costs will be reduced by declining income flows, by human death and displacement, and by reallocation of potentially available resources from education to other, equally pressing, demands.

If the impact of such events were to increase the additional annual costs of reaching UPE by 25% in four or five countries, between $0.4 - $0.5 billion would be added to the average annual costs of UPE across all countries. This would increase the projected total costs by 2% to 3%, but if the affected countries were among those which are expected to face financing gaps, it would represent an increase in the Bank's projected funding requirement of around one-fifth. This would be a minimum impact since the capacity to resource education systems in these countries would have been negatively affected by emergency.

How much is really needed to achieve EFA?

All recent studies on the costs for achieving primary schooling for all by 2015 appear to have understated the real situation.

The analysis in this chapter indicates that each of the recent studies of the costs of achieving primary schooling for all by 2015 appears to have understated them – in some cases, substantially so. It is clear that the World Bank study is, from a methodological standpoint, the strongest of the three. It has a transparent framework that allows the possibility of supplementary analysis in a helpful way. Its data requirements are not extensive, and the main cost parameters that affect the development of education systems are given a central place in its design and operation. The two other studies also have strengths – both of them use national-level data and employ a generally cautious and sensible approach to the ways in which education systems can be reformed. However, the data they use, particularly the financial information, appear highly variable, and in some cases, unreliable. The generally higher cost estimates that emerge from the Bank study are, in general terms, to be preferred.

Nevertheless, the World Bank analysis oversimplifies the cost side – partly by investigating only six-year systems, irrespective of their actual length, and by omitting a number of countries from the analysis which appear, prima facie, to be likely to have some difficulty in achieving the goals. In addition, the policy reforms proposed for the education systems in the countries covered by the study – which directly influence their expected costs – appear to give less weight to implementation difficulties than they might. This is particularly so as regards teacher salaries – where the proposed mechanisms for their reduction, relative to per capita income, would present a very demanding agenda for the highest cost countries.

Two other aspects of the study hold critical importance for the projected outcomes. The first concerns the revenue side. This chapter has argued that the revenue assumptions upon which the calculations of financing gaps are based are optimistic. A government completely committed to reforming its approach to the delivery of primary schooling would probably still have difficulty sustaining the real expenditure targets for primary schooling sought by the Bank over a fifteen-year period. Much depends, however, upon progress with economic growth in the countries concerned, because healthy and sustained income growth would more easily deliver the increased resources sought. The study is silent about the growth assumptions it employs, so it is not possible to assess this part of its analysis.

On balance, however, public resources available to primary schooling in these countries appear likely to grow at a slower rate than assumed in the study. This, together with the omissions on the cost side, suggest that the size of the financing gap, from these sources, is likely to emerge as being substantially larger than projected. A figure of $4.2 billion is suggested in the text, which is higher that that in the Bank paper by up to two-thirds.

This chapter has also shown, however, that there are at least three other major omissions from these cost estimates. The first concerns the demand side. There is a need to increase the incentives for families – particularly those in the poorest sections of the community – to enrol girls in school. The analysis suggests that the additional expenditures required might amount to $1.3 billion by 2015 in the countries concerned, which would increase the average annual funding gap by about $0.5 billion over the period. Similarly, the analysis suggests that the estimates for the resource requirements of responding to the HIV/AIDS pandemic were underestimated to the extent of approximately $0.4 billion. Finally, responding to the educational needs of countries in emergency situations might require additional resources of approximately $0.5 billion on an annual basis for those among the poorest countries falling victim to emergencies. All this implies an annual aid bill of the order of $5.6 billion per year being required to support the move to EFA, within the same kind of framework as that set out by the World Bank. This aggregate estimate for average annual aid requirements to support UPE with gender equality in good quality schools is more than double that given in the Bank document (World Bank, 2002*a*).

We are, then, some distance from being able to use the country-level resource requirement projections that are currently available as even a rough guide to aid requirements for securing EFA objectives. The national simulations should become the starting point for more country-level work, integrating new national planning effort and data to produce revised outcomes.

This chapter has shown that the 'bottom line' in all such approaches varies strongly with the assumptions used. All financing gap estimates are relatively small residuals that are sharply responsive to changes in the assumptions used to determine the size of the much larger aggregates of national expenditures and resources available. This implies that single-valued estimates need to be replaced by a range showing the extent to which conclusions change if the parameters turn out to be different. Applying this advice to the analysis presented in this chapter, it can be concluded that the level of required aid flows is almost certainly closer to $5.6 billion than to $2.5 billion. But more nationally informed work is needed to determine how closely accurate the former figure will turn out to be.

An annual aid bill of the order of $5.6 billion per year will be required to support the move to EFA.

Por crear
nos
a la
Calle
Queremos
local propio

Chapter 5

Meeting international commitments: the response to Dakar

The Dakar Framework for Action (World Education Forum 2000) declares a strong collective commitment to implementation of the EFA goals. Partners to that commitment comprise governments (in partnership with civil society institutions) in cooperation with regional and international agencies and institutions. The latter are expected to support the EFA process through resource mobilization, underpinned by a new global initiative. They are also expected to undertake 'consistent, coordinated and coherent' work with other partners in support of national EFA plans, based on comparative advantage. Strong national strategies must be supported with effective development cooperation. Countries with less-developed strategies, including countries in transition, those affected by conflict and post-crisis countries, must also be given the support they need to achieve more rapid progress towards education for all. The challenge is judged to be greatest in sub-Saharan Africa, in South Asia and in the least developed countries.

UNESCO has been requested to continue its mandated role in coordinating EFA partners and maintaining their collaborative momentum through the work of an annual, small and flexible High-Level Group and to facilitate the preparation of an annual monitoring report to assess progress on the EFA goals. The Organization has also been called upon to refocus its education programme in order to place the outcomes and priorities of Dakar at the heart of its work.

The purpose of this chapter is to assess the extent to which international commitments to EFA are being met. It begins by examining the recent record of aid provided by funding agencies for education in developing countries. Although there is good information covering the 1990s, owing to time-lags in reporting, more recent shifts in the composition of education aid in support of the EFA goals since 2000 are not easy to document. Accordingly, recent statements and commitments made by the international community in support of the EFA targets are also assessed here to determine both whether they reflect the Dakar process, and what their likely impact will be. The final sections of the chapter briefly consider the progress made with specific international programmes and initiatives, and include a review of UNESCO's role and responses since Dakar.

Total aid flows to developing countries

Aid flows to developing countries did not prosper during the last decade of the twentieth century.[1] Table 5.1 shows that they peaked in 1991 and declined thereafter. By 2000, grants and concessional loans to developing countries had fallen from US$60 billion to approximately US$50 billion. Of this amount, approximately 70% was from bilateral agencies. The largest proportion of multilateral assistance was from the World Bank (IDA), and the European Community. These two agencies together provided 64% of total multilateral assistance in 2000.[2] However, the real value of aid flows stood at only about 80% of their 1990/91 levels. This downward trend affected both bilateral and multilateral aid, although flows of the latter peaked slightly later in the decade.

1. More detailed accounts of the trends reported here can be found in Al-Samarrai (2002) and Colclough et. al. (forthcoming).

2. The other multilateral agencies in Table 5.1 have been included because they represent the larger multilaterals in terms of assistance or they have specific education programmes.

Table 5.1. Total official development assistance (ODA), net disbursements in billions of US$

	1990	1991	1992	1993	1994	1995	1996	1997	1998	1999	2000
Current prices											
Total	52.0	59.2	60.4	55.6	59.9	59.1	55.8	47.9	50.2	52.2	49.6
Bilateral	38.7	43.2	43.1	39.4	41.3	40.6	39.1	32.4	35.2	37.9	36.0
Mulitlateral	13.3	15.9	17.2	16.3	18.6	18.5	16.7	15.4	15.0	14.3	13.5
Constant 2000 prices											
Total	55.1	60.6	57.6	54.1	55.8	49.8	48.8	44.8	48.6	49.8	49.6
Bilateral	41.1	44.6	41.4	38.3	38.6	34.4	34.5	30.6	34.6	36.5	36.0
Mulitlateral o/w	14.0	16.1	16.3	15.8	17.2	15.5	14.2	14.2	13.9	13.3	13.5
UNICEF	0.6	0.6	0.7	0.8	0.8	0.7	0.6	0.5	0.5	0.5	0.6
IDA	4.2	4.5	4.7	4.4	5.3	0.4	5.1	5.0	4.7	4.3	4.2
Inter-American Development Bank	0.2	0.1	0.1	0.1	0.1	4.2	0.4	0.3	0.3	0.2	0.2
UNDP	1.0	1.0	0.8	0.7	0.5	0.2	0.5	0.6	0.6	0.5	0.4
African Development Fund	0.6	0.6	0.7	0.7	0.6	0.5	0.5	0.6	0.6	0.4	0.3
Asian Development Fund	1.2	1.1	0.9	0.9	1.1	1.0	1.0	1.0	1.0	0.9	0.9
European Community	2.5	3.2	3.6	3.5	4.0	3.6	4.1	4.4	4.3	4.3	4.4
Other	3.7	5.0	4.9	4.7	4.9	4.8	2.1	1.9	2.0	2.1	2.6

Notes: Official Development Assistance (ODA) consists in grants or concessional loans to developing countries. Net disbursements are defined as total disbursements less any repayments of loan principal during the same period. Other multilateral donors include other United Nations agencies, International Fund for Agricultural Development (IFAD), Arab Funds and parts of IMF assistance. The OECD Development Assistance Committee (DAC) deflators used for producing constant price estimates adjust for both inflation in the domestic currency and changes in the exchange rate between the domestic currency and US$ amounts. The currency effect tends to dominate for the period 1992–99.

Source: DAC online database, Table 2a.

Throughout this period, sub-Saharan Africa, South and Central Asia and Far East Asia received about 65% of total development assistance. However, the proportion of total aid going to Far East Asia increased following the financial crisis of 1997, while that for sub-Saharan Africa fell. The decline in the share of aid going to sub-Saharan Africa was particularly marked for multilateral assistance, falling from 50% in 1990 to 36% by 2000. Given the trends in overall development assistance, and these regional trends, total development assistance to sub-Saharan Africa declined by 14% in real terms, between 1990 and 2000.

Bilateral aid to education

As with total aid, the trend of bilateral aid flows to education has been downwards – from around US$5 billion at the start of the decade to less than US$4 billion by 2000 (Figure 5.1).[3] The most dramatic decline occurred in 2000, when commitments fell to US$3.5 billion, representing approximately a 30% decline in real terms from 1990 and accounting for about 7% of total bilateral aid.

The aggregate figures, however, hide major differences across the agencies. Five countries (France, Japan, Germany, the United States and the United Kingdom) accounted for between 75 and 80% of all bilateral aid commitments to education between 1990 and 2000 (Table 5.2). With the exceptions of Germany and Japan, where commitments remained relatively unchanged, real commitments to education for the other three major providers declined dramatically between the early and late 1990s. Moreover, while some countries did report increases, taken all together, real commitments declined over the period by approximately 16%.

Table 5.2 also shows the percentage of total aid commitments made to education. Again, wide differences between bilateral aid agencies are noticeable. Some countries (Australia, France, Ireland and New Zealand) have committed well above the bilateral average of 9% to 10% of total commitments, while others have committed far less (e.g. Denmark, Finland, Italy, Norway, Switzerland and the United States).

Figure 5.1. Bilateral ODA to education (1990–2000)

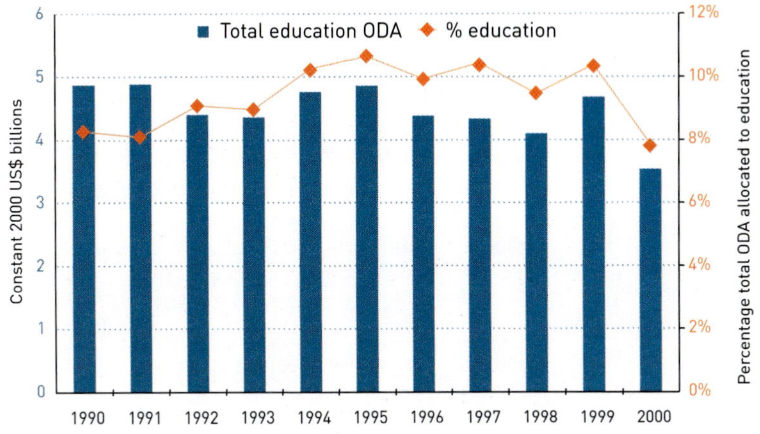

Source: DAC online database.

The final column of Table 5.2 shows the absolute percentage change in the proportion of total commitments allocated to education between 1990–92 and 1997–2000. A similar number of aid agencies reported a decline in the proportion of aid allocated to education as those who reported an increase, and the overall change between the early and the late 1990s was small. Accordingly, the fall in the volume of aid to education was similar to that of total aid flows, despite the inter-national commitments to increase aid to education that had been expressed at the World Conference on Education for All in 1990.

Reliable information on composition of aid to education is difficult to obtain. This is because of under-reporting and because a significant proportion of educational aid straddles each of the subsectors, and therefore cannot be allocated to just one. There are two particular problems with the available statistics. First, most agencies, including the Development Assistance Committee (DAC) of OECD, distinguish between 'basic' education and other subsectors (secondary, tertiary, etc). Although definitions of 'basic' education vary, that of DAC – which includes primary schooling, basic life skills for youth and adults, and early childhood education – is the most common formulation. In most definitions, literacy programmes are included in the notion of basic education. Because the statistics are reported in this manner, this chapter uses this definition to assess aid flows to basic education. It should, however, be recognized that much of the greater part of aid flows to basic education, classified in this way, are accounted for by support to primary schooling.

Total development assistance to sub-Saharan Africa declined by 14% in real terms between 1990 and 2000.

3. The data in these and subsequent tables, from the OECD DAC database, are for commitments, not disbursements. In recent years, the latter have been lower than the former by between 17% and 43%.

Table 5.2. Bilateral average annual official development assistance (ODA) commitments for education in millions of constant 2000 US$ (1990–2000)

	TOTAL			EDUCATION				EDUCATION AS % OF TOTAL			
	1990-1992	1993-1996	1997-2000	1990-1992	1993-1996	1997-2000	% change	1990-1992	1993-1996	1997-2000	% change
Australia	521	856	714	127	189	161	27	24	22	23	-2
Austria	628	473	422	87	77	85	-2	14	16	20	6
Belgium	484	404	447	76	49	51	-33	16	12	11	-4
Canada	1 661	1 524	1 295	136	111	120	-12	8	7	9	1
Denmark	636	828	733	38	38	43	13	6	5	6	0
Finland	466	186	209	14	8	16	14	3	4	8	5
France	5 945	5 008	4 280	1 512	1 253	1 186	-22	25	25	28	2
Germany	5 221	5 098	3 653	675	812	636	-6	13	16	17	4
Greece	n.a.	20	63	n.a.	7	7	n.a.	n.a.	34	10	n.a.
Ireland	27	86	133	7	15	24	250	25	18	18	-7
Italy	2 053	1 197	575	118	54	25	-79	6	5	4	-1
Japan	14401	14834	14898	930	1 051	952	2	6	7	6	0
Luxembourg	19	37	75	1	4	17	1 425	6	10	22	17
Netherlands	1 773	1 807	2005	186	97	147	-21	10	5	7	-3
New Zealand	66	65	86	19	22	22	19	29	34	26	-3
Norway	640	769	853	31	29	67	119	5	4	8	3
Portugal	198	149	218	33	31	20	-40	16	21	9	-7
Spain	937	608	785	46	53	99	114	5	9	13	8
Sweden	1 169	1 145	1 024	73	84	64	-12	6	7	6	0
Switzerland	626	576	558	50	27	18	-63	8	5	3	-5
United Kingdom	2 285	1 919	2 310	290	204	178	-39	13	11	8	-5
United States	18 308	8 657	8 569	533	395	223	-58	3	5	3	0
Total	58 068	46 247	43 906	4 981	4 608	4 161	-16	9	10	9	1

Notes: Official Development Assistance (ODA) consists of grants or concessional loans to developing countries.

Commitments are defined as firm obligations, expressed in writing and backed by the necessary funds, undertaken by a specific donor to provide specified assistance to a recipient country. Bilateral commitments are recorded as the total amount regardless of the time required for the completion of disbursements.

In the majority of cases, data for each year in a given period was available to calculate average annual commitments. Where this is not the case, average annual total and education commitments are calculated using the same years to ensure consistency.

Source: DAC online database, Table 5, Official Commitments (or Disbursements) by Sector, Bilateral and Regional Banks.

Secondly, the reporting of aid flows to each subsector of education is partial. For example, during the period 1993 to 1996, the 'big five' bilateral education agencies reported between 0% (France) and 83% (Germany) of their education commitments by sub-category. In all cases, this record improved by the later period (1997–2000), most donors having providing the information by this point. However, although under-reporting was much less marked than before, at the turn of the century the 'unspecified' category (representing aid which could not be apportioned to one of the subsectors) still represented 30% of reported education commitments.

Between the two periods shown in Table 5.3, the allocation of aid towards basic education increased in twelve of the eighteen agencies where data were available. Marked increases in the proportion of education aid allocated to basic education occurred in Denmark, Switzerland and the United Kingdom. These were compensated to some extent by large declines in Finland and Germany. Accordingly, the average allocation to basic education increased slightly between the two periods. Allocations to secondary education appear to have increased, with substantial reallocations from post-secondary education occurring in Austria and Italy.

Given the low levels of reporting of education subsector allocations, particularly during the first part of the decade, the data reported in Table 5.3 need to be interpreted cautiously. However, estimates based upon direct surveys of funding and technical assistance agencies suggest that by the mid-1990s about 20% of bilateral educational aid was committed for basic education (Bennel and Furlong, 1998; Bentall et al., 2000). These magnitudes are not inconsistent with the DAC data.

4. Since it is not possible to use the DAC data to explore the regional distribution of bilateral education commitments, the OECD's Creditor Reporting System (CRS) has been applied. The CRS suffers from lack of coverage: in 2000, only 70% of education commitments were recorded in the CRS database. These data are used in Figure 5.3.

Table 5.3. Composition of bilateral education assistance

	TOTAL EDUCATION ODA, 1993-1996					TOTAL EDUCATION ODA, 1997-2000					Change in allocation to:			
	% total education ODA reported by subsector	Allocation (%) to:				% total education ODA reported by subsector	Allocation (%) to:							
		Unspecified	Basic	Secondary	Post-secondary		Unspecified	Basic	Secondary	Post-secondary	Unspecified	Basic	Secondary	Post-secondary
Australia	100	7	8	5	80	100	9	20	8	64	1	12	3	-16
Austria	50	8	1	11	80	100	3	2	31	64	-6	2	21	-17
Belgium	72	36	3	9	52	100	26	5	13	57	-11	2	4	5
Canada	65	27	7	0	66	100	45	7	5	44	18	-1	5	-22
Denmark	98	65	8	17	10	100	53	27	18	2	-12	19	0	-8
Finland	90	42	41	0	16	100	60	25	5	10	18	-16	5	-6
France	0	–	–	–	–	69	32	22	20	25	–	–	–	–
Germany	83	53	21	7	19	100	7	12	18	62	-45	-8	11	43
Greece	100	100	0	0	0	100	49	0	0	50	-51	0	0	50
Ireland	0	–	–	–	–	39	100	0	0	0	–	–	–	–
Italy	100	10	2	4	83	100	57	1	24	19	46	-1	19	-65
Japan	19	39	14	16	31	51	57	16	10	18	18	1	-6	-13
Luxembourg	0	–	–	–	–	100	46	31	17	7	–	–	–	–
Netherlands	86	34	32	3	31	100	35	43	3	19	1	11	0	-12
New Zealand	70	0	0	4	95	69	2	13	6	79	1	13	2	-16
Norway	82	43	40	7	10	100	28	48	4	19	-14	8	-3	9
Portugal	58	17	5	19	59	100	24	5	19	52	7	0	0	-7
Spain	89	37	15	11	37	100	44	10	12	34	7	-4	1	-3
Sweden	77	31	51	1	16	100	24	56	3	17	-8	5	2	1
Switzerland	100	25	11	36	28	100	36	34	17	13	11	23	-18	-16
Unted Kingdom	47	65	8	5	23	100	61	27	6	6	-4	19	1	-16
United States	46	61	39	0	0	100	21	48	10	21	-40	9	10	21
DAC Total	41	42	19	7	32	80	30	21	14	34	-11	2	7	2

Notes: See notes to Table 2. The percentage of education ODA reported by subsector is the proportion of ODA in each period broken down into the subsectors (i.e. unspecified, basic, secondary and post-secondary) for each bilateral donor.

Source: DAC online database, Table 5, Official Commitments (or Disbursements) by Sector, Bilateral and Regional Banks.

Figure 5.2 shows the regional breakdown of these education commitments.[4] Africa received 47% of education commitments in 2000, representing a slightly greater proportion of aid to education than its share of total development assistance (37%). The reverse held for South Asia and Far East Asia, which received 23% of new education commitments but 34% of total development assistance in 2000. The greater concentration of education commitments to Africa are particularly marked, with almost 50% of all new bilateral education commitments being allocated to basic education in SSA in 2000.

In summary, bilateral aid to education appears to have declined since the mid-1990s – substantially so in 2000 – by which date bilateral education commitments stood at US$3.5 billion. The share of these commitments going to basic education appeared to have increased only slightly during the period, accounting for about 21% of aid to

Figure 5.2. Regional distribution of bilateral education commitments (2000)

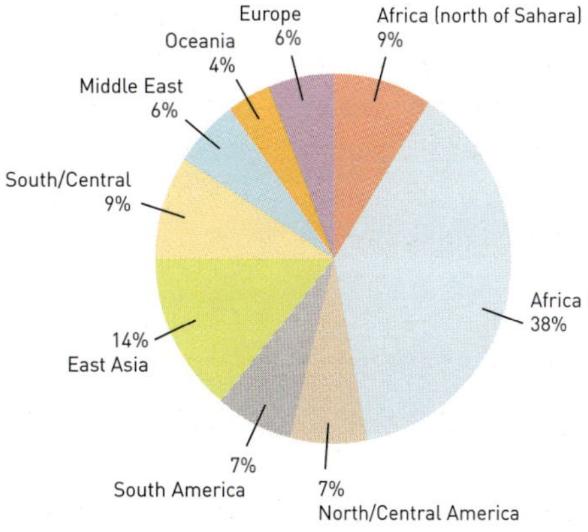

Note: In each region, a small percentage of commitments is not allocated to the sub-regions included in the graph; they have been allocated evenly over each sub-region.

Source: CRS Database, ODA/OA Commitments, Form 1, aggregated by DAC5 sectors, 1990–2001.

Marked increases in the proportion of education aid allocated to basic education occurred in Denmark, Switzerland and the United Kingdom.

education in the late 1990s. By contrast, commitments to secondary education increased substantially over this period.[5] Finally, in 2000, Africa received a larger share of education commitments than its share of overall development assistance.

Multilateral aid to education

As Table 5.1 showed, the World Bank and the European Council provide roughly similar levels of multilateral assistance, accounting for approximately 65% of total multilateral flows. However, a larger proportion of World Bank assistance has traditionally been allocated to the education sector and the Bank itself claims to be the largest external funder of education.[6] For this reason it is treated first, before exploring other multilateral aid to education.

World Bank assistance

The World Bank was certainly one of the major providers of concessional finance to education during 1990.[7] With the exception of 1997, IDA loans to education ranged from US$0.7 to 1.2 billion annually. However, after 1998, real IDA commitments to education fell to US$0.4 to 0.6 billion. IDA education commitments as a proportion of the total also declined over 1990 – from 13% to 10% of IDA commitments between the first and last three years shown in (Table 5.4.)

The World Bank does not regularly provide a breakdown of its education lending by subsector. Table 5.5 presents rough allocations to basic education (defined as before), based on the brief descriptions given for all projects in its Annual Reports. The data indicate that concessional commitments aimed exclusively at basic education increased from 32% to 52% between 1990–93 and 1994–97, but fell back to 33% between 1998 and 2001. If a broader definition is taken (to include loans which had any basic education component) a similar trend can be seen.[8]

Regional allocations of IDA education commitments are shown in Figure 5.3. As with bilateral education commitments, the main regions receiving World Bank education assistance are located in sub-Saharan Africa, South and Central Asia and Far East Asia. The figure shows that the share of commitments for sub-Saharan Africa has declined during the period. More importantly, the real value of IDA education support to this region fell by 37% between 1990–93 and 1998–2001.

Other multilateral assistance

Information on other multilateral assistance to education is difficult to compile. Using the DAC database, information on aid flows for some of the main multilaterals is presented in Table 5.6.

Table 5.4. World Bank commitments in billions of constant 2000 US$ (1990–2001)

	Total			Education			Education as % of total		
	IBRD	IDA	IBRD+IDA	IBRD	IDA	IBRD+IDA	IBRD	IDA	IBRD+IDA
1990	18.8	6.8	25.6	0.7	1.2	1.8	3	17	7
1991	19.6	7.5	27.1	1.8	0.9	2.7	9	12	10
1992	17.7	7.6	25.3	1.5	0.7	2.2	9	9	9
1993	19.3	7.7	27.0	1.1	1.2	2.3	6	15	8
1994	15.9	7.3	23.2	1.6	0.7	2.3	10	10	10
1995	18.4	6.2	24.6	1.4	0.9	2.3	8	14	9
1996	15.5	7.3	22.9	1.0	0.8	1.8	6	11	8
1997	15.2	4.9	20.1	0.8	0.3	1.1	5	6	5
1998	21.9	7.8	29.7	2.0	1.2	3.2	9	16	11
1999	22.7	7.0	29.7	0.8	0.6	1.4	4	8	5
2000	10.9	4.4	15.3	0.2	0.5	0.7	2	11	4
2001	10.3	6.6	16.9	0.4	0.4	0.8	4	6	5

Notes: DAC deflator for the United States used to produce constant price series.
Source: World Bank Annual Reports 1990–2001.

5. These results from the DAC database need to be interpreted with care, given the data issues alluded to earlier in this section.

6. See www.worldbank.org/education

7. For example, from 1990 to 1999 the World Bank committed US$8.5 billion in concessional (IDA) funds to education compared to US$13.5 billion for France and US$10.1 billion for Japan.

8. *The World Bank Annual Report 2001* suggests that from 1991 to 2000, basic education received approximately 44% of total education commitments (World Bank 2001*a*, p. 89). In addition, information contained on the World Bank website suggests that primary education received approximately 30% of all education lending (IDA and IBRD) between 1990–94 and 36% in 1995–99. (www.worldbank.org/education/primary.asp). These figures are broadly similar to those shown in Table 5.5. The website also indicates that the share of lending going to secondary education increased from 12% to 23% over the same period.

Table 5.5. World Bank commitments to basic education in billions of constant US$ (1990–2001)

	Loans exclusively basic				Loans to basic and some basic			
	IBRD	IDA	% total ed. IDA	% total	IBRD	IDA	% total ed. IDA	% total
1990-1993	1.25	0.95	32	24	2.11	2.33	54	49
1994-1997	1.43	1.08	52	34	1.99	2.22	73	56
1997-2001	0.89	1.05	33	32	1.33	2.05	50	55

Notes: The first column of percentages for the two sets of loans indicates the proportion of total IDA assistance for education that was assigned exclusively to basic education or basic and some basic education. The second column of percentages indicates the proportion of total assistance (IBRD+IDA) in any year which was assigned exclusively to basic education or basic and some basic education.

Source: Calculated from *World Bank Annual Reports*, 1990–2001.

The EC is by far the largest of these, committing US$0.4 billion to education in 2000. Education accounts for about 6% of total aid from these multilateral agencies – rather less than the bilateral shares, but similar to the World Bank.

In terms of allocations to education subsectors, data are only available for two of the multilateral donors shown in Table 5.6. UNICEF reports to DAC that all education assistance is committed to basic education (comprising primary and early childhood education). For the EC, approximately 50% of commitments went to basic education in 1995, increasing to 66% by 2000. This increase entailed a decline in the share of commitments going to secondary and post-secondary education during this period.

In terms of expenditures, UNESCO is an important support agency for education. Education programmes account for one-quarter of its budget, and their real value increased by 30% over 1990–2003, to approximately US$100 million per year. One source suggests that basic education accounted for between 3% and 50% of all UNESCO education commitments between 1991 and 1997, and, on average, 30% throughout the period (Bentall et al., 2000, p. 21).

In summary, just as with bilateral flows, multilateral aid to education declined sharply over the period from 1990–2001. World Bank IDA support for education appears to have been roughly halved since the mid-1990s, falling to US$0.4 billion in 2001. However, the proportion

Multilateral aid to education declined sharply over the period from 1990–2001.

Figure 5.3. IDA education commitments, percentage by region (1990s)

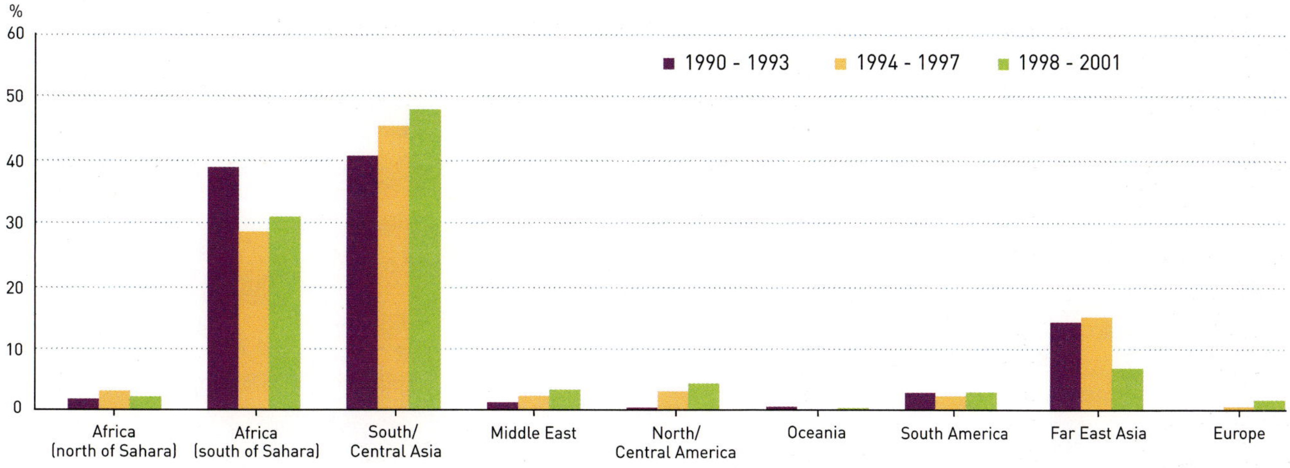

Note: The bars represent the proportion of total IDA education commitments allocated to each region for each of the three periods.

Source: Source: Calculated from *World Bank Annual Reports* 1990–2001.

Table 5.6. Multilateral official development assistance (ODA) commitments in millions of constant 2000 US$ (1995–2000)

	Total			Education							Education as % of total		
	1995	1998	2000	1995	1996	1997	1998	1999	2000	1995	1998	2000
Inter American Development Bank	699	633	442	19	10	46	45	28	30	3	7	7
African Development Fund	61	933	360	16	n.a.	115	145	96	46	26	16	13
Asian Development Fund	929	1 192	1 135	50	147	n.a.	121	96	89	5	10	8
European Community	1 450	n.a.	7 226	29	n.a.	n.a.	n.a.	n.a.	392	2	n.a.	5
UNICEF	n.a.	307	580	n.a.	n.a.	42	n.a.	44	52	n.a.	n.a.	9
Total	3 138	3 065	9 743	115	157	203	310	264	608	4	11	6

Notes: Official Development Assistance are grants or concessional loans to developing countries.
Commitments are defined as firm obligations, expressed in writing and backed by the necessary funds, undertaken by a specific donor to provide specified assistance to a recipient country.Commitments are recorded as the total amount regardless of the time required for the completion of disbursements.
No data was available for UNDP.
DAC deflator for the United States used for all multilateral agencies apart from the EC.

Source: DAC online database, Table 5, Official Commitments (or Disbursements) by Sector. Bilateral and Regional Banks.

allocated to basic education was higher than in the case of bilateral education commitments, and appears to have been maintained over the decade at about 40% (depending on the definitions used). The real value of IDA education commitments to South and West Asia, and particularly to sub-Saharan Africa, fell between the beginning and the end of the decade. Finally, the available data suggest that the real commitments to education from other multilateral agencies also declined after 1998. Over 60% of this assistance came from the European Union (EU), of which approximately two-thirds was allocated to basic education.

In 2002 the G8 adopted a series of recommendations to assist developing countries achieve universal primary education.

Total aid flows to education and the EFA goals

Table 5.7 draws together the information contained in previous figures and tables to provide estimates of total aid flows to education and to basic education in 1999 and 2000.[9] It shows that total assistance to education, from all bilateral and multilateral sources combined, stood at an estimated US$5.98 billion in 1999 and at US$4.72 billion in 2000. As regards its composition, the more optimistic estimates shown in the table suggest that external funding to basic education was about US$1.34 billion in 1999 and approximately US$1.45 billion in the year 2000. It has been seen in the analysis in Chapter 4 that this is equivalent to only about one-quarter of the additional external assistance likely to be needed each year to 2015, in order to achieve universal primary education alone.[10] Thus, aid to primary schooling would need to be quintupled – much of it concentrated in the countries of sub-Saharan Africa. Increases in external funding will, therefore, need to be focused upon that region to a much larger degree than has happened to date.[11] Because this takes account of universal primary education (UPE) with gender equity only, external-funding agencies would need to increase aid for EFA still more, if all six Dakar goals are to be achieved.

Recent international initiatives

A number of new international initiatives have, however, been announced in support of education since the World Education Forum in Dakar. Extensive lobbying by the Global Campaign for Education partly through UNESCO and the World Bank (Global Campaign for Education, 2002*b*; Murphy and Mundy, 2002), together with stronger coordination of the core EFA partners by UNESCO, made education an important part of the debate at the United Nations Special Session on Children and the World Summit on Sustainable Development, both held in 2002. Education has also been a central part of the deliberations of the G8 nations both before and after Dakar, but particularly at Okinawa in 2000 and at Genoa in 2001 (Japan, Government, 1999*a, b*; Japan, Ministry of Foreign Affairs, 2000; Italy, Government, 2001). At its most recent meeting in Kananaskis in 2002, the G8 focused upon fighting terrorism, on strengthening global economic growth and sustainable development and on building a new partnership for Africa's development. Under the chairmanship of Canada – a strong supporter of basic education – the G8 also adopted a series of recommendations to assist developing countries achieve universal primary education and equal access to education for girls with a special

9. A number of assumptions have been used in compiling Table 5.7 – e.g. in estimating the proportion of aid allocated to 'basic' education – that are detailed in the notes to the table. It should also be recalled that not all multilateral agencies are included. However, as Table 5.1 showed, those that are represented account for over 80% of all multilateral disbursements in 1999 and 2000. Furthermore, the agencies included in Table 5.7 are the main education aid providers.

10. The estimates in Chapter 4 suggested that annual additional external aid to support universal primary education (UPE) would be likely to amount to up to US$5.6 billion, if the goals of UPE, quality and gender were to be achieved by 2015.

11. See Figures 5.2 and 5.3.

Table 5.7.
Total bilateral and multilateral assistance to education in billions of constant 2000 US$ (1999 and 2000)

	Education		Basic education			
			1999		2000	
	1999	2000	high	low	high	low
Bilateral	4.68	3.52	0.67	0.67	0.82	0.82
Multilateral o/w	1.31	1.20	0.67	0.53	0.62	0.54
IDA	0.55	0.47	0.24	0.14	0.21	0.14
EC	0.39	0.39	0.26	0.26	0.26	0.26
UNESCO	0.10	0.12	0.03	0.04	0.04	0.04
Inter American Development Bank	0.03	0.03	0.01	0.01	0.01	0.01
Asian Development Fund	0.10	0.09	0.04	0.03	0.04	0.03
African Development Fund	0.10	0.05	0.04	0.01	0.02	0.01
UNICEF	0.04	0.05	0.04	0.04	0.05	0.05
Total	5.98	4.72	1.34	1.20	1.45	1.36

Notes: In 1999 (2000) 14.3% (23.4%) of bilateral education aid that was broken down into sub-categories was committed to basic education.
This figure is used to estimate total bilateral commitments to basic education in 1999 (2000).
IDA and UNESCO commitments are for fiscal years and therefore do not match exactly with calendar years.
Two estimates for the percentage of IDA education commitments allocated to basic education are used (a high estimate of 44% and a low estimate of 30% based on data provided in the text).
Due to lack of data, EC data for 2000 are used for 1999.
UNESCO data are budget figures derived from biennial figures in Table 7. It is assumed that 30% of UNESCO education aid goes to basic education.
The same high and low estimates for basic education, used to calculate IDA commitments to basic education, are used to estimate allocations from the Inter-American Development Bank, Asian Development Fund and African Development Fund.
It is assumed that all UNICEF education commitments go to basic education.
Source: Authors' calculations from tables and figures in this paper.

emphasis on sub-Saharan Africa (Canada, 2002*a, b, c, d, e*).

Education was also the particular focus of the spring meeting of the Development Committee of the World Bank in 2002, with specific reference to the Millennium Declaration and its development goals. The meeting was held in the context of a consensus on a new global approach to financing development that had been put together at the United Nations International Conference on Financing for Development at Monterrey in 2002 (United Nations 2002*b*).

The EU (European Council, 2002) and a number of its member countries have been redesigning their policies to strengthen the focus on education, basic education and/or Education for All. New regional initiatives, such as the New Partnership for Africa's Development (NEPAD), have had human resources development as a central priority (http://www.nepad.com).

The EU hailed the meetings on Finance for Development in Monterrey and on Sustainable Development in Johannesburg as a 'Global Deal' (Spain, 2002).[12] It involved a strengthened partnership in which the developing countries would assume greater responsibility for, and ownership of, their own development process, while the industrialized countries would recognize their own responsibilities for reducing global poverty. Investment in education and health, along with good governance and sound economic policies supporting entrepreneurship and enterprise, comprised the three strategic means that were seen as necessary for achieving sustainable development. These three items were also highlighted in the development compact proposed by the United States at Monterrey, based on the need to 'work with the flow of market principles' and the assumption that 'assistance works best when it is provided in the context of a strong commitment to market principles and a very strong economic policy framework' (U.S. Department of State, 2002).

The Monterrey 'consensus' resulted in new, stated commitments for official development assistance (ODA) from the EU, from its individual member states and from the G8 itself. The main pledges are summarized in Table 5.8. As announced at Monterrey, the new pledges for increased ODA amounted to US$12 billion per year by 2006 of which the EU is expected to raise an additional US$7 billion and the United States an additional US$5 billion. The commitments by the EU were stipulated in the context of achieving the 0.7% GNP target by its member states, set by the United Nations several decades ago. Some individual member countries have also set

The Monterrey 'consensus' resulted in new, stated commitments for official development assistance.

12. Also included in these meetings were the Fourth Ministerial Conference of the World Trade Organization held in Doha in 2001, which set a new development agenda in recognition of the need for special efforts to be made to integrate developing and, in particular, the least developed countries in the global economy (World Trade Organization, 2001).

Table 5.8. Stated new commitments for ODA, education and its regional distribution

	ODA overall	Education	Regional
G8	March 2002, new commitments announced at Monterrey to increase ODA by US$12 billion per year by 2006.[1]	March 2002, significantly increase support from bilateral agencies to countries that demonstrate strong policy and financial commitment to education.	March 2002, half or more of new ODA commitments could be for African nations that govern justly, invest in their own people and promote economic freedom. Fast-Track countries would be taken fully into account in efforts to achieve universal primary education.
EU	March 2002, an additional US$7 billion per year by 2006 which is at least US$20 billion extra for 2000–2006.[2]	April 2002, commission aid for education to be doubled. EU to mobilize US$1 billion per year for EFA. Collectively, the EU by 2006 will reach the target of at least 15% of its aid budget going to education (currently 11.3%).[3]	The least developed countries (LDCs) and low-income countries will be given priority.[4]
Belgium	March 2002, substantially increased ODA would reach 0.7% of GNP by 2010.[5]		
Canada	March 2002, the ODA growth rate of 8% per annum over recent years would continue by at least the same percentage or better in future.[5]	June 2002, double its investment in basic education in Africa by 2005, as part of support for G8 African Action Plan. Invest US$100 million annually by 2005 to help achieve UPE in Africa. Overall, resources for basic education will quadruple by 2005.[6]	March 2002, one-off, approximately US$340 million (Can$500 million) for the Africa action plan and additional measures to improve African countries' access to Canadian markets.[7]
Finland	March 2002, as a first step, increase to 0.4% of GNP by 2007.[8]		
Ireland	March 2002, reach 0.7% by 2007 and increase by 55% to meet interim target of 0.45% by 2002.[8]		
Japan		September 2002, separately from G8 EFA Action Plan, pledged an additional US$2 billion for education over the next five years.[9]	
Luxembourg	March 2002, pledged to increase from 0.74% toward 1% by 2005.[8]		
Netherlands	March 2002, continue to meet or exceed 0.7%.[8]	April 2002, committed 135 million euros for Education.[10]	
Norway	March 2002, increase from 0.92% to 1% of GDP by 2005.[8]	June 2002, pledged to increase ODA for basic education by 15%.[10]	
Sweden	March 2002, reaching 1%.[8]		
Switzerland	March 2002, increase ODA progressively to 0.4% by 2010.[8]		
United Kingdom		September 2002, significant increase in aid to education.[9]	Doubling aid (from _472 million) to Africa from 2001 to constitute US$1.5 billion (_1 billion) by 2006, excluding humanitarian aid and debt relief.[7]
United States	March 2002, additional US$5 billion annual increase over current levels of about US$10 billion to a running rate of US$15 billion per year by 2006. ODA to rise by US$1.7 billion in 2004, US$3.3 billion in 2005 and US$5.0 billion in 2006 and beyond.[8]	ODA for basic education to increase by 50% from 2001 to 2003.[11]	July 2002, pledged US$100 million more in education aid for Africa, representing US$20 million per year for five years. From 2001 to 2003, increase of 30% for Africa.[12]
World Bank		Increase IDA support for basic education by US$700 million.[13]	

Note: This table is based on information listed in the sources. It is indicative only, since it has not been possible to verify whether some of the commitments represent double counting.

Source:
1. United Nations, 2002*a*. The US$12 billion is equal to the commitments from the European Union and the United States. This estimate should be considered with caution because it includes assistance from non G-8 EU members, and does not include assistance committed by Japan and Canada. 2. Spain, 2002. EU ODA is to increase from the current level of 0.33% to an average 0.39% ODA target by 2006 towards the 0.7% target. Member countries not having reached this level individually will strive to reach at least 0.33% ODA/GNP by 2006. The translation of these targets into funding figures is shown in the table and represents the most modest assumption based on a low-growth scenario. 3. European Council, 2002. 4. European Commission, 2000. 5. United Nations, 2002*a*. 6. Canada, 2002*b*, *e*. 7. Oxfam, 2002. 8. United Nations, 2002*a*. 9. Oxfam, 2002; Murphy and Mundy, 2002. 10. Murphy and Mundy, 2002. 11. USAID, 2002*b*. 12. Murphy and Munday, 2002; USAID, 2002*b*. 13. Global Campaign for Education, 2002c.

ultimate and interim targets to achieve that same goal, while others, including Canada, Japan, Netherlands and Norway, have pledged significant increases in their assistance for basic education. New support has also been committed for Africa in the context of the G8 Africa Action Plan in response to NEPAD.

How do these commitments measure up to the financial challenge faced by developing countries attempting to achieve the Dakar goals? This question raises the matter of how to interpret the commitments summarized in the table. The extent to which the different undertakings of bilateral agencies are, or are not incorporated in EU or G8 pledges is not entirely clear. Nor is the available documentation from the agencies of much help in clarifying this. The US$12 billion appears to comprise the commitments made by the EU (US$7 billion) and US (US$5 billion). However, this incorporates aid from some EU countries that are not individual members of G8. Moreover, Canada and Japan, neither of which are member of EU, are also substantial providers of aid. Be that as it may, were the sum of US$12 billion to be spent in the same pattern as the current average across all sectors, US$1 billion would be made available to the education sector, of which US$0.3 billion would be allocated to 'basic' education.

In addition to the above, there are likely to be additional increases of total aid and/or support to basic education from European non-EU states – Norway and Switzerland – and from other non-G8 countries such as Australia and New Zealand. Given the size of their existing programmes it seems unlikely that these would together amount to more than US$0.1 billion per year in support of the EFA goals.

However, much more substantial additional pledges are indicated from Japan, which is increasing its aid to education by US$0.4 billion, separate from its G8 commitments. Furthermore, the World Bank has indicated an intention to increase IDA support to basic education by up to US$0.7 billion annually.

It seems, then, that in addition to whatever is implied by the G8 commitment, about US$1.2 billion additional annual assistance was pledged during 2002 to support basic education by the World Bank, Japan and the non-EU European States. In order to bridge the annual financing gap of up to US$5.6 billion anticipated in Chapter 4, approximately US$4.4 billion of the additional G8 pledges would need to be added to this to meet the UPE and gender goals in 2015. As indicated earlier, the costs of meeting the early childhood, adult literacy and life-skills goals have not been included in these figures. Even so, US$4.4 billion for EFA is vastly more than would be forthcoming if the sectoral distribution of the US$12 billion were allocated in a similar fashion to the existing pattern of support. It is also considerably more than the extra US$1 billion of support for basic education from EU that is suggested by the middle column of the table.

The costs of meeting the early childhood, adult literacy and life-skills goals have not been included in anyone's figures.

HIPC debt relief funding was an important source of additional finance for education in twenty-six countries in 2002. Although estimates vary it seems that average debt relief under this programme over the period 2001–2005 will amount to around US$1 billion per year, of which approximately 40% should be available for education spending. (World Bank 2002c; IMF 2002). On the other hand, since many of these countries would otherwise be in default, it is unclear what proportion of these funds represents genuine new resources to the nations concerned, if not to their education sectors.

The only other source of available aid support would be a redirection of existing educational aid to other subsectors. As the earlier sections of this chapter showed, this amounted to some US$3.3 billion in 2000 (Table 5.7), most of which originated from bilateral sources. It seems to be an inescapable conclusion, then, that the financing of EFA will not only require strong policy reform in the countries which are currently far from the goals, but also a very significant increase in the proposed levels of external finance for education together with some further redirection of bilateral assistance towards EFA (and away from other education subsectors), in those and other countries. This represents a very challenging agenda for all parties to the partnership.

The Fast-Track Initiative (FTI)

The emphasis on universal primary education – undoubtedly the most costly of the goals – is partly the consequence of the most visible initiative since Dakar influencing the 'Global Deal'. This is the Fast-Track Initiative (FTI), launched at the meeting of the Development Committee of the World Bank in April 2002 (World Bank Dev. Com., 2002*a*, *b*). Under this initiative, a first group of eighteen low-income and low-enrolment countries, each of which had a Poverty Reduction Strategy Paper (PRSP), were selected as recipients for early external assistance in achieving the education Millennium Development Goals (MDGs). The FTI is reflected in the recommendations of the G8 Task Force and in the new EU draft policy statement (European Commission, 2002*a*, 2002*b*; European Parliament, 2001).[13] It stipulates a set of key policy and financing norms against which countries' EFA plans may be evaluated and costed: the basis for gauging progress and for defining the rules of engagement between countries and their external partners. It has three main goals: (1) deeper developing-country commitment to education policy reform and the efficient use of resources; (2) increased and better coordinated aid from industrialized countries, to be provided within the framework of PRSPs; and (3) improved assessment based on improved data.

There may be a danger of ignoring countries which do not fulfil the criteria for eligibility to the FTI.

In designing the FTI, the analysis and conclusions of the World Bank's simulation analyses for forty-seven countries (World Bank 2002*a*) were drawn upon. The overall financial parameters of the FTI were based upon that analysis, and countries' reform programmes are expected to aim at achieving the revenue and efficiency 'norms' suggested by the study (as discussed in Chapter 4). In return, external partners would undertake to support the reforming countries (World Bank Dev. Com., 2002*a*, *b*, p. 7). Implementation was to be undertaken through a multi-partner consortium that would align the external financing needs of these countries with available financial support, which in turn would take into account existing programme designs, indicators and financing frameworks (World Bank, 2002*c*, p. 4).

The FTI has been widely welcomed and supported by core EFA partners, including UNESCO and UNICEF, by bilateral agencies, by regional organizations, such as the EU and by the Global Campaign for Education. Nevertheless, three types of concern have been expressed: (1) the speed and extent of domestic policy reform required both to improve efficiency and raise revenues may be too ambitious; (2) there may be a danger of ignoring countries which do not fulfil the criteria for eligibility to the FTI; and (3) its exclusive focus on the Millennium Development Goals may result in the remaining Dakar goals being overlooked.[14] It is also questionable whether the FTI quite lives up to the spirit of a 'Global Initiative', as defined in the Dakar Framework for Action (para. 11). This required the international community to assist national efforts in achieving EFA, based on six underlying dimensions of development cooperation and financing (UNESCO, 2001*i*).

As suggested by Figure 5.4, the six dimensions constitute a package, determined by country-specific conditions and based on a principle of inclusion rather than exclusion. Negotiated according to principles of transparency and ownership, it relies on institution and human-capacity building as concomitants to the process. Both the Global Deal and the FTI focus upon the Millennium Development Goals, accepting that investment in education is a core dimension of reducing and eliminating poverty. Although this notion is also fundamental to EFA in the Dakar Framework, the latter places much more emphasis upon education as a right, and upon basic education constituting the necessary foundation for lifelong learning, with all the implications that brings for personal and societal development.

The FTI is properly judged as a new funding mechanism with an emphasis upon urgent action. It is less satisfactory as a framework for medium to long-term education reform. As argued in Chapter 4, the FTI's proposed solutions in the form of norms and benchmarks have been derived from education system analysis isolated from a wider societal context.

13. Murphy and Mundy argue that the Initiative has such strong similarities with Oxfam's original Global Action Plan proposed in Dakar that there seems to be a line of influence (2002, p. 11).

14. It should be noted, however, that the World Bank is planning to extend the costing exercise to 'all the countries which have not yet achieved EFA' and broaden it to 'other EFA goals such as gender equality in primary and secondary education and adult literacy' (World Bank, 2002*c*, p. 4).

Figure 5.4. Diagrammatic representation of the Global Initiative

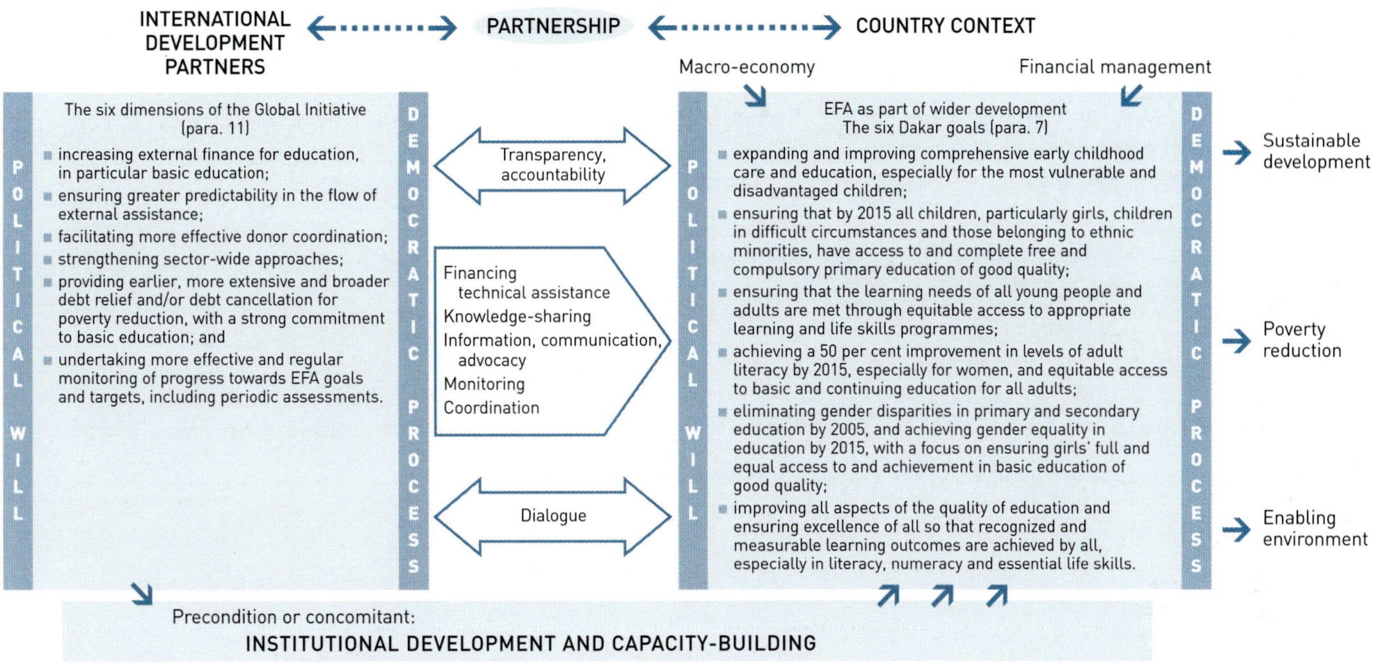

Source: UNESCO (2001*i*), adapted from Sida (2000), p. 30.

As regards country-choice, the FTI initially incorporated a limited number of countries having a 'credible' education plan aligned with a PRSP. They included some countries, such as Mozambique, where existing aid receipts appear to be beyond their domestic implementation capacity (Gustafsson, 2002). On the other hand, the FTI omitted a significant number of countries that could be considered as 'high priority' if aid effectiveness were interpreted in relation to highest need rather than highest efficiency. Table 5.9 compares the eighteen Fast-Track countries, five countries held in Fast-Track reserve (of which four are E-9 countries) and a group of fifteen other countries with poor development and education indicators.[15] As shown in the table, all three groups of countries have weak development and education indicators and clearly deserve external assistance. By contrast, those selected as initial FTI countries are, in fact, slightly better off than the other two groups. Table 5.9 indicates that the integration of the reserve countries into the Initiative could have a positive and strong impact upon global adult literacy rates and upon reducing the number of out-of-school children if these particular elements were specifically addressed. The 'other' country group not only have lower incomes than the FTI group, they also have higher rates of adult illiteracy, and much lower primary enrolment ratios. Attention to this 'other' group of countries would require the kind of flexibility implied by the Global Initiative and not necessarily insistence upon the existence of PRSPs in the countries concerned.

The emphasis placed by the FTI on UPE will make an important contribution to national development processes. However, its simple expansion may be to the cost of a more systemic approach focusing upon all six Dakar goals. Some have argued that an exclusive emphasis upon primary school enrolment and completion may come to dominate national educational agendas to the cost of more qualitative aspects of education reform (Gustafsson, 2002). Moreover, there is an obvious risk that the higher levels of external support entailed by FTI will increase aid dependency, as the extent of national ownership of plans and policies formulated via the PRSP instrument remains uncertain.

Existing aid receipts in Mozanbique appear to be beyond domestic implementation capacity.

15. This 'other' group comprises countries that were non Fast-Track, having the lowest net enrolment ratios in 2000. The full list of countries and their key development and education indicators are shown in Table 5.10.

Table 5.9. Comparison of Fast-Track Initiative and other low NER countries: key education and development indicators

Variables	Fast-Track	Reserve Fast-Track	Other Low NER	Total
Number of countries	18	5	15	38
Population (000) 1999	316 836.1	1 425 251.9	158 927.2	1 901 015.1
Average GNP per capita, current US$ 1999	470.0	372.5	381.8	423.1
Average GNP per capita PPP 1999	2 826.0	1 575.0	2 010.0	2 301.8
Average adult illiteracy rate (15+) 2000	38.8	46.8	43.4	41.7
Number of illiterates (15+) '(000) 2000	58 280.2	416 797.9	32 351.3	507 429.4
Average GER 1999	83.6	84.9	75.5	80.6
Average NER 1999	67.2	61.8	54.8	61.3
Estimated out-of-school children (000) 1999/2000	9 364.2	n.a.	6 403.9	15 768.1
Average public expenditure on primary education as a percentage of total public expenditure on education (latest from 1997–99)	55.2	45.6	45.3	49.6
Average public current expenditure in primary education as a percentage of GNP (latest from 1996–99)	2.3	1.2	2.3	2.1

Note: Country groups are as follows:

Fast-Track Initiative countries: Albania, Bolivia, Burkina Faso, Ethiopia, Gambia, Ghana, Guinea, Guyana, Honduras, Mauritania, Mozambique, Nicaragua, Niger, Uganda, United Republic of Tanzania, Viet Nam, Yemen, Zambia

Reserve Fast-Track countries: Bangladesh, Democratic Republic of the Congo, India, Nigeria, Pakistan

Other low NER countries: Bhutan, Burundi, Central African Republic, Chad, Comoros, Côte d'Ivoire, Djibouti, Eritrea, Haiti, Islamic Republic of Iran, Lesotho, Madagascar, Mali, Oman, Yugoslavia

Source: Tables 5.2. and 5.10.

Education is maintaining its place at the centre of the international development agenda.

In summary, education is maintaining its place at the centre of the international development agenda and the pledges made since Dakar represent an important reconfirmation of this fact. The high degree of attention paid to universal primary education is justifiable because of its centrality to the Dakar agenda and its clear requirement for extensive and effective external support. However, this has at least two implications: first, the financial pledges far from cover the financing needed to pay attention to the full Dakar agenda; second, the short-term support for universal primary education is designed somewhat in isolation from the longer-term developments needed for systemic reform. Unless a medium- to long-term perspective is adopted, this will limit the capacity of governments to plan flexibly. Therefore, the FTI does not amount to the broader Global Initiative requested in the Dakar Framework for Action. Further, it risks being dominated by the concerns of a minority of the core partners, rather than reflecting the 'consistent, coordinated, coherent work' (UNESCO, 2000*a*, para. 17) seen as essential by the World Education Forum.

International coordination

The World Education Forum mandated UNESCO to play a leading role in sustaining international support for EFA and promoting better coordination of the global effort to achieve the Dakar goals. In doing so, it set down both a technical and a political challenge. However, it also provided UNESCO with an important opportunity to demonstrate international leadership at a critical point in the global effort to realize the right to education and eliminate poverty.

As this Report demonstrates, UNESCO is active in promoting the importance of good data for effective policy through the UNESCO Institute for Statistics, in encouraging the development of EFA Plans, in establishing and contributing to Flagship Programmes, and in giving priority to basic education in its regular programmes. It has also helped start the development of an EFA agenda in Europe (Box 5.1). In these ways, UNESCO is infusing EFA throughout its normative and technical functions in a direct response to Dakar (UNESCO, 2000*a*, para. 20).

However, UNESCO is finding other aspects of its international role more challenging. This is partly because the objectives of exercising major influence on the world's political leaders and of mobilizing significant international resources for EFA are intrinsically difficult to achieve.

Nevertheless, over the period 2000–2002, UNESCO's interpretation of its mandate was conservative, with an emphasis on facilitating dialogue and promoting partnerships, rather than attempting to provide strong international leadership. Partnerships and alliances are important, but in the context of the international events outlined above, UNESCO has had the opportunity to be more openly proactive in analysing and arguing the case for global action in support of EFA.

UNESCO arranged for the High-Level Group to meet twice – in Paris in 2001 and Abuja in 2002. At the 2001 meeting, UNESCO was asked to facilitate the development of a comprehensive strategy for EFA (UNESCO 2001*g*). This was prepared and presented to the EFA Working Group in July 2002 (UNESCO 2002*b*[16]). UNESCO describes the strategy as a reference guide to the essential elements of EFA and to the definition of areas of potential mutual support. The strategy appears to be conceived as a broad framework for understanding, rather than as an agenda for international action.

Both in the High-Level Group and in the three meetings of the Working Group on Education for all, UNESCO has been mindful of the importance of broad geographical representation and the need to involve civil society organizations. It has tended to draw on politicians and on expertise from within the education sector and, in the case of the Working Group, on the services of officials carrying less political authority and weight. This is an understandable approach for UNESCO, given its responsibilities to its Member States, but it is questionable whether this way of working will provide the urgency and the political commitment or the action that the Dakar agreements demand. There clearly is a place for sharing information and building alliances. But this will not necessarily lead to increased influence on the world's political and development community.

Box 5.1. Education for all in Europe

UNESCO has supported a number of initiatives aimed at publicizing the six Dakar goals and their implications for educational development in Europe. EFA Forums have been established and national plans have been developed. A common theme is the need for European countries to provide education for marginalized and disadvantaged groups. Initiatives have stretched from Belarus, Bulgaria, Georgia, Moldova, Russia, South Caucasus, Ukraine to the Baltic States, Nordic countries and the United Kingdom.

The United Kingdom National Commission for UNESCO is organizing six conferences and seminars, each linked to one of the six EFA goals. The objectives of the series are to give an overview of progress worldwide and in the United Kingdom towards achievement of the goals and to consider the main obstacles and identify ways in which relevant United Kingdom experience can support achievement of the goals.

The Baltic States and the Nordic countries have made particular efforts to develop mutually supportive efforts nationally, regionally and internationally. A sub-regional conference on Education for All in the Baltic Sea Countries was held in Riga from 24–27 January 2002, with participation from Denmark, Estonia, Finland, Germany, Iceland, Latvia, Lithuania, Norway, Poland and Sweden and with observers from Belarus and the United Kingdom. The Conference was organized by the Ministry of Education and Science of the Republic of Latvia and the Latvian National Commission for UNESCO, in close cooperation with the UNESCO Secretariat in Paris, the Latvian National Committee for UNICEF, UNDP Latvia, the World Bank Mission in Latvia and the Latvian Adult Education Association.

The meeting agreed that the objectives of the Dakar Framework for Action provided direction for educational development in the individual countries, particularly concerning educational quality and basic education as the foundation for lifelong learning. It also recognized that broad civic participation in discussions through the institution of National Education Forums, or similar bodies, is critical to ensure a good quality of education for all. An informal EFA Coordination Working Group composed of representatives from Latvia, Lithuania and Sweden was formed to take the work forward.

UNESCO has played its part in the development of the FTI and the G8 Education Task Force. It has created the Dakar Follow Up Unit in UNESCO's Education Sector to manage EFA-related consultations. On behalf of the international community, it has facilitated the development of the independent Global EFA Monitoring Report. Recently, it was successful in promoting EFA at the World Summit on Sustainable Development. However, in order for UNESCO to play a truly influential international role it needs to be better resourced, in ways that harness both strong technical capability and authoritative policy analysis. In-house capacity is needed to analyse international developments, changing aid modalities and requirements, and comparative experience of education policy trends across the world.

16. UNESCO, An International Strategy to Operationalize the Dakar Framework for Action, Paris, UNESCO, 2002*b*.

Box 5.2. Learning to live together

Political events since September 2001 have further emphasized the absolute importance of universal basic education. Given the complexity of global problems, in particular the inequalities between and within countries, learning to live together has become a necessity for all regions of the world. This was the theme of the 46th International Conference on Education organized by the UNESCO International Bureau of Education (IBE) in 2001, which was attended by over 600 participants from 127 countries, including eighty ministers and vice-ministers of education and regional and non-governmental organizations and foundations. It is the particular focus of ongoing work at IBE.

The Conference agreed that achieving the objective of Education for All goes well beyond the achievement of universal schooling. Within each country, the search for social cohesion, the struggle against inequality, the respect for cultural diversity and access to information and communication technologies could be achieved through policies that focus on improving the quality of education.

Learning to live together means accepting the universality of certain values while respecting cultural diversity. Yet everyone must acquire, through education, values that are part of humanity's common heritage, as expressed in the International Declaration of Human Rights.

The International Bureau of Education's programme on 'Curriculum change and social cohesion in conflict-affected societies' in Bosnia-Herzegovina, Guatemala, Lebanon, Mozambique, Northern Ireland, Rwanda, Sri Lanka and Tajikistan aims at developing sustainable processes of change of the school curriculum to enhance social cohesion in divided and conflict-ridden societies. It takes the view that education per se is no guarantee for peace since violence and social exclusion can be embedded in education systems. It proposes the concept of 'peace-building education', which would analyse the structural causes and the wider social-political context of divisions and tensions.

In Afghanistan, basic training for curriculum and textbook development and printing capacity aims to strengthen both the Ministry of Education and the Ministry of Higher Education in their process of national educational reform. The project covers curriculum renewal, revision and modernization, development of materials and methodologies for human rights, peace and citizenship education and capacity building within the Ministry to design and produce printed materials.

Programme activities

UNESCO was the only organization specifically requested to place the outcomes and priorities of Dakar at the heart of its work although many other agencies in the United Nations system are developing EFA-related programmes. UNESCO responded by allocating 41% of its regular education programme budget for basic education. As part of its reform process, it brought Education for All into the work of all Divisions in the Education Sector, as well as to the other parts of the Organization. Cross-sectoral collaboration is illustrated by the cooperation between the Communication and Education sectors in distance education and between the Social Sciences and Education sectors in human rights.

UNESCO strongly advocates all of the six Dakar goals. Its programme activities notably include those which are assigned less importance by other international agencies: early childhood care and education, inclusive education, life skills, non-formal education and its synergies with formal education, adult education and literacy, and the quality of education. UNESCO has been interpreting the right to education through learning how to live together (Box 5.2). It has supported systemic development, for example, in its work with teachers and educational personnel (Box 5.3). It is also involved in a number of special focus areas, including education in emergency and crisis situations, school health and HIV/AIDS. Regionally, UNESCO was involved in planning, and organizing a range of meetings of ministers and of regional and sub-regional forums during 2001 and 2002.

Inter-agency Flagship Programmes

A range of inter-agency work is taking place through flagship programmes. An overview of all existing flagships is presented in Table 5.11. In the Communiqué of the first meeting of the High-Level Group, it was emphasized that 'multi-partner initiatives and programmes must be carefully synchronized with national priorities, form part of national EFA action plans, be properly coordinated by governments and pay special attention to the educational needs of out-of- school children' (UNESCO, 2001*b*). It appears from Table 5.11. that the common feature of the flagships is the fact that they cater to marginalized groups or countries. Although some have been linked with EFA planning processes at national level, most of them need to be strengthened in that regard.

In summary, programme activities, including the flagship programmes, indicate a concern with those areas of the Dakar agenda that are not the primary focus of the FTI. While constituting complementary agency efforts, they suggest a continued need to map the mandates and strengths of all EFA partners in order to ensure implementation of all the Dakar goals.

Box 5.3. National capacity-building of lead teacher training institutions in Africa

M. Siniscalco, in her study for the International Labour Office (ILO) and UNESCO, highlighted how declining working conditions and low salaries result in a declining number of teachers for the growing number of school children around the world. In order to improve the quality of education in Africa and support the achievement of the EFA goals, improvement of teacher training (TT) institutions in Africa is urgently needed.

UNESCO has launched a capacity-building programme for teacher training in Africa. It targets the lead teacher training institutions: *Écoles Normales (supérieures, d'Instituteurs des Écoles primaires, d'Institutrices des Jardins d'Enfants)*, university-level departments of teacher training and selected professional institutions that are the best national sources for quality education for the country and the training ground for future leaders in education.

The programme expects to assist the institutions in addressing more directly the challenges of teacher training as they relate to the development problems in the particular countries, especially those most in need. It also aims at creating a network to regroup the principal actors and the principal institutions in teacher training, and to bring forward the policy issue of teacher training development for Africa on the international agenda through ongoing communication with policy-makers, donors, the media and others.

Following an in-depth evaluation and analysis of the current conditions of the institutions in all forty-six Member States of sub-Saharan Africa during October-November 2002, the programme will begin to phase in the most urgently needed improvements of TT institutions. This will be based upon the recommendations of the evaluation and the priorities of the governments and the teacher training institutions. The immediate focus of the activities will be the *Écoles Normales Supérieures* that UNESCO played a fundamental role in establishing. Independent of the size of the country, only the lead teacher training institutions will be targeted. An analytic summary report of the evaluation results will be made available to major African mechanisms, such as MINEDAF VIII and NEPAD.

The activity will be carried out in partnership with the Commonwealth of Learning, International Council for Distance Education, Education International, World Confederation of Teachers, UNICEF, ILO, the Association for the Development of Education in Africa, relevant Working Groups on EFA and the World Council of Higher Education.

Source: From Siniscalco (2002).

Conclusions

This chapter has analysed the main trends in education aid between 1990 and 2001 and assessed the international commitments in support of Education for All made during the course of 2001–2002. It was shown that bilateral and multilateral aid to education declined towards the end of the 1990s. While there appears to have been a slight increase in the shares allocated to basic education, they too declined in real terms over the same period. Estimates of the additional external funding requirements necessary to achieve universal primary education suggest that current levels of assistance are far too low, particularly in view of the funding needs of all six Dakar goals. Achieving universal primary education alone will require a greater concentration on sub-Saharan Africa. Additional external funding for education, and particularly for universal primary education, was announced during 2002, but it is unclear whether this will lead to the very significant increases required. At the turn of the century, only 30% of educational aid was allocated to basic education. If the Dakar goals are to be met, further and sustained increases in educational aid are needed over the medium term, together with a significant redirection of educational aid towards the EFA sectors.

Major improvements have been made in the reporting of aid commitments to education, and particularly to basic education. However, there remains much room for further improvement in the coverage and quality of OECD DAC data. The priorities are to achieve greater conceptual clarity in reporting, and to provide much fuller information on education disbursements, including their subsectoral detail, in order to monitor actual aid flows.

Recent international commitments, initiatives and programmes demonstrate the cooperative spirit that exists among the international community as well as a widespread perception of the need for greater coherence and coordination at country levels. However, translating the commitments into real resources directed towards priority ends, and turning the language of coordination into real practice, remain some distance away. It is doubtful whether the international partners are yet working according to a commonly interpreted agenda as opposed to the separate mandates and strengths of their individual organizations. Further groundwork, therefore, remains essential in order to consolidate the individual initiatives into a movement that is enabled to focus upon all of the Dakar goals.

Translating international commitments into real resources remains some distance away.

Table 5.10. Comparison of Fast-Track and other low NER countries: key education and development indicators

Country	Population (000) 1999	GNP per capita (current US$ 1999)	GNP per capita PPP 1999	Adult illiteracy rate (15+) 2000	GER 1999	NER 1999	Estimated out-of-school children (000) 1999/2000	Public expenditure on primary education as % of total public expenditure on education (Latest from 1997–99)	Public current expenditure in primary education as % of GNP (Latest from 1996–99)
Fast-Track countries									
Albania	3 131	930	3 300	15.3	109.2	100.0	3.1	...	...
Bolivia	8 142	980	2 310	14.6	115.6	99.1	11.2	71.8	2.3
Burkina Faso	11 246	230	2 470	76.1	42.9	34.6	1 298.2	59.7	1.6
Ethiopia	61 388	100	1 410	60.9	70.8	87.3	...	...	4
Gambia	1 267	...	440	63.4	75.1	69.8	56.0	40.9	2
Ghana	18 893	390	...	28.4	87.7	...	...	66.7	2.6
Guinea	8 021	490	8 830	...	53.5	49.0	642.3	27.9	2
Guyana	757	860	3 640	1.5	88.3	40.0	...	...	5
Honduras	6 258	780	2 290	25.0	97.3	85.7	...	37.1	1.8
Mauritania	2 582	390	1 570	59.8	84.3	63.0	...	44.6	1.4
Mozambique	17 936	220	...	56.0	85.4	50.1	1 232.2	...	...
Nicaragua	4 938	390	2 000	33.5	104.4	79.4	163.8	74.1	2.2
Niger	10 455	190	...	84.0	32.4	21.2	1 408.4	...	1.4
Uganda	22 611	310	...	33.0	140.9	87.3	...	62	2
United Republic of Tanzania	34 285	...	...	25.0	63.0	46.7	3 542.6	65.2	1.5
Viet Nam	77 118	...	...	7.5	107.7	96.3	342.6	35.8	1
Yemen	17 620	...	...	53.6	68.0	...	...	80	4.4
Zambia	10 187	320	...	21.8	78.7	66.4	663.9	51.4	1.4
Reserve Fast-Track Country									
Bangladesh	134 584	350	1 500	60.0	96.5	81.4	...	42.7	1.2
Dem.Rep. of the Congo	49 581	...	770	38.6	60.7	58.7	...	...	...
India	992 686	440	2 240	42.8	100.9	71.1	...	37.1	1.1
Nigeria	110 845	250	...	36.0	70.3	35.9	...	...	1
Pakistan	137 556	450	1 790	56.8	96.0	...	...	57	1.3
Other low NER Country									
Bhutan	2 029	570	1 360	...	71.9	52.9	...	61.1	1.8
Burundi	6 255	120	...	52.0	62.5	44.5	631.7	37.3	2.7
Central African Republic	3 649	280	750	53.3	60.5	42.3	...	57	1.1
Chad	7 641	210	9 090	57.4	70.3	56.6	564.1	37.5	1
Comoros	685	400	790	44.1	83.8	54.8	50.4	17.4	0.5
Côte d'Ivoire	15 685	...	750	51.4	76.9	58.4	1 081.0	59.5	4.9
Djibouti	617	850	...	35.4	36.9	30.6	71.7	65.9	2.2
Eritrea	3 524	200	...	44.3	61.2	40.3	288.4	46.8	2.1
Haiti	8 016	490	1 450	50.2	126.0	86.8	...	38.3	0.7
Iran, Islamic Rep. of	69 244	...	...	24.0	87.6	74.6	2 398.9	34.4	2.5
Lesotho	2 008	590	1 170	16.6	103.5	58.5	146.4	41.6	8
Madagascar	15 512	250	720	33.5	101.8	66.4	729.3	37.8	0.8
Mali	11 039	240	...	74.4	50.0	39.9	...	68.1	1.9
Oman	2 457	...	...	28.3	73.3	65.1	150.5	31.6	1.3
Yugoslavia	10 567	...	...	...	65.9	50.6	291.5	...	...

Source: Annex, Table 1, (first seven columns); UNESCO, 2000*b* (last two columns).

Table 5.11. EFA Flagship Programmes

Title	Partners	Goals	Strategies	Activities and achievements
Flagship Programme on Early Childhood Regional Capacity-Building Initiative (Co-ordinated by UNICEF)	The Consultative Group on Early Childhood Care and Development (CG on ECCD) includes, among others: Aga Khan Foundation, Bernard van Leer Foundation, Christian Children's Fund, IADB, Save the Children Foundation (United States), UNICEF, UNESCO, USAID, World Bank, OECD, United Nations Family Unit.	Contribute to alleviating poverty by providing children, particularly those in disadvantaged situations, with early learning opportunities so that they grow up healthy, succeed in learning in school and become competent and productive members of society.	Establish/reinforce macro-policy structure of early childhood care and education in selected target countries. Establish regional policy forums for national policy-makers and decision-makers. Reinforce information management and networking in early childhood policy and practices.	Case studies on countries that have developed ECD strategies as part of their national EFA plans. Compiling and analyzing research studies that demonstrate the positive impact (both quantitative and qualitative) of ECD on broader EFA goals. Pilot programme on the financing of early childhood education. Improvement of existing and development of better ECCD indicators. Development of an ECD Flagship website. Achievement to date: Ongoing activities.
United Nations Girls' Education Initiative (UNGEI) (Coordinated by UNICEF)	DAW/DESA/UN, DGO, ILO, OCHA, UNAIDS, UNDP, UNESCO, UNFPA, UNHCR, UNICEF, UNIFEM, WFP, WHO, World Bank and non-governmental organizations such as the Forum of African Women Educationalists (FAWE).	Contribute to the elimination of gender discrimination and gender disparity in education systems through action at global, national, district and community levels.	Encourage and facilitate strategic action on girls' education by building political and resource commitments, ending the gender gap, ending gender bias and discrimination within education systems, helping girls' education in crisis, conflict and post-conflict situations, and eliminating ingrained gender bias that limits the demand for girls' education.	Advocacy and global action: by bringing the issue of girls' education to the agenda of various international meetings and conferences. Support to countries: taking action to promote girls' education-related content of CCAs and UNDAFs (e.g. development and introduction of a 'hands-on clinic' on the MDGs and their application through the CCA-UNDAF process in the Induction Programme for Resident Coordinators and a training module on girls' education as it relates to United Nations country teams and their work). Partnership building in order to ensure the mainstreaming of Girl's Education issues into the other inter-agency initiatives. Development of a supportive environment for country work: Organization of meetings with bilaterals in order to strengthen the global coalition for girls' education. Identification of capacity for different substantive components of girls' education. Posting of examples of good practice on DevLink website. Achievements to date: ▪ The United Nations Secretary-General's and other high-level international officials' commitment to promoting girls' education. ▪ Increase in number of requests for information and presentations on UNGEI. ▪ Six countries (from sub-Sah. Africa, S. Asia and the Arab States) expressed interest in participating in the Initiative, and working actively on improving the situation of girls' education. ▪ Significant steps towards including Girls' Education in the agenda of UNICEF, WFP, UNHCR, WFP, UNESCO, The World Bank, UNFPA, ILO, DESA. ▪ Gender issues mainstreamed in the work and materials developed by the Inter-Agency Network on Education in Emergencies.
The Initiative on Education in Situations of Emergency and Crisis (Coordinated by UNICEF, UNESCO, UNHCR, CARE and the Norwegian Refugee Council)	UNESCO, UNHCR, UNICEF, Norwegian Refugee Council, CARE International, Save the Children Alliance, other NGOs and bilateral agencies.	Assist Member States in situations of emergency and crisis to cope with their immediate education needs.	Support existing agencies and initiatives through the provision and sharing of information, learning materials, guidelines and training opportunities.	Information/experience sharing and research: promotion of greater donor understanding of education in emergencies, advocacy for education to be included in emergency response, advocacy for gender issues to be taken into account in emergency education initiatives, development of consensual guidelines on education in emergencies. Sensitization, advocacy. Training and capacity building. Achievements to date: ▪ Teaching and learning resources as well as documented best practices made available on the website of the Inter-Agency Network for Education in Emergencies (INEE). ▪ Comprehensive vision of educational needs adopted in the EFA Action plans of countries in emergency, crisis and reconstruction.

Table 5.11. (continued)

Title	Partners	Goals	Strategies	Activities and achievements
The Inter-Agency Initiative FRESH: Focusing Resources on Effective School Health - (Coordinated by UNESCO, UNICEF, WHO and the World Bank, in collaboration with Education International)	UNESCO, UNICEF, WHO, the World Bank and Education International, in collaboration with UNAIDS, FAO, WFP, Roll Back Malaria and others.	Increase awareness within the education community about the value of school health programmes as a strategy for achieving EFA.	Broaden the scope of school health programmes to include and make more effective the following four components: ▪ school policies, ▪ healthy, safe and secure learning environment, ▪ skills-based health education, and ▪ school-based health and nutrition services.	Advocacy at international and inter-agency meetings. Support to EFA Action Plans preparation: Sensitization and training seminars (in around sixty developing countries) for National EFA coordinators and Ministries of Education's personnel in charge of health education. Provision of FRESH consultants to support the EFA planning process in some countries in SSA and LAC regions. Launching of survey on finalized plans to verify whether HIV/AIDS and health education have been integrated. FRESH school health launched in 10 developing countries. Provision of sensitization textbooks for teachers, school personnel, communities and pupils. Achievements to date: 1. The convener agencies (UNESCO, UNICEF, WHO, World Bank and Education International) have been joined by new partners who are reinforcing the Initiative. 2. Integration of FRESH health components in the draft National EFA Action plans of fifteen countries of the Pacific Regions and six countries in sub-Saharan Africa.
The Impact of HIV/AIDS on Education	UNESCO, UNICEF, WHO, UNFPA, UNDP, World Bank, UNAIDS Secretariat, Education International, USAID, DFID, individual experts.	Mobilize commitment to preventive education and act as catalyst for the exchange of information about how education can be most effective in mitigating the effects of the HIV/AIDS crisis: reducing vulnerability and impact; interrupting transmission. Increase the Education Sector's contribution to two key and inter-linked targets: i) achieve 25% reduction in HIV infection rates among young people in most affected countries by 2005 and globally by 2010, and ii) ensure that by 2015, all children have access to and complete primary education of good quality.	Increase interagency cooperation by developing common approaches and frameworks, with a focus on work with children and young people at or near school age, as well as other educational settings. Facilitate the development of country level strategic plans for HIV/AIDS prevention and impact management in education systems, as part of an expanded global response to the pandemic.	Advocacy: Development of common advocacy approaches and materials. Advancement of knowledge and capacity building of key actors. Monitoring of progress on mitigating the impact of HIV/AIDS and on reducing vulnerability. Achievement to date: Development and adoption of a common strategic framework by all partners. (UNESCO leads the UNAIDS Inter-Agency Task Team on Education).
Teachers and Quality of Education (Coordinated by UNESCO, ILO, UNICEF and Education International) (Please also refer to Box 5.2 in Chapter 5, above.)	UNESCO, ILO, UNICEF, Education International and other partners.	Improvement of teachers' education, with the aim of enabling large numbers of teachers to provide quality basic education for all. Strengthened mechanisms for social dialogue in education by means of information sharing, consultation and negotiation on policies, financing, and teaching/learning conditions that ensure full participation of teachers, their organizations and other educational stakeholders in key reform decisions.	Strengthen high quality, relevant, and professional standard initial teacher education and lifelong professional development. Establish sub-regional,inter-ministerial and inter-sectoral processes for enriching the quality of teacher education reform in order to meet Dakar goals. Strengthen and institutionalize social dialogue mechanisms between education authorities and teachers' organizations.	Review of teacher education, recruitment and/or deployment, professional and material conditions and social dialogue mechanisms in the United Republic of Tanzania. This activity will be extended to six other pilot countries involved in the preparation of a Poverty Reduction Strategy Paper (PRSP) (two each in Africa, Asia and Latin America). Evaluation of selected Écoles Normales Supérieures in French-speaking Africa. Development of minimal sub-regional standards for qualifications for entry into the teaching profession in sub-regions where such common standards are desired but currently lacking. Achievement to date: ongoing activities.

Table 5.11. (continued)

Title	Partners	Goals	Strategies	Activities and achievements
Literacy in the framework of the United Nations Literacy Decade: Education for All (Facilitated by UNESCO)	UNESCO, UNICEF, World Bank, OECD.	Mobilize governments and civil society to recognize the importance of creating literate environments and providing quality non-formal learning opportunities.	Place literacy at the centre of all levels of national education systems. Adopt a two-pronged approach, giving equal importance to both formal and non-formal education modalities with synergy between the two. Promote an environment supportive of uses and culture of reading in schools and communities. Ensure community involvement in literacy programmes and their ownership by communities. Build partnership at all levels, particularly national. Develop systematic monitoring and evaluation processes at all levels, supported by research findings and databases.	Policy: development of a policy environment across communities, sectors, agencies and ministries that mainstreams the promotion of literacy. Programme modality: develop literacy programmes that cover the whole life cycle so as to ensure lifelong learning, are gender sensitive, and delivered through both non-formal and formal approaches. Capacity-building: ensure that partners and stakeholders are able to design and run these literacy programmes in a sustained manner. Research: undertake research activities that contribute to the formulation of literacy policies, the improvement of literacy programmes and the periodic review of progress towards Literacy for All. Community participation: take steps to secure community participation. Monitoring and evaluation: build functional monitoring information systems to provide reliable and meaningful information on literacy status, its use and its impact, and on literacy programmes performance and effectiveness. Achievement to date: this Flagship programme is still at a planning stage. The United Nations Literacy Decade will begin in 2003.
EFA and the Rights of Persons with Disabilities: Towards Inclusion (Facilitated by UNESCO)	Danish International Development Assistance, DfID, EENET, University of Manchester, Georgetown University Child Development Center, Inclusion International, International Council for Education of People with Visual Impairment, International Step by Step Association, International Working Group on Disability and Development, OECD, Rehabilitation International, UNESCO, University of Oslo, World Blind Union, World Federation of the Deaf.	Promote access to and completion of quality education for all children, youth, and adults with disabilities, and in that effort, incorporate the goals and approaches identified in the major conferences related to the rights of children, to equal opportunities for disabled people and EFA.	Serve as a technical resource for national, global and regional level activities. Mobilize resources. Assist the EFA monitoring process.	Support to the development and enhancement of national plans in regard to the right to education and the promotion of national policy and legislation that ensure the right to public education for all children with disabilities. Ensure that the right to education of people with disabilities is fully taken into account in all EFA activities and EFA flagships. Promote inter-agency and regional networking. Ensure dissemination of information about and respect for the principles of everyone's universal right to education. Promote international development assistance, the availability of assistance devices, the strengthening of human resources, and the like to support the education of persons with a disability. Develop disability-sensitive indicators to be used in monitoring EFA, to ensure that statistics reflect numbers of students with a disability who are receiving an education in regular schools and in special schools, as well as the number of children excluded from school. Support research to produce the data needed to inform governments and international financial institutions. Achievement to date: this flagship programme is still at a planning stage.
New flagship: Education for Rural People (Led by FAO)	FAO, UNESCO, ICRAF - World Agroforestry Centre of the CGIAR, IPGRI-International Plant Genetic Resources Institute, WFP, ILO, the Governments of Egypt and San Marino, Terre des Hommes, Italia and others.	Reducing the education gap among rural and urban populations.	Placing education of rural people at the core of national EFA plans and strengthen institutional capacity to do so. Expand access to and increase attendance in and completion of schools in rural areas by promoting and supporting initiatives that aim at improving children's nutrition and capacity to learn.	National level : technical support to countries willing to address the basic educational needs of rural people by formulating specific plans of action as part of the national plans on EFA. International level : i) Advocacy and mobilization of partnerships for education of the rural people concentrating on strategic global, regional and international events, and encouraging the same within countries. ii) Identification of capacities for different substantive components on education for rural people within partners institutions. iii) Support for exchange of good practices and knowledge on education for rural people. Achievement to date: this Flagship Programme was launched in September 2002.

©VU/Bertrand Desprez

Chapter 6

Prospects and opportunities

The EFA goals are of fundamental significance for development. This Report has shown that progress over the past ten years has been mixed. There are many cases of countries moving steadily towards achieving the goals. But there are others in which retrogression has been occurring, bringing real threats to the sustainability of the development process. New responses are needed if the future is to be any different. Accordingly, this chapter identifies some opportunities for national and international policy change. It synthesizes the major themes of the Report, and comments on some of the key issues they raise.

Progress

This Report has shown that progress towards the six Dakar goals is insufficient: the world is not on track to achieve education for all by 2015. This judgement is based upon a number of strands of evidence. The first of these derives from measurable trends in indicators. It will be recalled that three of the goals – universal primary education (UPE), gender equality and literacy – can presently be monitored quantitatively. Only 83 countries (accounting for just over one-third of the world's population) have already achieved the three goals or have a high chance of doing so by 2015 on the basis of recent trends. In 43 countries (with 37% of the world's population), at least one goal is likely to be missed, while a further 28 countries (with 28% of the world's population) are not on track to achieve any of them. Two-thirds of those in the latter category are in sub-Saharan Africa, but they also include India and Pakistan.

Progress towards the six Dakar goals is insufficient: the world is not on track to achieve education for all by 2015.

Of the three goals, literacy most frequently risks not being met: at present rates of progress, 79 countries will not be able to halve their rate of adult illiteracy by 2015. UPE is unlikely to be reached in 57 countries, 41 of which have recently even been moving in the wrong direction. The position is slightly better as regards the gender goals, with 86 countries having already achieved gender parity in primary enrolments, and a further 36 countries being close to doing so. With changes in policy – particularly selective demand-side financing – each of those countries has a reasonable chance of achieving gender parity by 2005. However, there are 31 countries, a majority of which are located in sub-Saharan Africa, which are at high risk of not achieving the goal by 2015. In those cases, even with sharp changes in policy, it is very unlikely that the 2005 goal will be reached.

The list of most vulnerable countries contains few surprises. For example, of the 28 at serious risk of not achieving any of the goals, 22 are also included in the World Bank's list of 47 'at risk' countries (World Bank, 2002*a*). However, there are some unexpected entries in the list of countries selected for the Fast-Track Initiative. For example, the 18 Fast-Track countries include only 6 – Burkina Faso, Ethiopia, Guinea, Mozambique, Niger and Zambia – of the 28 countries identified in Chapter 2 as being at serious risk of not achieving any of the three quantifiable goals. They also include 5 countries which are already on track towards achieving them (Albania, Bolivia, Guyana, Honduras and Viet Nam). Many of the excluded countries have lower incomes and school enrolments, and have less chance of achieving the goals than those in the Fast-Track group. It follows that a priority ranking based on need would not lead to the list of countries currently selected for Fast-Track treatment.

Planning

There is a range of evidence about the process of achieving the goals. National planning – one of the most critical aspects of this process – is under way, but not as universally as the World Education Forum in Dakar expected and required. Our information suggests that only 22 specially prepared EFA plans will be completed by the end of 2002. However, there are a good number of other countries where Poverty Reduction Strategy Paper (PRSP) processes have produced new documents of substance. In 15 of the 16 full PRSPs examined, education goals were explicitly incorporated in the analysis. Yet these documents usually fall well short of an integrated plan. Many governments, of course, have existing planning documents that already address at least some of the Dakar goals. Most of the 40 countries assessed for the purposes of this Monitoring Report had education plans or policy papers, half of which (18) specifically addressed some or all of the EFA goals. However, all but 4 of these were in place prior to the World Education Forum in Dakar. Thus, while many planning documents addressing the Goals are available, only a minority of them is a direct product of the Dakar Framework. Furthermore, some address only one or two goals (usually at least UPE) sometimes without setting a particular date for their achievement.

Planning at the national level is fundamentally important if adequate strategies of expansion and reform are to be designed. In many of the least developed countries (LDCs), which include those where the EFA agenda is at its most demanding, there is an urgent need for better data, and for expertise to be more consistently applied to planning tasks in government, and for the stronger engagement of civil society. The statistical base for many of the key planning parameters, such as enrolments, population, teachers and so on, is usually available. However, there are major priorities for producing better financial information, particularly on expenditures at subsectoral level and on private contributions. Also needed is serious exploration of the resource implications of alternative reform strategies in the light of existing and future financial and real resource constraints.

The national 'ownership' of planning documents and processes is fundamental to their effectiveness. While this is widely acknowledged internationally, it is clear that there has recently been a notable increase in international influence over such planning. The example of some PRSPs shows that external collaboration on planning initiatives can be made to work: at best, international engagement strengthens national planning processes. However, at worst, plans are prepared and shaped quickly, simply in response to the demands of funding agencies and their internal deadlines.

The latter phenomenon is not new, but it has, if anything, intensified. The external demands presently placed on governments to produce plans for different purposes are considerable. Although the Dakar requirement to produce EFA plans is being wisely interpreted in context-specific ways by most countries, the external demands for PRSPs, sector plans, comprehensive EFA plans and, in some cases, Fast-Track proposals, amount to a very demanding agenda. These potential overlaps and conflicts need to be resolved both generically and on a case-by-case basis.

Costs and resources

The costs of achieving EFA are large, but not beyond the means of most states. Most of the recent estimates have focused only upon the costs of achieving UPE. However, they have underestimated these costs because necessary policy measures to address the demand side – particularly in connection with gender issues – and to combat HIV/AIDS have been omitted or underemphasized. Further, the unusually high costs of responding to the educational needs of countries in situations of emergency have not been integrated in the macro balances.

For the same reasons, likely aid requirements have also been underestimated. Additionally, however, the revenue assumptions made by the most rigorous, and influential, of the recent studies (World Bank, 2002*a*) appear to be relatively optimistic as regards both growth prospects and reasonable expectations concerning the speed of reform. Both of these tendencies lead to the underestimation of the likely financing gaps in countries facing the most severe UPE challenges.

In rough terms, and after taking account of the above omissions, this Report estimates the financing gap at up to $5.6 billion, in comparison with the World Bank's figure of $2.5 billion. Our figure requires further analysis at the national level, in order to become firmer. Simulations for all countries are needed, using nationally-verified data in order to build up the macro estimates. In principle, the approach used by the Bank could be extended relatively easily for these purposes. In all such work, single-figure estimates for aid requirements are best avoided; a range of figures is required. If the impact of changing the assumptions – for marginal costs, policy reforms, economic growth and public resources available for education – is made plain, the sensitivity of projected outcomes to particular assumptions and policies can be better assessed.

The costs of achieving EFA are large, but not beyond the means of most countries.

This Report estimates the financing gap at up to $5.6 billion.

This Report has documented a startling decline in aid over the years 1990–2001, particularly in sub-Saharan Africa.

International cooperation

This Report has documented a startling decline in the real values of both total and education aid over the years 1990–2001, which was particularly heavily felt in sub-Saharan Africa. This, moreover, occurred over a period when aid agencies were promising much greater flows. A recent assessment of the reasons for slow-down in World Bank support to sub-Saharan Africa suggested that political turmoil in some of the larger countries, the weak absorptive capacity of key institutions throughout the region, and the reluctance of some governments to introduce (education) policy reforms were each partly to blame (World Bank, 2000*a*, p. 56).

The Bank paper also suggests that the decline in lending to Africa may have been influenced by the shift in lending priorities that occurred during the 1990s. In particular, the Bank itself may have focused 'staff resources too narrowly on basic education, at the expense of other subsectors and portfolio diversity' (*loc.cit.*). It is presumably implied that the primary sector needs more preparatory work, or is less able to absorb funds rapidly, than programmes focused upon higher levels of the education system.

Existing aid pledges are substantial, but they do not yet appear to be nearly sufficient to match the size of the gaps.

These questions assume particular significance in the context of the pledges to support primary and basic education which are currently required. As indicated above, requirements for aid financing of UPE alone may turn out to be as much as $5.6 billion per year. Chapter 5 showed that this would require aid flows in support of UPE to increase to four or five times the levels of the recent past, particularly towards sub-Saharan-Africa. Increased aid expenditure on basic education of this magnitude within the region would clearly be possible only by using modalities that were sharply changed from those used in the past.

There are indications that the climate for policy reform is better than during the 1990s, with governments being more willing to initiate a policy dialogue with agencies than was earlier the case. The increasing prominence of PRSPs as an aid instrument in the most indebted countries, and the introduction of the Fast-Track Initiative as a means of accelerating support to primary schooling, are both symptoms of that. In addition, new lending instruments in support of sector-wide strategies are being introduced by a number of agencies. As regards the World Bank, adjustable programme loans have been introduced. These are designed to support long-term sector-wide education development, with future loan tranches being activated by pre-determined policy triggers (and thus not needing the amount of preparation and negotiation required for new loans, nor, indeed, presentation to the Bank's Board). Equally, expanded debt relief under the debt initiative for the Heavily Indebted Poor Countries (HIPC) may provide additional support for basic education, although there are questions about the extent to which such resources are genuinely additional in some countries.

In these and other ways, the instruments used for securing rapid transfers of funds to support plans that are feasible, technically sound, and addressing the EFA goals in priority countries are being refined. However, there are challenges that must be addressed if the volume of resource transfers for EFA are to be transformed in the ways required.

First, although existing pledges of aid are substantial, their precise implications for additional funding of education remain unclear. Nevertheless, they do not yet appear to be nearly sufficient to match the size of the gaps suggested by Chapter 4. On the basis of the pledges summarized in Chapter 5, approximately $2.6 billion may be made available for basic education from European Union, the World Bank, Japan and other non-EU bilaterals, and from HIPC funds. This leaves a possible unfunded gap of $3 billion – rather more than double recent estimated aid to basic education. Even allowing for some shift in the composition of aid expenditures towards EFA goals (which is needed since in 2000 it accounted for only one-third of total aid to education), the overall increase in the amount of aid needed looks to be substantially greater than the amounts presently contemplated by the aid agencies. And there needs to be a much greater concentration of this aid in a relatively small number of countries.

Second, the expansion of the Fast-Track Initiative may be a very useful instrument to achieve such a change in focus. However, if so, the Initiative would need genuinely to gain the participation, and funding, of a broad cross-section of agencies, so as to allow its product, style and procedures not to be dominated by one participant in the programme. Furthermore, the criteria for inclusion would need to be broadened considerably if all countries at serious risk of not achieving EFA were to be included. The additional challenge will be to include countries in ways which secure country-ownership of the plans and programmes that are agreed by the countries themselves.

Increasingly, agencies are providing budget support to countries with well-designed poverty-reduction strategies and, in education, with credible plans. Under this mechanism, resources are provided in programme form, as direct support to public expenditures. Accounting procedures must be transparent, with acceptable financial control over the budget. Similar conditions apply to Fast-Track countries. The problem with this approach is that it tends to reward those countries with a stable political history and a developed policy tradition (or countries that are clearly making the transition to such status). Countries excluded from consideration because the criteria are not satisfied have demonstrable incentives to shift domestic governance in that direction. This inevitably means that a group of countries needing strong support are not, for other reasons, eligible to receive it.

This situation is not consistent with achieving the Dakar goals. In fact it needs to be reversed: instead of the countries with the weakest policy environments receiving least attention from the international community, they must receive most attention. The bigger the nature of the planning and implementation problems they manifest, the more assistance they should receive. Of course, the nature of this assistance would be different for each of the two groups. The countries with weak policy frameworks, planning capacity and implementation record would need to have more interaction with the agencies providing funds, and the conditions for their disbursement would be different.

This situation thus implies the need for a differentiated approach. The high risk, otherwise excluded countries, might be eligible for an 'Education Task Force', in which policy makers and stakeholders from the country and all resident agencies supporting education would participate. The brief of such a Task Force would be: i) to jointly prepare and agree a plan for EFA; ii) to design and approve its implementation mechanisms; iii) to cooperate closely in its implementation; and iv) to monitor and evaluate its progress and outcomes.

Task Forces would ideally be part of the EFA Forums, except that the international agencies providing resources would be invited to be full members. The roles and responsibilities of all participants would also be more tightly defined and action-oriented. Where EFA Forums did not exist, or where there was no significant agency presence in the country concerned, one of the multilateral agencies would stand ready to provide leadership in identifying other bilateral partners. Obviously a country would be free to accept or refuse the offer of a Task Force, but acceptance would be a condition for the receipt of enhanced levels of support under the initiative.

The most critical ingredient in national EFA plans, designed either as part of the Fast-Track Initiative, or in the context of broader agency support, is the extent to which governments genuinely embrace a process of national reform. This obviously goes far beyond, and raises much more difficult issues, than the decisions about what assumptions to incorporate in cost and revenue projections. The danger is that national governments may agree to reform proposals in financing documents that are acceptable to the agencies, even if the technical or the political capacity to implement them is absent. Typical reforms – for example, relative decline in teachers' salaries, increases in class-size, introduction of double-shift teaching, etc. – may be underpinned by a very strong logical case, yet may prove impossible to implement because of the power of particular interest groups. It will be critically important to take the planning process well beyond the level of a costing exercise, if the size of past gaps between plans and implementation patterns are not to recur.

The most critical ingredient in national EFA plans is the extent to which governments embrace a national reform process.

The quality of available data covering public spending on education has deteriorated in recent years.

Improving the availability and quality of data

The process of preparing this Report has highlighted the limitations of available data, both in terms of coverage and reliability. This is clear at two levels. First there are data which are critically important for the purposes of planning – such as data on unit costs – for which there are simply no reliable estimates available at the international level. It was shown in Chapter 4 that the cost estimates for achieving UPE in 2015 differed, on average, by a factor of 3 for each of the 45 individual countries included in three recent studies. Although the assumptions made by the studies about the value of future cost parameters were mainly the cause of such differences, an additional important source was the unit cost information available to each of the authors. Good public expenditure information that can be matched to particular levels of education is a *sine qua non* for financial projections. In principle, such information is not difficult to obtain, since all governments need it for their own internal accounting and auditing purposes. Significant efforts to improve and increase the coverage of internationally gathered information on public spending on education are needed. The evidence suggests that, if anything, the quality of available data covering these variables has deteriorated in recent years.

There is an urgent need to improve the quality and availability of a wide range of international data.

Second, there is an urgent need to improve the quality and availability of a wide range of international data. For example, regional averages have not been possible to estimate in many of the Annex tables, owing to there being too few observations in some regions. Furthermore, this Report has not been able to produce time-trends for a wide variety of basic statistics on national education systems. This is partly because of revisions to classification systems in education statistics, as the Technical Introduction to the Statistical Annex makes clear. However, it is partly because data collection methods changed between the mid- and late-1990s, making time-trends for a large number of variables difficult. By consequence, the coverage of the data presented in this Report is less useful for analytic purposes than it needs to be. In principle, an exercise to achieve comparability between contemporary data sets and those gathered in the early 1990s would be extremely valuable.

Third, the information available to monitor aid flows to education remains open to considerable improvement in quality and coverage. The main database held by the OECD DAC is provided by the agencies themselves. Coverage and reporting improved substantially during the last decade. However, even by 2000, almost one fifth of reported commitments were not shown by subsector. The information available on disbursements is partial, and covered only 70% of education aid by 2000. These problems mean that trends in aid to education can be analysed in only a partial fashion. The limitations often reflect the nature of agencies' own information systems. If donor commitments and disbursements in support of EFA goals are to be effectively monitored, more efforts in reporting complete and consistent information are urgently required.

EFA and the Millennium Development Goals

As argued in Chapter 1, EFA is important to the development of all facets of human well-being, whether these are conceived in terms of human rights, human capabilities or development opportunities. The Millenium Development Goals refer to only two of the EFA goals. This does not mean, however, that the other elements of EFA are unimportant in the collective endeavour to eliminate extreme poverty. UPE and the elimination of gender disparities are major priorities, but a broader EFA case can be made for the contribution of basic education to sustainable livelihoods, the reduction of child mortality, improvements in maternal health, the fight against HIV/AIDS, malaria and other diseases, and a sustainable environment. The MDG framework then, should be interpreted as an opportunity, and not as a narrowing of the agenda. In this context the development of the

FTI affords a chance to promote the broader objectives of EFA and to argue their case, rather than interpreting the specificity of the MDG targets as a constraint.

Future monitoring challenges

This Report has sought to initiate a sense of international accountability towards commitments that were made at the World Education Forum and thereafter. It will be important in future years to map – more clearly than has been possible here – the extent to which a significant shift in policy and practice in support of EFA by the leading development agencies occurs. Close cooperation with OECD-DAC will be important in this regard.

Changes in national policies and planning, and the extent of progress with policy reforms will continue to be central features of future reports. However, since the World Conference on Education for All (Jomtien, 1990) there has been some ambiguity as to whether EFA underpins a global EFA movement or whether it is primarily a vehicle for focusing on developing countries, where the challenge of enabling the poorest and most severely disadvantaged people to benefit from a basic education is the priority. The balance has been more towards the latter than the former position, and has been accentuated by the very strong international focus on UPE. This Report also reflects that balance (except in its coverage of educational statistics in the annexes), as does the reporting against the MDGs.

Nevertheless, many of the challenges of EFA extend well beyond developing countries.
The educational needs of those living in relative poverty in industrialized societies, questions of quality and relevance, of gender equality, of literacies responsive to the revolution in communications technology, and the challenge for education provided by the risks of drugs dependency are just some of the major issues deserving a wider, global treatment.
If EFA is treated as an issue specific to particular countries and regions of the world, it runs the danger of becoming partial, and perhaps more marginal, rather than a central educational priority worldwide. The EFA Global Monitoring Report will begin to redress this imbalance from 2003.

The challenges of EFA are not limited to the developing countries.

Annex

Technical introduction

The data on pupils, students, teachers and education expenditure presented in these annex tables are based on survey results reported to the UNESCO Institute for Statistics (UIS) for the school year 1999/2000. This school year includes countries with a calendar school year of 1999, and those with a school year stretching from 1999 into 2000. These education statistics refer to all formal schools in the country, including both public and private institutions, by levels of education. They are supplemented by demographic and economic statistics collected or produced by other international organizations, including the United Nations Population Division and the World Bank.

The majority of Member States report their data to UIS using standard questionnaires issued by the Institute. However, for some countries, education data are collected via surveys carried out under the auspices of the World Education Indicators project (WEI) funded by the World Bank, or are provided by the Organisation for Economic Cooperation and Development (OECD) countries) or Eurostat (East European countries that are part of the Trakai group). As an aid to the reader, symbols have been used in the tables to distinguish countries in these two categories from the other Member States: *o* for OECD countries; *w* for World Education Indicators Project (WEI) countries.

The indicators on access and participation presented here have been calculated using the population estimates produced by the United Nations Population Division. The results may differ from those published by individual countries or by other organizations such as OECD, or in the framework of projects like the WEI project, because of the difference between national population estimates and those of the United Nations. In this annex, the 1990 population-sensitive indicators, such as gross and net enrolment ratios, and gross and net intake ratio calculations were based on the 1998 United Nations Population Division revision, whereas the 1999 population figures were based on the 2000 United Nations revision. This means that indicators utilizing population data for 1990, and those using 1999, may not be comparable.

Differences in population revision reference dates may not be the only factor hindering the comparison of population-related indicators in 1990/91 and 1999/2000. In 1997 the International Standard Classification of Education (ISCED) was revised. At each of its annual regional workshops, UIS has worked with national statisticians to map their education system against the ISCED standard. The classification of programmes has come closer to the ISCED standard each year. The tables presented here use the classification agreed with national experts for the years 1998 and 1999. Please note that this was not the case with the 1990/91 data.

It should be noted that both actual and estimated data are presented throughout the annex tables. For some countries, 1998/99 data are presented when information for the 1999/00 school year was not available. In that case, a footnote has been inserted, and the data are in italics.

Footnotes to the tables, and the glossary which can be found at the end of the tables, will provide additional guides to help the reader interpret the data and information presented herein.

Symbols used in the tables

- * National estimate
- ** UNESCO Institute for Statistics (UIS) estimate
- ... Missing data
- o OECD countries
- w World Education Indicators (WEI) project countries
- – Magnitude nil, or no calculation

Composition of regions

World classification

- *Countries in transition*: Central Asia (minus Mongolia) and Central and Eastern Europe (minus Turkey).
- *Developed countries*: the North America and Western Europe region as well as Australia, Japan and New Zealand.
- *Developing countries*: Arab States and North Africa; East Asia and the Pacific (minus Australia, Japan and New Zealand); Latin America and the Caribbean; South and West Asia and Sub-Saharan Africa.

EFA regions

- Arab States and North Africa
  (20 countries/territories)
  Algeria, Bahrain, Djibouti, Egypt, Iraq, Jordan, Kuwait, Lebanon, Libyan Arab Jamahiriya, Mauritania, Morocco, Oman, Palestinian Autonomous Territories, Qatar, Saudi Arabia, Sudan, Syrian Arab Republic, Tunisia, United Arab Emirates, Yemen

- Central Asia *(9 countries)*
  Armenia, Azerbaijan, Georgia, Kazakhstan, Kyrgyzstan, Mongolia, Tajikistan, Turkmenistan, Uzbekistan

- Central and Eastern Europe *(20 countries)*
  Albania, Belarus, Bosnia and Herzegovina, Bulgaria, Czech Republic, Croatia, Estonia, Hungary, Latvia, Lithuania, Poland, Romania, Republic of Moldova, Russian Federation, Slovakia, Slovenia, The former Yugoslav Republic of Macedonia, Turkey, Ukraine, Yugoslavia

- East Asia and Pacific *(26 countries/territories)*
  Australia, Cambodia, China, Cook Islands, Democratic People's Republic of Korea, Fiji, Indonesia, Japan, Kiribati, Lao People's Democratic Republic, Malaysia, Marshall Islands, Myanmar, Nauru, Niue, New Zealand, Papua New Guinea, Philippines, Republic of Korea, Samoa, Solomon Islands, Thailand, Tonga, Tuvalu, Vanuatu, Viet Nam

- Latin America and The Caribbean
  (41countries/territories)
  Anguilla, Antigua and Barbuda, Aruba, Argentina, Bahamas, Barbados, Belize, Bermuda, Bolivia, British Virgin Islands, Brazil, Cayman Islands, Chile, Colombia, Costa Rica, Cuba, Dominica, Dominican Republic, Ecuador, El Salvador, Grenada, Guatemala, Guyana, Haiti, Honduras, Jamaica, Mexico, Montserrat, Netherlands Antilles, Nicaragua, Panama, Paraguay, Peru, Saint Kitts and Nevis, Saint Lucia, Saint Vincent and the Grenadines, Suriname, Trinidad and Tobago, Turks and Caicos Islands, Uruguay, Venezuela

- North America and Western Europe
  (26 countries)
  Andorra, Austria, Belgium, Canada, Cyprus, Denmark, Spain, Finland, France, Germany, Greece, Iceland, Ireland, Israel, Italy, Luxemburg, Malta, Monaco, Netherlands, Norway, Portugal, San Marino, Sweden, Switzerland, United Kingdom, United States

- South and West Asia *(9 countries)*
  Afghanistan, Bangladesh, Bhutan, India, Islamic Republic of Iran, Maldives, Nepal, Pakistan, Sri Lanka

- Sub-Saharan Africa *(45 countries)*
  Angola, Benin, Botswana, Burkina Faso, Burundi, Cameroon, Cape Verde, Central African Republic, Chad, Côte d'Ivoire, Comoros, Congo, Democratic Republic of the Congo, Equatorial Guinea, Eritrea, Ethiopia, Gabon, Gambia, Ghana, Guinea, Guinea-Bissau, Kenya, Lesotho, Liberia, Madagascar, Malawi, Mali, Mauritius, Mozambique, Namibia, Niger, Nigeria, Senegal, Sierra Leone, Togo, Uganda, Rwanda, Sao Tome and Principe, Seychelles, Somalia, South Africa, Swaziland, United Republic of Tanzania, Zambia, Zimbabwe

Table 1
Background statistics

Country or territory	POPULATION[1] Total (thousands)	Average annual growth rate (%)	Life expectancy at birth (M + F) (years)
	1999	1990–99	1999
Arab States and North Africa			
Algeria	29 755	2.0	71
Bahrain	627	2.8	73
Djibouti	617	2.3	47
Egypt[w]	66 693	1.9	67
Iraq	22 335	2.9	59
Jordan[w]	4 785	4.4	71
Kuwait	1 848	–1.6	77
Lebanon	3 438	2.7	70
Libyan Arab Jamahiriya	5 175	2.1	71
Mauritania	2 582	2.9	54
Morocco	29 334	2.0	67
Oman	2 457	3.6	73
Palestinian Autonomous Territories	3 074	...	...
Qatar	555	2.3	75
Saudi Arabia	19 644	2.7	72
Sudan	30 423	2.3	56
Syrian Arab Republic	15 778	2.7	69
Tunisia[w]	9 360	1.5	73
United Arab Emirates	2 558	2.7	75
Yemen	17 620	4.8	56
Central and Eastern Europe			
Albania	3 131	–0.5	72
Belarus	10 225	...	68
Bosnia and Herzegovina	3 846	–1.3	73
Bulgaria	8 039	–0.9	71
Croatia	4 653	0.3	73
Czech Republic[o]	10 285	...	75
Estonia	1 411	–1.2	71
Hungary[o]	10 020	–0.4	71
Latvia	2 435	–1.0	70
Lithuania	3 701	–0.1	72
Poland[o]	38 627	0.1	73
Republic of Moldova	4 305	...	67
Romania	22 479	–0.4	69
Russian Federation[w]	146 211	–0.2	66
Slovakia	5 394	0.3	...
Slovenia	1 991	0.4	75
The former Yugoslav Rep. of Macedonia	2 022	...	...
Turkey[o]	65 674	1.8	69
Ukraine	50 022	–0.4	67
Yugoslavia	10 567	...	...
Central Asia			
Armenia	3 788	0.7	74
Azerbaijan	7 982	1.2	72
Georgia	5 282	–0.4	73
Kazakhstan	16 258	...	...
Kyrgyzstan	4 848	1.1	...
Mongolia	2 509	1.4	67
Tajikistan	6 030	1.4	69
Turkmenistan	4 636	2.6	66
Uzbekistan	24 487	2.0	70
East Asia and the Pacific			
Australia[o]	18 933	1.3	79
Cambodia	12 766	3.2	54
China[w]	1 264 771	1.0	70

1. United Nations Population Division statistics.
2. World Bank statistics.

GNP[2]			AID AND POVERTY[2]		EXTERNAL DEBT[2]			
	GNP per capita							
Average annual growth rate (%)	US$ (current)	Purchasing parity power	Net aid per capita, current US$	Population below $1 per day (%)	Total debt service, current US$ (millions)	Total debt as % GNP	Public debt service as % of government current revenue	Total debt service as % exports
1990–99	1999	1999	1999	1999	1999	1999	1999	1999
3.1	1 540	4 880	3	<2	5 196	11.5	33.3	36.9
...	9 370	14 410	6	...	...	...	...	...
...	850	...	121	...	10	1.8	...	4.1
6.0	...	...	...	...	...	...	...	...
...	...	...	3	...	...	...	...	...
6.8	1 630	3 840	91	<2	526	6.6	20.5	9.6
...	16 870	18 530	4	...	...	...	...	...
...	3 910	4 510	45	...	770	4.4	12.8	...
...	...	...	...	...	...	...	...	...
5.5	390	1 570	85	28.6	106	11.4	...	28.4
3.8	1 200	3 400	24	<2	3 049	8.9	27.9	23.9
...	...	...	17	...	976	...	12.5	12.7
...	...	...	...	...	...	...	...	...
...	...	...	9	...	...	...	...	...
3.7	6 900	10 930	1	...	...	...	...	...
...	310	1 400	8	...	57	0.6	1.5	6.7
7.6	920	3 270	14	...	370	2.4	...	6.4
6.4	2 090	5 730	27	<2	1 534	7.6	22.5	15.9
...	...	...	1	...	...	...	...	...
4.6	...	...	...	...	...	...	...	...
2.2	930	3 300	144	...	23	0.6	...	2.3
-0.6	2 630	6 950	4	<2	202	0.8	3.7	3.1
...	1 200	...	278	...	191	4.0	...	...
-1.3	1 390	5 110	33	<2	1 152	9.4	14.4	19.0
-0.4	4 580	7 510	11	<2	1 893	9.6	9.8	21.5
1.1	5 130	13 080	32	<2	5 823	10.8	21.6	16.7
-0.8	3 490	8 470	60	<2	526	10.5	3.8	12.9
1.9	4 620	11 090	25	<2	7 480	16.1	17.4	26.4
-4.4	2 520	6 380	41	<2	372	5.6	2.0	12.1
-3.1	2 640	6 570	36	<2	662	6.4	5.9	15.2
5.2	4 010	8 460	31	<2	8 374	5.4	4.3	20.4
-9.8	410	2 130	25	11.3	211	17.5	34.0	28.7
-0.9	1 560	6 110	17	2.8	3 680	10.6	16.8	36.7
-4.2	1 750	7 190	13	7.1	12 000	6.6	10.7	14.1
1.9	...	...	...	...	...	...	...	...
3.1	9 980	16 200	16	<2	...	...	...	...
0.7	...	...	...	...	...	...	...	...
4.7	2 900	6 500	...	2.4	18 560	9.9	17.9	35.3
-8.1	760	3 390	11	2.9	2 805	9.1	17.2	16.4
...	...	...	...	...	...	...	...	...
-3.4	490	2 380	55	7.8	58	3.1	...	11.9
-6.8	570	2 430	21	<2	85	1.9	6.2	6.5
...	690	2 570	49	<2	109	3.7	24.0	11.5
-4.1	...	...	...	...	...	...	...	...
-3.5	...	...	...	...	...	...	...	...
1.4	390	1 710	93	13.9	26	2.9	10.9	4.8
...	170	980	20	...	69	6.7	10.5	10.2
-3.4	640	3 220	5	12.1	...	...	...	...
0.6	410	2 250	6	3.3	548	6.4	...	17.5
5.5	21 020	24 220	...	...	...	...	...	...
6.5	260	1 370	24	18.8	33	1.1	...	2.9
12.1	780	3 580	2	...	20 655	2.1	22.0	9.0

Table 1 (continued)

Country or territory	POPULATION[1] Total (thousands) 1999	Average annual growth rate (%) 1990–99	Life expectancy at birth (M + F) (years) 1999
Cook Islands	...	...	...
Democratic People's Rep. of Korea	22 110	...	...
Fiji	805	1.2	73
Indonesia[w]	209 287	1.5	66
Japan[o]	126 821	0.3	81
Kiribati	...	...	61
Lao People's Democratic Republic	5 156	...	...
Malaysia[w]	21 791	2.2	72
Marshall Islands	...	...	...
Myanmar	47 114	1.7	60
Nauru	...	...	...
New Zealand[o]	3 747	1.2	77
Niue	...	...	...
Papua New Guinea	4 701	2.5	58
Philippines[w]	74 184	2.2	69
Republic of Korea[o]	46 403	...	...
Samoa	158	−0.1	69
Solomon Islands	432	3.5	71
Thailand[w]	62 008	1.4	69
Tonga	...	...	71
Tuvalu	...	...	...
Vanuatu	192	...	...
Viet Nam	77 118	1.7	...
Latin America and the Caribbean			
Anguilla	...	...	...
Antigua and Barbuda	...	...	75
Argentina[w]	36 577	1.3	74
Aruba	...	...	...
Bahamas	300	1.8	73
Barbados	267	0.4	76
Belize	222	2.0	72
Bermuda	...	...	...
Bolivia	8 142	2.4	62
Brazil[w]	168 246	1.4	67
British Virgin Islands	...	...	...
Cayman Islands	...	...	...
Chile[w]	15 019	1.5	76
Colombia	41 400	1.9	70
Costa Rica	3 933	2.9	77
Cuba	11 158	0.5	76
Dominica	...	...	76
Dominican Republic	8 237	1.7	71
Ecuador	12 411	2.1	69
El Salvador	6 156	2.1	70
Grenada	...	...	72
Guatemala	11 090	2.7	65
Guyana	757	0.4	64
Haiti	8 016	1.7	53
Honduras	6 258	2.8	70
Jamaica[w]	2 555	0.8	75
Mexico[o]	97 356	1.8	72
Montserrat	...	...	...
Netherlands Antilles	213	1.4	76
Nicaragua	4 938	2.9	69
Panama	2 812	1.8	74
Paraguay[w]	5 358	2.7	70
Peru[w]	25 230	1.8	69
Saint Kitts and Nevis	...	...	71

1. United Nations Population Division statistics.
2. World Bank statistics.

GNP[2]			AID AND POVERTY[2]		EXTERNAL DEBT[2]			
	GNP per capita							
Average annual growth rate (%)	US$ (current)	Purchasing parity power	Net aid per capita, current US$	Population below $1 per day (%)	Total debt service, current US$ (millions)	Total debt as % GNP	Public debt service as % of government current revenue	Total debt service as % exports
1990–99	1999	1999	1999	1999	1999	1999	1999	1999
...	...	...	...	...	...	...	...	...
...	...	...	...	...	...	...	...	...
3.8	2 190	4 820	44	7.7	39	2.4	...	3.5
5.7	580	2 690	11	...	17 903	13.6	36.6	30.4
2.8	33 350	25 900	...	...	...	...	...	...
...	1 000	...	236	...	...	...	...	...
8.0	...	...	...	...	...	...	...	...
8.5	3 450	7 710	6	...	4 408	5.9	...	4.5
...	...	...	...	...	...	...	...	...
...	...	...	2	...	97	...	0.5	6.0
...	...	...	...	...	...	...	...	...
4.3	14 000	17 760	...	...	...	...	...	...
...	...	...	...	...	...	...	...	...
6.6	770	2 180	43	...	212	6.2	23.6	9.7
4.3	1 060	4 040	9	...	6 424	8.0	39.1	13.6
7.4	...	...	...	...	...	...	...	...
3.1	1 420	4 640	136	...	7	2.7	...	5.1
4.9	770	2 010	92	<2	11	3.3	...	4.8
6.0	2 000	5 970	17	...	16 210	13.7	20.9	21.8
...	1 680	...	213	...	4	2.8	...	10.9
...	...	...	...	...	...	...	...	...
2.7	...	...	...	...	...	...	...	...
9.3	...	...	...	...	...	...	...	...
...	...	...	...	...	...	...	...	...
4.9	8 710	9 510	159	...	...	...	...	...
6.8	7 550	11 990	3	...	25 681	9.3	30.5	75.8
...	...	...	–75	...	...	...	...	...
3.2	...	...	...	...	...	...	...	...
2.9	8 620	14 150	–8	...	...	...	...	...
5.6	2 850	4 810	200	...	44	6.4	...	11.0
...	...	...	...	...	...	...	...	...
5.6	980	2 310	70	14.4	444	5.5	17.3	28.8
4.1	3 870	6 910	1	11.6	68 067	13.3	...	112.8
...	...	...	...	...	...	...	...	...
...	...	...	...	...	...	...	...	...
8.3	4 600	8 550	5	<2	4 928	7.5	5.1	24.0
4.3	2 150	6 110	7	19.7	6 620	8.0	44.8	41.5
7.0	3 570	7 840	–2	12.6	549	4.0	15.1	6.5
...	...	...	5	...	...	...	...	...
3.4	...	...	...	...	10	4.4	...	6.6
7.4	1 950	5 270	24	3.2	378	2.3	11.7	3.9
3.3	1 330	2 840	12	20.2	1 701	9.9	...	26.2
6.5	1 910	4 320	30	21.0	341	2.8	13.6	7.3
4.6	3 490	6 460	106	...	14	3.9	...	6.0
5.8	1 680	3 660	26	10.0	416	2.3	...	10.3
7.2	860	3 640	105	...	103	16.6	...	...
0.2	490	1 450	34	...	50	1.2	9.2	8.8
4.6	780	2 290	131	24.3	496	9.4	...	18.5
1.8	2 600	3 390	–8	3.2	596	8.7	21.4	13.8
4.7	4 440	8 160	...	15.9	39 760	8.5	24.2	25.1
...	...	...	...	...	...	...	...	...
...	...	...	596	...	...	...	...	...
4.7	390	2 000	137	...	186	9.5	20.1	16.0
6.3	3 060	5 500	5	14.0	741	8.4	23.2	8.6
3.7	1 590	4 470	15	19.5	230	3.0	...	6.3
5.8	2 110	4 490	18	15.5	4 184	8.4	23.5	46.4
5.6	6 330	10 470	114	...	17	6.5	...	11.5

Table 1 (continued)

Country or territory	POPULATION[1] Total (thousands) 1999	Average annual growth rate (%) 1990–99	Life expectancy at birth (M + F) (years) 1999
Saint Lucia	146	...	72
Saint Vincent and the Grenadines	...	...	73
Suriname	415	0.4	70
Trinidad and Tobago	1 289	0.7	73
Turks and Caicos Islands	...	...	...
Uruguay[w]	3 313	0.7	74
Venezuela	23 706	2.2	...
North America and Western Europe			
Andorra	...	...	...
Austria[o]	8 085	0.5	78
Belgium[o]	10 232	0.3	78
Canada[o]	30 492	1.1	79
Cyprus	777	1.5	78
Denmark[o]	5 305	0.4	76
Finland[o]	5 164	0.4	77
France[o]	59 026	0.4	79
Germany[o]	82 026	0.4	77
Greece[o]	10 591	0.5	78
Iceland[o]	277	0.9	79
Ireland[o]	3 763	0.8	76
Israel[o]	5 910	3.0	78
Italy[o]	57 531	0.2	78
Luxembourg[o]	431	1.4	77
Malta	388	0.8	77
Monaco	...	...	...
Netherlands[o]	15 793	0.6	78
Norway[o]	4 449	0.5	78
Portugal[o]	9 996	0.1	75
San Marino	...	...	...
Spain[o]	39 892	0.2	78
Sweden[o]	8 850	0.4	79
Switzerland[o]	7 170	0.5	80
United Kingdom[o]	59 276	0.3	77
United States[o]	280 434	...	77
South and West Asia			
Afghanistan	21 202	5.0	46
Bangladesh	134 584	2.3	61
Bhutan	2 029	2.0	62
India[w]	992 686	1.8	63
Iran, Islamic Republic of	69 244	...	...
Maldives	282	3.0	68
Nepal	22 501	2.4	58
Pakistan	137 556	2.5	63
Sri Lanka[w]	18 747	1.1	73
Sub-Saharan Africa			
Angola	12 759	3.2	47
Benin	6 108	3.1	53
Botswana	1 524	2.3	39
Burkina Faso	11 246	2.5	45
Burundi	6 255	1.2	42
Cameroon	14 553	2.5	51
Cape Verde	417	2.3	69
Central African Republic	3 649	2.4	44
Chad	7 641	3.1	49
Comoros	685	3.0	61
Congo	2 930	3.1	...
Côte d'Ivoire	15 685	2.5	...

1. United Nations Population Division statistics.
2. World Bank statistics.

GNP[2]			AID AND POVERTY[2]		EXTERNAL DEBT[2]			
	GNP per capita							
Average annual growth rate (%)	US$ (current)	Purchasing parity power	Net aid per capita, current US$	Population below $1 per day (%)	Total debt service, current US$ (millions)	Total debt as % GNP	Public debt service as % of government current revenue	Total debt service as % exports
1990–99	1999	1999	1999	1999	1999	1999	1999	1999
4.4	3 860	5 250	167	…	19	3.1	…	5.0
4.9	2 640	5 020	143	…	15	4.7	12.4	8.1
4.9	1 950	3 690	87	…	…	…	…	…
4.4	4 670	7 710	20	12.4	454	7.2	…	13.1
…	…	…	…	…	…	…	…	…
5.1	6 230	8 860	7	<2	1 065	5.2	15.5	24.8
3.3	…	…	…	…	…	…	…	…
…	…	…	…	…	…	…	…	…
3.6	25 720	25 050	…	…	…	…	…	…
3.3	24 620	25 870	…	…	…	…	…	…
4.1	20 140	25 630	…	…	…	…	…	…
5.6	12 240	19 460	71	…	…	…	…	…
3.8	32 620	25 950	…	…	…	…	…	…
3.4	24 750	22 770	…	…	…	…	…	…
3.2	24 570	23 260	…	…	…	…	…	…
…	25 680	23 680	…	…	…	…	…	…
3.9	12 110	15 840	…	…	…	…	…	…
4.2	29 010	27 070	…	…	…	…	…	…
8.3	21 450	22 620	…	…	…	…	…	…
6.7	16 310	18 200	148	…	…	…	…	…
2.9	20 330	22 310	…	…	…	…	…	…
7.2	40 490	41 560	…	…	…	…	…	…
…	9 270	15 520	65	…	…	…	…	…
…	…	…	…	…	…	…	…	…
4.3	25 140	24 590	…	…	…	…	…	…
5.0	33 630	28 520	…	…	…	…	…	…
4.1	11 100	16 110	…	<2	…	…	…	…
…	…	…	…	…	…	…	…	…
3.9	14 920	18 110	…	…	…	…	…	…
3.0	27 400	22 660	…	…	…	…	…	…
2.1	38 440	29 060	…	…	…	…	…	…
3.7	23 640	22 420	…	…	…	…	…	…
4.7	32 370	32 370	…	…	…	…	…	…
…	…	…	…	…	…	…	…	…
6.3	350	1 500	…	…	718	1.6	14.5	9.2
7.9	570	1 360	…	…	7	1.6	8.1	5.1
7.2	440	2 240	…	…	10 108	2.3	15.1	15.3
5.6	…	…	…	…	…	…	…	…
…	1 950	4 060	…	…	18	3.3	9.5	4.0
6.4	230	1 290	…	…	107	2.1	19.4	7.9
5.6	450	1 790	…	…	2 935	5.2	18.0	29.4
6.8	820	3 250	…	…	674	4.4	19.5	9.9
1.6	240	1 890	30	…	1 000	36.2	…	18.7
6.3	370	660	35	…	70	3.0	…	10.0
6.1	3 040	1 010	38	…	82	1.8	…	2.4
6.0	230	2 470	36	…	61	2.5	…	15.5
-0.3	120	…	11	…	29	4.1	15.7	45.6
2.6	600	790	30	…	549	6.3	24.6	24.3
7.3	1 330	590	319	…	20	3.5	…	10.0
3.1	280	750	32	…	19	1.8	…	18.4
4.1	210	9 090	25	…	32	2.1	…	11.0
1.0	400	790	39	…	3	1.4	…	5.7
1.3	…	6 170	…	…	…	…	…	…
…	…	750	…	…	…	…	…	…

Table 1 (continued)

Country or territory	POPULATION[1] Total (thousands) 1999	Average annual growth rate (%) 1990–99	Life expectancy at birth (M + F) (years) 1999
Democratic Rep. of the Congo	49 581	...	...
Equatorial Guinea	444	2.6	51
Eritrea	3 524	1.4	50
Ethiopia	61 388	2.9	42
Gabon	1 199	2.8	53
Gambia	1 267	3.5	53
Ghana	18 893	2.5	58
Guinea	8 021	3.0	46
Guinea-Bissau	1 173	2.4	44
Kenya	30 029	2.7	48
Lesotho	2 008	2.0	45
Liberia	2 709	2.6	47
Madagascar	15 512	2.9	54
Malawi	11 030	1.8	39
Mali	11 039	2.6	43
Mauritius	1 152	1.0	71
Mozambique	17 936	3.1	43
Namibia	1 724	2.6	50
Niger	10 455	3.4	46
Nigeria	110 845	2.9	47
Rwanda	7 087	0.5	40
Sao Tome and Principe	...	...	65
Senegal	9 184	2.5	52
Seychelles	...	...	72
Sierra Leone	4 272	0.6	37
Somalia	8 418	1.8	48
South Africa	42 754	1.8	48
Swaziland	909	1.9	46
Togo	4 388	2.7	49
Uganda	22 611	3.1	42
United Republic of Tanzania	34 285	3.1	...
Zambia	10 187	2.7	38
Zimbabwe[w]	12 400	2.1	40
	sum	weighted average	
World	5 958 103	...	62
Countries in transition	49 714	...	...
Developed countries	70 799	...	...
Developing countries	549 827	...	...
Arab States and North Africa	268 660	...	65
Central and Eastern Europe	405 039	...	65
Central Asia	75 820	...	50
East Asia and the Pacific	1 998 497	...	65
Latin America and the Caribbean	505 521	...	66
North America and Western Europe	705 859	...	77
South and West Asia	1 398 831	...	60
Sub-Saharan Africa	599 877	...	39

1. United Nations Population Division statistics.
2. World Bank statistics.

	GNP[2]			AID AND POVERTY[2]		EXTERNAL DEBT[2]			
		GNP per capita							
	Average annual growth rate (%)	US$ (current)	Purchasing parity power	Net aid per capita, current US$	Population below $1 per day (%)	Total debt service, current US$ (millions)	Total debt as % GNP	Public debt service as % of government current revenue	Total debt service as % exports
	1990–99	1999	1999	1999	1999	1999	1999	1999	1999
	...	...	770	...	...	...	...	...	...
	...	920	880	45	...	5	1.1	...	0.4
	...	200	...	37	...	3	0.4	...	1.6
	5.2	100	1 410	10	...	155	2.4	...	16.4
	4.0	3 300	...	40	...	538	14.1	...	18.8
	4.8	...	440	...	...	...	...	...	...
	6.0	390	...	32	...	523	6.9	...	20.8
	5.6	490	8 830	33	...	128	3.8	26.5	15.6
	1.5	170	4 500	45	...	9	4.3	...	15.7
	3.5	360	1 430	11	...	704	6.8	...	25.9
	5.5	590	1 170	16	...	59	5.1	...	10.9
	...	...	...	31	...	3	...	...	...
	3.0	250	720	24	...	159	4.3	33.1	17.1
	5.2	190	2 670	44	...	69	3.9	...	12.7
	5.3	240	...	33	...	106	4.2	...	13.7
	6.6	3 580	...	36	...	262	6.2	17.5	9.8
	7.6	220	...	46	...	119	3.1	...	18.6
	5.3	2 070	...	103	...	...	...	...	...
	3.7	190	...	18	...	34	1.7	...	9.8
	4.1	250	...	1	...	1 052	3.4	...	6.8
	1.1	240	...	45	...	31	1.6	...	25.9
	...	270	...	190	...	4	10.2	...	29.1
	4.8	500	...	58	...	237	5.1	...	14.3
	...	7 020	...	163	...	26	4.3	8.4	5.4
	-3.9	130	...	15	...	22	3.4	16.0	29.5
	...	...	...	14	...	1	...	...	...
	3.0	3 160	...	13	...	4 290	3.4	2.8	12.2
	4.3	1 380	...	28	...	31	2.3	7.2	2.7
	3.1	320	...	16	...	45	3.2	...	8.9
	8.5	310	...	27	...	172	2.7	16.9	22.1
	4.5	...	...	...	...	...	...	...	...
	1.9	320	...	63	...	439	14.9	...	45.8
	4.1	490	...	20	...	648	12.6	...	27.3

		weighted average		median			median	median	median
	...	4 793	6 438	29.1	...	...	4.4	16.8	12.8
	...	...	...	...	...	...	...	...	...
	...	...	...	...	...	...	...	...	...
	...	...	...	...	...	...	...	...	...
	...	...	...	...	...	...	...	...	...
	...	2 179	6 439	...	...	...	9.3	12.6	16.7
	...	331	1 612	...	...	...	3.4	10.7	10.9
	...	...	...	...	...	...	...	...	...
	...	3 406	6 367	...	...	...	6.5	17.3	12.3
	...	26 485	26 527	...	...	...	...	...	...
	...	406	1 977	...	...	...	2.3	15.1	9.2
	...	452	...	32.5	...	...	3.5	...	15.5

Table 2
Adult literacy (age 15 and over)

Country or territory	ADULT LITERACY RATE (%) 1990 Total	1990 Male	1990 Female	2000 Total	2000 Male	2000 Female
Arab States and North Africa						
Algeria	52.9	64.3	41.3	66.7	76.3	57.0
Bahrain	82.1	86.8	74.6	87.5	90.9	82.6
Djibouti	53.0	66.8	39.7	64.6	75.6	54.4
Egypt[w]	47.1	60.4	33.6	55.3	66.6	43.8
Iraq	35.7	51.3	19.7	39.3	54.9	23.3
Jordan[w]	81.5	90.0	72.1	89.8	94.9	84.3
Kuwait	76.7	79.3	72.6	81.9	83.9	79.6
Lebanon	80.3	88.3	73.1	86.0	92.1	80.3
Libyan Arab Jamahiriya	68.1	82.8	51.1	79.9	90.8	68.1
Mauritania	34.8	46.3	23.9	40.2	50.7	30.1
Morocco	38.7	52.7	24.9	48.8	61.8	36.1
Oman	54.7	67.3	38.3	71.7	80.1	61.6
Palestinian Autonomous Territories	...	...	...	...	...	...
Qatar	77.0	77.4	76.0	81.2	80.4	83.1
Saudi Arabia	66.2	76.2	50.2	76.2	83.0	66.9
Sudan	45.8	60.0	31.5	57.7	69.2	46.2
Syrian Arab Republic	64.8	81.8	47.5	74.4	88.3	60.4
Tunisia[w]	59.1	71.6	46.5	71.0	81.4	60.6
United Arab Emirates	71.0	71.2	70.6	76.2	74.8	79.1
Yemen	32.7	55.2	12.9	46.4	67.5	25.3
Central and Eastern Europe						
Albania	77.0	86.8	66.7	84.7	92.1	77.0
Belarus	99.5	99.7	99.3	99.7	99.8	99.6
Bosnia and Herzegovina	...	...	...	...	...	...
Bulgaria	97.2	98.3	96.2	98.4	99.0	97.9
Croatia	96.9	99.0	94.9	98.3	99.3	97.3
Czech Republic[o]	...	...	...	...	...	...
Estonia	99.8	99.8	99.8	99.8	99.8	99.8
Hungary[o]	99.1	99.3	98.9	99.3	99.5	99.2
Latvia	99.8	99.8	99.8	99.8	99.8	99.8
Lithuania	99.3	99.5	99.1	99.6	99.7	99.5
Poland[o]	99.6	99.6	99.5	99.7	99.7	99.7
Republic of Moldova	97.5	99.1	96.1	98.9	99.5	98.3
Romania	97.1	98.6	95.6	98.1	99.0	97.3
Russian Federation[w]	99.2	99.6	98.9	99.6	99.7	99.4
Slovakia	...	...	...	...	...	...
Slovenia	99.6	99.6	99.5	99.6	99.7	99.6
The former Yugoslav Rep. of Macedonia	...	...	...	...	...	...
Turkey[o]	77.9	89.2	66.4	85.0	93.4	76.5
Ukraine	99.4	99.7	99.2	99.6	99.7	99.5
Yugoslavia	...	...	...	...	...	...
Central Asia						
Armenia	97.5	98.9	96.1	98.4	99.3	97.6
Azerbaijan	...	...	...	...	...	...
Georgia	...	...	...	...	...	...
Kazakhstan	98.8	99.5	99.2	99.4	99.7	99.1
Kyrgyzstan	...	...	...	...	...	...
Mongolia	97.8	98.5	97.1	98.4	98.6	98.3
Tajikistan	98.2	99.2	97.2	99.2	99.6	98.8
Turkmenistan	...	...	...	...	...	...
Uzbekistan	98.7	99.5	97.9	99.2	99.6	98.8
East Asia and the Pacific						
Australia[o]	...	...	...	...	...	...
Cambodia	62.0	77.7	48.8	68.0	80.2	57.2
China[w]	78.3	87.2	68.9	85.2	92.1	77.9

NUMBER OF ILLITERATES (15+)

(in thousands)

1990			2000		
Total	Male	Female	Total	Male	Female
6 804	2 588	4 218	6 571	2 360	4 211
59.9	27.0	33.1	57.3	25.1	32.1
135.8	42.0	97.9	127.0	39.0	90.8
17 866	6 752	11 116	19 613	7 374	12 253
6 198	2 377	3 821	8 125	3 057	5 070
320	91	229	300	78	220
317	169	148	238	130	103
347	98	250	337	91	246
775	223	553	701	168	533
715	287	428	890	360	530
9 090	3 465	5 624	9 988	3 702	6 286
433	177	257	402	155	246
...	...	...	...	...	...
74.3	53.4	21.0	77.8	57.0	21.2
2 968	1 210	1 840	2 760	1 092	1 723
7 792	2 859	4 948	7 881	2 857	5 019
2 273	592	1 680	2 449	566	1 879
2 081	726	1 355	1 928	621	1 307
410	297	113	459	345	117
3 994	1 243	2 750	4 914	1 444	3 525
509	149	361	336	88	248
42	10	32	29	9	20
...	...	...	...	...	...
195	59	136	106	33	73
113	17	95	66	12	54
...	...	...	...	...	...
2.5	1.2	1.3	2.5	1.2	1.3
78	29	49	56	21	36
4.3	1.9	2.4	4.3	1.9	2.4
20	6	13	13	5	8
119	48	71	84	38	46
80	14	66	38	7	31
519	121	398	342	86	257
857	202	655	535	159	376
...	...	...	...	...	...
6.8	2.9	3.9	6.0	2.6	3.4
...	...	...	...	...	...
8 077	1 981	6 097	6 993	1 539	5 453
237	55	182	160	46	113
...	...	...	...	...	...
62.6	12.7	49.9	45.8	10.1	35.9
...	...	...	...	...	...
...	...	...	...	...	...
136.0	29.0	107.0	72.4	19.6	53.0
...	...	...	...	...	...
29.0	9.9	19.1	25.7	11.4	14.3
55.0	12.4	42.6	29.7	7.7	22.0
...	...	...	...	...	...
163.7	32.0	131.7	125.6	31.5	94.1
...	...	...	...	...	...
2 025	543	1 482	2 352	689	1 660
181 331	54 922	126 409	141 903	38 424	103 499

Table 2 (continued)

Country or territory	ADULT LITERACY RATE (%)					
	1990			2000		
	Total	Male	Female	Total	Male	Female
Cook Islands	...	...	...	...	...	...
Democratic People's Rep. of Korea	...	...	...	...	...	...
Fiji	88.6	91.6	85.5	92.9	94.9	90.8
Indonesia[w]	79.5	86.7	72.5	86.8	91.8	81.9
Japan[o]	...	...	...	...	...	...
Kiribati	...	...	...	...	...	...
Lao People's Democratic Republic	56.5	70.3	42.8	64.8	76.2	53.4
Malaysia[w]	80.7	86.9	74.4	87.4	91.4	83.4
Marshall Islands	...	...	...	...	...	...
Myanmar	80.7	87.4	74.2	84.7	88.9	80.5
Nauru	...	...	...	...	...	...
New Zealand[o]	...	...	...	...	...	...
Niue	...	...	...	...	...	...
Papua New Guinea	56.6	64.4	48.2	63.9	70.6	56.8
Philippines[w]	91.7	92.2	91.2	94.9	95.1	94.8
Republic of Korea[o]	95.9	98.4	93.4	97.8	99.1	96.4
Samoa	98.0	98.5	97.4	98.6	98.9	98.3
Solomon Islands	...	...	...	...	...	...
Thailand[w]	92.4	95.3	89.5	95.5	97.1	93.9
Tonga	...	...	...	...	...	...
Tuvalu	...	...	...	...	...	...
Vanuatu	...	...	...	...	...	...
Viet Nam	90.4	94.0	87.1	92.5	94.5	90.7
Latin America and the Caribbean						
Anguilla	...	...	...	...	...	...
Antigua and Barbuda	...	...	...	...	...	...
Argentina[w]	95.7	95.9	95.6	96.8	96.8	96.8
Aruba	...	...	...	...	...	...
Bahamas	94.4	93.6	95.2	95.4	94.5	96.3
Barbados	99.4	99.4	99.3	99.7	99.7	99.7
Belize	89.1	90.0	88.2	93.2	93.3	93.2
Bermuda	...	...	...	...	...	...
Bolivia	78.1	86.8	69.8	85.4	91.9	79.2
Brazil[w]	82.0	82.9	81.2	86.9	87.0	86.8
British Virgin Islands	...	...	...	...	...	...
Cayman Islands	...	...	...	...	...	...
Chile[w]	94.0	94.4	93.6	95.8	95.9	95.6
Colombia	88.4	88.8	88.1	91.6	91.6	91.6
Costa Rica	93.9	93.9	93.8	95.6	95.5	95.6
Cuba	95.1	95.2	95.1	96.7	96.8	96.6
Dominica	...	...	...	...	...	...
Dominican Republic	79.4	79.8	79.0	83.7	83.7	83.7
Ecuador	87.6	90.2	85.1	91.6	93.2	89.9
El Salvador	72.4	76.1	69.1	78.7	81.5	76.1
Grenada	...	...	...	...	...	...
Guatemala	61.0	68.8	53.2	68.5	76.0	61.1
Guyana	97.2	98.0	96.4	98.5	98.9	98.1
Haiti	39.7	42.6	36.9	49.8	52.0	47.8
Honduras	68.1	68.9	67.3	75.0	74.9	75.0
Jamaica[w]	82.2	78.0	86.1	86.9	82.9	90.7
Mexico[o]	87.3	90.6	84.3	91.2	93.3	89.1
Montserrat	...	...	...	...	...	...
Netherlands Antilles	95.6	95.6	95.7	96.5	96.5	96.6
Nicaragua	62.7	62.7	62.8	66.5	66.2	66.7
Panama	89.0	89.7	88.4	91.9	92.5	91.2
Paraguay[w]	90.3	92.4	88.3	93.3	94.4	92.2
Peru[w]	85.5	92.0	79.1	89.9	94.7	85.2
Saint Kitts and Nevis	...	...	...	...	...	...

NUMBER OF ILLITERATES (15+) (in thousands)					
1990			2000		
Total	Male	Female	Total	Male	Female
...	...	...	...	...	...
...	...	...	...	...	...
51	19	32	39	14	25
23 927	7 734	16 124	19 377	6 018	13 306
...	...	...	...	...	...
...	...	...	...	...	...
1 010	338	680	1 064	354	716
2 190	750	1 440	1 846	636	1 211
...	...	...	...	...	...
4 913	1 589	3 319	4 897	1 740	3 161
...	...	...	...	...	...
...	...	...	...	...	...
...	...	...	...	...	...
949	406	543	1 040	443	594
2 986	1 397	1 590	2 395	1 161	1 235
1 307	255	1 052	831	159	673
1.91	0.74	1.18	1.28	0.54	0.74
...	...	...	...	...	...
2 842	855	1 996	2 081	647	1 440
...	...	...	...	...	...
...	...	...	...	...	...
...	...	...	...	...	...
3 897	1 200	2 651	3 901	1 419	2 463
...	...	...	...	...	...
...	...	...	...	...	...
964	448	517	849	409	440
...	...	...	...	...	...
9.6	5.4	4.2	9.8	5.8	4.1
1.2	0.5	0.7	0.7	0.3	0.4
11.3	5.3	6.0	9.5	4.7	4.7
...	...	...	...	...	...
846	249	598	733	199	535
17 358	8 127	9 232	15 885	7 690	8 195
...	...	...	...	...	...
...	...	...	...	...	...
550	248	302	461	216	245
2 584	1 226	1 359	2 368	1 152	1 216
119	59	59	121	62	59
398	196	202	294	141	153
...	...	...	...	...	...
895	445	450	910	462	448
775	307	468	706	283	423
835	346	489	862	359	503
...	...	...	...	...	...
1 843	740	1 104	2 020	768	1 251
13	4	9	8	3	5
2 323	1 061	1 263	2 428	1 111	1 318
851	414	436	934	467	467
274	163	110	231	146	84
6 469	2 357	4 112	5 845	2 161	3 684
...	...	...	...	...	...
6.0	2.8	3.2	5.6	2.7	2.9
764	373	391	975	481	494
170	81	89	159	74	86
237	94	143	224	94	130
1 935	525	1 409	1 735	448	1 287
...	...	...	...	...	...

Table 2 (continued)

Country or territory	ADULT LITERACY RATE (%) 1990 Total	1990 Male	1990 Female	2000 Total	2000 Male	2000 Female
Saint Lucia	...	...	...	...	...	...
Saint Vincent and the Grenadines	...	...	...	...	...	...
Suriname	...	...	...	...	...	...
Trinidad and Tobago	96.8	98.1	95.6	98.3	98.9	97.7
Turks and Caicos Islands	...	...	...	...	...	...
Uruguay[w]	96.5	96.0	97.0	97.6	97.1	98.0
Venezuela	88.9	90.1	87.7	92.5	93.0	92.0
North America and Western Europe						
Andorra	...	...	...	...	...	...
Austria[o]	...	...	...	...	...	...
Belgium[o]	...	...	...	...	...	...
Canada[o]	...	...	...	...	...	...
Cyprus	94.3	97.7	91.0	97.1	98.7	95.4
Denmark[o]	...	...	...	...	...	...
Finland[o]	...	...	...	...	...	...
France[o]	...	...	...	...	...	...
Germany[o]	...	...	...	...	...	...
Greece[o]	94.9	97.6	92.3	97.2	98.5	95.9
Iceland[o]	...	...	...	...	...	...
Ireland[o]	...	...	...	...	...	...
Israel[o]	91.4	94.9	88.0	94.8	97.0	92.7
Italy[o]	97.7	98.3	97.1	98.4	98.9	98.0
Luxembourg[o]	...	...	...	...	...	...
Malta	88.4	87.9	88.9	92.0	91.3	92.7
Monaco	...	...	...	...	...	...
Netherlands[o]	...	...	...	...	...	...
Norway[o]	...	...	...	...	...	...
Portugal[o]	87.2	90.9	83.8	92.2	94.7	89.9
San Marino	...	...	...	...	...	...
Spain[o]	96.3	97.8	94.8	97.6	98.5	96.8
Sweden[o]	...	...	...	...	...	...
Switzerland[o]	...	...	...	...	...	...
United Kingdom[o]	...	...	...	...	...	...
United States[o]	...	...	...	...	...	...
South and West Asia						
Afghanistan	...	...	...	...	...	...
Bangladesh	34.2	44.3	23.7	40.0	49.4	30.2
Bhutan	...	...	...	...	...	...
India[w]	49.3	61.9	35.9	57.2	68.4	45.4
Iran, Islamic Republic of	63.2	72.2	54.0	76.0	83.0	68.9
Maldives	94.8	95.0	94.6	96.9	97.0	96.8
Nepal	30.4	47.4	14.0	41.7	59.4	24.0
Pakistan	35.4	49.3	20.1	43.2	57.4	27.9
Sri Lanka[w]	88.7	92.9	84.7	91.6	94.4	89.0
Sub-Saharan Africa						
Angola	...	...	...	...	...	...
Benin	26.4	38.1	15.5	37.4	52.1	23.6
Botswana	68.1	65.7	70.3	77.2	74.5	79.8
Burkina Faso	16.3	25.0	8.0	23.9	33.9	14.1
Burundi	37.0	48.4	26.6	48.0	56.1	40.4
Cameroon	57.9	68.7	47.5	71.3	79.1	63.7
Cape Verde	63.8	76.2	54.3	73.8	84.5	65.7
Central African Republic	33.2	47.1	20.7	46.7	59.7	34.9
Chad	27.7	37.0	18.8	42.6	51.6	34.0
Comoros	53.8	61.4	46.4	55.9	63.2	48.7
Congo	67.1	77.1	57.9	80.7	87.5	74.4
Côte d'Ivoire	38.5	50.5	25.7	48.6	59.5	37.2

NUMBER OF ILLITERATES (15+)

(in thousands)

1990			2000		
Total	Male	Female	Total	Male	Female
...	...	...	...	...	...
...	...	...	...	...	...
...	...	...	...	...	...
26	8	18	17	5	12
...	...	...	...	...	...
80	44	37	61	35	26
1 340	599	741	1 189	554	635
...	...	...	...	...	...
...	...	...	...	...	...
...	...	...	...	...	...
...	...	...	...	...	...
29	6	23	18	4	14
...	...	...	...	...	...
...	...	...	...	...	...
...	...	...	...	...	...
...	...	...	...	...	...
419	94	324	256	67	189
...	...	...	...	...	...
...	...	...	...	...	...
267	78	190	225	64	162
1 103	386	717	778	271	507
...	...	...	...	...	...
32	16	16	25	13	12
...	...	...	...	...	...
...	...	...	...	...	...
...	...	...	...	...	...
1 013	341	672	654	210	444
...	...	...	...	...	...
1 186	339	847	807	240	568
...	...	...	...	...	...
...	...	...	...	...	...
...	...	...	...	...	...
...	...	...	...	...	...
...	...	...	...	...	...
41 908	18 480	23 309	50 558	22 035	28 445
...	...	...	...	...	...
272 388	105 800	166 639	286 951	109 367	177 689
12 059	4 706	7 272	10 552	3 819	6 696
6.0	3.0	3.0	5.1	2.6	2.5
7 439	2 885	4 481	7 922	2 808	5 065
41 169	17 082	23 993	46 702	17 980	28 871
1 302	434	839	1 167	401	745
...	...	...	...	...	...
1 773	724	1 049	2 106	782	1 322
212	106	106	203	109	94
3 876	1 626	2 268	4 504	1 817	2 723
1 949	761	1 187	1 734	691	1 047
2 683	979	1 704	2 432	875	1 555
70	20	51	68	18	50
1 112	417	695	1 129	408	719
2 297	974	1 323	2 423	1 000	1 423
129	53	76	177	73	104
401	134	266	313	98	215
4 141	1 756	2 365	4 761	1 953	2 795

Table 2 (continued)

Country or territory	ADULT LITERACY RATE (%)					
	1990			2000		
	Total	Male	Female	Total	Male	Female
Democratic Rep. of the Congo	47.5	61.4	34.4	61.4	73.1	50.2
Equatorial Guinea	73.3	85.8	61.1	83.2	92.5	74.4
Eritrea	46.4	58.5	34.8	55.7	67.3	44.5
Ethiopia	28.6	37.3	19.8	39.1	47.1	31.0
Gabon	...	...	...	...	...	...
Gambia	25.6	31.7	19.7	36.6	43.7	29.7
Ghana	58.5	70.1	47.2	71.6	80.3	63.2
Guinea						
Guinea-Bissau	27.2	42.3	12.9	38.4	54.1	23.5
Kenya	70.8	80.9	60.8	82.4	88.9	76.0
Lesotho	78.0	65.4	89.5	83.4	72.6	93.6
Liberia	39.2	55.4	22.8	53.5	70.2	36.7
Madagascar	58.0	66.4	49.8	66.5	73.6	59.7
Malawi	51.8	68.8	36.2	60.1	74.5	46.5
Mali	18.8	27.9	10.4	25.6	35.8	16.0
Mauritius	79.8	84.8	75.0	84.5	87.8	81.2
Mozambique	33.5	49.3	18.4	44.0	60.0	28.7
Namibia	74.9	77.4	72.4	82.0	82.8	81.2
Niger	11.4	18.0	5.1	16.0	23.8	8.5
Nigeria	48.7	59.4	38.4	64.0	72.2	56.1
Rwanda	53.3	62.9	44.0	66.8	73.6	60.4
Sao Tome and Principe	...	...	...	...	...	...
Senegal	28.4	38.2	18.6	37.4	47.3	27.7
Seychelles	...	...	...	...	...	...
Sierra Leone	...	...	...	...	...	...
Somalia	...	...	...	...	...	...
South Africa	81.2	82.2	80.2	85.2	86.0	84.6
Swaziland	71.6	73.7	69.9	79.6	80.8	78.6
Togo	44.2	60.5	28.7	57.1	72.3	42.5
Uganda	56.1	69.3	43.5	67.0	77.5	56.8
United Republic of Tanzania	62.9	75.5	51.0	75.0	83.9	66.5
Zambia	68.2	78.6	58.7	78.2	85.2	71.5
Zimbabwe[w]	80.7	86.6	75.0	88.7	92.8	84.6
	weighted average					
World	75.3	81.7	68.9	79.7	85.2	74.2
Developed countries and countries in transition	97.7	98.5	96.9	98.6	99.0	98.1
Developing countries	67.0	75.9	57.9	73.6	81.0	66.1
Arab States	50.2	63.8	35.8	60.1	71.7	47.8
Central and Eastern Europe	94.6	97.3	92.1	96.2	98.1	94.3
Central Asia	98.9	99.5	98.3	99.6	99.7	99.4
East Asia And the Pacific	80.2	88.0	72.1	86.5	92.4	80.5
Latin America And the Caribbean	85.1	86.8	83.4	88.9	89.9	87.9
North America and Western Europe	97.9	98.4	97.3	98.6	99.0	98.3
South And West Asia	47.5	59.7	34.5	55.3	66.4	43.6
Sub-Saharan Africa	49.2	59.3	39.5	60.3	68.9	52.0

NUMBER OF ILLITERATES (15+) (in thousands)					
1990			2000		
Total	Male	Female	Total	Male	Female
10256	3653	6602	10078	3437	6636
54	14	41	43	9	34
930	355	575	908	330	578
18822	8117	10752	21005	8996	12062
...	...	...	...	...	...
401	181	221	494	215	279
3438	1219	2218	3239	1112	2125
397	153	244	417	152	266
3479	1119	2367	3049	954	2102
219	166	54	205	166	41
640	237	403	776	251	524
2773	1094	1674	2957	1155	1799
2406	746	1660	2419	758	1659
3849	1655	2193	4548	1918	2627
150	56	94	134	52	82
5081	1889	3191	5741	2008	3728
196	84	112	178	83	96
3420	1568	1847	4564	2072	2483
23709	9324	14313	22510	8698	13715
1671	650	1021	1405	550	854
...	...	...	...	...	...
2863	1227	1636	3285	1365	1920
...	...	...	...	...	...
...	...	...	...	...	...
...	...	...	...	...	...
4215	1953	2262	4217	1956	2260
122	55	67	110	51	59
1047	363	684	1082	343	737
3924	1358	2561	3902	1324	2572
5142	1653	3490	4827	1528	3299
1384	459	909	1215	411	793
1071	368	701	784	249	532

sum	sum	sum	sum	sum	sum
879130	324914	554216	861966	313323	548643
21970	6660	15311	14895	4862	10033
857159	318254	538905	847071	308461	538610
62400	23118	39282	67473	24310	43162
16519	3833	12686	12518	2857	9661
480	98	383	222	73	149
232904	71924	160979	186404	53412	132992
41932	18243	23689	39254	17436	21819
11363	4024	7339	7873	2935	4938
382151	151980	230171	412242	159705	252538
131380	51693	79687	135980	52595	83385

Table 3
Youth literacy (age 15-24)

Country or territory	YOUTH LITERACY RATE (%)					
	1990			2000		
	Total	Male	Female	Total	Male	Female
Arab States and North Africa						
Algeria	77.3	86.1	68.1	88.5	93.2	83.6
Bahrain	95.6	96.2	95.0	98.4	98.2	98.6
Djibouti	73.2	82.2	64.2	84.0	88.7	79.4
Egypt[w]	61.3	70.9	51.0	69.7	76.4	62.6
Iraq	41.0	56.4	24.9	44.6	59.3	29.1
Jordan[w]	96.7	97.9	95.3	99.2	99.1	99.3
Kuwait	87.5	87.9	87.2	92.4	91.7	93.2
Lebanon	92.1	95.5	88.6	95.2	97.2	93.0
Libyan Arab Jamahiriya	91.0	98.9	82.7	96.5	99.8	93.0
Mauritania	45.8	55.5	36.1	48.9	57.1	40.6
Morocco	55.3	68.0	42.0	67.3	76.0	58.2
Oman	85.6	95.4	75.4	97.9	99.5	96.2
Palestinian Autonomous Territories	...	...	...	...	...	...
Qatar	90.3	88.3	93.0	94.8	92.6	97.1
Saudi Arabia	85.4	91.2	78.6	92.7	94.9	90.3
Sudan	65.0	75.6	54.0	77.2	82.8	71.5
Syrian Arab Republic	79.9	92.2	66.9	87.2	95.4	78.8
Tunisia[w]	84.1	92.8	75.2	93.3	97.4	89.1
United Arab Emirates	84.7	81.7	88.6	90.6	87.4	94.4
Yemen	50.0	73.5	25.0	65.0	82.9	46.2
Central and Eastern Europe						
Albania	94.8	97.4	91.9	97.8	99.1	96.4
Belarus	99.8	99.8	99.8	99.8	99.8	99.8
Bosnia and Herzegovina	...	...	...	...	...	...
Bulgaria	99.4	99.5	99.3	99.7	99.8	99.5
Croatia	99.6	99.7	99.6	99.8	99.8	99.8
Czech Republic[o]	...	...	...	...	...	...
Estonia	99.8	99.7	99.8	99.7	99.7	99.8
Hungary[o]	99.7	99.8	99.7	99.8	99.8	99.8
Latvia	99.8	99.8	99.8	99.8	99.8	99.8
Lithuania	99.8	99.8	99.8	99.8	99.8	99.8
Poland[o]	99.8	99.8	99.8	99.8	99.8	99.8
Republic of Moldova	99.8	99.8	99.8	99.8	99.8	99.8
Romania	99.3	99.3	99.2	99.6	99.5	99.7
Russian Federation[w]	99.8	99.8	99.8	99.8	99.8	99.8
Slovakia	...	...	...	...	...	...
Slovenia	99.8	99.7	99.8	99.8	99.8	99.8
The former Yugoslav Rep. of Macedonia	...	...	...	...	...	...
Turkey[o]	92.7	97.1	88.3	96.5	98.8	94.0
Ukraine	99.8	99.8	99.9	99.9	99.9	99.9
Yugoslavia	...	...	...	...	...	...
Central Asia						
Armenia	99.5	99.7	99.4	99.7	99.8	99.7
Azerbaijan	...	...	...	...	...	...
Georgia	...	...	...	...	...	...
Kazakhstan	99.8	99.8	99.8	99.8	99.8	99.8
Kyrgyzstan	...	...	...	...	...	...
Mongolia	98.9	98.7	99.1	99.0	98.7	99.3
Tajikistan	99.8	99.8	99.8	99.8	99.8	99.8
Turkmenistan	...	...	...	...	...	...
Uzbekistan	99.6	99.7	99.6	99.7	99.7	99.6
East Asia and the Pacific						
Australia[o]	...	...	...	...	...	...
Cambodia	73.5	81.5	65.6	79.1	83.9	74.3
China[w]	95.3	97.5	93.1	97.7	98.7	96.7

NUMBER OF ILLITERATES (15-24)
(in thousands)

1990			2000		
Total	Male	Female	Total	Male	Female
1 161	363	797	758	227	530
3.5	1.6	1.9	1.6	0.9	0.7
22.6	7.1	15.9	19.6	6.9	12.7
3 996	1 559	2 437	4 178	1 678	2 500
2 059	776	1 283	2 554	962	1 593
23.3	7.9	15.4	8.1	4.8	3.4
46.1	22.8	23.3	33.7	19.2	14.6
48.2	13.9	34.3	31.7	9.1	22.6
78.0	4.7	73.3	44.3	1.3	43.1
205	84	121	268	113	155
2 254	821	1 433	2 015	750	1 265
44.3	7.2	37.1	10.4	1.1	9.3
...	...	...	...	...	...
4.9	3.3	1.6	3.7	2.7	1.0
368	115	261	287	101	187
1 742	614	1 131	1 400	535	861
500	99	401	461	85	376
262	60	203	133	27	106
40.4	29.8	11.5	37.4	28.6	9.0
1 193	324	869	1 165	292	874
33.6	8.5	25.1	11.9	2.5	9.4
2.8	1.4	1.4	3.2	1.6	1.6
...	...	...	...	...	...
7.1	2.9	4.2	3.8	1.2	2.6
2.3	1.1	1.2	1.4	0.8	0.6
...	...	...	...	...	...
0.5	0.3	0.2	0.5	0.3	0.2
3.9	1.7	2.2	2.9	1.5	1.4
0.7	0.4	0.4	0.7	0.4	0.3
1.2	0.6	0.5	1.1	0.5	0.5
10.6	5.4	5.2	13.1	6.7	6.4
1.3	0.7	0.6	1.5	0.8	0.8
27.8	12.9	14.9	13.6	8.3	5.2
41.5	22.2	19.3	45.5	23.0	22.5
...	...	...	...	...	...
0.7	0.4	0.3	0.6	0.3	0.3
...	...	...	...	...	...
816	167	649	473	81	392
11.2	6.4	4.8	8.5	5.5	3.0
...	...	...	...	...	...
2.6	1.0	1.6	1.8	0.7	1.0
...	...	...	...	...	...
...	...	...	...	...	...
6.1	3.4	2.7	5.9	3.0	2.9
...	...	...	...	...	...
5.1	2.9	2.2	5.4	3.6	1.8
2.2	1.0	1.2	2.4	1.2	1.2
...	...	...	...	...	...
13.9	6.1	7.9	16.9	7.0	9.9
...	...	...	...	...	...
477	165	312	510	198	311
11 709	3 239	8 470	4 486	1 314	3 172

Table 3 (continued)

Country or territory	YOUTH LITERACY RATE (%)					
	1990			2000		
	Total	Male	Female	Total	Male	Female
Cook Islands	...	...	...	...	...	...
Democratic People's Rep. of Korea	...	...	...	...	...	...
Fiji	97.8	98.1	97.6	99.1	99.1	99.1
Indonesia[w]	95.0	96.6	93.4	97.7	98.3	97.1
Japan[o]	...	...	...	...	...	...
Kiribati	...	...	...	...	...	...
Lao People's Democratic Republic	70.1	79.5	60.6	77.9	84.9	70.8
Malaysia[w]	94.8	95.3	94.2	97.6	97.5	97.7
Marshall Islands	...	...	...	...	...	...
Myanmar	88.2	90.1	86.2	90.9	91.4	90.5
Nauru	...	...	...	...	...	...
New Zealand[o]	...	...	...	...	...	...
Niue	...	...	...	...	...	...
Papua New Guinea	68.6	74.4	62.4	75.7	79.8	71.3
Philippines[w]	97.3	97.1	97.4	98.7	98.5	98.9
Republic of Korea[o]	99.8	99.8	99.8	99.8	99.8	99.8
Samoa	99.0	99.1	98.9	99.4	99.4	99.4
Solomon Islands	...	...	...	...	...	...
Thailand[w]	98.1	98.6	97.6	98.9	99.4	98.4
Tonga	...	...	...	...	...	...
Tuvalu	...	...	...	...	...	...
Vanuatu	...	...	...	...	...	...
Viet Nam	94.1	94.5	93.6	95.2	95.0	95.4
Latin America and the Caribbean						
Anguilla	...	...	...	...	...	...
Antigua and Barbuda	...	...	...	...	...	...
Argentina[w]	98.2	98.0	98.4	98.6	98.3	98.8
Aruba	...	...	...	...	...	...
Bahamas	96.5	95.4	97.5	97.2	96.2	98.3
Barbados	99.8	99.8	99.8	99.8	99.8	99.8
Belize	96.0	95.4	96.7	98.0	97.3	98.7
Bermuda	...	...	...	...	...	...
Bolivia	92.6	96.2	89.0	95.8	98.0	93.6
Brazil[w]	91.8	90.5	93.1	95.3	94.0	96.7
British Virgin Islands	...	...	...	...	...	...
Cayman Islands	...	...	...	...	...	...
Chile[w]	98.1	97.9	98.3	98.9	98.7	99.0
Colombia	94.9	94.3	95.5	96.9	96.2	97.5
Costa Rica	97.4	97.1	97.7	98.3	98.0	98.6
Cuba	99.3	99.3	99.2	99.8	99.8	99.8
Dominica	...	...	...	...	...	...
Dominican Republic	87.5	86.8	88.2	91.1	90.4	91.9
Ecuador	95.5	96.0	94.9	97.2	97.5	96.9
El Salvador	83.8	85.1	82.6	88.2	89.0	87.3
Grenada	...	...	...	...	...	...
Guatemala	73.4	80.5	66.2	79.1	85.4	72.7
Guyana	99.8	99.8	99.8	99.8	99.8	99.8
Haiti	54.8	55.8	53.8	64.4	64.3	64.5
Honduras	79.7	78.5	80.8	85.1	83.5	86.6
Jamaica[w]	91.2	87.1	95.2	94.0	90.7	97.5
Mexico[o]	95.2	95.9	94.4	97.0	97.4	96.6
Montserrat	...	...	...	...	...	...
Netherlands Antilles	97.5	97.3	97.7	98.2	98.0	98.4
Nicaragua	68.2	67.7	68.7	71.6	71.0	72.3
Panama	95.3	95.7	94.8	96.7	97.1	96.3
Paraguay[w]	95.6	95.9	95.2	97.1	97.1	97.0
Peru[w]	94.5	96.9	92.1	96.7	98.2	95.2
Saint Kitts and Nevis	...	...	...	...	...	...

NUMBER OF ILLITERATES (15-24) (in thousands)					
1990			2000		
Total	Male	Female	Total	Male	Female
...	...	...	...	...	...
...	...	...	...	...	...
2.9	1.4	1.6	1.5	0.8	0.8
1 879	651	1 225	963	365	597
...	...	...	...	...	...
...	...	...	...	...	...
234	80	155	226	78	148
179	81	98	102	54	48
...	...	...	...	...	...
969	407	563	863	413	451
...	...	...	...	...	...
...	...	...	...	...	...
...	...	...	...	...	...
238	102	135	240	107	130
342	185	157	196	116	80
17.5	9.0	8.5	15.4	8.0	7.5
0.34	0.17	0.17	0.22	0.12	0.10
...	...	...	...	...	...
220	82	139	129	35	95
...	...	...	...	...	...
...	...	...	...	...	...
...	...	...	...	...	...
800	372	430	759	400	359
...	...	...	...	...	...
...	...	...	...	...	...
97	54	43	96	56	39
...	...	...	...	...	...
1.91	1.26	0.66	1.54	1.06	0.48
0.10	0.05	0.05	0.08	0.04	0.04
1.48	0.86	0.63	1.00	0.67	0.32
...	...	...	...	...	...
97	25	72	68	16	51
2 367	1 373	994	1 585	1 034	551
...	...	...	...	...	...
...	...	...	...	...	...
48	27	21	28	16	12
369	208	161	250	153	97
15.1	8.5	6.6	13.4	8.0	5.4
16.7	8.2	8.5	3.0	1.5	1.5
...	...	...	...	...	...
184	100	84	148	82	66
95	42	53	72	33	39
172	77	95	158	74	84
...	...	...	...	...	...
457	170	287	494	176	318
0.32	0.16	0.16	0.32	0.16	0.16
580	283	297	628	316	311
201	107	93	200	112	88
42.4	30.6	11.7	30.9	24.2	6.5
888	371	517	594	260	334
...	...	...	...	...	...
0.74	0.40	0.34	0.60	0.33	0.27
246	124	122	308	158	150
23	11	13	17	8	10
36	17	19	32	16	16
243	69	173	171	47	124
...	...	...	...	...	...

Table 3 (continued)

Country or territory	YOUTH LITERACY RATE (%) 1990 Total	1990 Male	1990 Female	2000 Total	2000 Male	2000 Female
Saint Lucia	...	...	...	...	...	...
Saint Vincent and the Grenadines	...	...	...	...	...	...
Suriname	...	...	...	...	...	...
Trinidad and Tobago	99.6	99.7	99.6	99.8	99.8	99.8
Turks and Caicos Islands	...	...	...	...	...	...
Uruguay[w]	98.7	98.3	99.1	99.1	98.8	99.4
Venezuela	96.0	95.4	96.6	98.0	97.3	98.6
North America and Western Europe						
Andorra	...	...	...	...	...	...
Austria[o]	...	...	...	...	...	...
Belgium[o]	...	...	...	...	...	...
Canada[o]	...	...	...	...	...	...
Cyprus	99.7	99.5	99.8	99.8	99.7	99.8
Denmark[o]	...	...	...	...	...	...
Finland[o]	...	...	...	...	...	...
France[o]	...	...	...	...	...	...
Germany[o]	...	...	...	...	...	...
Greece[o]	99.5	99.4	99.7	99.8	99.8	99.8
Iceland[o]	...	...	...	...	...	...
Ireland[o]	...	...	...	...	...	...
Israel[o]	98.7	99.0	98.4	99.4	99.5	99.3
Italy[o]	99.8	99.8	99.8	99.8	99.8	99.8
Luxembourg[o]	...	...	...	...	...	...
Malta	97.5	96.0	99.1	98.6	97.4	99.8
Monaco	...	...	...	...	...	...
Netherlands[o]	...	...	...	...	...	...
Norway[o]	...	...	...	...	...	...
Portugal[o]	99.5	99.5	99.6	99.8	99.8	99.8
San Marino	...	...	...	...	...	...
Spain[o]	99.6	99.6	99.6	99.8	99.8	99.8
Sweden[o]	...	...	...	...	...	...
Switzerland[o]	...	...	...	...	...	...
United Kingdom[o]	...	...	...	...	...	...
United States[o]	...	...	...	...	...	...
South and West Asia						
Afghanistan	...	...	...	...	...	...
Bangladesh	42.0	50.7	33.2	48.4	56.7	39.7
Bhutan	...	...	...	...	...	...
India[w]	64.3	73.4	54.2	72.6	79.7	64.8
Iran, Islamic Republic of	86.3	91.7	80.8	93.8	96.2	91.3
Maldives	98.1	98.1	98.1	99.1	99.0	99.1
Nepal	46.6	67.0	27.3	60.4	76.7	42.8
Pakistan	47.4	62.5	30.6	57.0	71.1	41.9
Sri Lanka[w]	95.1	95.9	94.2	96.8	97.0	96.6
Sub-Saharan Africa						
Angola	...	...	...	...	...	...
Benin	40.4	56.6	24.7	53.1	70.5	36.0
Botswana	83.3	79.3	87.2	88.3	84.5	92.1
Burkina Faso	24.9	35.7	14.0	34.6	45.8	23.3
Burundi	51.6	58.4	44.8	63.9	65.9	62.1
Cameroon	81.1	86.4	75.9	90.0	92.0	88.0
Cape Verde	81.5	87.1	76.2	88.0	91.3	84.8
Central African Republic	52.1	65.6	39.4	67.3	76.0	59.0
Chad	48.0	58.4	37.7	66.6	73.4	59.9
Comoros	56.7	63.8	49.6	58.6	65.3	51.8
Congo	92.5	94.9	90.3	97.4	98.1	96.8
Côte d'Ivoire	52.6	64.9	40.3	61.5	70.6	52.3

NUMBER OF ILLITERATES (15-24) (in thousands)					
1990			2000		
Total	Male	Female	Total	Male	Female
...	...	...	...	...	...
...	...	...	...	...	...
...	...	...	...	...	...
0.78	0.38	0.40	0.53	0.27	0.26
...	...	...	...	...	...
6.37	4.20	2.17	4.95	3.33	1.62
153	89	64	95	64	31
...	...	...	...	...	...
...	...	...	...	...	...
...	...	...	...	...	...
...	...	...	...	...	...
0.34	0.24	0.10	0.29	0.17	0.12
...	...	...	...	...	...
...	...	...	...	...	...
...	...	...	...	...	...
...	...	...	...	...	...
7.22	4.58	2.64	3.30	1.87	1.43
...	...	...	...	...	...
...	...	...	...	...	...
10.47	4.12	6.35	6.07	2.45	3.61
17.65	8.98	8.67	13.37	6.82	6.55
...	...	...	...	...	...
1.26	1.05	0.23	0.85	0.79	0.06
...	...	...	...	...	...
...	...	...	...	...	...
...	...	...	...	...	...
7.88	4.41	3.47	2.91	1.48	1.43
...	...	...	...	...	...
27.28	15.24	12.03	12.30	6.67	5.63
...	...	...	...	...	...
...	...	...	...	...	...
...	...	...	...	...	...
...	...	...	...	...	...
...	...	...	...	...	...
13 098	5 791	7 250	14 441	6 267	8 168
...	...	...	...	...	...
58 575	22 819	35 760	52 125	20 050	32 090
1 485	466	1 003	950	296	655
0.75	0.39	0.36	0.56	0.30	0.26
1 853	593	1 215	1 744	532	1 214
10 581	3 921	6 698	11 685	4 034	7 677
159	68	91	116	55	61
...	...	...	...	...	...
497	179	318	596	187	409
43	26	16	40	27	14
1 355	573	786	1 568	639	935
517	221	296	469	220	249
412	149	263	308	124	184
14	5	9	11	4	7
249	86	163	241	87	154
568	226	343	503	200	303
46	19	27	63	26	36
32	11	21	15	5	10
1 059	397	659	1 325	508	817

Table 3 (continued)

Country or territory	YOUTH LITERACY RATE (%) 1990 Total	1990 Male	1990 Female	2000 Total	2000 Male	2000 Female
Democratic Rep. of the Congo	68.9	80.3	57.6	81.7	88.4	74.9
Equatorial Guinea	92.7	96.6	88.8	96.9	98.5	95.4
Eritrea	60.9	72.5	49.3	70.2	80.1	60.4
Ethiopia	43.0	51.5	34.1	55.0	61.2	48.7
Gabon	...	...	...	...	...	...
Gambia	42.2	50.5	34.1	57.2	65.2	49.3
Ghana	81.8	88.2	75.4	91.1	93.6	88.6
Guinea	...	...	...	...	...	...
Guinea-Bissau	44.1	62.2	26.5	58.1	72.8	43.7
Kenya	89.8	92.9	86.7	95.1	96.0	94.2
Lesotho	87.2	77.2	97.1	90.5	82.7	98.5
Liberia	57.2	75.4	38.6	68.8	84.9	52.6
Madagascar	72.2	77.8	66.6	80.1	83.6	76.6
Malawi	63.2	75.7	51.2	71.1	81.0	61.0
Mali	27.6	38.3	17.1	36.1	47.3	25.1
Mauritius	91.1	91.2	91.1	93.8	93.3	94.3
Mozambique	48.8	66.1	31.7	60.6	75.1	46.2
Namibia	87.4	85.9	89.0	91.6	89.9	93.3
Niger	17.0	24.9	9.3	23.0	32.3	13.8
Nigeria	73.6	80.8	66.5	86.9	89.6	84.3
Rwanda	72.7	78.0	67.4	83.4	85.2	81.6
Sao Tome and Principe	...	...	...	...	...	...
Senegal	40.1	50.0	30.2	50.7	59.5	41.9
Seychelles	...	...	...	...	...	...
Sierra Leone	...	...	...	...	...	...
Somalia	...	...	...	...	...	...
South Africa	88.5	88.6	88.4	91.3	91.3	91.3
Swaziland	85.1	84.7	85.5	90.4	89.6	91.2
Togo	63.5	79.4	47.7	75.5	87.2	63.8
Uganda	70.1	79.8	60.5	78.7	85.4	72.1
United Republic of Tanzania	83.1	89.2	77.2	90.5	93.2	87.9
Zambia	81.2	86.4	76.2	88.2	90.8	85.5
Zimbabwe[w]	93.9	96.6	91.3	97.2	98.7	95.7
	weighted average					
World	84.2	88.2	80.0	86.8	89.9	83.4
Developed countries and countries in transition	99.6	99.6	99.5	99.7	99.7	99.7
Developing countries	80.8	85.7	75.7	84.2	88.0	80.1
Arab States	66.5	77.2	55.1	76.0	83.1	68.5
Central and Eastern Europe	98.4	99.2	97.5	99.1	99.6	98.6
Central Asia	99.7	99.7	99.7	99.7	99.7	99.7
East Asia And the Pacific	95.1	96.9	93.1	97.2	98.0	96.4
Latin America And the Caribbean	92.7	92.7	92.8	95.0	94.8	95.3
North America and Western Europe	99.5	99.6	99.4	99.7	99.7	99.6
South And West Asia	61.6	71.1	51.2	69.7	77.5	61.2
Sub-Saharan Africa	66.5	74.1	59.0	76.3	81.3	71.3

NUMBER OF ILLITERATES (15-24) (in thousands)					
1990			2000		
Total	Male	Female	Total	Male	Female
2 162	683	1 478	1 769	558	1 209
4.7	1.1	3.6	2.6	0.6	1.9
236	83	153	209	70	139
5 185	2 195	3 010	5 408	2 333	3 081
...	...	...	...	...	...
95	40	55	100	40	60
533	173	360	368	134	235
...	...	...	...	...	...
97	33	64	94	30	63
471	164	308	338	138	201
41	36	5	38	35	3
171	50	120	228	55	172
635	254	381	610	252	359
650	211	439	653	216	437
1 266	538	728	1 425	589	835
17.7	9.0	8.7	13.1	7.2	6.0
1 340	442	898	1 422	448	971
35.0	19.7	15.4	28.9	17.4	11.4
1 223	562	658	1 623	726	892
4 257	1 568	2 672	3 001	1 214	1 776
369	147	222	280	124	157
...	...	...	...	...	...
832	349	483	926	382	545
...	...	...	...	...	...
...	...	...	...	...	...
...	...	...	...	...	...
877	433	445	777	386	392
22.8	11.5	11.2	18.1	9.8	8.3
242	68	174	226	59	167
1 002	338	663	998	342	655
883	276	607	684	245	439
305	110	193	254	100	155
125	35	90	78	18	59

sum	sum	sum	sum	sum	sum
157 396	60 281	97 115	140 585	54 616	85 969
767	340	427	497	231	266
156 629	59 941	96 688	140 088	54 385	85 703
13 894	4 844	9 051	13 191	4 750	8 441
976	239	737	592	140	452
40	20	20	41	20	21
17 726	5 660	12 066	8 895	3 287	5 609
6 377	3 222	3 154	5 023	2 675	2 348
506	217	289	301	135	166
87 239	34 243	52 997	82 974	31 916	51 058
30 638	11 837	18 801	29 568	11 694	17 873

Table 4
Early Childhood Care and Education

Country or territory	GROSS ENROLMENT RATIO (GER) IN ECCE			
	1990[1]/91			GPI
	Total	Male	Female	F/M
Arab States and North Africa				
Algeria	...	...	...	...
Bahrain	27.1	26.6	27.6	1.04
Djibouti	0.7	0.6	0.8	1.46
Egypt[w]	6.1	6.1	6.1	1.00
Iraq	7.6	7.7	7.4	0.96
Jordan[w]	14.7	15.6	13.7	0.88
Kuwait	32.9	32.7	33.1	1.01
Lebanon	...	...	...	...
Libyan Arab Jamahiriya	...	...	...	...
Mauritania	...	...	...	...
Morocco	65.8	89.8	41.0	0.46
Oman	3.0	3.2	2.8	0.88
Palestinian Autonomous Territories	...	...	...	...
Qatar	27.3	28.2	26.4	0.94
Saudi Arabia	7.1	7.6	6.6	0.88
Sudan	18.4	23.4	13.2	0.56
Syrian Arab Republic	6.3	6.7	5.9	0.88
Tunisia[w]	7.8	...	...	...
United Arab Emirates	51.9	53.1	50.6	0.95
Yemen	0.8	0.8	0.8	0.94
Central and Eastern Europe				
Albania	58.6	...	...	...
Belarus	84.0	...	...	...
Bosnia and Herzegovina	...	...	...	...
Bulgaria	91.6	91.3	91.9	1.01
Croatia[2]	...	...	...	...
Czech Republic[o]	95.0	96.3	93.5	0.97
Estonia	75.1	75.7	74.5	0.98
Hungary[o]	113.4	115.4	111.4	0.97
Latvia	45.3	45.2	45.4	1.00
Lithuania	57.5	57.3	57.8	1.01
Poland[o]	46.7	...	...	...
Republic of Moldova	72.7	74.4	71.0	0.95
Romania	76.0	74.6	77.5	1.04
Russian Federation[w]	74.0	...	...	...
Slovakia	86.1	...	...	...
Slovenia	73.8	75.9	71.6	0.94
The former Yugoslav Rep. of Macedonia	...	...	...	...
Turkey[o]	4.6	4.7	4.4	0.94
Ukraine	85.0	88.4	81.5	0.92
Yugoslavia[2]	...	...	...	...
Central Asia				
Armenia	36.7	...	...	...
Azerbaijan	19.6	21.3	17.8	0.83
Georgia	59.0	...	...	...
Kazakhstan	72.3	...	...	...
Kyrgyzstan	33.5	33.2	33.9	1.02
Mongolia	39.1	35.0	43.3	1.23
Tajikistan	15.8	...	...	...
Turkmenistan	...	...	...	...
Uzbekistan	73.1	...	...	...
East Asia and the Pacific				
Australia[o]	71.3	71.3	71.3	1.00
Cambodia	5.3	5.6	5.1	0.91

1. Indicators for 1990/1991 and 1999/2000 may not be comparable. For further explanation, please see the Technical Introduction preceding these Annexes.
2. Enrolment ratios have not been calculated due to inconsistencies between enrolment and the United Nations population data.
3. Data in italics are for 1998/99.
4. Enrolment ratios have not been calculated due to lack of United Nations population data by age.

GROSS ENROLMENT RATIO (GER) IN ECCE				NEW ENTRANTS TO PRIMARY EDUCATION WITH ECCE EXPERIENCE AS %					
1999/2000			GPI	1998/99			1999/2000		
Total	Male	Female	F/M	Total	Male	Female	Total	Male	Female
2.8	2.8	2.8	0.99	1.5	1.5	1.5	1.4	1.4	1.4
36.9	37.7	36.1	0.96	…	…	…	65.4	64.9	66.0
0.4	0.3	0.4	1.25	2.3	1.1	3.9	…	…	…
11.4	11.7	11.2	0.95	…	…	…	…	…	…
5.7	5.7	5.7	1.00	…	…	…	…	…	…
30.6	32.0	29.1	0.91	…	…	…	38.7	40.8	36.5
…	…	…	…	87.2	87.8	86.5	85.6	88.6	82.5
66.8	67.6	65.9	0.98	…	…	…	…	…	…
4.9	5.0	4.9	0.98	…	…	…	…	…	…
…	…	…	…	…	…	…	…	…	…
58.0	74.4	41.0	0.55	…	…	…	…	…	…
4.8	5.2	4.5	0.87	…	…	…	…	…	…
39.1	40.0	38.1	0.95	…	…	…	49.2	50.2	48.1
28.6	29.7	27.5	0.92	…	…	…	…	…	…
5.2	5.4	4.9	0.90	…	…	…	…	…	…
22.2	23.0	21.5	0.94	51.3	46.5	56.8	45.6	81.5	…
8.5	8.9	8.0	0.90	…	…	…	…	…	…
15.8	15.9	15.7	0.99	…	…	…	…	…	…
78.4	78.8	78.1	0.99	90.0	90.0	90.0	75.6	73.9	77.5
0.9**	1.0**	0.8**	0.87	1.6	1.5	1.6	…	…	…
41.3	39.6	43.1	1.09	…	…	…	…	…	…
82.1	84.4	79.7	0.94	88.6	88.6	…	…	…	…
…	…	…	…	…	…	…	…	…	…
67.2	67.5	67.0	0.99	…	…	…	…	…	…
…	…	…	…	…	…	…	…	…	…
90.8	90.7	90.8	1.00	…	…	…	…	…	…
92.9	93.4	92.5	0.99	…	…	…	…	…	…
107.9	108.6	107.0	0.99	…	…	…	…	…	…
73.3	75.1	71.4	0.95	…	…	…	…	…	…
51.6	52.5	50.7	0.96	…	…	…	…	…	…
49.5	49.2	49.7	1.01	…	…	…	…	…	…
…	…	…	…	…	…	…	…	…	…
141.9	139.5	144.5	1.04	…	…	…	…	…	…
103.4	106.2	100.4	0.94	…	…	…	70.0	70.0	70.0
82.0	86.3	77.4	0.90	…	…	…	…	…	…
72.1	75.4	68.7	0.91	…	…	…	…	…	…
28.7	28.6	28.9	1.01	…	…	…	…	…	…
5.7	5.9	5.5	0.94	…	…	…	…	…	…
65.4	65.9	64.8	0.98	38.9	38.9	…	…	…	…
…	…	…	…	…	…	…	…	…	…
…	…	…	…	…	…	…	…	…	…
23.0	22.6	23.5	1.04	20.3	20.3	20.3	…	…	…
37.5	37.7	37.2	0.99	27.5	27.8	27.3	27.5	27.5	27.5
11.4	11.7	11.0	0.94	…	…	…	…	…	…
13.7	13.9	13.4	0.96	8.7	9.7	7.6	6.4	6.6	6.3
27.2	26.7	27.8	1.04	…	…	…	…	…	…
8.1	8.8	7.4	0.85	2.1	2.1	2.1	1.9	1.9	2.0
…	…	…	…	…	…	…	…	…	…
…	…	…	…	…	…	…	…	…	…
78.9	78.9	79.0	1.00	…	…	…	…	…	…
5.6	5.4	5.7	1.05	8.0	7.9	8.2	…	…	…

Table 4 (continued)

Country or territory	GROSS ENROLMENT RATIO (GER) IN ECCE 1990[1]/91 Total	Male	Female	GPI F/M
China[w]	22.7	22.7	22.6	0.99
Cook Islands	...	...	...	...
Democratic People's Rep. of Korea	...	...	...	...
Fiji	13.3	12.9	13.6	1.05
Indonesia[w]	18.4	...	...	...
Japan[o]	48.1	47.8	48.5	1.02
Kiribati	...	...	...	...
Lao People's Democratic Republic	7.2	7.7	6.7	0.87
Malaysia[w]	35.0	34.6	35.5	1.02
Marshall Islands	...	...	...	...
Myanmar	...	...	...	...
Nauru	...	...	...	...
New Zealand[o]	74.5	74.7	74.3	0.99
Niue	...	...	...	...
Papua New Guinea[3]	0.4	0.5	0.4	0.89
Philippines[w, 3]	12.1	...	...	...
Republic of Korea[o]	55.4	56.1	54.7	0.98
Samoa	...	...	...	...
Solomon Islands	31.8	32.1	31.5	0.98
Thailand[w]	43.3	43.0	43.5	1.01
Tonga	...	...	...	...
Tuvalu	...	...	...	...
Vanuatu	...	...	...	...
Viet Nam	28.0	...	...	...
Latin America and the Caribbean				
Anguilla[4]	...	...	...	...
Antigua and Barbuda[4]	...	...	...	...
Argentina[w]	...	...	...	...
Aruba[4]	...	...	...	...
Bahamas	...	...	...	...
Barbados	...	...	...	...
Belize	24.1	22.2	26.2	1.18
Bermuda	...	...	...	...
Bolivia	31.9	31.9	32.0	1.00
Brazil[w]	48.0	...	...	...
British Virgin Islands	...	...	...	...
Cayman Islands[4]	...	...	...	...
Chile[w]	82.4	82.0	82.8	1.01
Colombia	13.0	...	...	...
Costa Rica	61.0	60.7	61.3	1.01
Cuba	101.0	110.8	90.8	0.82
Dominica	...	...	...	...
Dominican Republic	...	...	...	...
Ecuador[3]	41.9	...	...	...
El Salvador[3]	...	...	...	...
Grenada	...	...	...	...
Guatemala	...	...	...	...
Guyana[3]	68.9	67.8	70.1	1.03
Haiti[3]	33.9	34.7	33.0	0.95
Honduras	...	...	...	...
Jamaica[w]	78.1	76.9	79.4	1.03
Mexico[o]	64.5	63.6	65.4	1.03
Montserrat[4]	...	...	...	...
Netherlands Antilles	...	...	...	...
Nicaragua	12.1	11.6	12.6	1.09
Panama	53.0	53.0	52.9	1.00
Paraguay[w]	27.1	26.7	27.6	1.03

1. Indicators for 1990/1991 and 1999/2000 may not be comparable. For further explanation, please see the Technical Introduction preceding these Annexes.
2. Enrolment ratios have not been calculated due to inconsistencies between enrolment and the United Nations population data.
3. Data in italics are for 1998/99.
4. Enrolment ratios have not been calculated due to lack of United Nations population data by age.

GROSS ENROLMENT RATIO (GER) IN ECCE				NEW ENTRANTS TO PRIMARY EDUCATION WITH ECCE EXPERIENCE AS %					
1999/2000			GPI	1998/99			1999/2000		
Total	Male	Female	F/M	Total	Male	Female	Total	Male	Female
39.5	40.4	38.5	0.95	...	...	...	...	...	...
...	...	...	...	...	...	...	...	...	...
...	...	...	...	...	...	...	...	...	...
15.4**	15.2**	15.5**	1.02	...	...	...	...	...	...
18.6	18.3	18.9	1.04	...	...	...	...	...	...
83.5	83.5**	83.6**	1.00	...	...	...	...	...	...
...	...	...	...	...	...	...	...	...	...
8.0	7.6	8.4	1.10	...	...	...	...	...	...
51.8	50.9	52.8	1.04	...	...	...	90.4	89.0	91.8
...	...	...	...	...	...	...	...	...	...
1.9**	...	...	...	...	...	...	...	...	...
...	...	...	...	...	...	...	...	...	...
57.8	57.8	57.9	1.00	...	...	...	...	...	...
...	...	...	...	12.2	11.1	14.3	...	...	...
18.9	*19.4*	*18.3*	*0.94*	24.3	24.1	24.5	...	...	...
30.7	*30.0*	*31.5*	*1.05*	...	...	...	...	...	...
78.8	79.2	78.4	0.99	...	...	...	...	...	...
35.4	33.8	37.0	1.10	...	...	...	...	...	...
...	...	...	...	...	...	...	...	...	...
83.5	84.0	83.0	0.99	...	...	...	94.5	92.5	96.7
...	...	...	...	66.1	51.7	82.2	26.2**	30.2**	21.5**
...	...	...	...	...	...	...	...	...	...
73.1	69.9	76.5	1.10	100.0	100.0	100.0	...	...	...
40.3	41.1	39.5	0.96	...	...	...	...	...	...
...	...	...	...	100.0	100.0	100.0	100.0	100.0	100.0
...	...	...	...	...	...	...	96.0	94.2	96.6
57.4	56.7	58.1	1.02	...	...	...	...	...	...
...	...	...	...	84.9	84.7	85.1	82.9	86.0	79.7
...	...	...	...	...	...	...	...	...	...
79.1	77.5	80.7	1.04	...	...	...	100.0	100.0	100.0
30.9	30.5	31.3	1.03	...	...	...	...	...	...
...	...	...	...	...	...	...	...	...	...
45.3**	45.0**	45.7**	1.02	...	...	...	49.5	49.5	49.4
59.7	59.7	59.7	1.00	...	...	...	...	...	...
...	...	...	...	...	...	...	...	...	...
...	...	...	...	86.9**	91.3**	82.4**	90.0**	90.0**	90.0**
76.7	77.0	76.4	0.99	...	...	...	...	...	...
35.9	35.6	36.3	1.02	...	...	...	...	...	...
81.9	82.1	81.6	0.99	...	...	...	77.3	77.0	77.7
107.6	105.5	109.9	1.04	99.1	98.8	99.3	96.2	96.4	96.0
...	...	...	...	...	...	...	...	...	...
37.4	37.2	37.7	1.01	...	...	...	...	...	...
65.6	64.7	66.5	1.03	44.9	44.0	45.9	...	...	...
40.0	*39.2*	*40.9*	*1.04*	...	...	...	...	...	...
...	...	...	...	...	...	...	...	...	...
45.8	46.0	45.5	0.99	...	...	...	...	...	...
119.7	*120.0*	*119.4*	*1.00*	...	...	...	...	...	...
64.3	*63.2*	*65.3*	*1.03*	...	...	...	...	...	...
...	...	...	...	...	...	...	...	...	...
88.1	86.6	89.7	1.04	...	...	...	...	...	...
76.3	75.3	77.4	1.03	...	...	...	...	...	...
...	...	...	...	...	...	...	100.0	100.0	100.0
98.0	97.5	98.5	1.01	...	...	...	100.0	100.0	100.0
26.5	26.0	27.1	1.04	...	...	...	...	...	...
40.5	40.1	40.9	1.02	...	...	...	76.5	75.2	77.8
83.0	81.9	84.1	1.03	...	...	...	57.4	56.0	58.9

Table 4 (continued)

Country or territory	GROSS ENROLMENT RATIO (GER) IN ECCE 1990[1]/91 Total	Male	Female	GPI F/M
Peru[w]	29.9	...	...	...
Saint Kitts and Nevis[4]	...	...	...	...
Saint Lucia	...	...	...	...
Saint Vincent and the Grenadines	...	...	...	...
Suriname[3]	79.4	80.5	78.3	0.97
Trinidad and Tobago	8.8	8.8	8.9	1.01
Turks and Caicos Islands[4]	...	...	...	...
Uruguay[w]	42.7	42.2	43.1	1.02
Venezuela	40.8	40.4	41.2	1.02
North America and Western Europe				
Andorra	...	...	...	...
Austria[o]	70.0	70.5	69.4	0.98
Belgium[o]	105.1	105.2	105.0	1.00
Canada[o]	60.4	60.6	60.2	0.99
Cyprus[2]	...	...	...	...
Denmark[o]	99.0	99.3	98.8	1.00
Finland[o]	33.6	...	...	...
France[o]	83.3	83.5	83.1	1.00
Germany[o]	...	...	...	...
Greece[o]	56.4	56.3	56.5	1.00
Iceland[o]	...	...	...	...
Ireland[o]	101.5	102.3	100.7	0.98
Israel[o]	82.7	...	...	...
Italy[o]	93.4	92.9	93.9	1.01
Luxembourg[o]	91.7	...	...	...
Malta[3]	103.8	108.2	99.3	0.92
Monaco	...	...	...	...
Netherlands[o]	99.2	98.6	99.9	1.01
Norway[o]	88.3	...	...	...
Portugal[o]	52.9	53.2	52.6	0.99
San Marino	...	...	...	...
Spain[o]	59.4	58.6	60.3	1.03
Sweden[o]	64.7	...	...	...
Switzerland[o]	59.7	59.7	59.8	1.00
United Kingdom[o]	52.4	51.9	52.9	1.02
United States[o]	62.6	63.5	61.6	0.97
South and West Asia				
Afghanistan	...	...	...	...
Bangladesh[3]	...	...	...	...
Bhutan	...	...	...	...
India[w]	3.4	3.6	3.2	0.90
Iran, Islamic Republic of	12.5	12.8	12.1	0.95
Maldives	...	...	...	...
Nepal	...	...	...	...
Pakistan	...	...	...	...
Sri Lanka[w]	...	...	...	...
Sub-Saharan Africa				
Angola	53.9	71.2	36.6	0.51
Benin	2.6	2.8	2.4	0.83
Botswana	...	...	...	...
Burkina Faso	0.7	0.7	0.7	1.02
Burundi	...	...	...	...
Cameroon	12.7	12.7	12.8	1.01
Cape Verde	...	...	...	...
Central African Republic	5.7	...	...	...
Chad	...	...	...	...

1. Indicators for 1990/1991 and 1999/2000 may not be comparable. For further explanation, please see the Technical Introduction preceding these Annexes.
2. Enrolment ratios have not been calculated due to inconsistencies between enrolment and the United Nations population data.
3. Data in italics are for 1998/99.
4. Enrolment ratios have not been calculated due to lack of United Nations population data by age.

GROSS ENROLMENT RATIO (GER) IN ECCE				NEW ENTRANTS TO PRIMARY EDUCATION WITH ECCE EXPERIENCE AS %					
1999/2000			GPI	1998/99			1999/2000		
Total	Male	Female	F/M	Total	Male	Female	Total	Male	Female
59.0	58.3	59.7	1.02	...	...	...	...	...	...
...	...	...	...	...	...	...	98.2	98.1	98.4
63.6	60.9	66.5	1.09	...	...	...	...	...	...
...	...	...	...	...	...	...	...	...	...
88.9	...	...	...	...	...	...	...	...	...
60.2	60.4**	60.0**	0.99	...	...	...	...	...	...
...	...	...	...	...	...	...	100.0	100.0	100.0
59.2	58.5	59.8	1.02	...	...	...	100.0	100.0	100.0
48.1**	47.7**	48.6**	1.02	...	...	...	...	...	...
...	...	...	...	...	...	...	...	...	...
81.4	81.4	81.3	1.00	...	...	...	...	...	...
111.5	112.1	110.8	0.99	...	...	...	...	...	...
64.2	64.4	64.0	0.99	...	...	...	...	...	...
...	...	...	...	...	...	...	...	...	...
91.7	91.7	91.7	1.00	...	...	...	...	...	...
49.0	49.1	48.8	0.99	...	...	...	...	...	...
84.4	84.5	84.3	1.00	...	...	...	...	...	...
96.2	98.1	94.3	0.96	...	...	...	...	...	...
72.2	71.4	73.0	1.02	...	...	...	...	...	...
83.3	83.5	83.1	0.99	...	...	...	...	...	...
3.1	2.8	3.4	1.20	...	...	...	...	...	...
78.4	78.7	78.2	0.99	...	...	...	...	...	...
95.5	95.5	95.4	1.00	...	...	...	...	...	...
117.1	132.1	101.2	0.77	...	...	...	...	...	...
102.3	*102.4*	*102.2*	*1.00*	...	...	...	...	...	...
...	...	...	...	...	...	...	...	...	...
97.7	98.3	97.1	0.99	...	...	...	...	...	...
77.4	75.3	79.7	1.06	...	...	...	...	...	...
68.1	68.1	68.2	1.00	...	...	...	...	...	...
...	...	...	...	...	...	...	...	...	...
74.4	73.9	75.0	1.02	...	...	...	...	...	...
73.9	74.1	73.7	0.99	...	...	...	...	...	...
94.6	95.2	94.0	0.99	...	...	...	...	...	...
79.1	79.1	79.0	1.00	...	...	...	...	...	...
57.2	56.8	57.6	1.01	...	...	...	...	...	...
...	...	...	...	...	...	...	...	...	...
*23.8***	*22.4***	*25.2***	*1.13*	...	...	...	...	...	...
...	...	...	...	...	...	...	...	...	...
30.0	30.1	29.9	0.99	...	...	...	...	...	...
14.4	14.0	14.8	1.06	...	...	...	...	...	...
47.5	47.6	47.4	1.00	...	...	...	88.6	88.4	88.8
..	...	...	...	...	...	...	...	...	...
9.3	13.6	4.8	0.36	...	...	...	...	...	...
...	...	...	...	...	...	...	...	...	...
...	...	...	...	...	...	...	...	...	...
6.9	7.1	6.7	0.94	...	...	...	...	...	...
...	...	...	...	27.0**	24.3**	29.9**	...	...	...
1.6*	1.6*	1.6*	1.02	2.8	2.5	3.2	...	...	...
0.9*	0.9*	0.8*	0.95	...	...	...	...	...	...
10.2	9.6	10.8	1.13	...	...	...	...	...	...
...	...	...	...	...	...	...	...	...	...
...	...	...	...	...	...	...	...	...	...
...	...	...	...	...	...	...	...	...	...

Table 4 (continued)

Country or territory	GROSS ENROLMENT RATIO (GER) IN ECCE 1990[1]/91 Total	Male	Female	GPI F/M
Comoros	...	...	...	...
Congo	2.6	2.6	2.6	0.99
Côte d'Ivoire	0.9	1.0	0.9	0.95
Democratic Rep. of the Congo	...	...	...	...
Equatorial Guinea	...	...	...	...
Eritrea	...	...	...	...
Ethiopia	1.6	1.6	1.6	0.99
Gabon	...	...	...	...
Gambia	...	...	...	...
Ghana[3]	...	...	...	...
Guinea	...	...	...	...
Guinea-Bissau	...	...	...	...
Kenya[3]	33.9	31.5	36.3	1.15
Lesotho[3]	...	...	...	...
Liberia	...	...	...	...
Madagascar	...	...	...	...
Malawi	...	...	...	...
Mali[3]	...	...	...	...
Mauritius	56.1	56.4	55.8	0.99
Mozambique	...	...	...	...
Namibia	14.4	13.5	15.4	1.15
Niger	1.5	1.6	1.4	0.91
Nigeria	...	...	...	...
Rwanda	...	...	...	...
Sao Tome and Principe	...	...	...	...
Senegal	2.4	2.4	2.5	1.04
Seychelles[4]	...	...	...	...
Sierra Leone	...	...	...	...
Somalia	...	...	...	...
South Africa	18.9	18.6	19.1	1.02
Swaziland	16.6	11.8	21.3	1.80
Togo	3.1	3.1	3.0	0.98
Uganda	...	...	...	...
United Republic of Tanzania	...	...	...	...
Zambia[3]	...	...	...	...
Zimbabwe[w]	...	...	...	...

1. Indicators for 1990/1991 and 1999/2000 may not be comparable. For further explanation, please see the Technical Introduction preceding these Annexes.
2. Enrolment ratios have not been calculated due to inconsistencies between enrolment and the United Nations population data.
3. Data in italics are for 1998/99.
4. Enrolment ratios have not been calculated due to lack of United Nations population data by age.

GROSS ENROLMENT RATIO (GER) IN ECCE				NEW ENTRANTS TO PRIMARY EDUCATION WITH ECCE EXPERIENCE AS %					
1999/2000			GPI	1998/99			1999/2000		
Total	Male	Female	F/M	Total	Male	Female	Total	Male	Female
1.7	1.6	1.8	1.08	4.0	4.5	3.5	99.8	99.8	...
2.7	2.2	3.2	1.47	...	...	...	...	...	...
2.7**	2.8**	2.7**	0.97	...	...	...	...	...	...
...	...	...	...	...	...	...	...	...	...
30.0**	29.3**	30.7**	1.05	...	...	...	...	...	...
5.5	5.7	5.3	0.93	...	...	...	...	...	...
1.7	1.8	1.7	0.93	...	...	...	...	...	...
...	...	...	...	...	...	...	...	...	...
28.3**	29.8**	26.8**	0.90	27.5	27.2	27.8	...	...	...
57.1	*57.3*	*56.9*	*0.99*	...	...	...	...	...	...
...	...	...	...	...	...	...	...	...	...
3.9	3.8	4.0	1.05	...	...	...	...	...	...
38.4	*37.1*	*39.7*	*1.07*	...	...	...	...	...	...
21.8	*20.3*	*23.3*	*1.15*	...	...	...	...	...	...
69.5	73.7	65.3	0.89	...	...	...	25.8	20.3	31.5
3.4	3.3	3.4	1.02	...	...	...	...	...	...
...	...	...	...	...	...	...	...	...	...
2.4	*1.9*	*2.9*	*1.53*	...	...	...	...	...	...
96.1	95.2	97.0	1.02	97.0	...	...	...	...	...
...	...	...	...	...	...	...	...	...	...
64.7	60.2	69.3	1.15	...	...	...	...	...	...
0.9	0.9	1.0	1.02	...	...	...	...	...	...
...	...	...	...	...	...	...	...	...	...
...	...	...	...	...	...	...	...	...	...
...	...	...	...	...	...	...	...	...	...
3.0	2.9	3.0	1.06	...	...	...	...	...	...
...	...	...	...	100.0	100.0	100.0	100.0	100.0	100.0
4.0	3.9	4.2	1.07	...	...	...	5.3	4.8	5.9
...	...	...	...	...	...	...	...	...	...
21.8	21.8	21.8	1.00	...	...	...	...	...	...
...	...	...	...	...	...	...	...	...	...
2.2	2.2	2.3	1.06	...	...	...	...	...	...
2.8	2.8	2.8	1.00	2.5	4.9	...	...	...	...
...	...	...	...	...	...	...	...	...	...
*2.3**	*2.1**	*2.5**	*1.21*	8.5	7.7	9.4	...	...	...
...	...	...	...	...	...	...	...	...	...

Table 5
Access to primary education

Country or territory	Entrance-age population 1999 (thousands)	GROSS INTAKE RATE (GIR) IN PRIMARY EDUCATION 1990[1]/91 Total	Male	Female	GPI F/M	1999/2000 Total	Male	Female	GPI F/M
Arab States and North Africa									
Algeria[3]	701	101.3	106.0	96.3	0.91	102.5	103.8	101.2	0.98
Bahrain	13	107.9	106.7	109.1	1.02	98.3	98.1	98.6	1.00
Djibouti	19	35.9	37.9	33.9	0.90	32.5	36.7	28.2	0.77
Egypt[w]	1 557	...	...	...	...	95.6**	97.4**	93.8**	0.96
Iraq	610	...	...	...	...	116.3	123.2	109.2	0.89
Jordan[w]	125	...	...	...	...	105.6	105.3	105.8	1.00
Kuwait[3]	35	...	...	...	...	*86.3*	*87.4*	*85.1*	*0.97*
Lebanon[3]	77	...	...	...	...	87.0	88.1	85.8	0.97
Libyan Arab Jamahiriya	105	...	...	...	...	...	...	...	...
Mauritania	77	53.3	60.3	46.1	0.76	...	...	...	...
Morocco	684	76.1	87.1	64.7	0.74	106.9	109.7	104.1	0.95
Oman[3]	75	88.5	90.0	86.9	0.97	68.9	69.0	68.7	1.00
Palestinian Autonomous Territories	93	...	...	...	...	110.4	110.4	110.4	1.00
Qatar[3]	10	54.1	53.5	54.7	1.02	*113.6*	*115.3*	*111.7*	*0.97*
Saudi Arabia	587	73.0	74.7	71.2	0.95	66.7	67.3	66.0	0.98
Sudan	833	56.0	63.7	48.2	0.76	53.7	59.0	48.1	0.82
Syrian Arab Republic[3]	419	102.9	105.8	99.8	0.94	*108.1*	*111.2*	*104.8*	*0.94*
Tunisia[w]	190	101.2	103.0	99.3	0.96	104.9	104.9	105.0	1.00
United Arab Emirates	44	98.7	100.8	96.5	0.96	108.1	108.2	107.9	1.00
Yemen[3]	611	...	...	...	...	*75.6*	*88.8*	*63.7*	*0.72*
Central and Eastern Europe									
Albania	65	103.6	102.1	105.3	1.03	101.3	102.0	100.6	0.99
Belarus	122	97.5	...	...	...	99.5	98.6	100.3	1.02
Bosnia and Herzegovina	46	...	...	...	...	...	...	...	...
Bulgaria	90	95.6	94.6	96.5	1.02	99.6	100.8	98.4	0.98
Croatia[2]	54	...	...	...	...	...	...	...	...
Czech Republic[o]	119	104.8	...	...	...	102.6	102.3	102.9	1.01
Estonia	17	...	...	...	...	102.1	102.6	101.5	0.99
Hungary[o]	120	98.5	94.4	102.9	1.09	101.8	103.5	100.0	0.97
Latvia[3]	30	...	...	...	...	*98.9*	*95.8*	*102.2*	*1.07*
Lithuania[3]	51	...	...	...	...	*101.1*	*101.4*	*100.8*	*0.99*
Poland[o]	515	100.1	99.0	101.3	1.02	98.1	98.5**	97.6**	0.99
Republic of Moldova	69	...	...	...	...	...	...	...	...
Romania[3]	260	84.8	85.0	84.6	1.00	*93.7*	*94.1*	*93.3*	*0.99*
Russian Federation[w, 3]	1 582	...	...	...	...	*93.8*	*94.3***	*93.3***	*0.99*
Slovakia	72	...	...	...	...	102.0	102.6	101.4	0.99
Slovenia[3]	21	...	...	...	...	*95.2*	*95.6*	*94.9*	*0.99*
The former Yugoslav Rep. of Macedonia[3]	31	...	...	...	...	...	...	...	...
Turkey[o]	1 427	93.0	96.2	89.6	0.93	101.5	106.9	96.0	0.90
Ukraine	586	100.8	...	...	...	...	...	...	...
Yugoslavia[2]	142	...	...	...	...	...	...	...	...
Central Asia									
Armenia	67	...	...	...	...	...	...	...	...
Azerbaijan[3]	174	...	...	...	...	95.5	93.9	97.2	1.04
Georgia	71	...	...	...	...	...	...	...	...
Kazakhstan	298	...	...	...	...	...	...	...	...
Kyrgyzstan	113	...	...	...	...	...	...	...	...
Mongolia	62	...	...	...	...	...	...	...	...
Tajikistan	163	...	...	...	...	...	...	...	...
Turkmenistan	120	...	...	...	...	...	...	...	...
Uzbekistan	625	...	...	...	...	...	...	...	...
East Asia and the Pacific									
Australia[o]	266	103.4	104.2	102.7	0.99	...	...	...	...
Cambodia	377	...	...	...	...	121.9	125.9	117.8	0.94

1. Indicators for 1990/1991 and 1999/2000 may not be comparable. For further explanation, please see the Technical Introduction preceding these Annexes.
2. Enrolment ratios have not been calculated due to inconsistencies between enrolment and the United Nations population data.
3. Data in italics are for 1998/99.
4. Enrolment ratios have not been calculated due to lack of United Nations population data by age.

NET INTAKE RATE (NIR) IN PRIMARY EDUCATION				SCHOOL LIFE EXPECTANCY Expected number of years of formal schooling							
1999/2000			GPI	1990[1]/91			GPI	1999/2000			GPI
Total	Male	Female	F/M	Total	Male	Female	F/M	Total	Male	Female	F/M
79.1	80.5	77.6	0.96	7	7	6	0.84	*12*	...	...	...
80.3	79.1	81.6	1.03	8	7	8	1.04	...	...	...	...
25.4	29.2	21.5	0.74	...	...	...	...	...	...	...	...
75.6	77.2	73.9	0.96	...	...	...	...	...	...	...	...
86.7	90.4	82.9	0.92	...	...	...	...	9	10	8	0.75
70.6	69.9	71.4	1.02	9	8	9	1.04	...	...	...	...
54.9	*56.7*	*53.1*	*0.94*	...	...	...	...	*9*	*8***	*9*	*1.11*
8.1	7.4	8.8	1.19	...	...	...	...	*13*	*13*	*13*	*1.03*
...	...	...	...	...	...	...	...	...	...	...	...
...	...	...	...	...	...	...	...	...	...	...	...
58.5	60.2	56.6	0.94	7	8	5	0.69	8	9	7	0.82
56.1	56.1	56.2	1.00	8	9	8	0.87	*9*	*9*	*9*	*0.96*
90.7	90.3	91.2	1.01	...	...	...	...	12	12	12	1.02
...	...	...	...	12	11	13	1.17	*13*	*12***	*14*	*1.14*
42.7	50.9	34.2	0.67	8	8	7	0.87	...	...	...	...
28.0	29.5	26.4	0.89	...	...	...	...	...	...	...	...
61.0	*61.6*	*60.4*	*0.98*	10	11	9	0.82	9	...	...	...
81.7	81.2	82.2	1.01	7	8	7	0.87	14	14	14	1.00
55.9	56.1	55.7	0.99	11	10	11	1.09	...	...	...	...
25.5	*30.1*	*20.7*	*0.69*	...	...	...	...	*8*	*11*	*5*	*0.47*
...	...	...	...	...	...	...	...	...	...	...	...
81.2	81.8	80.6	0.99	...	...	...	...	...	...	...	...
...	...	...	...	...	...	...	...	...	...	...	...
...	...	...	...	10	10	11	1.08	13	12	13	1.04
...	...	...	...	...	...	...	...	...	...	...	...
...	...	...	...	...	...	...	...	14	13	14	1.00
...	...	...	...	...	...	...	...	14	14	15	1.07
...	...	...	...	9	9	9	1.07	14	13	14	1.03
...	...	...	...	...	...	...	...	11	11	11	1.01
...	...	...	...	...	...	...	...	12	12	12	0.99
...	...	...	...	10	9	10	1.10	14	14	15	1.05
...	...	...	...	...	...	...	...	...	...	...	...
...	...	...	...	...	...	...	...	...	...	...	...
...	...	...	...	...	...	...	...	...	...	...	...
...	...	...	...	...	...	...	...	...	...	...	...
...	...	...	...	...	...	...	...	*14*	*14***	*15*	*1.07*
...	...	...	...	9	9	9	0.99	*12*	*12*	*12*	*1.01*
...	...	...	...	8	15	...	...	...	...	...	...
...	...	...	...	...	...	...	...	...	...	...	...
...	...	...	...	...	...	...	...	...	...	...	...
...	...	...	...	...	...	...	...	...	...	...	...
11.7	*11.5*	*11.8*	*1.03*	...	...	...	...	*11*	*11***	*10*	*0.99*
...	...	...	...	...	...	...	...	...	...	...	...
...	...	...	...	...	...	...	...	...	...	...	...
...	...	...	...	...	...	...	...	...	...	...	...
...	...	...	...	...	...	...	...	8	7	8	1.13
...	...	...	...	...	...	...	...	...	...	...	...
...	...	...	...	...	...	...	...	...	...	...	...
...	...	...	...	...	...	...	...	...	...	...	...
...	...	...	...	13	13	13	1.03	17	16	17	1.02
69.5	71.4	67.5	0.95	...	...	...	...	7	8	6	0.82

Table 5 (continued)

Country or territory	Entrance-age population 1999 (thousands)	GROSS INTAKE RATE (GIR) IN PRIMARY EDUCATION 1990[1]/91 Total	Male	Female	GPI F/M	1999/2000 Total	Male	Female	GPI F/M
China[w]	20 533	106.6	94.6	119.8	1.27	99.6	98.8	100.5	1.02
Cook Islands[4]	...	...	...	...	...	...	...	...	...
Democratic People's Rep. of Korea	414	...	...	...	...	...	...	...	...
Fiji[3]	18	...	...	...	...	*122.3***	*123.6***	*121.0***	*0.98*
Indonesia[w]	4 340	111.0	92.8	129.7	1.40	109.6**	113.2**	105.8**	0.93
Japan[o, 3]	1 190	102.3	102.1	102.5	1.00	*101.6*	*101.7*	*101.5*	*1.00*
Kiribati	...	...	...	...	...	...	...	...	...
Lao People's Democratic Republic	150	...	...	...	...	124.5	132.0	116.8	0.88
Malaysia[w, 3]	541	94.6	94.6	94.6	1.00	*95.2*	*95.5*	*94.9*	*0.99*
Marshall Islands[4]	...	...	...	...	...	...	...	...	...
Myanmar	1 092	...	...	...	...	111.7	109.8	113.6	1.03
Nauru	...	...	...	...	...	...	...	...	...
New Zealand[o]	60	104.2	104.7	103.7	0.99	98.5	98.6	98.4	1.00
Niue	...	...	...	...	...	...	...	...	...
Papua New Guinea[3]	131	98.1	105.7	90.3	0.85	*97.8*	*102.0*	*93.2*	*0.91*
Philippines[w, 3]	1 932	...	...	...	...	*133.5*	*136.9*	*130.0*	*0.95*
Republic of Korea[o]	680	97.7	97.5	98.0	1.00	105.9	105.5	106.4	1.01
Samoa	4	...	...	...	...	114.6	116.8	112.2	0.96
Solomon Islands	13	86.0	85.1	87.0	1.02	...	...	...	...
Thailand[w]	1 079	109.0	111.0	106.9	0.96	91.1	94.1	88.0	0.94
Tonga	...	...	...	...	...	...	...	...	...
Tuvalu	...	...	...	...	...	...	...	...	...
Vanuatu	5	...	...	...	...	107.6**	107.3**	108.0**	1.01
Viet Nam	1 846	...	...	...	...	107.8	110.0**	105.5**	0.96
Latin America and the Caribbean									
Anguilla[4]	...	...	...	...	...	...	...	...	...
Antigua and Barbuda[4]	...	...	...	...	...	...	...	...	...
Argentina[w]	685	...	...	...	...	114.0	113.9	114.2	1.00
Aruba[4]	...	...	...	...	...	...	...	...	...
Bahamas[3]	6	110.3	...	...	...	*114.9*	*119.7*	*109.8*	*0.92*
Barbados	4	...	...	...	...	102.0	101.5	102.5	1.01
Belize	6	158.7	160.7	156.6	0.97	137.6	140.7	134.4	0.96
Bermuda	...	...	...	...	...	...	...	...	...
Bolivia	224	139.6	140.2	138.9	0.99	126.8**	126.2**	127.5**	1.01
Brazil[w, 3]	3 250	...	...	...	...	*128.7*	...	...	...
British Virgin Islands[4]	...	...	...	...	...	...	...	...	...
Cayman Islands[4]	...	...	...	...	...	...	...	...	...
Chile[w]	293	104.8	106.3	103.3	0.97	96.7	97.3	96.2	0.99
Colombia	946	125.4	118.0	133.2	1.13	134.0	136.9	131.0	0.96
Costa Rica	85	101.5	81.6	122.2	1.50	102.4	102.6	102.2	1.00
Cuba[3]	158	100.4	100.7	100.1	0.99	96.5	96.4	96.7	1.00
Dominica[4]	...	...	...	...	...	...	...	...	...
Dominican Republic	185	...	...	...	...	141.7	147.9	135.2	0.91
Ecuador[3]	287	...	...	...	...	*131.5*	*131.8*	*131.1*	*1.00*
El Salvador[3]	148	...	...	...	...	*127.8*	*130.2*	*125.4*	*0.96*
Grenada	...	...	...	...	...	...	...	...	...
Guatemala	325	...	...	...	...	131.0	133.5	128.4	0.96
Guyana[3]	15	88.1	88.9	87.2	0.98	*120.4*	*117.3*	*123.6*	*1.05*
Haiti[3]	211	59.3	60.5	58.2	0.96	...	...	...	...
Honduras	179	...	...	...	...	...	...	...	...
Jamaica[w]	55	95.2	96.7	93.8	0.97	100.5	100.7	100.4	1.00
Mexico[o]	2 206	120.2	99.3	141.8	1.43	113.4	113.2	113.7	1.00
Montserrat	...	...	...	...	...	...	...	...	...
Netherlands Antilles[3]	4	...	...	...	...	*124.6*	*129.7*	*119.3*	*0.92*
Nicaragua	142	...	...	...	...	142.7	146.2	139.2	0.95
Panama	60	115.7	119.5	111.7	0.93	113.9	114.3	113.5	0.99

1. Indicators for 1990/1991 and 1999/2000 may not be comparable. For further explanation, please see the Technical Introduction preceding these Annexes.
2. Enrolment ratios have not been calculated due to inconsistencies between enrolment and the United Nations population data.
3. Data in italics are for 1998/99.
4. Enrolment ratios have not been calculated due to lack of United Nations population data by age.

NET INTAKE RATE (NIR) IN PRIMARY EDUCATION				SCHOOL LIFE EXPECTANCY Expected number of years of formal schooling							
1999/2000			GPI	1990[1]/91			GPI	1999/2000			GPI
Total	Male	Female	F/M	Total	Male	Female	F/M	Total	Male	Female	F/M
...	...	...	...	6	7	6	0.92	...	...	...	...
...	...	...	...	...	...	...	...	...	...	...	...
...	...	...	...	...	...	...	...	...	...	...	...
80.5**	81.0**	79.9**	*0.99*	...	...	...	...	...	...	...	...
40.1**	41.0**	39.2**	0.95	9	9	9	0.95	...	...	...	...
...	...	...	...	13	18	7	...	14	14	14	0.98
...	...	...	...	...	...	...	...	...	...	...	...
59.3	60.0	58.6	0.98	...	...	...	...	8	9	7	0.79
95.2	*95.5*	*94.9*	*0.99*	...	...	...	...	11	11	12	1.05
...	...	...	...	...	...	...	...	...	...	...	...
81.1	79.7	82.5	1.03	...	...	...	...	...	...	...	...
...	...	...	...	...	...	...	...	...	...	...	...
...	...	...	...	14	14	15	1.01	...	...	...	...
...	...	...	...	...	...	...	...	...	...	...	...
97.8	*102.0*	*93.2*	*0.91*	...	...	...	...	*6*	*6*	*6*	*0.89*
46.6**	47.7**	45.3**	*0.95*	...	...	...	...	...	...	...	...
...	...	...	...	13	13	12	0.88	...	...	...	...
84.3	83.6	85.0	1.02	...	...	...	...	12	12	12	1.05
...	...	...	...	...	...	...	...	...	...	...	...
54.0	56.0	52.0	0.93	...	...	...	...	11	11	11	1.02
...	...	...	...	...	...	...	...	...	...	...	...
...	...	...	...	...	...	...	...	...	...	...	...
...	...	...	...	...	...	...	...	...	...	...	...
87.3	...	...	...	...	...	...	...	10	11	...	...
...	...	...	...	...	...	...	...	...	...	...	...
...	...	...	...	...	...	...	...	...	...	...	...
92.2**	92.1**	92.3**	1.00	...	...	...	...	14	14	15	1.11
...	...	...	...	...	...	...	...	...	...	...	...
...	...	...	...	...	...	...	...	...	...	...	...
81.5	80.0	83.0	1.04	...	...	...	...	*12*	*12*	*13*	*1.11*
...	...	...	...	...	...	...	...	...	...	...	...
...	...	...	...	...	...	...	...	...	...	...	...
68.0**	67.7**	68.4**	1.01	9	8	7	0.91	...	...	...	...
68.8**	...	...	...	9	18	...	...	13	13	14	1.03
...	...	...	...	...	...	...	...	...	...	...	...
...	...	...	...	...	...	...	...	...	...	...	...
37.1**	36.7**	37.4**	1.02	8	16	...	...	14	14	13	0.98
62.5**	64.4**	60.7**	0.94	...	...	...	...	...	...	...	...
59.1	58.2	60.1	1.03	9	8	8	1.00	...	...	...	...
90.3	*90.4*	*90.1*	*1.00*	11	10	11	1.08	12	12	12	1.02
...	...	...	...	...	...	...	...	...	...	...	...
60.0	59.7	60.2	1.01	...	...	...	...	...	...	...	...
82.3	*81.9*	*82.9*	*1.01*	...	...	...	...	...	...	...	...
...	...	...	...	...	...	...	...	...	...	...	...
...	...	...	...	...	...	...	...	...	...	...	...
...	...	...	...	...	...	...	...	...	...	...	...
...	...	...	...	10	10	10	1.02	...	...	...	...
43.1	*37.2*	*49.1*	*1.32*	5	5	5	0.93	...	...	...	...
...	...	...	...	...	...	...	...	...	...	...	...
82.2**	80.1**	84.3**	1.05	6	6	6	0.99	11	11	11	1.05
...	...	...	...	10	20	...	...	12	12	11	0.98
...	...	...	...	...	...	...	...	...	...	...	...
...	...	...	...	...	...	...	...	12	12	12	1.03
39.8	40.8	38.7	0.95	8	7	8	1.12	...	...	...	...
85.5**	85.1**	86.0**	1.01	8	7	6	0.96	...	...	...	...

Table 5 (continued)

Country or territory	Entrance-age population 1999 (thousands)	GROSS INTAKE RATE (GIR) IN PRIMARY EDUCATION 1990[1]/91 Total	Male	Female	GPI F/M	1999/2000 Total	Male	Female	GPI F/M
Paraguay[w]	146	119.5	121.8	117.2	0.96	120.8	122.9	118.6	0.96
Peru[w]	572	...	...	...	...	127.9	127.5	128.2	1.01
Saint Kitts and Nevis[4]	...	...	...	...	...	...	...	...	...
Saint Lucia	3	...	...	...	...	110.3	110.1	110.5	1.00
Saint Vincent and the Grenadines[4]	...	...	...	...	...	...	...	...	...
Suriname	8	...	...	...	...	...	...	...	...
Trinidad and Tobago[3]	20	87.9	89.7	86.1	0.96	96.0	98.0	93.9	0.96
Turks and Caicos Islands[4]	...	...	...	...	...	...	...	...	...
Uruguay[w]	56	100.5	100.2	100.8	1.01	107.3	107.2	107.4	1.00
Venezuela	551	114.5	116.9	112.0	0.96	103.0**	103.8**	102.3**	0.99
North America and Western Europe									
Andorra	95	99.3	99.9	98.6	0.99	...	...	...	...
Austria[o]	123	94.1	92.7	95.7	1.03	106.1**	107.3**	104.8**	1.0
Belgium[o]	408	107.1	109.6	104.6	0.95	...	...	...	...
Canada[o, 3]	13	87.7	88.6	86.7	0.98	*102.8*	*103.4*	*102.2*	*1.0*
Cyprus[2]	68	...	...	...	...	...	...	...	...
Denmark[o]	66	102.0	102.1	101.9	1.00	102.0	102.3	101.6	1.0
Finland[o]	721	100.7	94.1	107.5	1.14	101.2	102.1	100.4	1.0
France[o]	833	...	...	...	...	97.7	98.3**	97.1**	1.0
Germany[o, 3]	104	96.7	97.0	96.4	0.99	100.4	100.5	100.3	1.0
Greece[o]	5	...	...	...	...	...	...	...	...
Iceland[o]	52	98.4	98.8	98.0	0.99	99.2	97.2	101.4	1.0
Ireland[o]	110	99.0	97.4	100.6	1.03	99.1	99.5	98.7	1.0
Israel[o]	557	98.8	99.3	98.2	0.99	...	...	...	...
Italy[o]	6	...	...	...	...	100.2	100.5	99.9	1.0
Luxembourg[o]	5	102.7	105.2	100.1	0.95	99.0**	99.3**	98.7**	1.0
Malta[3]	...	...	...	...	...	*102.0*	*102.0*	*102.1*	*1.0*
Monaco	200	...	...	...	...	...	...	...	...
Netherlands[o]	62	98.4	99.1	97.7	0.99	98.5	99.0	98.0	1.0
Norway[o, 3]	112	217.8	217.8	217.8	1.00	*100.3*	*101.0*	*99.5*	*1.0*
Portugal[o]	...	...	...	...	...	...	...	...	...
San Marino	394	107.9	108.4	107.4	0.99	...	...	...	...
Spain[o, 3]	123	98.3	98.7	97.9	0.99	*104.1*	*103.7*	*104.5*	*1.0*
Sweden[o, 3]	84	98.0	96.9	99.2	1.02	*103.9*	*104.8*	*102.9*	*1.0*
Switzerland[o]	767	...	...	...	...	97.3	95.4	99.3	1.0
United Kingdom[o]	4 178	105.4	106.5	104.2	0.98	...	...	...	...
United States[o]	589	...	...	...	...	...	...	...	...
South and West Asia									
Afghanistan	589	...	...	...	...	...	...	...	...
Bangladesh[3]	3 578	100.3	106.9	93.1	0.87	*136.5***	*139.1***	*133.8***	*0.96*
Bhutan	60	...	...	...	...	...	...	...	...
India[w]	22 748	...	...	...	...	130.3	141.3	118.6	0.84
Iran, Islamic Republic of	1 807	112.3	113.6	111.0	0.98	79.1	79.0	79.2	1.00
Maldives	8	...	...	...	...	98.6	98.1	99.3	1.01
Nepal	632	...	...	...	...	...	...	...	...
Pakistan	4 022	...	...	...	...	...	...	...	...
Sri Lanka[w, 3]	330	98.8	98.8	98.8	1.00	*104.7*	*104.5*	*104.9*	*1.00*
Sub-Saharan Africa									
Angola	413	...	...	...	...	64.0**	68.8**	59.2**	0.86
Benin	193	75.9	102.9	49.1	0.48	123.9	140.9	106.9	0.76
Botswana	44	117.5	116.8	118.3	1.01	115.1	115.7	114.4	0.99
Burkina Faso	356	32.5	39.5	25.5	0.64	45.0	52.4	37.6	0.72
Burundi	197	68.3	73.0	63.5	0.87	69.8	77.1	62.4	0.81
Cameroon	431	85.1	90.2	79.9	0.89	81.3	88.3	74.3	0.84
Cape Verde[3]	11	...	...	...	...	*118.9*	*118.6*	*119.1*	*1.00*

1. Indicators for 1990/1991 and 1999/2000 may not be comparable. For further explanation, please see the Technical Introduction preceding these Annexes.
2. Enrolment ratios have not been calculated due to inconsistencies between enrolment and the United Nations population data.
3. Data in italics are for 1998/99.
4. Enrolment ratios have not been calculated due to lack of United Nations population data by age.

NET INTAKE RATE (NIR) IN PRIMARY EDUCATION				SCHOOL LIFE EXPECTANCY Expected number of years of formal schooling							
1999/2000			GPI	1990[1]/91			GPI	1999/2000			GPI
Total	Male	Female	F/M	Total	Male	Female	F/M	Total	Male	Female	F/M
68.7	67.4	70.0	1.04	7	7	7	0.95	...	...	...	...
84.7	84.7	84.7	1.00	...	...	...	...	...	...	...	...
...	...	...	...	...	...	...	...	...	...	...	...
22.7	21.6	23.9	1.11	...	...	...	...	...	...	...	...
...	...	...	...	...	...	...	...	...	...	...	...
...	...	...	...	...	...	...	...	...	...	...	...
89.8	*85.6*	*94.0*	*1.10*	11	11	11	1.01	*11*	*11*	*12*	*1.03*
...	...	...	...	...	...	...	...	...	...	...	...
44.9	44.5	45.4	1.02	...	...	...	...	14	13	14	1.11
63.5	63.0	64.0	1.02	10	9	9	1.03	...	...	...	...
...	...	...	...	...	...	...	...	...	...	...	...
...	...	...	...	8	8	8	1.00	15	15	15	0.99
...	...	...	...	17	16	17	1.05	16	16	16	1.02
...	...	...	...	6	6	6	1.01	15	14	15	1.06
...	...	...	...	...	...	...	...	...	...	...	...
86.9	85.5	88.2	1.03	7	7	8	1.15	16	15	16	1.06
...	...	...	...	7	7	8	1.03	17	16	17	1.06
...	...	...	...	...	...	...	...	15	15	16	1.03
...	...	...	...	12	12	13	1.03	*15.5*	*15*	*15*	*0.98*
100.0	100.0	100.0	1.00	...	...	...	...	14	14	14	1.02
...	...	...	...	12	12	12	1.01	16	15	17	1.10
...	...	...	...	...	...	...	...	15	14	15	1.06
...	...	...	...	...	...	...	...	15	14	15	1.06
...	...	...	...	...	...	...	...	15	14	15	1.02
...	...	...	...	12	12	12	1.05	13	13**	13	1.04
...	...	...	...	...	...	...	...	...	...	...	...
...	...	...	...	12	11	12	1.03	...	...	...	...
...	...	...	...	12	12	13	1.06	16	16	16	0.98
...	...	...	...	12	12	13	1.06	17	16	18	1.08
...	...	...	...	...	...	...	...	15	15	16	1.07
...	...	...	...	13	13	13	1.04	...	...	...	...
...	...	...	...	11	11	12	1.07	15	15	16	1.04
...	...	...	...	11	11	11	0.97	16	15	17	1.12
...	...	...	...	13	13	13	1.02	15	16	15	0.93
...	...	...	...	15	15	16	1.05	16	16	17	1.05
...	...	...	...	...	...	...	...	15	15	16	1.06
...	...	...	...	...	...	...	...	...	...	...	...
*73.5***	*74.9***	*72.0***	*0.96*	4	4	3	0.80	...	...	...	...
...	...	...	...	...	...	...	...	...	...	...	...
...	...	...	...	...	...	...	...	...	...	...	...
38.4	38.7	38.0	0.98	...	...	...	...	...	...	...	...
...	...	...	...	...	...	...	...	12	12	12	1.01
...	...	...	...	...	...	...	...	...	...	...	...
...	...	...	...	...	...	...	...	...	...	...	...
...	...	...	...	...	...	...	...	...	...	...	...
17.5**	18.3**	16.6**	0.91	...	...	...	...	...	...	...	...
...	...	...	...	...	...	...	...	7	9	5	0.60
23.7	21.7	25.7	1.18	10	10	11	1.07	12	12	12	1.00
20.6	24.3	16.8	0.69	...	...	...	...	...	...	...	...
27.9	29.5	26.4	0.89	...	...	...	...	...	...	...	...
...	...	...	...	...	...	...	...	...	...	...	...
76.7	*74.8*	*78.7*	*1.05*	...	...	...	...	...	...	...	...

Table 5 (continued)

Country or territory	Entrance-age population 1999 (thousands)	GROSS INTAKE RATE (GIR) IN PRIMARY EDUCATION 1990[1]/91 Total	Male	Female	GPI F/M	1999/2000 Total	Male	Female	GPI F/M
Central African Republic[3]	107	59.5	68.7	50.5	0.74	*42.1***	*48.8***	*35.3***	*0.72*
Chad	239	55.2	69.4	41.2	0.59	80.9	93.9	67.8	0.72
Comoros[3]	20	...	...	...	...	76.5**	83.6**	69.2**	0.83
Congo[3]	92	94.2	100.3	88.3	0.88	*34.8*	*36.1*	*33.7*	*0.93*
Côte d'Ivoire[3]	434	57.0	64.6	49.4	0.76	*70.7*	*78.3*	*63.0*	*0.80*
Democratic Rep. of the Congo[3]	1648	69.1	75.6	62.5	0.83	*48.3*	*46.5*	*50.0*	*1.08*
Equatorial Guinea	13	...	...	...	...	...	...	...	...
Eritrea[3]	103	29.0	...	...	...	67.1	74.5	59.7	0.80
Ethiopia[3]	1803	49.3	59.8	39.0	0.65	98.5	113.6	83.3	0.73
Gabon	32	...	...	...	...	...	...	...	...
Gambia	33	...	...	...	...	110.0	113.4	106.6	0.94
Ghana[3]	529	82.4	87.4	77.3	0.88	*89.6*	*92.7*	*86.5*	*0.93*
Guinea[3]	225	43.0	57.4	28.3	0.49	64.1	68.7	59.3	0.86
Guinea-Bissau[3]	33	...	...	...	...	111.6	127.8	95.4	0.75
Kenya	860	119.9	122.0	117.7	0.96	*112.9*	*116.5*	*109.3*	*0.94*
Lesotho	53	113.1	111.2	115.0	1.03	96.2	95.1	97.3	1.02
Liberia[3]	64	...	...	...	...	*135.8*	*156.6*	*114.9*	*0.73*
Madagascar[3]	466	102.5	98.6	106.6	1.08	112.4	114.5	110.2	0.96
Malawi	348	101.0	104.6	97.4	0.93	...	...	...	...
Mali[3]	323	26.7	33.7	19.7	0.59	*55.0*	*62.8*	*47.1*	*0.75*
Mauritius	22	99.0	98.9	99.1	1.00	99.0	97.3	100.7	1.04
Mozambique	528	73.3	81.2	65.5	0.81	101.6	110.4	92.7	0.84
Namibia	53	...	...	...	...	103.3	102.0	104.7	1.03
Niger	330	27.4	34.9	20.1	0.58	44.1	52.3	35.7	0.68
Nigeria	3403	111.7	125.6	97.6	0.78	...	...	...	...
Rwanda	203	94.1	94.6	93.6	0.99	161.8	162.4	161.3	0.99
Sao Tome and Principe[4]	...	...	...	...	...	...	...	...	...
Senegal	271	64.4	...	...	...	90.3	92.1	88.4	0.96
Seychelles[4]	...	...	...	...	...	...	...	...	...
Sierra Leone	123	...	...	...	...	80.4	81.7	79.1	0.97
Somalia	240	...	...	...	...	...	...	...	...
South Africa	947	...	...	...	...	127.0	127.7	126.2	0.99
Swaziland	26	127.0	129.8	124.3	0.96	118.2	120.7	115.6	0.96
Togo[3]	132	96.1	109.3	83.0	0.76	103.0	109.1	96.9	0.89
Uganda	746	112.5	120.8	104.1	0.86	...	...	...	...
United Republic of Tanzania	1023	79.2	80.2	78.1	0.97	69.8	70.1	69.5	0.99
Zambia	312	...	...	...	...	80.7	79.9	81.6	1.02
Zimbabwe[w]	387	132.5	133.2	131.9	0.99	102.9	104.6	101.3	0.97

	sum	median	median	median		median	median	median	
World	120736	98.8	98.8	98.1	...	102.0	102.3	101.3	...
Countries in transition	...	...	...	...	...	...	...	...	...
Developed countries	...	...	...	...	...	...	...	...	...
Developing countries	...	...	...	...	...	...	...	...	...
Arab States and North Africa	6864	76.1	87.1	72.3	...	100.4	100.9	99.9	...
Central and Eastern Europe	5420	98.0	94.6	96.5	...	99.6	100.8	100.0	...
Central Asia	1693	...	...	...	...	...	...	...	...
East Asia and the Pacific	34673	102.9	99.8	102.6	...	107.7	108.6	106.1	...
Latin America and the Caribbean	10831	112.4	100.5	111.8	...	117.6	117.3	114.2	...
North America and Western Europe	9671	99.1	99.2	99.4	...	100.3	100.5	100.3	...
South and West Asia	33772	...	...	...	...	117.5	121.8	111.7	...
Sub-Saharan Africa	17812	82.4	94.6	83.0	...	96.2	95.1	88.4	...

1. Indicators for 1990/1991 and 1999/2000 may not be comparable. For further explanation, please see the Technical Introduction preceding these Annexes.
2. Enrolment ratios have not been calculated due to inconsistencies between enrolment and the United Nations population data.
3. Data in italics are for 1998/99.
4. Enrolment ratios have not been calculated due to lack of United Nations population data by age.

NET INTAKE RATE (NIR) IN PRIMARY EDUCATION				SCHOOL LIFE EXPECTANCY Expected number of years of formal schooling							
1999/2000			GPI	1990[1]/91			GPI	1999/2000			GPI
Total	Male	Female	F/M	Total	Male	Female	F/M	Total	Male	Female	F/M
...	...	...	...	4	5	3	0.61	...	...	...	...
27.4	31.6	23.2	0.73	...	...	...	...	...	...	...	...
_15.5_	_15.7_	_15.3_	_0.97_	...	...	...	...	...	...	...	...
...	...	...	...	...	...	...	...	...	...	...	...
_28.9_	_32.2_	_25.6_	_0.79_	4	9	...	...	...	...	...	...
_21.8_	_20.8_	_22.7_	_1.09_	5	5	4	0.73	_4_	...	...	...
...	...	...	...	...	...	...	...	...	...	...	...
20.1	21.7	18.6	0.86	...	...	...	...	_5_	_5_	_4_	_0.76_
24.6	27.2	22.1	0.81	...	...	...	...	_4_	_5_	_3_	_0.60_
...	...	...	...	...	...	...	...	...	...	...	...
42.7*	...	...	...	...	...	...	...	...	...	...	...
...	...	...	...	...	...	...	...	...	...	...	...
_20.4_	_21.9_	_18.9_	_0.86_	...	...	...	...	...	...	...	...
_33.5**_	_37.8**_	_29.2**_	_0.77_	...	...	...	...	...	...	...	...
...	...	...	...	...	...	...	...	...	...	...	...
25.4	24.5	26.2	1.07	10	9	11	1.25	10	9	10	1.12
_47.0**_	_56.9**_	_37.1**_	_0.65_	...	...	...	...	9	12	7	0.59
_54.3**_	_59.4**_	_49.3**_	_0.83_	...	...	...	...	_6_	_6_	_6_	_0.96_
...	...	...	...	6	7	5	0.80	...	...	...	...
...	...	...	...	...	...	...	...	...	...	...	...
25.3	24.7	26.0	1.05	10	10	10	1.00	...	...	...	...
17.6	18.3	17.0	0.93	4	7	...	...	5	6	4	0.72
58.8**	57.0**	60.5**	1.06	...	...	...	...	12	12	12	1.03
28.5	33.8	23.0	0.68	...	...	...	...	...	...	...	...
...	...	...	...	...	...	...	...	...	...	...	...
...	...	...	...	6	6	6	0.96	...	...	...	...
...	...	...	...	...	...	...	...	...	...	...	...
39.9	...	...	...	...	...	...	...	...	...	...	...
...	...	...	...	...	...	...	...	...	...	...	...
80.2	81.6	78.9	0.97	...	...	...	...	...	...	...	...
...	...	...	...	...	...	...	...	...	...	...	...
...	...	...	...	...	...	...	...	...	...	...	...
50.0	48.5	51.4	1.06	8	8	8	0.94	...	...	...	...
43.4	46.1	40.8	0.88	9	11	6	0.56	_11_	_12_	_8_	_0.71_
77.8	77.1	78.5	1.02	...	...	...	...	...	...	...	...
13.3	12.3	14.4	1.17	5	5	5	0.97	5	5	5	0.97
35.9	34.5	37.3	1.08	...	...	...	...	7	7	7	0.88
39.6	38.6	40.5	1.05	...	...	...	...	...	...	...	...

median	median	median		median	median	median		median	median	median	
55.4	56.8	54.4	...	9	9	9	...	12	12	13	...
...	...	...	...	...	...	...	...	...	...	...	...
...	...	...	...	...	...	...	...	...	...	...	...
...	...	...	...	...	...	...	...	...	...	...	...
58.5	60.2	56.6	...	8	8	8	...	9	11	9	...
...	...	...	...	9	9	9	...	13	13	13	...
...	...	...	...	...	...	...	...	9	9	9	...
80.5	75.6	73.7	...	13	13	10	...	11	11	11	...
68.4	67.4	68.4	...	9	8	8	...	12	12	13	...
...	...	...	...	12	12	12	...	15	15	16	...
...	...	...	...	4	4	3	...	12	12	12	...
28.5	31.6	26.0	...	6	8	6	...	7	8	6	...

Table 6
Participation in primary education

Country or territory	Age group	School-age population (thousands)		GROSS ENROLMENT RATIO (GER) IN PRIMARY EDUCATION			
				1990[1]/91			GPI
	1999	1990	1999	Total	Male	Female	F/M
Arab States and North Africa							
Algeria	6-11	4 182	4 235	100.2	108.4	91.6	0.85
Bahrain	6-11	61	76	110.0	110.0	110.1	1.00
Djibouti	6-11	83	103	38.1	44.6	31.6	0.71
Egypt[w]	6-10	7 422	7 951	93.8	101.4	85.8	0.85
Iraq	6-11	2 990	3 583	111.3	120.3	101.8	0.85
Jordan[w]	6-11	1 307	718	...	...	...	...
Kuwait	6-9	208	165	60.2	61.7	58.7	0.95
Lebanon	6-10	288	384	...	...	...	...
Libyan Arab Jamahiriya	6-11	1 117	677	105.2	108.5	101.7	0.94
Mauritania[3]	6-11	344	422	48.7	55.9	41.3	0.74
Morocco	6-11	3 713	4 058	66.9	79.0	54.3	0.69
Oman	6-11	305	431	86.1	90.3	81.8	0.91
Palestinian Autonomous Territories	6-9	...	357	...	...	...	...
Qatar	6-11	50	59	97.3	100.5	94.0	0.93
Saudi Arabia	6-11	2 561	3 340	73.3	78.2	68.2	0.87
Sudan	6-11	3 871	4 663	52.8	60.3	45.2	0.75
Syrian Arab Republic	6-11	2 263	2 620	108.4	114.2	102.3	0.90
Tunisia[w]	6-11	1 241	1 196	113.3	119.6	106.6	0.89
United Arab Emirates[3]	6-11	219	289	104.3	105.8	102.8	0.97
Yemen[3]	6-11	2 964	3 152	...	...	...	...
Central and Eastern Europe							
Albania	6-9	550	259	100.2	100.1	100.3	1.00
Belarus	6-10	649	543	94.8	...	...	...
Bosnia and Herzegovina	6-9	275	201	...	...	...	...
Bulgaria	7-10	984	379	97.6	98.8	96.3	0.97
Croatia[2]	6-9	509	221	...	...	...	...
Czech Republic[o]	6-10	566	620	96.4	96.2	96.5	1.00
Estonia	7-12	115	120	110.7	112.3	109.1	0.97
Hungary[o]	7-10	1 196	484	94.5	94.6	94.5	1.00
Latvia	7-10	152	133	94.2	94.5	93.9	0.99
Lithuania	7-10	223	216	90.7	92.9	88.4	0.95
Poland[o]	7-12	5 276	3 366	98.3	98.8	97.8	0.99
Republic of Moldova	7-10	324	297	93.1	93.0	93.1	1.00
Romania	7-10	1 373	1 165	91.3	91.2	91.4	1.00
Russian Federation[w, 3]	6-9	6 958	7 240	109.2	109.2	109.1	1.00
Slovakia	6-9	360	301	...	...	...	...
Slovenia[3]	7-10	103	90	108.3	...	...	...
The former Yugoslav Rep. of Macedonia	7-10	269	126	99.3	100.1	98.5	0.98
Turkey[o, 3]	6-11	6 924	7 776	99.1	102.0	96.0	0.94
Ukraine	6-9	4 496	2 556	88.8	88.9	88.7	1.00
Yugoslavia[2]	7-10	648	591	...	...	...	...
Central Asia							
Armenia	7-10	217	284	...	...	...	...
Azerbaijan	6-9	464	709	113.7	114.2	113.3	0.99
Georgia	6-9	362	303	97.3	97.4	97.2	1.00
Kazakhstan	7-10	1 371	1 256	87.3	...	...	...
Kyrgyzstan	6-9	319	459	111.1	110.9	111.2	1.00
Mongolia	8-11	171	257	97.2	96.1	98.3	1.02
Tajikistan	7-10	558	662	91.0	91.9	90.0	0.98
Turkmenistan	7-10	370	476	...	...	...	...
Uzbekistan	6-9	2 184	2 533	81.4	82.2	80.7	0.98
East Asia and the Pacific							
Australia[o]	5-11	1 470	1 863	107.7	108.0	107.4	0.99
Cambodia	6-11	1 099	2 195	120.9	...	...	...

1. Indicators for 1990/1991 and 1999/2000 may not be comparable. For further explanation, please see the Technical Introduction preceding these Annexes.
2. Enrolment ratios have not been calculated due to inconsistencies between enrolment and the United Nations population data.
3. Data in italics are for 1998/99.
4. Enrolment ratios have not been calculated due to lack of United Nations population data by age.

GROSS ENROLMENT RATIO (GER) IN PRIMARY EDUCATION				NET ENROLMENT RATIO (NER) IN PRIMARY EDUCATION				PRIMARY PUPILS					
1999/2000			GPI	1999/2000			GPI	under age (%) 1999/2000			over age (%) 1999/2000		
Total	Male	Female	F/M	Total	Male	Female	F/M	Total	Male	Female	Total	Male	Female
114.4	118.9	109.6	0.92	97.2	98.8	95.6	0.97	2.5	2.4	2.7	12.5	14.5	10.1
102.5	102.2	102.7	1.00	94.0	92.6	95.5	1.03	2.3	2.4	2.2	6.0	7.1	4.8
36.9	42.5	31.2	0.73	30.6	34.8	26.3	0.75	0.9	0.9	0.8	16.2	17.2	14.8
100.0**	103.8**	96.0**	0.93	92.3**	95.0**	89.5**	0.94	1.2**	1.2**	1.2**	6.5**	7.3**	5.6**
101.6	111.4	91.3	0.82	93.1	100.0	85.7	...	...	...	...	6.4	8.3	6.2
100.8	100.6**	101.0**	1.00	93.6	93.2	93.9	1.01	5.5	5.6	5.4	1.7	1.8**	1.6**
84.8	85.3	84.3	0.99	66.4	68.1	64.6	0.95	5.7	3.5	8.0	16.0	16.7	15.4
100.2	102.3	98.0	0.96	70.9	70.8	71.1	1.00	0.1	0.1	0.1	29.1	30.7	27.4
...	...	...	...	...	...	...	...	...	...	...	...	...	...
84.3	86.8	81.8	0.94	...	...	...	...	_1.0**_	_1.1**_	_1.0**_	_26.6**_	_26.5**_	_26.7_
90.4	98.0	82.5	0.84	74.5	79.0	69.8	0.88	0.4	0.4	0.4	17.2	19.1	15.0
73.3	75.1	71.4	0.95	65.1	65.6	64.6	0.98	2.1	2.1	2.0	9.1	10.6	7.5
108.6	108.2	109.0	1.01	99.1	98.9	99.4	1.00	5.5	5.4	5.5	3.2	3.2	3.3
...	...	...	...	...	...	...	...	5.8	6.0	5.6	4.3	6.1	2
68.4	69.7	67.1	0.96	57.9	60.0	55.8	0.93	0.8	1.1	0.5	14.5	12.8	16.3
55.0	59.3	50.6	0.85	44.7	48.6	40.7	0.84	0.4	0.2	0.5	18.4	17.9	19.0
...	...	...	...	...	...	...	...	5.8	5.8	5.7	4.9	5.4	4.3
118.2	121.2	115.0	0.95	98.2	99.2	97.1	0.98	1.6	1.6	1.7	15.3	16.6	13.8
94.4	94.6	94.2	1.00	78.2	77.9	78.6	1.01	_7.5_	_7.3_	_7.6_	_9.7_	_10.3_	_9.0_
...	...	...	...	...	...	...	...	_1.1_	_1.2_	_1_	_20.6_	_21.9_	_18.0_
109.2	109.7	108.7	0.99	100.0	100.0	100.0	1.00	...	...	...	6.6	6.7	6.5
110.5	111.8	109.2	0.98	...	...	...	...	...	...	...	...	...	...
...	...	...	...	...	...	...	...	...	...	...	...	...	...
103.5	104.9	102.1	0.97	95.4	96.2	94.5	0.98	2.4	2.3	2.5	5.5	6.0	5.0
...	...	...	...	...	...	...	...	...	...	...	20.1	20.6	19.6
104.1	104.4	103.8	0.99	90.4	90.4	90.4	...	...	...	...	13.1	13.4	12.9
102.8	104.6	100.9	0.96	97.6	98.5	96.6	0.98	1.5	1.2	1.8	3.6	4.7	2.4
103.4	104.2	102.6	0.98	89.8	90.0	89.6	1.00	8.6	8.2	8.9	4.6	5.4	3.7
101.2	102.0	100.4	0.98	93.1	93.3	92.9	1.00	0.8	0.7	1.0	7.2	7.9	6.5
100.8	101.2	100.5	0.99	94.2	94.3	94.2	1.00	2.4	2.0	2.8	4.2	4.9	3.4
101.0**	102.4**	99.5**	0.97	96.6**	96.7**	96.6**	1.00	0.1**	0.1**	0.1**	3.6**	4.8**	2.4**
...	...	...	...	...	...	...	...	...	...	...	...	...	...
102.1	103.0	101.1	0.98	93.2	93.4	93.0	1.00	3.4	3.3	3.4	5.3	6.0	4.6
84.8	85.1	84.5	0.99	...	...	...	...	...	...	...	...	...	...
102.8	103.5	102.2	0.99	...	...	...	...	...	...	...	...	...	...
...	...	...	...	...	...	...	...	...	_1.7_	_2_	_1.8_	_2.2_	_1.5_
100.4	100.7	100.0	0.99	93.6	94.0	93.1	0.99	5.4	5.3	1.4	1.4	1.4	1.4
100.9**	105.5**	96.2**	0.91	...	...	...	...	_0.7_	_0.7_	_0.8_	...	...	...
...	...	...	...	...	...	...	...	...	...	...	...	...	...
...	...	...	...	...	...	...	...	...	...	...	23.2**	23.3**	20.1**
...	...	...	...	...	...	...	...	...	...	...	...	...	...
98.3	97.4	99.2	1.02	...	...	...	...	...	...	...	5.0*	5.6*	4.5*
98.5	98.5	98.5	1.00	...	...	...	...	...	...	...	...	...	...
96.2	95.9	96.4	1.01	...	...	...	...	...	...	...	...	18.4*	...
101.6	103.0	100.3	0.97	82.1	82.5	81.6	...	...	...	...	19.3	19.9	16.5
98.5	96.7	100.4	1.04	89.5	87.9	91.2	1.04	4.8	4.3	5.2	4.4	4.7	4.0
104.6	108.5	100.6	0.93	86.5**	89.8**	83.2**	...	17.3**	17.3**	17.2**	...	...	...
...	...	...	...	...	...	...	...	...	...	...	...	...	...
...	...	...	...	...	...	...	...	...	...	...	...	...	...
101.2	101.1	101.2	1.00	94.9	94.5	95.4	1.01	0.2	0.2	0.2	6.0	6.4	5.5
102.4	109.5	95.2	0.87	88.6	93.9	83.1	0.88	0.4	0.4	0.4	13.1	13.8	12.3

Table 6 (continued)

Country or territory	Age group	School-age population (thousands)		GROSS ENROLMENT RATIO (GER) IN PRIMARY EDUCATION			
				1990[1]/91			GPI
	1999	1990	1999	Total	Male	Female	F/M
China[w]	6-11	97 812	132 703	125.2	129.6	120.3	0.93
Cook Islands[4]	5-10	...	...	...	...	...	...
Democratic People's Rep. of Korea	6-9	1 360	1 634	...	...	...	...
Fiji[3]	6-11	115	105	125.2	...	...	...
Indonesia[w]	7-12	25 831	26 140	115.2	116.7	113.6	0.97
Japan[o]	6-11	9 399	7 435	99.7	99.6	99.9	1.00
Kiribati	6-12	...	...	...	...	...	...
Lao People's Democratic Republic	6-10	549	721	105.0	117.6	92.1	0.78
Malaysia[w, 3]	6-11	2 620	2 997	93.7	93.8	93.6	1.00
Marshall Islands[3, 4]	6-11	...	...	...	...	...	...
Myanmar	5-9	5 058	5 341	106.5	108.3	104.6	0.97
Nauru	6-11	...	...	...	...	...	...
New Zealand[o]	5-10	302	358	105.6	106.4	104.7	0.98
Niue	5-10	...	...	...	...	...	...
Papua New Guinea	7-12	577	706	71.9	77.9	65.6	0.84
Philippines[w]	6-11	9 370	11 200	111.3	113.2	109.3	0.97
Republic of Korea[o]	6-11	4 639	4 002	104.9	104.6	105.3	1.01
Samoa[3]	5-10	29	27	121.9	116.9	127.4	1.09
Solomon Islands	6-11	56	72	84.5	90.7	77.8	0.86
Thailand[w]	6-11	7 023	6 524	99.1	100.0	98.0	0.98
Tonga	5-10	...	...	...	...	...	...
Tuvalu	6-11	...	...	...	...	...	...
Vanuatu[3]	6-11	25	32	96.1	98.4	93.6	0.95
Viet Nam	6-10	8 616	9 340	102.9	...	...	...
Latin America and the Caribbean							
Anguilla[4]	5-11	...	...	...	...	...	...
Antigua and Barbuda[4]	5-11	...	...	...	...	...	...
Argentina[w]	6-11	4 673	4 053	106.3	...	...	...
Aruba[4]	6-11	...	...	...	...	...	...
Bahamas	5-10	32	37	101.5	...	...	...
Barbados	5-10	30	23	93.0	93.0	93.0	1.00
Belize	5-10	43	35	110.8	112.1	109.5	0.98
Bermuda	5-10	...	...	...	...	...	...
Bolivia	6-11	1 350	1 260	94.7	99.0	90.4	0.91
Brazil[w]	7-10	27 239	13 207	106.3	...	...	...
British Virgin Islands[4]	5-11	...	...	...	...	...	...
Cayman Islands[4]	5-10	...	...	...	...	...	...
Chile[w]	6-11	1 993	1 743	99.9	100.6	99.1	0.98
Colombia	6-10	4 155	4 589	102.2	95.3	109.4	1.15
Costa Rica	6-11	432	514	100.7	101.4	100.0	0.99
Cuba	6-11	909	1 005	97.7	99.1	96.1	0.97
Dominica[4]	5-11	...	...	...	...	...	...
Dominican Republic	6-11	1 333	1 123	96.6	...	...	...
Ecuador	6-11	1 585	1 690	116.5	...	...	...
El Salvador[3]	7-12	1 245	846	81.1	80.7	81.6	1.01
Grenada	5-11	...	...	...	...	...	...
Guatemala	7-12	1 501	1 829	77.6	...	...	...
Guyana[3]	6-11	107	91	97.7	98.5	96.9	0.98
Haiti[3]	6-11	1 162	1 304	74.4	76.4	72.5	0.95
Honduras	7-12	822	1 013	...	...	...	...
Jamaica[w]	6-11	335	331	101.3	101.8	100.9	0.99
Mexico[o]	6-11	12 643	13 014	113.9	115.3	112.4	0.98
Montserrat	5-11	...	...	...	...	...	...
Netherlands Antilles	6-11	20	22	...	...	...	...
Nicaragua	7-12	677	795	93.5	90.8	96.3	1.06
Panama	6-11	330	358	106.2	108.3	104.1	0.96

1. Indicators for 1990/1991 and 1999/2000 may not be comparable. For further explanation, please see the Technical Introduction preceding these Annexes.
2. Enrolment ratios have not been calculated due to inconsistencies between enrolment and the United Nations population data.
3. Data in italics are for 1998/99.
4. Enrolment ratios have not been calculated due to lack of United Nations population data by age.

GROSS ENROLMENT RATIO (GER) IN PRIMARY EDUCATION				NET ENROLMENT RATIO (NER) IN PRIMARY EDUCATION				PRIMARY PUPILS					
1999/2000			GPI	1999/2000			GPI	under age (%) 1999/2000			over age (%) 1999/2000		
Total	Male	Female	F/M	Total	Male	Female	F/M	Total	Male	Female	Total	Male	Female
106.4	105.2	107.8	1.02	93.2**	91.8**	94.7**	1.03	0.1**	0.1**	0.1**	12.3**	12.6**	12.0**
...	...	...	...	...	...	...	...	7.2	7.3	7.1	...	...	...
...	...	...	...	...	...	...	...	...	...	...	...	...	...
...	...	...	...	...	...	...	...	4.0*	3.9**	4**	6.0**	6.6**	5.3**
107.9**	109.7**	106.0**	0.97	91.3**	92.9**	89.7**	0.97	10.3**	10.6**	9.9**	5.1**	4.8**	5.4**
101.3	101.3	101.2	1.00	100.0	100.0	100.0	1.00	...	...	...	...	...	...
...	...	...	...	...	...	...	...	...	...	...	...	...	...
115.3	124.3	106.0	0.85	81.8	85.2	78.2	0.92	...	...	...	29.1	29.8	26.2
101.4	102.4	100.4	0.98	100.0**	100.0**	100.0**	1.00	...	...	...	0.0**	0.4**	0.0**
...	...	...	...	...	...	...	...	1.5	1.6	1.5	...	...	...
91.0	91.4	90.5	0.99	83.2	83.5	82.9	0.99	...	...	...	8.5	8.6	6.2
...	...	...	...	...	...	...	...	...	...	...	...	...	...
100.8	101.0	100.7	1.00	100.0	100.0	100.0	1.00	...	...	...	...	0.9	0.7
...	...	...	...	...	...	...	...	...	...	...	...	...	...
...	...	...	...	...	...	...	...	...	...	...	...	...	...
...	...	...	...	...	...	...	...	...	...	...	...	...	...
98.6	98.0	99.3	1.01	97.3	96.7	97.9	1.01	0.2	0.2	0.3	1.1	1.1	1.1
102.5	104.2	100.8	0.97	96.6	97.1	96.0	0.99	...	...	...	3.3	4.9	2.7
...	...	...	...	...	...	...	...	...	...	...	...	...	...
93.5	95.7	91.2	0.95	81.4	83.1	79.6	0.96	...	...	...	10.8	13.1	12.7
...	...	...	...	...	...	...	...	...	...	...	...	...	...
...	...	...	...	...	...	...	...	...	...	...	...	...	...
117.1	113.1	121.6	1.08	96.1**	99.9**	91.9**	0.92**	2.5**	2.5**	2.6	15.5**	9.1**	22.0**
107.7	111.1	104.3	0.94	96.3	...	...	...	0.1	...	...	10.6	...	...
...	...	...	...	...	...	...	...	2.3	2.1	2.6	...	...	...
...	...	...	...	...	...	...	...	...	...	...	...	...	...
118.9	118.8	119.0	1.00	100.0	100.0	100.0	1.00	0.4	0.4	0.4	10.1	9.9	10.2
...	...	...	...	...	...	...	...	0.2	0.2	0.3	...	...	...
...	...	...	...	...	...	...	...	...	...	...	4.2	5.5	2.8
108.7	109.4	108.0	0.99	89.7	89.4	90.0	1.01	0.2	0.2	0.3	17.3	5.6**	16.4
127.5	129.8	125.1	0.96	100.0	100.0	100.0	1.00	3.7	3.5	3.9	14.5	16.0	12.9
...	...	...	...	...	...	...	...	...	...	...	...	...	...
115.6**	116.6**	114.7**	0.98	99.1**	99.0**	99.2**	1.00**	1.3**	1.3**	1.3**	13.0**	13.7**	12.2**
166.0	169.8	161.9	0.95	96.5	99.8	93.2	0.93	2.6	2.7	2.5	39.2	38.6	39.9
...	...	...	...	...	...	...	...	3.2	2.9	3.5	...	...	...
...	...	...	...	...	...	...	...	7.2	7.1	7.3	...	...	...
106.9	109.2	104.5	0.96	88.9	89.4	88.4	0.99	0.7	0.9	0.5	16.3	17.5	15.0
112.5	112.6	112.4	1.00	88.1	88.2**	88.1**	1.00**	2.2**	2.2**	2.2**	19.5	19.5**	19.5**
107.5	109.0	106.0	0.97	91.3	91.4	91.1	1.00	0.3	0.3	0.3	14.8	15.8	13.7
104.0	106.1	101.8	0.96	99.2	99.9	98.5	0.99	0.1	0.1	0.1	4.5	5.7	3.1
...	...	...	...	...	...	...	...	2.9	2.9	2.8	...	...	...
124.7**	126.4**	123.0**	0.97	90.6**	89.8**	91.4**	1.02**	1.3**	1.2**	1.5**	26.0**	27.7**	24.2**
113.9	114.3	113.5	0.99	97.7	97.4	98.0	1.01	2.5	2.4	2.5	11.7	12.3	11.1
...	...	...	...	...	...	...	...	2	0.9	2	25.9*	33.3	18.0
...	...	...	...	...	...	...	...	...	...	...	...	...	...
99.8	105.3	94.0	0.89	81.0	83.3	78.5	0.94	3.7	3.5	3.8	15.2	17.4	12.7
...	...	...	...	...	...	...	...	16.2	14.5	18	...	...	...
...	...	...	...	...	...	...	...	...	...	...	46.1**	47.3**	46.3
...	...	...	...	...	...	...	...	...	8.0	...	...	...	...
98.7	95.6	101.9	1.07	94.2	94.3	94.1	1.00	0.4	0.2	0.5	4.2	1.1	7.4
113.5	114.1	112.8	0.99	100.0	100.0	100.0	1.00	1.5	1.4	1.5	7.7	8.7	6.7
...	...	...	...	...	...	...	...	...	...	...	...	...	...
112.8	114.9	110.7	0.96	95.0	94.6	95.5	1.01	0.4	0.2	0.6	15.4	17.5	13.1
104.4	104.1	104.8	1.01	79.4	79.0	79.8	1.01	10.0	9.8	10.2	14.0	14.3	13.7
109.9	111.4	108.2	0.97	98.0	98.1	97.9	1.00	0.4	0.4	0.4	10.4	11.6	9.1

Table 6 (continued)

Country or territory	Age group	School-age population (thousands)		GROSS ENROLMENT RATIO (GER) IN PRIMARY EDUCATION			
				1990[1]/91			GPI
	1999	1990	1999	Total	Male	Female	F/M
Paraguay[w]	6-11	652	843	105.4	107.2	103.5	0.97
Peru[w]	6-11	3 254	3 410	118.5	...	...	...
Saint Kitts and Nevis[4]	5-11	...	...	...	...	...	...
Saint Lucia	5-11	...	22	...	...	...	...
Saint Vincent and the Grenadines[4]	5-11	...	...	...	...	...	...
Suriname	6-11	60	52	100.2	100.4	100.1	1.00
Trinidad and Tobago	5-11	201	162	96.7	97.0	96.3	0.99
Turks and Caicos Islands[4]	6-11	...	...	...	...	...	...
Uruguay[w]	6-11	319	327	108.6	109.2	107.9	0.99
Venezuela	6-11	4 235	3 267	95.7	94.3	97.2	1.03
North America and Western Europe							
Andorra	6-10	...	...	...	...	...	...
Austria[o]	6-9	363	380	101.9	101.9	101.9	1.00
Belgium[o]	6-11	716	737	100.5	99.8	101.3	1.02
Canada[o, 3]	6-11	2 307	2 463	103.0	103.9	102.0	0.98
Cyprus[2]	6-11	70	78	...	...	...	...
Denmark[o]	7-12	346	377	98.3	98.2	98.3	1.00
Finland[o]	7-12	395	386	98.8	99.1	98.5	0.99
France[o]	6-10	3 825	3 694	108.5	109.3	107.6	0.99
Germany[o]	6-9	3 393	3 470	101.1	...	...	...
Greece[o]	6-11	832	651	97.8	98.1	97.5	0.99
Iceland[o]	6-12	29	31	101.3	...	...	...
Ireland[o]	6-11	405	329	102.8	102.6	103.1	1.00
Israel[o]	6-11	764	648	94.9	93.4	96.4	1.03
Italy[o]	6-10	2 963	2 797	103.1	103.3	103.0	1.00
Luxembourg[o]	6-11	26	32	90.6	87.2	94.2	1.08
Malta[3]	5-10	34	32	109.7	111.7	107.5	0.96
Monaco	6-10	...	...	...	...	...	...
Netherlands[o]	6-11	1 057	1 185	102.4	100.8	104.0	1.03
Norway[o]	6-12	308	415	100.4	100.5	100.4	1.00
Portugal[o]	6-11	826	661	123.4	126.3	120.4	0.95
San Marino	6-10	...	...	...	...	...	...
Spain[o]	6-11	2 598	2 421	108.6	109.1	107.9	0.99
Sweden[o]	7-12	580	709	99.8	99.7	99.9	1.00
Switzerland[o]	7-12	447	501	90.3	89.7	90.9	1.01
United Kingdom[o]	5-10	4 350	4 670	104.2	102.9	105.5	1.03
United States[o]	6-11	21 925	24 888	102.3	103.2	101.4	0.98
South and West Asia							
Afghanistan	7-12	2 302	3 290	27.0	34.6	19.0	0.55
Bangladesh[3]	6-10	16 683	17 481	71.6	76.5	66.3	0.87
Bhutan[2, 3]	6-12	304	392	...	...	...	...
India[w]	6-11	101 968	133 579	97.2	109.9	83.5	0.76
Iran, Islamic Republic of	6-10	8 351	9 455	112.2	118.1	106.0	0.90
Maldives	6-12	32	55	...	...	...	...
Nepal	6-10	2 589	2 991	107.7	132.2	81.1	0.61
Pakistan	5-9	16 448	19 136	60.7	81.5	39.0	0.48
Sri Lanka[w, 3]	5-9	1 994	1 689	105.9	107.0	104.8	0.98
Sub-Saharan Africa							
Angola	6-9	1 080	1 555	91.7	95.5	87.9	0.92
Benin	6-11	843	1 085	58.1	77.8	38.5	0.49
Botswana	6-12	250	297	113.2	109.3	117.1	1.07
Burkina Faso	7-12	1 513	1 986	33.3	40.9	25.7	0.63
Burundi	7-12	870	1 137	72.8	79.4	66.2	0.83
Cameroon	6-11	1 942	2 456	101.1	108.8	93.4	0.86
Cape Verde	6-11	58	64	121.3	...	...	...

1. Indicators for 1990/1991 and 1999/2000 may not be comparable. For further explanation, please see the Technical Introduction preceding these Annexes.
2. Enrolment ratios have not been calculated due to inconsistencies between enrolment and the United Nations population data.
3. Data in italics are for 1998/99.
4. Enrolment ratios have not been calculated due to lack of United Nations population data by age.

GROSS ENROLMENT RATIO (GER) IN PRIMARY EDUCATION				NET ENROLMENT RATIO (NER) IN PRIMARY EDUCATION				PRIMARY PUPILS					
1999/2000			GPI	1999/2000			GPI	under age (%) 1999/2000			over age (%) 1999/2000		
Total	Male	Female	F/M	Total	Male	Female	F/M	Total	Male	Female	Total	Male	Female
113.4	115.4	111.4	0.97	91.5	91.3	91.7	1.00	0.5	0.4	0.5	18.9	20.4	17.2
127.6	128.2	126.9	0.99	100.0**	100.0**	100.0**	1.00	1.0**	1.0**	1.1**	17.0**	17.3**	16.8**
...	...	...	...	...	...	...	...	3.5	3.4	3.6	...	...	...
114.5**	117.5**	111.3**	0.95	95.7	94.9	96.4	1.02	...	...	...	16.4**	17.5**	13.4**
...	...	...	...	...	...	...	...	3.9	3.7	4.0	...	...	...
...	...	...	...	...	...	...	...	...	...	...	...	...	...
104.0	104.7	103.4	0.99	92.9	93.1	92.8	1.00	1.9	1.8	1.9	8.9	9.3	8.4
...	...	...	...	...	...	...	...	3.5	3.4	3.6	...	...	...
112.1	112.8	111.3	0.99	93.6**	93.1**	94.2**	1.01	...	...	...	16.5**	15.7**	15.4**
101.9**	102.7**	101.0**	0.98	88.0	83.9	92.2	1.10	1.9	1.9	1.9	11.7**	17.1**	6.4**
...	...	...	...	...	...	...	...	...	...	...	...	...	...
103.2	103.7	102.6	0.99	90.8	90.3	91.3	1.01	...	...	...	12.0	12.9	9.0
104.9	105.4	104.5	0.99	100.0**	100.0**	100.0**	1.00	0.2**	0.1**	0.2**	4.0**	4.4**	3.5**
98.6	98.5	98.8	1.00	98.6	98.5	98.8	1.00	_0.2_	_0.2_	_0.17_	_0.7_	_0.7_	_0.7_
...	...	...	...	...	...	...	...	0.3	0.3	0.3	1.2	1.3	1.1
101.9	102.0	101.7	1.00	99.3	99.3	99.4	1.00	0.8	0.6	1.0	1.7	2.2	1.2
100.5	100.8	100.2	0.99	100.0	100.0	100.0	1.00	0.2	0.1	0.2	0.4	0.4	0.3
105.2	105.8	104.5	0.99	100.0	100.0	100.0	1.00	0.3	0.2	0.3	4.6	5.2	3.9
105.4	105.5	105.2	1.00	...	...	...	...	...	...	...	16.0	17.0	16.8
99.1	99.2	98.9	1.00	96.8	96.9	96.7	1.00	0.5	0.5	0.5	1.8	1.9	1.7
101.3	102.0	100.7	0.99	100.0	100.0	100.0	1.00	0.0	0.0	0.1	0.1	0.1	0.1
119.4	119.8	119.0	0.99	90.2**	90.2**	90.2**	1.00	19.2**	18.8**	19.5**	5.3**	5.9**	4.7**
114.1	114.6	113.5	0.99	100.0**	100.0**	100.0**	1.00	0.3**	0.4**	0.1**	11.0**	11.2**	10.9**
101.4	101.6	101.2	1.00	99.7	99.9	99.5	1.00	0.4	0.4	0.4	1.3	1.3	1.3
100.3	99.5	101.2	1.02	96.0	94.9	97.2	1.02	0.6	0.6	0.6	3.7	4.1	3.4
...	...	...	...	...	...	...	...	...	...	...	_4.8_	_5.3_	_6.2_
...	...	...	...	...	...	...	...	...	...	...	...	...	...
107.9	109.1	106.7	0.98	99.9	100.0	99.4	0.99	...	...	...	7.4	4.3	6.9
101.2	101.1	101.4	1.00	100.0	100.0	100.0	1.00	...	...	...	...	...	...
122.7	125.3	120.0	0.96	100.0	100.0	100.0	1.00	...	...	...	14.7	14.4	15.1
...	...	...	...	...	...	...	...	...	...	...	...	...	...
104.9	105.2	104.6	0.99	100.0	100.0	100.0	1.00	...	...	...	0.6	1.1	2.0
109.4	108.1	110.8	1.03	100.0	100.0	100.0	1.00	0.6	0.6	0.7	6.0	4.7	7.4
107.5	108.0	107.0	0.99	99.2	99.5	98.9	0.99	5.7	5.5	5.8	2.1	2.4	1.8
99.2	99.1	99.2	1.00	99.2	99.1	99.2	1.00	...	...	...	...	...	...
100.3	101.2	99.5	0.98	94.6	94.7	94.6	1.00	0.9	1.0	0.9	4.7	5.5	4.0
...	...	...	...	...	...	...	...	...	...	...	...	...	...
...	...	...	...	...	...	...	...	_10.9*_	_11.0*_	_10.9**_	_15.2**_	_15.1**_	_15.3_
...	...	...	...	...	...	...	...	_0.4_	_0.3_	_0.3_	_24.4_	_25.8_	_22.8_
100.9	108.9	92.4	0.85	...	...	...	...	...	...	...	...	...	...
87.6	89.4	85.8	0.96	74.6	75.3	73.9	0.98	...	...	...	12.6	13.5	13.8
133.7	133.2	134.2	1.01	99.8	99.5	100.0	1.00	0.5	0.5	0.5	24.9	24.8	25.0
126.4	140.0	111.7	0.80	...	...	...	...	...	...	...	...	...	...
96.0	116.7	73.9	0.63	...	...	...	...	...	...	...	...	...	...
...	...	...	...	...	...	...	...	...	...	...	_8.4_	_7.9_	_6.9_
64.4*	69.0*	59.9*	0.87	27.3**	29.2**	25.4**	0.87	1.3**	0.3**	1.6**	53.3**	53.5**	52.9**
85.9	102.7	69.1	0.67	70.3**	83.2**	57.3**	0.69	2.5**	2.1**	3.0**	15.7**	16.8**	14.1**
108.4	...	...	...	83.6	...	...	...	0.2	0.2**	0.2**	22.7	25.0	21.7
42.9	50.5**	35.2**	0.70	34.6	40.9	28.3	0.69	7.8	7.4**	8.4**	11.5	11.6**	11.3**
62.5*	69.4*	55.5*	0.80	44.5**	49.4**	39.6**	0.80	4.4**	2.6**	6.6**	24.4**	26.2**	22.1**
91.1	98.2	83.9	0.85	...	...	...	...	...	...	...	...	...	...
...	...	...	...	...	...	...	...	0.5	0.5	0.5	31.0	31.9	30.0

Table 6 (continued)

Country or territory	Age group	School-age population (thousands)		GROSS ENROLMENT RATIO (GER) IN PRIMARY EDUCATION			
				1990[1]/91			GPI
	1999	1990	1999	Total	Male	Female	F/M
Central African Republic	6-11	474	597	65.0	79.8	50.6	0.63
Chad	6-11	966	1 300	54.4	75.4	33.6	0.45
Comoros	6-11	97	112	75.1	86.9	63.1	0.73
Congo	6-11	373	500	132.5	140.9	124.3	0.88
Côte d'Ivoire	6-11	2 110	2 597	67.1	78.5	55.6	0.71
Democratic Rep. of the Congo[3]	6-11	6 486	8 909	70.3	80.8	59.9	0.74
Equatorial Guinea[3]	7-11	46	59	...	...	...	...
Eritrea	7-11	452	483	...	...	...	...
Ethiopia	7-10	7 552	6 886	32.7	38.9	26.2	0.67
Gabon	6-11	126	179	...	...	...	...
Gambia	7-12	135	185	63.9	76.3	51.6	0.68
Ghana[3]	6-11	2 584	3 067	75.3	82.2	68.4	0.83
Guinea[3]	7-12	935	1 259	37.1	50.1	23.7	0.47
Guinea-Bissau	7-12	143	182	...	...	...	...
Kenya	6-12	5 676	6 055	95.0	96.6	93.3	0.97
Lesotho	6-12	315	353	111.8	100.4	123.4	1.23
Liberia	6-11	423	394	...	...	...	...
Madagascar	6-10	1 526	2 169	102.9	102.8	103.1	1.00
Malawi	6-9	2 064	1 321	67.9	73.8	61.8	0.84
Mali[3]	7-12	1 495	1 790	26.5	33.5	19.4	0.58
Mauritius	6-11	126	123	109.2	109.0	109.5	1.00
Mozambique	6-10	1 883	2 470	66.9	76.5	57.4	0.75
Namibia	6-12	243	339	129.3	123.2	135.4	1.10
Niger	7-12	1 280	1 787	28.8	36.9	20.8	0.56
Nigeria[3]	6-11	14 891	19 009	91.4	103.7	79.0	0.76
Rwanda	7-12	1 580	1 170	69.6	70.4	68.9	0.98
Sao Tome and Principe[3, 4]	7-12	...	...	...	...	...	...
Senegal	7-12	1 202	1 513	58.9	67.9	49.8	0.73
Seychelles[4]	6-11	...	...	...	...	...	...
Sierra Leone	6-11	761	679	50.2	59.6	41.1	0.69
Somalia	6-12	1 726	1 645	...	...	...	...
South Africa[3]	7-13	5 715	6 686	121.6	122.7	120.6	0.98
Swaziland	6-12	150	171	111.3	113.9	108.7	0.95
Togo	6-11	591	739	109.4	132.3	86.5	0.65
Uganda[3]	6-12	3 370	4 656	71.3	79.2	63.3	0.80
United Republic of Tanzania	7-13	4 847	6 646	69.7	70.3	69.1	0.98
Zambia	7-13	1 480	1 976	98.7	...	...	...
Zimbabwe[w]	6-12	1 829	2 548	115.7	116.6	114.8	0.98

		sum		weighted average			
World	...	601 885	680 494	99.5	105.7	93.1	0.88
Countries in transition	...	30 870	25 590	91.7	91.8	91.6	1.00
Developed countries	...	59 627	61 101	104.6	104.6	104.6	1.00
Developing countries	...	511 387	593 804	99.4	106.6	91.8	0.86
Arab States and North Africa	...	35 190	38 479	80.4	89.7	70.8	0.79
Central and Eastern Europe	...	31 950	26 684	101.8	103.9	99.6	0.96
Central Asia	...	6 015	6 939	87.1	86.4	87.8	1.02
East Asia and the Pacific	...	175 952	213 396	116.8	119.9	113.5	0.95
Latin America and the Caribbean	...	71 339	56 965	104.3	105.4	103.1	0.98
North America and Western Europe	...	48 560	51 555	105.4	105.4	105.3	1.00
South and West Asia	...	150 672	188 069	91.7	104.2	78.4	0.75
Sub-Saharan Africa	...	82 207	98 408	77.5	86.7	68.3	0.79

1. Indicators for 1990/1991 and 1999/2000 may not be comparable. For further explanation, please see the Technical Introduction preceding these Annexes.
2. Enrolment ratios have not been calculated due to inconsistencies between enrolment and the United Nations population data.
3. Data in italics are for 1998/99.
4. Enrolment ratios have not been calculated due to lack of United Nations population data by age.

GROSS ENROLMENT RATIO (GER) IN PRIMARY EDUCATION				NET ENROLMENT RATIO (NER) IN PRIMARY EDUCATION				PRIMARY PUPILS					
1999/2000			GPI	1999/2000			GPI	under age (%) 1999/2000			over age (%) 1999/2000		
Total	Male	Female	F/M	Total	Male	Female	F/M	Total	Male	Female	Total	Male	Female
...	...	...	...	...	...	...	...	...	...	...	6.9**	7.8**	5.7**
70.3	87.4	53.1	0.61	56.6	68.7	44.6	0.65	1.6	1.5	1.6	17.9	20.0	14.4
83.8	91.0**	76.4**	0.84	54.8**	59.6**	49.9**	0.84	1.3**	1.2**	1.5**	33.3**	33.3**	33.2**
83.8	88.2	79.4	0.90	...	...	...	...	...	...	...	...	...	...
76.9**	88.2**	65.6**	0.74	58.4**	66.5**	50.2**	0.75	7.5**	6.9**	8.2**	16.6**	17.6**	15.3**
...	...	...	...	...	...	...	...	1.1	...	2	...	30.8**	26.6**
124.8**	137.2**	112.4**	0.82	79.0**	87.5**	70.4**	0.80	0.3**	0.3**	0.2**	35.1**	34.7**	37.3**
61.2	67.3	55.1	0.82	40.3	43.3	37.4	0.86	2.1	2.0	2.3	32.0	33.6	29.9
70.8	84.8	56.7	0.67	...	...	...	...	1.1	1.0	1.2	55.0	58.4	49.9
151.5**	151.9**	151.0**	0.99	...	...	...	...	...	...	...	...	...	...
75.1	79.1	71.2	0.90	69.8	74.6	64.9	0.87	2.6	2.5	2.8	3.8	2.4	5.4
...	...	...	...	...	...	...	...	3.2	3.2	3	32.3	34.8	29.5
62.8	74.5	50.7	0.68	49.0	56.4	41.4	0.73	1.9	1.7	2	20.6	23.2	16.3
82.7	99.1	66.3	0.67	53.5	62.6	44.5	0.71	3.4	3.1	3.8	31.8	33.7	29.1
...	...	...	...	...	...	...	...	...	...	...	...	...	...
103.5	99.0	108.2	1.09	58.5	54.7	62.3	1.14	0.6	0.6	0.6	42.9	44.1	41.8
118.0	136.7	99.3	0.73	...	...	...	...	0.4	0.5	0.2**	29.0	21.4	43.0
101.8	103.8	99.8	0.96	66.4	66.1	66.7	1.01	1.6	1.5	1.7	33.2	34.9	31.5
158.1	157.9	158.3	1.00	...	...	...	...	1.2**	1.2**	1.3**	55.4**	57.2**	53.6**
...	...	...	...	...	...	...	...	7**	6.8**	8**	14.3**	15.1**	13.1**
108.4	108.3	108.6	1.00	94.2	94.1	94.3	1.00	12.0	11.8	12.1	1.2	1.3	1.1
85.4	97.9	72.9	0.75	50.1	54.7	45.6	0.83	...	...	...	38.9	44.1	37.5
113.2	112.4	114.1	1.02	79.7	76.9	82.5	1.07	0.1	0.0	0.1	29.6	31.6	27.6
32.4	38.7	26.0	0.67	21.2	20.6	21.8	1.06	3.1	2.8	3.5	31.6	44.0	12.4
...	...	...	...	...	...	...	...	5.4	...	...	...	...	...
122.4	123.8	120.9	0.98	97.3**	97.1**	97.5**	1.00	2.1**	2.1**	2.2**	18.3**	19.5**	17.2**
...	...	...	...	...	...	...	...	4.5	4.4**	5	...	...	...
73.2	78.4	67.9	0.87	61.7**	65.6**	57.8**	0.88	3.8**	3.9**	3.8**	11.8**	12.5**	11.1**
...	...	...	...	...	...	...	...	11.1	11.2	11.1	...**	...**	...**
65.2	67.8	62.7	0.92	65.2	67.8	62.7	0.93	...	...	...	0.0	...	...
...	...	...	...	...	...	...	...	...	...	...	...	...	...
118.7	120.8	116.6	0.96	...	...	...	...	8.7	8.6	9	11.5*	13.2*	9.7*
124.6	128.0	121.2	0.95	92.8	92.1	93.6	1.02	1.2	1.1	1.3	24.4	27.2	21.5
123.8	138.6	108.8	0.78	91.4	100.0	82.0	0.82	5.4	5.0	5.9	20.8	22.3	18.8
140.9	145.7	136.1	0.93	...	...	...	...	8**	0.1**	0.1**	29.5**	32.9**	25.7**
63.0	62.9	63.2	1.00	46.7	45.8	47.6	1.04	0.1	0.1	0.1	25.8	27.1	24.6
78.7	81.3	76.1	0.94	66.4	67.2	65.6	0.98	1.5	1.2	1.7	14.2	16.2	12.1
96.6	98.1	95.0	0.97	80.2	79.9	80.4	1.01	1.8	1.7	1.9	15.2	16.8	13.4

weighted average				weighted average				median					
100.3	104.0	96.5	0.93	83.0	85.6	80.3	0.94	1.6	1.5	1.8	12.5	13.3	12.2
90.8	91.4	90.1	0.99	79.0	79.2	78.8	1.00	...	...	...	...	...	...
102.0	102.5	101.5	0.99	97.0	96.9	97.0	1.00	...	...	...	...	...	...
100.6	104.7	96.2	0.92	81.8	84.7	78.7	0.93	...	...	...	...	...	...
91.1	97.0	85.0	0.88	78.9	83.0	74.7	0.90	1.9	1.8	1.9	12.5	12.8	10.1
94.4	96.1	92.6	0.96	86.6	87.8	85.3	0.97	2.4	1.7	2.0	5.4	5.7	4.8
88.5	89.0	88.0	0.99	69.4	69.6	69.1	0.99	...	...	...	...	...	...
105.7	105.5	105.9	1.00	92.9	92.5	93.3	1.01	...	...	...	...	...	...
126.0	127.5	124.5	0.98	96.1	96.5	95.8	0.99	1.9	1.8	1.9	15.0	15.9	13.1
102.1	102.7	101.6	0.99	96.4	96.4	96.4	1.00	0.4	0.4	0.4	4.0	4.3	3.5
99.2	107.8	90.0	0.84	78.8	85.9	71.3	0.83	...	...	...	15.2	15.1	15.3
81.2	86.0	76.3	0.89	56.9	59.1	54.7	0.93	2.1	1.7	2.0	24.4	26.7	21.9

Table 7
Particpation in secondary education

Country or territory	Age group 1999	School-age population (thousands) 1999	GROSS ENROLMENT RATIO (GER) IN SECONDARY EDUCATION 1990/91[1] Total	Male	Female	GPI F/M
Arab States and North Africa						
Algeria	12-17	4 212	60.8	67.3	54.1	0.80
Bahrain	12-17	64	99.7	98.1	101.3	1.03
Djibouti	12-18	96	11.9	14.4	9.4	0.65
Egypt[w]	11-16	9 611	76.2	83.8	68.1	0.81
Iraq	12-17	3 195	47.0	57.1	36.4	0.64
Jordan[w]	12-17	666	44.6	43.7	45.6	1.04
Kuwait[3]	10-17	432	42.9	43.3	42.5	0.98
Lebanon[3]	11-17	490	...	...	...	...
Libyan Arab Jamahiriya[3]	12-17	810	86.0	...	...	...
Mauritania	12-17	356	13.7	18.6	8.7	0.47
Morocco	12-17	3 918	35.3	40.6	29.7	0.73
Oman	12-17	358	45.7	51.2	40.1	0.78
Palestinian Autonomous Territories	10-17	592	...	...	...	...
Qatar[3]	12-17	51	80.7	77.1	84.5	1.10
Saudi Arabia	12-17	2 719	44.0	48.6	39.2	0.81
Sudan	12-16	3 401	24.0	26.9	21.1	0.78
Syrian Arab Republic[3]	12-17	2 535	51.9	59.8	43.7	0.73
Tunisia[w]	12-18	1 459	44.9	50.0	39.5	0.79
United Arab Emirates	12-17	282	67.0	63.0	71.6	1.14
Yemen[3]	12-17	2 268	...	...	...	...
Central and Eastern Europe						
Albania	10-17	480	78.3	84.0	72.2	0.86
Belarus	11-15	1 181	93.0	...	...	...
Bosnia and Herzegovina	10-17	487	...	...	...	...
Bulgaria	11-17	756	75.2	73.7	76.8	1.04
Croatia[2]	10-17	500	...	...	...	...
Czech Republic[o]	11-18	1 089	91.2	92.5	89.7	0.97
Estonia	13-17	109	101.9	97.6	106.6	1.09
Hungary[o]	11-18	1 016	78.6	78.2	78.9	1.01
Latvia	11-18	300	92.7	92.7	92.8	1.00
Lithuania	11-18	451	91.9	...	...	...
Poland[o]	13-18	3 978	81.5	79.6	83.4	1.05
Republic of Moldova	11-17	581	80.0	76.7	83.4	1.09
Romania	11-18	2 776	92.0	92.5	91.5	0.99
Russian Federation[w]	10-16	16 921	93.3	90.6	96.1	1.06
Slovakia	10-18	776	...	...	...	...
Slovenia[3]	11-18	217	91.1	...	...	...
The former Yugoslav Rep. of Macedonia[3]	11-18	265	55.7	56.0	55.5	0.99
Turkey[o]	12-17	7 570	47.3	57.5	36.6	0.64
Ukraine[3]	10-16	5 333	92.8	...	...	...
Yugoslavia[2]	11-18	1 294	...	...	...	...
Central Asia						
Armenia	11-16	459	...	...	...	...
Azerbaijan	10-16	1 179	89.9	89.9	89.9	1.00
Georgia	10-16	601	94.9	96.1	93.5	0.97
Kazakhstan	11-17	2 303	98.0	96.7	99.4	1.03
Kyrgyzstan[3]	10-16	784	100.1	98.9	101.3	1.02
Mongolia	12-17	365	82.4	77.2	87.7	1.14
Tajikistan	11-17	1 052	102.1	...	...	...
Turkmenistan	11-17	745	...	...	...	...
Uzbekistan	10-16	4 216	99.4	103.8	94.9	0.91
East Asia and the Pacific						
Australia[o]	12-17	1 593	81.7	80.1	83.4	1.04
Cambodia	12-17	2 035	32.1	44.7	19.3	0.43

1. Indicators for 1990/1991 and 1999/2000 may not be comparable. For further explanation, please see the Technical Introduction preceding these Annexes.
2. Enrolment ratios have not been calculated due to inconsistencies between enrolment and the United Nations population data.
3. Data in italics are for 1998/99.
4. Enrolment ratios have not been calculated due to lack of United Nations population data by age.

GROSS ENROLMENT RATIO (GER) IN SECONDARY EDUCATION				NET ENROLMENT RATIO (NER) IN SECONDARY EDUCATION							
1999/2000			GPI	1990[1]/91			GPI	1999/2000			GPI
Total	Male	Female	F/M	Total	Male	Female	F/M	Total	Male	Female	F/M
66.9	64.7	69.2	1.07	53.7	59.6	47.5	0.80	58.5**	57.3**	59.8**	1.04
102.0	99.2	105.0	1.06	84.9	83.7	86.1	1.03	81.6	76.9	86.6	1.13
14.7	12.9	16.6	1.29	...	...	...	...	...	...	...	...
83.5**	86.2**	80.7**	0.94	...	...	...	...	79.0**	81.3**	76.7**	0.94
38.3	47.1	29.1	0.62	...	...	...	...	33.0	39.6	26.0	0.66
87.7	86.4**	89.0**	1.03	...	...	...	...	75.9	73.4	78.5	1.07
55.6	55.1	56.1	1.02	...	...	...	...	_49.7_	_49.2_	_50.2_	_1.02_
78.2	74.9	81.6	1.09	...	...	...	...	_70.2**_	_67.2**_	_73.3**_	_1.09_
_79.3_	_75.1**_	_83.5**_	_1.11_	...	...	...	...	...	...	...	...
18.4	21.4	15.4	0.72	...	...	...	...	...	...	...	...
39.3	43.6	35.0	0.80	...	...	...	...	29.9	32.7	27.0	0.83
67.8	68.3	67.3	0.98	...	...	...	...	58.5	58.3	58.8	1.01
80.7	78.4	83.0	1.06	...	...	...	...	76.9	74.7	79.3	1.06
_92.4_	_78.4_	_107.0_	_1.36_	67.1	64.1	70.4	1.10	_78.0_	_74.6_	_81.6_	_1.10_
68.5	71.9	64.8	0.90	31.2	34.3	28.0	0.82	...	...	...	...
28.8	21.7	36.2	1.67	...	...	...	...	...	...	...	...
_42.0_	_44.4_	_39.5_	_0.89_	45.8	52.5	39.0	0.74	_37.6_	_39.2_	_35.9_	_0.92_
74.6	73.0	76.2	1.04	...	...	...	...	67.9**	65.9**	69.9**	1.06
74.4	69.6	79.8	1.15	59.2	55.7	63.1	1.13	67.5	63.4	72.1	1.14
_47.6_	_68.6_	_25.4_	_0.37_	...	...	...	...	_37.0*_	_52.1*_	_21.1*_	_0.40_
75.8	74.6	77.0	1.03	...	...	...	...	71.5	70.4	72.6	1.03
94.2	95.7	92.7	0.97	...	...	...	...	...	...	...	...
...	...	...	...	...	...	...	...	...	...	...	...
92.0	93.1	90.9	0.98	63.3	62.0	64.7	1.04	85.8	86.6	84.8	0.98
...	...	...	...	...	...	...	...	...	...	...	...
87.9	87.2	88.7	1.02	...	...	...	...	84.3	83.9	84.8	1.01
107.0	105.5	108.5	1.03	...	...	...	...	90.0	87.5	92.6	1.06
98.6	98.2	99.0	1.01	74.8	73.3	76.3	1.04	87.2	86.8	87.6	1.01
88.9	87.8	90.0	1.03	...	...	...	...	84.2	83.3	85.2	1.02
93.4	115.3	70.7	0.61	...	...	...	...	87.7	87.3	88.1	1.01
98.4**	98.8**	98.1**	0.99	75.8	72.8	79.0	1.08	88.1**	86.0**	90.4**	1.05
...	...	...	...	...	...	...	...	...	...	...	...
80.2	79.6	80.8	1.01	...	...	...	...	75.9	75.0	76.9	1.02
81.9	79.1	84.8	1.07	...	...	...	...	...	...	...	...
86.6	85.8	87.4	1.02	...	...	...	...	...	...	...	...
_98.8_	_97.4_	_100.2_	_1.03_	...	...	...	...	_89.5_	_88.0_	_91.1_	_1.04_
83.6	85.0	82.2	0.97	...	...	...	...	_78.8**_	_79.9**_	_77.7**_	_0.97_
57.7**	67.3**	47.7**	0.71	41.4	...	...	...	...	...	...	...
_92.8_	_86.5*_	_99.3*_	_1.15_	...	...	...	...	...	...	...	...
...	...	...	...	...	...	...	...	...	...	...	...
...	...	...	...	...	...	...	...	...	...	...	...
80.2	80.0	80.3	1.00	...	...	...	...	78.0**	77.6**	78.3**	1.01
77.7	77.1	78.3	1.02	...	...	...	...	54.4**	52.6**	56.3**	1.07
87.0	86.7	87.2	1.01	...	...	...	...	...	...	...	...
_83.0_	_82.0_	_84.1_	_1.03_	...	...	...	...	...	...	...	...
64.4	58.0	71.0	1.23	...	...	...	...	59.0	52.9	65.2	1.23
76.0	81.8	70.0	0.86	...	...	...	...	...	...	...	...
...	...	...	...	...	...	...	...	...	...	...	...
...	...	...	...	...	...	...	...	...	...	...	...
156.4	156.2	156.7	1.00	78.6	76.9	80.4	1.05	86.8**	86.0**	87.8**	1.02
17.3	22.2	12.2	0.55	...	...	...	...	15.6	19.9	11.2	0.56

Table 7 (continued)

Country or territory	Age group	School-age population (thousands)	GROSS ENROLMENT RATIO (GER) IN SECONDARY EDUCATION			
			1990/91[1]			GPI
	1999	1999	Total	Male	Female	F/M
China[w]	12-17	129 709	48.7	55.3	41.7	0.75
Cook Islands[4]	11-18	...	...	...	...	...
Democratic People's Rep. of Korea	10-15	782	...	...	...	...
Fiji	12-18	122	56.2	...	...	...
Indonesia[w]	13-18	25 990	44.0	48.2	39.7	0.82
Japan[o]	12-17	8 606	97.1	96.3	98.0	1.02
Kiribati	13-18	...	...	...	...	...
Lao People's Democratic Republic	11-16	744	25.2	31.1	19.2	0.62
Malaysia[w]	12-16	2 203	56.3	54.5	58.2	1.07
Marshall Islands[4]	12-17	...	...	...	...	...
Myanmar[3]	10-15	5 961	22.7	22.8	22.5	0.99
Nauru	12-17	...	...	...	...	...
New Zealand[o]	11-17	387	89.1	88.3	89.8	1.02
Niue	11-16	...	...	...	...	...
Papua New Guinea[3]	13-18	642	12.4	14.9	9.8	0.66
Philippines[w, 3]	12-15	6 852	73.2	73.5	72.9	0.99
Republic of Korea[o]	12-17	4 287	89.8	91.1	88.5	0.97
Samoa	11-17	29	36.1	32.8	39.9	1.22
Solomon Islands	12-18	69	14.1	17.3	10.8	0.62
Thailand[w]	12-17	6 881	30.1	30.6	29.6	0.97
Tonga	11-16	...	...	...	...	...
Tuvalu	12-17	...	...	...	...	...
Vanuatu	12-19	35	16.8	19.0	14.5	0.76
Viet Nam	11-17	12 193	32.0	...	...	...
Latin America and the Caribbean						
Anguilla[4]	12-16	...	...	...	...	...
Antigua and Barbuda[4]	12-16	...	...	...	...	...
Argentina[w]	12-17	3 973	71.1	...	...	...
Aruba[4]	12-16	...	...	...	...	...
Bahamas	11-16	34	...	...	...	...
Barbados	11-15	21	...	...	...	...
Belize	11-16	32	41.3	38.9	43.8	1.13
Bermuda	11-17	...	...	...	...	...
Bolivia	12-17	1 074	36.6	39.5	33.6	0.85
Brazil[w]	11-17	24 197	38.4	...	...	...
British Virgin Islands[4]	12-16	...	...	...	...	...
Cayman Islands[4]	11-16	...	...	...	...	...
Chile[w]	12-17	1 597	73.5	70.5	76.5	1.08
Colombia	11-16	5 060	49.8	46.8	52.8	1.13
Costa Rica	12-16	418	41.6	40.6	42.7	1.05
Cuba	12-17	965	88.9	83.0	95.0	1.14
Dominica[4]	12-16	...	...	...	...	...
Dominican Republic	12-17	1 105	...	...	...	...
Ecuador	12-17	1 619	55.3	...	...	...
El Salvador[3]	13-18	797	26.4	25.6	27.2	1.06
Grenada[4]	12-16	...	...	...	...	...
Guatemala	13-17	1 331	...	...	...	...
Guyana[3]	12-16	80	83.4	80.6	86.2	1.07
Haiti	12-18	1 437	20.9	21.4	20.4	0.96
Honduras	13-17	740	...	...	...	...
Jamaica[w]	12-16	274	65.3	63.6	67.1	1.06
Mexico[o]	12-17	12 389	53.3	53.0	53.5	1.01
Montserrat	12-16	...	...	...	...	...
Netherlands Antilles	12-16	17	...	...	...	...
Nicaragua	13-17	606	40.5	34.2	46.7	1.36
Panama	12-17	335	62.6	60.5	64.7	1.07
Paraguay[w]	12-17	747	30.9	30.3	31.6	1.04

1. Indicators for 1990/1991 and 1999/2000 may not be comparable. For further explanation, please see the Technical Introduction preceding these Annexes.
2. Enrolment ratios have not been calculated due to inconsistencies between enrolment and the United Nations population data.
3. Data in italics are for 1998/99.
4. Enrolment ratios have not been calculated due to lack of United Nations population data by age.

GROSS ENROLMENT RATIO (GER) IN SECONDARY EDUCATION				NET ENROLMENT RATIO (NER) IN SECONDARY EDUCATION							
1999/2000			GPI	1990[1]/91			GPI	1999/2000			GPI
Total	Male	Female	F/M	Total	Male	Female	F/M	Total	Male	Female	F/M
62.8	65.9**	59.5**	0.90	...	...	...	...	...	...	...	...
...	...	...	...	...	...	...	...	...	...	...	...
...	...	...	...	...	...	...	...	...	...	...	...
...	...	...	...	...	...	...	...	...	...	...	...
54.9**	56.2**	53.5**	0.95	37.9	40.3	35.4	0.88	47.5**	48.6**	46.4**	0.96
102.1	101.5	102.6	1.01	96.8	...	...	...	100.0**	100.0**	100.0**	1.00
...	...	...	...	...	...	...	...	...	...	...	...
35.6	41.7	29.3	0.70	...	...	...	...	28.6	31.9	25.1	0.79
98.8	94.2	103.7	1.10	...	...	...	...	88.8	84.7	93.2	1.10
...	...	...	...	...	...	...	...	...	...	...	...
*34.9***	*34.9***	*34.8***	*1.00*	...	...	...	...	...	...	...	...
...	...	...	...	...	...	...	...	...	...	...	...
112.9	110.0	116.1	1.06	85.0	84.2	85.9	1.02	...	...	...	...
...	...	...	...	...	...	...	...	...	...	...	...
21.2	*23.6*	*18.3*	*0.78*	...	...	...	...	*21.3**	*23.8**	*18.5**	*0.78*
75.9	*72.6*	*79.4*	*1.09*	...	...	...	...	*50.9*	*48.7*	*53.1*	*1.09*
97.4	97.6	97.2	1.00	85.8	86.8	84.7	0.98	94.4	94.5	94.2	1.00
76.0	72.9	79.5	1.09	...	...	...	...	68.4	64.7	72.6	1.12
...	...	...	...	...	...	...	...	...	...	...	...
79.0	78.1	79.9	1.02	...	...	...	...	55.4	54.3	56.5	1.04
...	...	...	...	...	...	...	...	...	...	...	...
...	...	...	...	...	...	...	...	...	...	...	...
28.5	31.0	25.8	0.83	...	...	...	...	22.6	23.7	21.5	0.91
64.6	67.7	61.4	0.91	...	...	...	...	61.3	64.4**	58.3**	0.91
...	...	...	...	...	...	...	...	...	...	...	...
...	...	...	...	...	...	...	...	...	...	...	...
93.7	90.6	96.9	1.07	...	...	...	...	76.0	72.9	79.2	1.09
...	...	...	...	...	...	...	...	...	...	...	...
...	...	...	...	...	...	...	...	...	...	...	...
101.1	99.2	103.1	1.04	...	...	...	...	70.7	70.1	71.2	1.02
71.6	71.7	71.6	1.00	28.9	27.3	30.5	1.11	36.0	32.1	40.0	1.25
...	...	...	...	...	...	...	...	...	...	...	...
78.5**	81.2**	75.7**	0.93	29.4	31.7	27.0	0.85	...	...	...	...
103.2	98.0	108.7	1.11	15.5	...	...	...	68.5	65.7	71.3	1.08
...	...	...	...	...	...	...	...	...	...	...	...
...	...	...	...	...	...	...	...	...	...	...	...
87.5	86.6	88.4	1.02	54.6	...	...	...	71.8	70.5	73.1	1.04
70.9	67.3	74.7	1.11	...	...	...	...	54.3	51.5**	57.1**	1.11
50.9	48.1	53.9	1.12	35.7	34.5	37.0	1.07	43.4	40.8	46.0	1.13
81.9	80.2	83.7	1.04	68.9	64.4	73.7	1.14	79.7	78.1	81.3	1.04
...	...	...	...	...	...	...	...	...	...	...	...
66.4**	59.9**	73.3**	1.22	...	...	...	...	40.0**	35.2**	45.0**	1.28
56.7	56.2	57.1	1.02	...	...	...	...	46.9	46.2	47.6	1.03
49.8	*50.0*	*49.6*	*0.99*	...	...	...	...	...	...	...	...
...	...	...	...	...	...	...	...	...	...	...	...
32.7	34.9	30.4	0.87	...	...	...	...	18.4**	18.5**	18.3**	0.99
81.0	*80.3*	*81.7*	*1.02*	70.6	68.3	72.9	1.07	...	...	...	...
...	...	...	...	...	...	...	...	...	...	...	...
...	...	...	...	...	...	...	...	...	...	...	...
83.6	85.1	82.0	0.96	63.6	61.7	65.4	1.06	74.7**	73.1**	76.3**	1.04
73.4	72.0	74.9	1.04	44.8	...	...	...	57.4**	57.2**	57.6**	1.01
...	...	...	...	...	...	...	...	...	...	...	...
83.1	78.5	87.8	1.12	...	...	...	...	63.3	59.0	67.6	1.15
60.2**	55.2**	65.4**	1.19	...	...	...	...	...	...	...	...
68.7	66.5	71.0	1.07	50.8	48.2	53.4	1.11	60.9**	58.2**	63.7**	1.09
56.9	55.8	58.0	1.04	25.8	25.4	26.3	1.04	45.0**	43.8**	46.3**	1.06

Table 7 (continued)

Country or territory	Age group 1999	School-age population (thousands) 1999	GROSS ENROLMENT RATIO (GER) IN SECONDARY EDUCATION 1990/91[1] Total	Male	Female	GPI F/M
Peru[w, 3]	12-16	2 758	67.3	...	...	...
Saint Kitts and Nevis[4]	12-16	...	...	...	...	...
Saint Lucia	12-16	15	...	...	...	...
Saint Vincent and the Grenadines[4]	12-16	...	...	...	...	...
Suriname[3]	12-16	49	52.1	48.5	55.7	1.15
Trinidad and Tobago	12-16	142	80.4	78.5	82.3	1.05
Turks and Caicos Islands[4]	12-16	...	...	...	...	...
Uruguay[w]	12-17	310	81.3	...	...	...
Venezuela	12-16	2 566	34.7	29.2	40.3	1.38
North America and Western Europe						
Andorra	11-17	...	...	...	...	...
Austria[o]	10-17	756	103.7	107.2	100.1	0.93
Belgium[o]	12-17	728	102.9	102.5	103.4	1.01
Canada[o]	12-17	2 448	100.7	100.7	100.7	1.00
Cyprus[2]	12-17	77	...	...	...	...
Denmark[o]	13-18	332	109.2	108.5	109.8	1.01
Finland[o]	13-18	394	116.4	106.3	126.9	1.19
France[o]	11-17	5 455	98.5	96.0	101.2	1.05
Germany[o]	10-18	8 387	98.3	99.6	97.0	0.97
Greece[o]	12-17	781	93.3	94.2	92.3	0.98
Iceland[o]	13-19	30	99.6	101.4	97.8	0.96
Ireland[o]	12-16	321	100.5	96.2	105.1	1.09
Israel[o]	12-17	632	85.4	82.2	88.7	1.08
Italy[o]	11-18	4 748	82.8	83.0	82.6	1.00
Luxembourg[o]	12-18	35	74.6	...	...	...
Malta[3]	11-17	41	84.2	86.8	81.4	0.94
Monaco	11-17	...	...	...	...	...
Netherlands[o]	12-17	1 111	119.5	124.1	114.7	0.92
Norway[o]	13-18	318	103.0	101.4	104.6	1.03
Portugal[o]	12-17	742	67.4	62.5	72.4	1.16
San Marino	...	...	...	...	...	...
Spain[o]	12-17	2 877	104.1	100.9	107.5	1.07
Sweden[o]	13-18	611	90.2	88.2	92.3	1.05
Switzerland[o]	13-19	550	99.1	101.7	96.4	0.95
United Kingdom[o]	11-17	5 278	85.5	83.0	88.1	1.06
United States[o]	12-17	23 876	93.1	92.5	93.8	1.01
South and West Asia						
Afghanistan	...	...	8.9	...	...	...
Bangladesh	11-15	16 169	19.0	25.1	12.7	0.51
Bhutan[2]	13-16	191	...	...	...	...
India[w]	12-16	104 269	44.4	55.0	32.9	0.60
Iran, Islamic Republic of	11-16	11 470	55.2	63.7	46.4	0.73
Maldives	13-17	35	...	...	...	...
Nepal	11-15	2 596	33.1	46.0	19.6	0.43
Pakistan	10-14	16 823	22.7	29.8	14.8	0.50
Sri Lanka[w, 3]	10-17	2 925	73.8	70.7	76.9	1.09
Sub-Saharan Africa						
Angola	10-16	2 196	12.4	...	...	...
Benin	12-18	1 052	11.9	16.9	6.9	0.41
Botswana	13-17	194	42.7	40.5	45.0	1.11
Burkina Faso	13-19	1 901	7.2	9.3	4.9	0.53
Burundi[3]	13-19	1 067	5.6	7.1	4.1	0.58
Cameroon[3]	12-18	2 431	28.0	32.7	23.2	0.71
Cape Verde	12-17	59	20.6	...	...	...
Central African Republic	12-18	578	11.7	17.1	6.7	0.39
Chad	12-18	1 195	7.8	13.1	2.6	0.20

1. Indicators for 1990/1991 and 1999/2000 may not be comparable. For further explanation, please see the Technical Introduction preceding these Annexes.
2. Enrolment ratios have not been calculated due to inconsistencies between enrolment and the United Nations population data.
3. Data in italics are for 1998/99.
4. Enrolment ratios have not been calculated due to lack of United Nations population data by age.

GROSS ENROLMENT RATIO (GER) IN SECONDARY EDUCATION				NET ENROLMENT RATIO (NER) IN SECONDARY EDUCATION							
1999/2000			GPI	1990[1]/91			GPI	1999/2000			GPI
Total	Male	Female	F/M	Total	Male	Female	F/M	Total	Male	Female	F/M
80.8	*83.1*	*78.4*	*0.94*	...	...	...	...	*61.5*	*62.2*	*60.7*	*0.98*
...	...	...	...	...	...	...	...	...	...	...	...
94.3	84.8**	103.6**	1.22	...	...	...	...	64.0	48.1	79.5	1.65
...	...	...	...	...	...	...	...	...	...	...	...
50.7	...	...	...	...	...	...	...	...	...	...	...
78.4	75.0	81.9	1.09	...	...	...	...	63.8	60.9	66.9	1.10
...	...	...	...	...	...	...	...	...	...	...	...
91.6	84.4	99.0	1.17	...	...	...	...	77.4**	74.3**	80.6**	1.08
59.3**	54.2**	64.6**	1.19	18.6	14.9	22.4	1.50	50.4	45.9	55.0	1.20
...	...	...	...	...	...	...	...	...	...	...	...
99.1	101.0	97.0	0.96	...	...	...	...	88.8**	89.0**	88.5**	0.99
145.4	138.4	152.6	1.10	87.7	86.2	89.2	1.03	95.0**	94.6**	95.5**	1.01
102.6	101.9	103.4	1.02	88.7	88.4	89.0	1.01	97.9	97.6	98.2	1.01
...	...	...	...	...	...	...	...	...	...	...	...
128.2	125.3	131.3	1.05	86.8	85.7	88.0	1.03	89.5	88.2	90.8	1.03
124.5	119.0	130.2	1.09	93.0	92.2	93.9	1.02	95.1**	94.4**	95.9**	1.02
108.7	108.5	108.9	1.00	...	...	...	...	92.6	91.6	93.5	1.02
99.0	99.5	98.5	0.99	...	...	...	...	87.7**	87.4**	88.0**	1.01
94.6	93.2	96.1	1.03	82.7	81.9	83.4	1.02	86.0	84.3	87.8	1.04
108.8	104.7	113.1	1.08	...	...	...	...	76.3	74.9	77.8	1.04
123.1	119.0	127.4	1.07	79.9	78.1	81.9	1.05	99.8**	97.4**	100.0**	1.03
93.0	92.9	93.1	1.00	...	...	...	...	88.1**	87.3**	88.9**	1.02
92.8	94.8	90.7	0.96	...	...	...	...	87.6**	89.0**	86.1**	0.97
95.3	92.8	97.8	1.05	...	...	...	...	82.4	80.2	84.7	1.06
90.4	*95.2*	*85.4*	*0.90*	79.6	79.8	79.4	0.99	*79.2***	*81.2***	*77.2***	*0.95*
...	...	...	...	...	...	...	...	...	...	...	...
124.1	126.6	121.5	0.96	83.6	82.7	84.6	1.02	91.9**	91.9**	92.0**	1.00
117.0	115.6	118.4	1.02	87.7	87.0	88.4	1.02	95.5**	95.0**	96.0**	1.01
112.0	108.4	115.8	1.07	...	...	...	...	87.3**	84.1**	90.7**	1.08
...	...	...	...	...	...	...	...	...	...	...	...
112.8	109.7	116.2	1.06	...	...	...	...	90.8**	89.5**	92.2**	1.03
152.8	135.1	171.5	1.27	85.3	84.7	85.8	1.01	96.1	94.4	97.9	1.04
99.9	103.5	96.2	0.93	79.8	82.3	77.2	0.94	88.4	91.1	85.6	0.94
157.2	145.8	169.3	1.16	79.1	77.1	81.2	1.05	93.6	92.5	94.7	1.02
94.6	94.3	95.0	1.01	85.8	85.0	86.6	1.02	87.4	86.5	88.4	1.02
...	...	...	...	...	...	...	...	...	...	...	...
53.7	51.7	55.9	1.08	18.0	23.7	12.2	0.51	...	...	...	...
...	...	...	...	...	...	...	...	...	...	...	...
49.9	58.9	40.2	0.68	...	...	...	...	...	...	...	...
80.0	83.1	76.8	0.92	...	...	...	...	...	...	...	...
42.7	41.4	44.2	1.07	...	...	...	...	31.4	29.5	33.3	...
53.9	62.3	44.9	0.72	...	...	...	...	...	...	...	...
39.0	45.8	31.9	0.70	...	...	...	...	...	...	...	...
*72.1***	*69.9***	*74.5***	*1.07*	...	...	...	...	...	...	...	...
15.5**	17.5**	13.4**	0.77	...	...	...	...	...	...	...	...
21.8	30.1	13.5	0.45	...	...	...	...	17.4	23.8	11.0	0.46
81.8	78.2	85.4	1.09	33.5	30.6	36.5	1.19	58.8**	54.5**	63.1**	1.16
10.0	12.2	7.8	0.64	...	...	...	...	8.3**	10.1**	6.6**	0.65
*7.1***	*8.1***	*6.1***	*0.75*	...	...	...	...	...	...	...	...
*19.6***	*22.0***	*17.2***	*0.78*	...	...	...	...	...	...	...	...
68.6**	...	...	...	...	...	...	...	...	...	...	...
...	...	...	...	...	...	...	...	...	...	...	...
11.5	17.9	5.1	0.28	...	...	...	...	7.7	11.8	3.7	0.31

Table 7 (continued)

Country or territory	Age group	School-age population (thousands)	GROSS ENROLMENT RATIO (GER) IN SECONDARY EDUCATION			
			1990/91[1]			GPI
	1999	1999	Total	Male	Female	F/M
Comoros	12-18	118	17.5	21.2	13.8	0.65
Congo	12-18	456	52.9	62.5	43.8	0.70
Côte d'Ivoire[3]	12-18	2 788	22.0	29.8	14.3	0.48
Democratic Rep. of the Congo[3]	12-17	6 939	...	...	...	...
Equatorial Guinea	12-18	67	...	...	...	...
Eritrea	12-17	480	...	...	...	...
Ethiopia	11-18	11 197	14.2	15.9	12.5	0.79
Gabon[3]	12-18	165	...	...	...	...
Gambia[3]	12-17	156	18.8	25.4	12.3	0.49
Ghana[3]	12-17	2 802	36.4	44.6	28.2	0.63
Guinea[3]	13-19	1 267	10.0	14.9	4.9	0.33
Guinea-Bissau	13-17	126	...	...	...	...
Kenya	13-17	3 987	24.1	27.6	20.6	0.75
Lesotho	13-18	263	25.3	20.3	30.4	1.50
Liberia	13-19	524	...	...	...	...
Madagascar[3]	11-17	2 496	18.0	18.2	17.9	0.98
Malawi[3]	10-17	2 161	7.7	10.6	4.9	0.46
Mali[3]	13-18	1 483	7.0	9.3	4.6	0.50
Mauritius	12-16	97	52.9	52.7	53.1	1.01
Mozambique	11-15	2 127	7.6	9.7	5.5	0.57
Namibia	13-17	194	43.8	38.6	49.0	1.27
Niger[3]	13-19	1 633	6.6	9.4	3.9	0.41
Nigeria	12-17	15 906	24.9	28.5	21.2	0.74
Rwanda	13-18	1 071	8.0	9.1	6.9	0.75
Sao Tome and Principe[4]	13-18	...	...	...	...	...
Senegal	13-18	1 248	16.2	21.2	11.2	0.53
Seychelles[4]	12-16	...	...	...	...	...
Sierra Leone	12-17	572	17.3	22.1	12.6	0.57
Somalia	...	699	...	...	...	...
South Africa	14-18	4 698	74.3	68.9	79.7	1.16
Swaziland[3]	13-17	103	44.3	45.2	43.4	0.96
Togo	12-18	715	23.6	35.3	11.9	0.34
Uganda	13-18	3 157	13.2	16.9	9.5	0.56
United Republic of Tanzania	14-19	4 692	4.9	5.8	4.1	0.70
Zambia[3]	14-18	1 171	23.0	...	...	...
Zimbabwe[w]	13-18	...	...	...	...	...
		Total	**weighted average**			
World	...	670 340	50.7	55.4	46.1	0.83
Countries in transition	...	49 714	87.4	86.9	88.5	1.02
Developed countries	...	70 799	94.4	93.8	95.5	1.02
Developing countries	...	549 827	41.2	47.1	35.2	0.75
Arab States and North Africa	...	37 515	50.5	56.6	44.3	0.78
Central and Eastern Europe	...	46 082	79.3	80.4	78.7	0.98
Central Asia	...	11 704	87.3	88.5	86.4	0.98
East Asia and the Pacific	...	209 117	50.2	54.3	45.6	0.84
Latin America and the Caribbean	...	64 687	48.6	47.9	49.6	1.04
North America and Western Europe	...	60 526	94.3	93.8	95.3	1.02
South and West Asia	...	154 478	39.6	49.2	29.8	0.61
Sub-Saharan Africa	...	86 232	20.1	22.6	17.8	0.79

1. Indicators for 1990/1991 and 1999/2000 may not be comparable. For further explanation, please see the Technical Introduction preceding these Annexes.
2. Enrolment ratios have not been calculated due to inconsistencies between enrolment and the United Nations population data.
3. Data in italics are for 1998/99.
4. Enrolment ratios have not been calculated due to lack of United Nations population data by age.

GROSS ENROLMENT RATIO (GER) IN SECONDARY EDUCATION				NET ENROLMENT RATIO (NER) IN SECONDARY EDUCATION							
1999/2000			GPI	1990[1]/91			GPI	1999/2000			GPI
Total	Male	Female	F/M	Total	Male	Female	F/M	Total	Male	Female	F/M
20.6**	22.6**	18.5**	0.82	...	...	...	...	...	...	...	...
...	...	...	...	...	...	...	...	...	...	...	...
21.7**	28.3**	15.1**	0.53	...	...	...	...	...	...	...	...
18.4**	24.1**	12.6**	0.52	...	...	...	...	11.7**	14.8**	8.6**	0.58
31.2**	43.2**	19.2**	0.44	...	...	...	...	26.1**	38.3**	13.9**	0.36
28.2	33.2	23.1	0.70	...	...	...	...	22.5	25.0	20.1	0.80
5.2	6.2	4.2	0.68	...	...	...	...	...	...	...	...
54.4	58.3	50.5	0.87	...	...	...	...	...	...	...	...
27.0	31.1	23.0	0.74	...	...	...	...	23.4	27.3	19.6	0.72
37.3	41.9	32.7	0.78	...	...	...	...	26.1	29.0	23.2	0.80
13.8**	20.1**	7.3**	0.36	...	...	...	...	11.9**	17.1**	6.5**	0.38
20.4	26.4	14.4	0.54	...	...	...	...	...	...	...	...
29.9**	31.5**	28.2**	0.90	...	...	...	...	...	...	...	...
28.0	23.6	32.4	1.37	...	...	...	...	19.6	15.1	24.2	1.61
22.5	26.6	18.4	0.69	...	...	...	...	20.3	23.7	16.9	0.71
14.3**	14.6**	14.0**	0.96	...	...	...	...	11.5**	11.3**	11.6**	1.03
45.2**	50.3**	40.0**	0.80	...	...	...	...	...	...	...	...
15.0	19.8	10.3	0.52	5.3	6.9	3.8	0.55	...	...	...	...
107.3	108.3	106.3	0.98	...	...	...	...	72.5	71.1	73.9	1.04
13.9	16.6	11.3	0.68	...	...	...	...	7.3	8.5	6.2	0.73
59.8	56.3	63.3	1.12	...	...	...	...	34.2	28.5	39.9	1.40
6.5**	7.8**	5.1**	0.65	5.8	8.2	3.5	0.43	5.8**	6.9**	4.5**	0.65
...	...	...	...	...	...	...	...	...	...	...	...
12.1	12.4	11.8	0.95	7.1	8.1	6.1	0.76	...	...	...	...
...	...	...	...	...	...	...	...	...	...	...	...
19.5	23.7	15.3	0.64	...	...	...	...	...	...	...	...
...	...	...	...	...	...	...	...	...	...	...	...
23.9	26.4	21.6	0.82	...	...	...	...	23.9	26.4	21.6	0.82
...	...	...	...	...	...	...	...	...	...	...	...
90.2	132.8	48.0	0.36	...	...	...	...	...	...	...	...
60.0**	59.9**	60.2**	1.01	...	...	...	...	37.3**	40.0**	34.6**	0.86
36.2**	50.2**	22.2**	0.44	18.2	26.5	9.9	0.38	23.1	32.1	14.0	0.44
...	...	...	...	...	...	...	...	...	...	...	...
5.3	5.7	4.9	0.86	...	...	...	...	4.8**	4.9**	4.6**	0.95
25.5	28.7	22.2	0.77	...	...	...	...	20.7**	22.5**	18.9**	0.84
45.3	48.1	42.5	0.88	...	...	...	...	42.3	44.4	40.2	0.91

weighted average								median	median	median	
62.3	64.6	60.0	0.93	...	...	...	...	67.9	64.7	71.3	...
74.4	73.0	75.9	1.04	...	...	...	...	...	...	...	...
106.6	105.1	107.9	1.03	...	...	...	...	...	...	...	...
55.5	58.6	52.3	0.89	...	...	...	...	...	...	...	...
60.3	62.6	57.7	0.92	...	...	...	...	67.5	63.4	69.9	...
79.4	79.3	79.7	1.00	...	...	...	...	85.0	84.9	85.0	...
43.5	43.7	43.3	0.99	...	...	...	...	...	...	...	...
64.9	66.9	62.9	0.94	...	...	...	...	55.4	54.3	56.5	...
82.5	79.6	85.9	1.08	...	...	...	...	61.5	58.2	63.7	...
105.9	104.3	107.2	1.03	...	...	...	...	88.8	89.0	90.7	...
51.9	58.8	44.3	0.75	...	...	...	...	...	...	...	...
24.3	26.4	22.4	0.85	...	...	...	...	20.7	23.8	16.9	...

Table 8
Human resources

Country or territory	PRE-PRIMARY EDUCATION							
	Trained teachers (%)				Pupil/teacher ratio		Female teachers (%)	
	1998/99		1999/2000					
	Total	Female	Total	Female	1990/91	1999/00	1990/91	1999/00
Arab States and North Africa								
Algeria	...	...	...	...	...	27	...	87.9
Bahrain	18.3	18.3	...	...	26	21**	100.0	99.7**
Djibouti	...	...	...	...	...	36**	...	100.0**
Egypt[w]	...	...	...	...	25	24**	95.4	98.6**
Iraq	...	...	...	...	18	15	100.0	100.0
Jordan[w]	...	...	...	...	23	22	99.9	99.8
Kuwait	100.0	100.0	...	...	16	16	100.0	99.9
Lebanon	...	...	...	...	...	14	...	81.4
Libyan Arab Jamahiriya	...	...	...	...	...	...	...	...
Mauritania	...	...	...	...	...	...	...	...
Morocco	...	...	...	...	20	18	20.3	43.2
Oman	92.5	92.5	...	...	20	19	100.0	100.0
Palestinian Autonomous Territories	...	...	...	...	...	22	...	99.3
Qatar	...	...	...	...	18	...	99.3	72.2
Saudi Arabia	...	...	...	...	14	10	100.0	100.0
Sudan	...	...	...	...	35	30	46.8	84.5
Syrian Arab Republic	87.1	87.1	...	...	27	...	98.2	...
Tunisia[w]	...	...	...	...	26	20	...	96.0
United Arab Emirates	59.3	59.3	...	...	21	19	98.9	99.8
Yemen	...	...	...	...	15	17**	...	93.0**
Central and Eastern Europe								
Albania	...	...	...	...	23	21	100.0	100.0
Belarus	...	...	...	...	7	5	...	...
Bosnia and Herzegovina	...	...	...	...	...	...	...	...
Bulgaria	...	...	...	...	11	11	100.0	99.0
Croatia	76.3	76.3	79.2	79.2	13	13	...	99.7
Czech Republic[o]	...	...	...	...	11	18	100.0	99.7
Estonia	...	...	...	...	7	8	...	99.8
Hungary[o]	...	...	...	...	12	12	99.7	100.0
Latvia	...	...	...	...	9	44	...	98.0
Lithuania	...	...	...	...	7	8	100.0[e]	99.3
Poland[o]	...	...	...	...	14	12	...	...
Republic of Moldova	...	...	...	...	9	...	100.0	...
Romania	...	...	...	...	20	17	100.0	0.1
Russian Federation[w]	...	...	...	...	9	7	...	98.7**
Slovakia	...	...	...	...	12	10	...	99.9
Slovenia	...	...	...	...	11	...	99.0	...
The former Yugoslav Rep. of Macedonia	...	...	...	...	...	11	...	99.5
Turkey[o]	...	...	...	...	17	16	99.6	68.2**
Ukraine	...	...	...	...	9	...	...	...
Yugoslavia	95.5	95.5	...	...	...	14	...	...
Central Asia								
Armenia	...	...	...	...	9	...	...	...
Azerbaijan	...	...	...	...	7	10	100.0	100.0
Georgia	...	...	...	...	7	11	100.0[e]	100.0
Kazakhstan	...	...	...	...	11	8	...	...
Kyrgyzstan	...	...	...	...	...	12	...	100.0
Mongolia	...	...	...	...	26	26	...	99.2
Tajikistan	...	...	...	...	10	10	...	90.8**
Turkmenistan	...	...	...	...	...	...	...	...
Uzbekistan	...	...	...	...	15	...	...	...
East Asia and the Pacific								
Australia[o]	...	...	...	...	...	...	...	...
Cambodia	...	...	...	...	17	28	82.1	99.3
China[w]	...	...	...	...	26	27	96.3	93.6

PRIMARY EDUCATION								LOWER SECONDARY EDUCATION							
Trained teachers (%)				Pupil/teacher ratio		Female teachers (%)		Trained teachers (%)				Pupil/teacher ratio		Female teachers (%)	
1998/99		1998/99						1998/99		1998/99					
Total	Female	Total	Female	1990/91	1999/00	1990/91	1999/00	Total	Female	Total	Female	1998/99	1999/00	1990/91	1999/00
93.7	95.7	...	...	28	28	39.1	46.1	99.9	99.9	...	99.9	19	19	43.0	49.6
...	...	...	...	19	18**	54.3[e]	74.6**	...	...	...	...	13**	15**	54.2	57.5**
...	...	...	...	43	32**	37.1	18.5**	...	...	...	...	28	31**	...	19.1**
...	...	...	...	24	23**	51.6[e]	52.4**	...	...	...	...	...	...	43.9	42.5**
...	...	...	...	25	21	70.1	72.5	...	...	...	...	...	22	...	76.6
...	...	...	...	25	...	61.7	...	...	...	...	...	...	...	...	...
100.0	100.0	...	...	18	14	61.4	73.9	100.0	100.0	...	100.0	12	12	53.5	58.0
...	...	...	...	...	19	...	80.9	...	...	...	...	11	17	...	60.8**
...	...	...	...	14	...	...	...	...	...	...	...	8	...	...	...
...	...	...	...	45	45	17.8	26.4	...	...	...	...	28**	42	...	15.4
...	...	...	...	27	29	37.2	36.5	...	...	...	...	19	19	32.4	34.5**
99.6	99.4	...	...	28	25	47.0	54.1	99.9	99.9	...	99.9	19	19	40.3	47.6
...	...	...	...	...	31**	...	50.9**	...	...	...	...	31**	33**	...	52.7**
...	...	...	...	11	...	72.4	...	...	...	...	...	13	...	56.3	...
...	...	...	...	16	12	47.5	52.9	...	...	...	...	12	12	38.1	49.6
62.4**	47.0**	...	...	34	27**	51.0	62.7**	...	...	...	...	26**	27**	40.0	62.7**
92.2	95.0	...	...	25	...	64.1	...	...	...	...	...	34**	...	...	...
...	...	...	...	28	23	44.8	49.7	...	...	...	...	17	23	...	46.0
71.0	69.7	...	...	18	17	64.3	73.7	53.5	60.1	...	60.1	14	14	...	56.4
...	...	...	...	...	...	...	...	...	...	...	...	12**	...	...	...
...	...	...	...	19	...	55.0	...	...	...	...	...	...	...	...	53.5
...	...	...	...	...	18	...	99.1	...	...	...	...	...	7	...	...
...	...	...	...	...	...	...	...	...	...	...	...	...	...	...	...
...	...	...	...	15	17	77.3	89.2	...	...	...	...	13	...	...	77.8
...	...	...	...	19	19	75.3	89.3	...	...	...	...	14	13	...	68.1
...	...	...	...	23	17	...	84.4	...	...	...	...	19	17**	...	82.4
...	...	...	...	...	14	...	85.7	...	...	...	...	11	...	...	84.6
...	...	...	...	12	11	83.5	84.9	...	...	...	...	11	11	...	84.5
...	...	...	...	15	15	...	96.6	...	...	...	...	10	...	...	83.8
...	...	...	...	18	16	93.6	98.1	...	...	...	...	11**	...	...	80.2
...	...	...	...	16	...	...	...	...	...	...	...	...	...	...	...
...	...	...	...	23	...	97.4	...	...	...	...	...	...	...	...	...
...	...	...	...	22	...	84.0	...	...	...	...	...	12	...	66.8	24.5
...	...	...	...	22	19	98.8	98.7	...	...	...	...	12**	12**	...	81.6**
...	...	...	...	...	18	...	90.3	...	...	...	...	13	13**	...	75.6
...	...	...	...	...	...	...	...	...	...	...	...	14	...	...	...
...	...	...	...	21	22	...	66.7	...	...	...	...	16	...	...	46.4
...	...	...	...	30	...	43.3	...	...	...	...	...	...	...	34.9	...
...	...	...	...	22	...	98.0[e]	...	...	...	...	...	...	...	...	...
100.0**	100.0**	...	...	...	20	...	81.8	100.0**	100.0**	...	100.0**	17**	14	...	61.7
...	...	...	...	...	...	...	...	...	...	...	...	...	...	...	...
...	...	...	...	...	19	...	82.8	...	...	...	...	8**	8**	...	63.6**
...	...	...	...	17	17	92.3	94.7	...	...	...	...	...	9	...	76.7
...	...	...	...	21	...	96.3	...	...	...	...	...	...	...	...	...
...	...	...	...	16	24	80.5	94.3	...	...	...	...	10	10	...	70.5
...	...	...	...	28	33	89.7	93.8	...	...	...	...	19	20	...	68.7
...	...	...	...	21	22	48.6	59.1	...	...	...	...	...	17**	...	29.3**
...	...	...	...	...	...	...	...	...	...	...	...	...	...	...	...
...	...	...	...	24	...	78.7	...	...	...	...	...	...	...	...	...
...	...	...	...	...	...	...	...	...	...	...	...	...	...	...	...
...	...	...	...	33	50	30.7	38.5	...	...	...	...	16	17	27.8	28.0
...	...	...	...	22	20	43.2	50.3**	...	...	...	...	...	...	32.7	41.7**

Table 8 (continued)

Country or territory	PRE-PRIMARY EDUCATION: Trained teachers (%) 1998/99 Total	Female	1999/2000 Total	Female	Pupil/teacher ratio 1990/91	1999/00	Female teachers (%) 1990/91	1999/00
Cook Islands	...	...	...	...	...	14	...	100.0
Democratic People's Rep. of Korea	...	...	...	...	...	...	...	...
Fiji	...	...	...	...	20	...	...	...
Indonesia[w]	...	...	...	...	17	17	...	98.1
Japan[o]	...	...	...	...	18	31	88.8	...
Kiribati	...	...	...	...	...	...	...	...
Lao People's Democratic Republic	...	...	...	...	20	17	100.0	99.7
Malaysia[w]	...	...	...	...	31	...	...	...
Marshall Islands	...	...	...	...	...	...	...	...
Myanmar	...	...	...	...	...	...	...	...
Nauru	...	...	...	...	...	...	...	...
New Zealand[o]	...	...	...	...	...	15	...	98.5
Niue	...	...	...	...	...	11	...	100.0
Papua New Guinea	...	...	...	...	...	...	...	...
Philippines[w]	...	...	...	...	41	...	...	...
Republic of Korea[o]	...	...	...	...	22	24	93.5	99.8
Samoa	...	...	...	...	...	...	...	...
Solomon Islands	...	...	...	...	...	...	...	...
Thailand[w]	...	...	...	...	23	25	...	79.3
Tonga	...	...	...	...	...	18	...	100.0
Tuvalu	...	...	...	...	...	...	...	...
Vanuatu	...	...	...	...	...	10	...	98.6
Viet Nam	42.7	42.7	49.2	49.2	23	22	...	100.0
Latin America and the Caribbean								
Anguilla	...	...	45.5	45.5	...	14	...	100.0
Antigua and Barbuda	...	...	45.1	45.1	...	6	...	100.0
Argentina[w]	...	...	...	...	...	24	...	95.8
Aruba	...	...	100.0	100.0	...	27	...	100.0
Bahamas	...	...	...	...	...	...	...	...
Barbados	...	...	...	...	...	17**	...	100.0**
Belize	...	...	1.0	...	18	19	99.4	97.9**
Bermuda	...	...	...	...	...	...	...	...
Bolivia	...	...	...	...	42	42**	95.6	93.1**
Brazil[w]	...	...	...	...	21	19	...	98.1
British Virgin Islands	...	...	24.4	24.4	...	13	...	100.0
Cayman Islands	...	...	...	100.0	...	12	...	100.0
Chile[w]	...	...	...	...	24	...	...	98.7
Colombia	...	...	...	...	24	18	...	94.5
Costa Rica	...	...	...	...	23	19	...	96.7
Cuba	...	...	100.0	100.0	24	34	100.0	100.0
Dominica	75.0	75.0	100.0	100.0	22	15	100.0	265.2
Dominican Republic	...	...	...	...	...	22	...	94.0
Ecuador	...	...	...	...	18	15	...	87.7
El Salvador	...	...	...	...	...	...	...	...
Grenada	...	...	...	...	...	19	...	100.0
Guatemala	...	...	...	...	...	26	...	...
Guyana	...	...	...	...	23	...	98.9	...
Haiti	...	...	...	...	...	...	...	...
Honduras	...	...	...	...	...	...	...	...
Jamaica[w]	...	...	...	...	32	22	...	...
Mexico[o]	...	...	...	...	26	22	98.5*	...
Montserrat	...	...	100.0	100.0	...	15	...	100.0
Netherlands Antilles	...	...	100.0	100.0	...	20	...	80.1
Nicaragua	...	...	...	...	33	26	98.7	97.1
Panama	...	...	36.4	36.5	22	20	98.1	...
Paraguay[w]	...	...	...	...	...	...	...	...
Peru[w]	...	...	...	...	25	...	...	...
Saint Kitts and Nevis	...	...	...	...	...	9	...	100.0

PRIMARY EDUCATION								LOWER SECONDARY EDUCATION							
Trained teachers (%)				Pupil/teacher ratio		Female teachers (%)		Trained teachers (%)				Pupil/teacher ratio		Female teachers (%)	
1998/99		1998/99						1998/99		1999/2000					
Total	Female	Total	Female	1990/91	1999/00	1990/91	1999/00	Total	Female	Total	Female	1998/99	1999/00	1990/91	1999/00
...	...	...	...	...	18	...	86.1	...	...	...	...	...	...	...	...
...	...	...	...	...	...	...	...	...	...	...	...	...	22	...	...
...	...	...	...	34	...	...	...	...	...	...	...	26**	...	...	...
...	...	...	...	23	22**	50.5	53.7**	...	...	...	...	...	17**	39.4	44.1**
...	...	...	...	21	21	58.4	...	...	...	...	...	16	16	37.0	...
...	...	...	...	29	...	57.4	...	...	...	...	...	...	...	...	...
...	...	...	...	27	30	37.8	43.4	...	...	...	...	20	22	...	40.9
...	...	...	...	20	20	56.8	63.9	...	...	...	...	...	...	...	...
...	...	...	...	...	...	...	...	...	...	...	...	28	...	...	...
...	...	...	...	48	33	61.8	74.7	...	...	...	...	28	30	71.3	...
...	...	...	...	...	...	...	...	...	...	...	...	...	...	...	...
...	...	...	...	18	15	78.6	78.2	...	...	...	...	...	14	60.8	58.8
...	...	...	...	...	...	...	...	...	...	...	...	24	...	...	...
...	...	...	...	32	...	32.3	...	...	...	...	...	23	...	...	...
...	...	...	...	33	...	...	...	...	...	...	...	41	...	...	...
...	...	...	...	36	32	50.1	66.8	...	...	...	...	...	...	46.2	56.2
...	...	...	...	24	24**	63.8[e]	72.2**	...	...	...	...	...	26**	...	72.5**
...	...	...	...	19	...	...	...	...	...	...	...	...	...	...	...
...	...	...	...	22	21	...	63.6	...	...	...	...	...	23	...	58.3
...	...	...	...	24	21	68.9	67.2	...	...	...	...	...	...	...	48.4
...	...	...	...	21	...	72.2	...	...	...	...	...	...	...	...	...
...	...	...	...	27	23	40.0[e]	44.0	...	...	...	...	29	30	...	46.5
77.6	78.4	80.0	81.6	35	30	...	77.9	86.0	86.9	86.3	86.9	29	28	...	69.5
...	...	77.9	...	...	20	...	89.6	...	...	...	...	16**	17**	...	67.5**
...	...	46.9	43.7	...	19	...	78.7	...	...	40.7	...	...	11	...	71.1
...	...	...	...	...	22	...	88.4	...	...	...	...	14	13	...	73.2
...	...	100.0	100.0	...	19	...	77.8	...	...	...	...	20**	16**	...	48.2**
...	...	...	...	...	...	...	...	...	...	...	...	...	...	...	...
...	...	...	...	18	17**	72.0[e]	74.7**	...	...	...	...	15**	17**	...	56.4**
...	...	54.1	...	26	23	69.9[e]	63.9	...	...	54.3	...	26**	23	...	64.2
...	...	...	...	...	...	...	...	...	...	...	...	...	...	...	...
...	...	...	...	25	25**	57.3	61.1**	...	...	...	...	...	24**	...	61.6**
...	...	...	...	23	27	...	92.6	...	...	...	...	...	23	...	84.2
...	...	89.0	67.1	19	18	...	87.2	...	...	...	...	...	14**	...	65.0**
...	...	100.0	100.0	...	14	...	86.9	...	...	100.0	...	10	11	...	56.0
...	...	...	...	29	33	74.6[e]	77.1	...	...	...	...	27	32	...	77.6
...	...	...	...	30	24	...	77.0	...	...	...	...	...	18**	...	49.5**
...	...	...	...	32	27	...	80.3	...	...	...	...	...	19**	...	50.9**
...	...	100.0	100.0	13	11	78.9	83.2	...	...	86.6	...	12	13	59.9	68.3
64.0	68.4	64.6	67.6	29	20	80.6	80.1	44.4**	...	40.8**	...	28**	21**	...	66.9**
...	...	...	...	...	53**	...	81.6**	...	...	...	...	15**	15**	...	65.6**
...	...	...	...	30	23	...	67.6	...	...	...	...	17**	12**	...	50.0**
...	...	...	...	...	...	...	...	...	...	...	...	...	...	...	...
...	...	...	...	...	21	...	76.2	...	...	...	...	18**	19**	...	61.1**
...	...	...	...	...	38	...	...	...	...	...	...	...	15	...	...
...	...	...	...	30	...	76.1	...	...	...	...	...	18**	...	...	...
...	...	...	...	36	...	44.7	...	...	...	...	...	...	...	...	...
...	...	...	...	...	...	...	...	...	...	...	...	...	...	...	...
...	...	...	...	34	30	...	...	...	...	...	...	...	19**	...	...
...	...	...	...	31	25	...	...	...	...	...	...	23	22	...	...
...	...	85.0	93.3	...	17	...	75.0	...	...	...	...	11**	11**	...	68.8**
...	...	100.0	100.0	...	18	...	69.1	...	...	100.0	...	16	6	...	51.2
...	...	...	...	33	34	86.9	83.2	...	...	...	...	...	31	...	52.5**
...	...	...	...	23	26	74.8[e]	...	...	...	74.1	...	...	22	56.3	55.5
...	...	...	...	25	...	...	...	...	...	...	...	10**	...	...	...
...	...	...	...	29	...	...	...	...	...	...	...	17**	...	...	...
...	...	...	...	22	19	73.5[e]	82.6	...	...	...	...	...	14**	...	55.9**

Table 8 (continued)

Country or territory	PRE-PRIMARY EDUCATION							
	Trained teachers (%)				Pupil/teacher ratio		Female teachers (%)	
	1998/99		1999/2000					
	Total	Female	Total	Female	1990/91	1999/00	1990/91	1999/00
Saint Lucia	...	...	...	...	16	12	...	97.5**
Saint Vincent and the Grenadines	...	...	...	...	14	...	100.0	...
Suriname	...	...	...	...	25	...	100.0	...
Trinidad and Tobago	...	...	...	...	14	13	96.2[e]	76.0**
Turks and Caicos Islands	...	...	...	...	...	18**	...	100.0**
Uruguay[w]	...	...	...	...	30	31	...	98.0**
Venezuela	...	...	...	...	24	...	98.7	...
North America and Western Europe								
Andorra	...	...	...	...	...	...	...	...
Austria[o]	...	...	...	...	21	16**	99.6	98.8**
Belgium[o]	...	...	...	...	...	13**	...	82.5**
Canada[o]	...	...	...	...	31	15	69.8	68.0
Cyprus	...	...	...	...	23	18	99.2	86.4
Denmark[o]	...	...	...	...	...	5	...	92.0
Finland[o]	...	...	...	...	...	12	...	96.5
France[o]	...	...	...	...	...	19**	...	80.0**
Germany[o]	...	...	...	...	...	19	...	95.0
Greece[o]	...	...	...	...	16	16**	99.8	...
Iceland[o]	...	...	...	...	...	5	...	98.5
Ireland[o]	...	...	...	...	28	18**	76.7	92.4**
Israel[o]	...	...	...	...	...	...	...	...
Italy[o]	...	...	...	...	14	13	99.1	99.3
Luxembourg[o]	...	...	...	...	17	...	...	...
Malta	...	...	...	...	16	...	100.0	...
Monaco	...	...	...	...	19	...	63.8	...
Netherlands[o]	...	...	...	...	17	...	100.0	...
Norway[o]	...	...	...	...	4	5	95.2	95.0
Portugal[o]	...	...	...	...	19	18	97.9	99.1
San Marino	...	...	...	...	7	8	100.0	99.2
Spain[o]	...	...	...	...	25	16	95.3	94.9
Sweden[o]	...	...	...	...	...	13	...	96.7
Switzerland[o]	...	...	...	...	...	16**	...	99.4**
United Kingdom[o]	...	...	...	...	26	23	95.5	95.3
United States[o]	...	...	...	...	...	21	...	94.7
South and West Asia								
Afghanistan	...	...	...	...	...	...	...	...
Bangladesh	...	...	...	...	...	...	...	...
Bhutan	...	...	...	...	...	22	...	30.8
India[w]	...	...	...	...	...	...	...	...
Iran, Islamic Republic of	...	...	...	...	27	39**	99.8	96.8**
Maldives	...	...	47.0	47.2	...	31	...	90.5
Nepal	...	...	...	...	...	...	...	...
Pakistan	...	...	...	...	...	...	...	...
Sri Lanka[w]	...	...	...	...	...	...	...	...
Sub-Saharan Africa								
Angola	...	...	...	...	...	...	...	...
Benin	100.0	100.0	69.5	62.4	23	39	54.8	61.2
Botswana	...	...	...	...	...	...	...	...
Burkina Faso	...	...	...	...	28	40**	85.0	87.0**
Burundi	...	...	...	...	...	28*	...	98.9**
Cameroon	...	...	...	...	26	22	99.9	98.9
Cape Verde	...	...	...	...	...	...	...	...
Central African Republic	...	...	...	...	...	...	...	...
Chad	...	...	...	...	...	...	...	...
Comoros	...	...	...	...	...	26	...	...
Congo	...	...	77.8	77.8	9	10	100.0	100.0
Côte d'Ivoire	...	...	...	...	...	...	...	...

PRIMARY EDUCATION								LOWER SECONDARY EDUCATION							
Trained teachers (%)				Pupil/teacher ratio		Female teachers (%)		Trained teachers (%)				Pupil/teacher ratio		Female teachers (%)	
1998/99		1998/99						1998/99		1999/2000					
Total	Female	Total	Female	1990/91	1999/00	1990/91	1999/00	Total	Female	Total	Female	1998/99	1999/00	1990/91	1999/00
...	...	...	...	29	23**	82.9[e]	82.9**	...	...	...	...	19**	16	...	62.3
...	...	...	...	20	25**	66.7	...	...	...	...	...	...	25**	...	64.8**
...	...	...	...	22	...	84.1	...	...	...	...	...	15**	...	...	...
...	...	76.1	75.4	26	21	70.3	75.8	...	...	...	...	50**	54**	...	57.7**
...	...	...	...	...	19**	...	93.5**	...	...	...	...	...	9**	...	62.5**
...	...	...	...	22	20	...	92.0**	...	...	...	...	14	11	...	75.0**
...	...	...	...	23	...	74.5	...	...	...	...	...	...	...**	...	...
...	...	...	...	...	...	...	...	...	...	...	...	...	...	...	...
...	...	...	...	11	13**	81.7	88.5**	...	...	...	...	9	9**	...	63.8**
...	...	...	...	...	13**	...	82.5**	...	...	...	...	...	...	...	...
...	...	...	...	15	15	68.7	68.0	...	...	...	...	15	15	53.2	68.0
...	...	...	...	21	15	60.0	58.9	...	...	...	...	14**	...	...	...
...	...	...	...	...	10	...	64.0	...	...	...	...	10	10	...	64.0
...	...	...	...	...	16	...	70.9	...	...	...	...	10	10	...	69.6
...	...	...	...	...	19**	...	80.0**	...	...	...	...	12	14	62.6	64.1
...	...	...	...	...	15	...	81.2	...	...	...	...	15	14	...	58.7
...	...	...	...	19	13**	52.2	...	...	...	...	...	10	10**	62.3	...
...	...	...	...	...	11**	...	77.5**	...	...	...	...	11**	11**	...	77.6**
...	...	...	...	27	22**	76.6	73.6**	...	...	...	...	...	...	...	...
...	...	...	...	15	...	82.0[e]	...	...	...	...	...	12	...	...	...
...	...	...	...	12	11	90.6	94.8	...	...	...	...	10	10	71.0	72.8
...	...	...	...	13	...	50.8	...	...	...	...	...	...	...	...	...
...	...	...	...	21	...	79.3	...	...	...	...	...	9	...	...	...
...	...	...	...	...	...	...	...	...	...	...	...	...	...	54.3	...
...	...	...	...	17	...	53.0	...	...	...	...	...	...	14**	...	...
...	...	...	...	...	...	...	...	...	...	...	...	4	...	...	...
...	...	...	...	14	13	81.5	82.1	...	...	...	...	...	11**	...	70.0
...	...	...	...	6	5	89.4	91.0	...	...	...	...	...	...	67.2	69.8
...	...	...	...	22	15	72.7	69.1	...	...	...	...	...	18**	53.1	51.4**
...	...	...	...	10	12	76.9[e]	80.4	...	...	...	...	13	12	...	61.9
...	...	...	...	...	14**	...	72.4**	...	...	...	...	10	10**	...	45.0**
...	...	...	...	20	19	78.0	81.1	...	...	...	...	16	16	53.5	58.8
...	...	...	...	...	15	...	86.5	...	...	...	...	16	16	...	60.2
...	...	...	...	41	...	58.7	...	...	...	...	...	...	...	...	...
...	...	...	...	63	...	19.4	19.3**	...	...	...	...	...	30**	9.7	16.4**
...	...	100.0	100.0	...	42	...	32.0	...	...	100.0	...	40	35	...	32.1
...	...	...	...	47	43*	28.0[e]	44.2**	...	...	...	...	...	...	...	...
...	...	...	...	31	26**	52.9	53.9**	...	...	...	...	27**	27**	43.4	45.6**
...	...	66.7	64.5	...	24	...	59.7	...	...	79.2	...	17*	18	...	25.3
...	...	...	...	39	38	...	23.8	...	...	...	...	38	37	...	13.4
...	...	...	...	43	55	26.5[e]	34.7	...	...	...	...	27	23	...	37.6
...	...	...	...	29	...	...	...	...	...	...	...	...	...	...	...
...	...	...	...	32	27**	...	29.8**	...	...	...	...	22**	17**	...	29.3**
...	...	65.0	70.0	36	53	24.7	21.9	33.9	41.2	39.2	41.2	25	34	...	11.5
91.8	92.9	90.2	92.3	32	27	79.8	81.2	75.1**	73.1**	82.1	73.1**	19**	14	...	46.6
...	...	...	...	57	49	27.0	24.5**	...	...	...	...	31**	33**	...	16.6**
...	...	...	...	67	57*	46.2	57.0**	...	...	...	...	18**	...	...	...
...	...	...	...	51	69	30.0	36.6	...	...	...	...	31*	31**	...	...
...	...	...	...	...	...	...	...	...	...	...	...	24**	...	...	...
...	...	...	...	77	...	24.9	...	...	...	...	...	...	...	...	...
...	...	43.6	...	66	69	5.9	9.6	...	...	...	...	42	37	...	4.3**
...	...	...	...	37	...	...	25.0**	...	...	...	...	...	13	...	...
...	...	64.6	72.5	65	60	32.4	36.5	...	...	...	...	26	24	...	...
...	...	...	...	37	...	18.2[e]	...	...	...	...	...	37	...	...	...

Table 8 (continued)

Country or territory	PRE-PRIMARY EDUCATION							
	Trained teachers (%)				Pupil/teacher ratio		Female teachers (%)	
	1998/99		1999/2000					
	Total	Female	Total	Female	1990/91	1999/00	1990/91	1999/00
Democratic Rep. of the Congo	...	...	...	...	...	...	...	...
Equatorial Guinea	...	...	...	...	...	28**	...	82.2**
Eritrea	64.8	64.8	69.1	69.7	...	37	...	97.8
Ethiopia	63.0	63.0	61.2	62.0	35	35	93.5	93.2
Gabon	...	...	...	...	...	...	...	...
Gambia	...	...	...	...	...	...	...	...
Ghana	29.2	29.2	...	...	...	...	...	...
Guinea	...	...	...	...	...	...	...	...
Guinea-Bissau	...	...	22.7	21.1	...	21	...	73.2
Kenya	42.1	42.1	...	...	39	...	99.1	...
Lesotho	...	...	...	...	...	...	...	...
Liberia	...	...	...	...	...	36	...	70.0
Madagascar	...	...	...	...	...	18**	...	98.8**
Malawi	...	...	...	...	...	...	...	...
Mali	...	...	...	...	...	...	...	...
Mauritius	100.0	100.0	100.0	100.0	18	16	100.0	100.0
Mozambique	...	...	...	...	...	...	...	...
Namibia	...	...	77.1	86.4	...	27	...	87.6
Niger	...	...	96.0	96.1	37	18	100.0	98.9
Nigeria	...	...	...	...	...	...	...	...
Rwanda	...	...	...	...	...	...	...	...
Sao Tome and Principe	...	...	...	...	...	...	...	...
Senegal	...	...	...	...	26	19	75.2	51.7
Seychelles	88.1	88.1	85.7	85.6	20	16	100.0[e]	99.5
Sierra Leone	...	...	49.7	23.7	...	24	...	90.0
Somalia	...	...	...	...	...	...	...	...
South Africa	65.8**	65.8**	...	...	...	...	...	79.1**
Swaziland	...	...	...	...	19	...	...	...
Togo	...	...	...	...	29	17	100.0	97.3
Uganda	...	...	85.6	89.4	...	25	...	69.8
United Republic of Tanzania	...	...	...	...	...	...	...	...
Zambia	100.0	100.0	...	...	...	...	...	...
Zimbabwe[w]	...	...	...	...	...	...	...	...

PRIMARY EDUCATION								LOWER SECONDARY EDUCATION							
Trained teachers (%)				Pupil/teacher ratio		Female teachers (%)		Trained teachers (%)				Pupil/teacher ratio		Female teachers (%)	
1998/99		1998/99						1998/99		1999/2000					
Total	Female	Total	Female	1990/91	1999/00	1990/91	1999/00	Total	Female	Total	Female	1998/99	1999/00	1990/91	1999/00
...	...	...	...	40	...	24.0[e]	...	...	...	...	...	15**	...	...	...
...	...	...	...	...	43**	...	23.7**	...	...	...	...	26	27**	...	3.9**
72.8	69.1	72.0	62.1	...	48	...	37.4	37.7	58.4	49.2	58.4	55	57	14.4	12.7
...	...	...	...	36	...	23.9	...	...	...	...	...	...	...	10.8	...
...	...	...	...	...	...	...	...	...	...	...	...	29**	...	...	...
72.5	72.4**	62.9	...	31	33	30.8[e]	25.2	80.9**	80.6**	77.3	80.6**	26	24	...	16.6
71.8	88.5	...	...	29	...	35.8	...	83.7	97.4	...	97.4	20	...	26.8	...
...	...	...	...	40	46	22.5	25.9	...	...	...	...	31	34	...	9.0
...	...	35.1	42.4	...	44	...	20.2	...	...	...	...	...	22**	...	4.4**
96.6	97.3	...	...	31	...	37.5	...	92.5**	95.6**	...	95.6**	26**	...	...	...
43.9	44.5	78.0	80.5	55	...	79.9	80.2	84.1**	84.2**	...	84.2**	24**	...	...	...
...	...	...	...	...	36	...	28.0	...	...	...	...	16	11	...	22.0
...	...	...	...	40	48	...	60.7	...	...	...	...	20	21	...	...
53.6**	50.0**	53.5	50.0	61	46	31.3	40.0	53.6**	50.0**	33.4	50.0**	61**	35	...	21.7
...	...	...	...	47	...	25.3[e]	23.9	...	...	...	...	31*	35	14.2	16.8
100.0	100.0	100.0	100.0	21	26	44.1[e]	53.8	...	...	...	...	10	...	...	...
32.7	32.9	65.0	67.9	55	61	23.1[e]	25.3	75.8**	86.2**	...	86.2**	36	32	17.6	18.4**
29.1	29.2	29.3	30.4	...	32	...	67.1	...	...	59.3	...	...	25	...	45.2
...	...	97.1	96.9	42	41	32.6	32.4	...	...	...	...	36	36	21.5	22.5**
...	...	...	...	41	...	42.9	...	...	...	...	...	...	...	...	...
...	...	...	...	57	54	46.3	53.0	...	...	...	...	...	...	...	...
...	...	...	...	...	...	...	...	...	...	...	...	...	...	...	...
...	...	...	...	53	51	26.9[e]	23.0	...	...	...	...	33**	31	...	...
83.7	84.5	82.3	83.4	...	15	...	84.6	87.5**	89.7**	...	89.7**	10**	...	...	...
...	...	60.7	57.6	35	30	...	40.1	...	...	89.8	...	...	...	...	43.1
...	...	...	...	...	...	...	...	...	...	...	...	...	...	...	...
63.1**	62.4**	63.3	62.5	...	35	...	78.1	89.1**	92.5**	...	92.5**	30**	...	...	...
91.1	91.8	91.1	91.8	33	33	79.2	75.4	99.2**	98.7**	...	98.7**	18**	...	...	...
...	...	...	...	58	37	18.8	13.2	...	...	...	...	46	38	11.1	10.6**
45.0**	46.0**	...	...	29	59	29.8	...	...	...	...	...	19**	...	...	...
44.1	44.0	100.0	100.0	35	40	41.3	45.3	...	...	90.5	...	19**	18	...	27.7
88.8	91.7	94.2	95.2	44	47	...	48.9	82.0	79.4	81.4	79.4	42	...	...	23.0
...	...	...	...	36	41	39.2	47.3	...	...	...	...	...	...	...	...

Table 9
Internal efficiency: repetition rates

Country or territory	REPETITION RATES BY GRADE IN PRIMARY EDUCATION 1999/2000					
	Grade 1			Grade 2		
	Total	Male	Female	Total	Male	Female
Arab States and North Africa						
Algeria	12.5	14.2	10.5	10.1	12.3	7.7
Bahrain	4.8	4.0	5.5	4.1	4.5	3.7
Djibouti	8.7	9.3	8.0	10.0	10.2	9.6
Egypt[w]	...	...	...	...	...	...
Iraq	10.8	11.8	9.6	10.7	12.2	8.8
Jordan[w]	0.3	0.3	0.3	0.2	0.2	0.2
Kuwait	3.8	3.5	4.1	2.8	2.7	3.0
Lebanon	4.3	5.0	3.5	10.1	11.7	8.4
Libyan Arab Jamahiriya	...	...	...	...	...	...
Mauritania	...	...	...	...	...	...
Morocco	16.5	17.1	15.8	11.9	13.4	10.0
Oman	8.1	8.2	8.0	8.1	8.5	7.8
Palestinian Autonomous Territories	1.1	1.0	1.2	1.3	1.4	1.2
Qatar	...	...	...	...	...	...
Saudi Arabia	6.2	7.1	5.2	3.4	5.0	1.6
Sudan	11.0	10.4	11.8	10.0	8.6	11.7
Syrian Arab Republic	...	...	...	...	...	...
Tunisia[w]	11.9	13.0	10.8	12.7	14.2	11.1
United Arab Emirates	3.4	3.2	3.6	3.3	3.3	3.2
Yemen	...	...	...	...	...	...
Central and Eastern Europe						
Albania	5.4	6.1	4.7	4.0	4.6	3.2
Belarus	1.6	...	...	0.4	...	...
Bosnia and Herzegovina	...	...	...	...	...	...
Bulgaria	2.6	2.9	2.2	4.4	5.2	3.6
Croatia	1.1	1.2	0.9	0.3	0.4	0.3
Czech Republic[o]	1.5	1.7	1.4	1.1	1.2	1.0
Estonia	1.9	2.5	1.2	1.5	2.0	0.8
Hungary[o]	3.8	3.7	3.8	1.8	1.8	1.8
Latvia	...	...	...	...	...	...
Lithuania	...	...	...	...	...	...
Poland[o]	1.1	1.1**	1.1**	0.5	0.5**	0.5**
Republic of Moldova	...	...	...	...	...	...
Romania	...	...	...	...	...	...
Russian Federation[w]	...	...	...	...	...	...
Slovakia	4.7	5.1	4.2	1.9	2.3	1.6
Slovenia	...	...	...	...	...	...
The former Yugoslav Rep. of Macedonia	...	...	...	...	...	...
Turkey[o]	...	...	...	...	...	...
Ukraine	...	...	...	...	...	...
Yugoslavia	...	...	...	...	...	...
Central Asia						
Armenia	...	...	...	...	...	...
Azerbaijan	0.5	0.5	0.5	0.5	0.5	0.5
Georgia	...	...	...	...	...	...
Kazakhstan	...	...	...	...	...	...
Kyrgyzstan	...	...	...	...	...	...
Mongolia	...	...	...	...	...	...
Tajikistan	...	...	...	...	...	...
Turkmenistan	...	...	...	...	...	...
Uzbekistan	...	...	...	...	...	...
East Asia and the Pacific						
Australia[o]	...	...	...	...	...	...
Cambodia	37.0	38.1	35.8	...	...	...
China[w]	2.1	2.4	1.9	0.7	0.8	0.6

NB. Twelve countries apply a seven-year primary-school cycle: Bhutan, Botswana, Kenya, Lesotho, Namibia, South Africa, Swaziland, Trinidad and Tobago, Uganda, United Republic of Tanzania, Zambia and Zimbabwe

REPETITION RATES BY GRADE IN PRIMARY EDUCATION 1999/2000

Grade 3			Grade 4			Grade 5			Grade 6		
Total	Male	Female	Total	Male	Female	Total	Male	Female	Total	Male	Female
11.6	14.4	8.3	12.3	15.5	8.7	13.4	17.0	9.4	25.0	28.9	20.3
3.9	4.6	3.3	4.3	5.4	3.0	4.5	5.7	3.3	4.3	5.8	2.7
9.9	9.3	10.7	9.9	9.3	10.7	9.4	9.3	9.5	32.4	33.6	30.4
...	...	...	...	...	...	...	...	...	...	...	...
10.6	12.4	8.4	12.6	14.7	9.8	21.9	24.8	17.9	6.0	7.6	3.8
0.2	0.2	0.1	0.6	0.5	0.7	1.3	1.2	1.4	1.4	1.4	1.3
4.1	4.3	3.9	2.7	3.0	2.3	...	...	...	...	...	...
10.6	12.2	8.9	8.7	9.9	7.5	8.2	9.3	7.2	...	...	...
...	...	...	...	...	...	...	...	...	...	...	...
...	...	...	...	...	...	...	...	...	...	...	...
13.1	15.1	10.6	11.3	13.4	8.6	9.8	11.9	7.0	7.7	9.4	5.2
7.0	8.1	5.8	8.3	11.1	5.2	6.5	8.4	4.4	5.5	7.7	2.9
2.4	2.5	2.3	3.5	3.9	3.2	...	...	...	...	...	...
...	...	...	...	...	...	...	...	...	...	...	...
5.9	7.8	3.8	6.5	7.6	5.3	6.4	8.0	4.6	2.5	3.3	1.5
11.4	11.5	11.3	12.7	12.3	13.2	12.0	12.1	11.9	10.8	11.1	10.4
...	...	...	...	...	...	...	...	...	...	...	...
14.4	16.6	12.0	12.5	14.5	10.3	18.3	20.3	16.0	26.0	27.1	24.8
2.5	2.8	2.2	4.3	6.1	2.4	4.2	5.6	2.6	2.6	3.7	1.5
...	...	...	...	...	...	...	...	...	...	...	...
3.0	3.6	2.4	3.4	4.0	2.8	...	...	...	...	...	...
0.3	...	...	0.2	...	...	...	...	...	...	...	...
...	...	...	...	...	...	...	...	...	...	...	...
2.8	3.4	2.2	2.8	3.6	2.0	...	...	...	...	...	...
0.2	0.3	0.2	0.2	0.2	0.2	...	...	...	...	...	...
1.0	1.2	0.8	1.2	1.5	0.9	1.2	1.5	0.9	...	...	...
2.0	2.8	1.1	2.0	2.9	1.1	2.3	3.5	1.1	4.1	6.0	2.0
1.3	1.3	1.4	1.5	1.5	1.5	...	...	...	...	...	...
...	...	...	...	...	...	...	...	...	...	...	...
...	...	...	...	...	...	...	...	...	...	...	...
0.4	0.4**	0.4**	0.8	0.8	0.8	1.1	1.1	1.1	1.1	1.1	1.1
...	...	...	...	...	...	...	...	...	...	...	...
...	...	...	...	...	...	...	...	...	...	...	...
...	...	...	...	...	...	...	...	...	...	...	...
1.5	1.7	1.2	1.7	1.9	1.5	...	...	...	...	...	...
...	...	...	...	...	...	...	...	...	...	...	...
...	...	...	...	...	...	...	...	...	...	...	...
...	...	...	...	...	...	...	...	...	...	...	...
...	...	...	...	...	...	...	...	...	...	...	...
...	...	...	...	...	...	...	...	...	...	...	...
...	...	...	...	...	...	...	...	...	...	...	...
0.4	0.4	0.4	0.5	0.5	0.5	...	...	...	...	...	...
...	...	...	...	...	...	...	...	...	...	...	...
...	...	...	...	...	...	...	...	...	...	...	...
...	...	...	...	...	...	...	...	...	...	...	...
...	...	...	...	...	...	...	...	...	...	...	...
...	...	...	...	...	...	...	...	...	...	...	...
...	...	...	...	...	...	...	...	...	...	...	...
...	...	...	...	...	...	...	...	...	...	...	...
...	...	...	...	...	...	...	...	...	...	...	...
...	...	...	...	...	...	...	...	...	...	...	...
0.5	0.6	0.4	0.4	0.4	0.3	0.2	0.2	0.1	0.1	0.1	0.0

Table 9 (continued)

Country or territory	REPETITION RATES BY GRADE IN PRIMARY EDUCATION 1999/2000					
	Grade 1			Grade 2		
	Total	Male	Female	Total	Male	Female
Cook Islands	5.2	...	...	0.5	...	...
Democratic People's Rep. of Korea	...	...	...	...	...	...
Fiji	...	...	...	...	...	...
Indonesia[w]	11.8**	11.7**	11.9**	7.4**	7.3**	7.5**
Japan[o]	...	...	...	...	...	...
Kiribati	...	...	...	...	...	...
Lao People's Democratic Republic	33.8	34.9	32.6	19.6	21.5	17.4
Malaysia[w]	...	...	...	...	...	...
Marshall Islands	...	...	...	...	...	...
Myanmar	1.0	1.0	1.0	0.5	0.5	0.5
Nauru	...	...	...	...	...	...
New Zealand[o]	...	...	...	...	...	...
Niue	...	...	...	...	...	...
Papua New Guinea	...	...	...	...	...	...
Philippines[w]	...	...	...	...	...	...
Republic of Korea[o]	...	...	...	...	...	...
Samoa	2.8	3.1	2.5	0.7	1.0	0.4
Solomon Islands	...	...	...	...	...	...
Thailand[w]	9.7	9.4	9.9	3.9	3.9	4.0
Tonga	...	...	...	...	...	...
Tuvalu	...	...	...	...	...	...
Vanuatu	11.3**	11.3**	11.2**	10.7**	11.4**	10.0**
Viet Nam	6.9	7.8**	6.0**	3.7	...	...
Latin America and the Caribbean						
Anguilla	...	...	...	...	...	...
Antigua and Barbuda	...	...	...	...	...	...
Argentina[w]	9.6	10.9	8.3	6.6	7.7	5.5
Aruba	14.2	17.9	10.1	8.5	9.6	7.1
Bahamas	...	...	...	...	...	...
Barbados	...	...	...	...	...	...
Belize	12.8	13.8	11.7	8.4	9.1	7.6
Bermuda	...	...	...	...	...	...
Bolivia	3.0**	3.0**	2.9**	2.3**	2.3**	2.3**
Brazil[w]	...	...	...	...	...	...
British Virgin Islands	3.1	3.5	2.6	1.4	1.5	1.4
Cayman Islands	...	...	...	...	...	...
Chile[w]	1.2	1.3	1.0	4.6	5.2	3.9
Colombia	9.5	10.3	8.6	4.9	5.3	4.4
Costa Rica	16.0	17.9	13.9	10.4	11.7	8.9
Cuba	3.5	5.6	1.3	2.6	3.2	1.9
Dominica	5.1	...	...	0.8	...	...
Dominican Republic	2.7	3.1	2.2	3.0	3.5	2.3
Ecuador	...	...	...	...	...	...
El Salvador	...	...	...	...	...	...
Grenada	...	...	...	...	...	...
Guatemala	26.1	26.8	25.3	13.8	15.0	12.6
Guyana	...	...	...	...	...	...
Haiti	...	...	...	...	...	...
Honduras	...	...	...	...	...	...
Jamaica[w]	5.0	6.3	3.5	2.4	3.1	1.6
Mexico[o]	10.7	11.9	9.3	8.6	10.0	7.1
Montserrat	4.2	...	...	...	...	...
Netherlands Antilles	...	...	...	...	...	...
Nicaragua	7.4	8.1	6.7	4.3	4.8	3.7
Panama	10.9	12.2	9.4	9.3	10.7	7.8
Paraguay[w]	13.7	14.7	12.6	10.3	11.8	8.6
Peru[w]	5.4	5.5	5.2	17.5	17.8	17.2
Saint Kitts and Nevis	...	...	...	...	...	...

NB. Twelve countries apply a seven-year primary-school cycle: Bhutan, Botswana, Kenya, Lesotho, Namibia, South Africa, Swaziland, Trinidad and Tobago, Uganda, United Republic of Tanzania, Zambia and Zimbabwe

REPETITION RATES BY GRADE IN PRIMARY EDUCATION 1999/2000

Grade 3			Grade 4			Grade 5			Grade 6		
Total	Male	Female	Total	Male	Female	Total	Male	Female	Total	Male	Female
0.3	...	...	2.7	...	...	1.8	...	...	3.4	...	...
...	...	...	...	...	...	...	...	...	...	...	...
...	...	...	...	...	...	...	...	...	...	...	...
6.1**	6.1**	6.2**	4.6**	4.6**	4.7**	3.2**	3.2**	3.2**	0.4**	0.4**	0.4**
...	...	...	...	...	...	...	...	...	...	...	...
...	...	...	...	...	...	...	...	...	...	...	...
11.6	13.3	9.7	7.8	9.6	5.7	6.8	8.4	4.9	...	...	...
...	...	...	...	...	...	...	...	...	...	...	...
...	...	...	...	...	...	...	...	...	...	...	...
0.4	0.4	0.4	0.3	0.3	0.3	0.2	0.2	0.2	...	...	...
...	...	...	...	...	...	...	...	...	...	...	...
...	...	...	...	...	...	...	...	...	...	...	...
...	...	...	...	...	...	...	...	...	...	...	...
...	...	...	...	...	...	...	...	...	...	...	...
...	...	...	...	...	...	...	...	...	...	...	...
...	...	...	...	...	...	...	...	...	...	...	...
0.4	0.3	0.6	0.6	0.7	0.4	0.5	0.5	0.5	0.4	0.3	0.4
...	...	...	...	...	...	...	...	...	...	...	...
2.1	2.0	2.1	2.1	2.1	2.2	1.9	1.9	1.9	1.2	1.2	1.2
...	...	...	...	...	...	...	...	...	...	...	...
...	...	...	...	...	...	...	...	...	...	...	...
9.9**	10.5**	8.6**	8.8**	9.6**	7.9**	7.8**	9.6**	6.3**	17.0**	17.1**	16.9**
2.6	...	...	2.5	...	...	0.5	...	...	...	...	...
...	...	...	...	...	...	...	...	...	...	...	...
...	...	...	...	...	...	...	...	...	...	...	...
5.9	7.0	4.8	5.0	6.0	4.0	4.2	5.1	3.3	3.4	4.2	2.6
8.2	10.9	5.3	6.2	7.6	4.8	4.8	6.1	3.5	2.9	3.3	2.6
...	...	...	...	...	...	...	...	...	...	...	...
...	...	...	...	...	...	...	...	...	...	...	...
9.3	10.6	7.9	8.8	9.9	7.8	8.3	9.4	7.0	8.4	9.7	7.0
...	...	...	...	...	...	...	...	...	...	...	...
2.3**	2.4**	2.2**	2.3**	2.3**	2.2**	1.9**	2.0**	1.8**	2.9**	3.3**	2.5**
...	...	...	...	...	...	...	...	...	...	...	...
2.0	1.7	2.4	1.5	...	...	1.8	...	...	2.9	...	...
...	...	...	...	...	...	...	...	...	...	...	...
1.1	1.3	0.8	2.2	2.7	1.7	2.6	3.3	1.9	3.0	3.7	2.2
4.0	4.4	3.6	3.0	3.3	2.7	2.1	2.5	1.8	...	...	...
8.5	9.6	7.4	9.8	11.3	8.3	8.1	9.4	6.7	1.1	1.3	0.9
2.5	3.2	1.8	1.6	2.1	1.0	0.8	1.1	0.5	0.2	0.3	0.1
0.5	...	...	0.7	...	...	0.7	...	...	0.8	...	...
11.0	13.0	8.7	5.4	6.6	4.2	3.8**	4.9**	2.8**	3.2**	4.1**	2.2**
...	...	...	...	...	...	...	...	...	...	...	...
...	...	...	...	...	...	...	...	...	...	...	...
...	...	...	...	...	...	...	...	...	...	...	...
10.8	12.0	9.4	8.0	9.3	6.3	5.0	5.8	4.0	2.9	3.3	2.5
...	...	...	...	...	...	...	...	...	...	...	...
...	...	...	...	...	...	...	...	...	...	...	...
...	...	...	...	...	...	...	...	...	...	...	...
1.9	2.6	1.2	11.8	15.7	7.5	1.7	2.2	1.3	6.3	7.2	5.4
6.9	8.1	5.7	5.0	6.0	3.9	3.5	4.3	2.6	1.0	1.2	0.9
...	...	...	...	...	...	...	...	...	...	...	...
...	...	...	...	...	...	...	...	...	...	...	...
4.0	4.5	3.5	4.2	5.0	3.5	2.8	3.3	2.3	2.6	3.1	2.1
6.8	8.0	5.5	4.5	5.5	3.4	3.3	4.1	2.4	1.3	1.6	1.0
7.9	9.0	6.6	5.6	6.6	4.6	3.6	4.2	2.9	1.7	2.2	1.2
15.6	15.9	15.3	10.7	11.0	10.3	6.8	7.3	6.2	3.3	3.5	3.1
...	...	...	...	...	...	...	...	...	...	...	...

Table 9 (continued)

Country or territory	REPETITION RATES BY GRADE IN PRIMARY EDUCATION 1999/2000					
	Grade 1			Grade 2		
	Total	Male	Female	Total	Male	Female
Saint Lucia	...	...	...	...	...	...
Saint Vincent and the Grenadines	...	...	...	...	...	...
Suriname	...	...	...	...	...	...
Trinidad and Tobago	8.8	10.4	7.0	4.4	5.5	3.3
Turks and Caicos Islands	0.6	...	...	1.3	...	...
Uruguay[w]	14.5	16.7	12.1	10.2	12.0	8.3
Venezuela	9.2**	10.6**	7.6**	7.8	9.3	6.2
North America and Western Europe						
Andorra	...	...	...	...	...	...
Austria[o]	1.8**	2.1**	1.5**	1.7**	1.9**	1.5**
Belgium[o]	...	...	...	...	...	...
Canada[o]	...	...	...	...	...	...
Cyprus	...	...	...	...	...	...
Denmark[o]	...	...	...	...	...	...
Finland[o]	0.8	1.2	0.5	0.9	1.2	0.6
France[o]	5.8	5.8**	5.8**	6.3	6.3**	6.3**
Germany[o]	1.9	2.0	1.7	2.4	2.6	2.2
Greece[o]	...	...	...	...	...	...
Iceland[o]	...	...	...	...	...	...
Ireland[o]	1.5	1.6	1.4	3.5	3.9	3.0
Israel[o]	...	...	...	...	...	...
Italy[o]	0.6	0.7	0.4	0.5	0.6	0.3
Luxembourg[o]	5.0**	5.0**	5.0**	5.0**	5.0**	5.0**
Malta	...	...	...	...	...	...
Monaco	...	...	...	...	...	...
Netherlands[o]	...	...	...	...	...	...
Norway[o]	...	...	...	...	...	...
Portugal[o]	...	...	...	...	...	...
San Marino	...	...	...	...	...	...
Spain[o]	...	...	...	...	...	...
Sweden[o]	...	...	...	...	...	...
Switzerland[o]	1.2	1.3	1.0	2.5	2.6	2.4
United Kingdom[o]	...	...	...	...	...	...
United States[o]	...	...	...	...	...	...
South and West Asia						
Afghanistan	...	...	...	...	...	...
Bangladesh	...	...	...	...	...	...
Bhutan	14.9	15.8	14.0	14.1	14.7	13.3
India[w]	4.0	3.9	4.1	2.9	2.9	3.0
Iran, Islamic Republic of	9.1	10.2	7.9	6.2	7.6	4.7
Maldives	4.9	6.0	3.7	...	...	...
Nepal	...	...	...	...	...	...
Pakistan	...	...	...	...	...	...
Sri Lanka[w]	...	...	...	...	...	...
Sub-Saharan Africa						
Angola	31.1**	30.6**	31.6**	31.0**	30.8**	31.3**
Benin	...	...	...	...	...	...
Botswana	3.9	4.4	3.4	2.3	2.6	2.0
Burkina Faso	11.7	11.8	11.6	12.6	12.7	12.4
Burundi	27.4	26.4	28.5	20.6	20.5	20.7
Cameroon	29.7	29.8	29.6	23.1	23.3	22.9
Cape Verde	...	...	...	...	...	...
Central African Republic	...	...	...	...	...	...
Chad	29.6	29.6	29.6	25.7	25.6	25.7
Comoros	32.4**	32.3**	32.5**	26.4**	26.4**	26.5**
Congo	...	...	...	...	...	...
Côte d'Ivoire	...	...	...	...	...	...

NB. Twelve countries apply a seven-year primary-school cycle: Bhutan, Botswana, Kenya, Lesotho, Namibia, South Africa, Swaziland, Trinidad and Tobago, Uganda, United Republic of Tanzania, Zambia and Zimbabwe

REPETITION RATES BY GRADE IN PRIMARY EDUCATION 1999/2000

Grade 3			Grade 4			Grade 5			Grade 6		
Total	Male	Female	Total	Male	Female	Total	Male	Female	Total	Male	Female
...	...	...	...	...	...	...	...	...	...	...	...
...	...	...	...	...	...	...	...	...	...	...	...
...	...	...	...	...	...	...	...	...	...	...	...
4.3	5.2	3.4	3.5	4.2	2.7	4.4	5.1	3.7	6.4	7.1	5.7
1.5	...	...	0.6	...	...	...	...	...	...	...	...
7.7	9.1	6.3	6.4	7.6	5.2	4.9	5.9	4.0	2.5	3.0	2.0
8.8	10.6	6.7	6.6	8.1	5.0	4.4	7.1	2.7	1.9	2.4	1.4
...	...	...	...	...	...	...	...	...	...	...	...
1.4**	1.7**	1.1**	1.2**	1.4**	1.0**	...	...	...	...	...	...
...	...	...	...	...	...	...	...	...	...	...	...
...	...	...	...	...	...	...	...	...	...	...	...
...	...	...	...	...	...	...	...	...	...	...	...
...	...	...	...	...	...	...	...	...	...	...	...
0.4	0.5	0.3	0.2	0.3	0.2	0.2	0.2	0.1	0.2	0.2	0.1
3.1	3.1**	3.1**	2.5	2.5**	2.5**	3.4	3.4**	3.4**	...	...	...
1.6	1.8	1.4	1.1	1.3	1.0	...	...	...	...	...	...
...	...	...	...	...	...	...	...	...	...	...	...
...	...	...	...	...	...	...	...	...	...	...	...
2.4	2.7	2.2	1.4	1.6	1.1	1.1	1.2	1.0	1.0	1.0	1.0
...	...	...	...	...	...	...	...	...	...	...	...
0.3	0.4	0.2	0.3	0.4	0.2	0.5	0.6	0.4	...	...	...
5.0**	5.0**	5.0**	5.0**	5.0**	5.0**	5.0**	5.0**	5.0**	5.0**	5.0**	5.0**
...	...	...	...	...	...	...	...	...	...	...	...
...	...	...	...	...	...	...	...	...	...	...	...
...	...	...	...	...	...	...	...	...	...	...	...
...	...	...	...	...	...	...	...	...	...	...	...
...	...	...	...	...	...	...	...	...	...	...	...
...	...	...	...	...	...	...	...	...	...	...	...
...	...	...	...	...	...	...	...	...	...	...	...
...	...	...	...	...	...	...	...	...	...	...	...
2.2	2.3	2.0	1.9	2.1	1.6	1.6	1.9	1.3	1.0	1.2	0.8
...	...	...	...	...	...	...	...	...	...	...	...
...	...	...	...	...	...	...	...	...	...	...	...
...	...	...	...	...	...	...	...	...	...	...	...
...	...	...	...	...	...	...	...	...	...	...	...
12.5	12.9	11.9	9.8	10.4	9.1	13.2	13.6	12.7	11.5	11.2	11.9
5.0	4.9	5.3	4.4	4.5	4.3	3.9	4.0	3.8	4.9	5.1	4.7
4.2	5.4	2.9	4.7	6.1	3.1	3.1	4.1	2.0	...	...	...
...	...	...	...	...	...	...	...	...	...	...	...
...	...	...	...	...	...	...	...	...	...	...	...
...	...	...	...	...	...	...	...	...	...	...	...
...	...	...	...	...	...	...	...	...	...	...	...
28.6**	28.9**	28.3**	22.6**	22.5**	22.7**	...	...	...	...	...	...
...	...	...	...	...	...	...	...	...	...	...	...
1.9	2.1	1.7	10.5	12.6	8.3	1.4	1.7	1.1	1.3	1.4	1.2
16.6	17.0	16.1	15.2	15.2	15.3	16.3	15.4	17.7	35.1	34.5	36.1
18.5	18.0	19.3	21.2	20.7	21.8	31.2	30.6	31.9	38.7	38.0	39.6
30.7	30.9	30.5	23.5	23.4	23.5	27.1	27.3	26.9	25.3	25.7	24.9
...	...	...	...	...	...	...	...	...	...	...	...
...	...	...	...	...	...	...	...	...	...	...	...
21.7	21.6	22.0	21.0	20.5	21.9	15.1	15.0	15.2	25.7	26.6	23.3
25.1**	26.7**	23.2**	20.8**	21.3**	20.3**	19.6**	20.3**	18.7**	26.5**	26.3**	26.8**
...	...	...	...	...	...	...	...	...	...	...	...
...	...	...	...	...	...	...	...	...	...	...	...

Table 9 (continued)

Country or territory	REPETITION RATES BY GRADE IN PRIMARY EDUCATION 1999/2000					
	Grade 1			Grade 2		
	Total	Male	Female	Total	Male	Female
Democratic Rep. of the Congo	...	...	...	...	...	...
Equatorial Guinea	8.6**	4.6**	13.5**	17.1**	15.4**	19.7**
Eritrea	24.3	24.0	24.7	15.0	15.3	14.7
Ethiopia	9.1	8.7	9.8	5.1	4.8	5.6
Gabon	...	...	...	...	...	...
Gambia	...	...	...	...	...	...
Ghana	...	...	...	...	...	...
Guinea	20.0	20.2	19.9	20.5	19.8	21.4
Guinea-Bissau	23.3	23.3	23.2	26.3	25.5	27.3
Kenya	...	...	...	...	...	...
Lesotho	24.2	26.7	21.5	23.6	26.7	20.3
Liberia	2.3	2.3	2.4	2.0	1.9	2.2
Madagascar	34.2	35.2	33.1	24.4	25.8	23.0
Malawi	17.9	18.1	17.8	16.2	16.5	15.9
Mali	...	...	...	...	...	...
Mauritius	...	...	...	...	...	...
Mozambique	25.4	25.2	25.7	24.5	24.2	24.9
Namibia	13.9	15.5	12.2	11.2	13.1	9.3
Niger	1.4	1.3	1.4	7.0	6.9	7.0
Nigeria	...	...	...	...	...	...
Rwanda	37.6	37.9	37.3	22.8	16.3	29.5
Sao Tome and Principe	...	...	...	...	...	...
Senegal	8.8	8.8	8.7	11.4	11.5	11.3
Seychelles	...	...	...	...	...	...
Sierra Leone	...	...	...	...	...	...
Somalia	...	...	...	...	...	...
South Africa	10.7	12.0	9.2	9.9	11.3	8.3
Swaziland	19.1	21.9	16.0	17.3	20.1	14.1
Togo	33.8	34.4	33.1	28.5	28.8	28.2
Uganda	1.8	1.8	1.7	1.3	1.3	1.3
United Republic of Tanzania	3.2	3.2	3.2	2.1	2.1	2.1
Zambia	4.3	4.4	4.1	4.3	4.4	4.3
Zimbabwe[w]	...	...	...	...	...	...

	median	median	median	median	median	median
World	7.2	8.2	7.6	5.1	7.1	5.9
Countries in transition	...	...	...	...	...	...
Developed countries	...	...	...	...	...	...
Developing countries	...	...	...	...	...	...
Arab States and North Africa	7.1	7.6	6.7	9.1	8.6	7.7
Central and Eastern Europe	1.9	2.7	1.8	1.5	1.9	1.3
Central Asia	...	...	...	...	...	...
East Asia and the Pacific	8.3	9.4	9.9	3.7	3.9	4.0
Latin America and the Caribbean	8.8	10.5	7.9	5.8	8.4	5.8
North America and Western Europe	...	...	...	...	...	...
South and West Asia	...	...	...	...	...	...
Sub-Saharan Africa	19.1	20.2	17.8	17.1	16.3	15.9

NB. Twelve countries apply a seven-year primary-school cycle: Bhutan, Botswana, Kenya, Lesotho, Namibia, South Africa, Swaziland, Trinidad and Tobago, Uganda, United Republic of Tanzania, Zambia and Zimbabwe

REPETITION RATES BY GRADE IN PRIMARY EDUCATION 1999/2000

Grade 3			Grade 4			Grade 5			Grade 6		
Total	Male	Female	Total	Male	Female	Total	Male	Female	Total	Male	Female
...	...	...	...	...	...	...	...	...	...	...	...
16.1**	16.6**	15.6**	14.7**	14.5**	14.9**	12.2**	10.8**	13.8**	...	...	...
18.0	17.2	18.9	22.3	21.0	23.8	13.4	12.7	14.3	...	...	...
4.7	4.1	5.5	5.6	4.8	7.0	...	...	...	...	...	...
...	...	...	...	...	...	...	...	...	...	...	...
...	...	...	...	...	...	...	...	...	...	...	...
...	...	...	...	...	...	...	...	...	...	...	...
25.7	24.7	27.1	21.7	20.6	23.5	23.2	22.1	25.0	32.4	31.9	33.6
23.8	23.6	24.1	23.3	22.6	24.4	20.1	20.1	20.2	27.2	26.2	29.0
...	...	...	...	...	...	...	...	...	...	...	...
20.8	23.8	17.7	20.9	23.6	18.3	16.7	19.5	14.4	12.4	13.8	11.3
2.8	1.4	34.9	4.5	3.8	5.6	5.5	4.2	8.8	4.7	3.2	9.4
26.2	26.9	25.5	21.2	21.4	21.1	24.8	24.5	25.2	...	...	...
15.1	15.4	14.9	11.6	11.7	11.4	...	...	...	...	...	...
...	...	...	...	...	...	...	...	...	...	...	...
...	...	...	...	...	...	...	...	...	...	...	...
24.4	23.6	25.5	20.2	19.3	21.5	18.8	18.3	19.7	...	...	...
12.6	14.9	10.1	17.0	19.4	14.5	13.7	15.3	12.0	8.8	9.2	8.3
11.4	11.4	11.4	11.5	11.6	11.3	15.0	14.9	15.0	37.7	38.1	37.0
...	...	...	...	...	...	...	...	...	...	...	...
30.6	30.3	30.9	33.9	33.2	34.6	36.4	35.2	37.6	30.3	29.6	31.1
...	...	...	...	...	...	...	...	...	...	...	...
12.1	12.1	12.1	12.0	12.0	12.0	14.8	14.4	15.3	28.8	28.4	29.5
...	...	...	...	...	...	...	...	...	...	...	...
...	...	...	...	...	...	...	...	...	...	...	...
...	...	...	...	...	...	...	...	...	...	...	...
10.0	11.5	8.3	10.6	12.2	8.9	9.5	10.8	8.1	8.4	9.3	7.5
19.6	23.2	15.6	17.9	21.0	14.9	16.2	17.4	14.9	16.3	17.5	15.1
29.7	29.5	30.0	22.7	22.7	22.7	24.2	24.4	24.0	14.5	14.4	14.6
1.3	1.3	1.2	7.8	7.8	7.8	8.4	8.3	8.5	9.2	9.1	9.4
1.4	1.4	1.4	12.4	12.3	12.5	0.1	0.1	0.0	0.0	0.0	0.0
4.4	4.5	4.3	5.7	5.8	5.6	5.6	5.8	5.4	7.3	7.4	7.2
...	...	...	...	...	...	...	...	...	...	...	...

median	median	median	median	median	median	median	median	median	median	median	median
5.0	7.4	5.5	5.6	7.6	5.2	5.0	6.0	4.5	4.3	5.5	3.5
...	...	...	...	...	...	...	...	...	...	...	...
...	...	...	...	...	...	...	...	...	...	...	...
...	...	...	...	...	...	...	...	...	...	...	...
8.4	8.7	7.1	8.5	9.6	6.4	8.8	9.3	7.1	6.0	7.7	3.8
1.3	1.5	1.1	1.5	1.7	1.3	...	...	...	...	...	...
...	...	...	...	...	...	...	...	...	...	...	...
2.1	2.0	2.1	2.5	2.1	2.2	1.8	1.9	1.9	...	...	...
6.4	8.0	5.4	5.0	6.6	4.2	3.6	4.9	2.8	2.9	3.3	2.2
...	...	...	...	...	...	...	...	...	...	...	...
...	...	...	...	...	...	...	...	...	...	...	...
18.0	17.2	17.7	17.9	19.4	15.3	15.6	15.3	15.1	20.8	21.6	19.2

Table 10
Internal efficiency: survival rates

Country or territory	SURVIVAL RATES AT GRADE 4							
	1990/91			GPI	1998/99			GPI
	Total	Male	Female	F/M	Total	Male	Female	F/M
Arab States and North Africa								
Algeria	97.2	97.4	97.0	1.00	97.2	96.6	97.8	1.01
Bahrain	91.9	91.4	92.4	1.01	97.6	97.6	97.5	1.00
Djibouti	...	...	...	...	81.1	75.8	88.8	1.17
Egypt[w]	...	...	...	...	...	...	...	...
Iraq	...	...	...	...	...	...	...	...
Jordan[w]	...	...	...	...	98.4	98.4	98.4	1.00
Kuwait	...	...	...	...	94.0	92.9	95.1	1.02
Lebanon	...	...	...	...	94.5	90.0	99.6	1.11
Libyan Arab Jamahiriya	...	...	...	...	...	...	...	...
Mauritania	81.4	81.1	82.0	1.01	...	...	...	...
Morocco	81.7	81.7	81.7	1.00	86.8	86.9	86.8	1.00
Oman	...	...	...	...	97.1	97.7	96.5	0.99
Palestinian Autonomous Territories	...	...	...	...	...	...	...	...
Qatar	73.1	74.9	71.4	0.95	...	...	...	...
Saudi Arabia	87.5	86.7	88.5	1.02	96.8	96.6	97.1	1.01
Sudan	...	...	...	...	83.4**	85.1**	81.5**	0.96
Syrian Arab Republic	99.5	99.8	99.3	0.99	...	...	...	...
Tunisia[w]	92.0	97.4	85.8	0.88	95.1	94.9	95.4	1.01
United Arab Emirates	84.8	85.1	84.6	0.99	94.1	94.6	93.5	0.99
Yemen	...	...	...	...	...	...	...	...
Central and Eastern Europe								
Albania	...	...	...	...	...	...	...	...
Belarus	...	...	...	...	...	...	...	...
Bosnia and Herzegovina	...	...	...	...	...	...	...	...
Bulgaria	92.2	92.3	92.1	1.00	92.9	92.6	93.3	1.01
Croatia	...	...	...	...	...	...	...	...
Czech Republic[o]	...	...	...	...	98.5	98.2	98.9	1.01
Estonia	...	...	...	...	...	...	...	...
Hungary[o]	...	...	...	...	96.8	95.7	97.9	1.02
Latvia	...	...	...	...	...	...	...	...
Lithuania	...	...	...	...	...	...	...	...
Poland[o]	...	...	...	...	...	...	...	...
Republic of Moldova	...	...	...	...	...	...	...	...
Romania	...	...	...	...	...	...	...	...
Russian Federation[w]	...	...	...	...	...	...	...	...
Slovakia	...	...	...	...	96.9	96.3	97.6	1.01
Slovenia	...	...	...	...	...	...	...	...
The former Yugoslav Rep. of Macedonia	...	...	...	...	...	...	...	...
Turkey[o]	98.6	98.9	98.3	0.99	...	...	...	...
Ukraine	...	...	...	...	...	...	...	...
Yugoslavia	...	...	...	...	...	...	...	...
Central Asia								
Armenia	...	...	...	...	...	...	...	...
Azerbaijan	...	...	...	...	98.4	97.5	99.4	1.02
Georgia	...	...	...	...	...	...	...	...
Kazakhstan	...	...	...	...	...	...	...	...
Kyrgyzstan	...	...	...	...	...	...	...	...
Mongolia	...	...	...	...	...	...	...	...
Tajikistan	...	...	...	...	...	...	...	...
Turkmenistan	...	...	...	...	...	...	...	...
Uzbekistan	...	...	...	...	...	...	...	...
East Asia and the Pacific								
Australia[o]	...	...	...	...	...	...	...	...
Cambodia	...	...	...	...	...	...	...	...
China[w]	...	...	...	...	99.4	99.1	99.7	1.01

SURVIVAL RATES AT GRADE 5								TRANSITION TO SECONDARY			
1990/91			GPI	1998/99			GPI	1998/99			GPI
Total	Male	Female	F/M	Total	Male	Female	F/M	Total	Male	Female	F/M
94.5	95.1	93.9	0.99	95.0	93.9	96.1	1.02	66.3	62.0	71.3	1.15
89.2	88.6	89.9	1.01	95.8	95.3	96.3	1.01	98.4	97.0	99.9	1.03
...	...	...	...	76.7	71.2	84.9	1.19	...	...	...	...
...	...	...	...	...	...	...	...	...	...	...	...
...	...	...	...	...	...	...	...	82.3	90.8	71.4	0.79
...	...	...	...	97.7	98.0	97.4	0.99	97.1	97.1	97.2	1.00
...	...	...	...	...	...	...	...	...	...	...	...
...	...	...	...	91.3	88.2	94.8	1.07	...	...	...	...
...	...	...	...	...	...	...	...	...	...	...	...
75.3	75.6	75.0	0.99	...	...	...	...	...	...	...	...
75.1	74.6	75.9	1.02	81.9	81.7	82.0	1.00	80.7	...	...	...
96.9	97.3	96.5	0.99	93.7	93.7	93.8	1.00	94.6	92.7	96.6	1.04
...	...	...	...	...	...	...	...	96.2	95.0	97.5	1.03
64.1	63.4	64.9	1.02	...	...	...	...	...	...	...	...
82.9	81.8	84.2	1.03	95.3	95.2	95.4	1.00	...	...	...	...
...	...	...	...	86.8**	85.6**	88.2**	1.03	80.8**	86.0**	75.7**	0.88
96.0	96.8	95.1	0.98	...	...	...	...	...	...	...	...
86.6	93.9	77.9	0.83	92.1	91.4	92.9	1.02	68.0**	66.6**	69.6**	1.04
80.0	80.3	79.8	0.99	92.4	92.8	91.9	0.99	96.0	94.6	97.5	1.03
...	...	...	...	...	...	...	...	...	...	...	...
...	...	...	...	...	...	...	...	...	...	...	...
...	...	...	...	...	...	...	...	...	...	...	...
...	...	...	...	...	...	...	...	...	...	...	...
90.6	91.0	90.2	0.99	...	...	...	...	...	...	...	...
...	...	...	...	...	...	...	...	...	...	...	...
...	...	...	...	98.3	98.0	98.6	1.01	...	...	...	...
...	...	...	...	...	...	...	...	...	...	...	...
...	...	...	...	...	...	...	...	99.3	99.9	98.6	0.99
...	...	...	...	...	...	...	...	...	...	...	...
...	...	...	...	...	...	...	...	...	...	...	...
...	...	...	...	...	...	...	...	...	...	...	...
...	...	...	...	...	...	...	...	...	...	...	...
...	...	...	...	...	...	...	...	...	...	...	...
...	...	...	...	...	...	...	...	...	...	...	...
...	...	...	...	...	...	...	...	98.6**	98.5**	98.8**	1.00
...	...	...	...	...	...	...	...	...	...	...	...
...	...	...	...	...	...	...	...	...	...	...	...
97.6	98.1	97.1	0.99	...	...	...	...	...	...	...	...
...	...	...	...	...	...	...	...	...	...	...	...
...	...	...	...	...	...	...	...	...	...	...	...
...	...	...	...	...	...	...	...	...	...	...	...
...	...	...	...	...	...	...	...	...	...	...	...
...	...	...	...	...	...	...	...	...	...	...	...
...	...	...	...	...	...	...	...	...	...	...	...
...	...	...	...	...	...	...	...	...	...	...	...
...	...	...	...	...	...	...	...	...	...	...	...
...	...	...	...	...	...	...	...	...	...	...	...
...	...	...	...	...	...	...	...	...	...	...	...
...	...	...	...	...	...	...	...	...	...	...	...
...	...	...	...	...	...	...	...	...	...	...	...
...	...	...	...	...	...	...	...	...	...	...	...
...	...	...	...	97.3	97.1	97.6	1.00	...	...	...	...

Table 10 (continued)

Country or territory	SURVIVAL RATES AT GRADE 4							
	1990/91			GPI	1998/99			GPI
	Total	Male	Female	F/M	Total	Male	Female	F/M
Cook Islands	...	...	...	...	55.6	...	...	...
Democratic People's Rep. of Korea	...	...	...	...	...	...	...	...
Fiji	...	...	...	...	...	...	...	...
Indonesia[w]	...	...	...	...	...	...	...	...
Japan[o]	...	...	...	...	...	...	...	...
Kiribati	...	...	...	...	...	...	...	...
Lao People's Democratic Republic	...	...	...	...	60.5	60.6	60.4	1.00
Malaysia[w]	...	...	...	...	...	...	...	...
Marshall Islands	...	...	...	...	...	...	...	...
Myanmar	...	...	...	...	73.9*	82.1*	67.0*	0.82
Nauru	...	...	...	...	...	...	...	...
New Zealand[o]	...	...	...	...	...	...	...	...
Niue	...	...	...	...	...	...	...	...
Papua New Guinea	...	...	...	...	...	...	...	...
Philippines[w]	...	...	...	...	...	...	...	...
Republic of Korea[o]	...	...	...	...	...	...	...	...
Samoa	...	...	...	...	82.8	81.6	84.3	1.03
Solomon Islands	...	...	...	...	...	...	...	...
Thailand[w]	...	...	...	...	97.9	96.3	99.6	1.03
Tonga	...	...	...	...	...	...	...	...
Tuvalu	...	...	...	...	...	...	...	...
Vanuatu	...	...	...	...	...	...	...	...
Viet Nam	...	...	...	...	87.3	...	...	...
Latin America and the Caribbean								
Anguilla	...	...	...	...	...	...	...	...
Antigua and Barbuda	...	...	...	...	...	...	...	...
Argentina[w]	...	...	...	...	96.6	95.6	97.5	1.02
Aruba	...	...	...	...	97.3	97.6	96.9	0.99
Bahamas	...	...	...	...	...	...	...	...
Barbados	...	...	...	...	...	...	...	...
Belize	69.6	70.5	68.5	0.97	79.6	76.9	82.5	1.07
Bermuda	...	...	...	...	...	...	...	...
Bolivia	...	...	...	...	84.1**	84.4**	83.8**	0.99
Brazil[w]	...	...	...	...	...	...	...	...
British Virgin Islands	...	...	...	...	...	...	...	...
Cayman Islands	...	...	...	...	...	...	...	...
Chile[w]	...	...	...	...	...	...	...	...
Colombia	64.8	70.9	59.8	0.84	72.0	69.4	74.8	1.08
Costa Rica	86.9	85.4	88.5	1.04	...	...	...	...
Cuba	...	...	...	...	...	...	...	...
Dominica	...	...	...	...	91.8	...	...	...
Dominican Republic	...	...	...	...	79.8**	77.0**	82.9**	1.08
Ecuador	...	...	...	...	...	...	...	...
El Salvador	...	...	...	...	...	...	...	...
Grenada	...	...	...	...	...	...	...	...
Guatemala	...	...	...	...	...	...	...	...
Guyana	...	...	...	...	...	...	...	...
Haiti	...	...	...	...	...	...	...	...
Honduras	...	...	...	...	...	...	...	...
Jamaica[w]	...	...	...	...	...	...	...	...
Mexico[o]	...	...	...	...	91.2	90.4	92.0	1.02
Montserrat	...	...	...	...	...	...	...	...
Netherlands Antilles	...	...	...	...	...	...	...	...
Nicaragua	...	...	...	...	63.0	60.6	65.6	1.08
Panama	...	...	...	...	...	...	...	...
Paraguay[w]	78.4	77.4	79.5	1.03	81.3	80.7	81.9	1.01
Peru[w]	...	...	...	...	89.9	90.0	89.7	1.00
Saint Kitts and Nevis	...	...	...	...	...	...	...	...

SURVIVAL RATES AT GRADE 5								TRANSITION TO SECONDARY			
1990/91			GPI	1998/99			GPI	1998/99			GPI
Total	Male	Female	F/M	Total	Male	Female	F/M	Total	Male	Female	F/M
...	...	...	...	51.5	...	...	...	...	...	...	...
...	...	...	...	...	...	...	...	...	...	...	...
...	...	...	...	...	...	...	...	...	...	...	...
...	...	...	...	...	...	...	...	...	...	...	...
...	...	...	...	...	...	...	...	...	...	...	...
...	...	...	...	...	...	...	...	...	...	...	...
...	...	...	...	54.2	54.8	53.5	0.98	...	...	...	...
...	...	...	...	...	...	...	...	...	...	...	...
...	...	...	...	...	...	...	...	...	...	...	...
...	...	...	...	68.6*	76.0*	62.2*	0.82	...	...	...	...
...	...	...	...	...	...	...	...	...	...	...	...
...	...	...	...	...	...	...	...	...	...	...	...
...	...	...	...	...	...	...	...	...	...	...	...
...	...	...	...	...	...	...	...	...	...	...	...
...	...	...	...	...	...	...	...	...	...	...	...
...	...	...	...	...	...	...	...	...	...	...	...
...	...	...	...	82.6	89.0	77.3	0.87	...	...	...	...
...	...	...	...	...	...	...	...	...	...	...	...
...	...	...	...	97.1	95.6	98.8	1.03	90.7	89.8	91.7	1.02
...	...	...	...	...	...	...	...	...	...	...	...
...	...	...	...	...	...	...	...	...	...	...	...
...	...	...	...	...	...	...	...	...	...	...	...
...	...	...	...	82.8	...	...	...	...	...	...	...
...	...	...	...	...	...	...	...	...	...	...	...
...	...	...	...	...	...	...	...	...	...	...	...
...	...	...	...	94.7	93.3	96.1	1.03	94.1**	92.7**	95.5**	1.03
...	...	...	...	96.8	97.4	96.2	0.99	...	...	...	...
...	...	...	...	...	...	...	...	...	...	...	...
...	...	...	...	...	...	...	...	...	...	...	...
67.4	68.9	65.9	0.96	77.8	76.2	79.5	1.04	...	...	...	...
...	...	...	...	...	...	...	...	...	...	...	...
...	...	...	...	82.2**	83.2**	81.2**	0.98	...	...	...	...
...	...	...	...	...	...	...	...	...	...	...	...
...	...	...	...	...	...	...	...	...	...	...	...
...	...	...	...	...	...	...	...	99.1*	100.0*	97.8*	0.97
...	...	...	...	...	...	...	...	95.5**	94.2**	96.8**	1.03
62.1	79.9	50.2	0.63	69.0	66.0	72.2	1.09	...	...	...	...
82.4	80.8	84.1	1.04	...	...	...	...	...	...	...	...
...	...	...	...	...	...	...	...	...	...	...	...
...	...	...	...	91.1	...	...	...	89.2	90.3	88.3	0.98
...	...	...	...	83.5**	79.8**	87.6**	1.10	...	...	...	...
...	...	...	...	...	...	...	...	...	...	...	...
...	...	...	...	...	...	...	...	...	...	...	...
...	...	...	...	...	...	...	...	...	...	...	...
...	...	...	...	...	...	...	...	...	...	...	...
93.1	93.7	92.4	0.99	...	...	...	...	...	...	...	...
...	...	...	...	...	...	...	...	...	...	...	...
...	...	...	...	...	...	...	...	...	...	...	...
...	...	...	...	...	...	...	...	96.1**	97.8**	94.5**	0.97
...	...	...	...	89.0	88.0	90.0	1.02	...	...	...	...
...	...	...	...	...	...	...	...	...	...	...	...
...	...	...	...	...	...	...	...	51.1	46.8	55.0	1.18
...	...	...	...	55.0	52.3	57.9	1.11	...	...	...	...
...	...	...	...	...	...	...	...	...	...	...	...
70.5	69.1	71.9	1.04	75.5	74.7	76.4	1.02	89.6**	89.7**	89.5**	1.00
...	...	...	...	87.9	88.2	87.6	0.99	...	...	...	...
...	...	...	...	...	...	...	...	...	...	...	...

Table 10 (continued)

Country or territory	SURVIVAL RATES AT GRADE 4							
	1990/91			GPI	1998/99			GPI
	Total	Male	Female	F/M	Total	Male	Female	F/M
Saint Lucia	...	...	...	...	...	...	...	...
Saint Vincent and the Grenadines	...	...	...	...	...	...	...	...
Suriname	...	...	...	...	...	...	...	...
Trinidad and Tobago	...	...	...	...	...	...	...	...
Turks and Caicos Islands	...	...	...	...	...	...	...	...
Uruguay[w]	96.3	95.4	97.3	1.02	86.8	85.6	88.2	1.03
Venezuela	90.1	87.4	93.1	1.07	94.0	91.8	96.3	1.05
North America and Western Europe								
Andorra	...	...	...	...	...	...	...	...
Austria[o]	...	...	...	...	96.6**	95.5**	97.9**	1.03
Belgium[o]	...	...	...	...	...	...	...	...
Canada[o]	...	...	...	...	...	...	...	...
Cyprus	...	...	...	...	...	...	...	...
Denmark[o]	...	...	...	...	...	...	...	...
Finland[o]	...	...	...	...	...	...	...	...
France[o]	...	...	...	...	98.5	98.3**	98.7**	1.00
Germany[o]	...	...	...	...	99.5	99.2	99.8	1.01
Greece[o]	...	...	...	...	...	...	...	...
Iceland[o]	...	...	...	...	...	...	...	...
Ireland[o]	...	...	...	...	95.9	94.5	97.4	1.03
Israel[o]	...	...	...	...	...	...	...	...
Italy[o]	...	...	...	...	...	...	...	...
Luxembourg[o]	...	...	...	...	...	...	...	...
Malta	...	...	...	...	...	...	...	...
Monaco	88.3	93.0	83.4	0.90	...	...	...	...
Netherlands[o]	...	...	...	...	...	...	...	...
Norway[o]	...	...	...	...	...	...	...	...
Portugal[o]	...	...	...	...	...	...	...	...
San Marino	...	...	...	...	...	...	...	...
Spain[o]	...	...	...	...	...	...	...	...
Sweden[o]	...	...	...	...	...	...	...	...
Switzerland[o]	...	...	...	...	...	...	...	...
United Kingdom[o]	...	...	...	...	...	...	...	...
United States[o]	...	...	...	...	...	...	...	...
South and West Asia								
Afghanistan	...	...	...	...	...	...	...	...
Bangladesh	...	...	...	...	...	...	...	...
Bhutan	...	...	...	...	...	...	...	...
India[w]	...	...	...	...	63.1	64.2	61.7	0.96
Iran, Islamic Republic of	92.5	92.8	92.2	0.99	...	...	...	...
Maldives	...	...	...	...	...	...	...	...
Nepal	...	...	...	...	...	...	...	...
Pakistan	...	...	...	...	...	...	...	...
Sri Lanka[w]	96.8	96.6	97.0	1.00	...	...	...	...
Sub-Saharan Africa								
Angola	...	...	...	...	15.5**	14.9**	16.3**	1.09
Benin	62.8	62.5	63.5	1.02	...	...	...	...
Botswana	97.3	95.6	99.0	1.03	89.4	87.6	91.3	1.04
Burkina Faso	72.0	72.5	71.2	0.98	76.6	75.6	78.0	1.03
Burundi	65.3	67.5	62.8	0.93	...	...	...	...
Cameroon	...	...	...	...	...	...	...	...
Cape Verde	...	...	...	...	...	...	...	...
Central African Republic	38.3	39.4	36.6	0.93	...	...	...	...
Chad	63.6	69.3	53.5	0.77	65.1	67.7	61.0	0.90
Comoros	...	...	...	...	...	...	...	...
Congo	74.6	69.9	80.2	1.15	...	...	...	...
Côte d'Ivoire	78.0	79.0	76.5	0.97	...	...	...	...

SURVIVAL RATES AT GRADE 5								TRANSITION TO SECONDARY			
1990/91			GPI	1998/99			GPI	1998/99			GPI
Total	Male	Female	F/M	Total	Male	Female	F/M	Total	Male	Female	F/M
...	...	...	...	...	...	...	...	...	...	...	...
...	...	...	...	...	...	...	...	...	...	...	...
...	...	...	...	...	...	...	...	...	...	...	...
...	...	...	...	...	...	...	...	...	...	...	...
...	...	...	...	...	...	...	...	...	...	...	...
94.5	93.2	95.8	1.03	85.8	82.8	89.1	1.08	76.4**	67.5**	86.0**	1.27
86.1	82.5	89.8	1.09	...	...	...	...	...	...	...	...
...	...	...	...	...	...	...	...	...	...	...	...
...	...	...	...	...	...	...	...	...	...	...	...
...	...	...	...	...	...	...	...	...	...	...	...
...	...	...	...	...	...	...	...	...	...	...	...
...	...	...	...	...	...	...	...	...	...	...	...
...	...	...	...	...	...	...	...	100.0	100.0	100.0	1.00
...	...	...	...	...	...	...	...	100.0	100.0	100.0	1.01
...	...	...	...	98.0	98.4**	97.5**	0.99	98.7**	99.1**	98.3**	0.99
...	...	...	...	...	...	...	...	99.6	99.6	99.6	1.00
...	...	...	...	...	...	...	...	...	...	...	...
...	...	...	...	...	...	...	...	...	...	...	...
...	...	...	...	95.1	93.7	96.6	1.03	85.6**	85.9**	85.2**	0.99
...	...	...	...	...	...	...	...	...	...	...	...
...	...	...	...	...	...	...	...	100.0	...	...	...
...	...	...	...	...	...	...	...	...	...	...	...
...	...	...	...	...	...	...	...	...	...	...	...
82.9	92.4	74.5	0.81	...	...	...	...	...	...	...	...
...	...	...	...	...	...	...	...	...	...	...	...
...	...	...	...	...	...	...	...	...	...	...	...
...	...	...	...	...	...	...	...	...	...	...	...
...	...	...	...	...	...	...	...	...	...	...	...
...	...	...	...	...	...	...	...	...	...	...	...
...	...	...	...	...	...	...	...	...	...	...	...
79.7	80.4	79.0	0.98	...	...	...	...	100.0	100.0	100.0	1.00
...	...	...	...	...	...	...	...	...	...	...	...
...	...	...	...	...	...	...	...	...	...	...	...
...	...	...	...	...	...	...	...	...	...	...	...
...	...	...	...	...	...	...	...	...	...	...	...
...	...	...	...	...	...	...	...	...	...	...	...
...	...	...	...	59.7	62.0	56.7	0.91	...	...	...	...
89.9	90.7	89.1	0.98	...	...	...	...	...	...	...	...
...	...	...	...	...	...	...	...	...	...	...	...
...	...	...	...	...	...	...	...	...	...	...	...
...	...	...	...	...	...	...	...	...	...	...	...
94.4	94.0	94.8	1.01	...	...	...	...	...	...	...	...
...	...	...	...	3.7**	3.4**	4.1**	1.22	...	...	...	...
55.1	54.6	55.9	1.02	...	...	...	...	...	...	...	...
...	...	...	...	87.6	84.2	91.1	1.08	...	...	...	...
69.7	70.9	67.8	0.96	68.3	66.9	70.4	1.05	...	...	...	...
61.8	65.3	58.0	0.89	...	...	...	...	...	...	...	...
...	...	...	...	...	...	...	...	...	...	...	...
...	...	...	...	...	...	...	...	...	...	...	...
24.0	25.0	22.5	0.90	...	...	...	...	...	...	...	...
53.1	58.3	43.7	0.75	55.1	58.1	50.0	0.86	...	...	...	...
...	...	...	...	...	...	...	...	...	...	...	...
62.7	58.6	67.4	1.15	...	...	...	...	...	...	...	...
73.0	75.0	70.2	0.94	...	...	...	...	...	...	...	...

Table 10 (continued)

Country or territory	SURVIVAL RATES AT GRADE 4							
	1990/91			GPI	1998/99			GPI
	Total	Male	Female	F/M	Total	Male	Female	F/M
Democratic Rep. of the Congo	63.3	66.6	59.2	0.89	...	...	...	...
Equatorial Guinea	...	...	...	...	20.2**	16.6**	25.0**	1.50
Eritrea	...	...	...	...	97.7	98.2	97.0	0.99
Ethiopia	...	...	...	...	56.9	56.2	58.0	1.03
Gabon	...	...	...	...	...	...	...	...
Gambia	...	...	...	...	...	...	...	...
Ghana	84.0	84.5	83.4	0.99	...	...	...	...
Guinea	68.4	73.0	59.0	0.81	94.2	99.4	87.2	0.88
Guinea-Bissau	...	...	...	...	...	...	...	...
Kenya	...	...	...	...	...	...	...	...
Lesotho	76.7	66.8	86.4	1.29	76.2	71.0	81.5	1.15
Liberia	...	...	...	...	90.1	...	...	...
Madagascar	30.9	31.0	30.9	1.00	59.4	58.8	60.0	1.02
Malawi	67.4	75.3	59.2	0.79	...	...	...	...
Mali	78.5	75.3	84.0	1.12	...	...	...	...
Mauritius	...	...	...	...	...	...	...	...
Mozambique	43.6	47.9	38.4	0.80	57.4	60.9	53.1	0.87
Namibia	...	...	...	...	89.3	87.2	91.5	1.05
Niger	71.3	71.1	71.7	1.01	69.1	69.9	68.0	0.97
Nigeria	...	...	...	...	...	...	...	...
Rwanda	68.5	68.1	68.9	1.01	58.1	59.8	56.3	0.94
Sao Tome and Principe	...	...	...	...	...	...	...	...
Senegal	...	...	...	...	72.5	...	...	...
Seychelles	...	...	...	...	...	...	...	...
Sierra Leone	...	...	...	...	...	...	...	...
Somalia	...	...	...	...	...	...	...	...
South Africa	76.3	73.6	79.1	1.08	79.2	79.2	79.3	1.00
Swaziland	80.4	79.0	81.8	1.04	81.3**	76.3**	86.5**	1.13
Togo	58.4	62.0	53.4	0.86	59.3	61.2	56.9	0.93
Uganda	...	...	...	...	56.2**	55.1**	57.4**	1.04
United Republic of Tanzania	84.2	83.2	85.1	1.02	86.5	85.6	87.4	1.02
Zambia	...	...	...	...	85.9	91.2	80.6	0.88
Zimbabwe[w]	...	...	...	...	...	...	...	...

SURVIVAL RATES AT GRADE 5								TRANSITION TO SECONDARY			
1990/91			GPI	1998/99			GPI	1998/99			GPI
Total	Male	Female	F/M	Total	Male	Female	F/M	Total	Male	Female	F/M
54.7	58.5	50.1	0.86	...	...	...	...	...	...	...	...
...	...	...	...	16.3**	14.2**	19.0**	1.33	...	...	...	...
...	...	...	...	95.3	97.5	92.8	0.95	84.5	86.9	81.5	0.94
...	...	...	...	...	...	...	...	84.5	...	...	...
...	...	...	...	...	...	...	...	...	...	...	...
...	...	...	...	...	...	...	...	...	...	...	...
80.5	81.4	79.4	0.98	...	...	...	...	...	...	...	...
58.8	63.9	48.5	0.76	86.9	92.5	79.1	0.86	...	...	...	...
...	...	...	...	...	...	...	...	...	...	...	...
...	...	...	...	...	...	...	...	...	...	...	...
70.7	58.2	82.7	1.42	68.4	60.6	76.1	1.25	...	...	...	...
...	...	...	...	33.4	...	...	...	...	...	...	...
21.7	22.2	21.2	0.95	51.1	50.7	51.6	1.02	...	...	...	...
64.5	71.3	57.4	0.80	...	...	...	...	...	...	...	...
72.5	73.7	70.2	0.95	...	...	...	...	...	...	...	...
...	...	...	...	...	...	...	...	...	...	...	...
32.9	37.0	28.1	0.76	46.2	49.4	42.1	0.85	...	...	...	...
...	...	...	...	83.4	79.8	87.1	1.09	83.6	82.8	84.2	1.02
62.4	61.0	65.0	1.06	61.3	62.1	60.2	0.97	...	...	...	...
...	...	...	...	...	...	...	...	...	...	...	...
60.0	61.0	58.9	0.97	45.4	47.9	42.8	0.89	...	...	...	...
...	...	...	...	...	...	...	...	...	...	...	...
...	...	...	...	76.7	...	...	...	...	...	...	...
...	...	...	...	...	...	...	...	...	...	...	...
...	...	...	...	...	...	...	...	...	...	...	...
...	...	...	...	...	...	...	...	...	...	...	...
75.3	72.1	78.7	1.09	75.9	75.1	76.7	1.02	92.2	91.1	93.2	1.02
76.2	74.3	78.1	1.05	75.5**	70.4**	80.8**	1.15	...	...	...	...
50.7	55.0	44.6	0.81	51.6	54.2	48.4	0.89	...	...	...	...
...	...	...	...	44.7**	43.9**	45.5**	1.04	...	...	...	...
78.9	77.1	80.7	1.05	80.9	78.6	83.3	1.06	...	...	...	...
...	...	...	...	78.2	83.5	73.0	0.87	...	...	...	...
...	...	...	...	...	...	...	...	...	...	...	...

Table 11
Education finance

Country or territory	Public current expenditure on primary education as % of GNP		Public current expenditure per pupil on primary education as % of GNP per capita	
	1990/91	1999/2000	1990[1]/91	1999/2000
Arab States and North Africa				
Algeria	...	...	...	...
Bahrain	...	...	...	...
Djibouti	...	...	...	...
Egypt[w]	...	...	...	...
Iraq	...	...	...	...
Jordan[w]	...	...	...	...
Kuwait	1.49	...	...	...
Lebanon	...	...	...	...
Libyan Arab Jamahiriya	...	...	...	...
Mauritania	1.35	0.65	16.1	4.7
Morocco	...	...	...	...
Oman	...	...	...	...
Palestinian Autonomous Territories	...	...	...	...
Qatar	...	...	...	...
Saudi Arabia	...	...	...	...
Sudan	...	...	...	...
Syrian Arab Republic	...	...	...	...
Tunisia[w]	...	...	...	...
United Arab Emirates	...	...	...	...
Yemen	...	...	...	...
Central and Eastern Europe				
Albania	...	...	...	...
Belarus	1.56	...	...	...
Bosnia and Herzegovina	...	...	...	...
Bulgaria	2.64	...	...	...
Croatia	...	...	...	...
Czech Republic[o]	...	...	...	...
Estonia	...	...	...	...
Hungary[o]	2.31	...	21.2	...
Latvia	...	...	...	...
Lithuania	...	...	...	...
Poland[o]	1.76	...	...	...
Republic of Moldova	...	...	...	...
Romania	1.25	...	23.1	...
Russian Federation[w]	...	...	...	...
Slovakia	...	...	...	...
Slovenia	...	...	...	...
The former Yugoslav Rep. of Macedonia	...	...	...	...
Turkey[o]	...	...	...	...
Ukraine	...	...	...	...
Yugoslavia	...	...	...	...
Central Asia				
Armenia	...	...	...	...
Azerbaijan	...	...	...	...
Georgia	...	...	...	...
Kazakhstan	...	...	...	...
Kyrgyzstan	...	...	...	...
Mongolia	...	...	...	...
Tajikistan	...	...	...	...
Turkmenistan	...	...	...	...
Uzbekistan	...	...	...	...
East Asia and the Pacific				
Australia[o]	...	...	...	...
Cambodia	...	...	...	...
China[w]	...	...	...	...

1. Indicators for 1990/1991 and 1999/2000 may not be comparable.
For further explanation, please see the Technical Introduction preceding these Annexes.

Public current expenditure on primary education as % of current expenditure on education		Total public expenditure as % of GNP		Total public expenditure on education as % of total government expenditure		Public current expenditure on education as % of total expenditure on education	
1990/91	1999/2000	1990/91	1999/2000	1990/91	1999/2000	1990/91	1999/2000
...	...	5.5	...	21.1	...	84.6	...
30.4	...	5.0	3.7	14.6	...	94.3	...
58.0	...	...	...	10.5	...	100.0	...
...	...	3.8	4.1**	...	...	86.4	...
...	...	...	...	...	...	...	81.7
...	...	8.9	5.1	17.1	5.0	70.7	...
43.1	...	3.5	...	3.4	...	...	...
...	...	...	1.9	...	...	...	89.6
...	...	...	...	...	...	...	68.4
33.3	...	...	3.1**	...	...	...	...
34.8	...	5.5	5.2	26.1	...	90.8	91.2
54.1	...	3.5	...	11.1	...	92.0	...
...	...	...	...	...	...	...	...
...	...	3.4	...	...	...	97.3	...
78.8	...	6.0	9.3**	17.8	...	94.4	...
...	...	0.9	...	2.8	...	...	...
38.5	...	4.3	3.5	17.3	...	...	...
39.8	...	6.2	7.8**	13.5	17.7**	87.8	...
...	...	1.7	...	14.6	...	95.4	92.3
...	...	...	...	...	...	...	...
...	...	5.8	...	...	...	...	...
38.1	...	4.9	6.0	...	...	84.0	...
...	...	...	...	...	...	...	...
50.5	...	5.6	...	...	...	92.6	...
...	...	...	4.3**	...	...	...	...
...	...	...	4.4	...	9.7	...	...
...	...	...	7.6	...	...	...	...
41.8	...	6.1	4.8	7.8	12.8	90.4	...
...	...	3.8	6.3	10.8	...	91.1	...
...	...	4.6	...	13.8	...	93.9	...
32.9	...	...	5.1	...	11.4	...	...
...	...	...	...	...	...	78.9	...
45.0	...	2.8	3.6**	7.3	...	98.4	...
...	...	3.5	4.7	...	...	...	...
...	...	5.1	4.4	...	13.8	...	...
...	...	...	...	...	...	...	...
...	...	...	4.2**	...	...	...	...
58.1	...	2.1	4.0	...	...	89.1	...
38.9	...	5.0	...	19.7	...	80.2	...
...	...	...	5.1**	...	...	...	...
...	...	7.3	...	20.5	...	...	...
...	...	7.0	4.3	23.5	24.4	...	99.2
...	...	...	...	...	...	...	...
...	...	3.2	...	17.6	...	...	...
...	...	8.3	...	22.5	...	88.5	...
...	...	12.9	...	17.6	...	...	...
...	...	9.7	2.2	24.7	11.8	91.8	90.0
...	...	4.3	...	21.0	...	...	...
...	...	9.5	...	20.4	...	79.8	...
...	...	5.3	4.6	14.8	...	92.4	...
...	...	...	1.1	...	8.7	...	...
...	...	2.3	2.1	12.8	...	93.2	...

Table 11 (continued)

Country or territory	Public current expenditure on primary education as % of GNP		Public current expenditure per pupil on primary education as % of GNP per capita	
	1990/91	1999/2000	1990[1]/91	1999/2000
Cook Islands	...	...	...	...
Democratic People's Rep. of Korea	...	...	...	...
Fiji	...	...	...	...
Indonesia[w]	...	...	...	...
Japan[o]	...	...	...	...
Kiribati	...	...	...	...
Lao People's Democratic Republic	...	...	...	...
Malaysia[w]	...	...	...	...
Marshall Islands	...	...	...	...
Myanmar	...	...	...	...
Nauru	...	...	...	...
New Zealand[o]	1.68	...	18.1	...
Niue	...	...	...	...
Papua New Guinea	...	...	...	...
Philippines[w]	...	...	...	...
Republic of Korea[o]	1.36	...	12.0	...
Samoa	...	1.31**	...	...
Solomon Islands	...	...	...	...
Thailand[w]	1.68	...	34.7	...
Tonga	...	...	...	...
Tuvalu	...	...	...	...
Vanuatu	...	2.35	...	...
Viet Nam	...	...	...	...
Latin America and the Caribbean				
Anguilla	...	...	...	...
Antigua and Barbuda	...	...	...	...
Argentina[w]	...	...	...	...
Aruba	...	...	...	...
Bahamas	...	...	...	...
Barbados	...	1.67	...	18.2
Belize	2.74	3.17	11.3	...
Bermuda	1.09	...	...	...
Bolivia	...	1.99**	...	11.1**
Brazil[w]	...	...	...	...
British Virgin Islands	...	...	...	...
Cayman Islands	...	...	...	...
Chile[w]	1.35	...	8.9	...
Colombia	...	...	...	...
Costa Rica	...	2.60	...	17.6
Cuba	...	2.24	...	...
Dominica	...	...	...	...
Dominican Republic	...	...	...	...
Ecuador	...	0.44	...	...
El Salvador	...	...	...	...
Grenada	...	...	...	...
Guatemala	0.37	...	2.8	...
Guyana	...	...	...	...
Haiti	0.77	...	5.8	...
Honduras	...	...	...	...
Jamaica[w]	1.62	...	12.3	...
Mexico[o]	0.62	...	...	...
Montserrat	...	...	...	...
Netherlands Antilles	...	...	...	...
Nicaragua	...	...	...	...
Panama	...	2.27	...	...
Paraguay[w]	0.49	...	3.0	...
Peru[w]	...	...	...	...
Saint Kitts and Nevis	...	...	...	...

1. Indicators for 1990/1991 and 1999/2000 may not be comparable.
For further explanation, please see the Technical Introduction preceding these Annexes.

Public current expenditure on primary education as % of current expenditure on education		Total public expenditure as % of GNP		Total public expenditure on education as % of total government expenditure		Public current expenditure on education as % of total expenditure on education	
1990/91	1999/2000	1990/91	1999/2000	1990/91	1999/2000	1990/91	1999/2000
...	51.1	...	...	...	...	...	98.4
...	...	...	...	...	...	...	...
...	...	4.7	5.1**	...	...	99.1	...
...	...	1.0	1.3	...	...	69.0	...
...	...	...	3.5	...	9.3	...	...
...	...	5.4	...	18.3	...	100.0	...
...	...	...	...	...	...	...	...
34.3	...	5.5	6.0	18.3	25.2	77.3	...
...	...	...	...	...	...	...	...
...	...	...	0.5	...	...	...	63.8
...	...	...	...	...	...	...	95.3**
26.9	...	6.5	7.4	...	...	95.5	...
...	...	...	...	...	...	...	99.7**
...	...	...	10.0**	...	...	...	...
...	...	2.9	...	10.1	...	92.4	...
44.3	...	3.5	3.8	22.4	...	89.2	...
52.6	34.0**	4.2	3.9	10.7	...	94.0	99.9
...	...	...	3.6**	...	...	...	...
56.0	...	3.6	5.2	20.0	...	83.6	...
...	...	...	...	...	...	...	...
35.9	...	...	...	16.2	...	100.0	...
59.8	38.9	4.4	7.2	...	...	100.0	83.7
...	...	2.1	...	7.5	...	90.3	...
...	...	...	...	...	...	...	...
...	...	...	3.5	...	...	...	100.0
3.4	...	1.1	4.6	10.9	13.3	96.0	...
...	30.0	5.0	...	18.0	13.8	81.2	89.4
...	...	4.3	...	17.8	...	89.2	...
37.5	28.6	7.9	6.4	22.2	18.5	81.0	91.4
60.3	61.7	4.8	5.4	18.5	...	94.4	96.0
35.7	...	3.3	...	14.5	...	92.5	...
...	40.8**	2.5	5.8	...	...	...	84.3
...	...	...	5.1	...	12.3	...	...
35.5	...	...	...	12.2	...	89.2	...
...	...	...	...	...	...	...	...
52.2	...	2.7	4.3	10.4	17.0	97.0	...
39.3	...	2.6	...	16.0	...	89.8	...
...	47.2	4.6	5.5	20.8	...	96.9	99.6
18.2	29.4	6.6	7.7	12.3	...	93.1	99.3
...	...	...	5.6**	...	...	...	...
...	...	...	...	...	...	...	...
34.4	43.4	3.1	2.5	17.2	...	92.4	...
...	...	2.0	2.4**	16.6	...	...	...
...	...	5.4	4.8**	13.2	...	100.0	...
29.5	...	1.4	1.6	11.8	...	90.0	88.5
...	...	4.8	4.6**	4.4	...	82.7	...
53.0	...	1.5	...	20.0	...	99.9	...
...	...	...	...	...	...	...	...
34.7	...	5.4	6.3	12.8	10.8	86.7	...
26.7	...	3.7	4.6	12.8	22.6	62.4	...
23.8	...	...	...	...	...	...	47.3
36.7	...	...	...	...	14.0	...	93.8
...	...	3.4	4.0**	9.7	...	...	...
37.0	37.5	4.9	6.3	20.9	...	97.3	96.1
43.9	...	1.1	4.8	9.1	8.8	97.4	...
...	...	2.3	3.5	...	21.1	...	...
...	...	2.8	...	...	...	100.0	...

Table 11 (continued)

Country or territory	Public current expenditure on primary education as % of GNP		Public current expenditure per pupil on primary education as % of GNP per capita	
	1990/91	1999/2000	1990[1]/91	1999/2000
Saint Lucia	2.57	2.43	10.5	12.8
Saint Vincent and the Grenadines	...	...	...	...
Suriname	...	...	...	...
Trinidad and Tobago	1.55	1.53	9.8	11.7
Turks and Caicos Islands	...	...	...	...
Uruguay[w]	...	...	...	...
Venezuela	0.52	...	2.5	...
North America and Western Europe				
Andorra	...	...	...	...
Austria[o]	0.88	...	18.1	...
Belgium[o]	...	...	...	...
Canada[o]	...	...	...	...
Cyprus	1.11	1.58	12.0	18.6
Denmark[o]	...	...	...	...
Finland[o]	...	...	...	...
France[o]	0.89	...	11.9	...
Germany[o]	...	...	10.0	...
Greece[o]	0.65	...	7.9	...
Iceland[o]	...	...	...	...
Ireland[o]	1.55	...	12.1	...
Israel[o]	2.02	...	13.0	...
Italy[o]	0.83	...	15.3	...
Luxembourg[o]	...	...	...	...
Malta	...	...	...	...
Monaco	...	...	...	...
Netherlands[o]	0.92	...	12.0	...
Norway[o]	...	...	...	...
Portugal[o]	1.64	...	15.5	...
San Marino	...	...	...	...
Spain[o]	0.91	...	11.9	...
Sweden[o]	3.36	...	48.3	...
Switzerland[o]	2.02	...	33.5	...
United Kingdom[o]	1.22	...	15.2	...
United States[o]	...	...	...	...
South and West Asia				
Afghanistan	...	...	...	...
Bangladesh	...	0.61**	...	4.4**
Bhutan	...	0.81**	...	7.8**
India[w]	...	...	...	...
Iran, Islamic Republic of	...	1.15	...	8.7
Maldives	...	...	...	...
Nepal	...	...	...	...
Pakistan	...	...	...	...
Sri Lanka[w]	...	...	...	...
Sub-Saharan Africa				
Angola	...	...	...	...
Benin	...	...	...	...
Botswana	...	...	...	...
Burkina Faso	...	...	...	...
Burundi	...	1.43**	...	13.6**
Cameroon	...	...	...	...
Cape Verde	...	...	...	...
Central African Republic	...	...	...	...
Chad	...	...	...	...
Comoros	...	...	...	...
Congo	...	1.83	...	12.9
Côte d'Ivoire	...	2.06	...	16.1

1. Indicators for 1990/1991 and 1999/2000 may not be comparable.
For further explanation, please see the Technical Introduction preceding these Annexes.

Public current expenditure on primary education as % of current expenditure on education		Total public expenditure as % of GNP		Total public expenditure on education as % of total government expenditure		Public current expenditure on education as % of total expenditure on education	
1990/91	1999/2000	1990/91	1999/2000	1990/91	1999/2000	1990/91	1999/2000
47.9	38.7	...	8.0	...	21.3	...	78.5
64.1	...	6.7	7.1**	13.8	...	75.3	...
60.5	...	8.3	6.7**	...	...	99.6	...
42.4	39.8	4.0	4.0	11.6	...	92.2	95.4
...	29.7	...	...	...	17.4	...	72.8
37.5	...	3.1	2.8	15.9	...	91.8	...
20.2	...	3.1	...	12.0	...	...	...
...	...	...	...	...	...	...	...
17.7	...	5.4	6.4	7.6	12.4	92.4	...
23.3	...	5.0	5.8	...	11.6	98.8	...
...	...	6.8	5.7	14.2	...	92.6	...
34.2	33.9	3.4	5.4	11.3	...	94.9	86.2
...	...	...	8.0	...	14.9	...	...
27.9	...	5.7	6.3	11.9	12.5	93.0	...
17.6	...	5.4	5.8	...	11.5	93.1	...
...	...	...	4.7	...	9.7	...	...
28.2	...	2.5	3.6	...	7.0	94.1	...
59.5	...	5.6	...	...	...	73.9	...
29.0	...	5.6	5.0	10.2	13.2	95.0	...
33.7	...	6.5	7.6	11.3	...	92.2	...
26.6	...	3.2	4.6	...	9.5	98.9	...
...	...	2.6	4.0**	10.4	8.5**	...	...
25.1	...	4.0	4.9**	8.3	...	94.4	...
...	...	...	...	...	...	...	...
16.3	...	6.0	4.8	14.8	10.4	95.1	...
39.5	...	7.3	7.4	14.6	15.6	86.3	...
42.3	...	4.2	5.9	...	13.1	91.7	...
32.2	...	...	...	...	...	98.5	...
23.3	...	4.4	4.6	9.4	11.3	88.7	...
47.6	...	7.7	7.9	13.8	13.6	91.8	...
46.3	...	4.9	5.2	18.7	15.2	88.8	...
26.1	...	4.9	4.4	...	11.4	94.9	...
38.9	...	5.2	5.0	12.3	...	90.5	...
87.6	...	...	...	...	...	93.2	...
45.6	41.4**	1.5	2.3**	10.3	...	79.1	62.6**
...	56.9**	...	...	...	...	...	48.3**
38.9	...	3.9	2.9	12.2	12.6	98.7	...
33.2	27.1	4.1	4.6	22.4	18.3	82.5	91.4
...	...	6.3	...	10.0	...	...	...
48.2	...	2.0	2.9**	8.5	13.2**	...	...
...	...	2.7	...	7.4	...	80.9	...
...	...	2.7	...	8.1	...	81.5	...
96.3	...	4.9	5.2**	10.7	...	89.9	88.7**
...	...	...	2.6**	...	...	...	93.8**
...	...	6.9	9.3**	17.0	...	71.3	...
...	...	2.7	...	...	...	...	...
46.8	38.9**	3.4	3.9**	16.7	...	97.0	94.2**
70.5	...	3.4	2.5	19.6	9.8	90.7	85.8
...	...	...	...	...	...	...	...
52.7	...	2.2	...	...	...	96.9	...
...	...	...	2.0**	...	...	...	...
42.4	...	...	3.5	...	23.5	...	...
...	35.9	6.0	5.5	14.4	12.6	97.4	92.9
...	43.4	...	6.4	...	40.8	...	74.0

Table 11 (continued)

Country or territory	Public current expenditure on primary education as % of GNP 1990/91	1999/2000	Public current expenditure per pupil on primary education as % of GNP per capita 1990[1]/91	1999/2000
Democratic Rep. of the Congo	...	...	...	...
Equatorial Guinea	...	...	...	...
Eritrea	...	...	...	...
Ethiopia	1.51	...	31.5	...
Gabon	...	1.27**	...	5.6**
Gambia	1.33	...	14.2	...
Ghana	...	...	...	...
Guinea	...	...	...	...
Guinea-Bissau	...	...	...	...
Kenya	3.16	...	13.6	...
Lesotho	...	3.12	...	17.2
Liberia	...	...	...	...
Madagascar	...	...	...	...
Malawi	1.14	...	6.6	...
Mali	...	1.33**	...	18.0
Mauritius	1.24	...	9.5	...
Mozambique	1.04	...	11.7	...
Namibia	...	...	...	...
Niger	...	...	...	...
Nigeria	...	...	...	...
Rwanda	...	...	...	...
Sao Tome and Principe	...	...	...	...
Senegal	1.73	...	17.9	...
Seychelles	...	...	...	...
Sierra Leone	...	...	...	...
Somalia	...	...	...	...
South Africa	...	2.64	...	14.0
Swaziland	1.39	...	6.7	...
Togo	1.59	1.70**	8.5	...
Uganda	...	...	...	...
United Republic of Tanzania	...	...	...	...
Zambia	...	...	...	...
Zimbabwe[w]	4.29	...	20.8	...
	median	median	median	median
World	1.4	1.7	12.0	12.9
Countries in transition	...	...	...	...
Developed countries	...	...	...	...
Developing countries	...	...	...	...
Arab States and North Africa	...	...	...	...
Central and Eastern Europe	...	...	...	...
Central Asia	...	...	...	...
East Asia and the Pacific	...	...	...	...
Latin America and the Caribbean	...	...	...	...
North America and Western Europe	1.1	...	12.5	...
South and West Asia	...	...	...	...
Sub-Saharan Africa	...	...	...	...

1. Indicators for 1990/1991 and 1999/2000 may not be comparable.
For further explanation, please see the Technical Introduction preceding these Annexes.

Public current expenditure on primary education as % of current expenditure on education		Total public expenditure as % of GNP		Total public expenditure on education as % of total government expenditure		Public current expenditure on education as % of total expenditure on education	
1990/91	1999/2000	1990/91	1999/2000	1990/91	1999/2000	1990/91	1999/2000
...	...	...	...	...	...	...	...
...	...	...	2.0**	...	...	...	84.5**
...	...	...	...	...	...	...	84.5
53.9	...	3.4	...	9.4	...	82.4	...
...	38.6**	...	3.8**	...	...	...	87.3**
41.6	...	4.1	...	14.6	5.7	77.1	...
29.2	...	3.3	4.2**	24.3	...	86.7	...
...	...	...	2.1**	...	...	...	50.0**
...	...	...	2.3	...	4.8	...	...
50.3	...	7.1	6.8	17.0	...	90.4	97.8
...	46.5	3.7	7.9	12.2	18.5	82.1	84.6
...	...	...	...	...	...	...	...
49.1	...	2.2	5.9**	...	...	90.8	...
44.7	...	3.4	4.1**	11.1	...	75.3	...
...	48.9**	...	3.0**	...	...	...	89.6**
37.5	...	3.6	3.5	11.8	...	93.0	100.0
49.8	...	4.1	...	12.0	...	63.7	...
...	...	7.5	...	...	...	...	...
...	...	3.2	2.1**	18.6	...	...	...
...	...	1.0	0.7**	...	...	85.0	...
...	...	...	...	...	...	...	...
...	...	...	...	...	...	...	...
43.0	...	4.1	3.5**	26.9	...	99.4	...
28.2	...	8.1	7.9**	14.8	...	100.0	...
...	...	...	...	...	...	...	...
...	...	...	...	...	...	...	...
75.6	47.9	6.5	5.9	...	...	89.0	94.3
31.1	...	5.5	6.2	19.5	...	81.9	100.0
30.4	36.8**	5.6	4.8	26.4	26.2	93.0	96.7
...	...	1.5	2.3**	11.5	...	91.8	...
...	...	3.4	...	11.4	...	87.9	...
...	...	2.6	...	8.7	...	87.0	...
54.1	...	8.0	11.1**	...	...	99.2	...

median	median	median	median	median	median	median	median
38.9	38.9	4.2	4.7	13.8	12.8	91.8	90.6
...	...	...	...	...	...	...	...
...	...	...	...	...	...	...	...
...	...	...	...	...	...	...	...
39.8	...	4.3	4.1	14.6	...	92.0	...
41.8	...	4.9	4.7	...	...	90.4	...
...	...	7.8	...	20.7	...	...	...
44.3	...	4.2	3.9	15.5	...	92.8	...
37.0	38.7	3.4	4.8	13.5	...	92.4	92.6
28.6	...	5.2	5.3	11.6	11.6	93.0	...
45.6	...	2.7	...	10.0	...	82.0	...
46.8	...	3.6	3.9	14.6	...	89.9	89.6

Table 12
Private enrolment

Country or territory	PRIVATE ENROLMENT AS % OF TOTAL ENROLMENT					
	Pre-primary education		Primary education		Secondary general education	
	1990/91	1999/2000	1990/91	1999/2000	1990/91	1999/2000
Arab States and North Africa						
Algeria	...	...	...	0.0	...	...
Bahrain	100.0	99.3	13.2	19.1	8.8	15.8
Djibouti	100.0	100.0	8.9	6.8	15.7	11.1
Egypt[w]	86.6	51.2	5.8	7.9	...	...
Iraq	...	...	...	...	...	...
Jordan[w]	98.5	99.6	22.9	30.0	6.1	...
Kuwait	9.3	26.0	25.0	31.1	...	27.9
Lebanon	...	76.5	...	65.5	...	52.0
Libyan Arab Jamahiriya	...	...	...	...	...	...
Mauritania	...	...	0.7	2.8	2.5	...
Morocco	100.0	100.0	3.6	4.7	2.7	3.1
Oman	100.0	100.0	1.7	4.5	0.7	...
Palestinian Autonomous Territories	100.0	99.8	...	8.7	...	4.6
Qatar	100.0	100.0	23.4	...	12.3	...
Saudi Arabia	78.7	49.9	4.1	6.4	2.8	...
Sudan	...	90.4	1.0	2.4	21.0	8.3
Syrian Arab Republic	61.2	...	3.5	...	5.6	...
Tunisia[w]	...	...	0.5	...	12.0	...
United Arab Emirates	63.8	68.2	32.2	45.0	20.6	32.0
Yemen	...	...	...	...	...	...
Central and Eastern Europe						
Albania	...	...	...	...	...	...
Belarus	...	0.0	...	0.1	...	0.2
Bosnia and Herzegovina	...	...	...	...	...	...
Bulgaria	...	0.2	...	0.3	...	...
Croatia	...	5.8	...	0.2	...	0.9
Czech Republic[o]	...	1.5	...	0.9	...	2.8
Estonia	...	0.9	...	1.3	...	...
Hungary[o]	0.1	3.4	...	5.1	...	...
Latvia	...	1.0	...	0.9	...	...
Lithuania	...	0.0	...	0.3	...	0.0
Poland[o]	...	3.9	0.1	...	0.4	9.3
Republic of Moldova	...	...	...	...	...	...
Romania	...	0.6	...	0.0	...	0.0
Russian Federation[w]	...	0.0	...	3.0	...	0.0
Slovakia	...	0.5	...	3.9	...	6.2
Slovenia	...	...	...	...	...	...
The former Yugoslav Rep. of Macedonia	...	0.0	...	0.0	...	...
Turkey[o]	5.6	5.8	0.6	...	2.8	4.6
Ukraine	...	...	...	...	...	...
Yugoslavia	...	...	...	...	...	...
Central Asia						
Armenia	...	...	...	...	...	...
Azerbaijan	...	...	...	...	...	...
Georgia	...	0.2	...	1.8	...	1.2
Kazakhstan	...	13.0	...	0.5	...	0.6
Kyrgyzstan	...	1.0	...	2.0	...	2.0
Mongolia	...	3.7	...	0.9	...	0.2
Tajikistan	...	...	...	...	...	...
Turkmenistan	...	...	...	...	...	...
Uzbekistan	...	...	...	...	...	...
East Asia and the Pacific						
Australia[o]	26.2	...	24.9	26.9	31.9	...
Cambodia	...	22.5	...	1.6	...	0.6
China[w]	...	0.0	...	0.0	...	0.0

Table 12 (continued)

Country or territory	PRIVATE ENROLMENT AS % OF TOTAL ENROLMENT					
	Pre-primary education		Primary education		Secondary general education	
	1990/91	1999/2000	1990/91	1999/2000	1990/91	1999/2000
Cook Islands	...	24.6	...	15.0	...	12.6
Democratic People's Rep. of Korea	...	...	...	...	...	...
Fiji	100.0	...	...	...	...	...
Indonesia[w]	99.6	99.0	17.6	...	49.2	...
Japan[o]	78.1	65.0	0.7	0.9	16.5	...
Kiribati	...	...	...	...	...	...
Lao People's Democratic Republic	...	16.6	...	2.0	...	0.9
Malaysia[w]	59.9	48.7	0.3	5.7	6.2	...
Marshall Islands	...	...	...	...	...	...
Myanmar	...	...	...	...	...	...
Nauru	...	...	...	...	...	...
New Zealand[o]	0.4	24.4	2.5	2.1	4.9	...
Niue	...	...	...	...	...	...
Papua New Guinea	100.0	...	2.4	...	...	...
Philippines[w]	58.2	...	6.7	...	36.4	...
Republic of Korea[o]	69.3	75.4	1.4	1.5	45.2	...
Samoa	...	100.0	11.7	15.8	...	31.9
Solomon Islands	...	...	11.7	...	...	...
Thailand[w]	...	18.7	9.6	13.1	16.2	...
Tonga	...	100.0	7.4	7.1	77.7	74.5
Tuvalu	...	...	...	...	...	...
Vanuatu	...	100.0	22.4	3.8	...	25.8
Viet Nam	...	51.1	...	0.3	...	11.3
Latin America and the Caribbean						
Anguilla	...	100.0	...	6.4	...	...
Antigua and Barbuda	...	100.0	...	38.2	...	23.2
Argentina[w]	...	28.1	...	19.5	...	...
Aruba	...	81.8	...	82.4	...	88.9
Bahamas	...	...	...	...	...	...
Barbados	...	16.5	...	9.8	...	6.3
Belize	...	1.8	...	87.0	...	79.1
Bermuda	...	...	...	...	...	...
Bolivia	9.8	...	10.4	...	25.9	...
Brazil[w]	33.6	27.9	14.2	8.1	34.7	...
British Virgin Islands	100.0	100.0	15.3	16.3	...	2.8
Cayman Islands	...	93.2**	...	37.2	...	25.0
Chile[w]	47.7	45.0	38.8	43.2	49.0	...
Colombia	...	44.7	15.2	19.6	...	32.4
Costa Rica	10.9	9.8	4.7	6.8	7.9	17.7
Cuba	...	0.0	...	0.0	...	0.0
Dominica	100.0	100.0	4.0	26.3	...	43.5
Dominican Republic	...	45.5	...	...	...	...
Ecuador	...	39.3	...	21.8	...	25.6
El Salvador	...	...	...	...	...	24.9
Grenada	...	...	8.7	...	...	...
Guatemala	...	21.6	...	14.9	...	47.7
Guyana	...	...	...	...	...	...
Haiti	86.0	...	67.0	...	...	...
Honduras	...	...	5.8	...	...	...
Jamaica[w]	84.1	...	...	...	5.8	2.7
Mexico[o]	8.5	9.4	6.2	7.4	16.6	12.1
Montserrat	...	14.0	...	37.0	...	...
Netherlands Antilles	...	74.5	...	74.8	...	78.0
Nicaragua	24.0	17.5	12.6	16.8	...	32.9
Panama	26.7	23.0	7.8	9.1	15.7	21.7
Paraguay[w]	54.7	28.7	15.0	15.0	21.9	...
Peru[w]	18.1	14.5	12.6	12.6	14.6	...

Table 12 (continued)

Country or territory	PRIVATE ENROLMENT AS % OF TOTAL ENROLMENT					
	Pre-primary education		Primary education		Secondary general education	
	1990/91	1999/2000	1990/91	1999/2000	1990/91	1999/2000
Saint Kitts and Nevis	...	71.8	...	14.6	...	3.1
Saint Lucia	100.0	100.0	1.8	...	12.0	4.0
Saint Vincent and the Grenadines	100.0	...	3.2	4.2	...	...
Suriname	...	...	...	...	...	...
Trinidad and Tobago	...	...	...	5.4	...	13.6
Turks and Caicos Islands	...	51.4	...	17.8	...	9.1
Uruguay[w]	29.8	22.0	16.2	14.2	14.0	...
Venezuela	15.3	...	13.7	...	25.9	...
North America and Western Europe						
Andorra	...	...	...	...	...	...
Austria[o]	25.9	25.6	4.0	4.2	9.4	2.4
Belgium[o]	56.8	54.4	56.0	54.4	65.8	...
Canada[o]	4.2	7.9	3.7	6.5	5.8	6.7
Cyprus	67.9	52.3	4.8	4.1	13.1	...
Denmark[o]	9.1	2.7	...	10.8	41.4	15.8
Finland[o]	...	9.8	0.9	1.1	5.9	5.8
France[o]	12.3	12.6	14.8	14.6	22.0	20.9
Germany[o]	...	58.8	...	2.2	...	7.2
Greece[o]	4.9	3.4	7.1	7.0	5.4	5.6
Iceland[o]	...	6.1	...	1.4	...	0.4
Ireland[o]	1.8	48.4	1.5	1.4	0.4	...
Israel[o]	...	6.8	...	...	...	...
Italy[o]	29.4	29.4	7.1	6.6	6.4	...
Luxembourg[o]	...	5.3	0.7	6.8	...	22.1
Malta	37.6	...	29.2	...	23.3	...
Monaco	33.0	27.1	33.8	30.1	25.0	28.6
Netherlands[o]	68.6	68.3	68.7	68.6	82.9	75.1
Norway[o]	36.0	40.1	1.2	1.5	5.2	4.4
Portugal[o]	64.1	49.9	6.7	9.6	8.2	9.6
San Marino	...	...	...	...	...	...
Spain[o]	38.9	33.0	34.9	33.4	30.5	30.0
Sweden[o]	...	11.7	0.9	3.4	1.2	2.7
Switzerland[o]	5.3	7.3	2.4	3.3	5.8	7.7
United Kingdom[o]	6.0	...	...	...	...	...
United States[o]	37.6	35.0	10.4	11.6	9.6	...
South and West Asia						
Afghanistan	...	...	...	...	...	...
Bangladesh	...	...	15.2	...	...	...
Bhutan	...	100.0	...	1.7	...	0.4
India[w]	...	...	...	17.9	...	...
Iran, Islamic Republic of	...	12.7	0.1	3.3	0.3	5.4
Maldives	...	30.0	...	2.9	...	20.5
Nepal	...	...	...	12.3	...	26.3
Pakistan	...	35.3	...	34.8	...	22.4
Sri Lanka[w]	...	...	1.5	...	2.5	...
Sub-Saharan Africa						
Angola	...	...	...	...	...	...
Benin	8.0	23.0	3.4	10.1	...	12.0
Botswana	...	...	5.2	4.7	68.9	4.2
Burkina Faso	29.4	...	8.6	11.4	41.1	30.9
Burundi	...	...	0.8	...	...	...
Cameroon	36.3	44.6	25.2	27.3	42.8	31.6**
Cape Verde	...	...	...	...	...	...
Central African Republic	...	...	...	...	4.1	...
Chad	...	...	6.0	27.8	...	15.3
Comoros	...	100.0	...	10.7	...	52.1**
Congo	...	86.5	...	15.2	...	14.0

Table 12 (continued)

Country or territory	PRIVATE ENROLMENT AS % OF TOTAL ENROLMENT					
	Pre-primary education		Primary education		Secondary general education	
	1990/91	1999/2000	1990/91	1999/2000	1990/91	1999/2000
Côte d'Ivoire	66.5	...	10.4	...	...	...
Democratic Rep. of the Congo	...	...	...	...	...	...
Equatorial Guinea	...	...	...	...	...	...
Eritrea	...	94.6	31.4	10.1	...	5.6
Ethiopia	100.0	100.0	12.5	6.5	...	2.1
Gabon	...	...	...	...	...	29.3
Gambia	...	...	...	3.2	...	28.7
Ghana	...	...	7.3	...	...	7.1
Guinea	...	...	2.4	16.1	4.1	8.1**
Guinea-Bissau	...	62.2	...	19.4	...	13.2
Kenya	...	...	...	...	...	...
Lesotho	...	...	100.0	...	...	...
Liberia	...	18.0	...	22.0	...	41.1
Madagascar	...	93.0	17.8	22.6	...	45.0
Malawi	...	...	7.2	...	...	7.1
Mali	...	...	3.3	9.1	...	6.9
Mauritius	...	84.7	...	23.8	79.4	74.6
Mozambique	...	...	...	1.6	...	6.4
Namibia	...	100.0	...	4.1	...	4.4
Niger	22.5	36.3	2.8	4.3	7.3	15.6
Nigeria	...	...	...	...	...	...
Rwanda	...	...	0.7	0.0	24.1	46.4
Sao Tome and Principe	...	...	...	...	...	...
Senegal	57.7	69.2	9.2	10.6	...	26.5
Seychelles	...	5.1	...	4.7	...	3.2
Sierra Leone	...	100.0	...	1.1	...	...
Somalia	...	...	...	...	...	...
South Africa	...	26.0	0.8	1.7	...	2.4
Swaziland	...	...	...	...	...	...
Togo	50.6	52.2	24.9	36.9	17.0	18.4
Uganda	...	100.0	...	4.7	...	...
United Republic of Tanzania	...	...	0.2	0.2	49.8	43.1
Zambia	...	...	...	...	...	...
Zimbabwe[w]	...	...	87.8	88.1	...	38.8

Table 13
Out-of-school children

Country or territory	ESTIMATED OUT-OF-SCHOOL CHILDREN (IN THOUSANDS) 1998/99 Total	Male	Female	% Female	1999/2000 Total	Male	Female	% Female
Arab States and North Africa								
Algeria	134.7	27.9	106.8	79.3	117.4	26.2	91.1	77.6
Bahrain	2.8	1.8	1.1	37.5	4.6	2.9	1.7	36.6
Djibouti	69.0	32.2	36.8	53.4	71.7	33.8	37.9	52.8
Egypt[w]	585.1	173.2	411.9	70.4	610.7	204.8	406.0	66.5
Iraq	246.3	...	...	...	248.7	...	...	...
Jordan[w]	54.2	28.9	25.2	46.6	46.2	24.9	21.3	46.0
Kuwait	61.4	30.5	30.9	50.3	55.6	26.8	28.8	51.9
Lebanon	101.9	49.8	52.1	51.2	111.5	57.1	54.4	48.8
Libyan Arab Jamahiriya	...	...	...	...	...	...	...	...
Mauritania	...	...	...	...	...	...	...	...
Morocco	1 214.4	508.9	705.6	58.1	1 035.7	434.4	601.3	58.1
Oman	143.0	71.2	71.8	50.2	150.5	75.3	75.2	50.0
Palestinian Autonomous Territories	31.8	27.3	4.5	14.2	3.1	2.0	1.1	35.3
Qatar	...	...	...	...	...	...	...	...
Saudi Arabia	1 383.1	674.1	709.0	51.3	1 404.7	682.4	722.4	51.4
Sudan	2 522.7	1 194.6	1 328.2	52.6	2 576.3	1 219.8	1 356.4	52.7
Syrian Arab Republic	...	...	...	...	...	...	...	...
Tunisia[w]	36.6	11.1	25.5	69.6	21.8	5.2	16.7	76.3
United Arab Emirates	57.0	31.1	25.9	45.4	63.0	33.2	29.8	47.3
Yemen	...	...	...	...	...	...	...	...
Central and Eastern Europe								
Albania	3.1	1.5	1.6	51.3	...	...	...	...
Belarus	...	...	...	...	...	...	...	...
Bosnia and Herzegovina	...	...	...	...	...	...	...	...
Bulgaria	13.3	5.1	8.2	61.4	17.6	7.4	10.2	58.1
Croatia[1]	...	...	...	...	...	...	...	...
Czech Republic[o]	61.6	32.7	28.9	47.0	59.6	30.6	29.0	48.6
Estonia	4.7	1.7	3.0	63.0	2.9	0.9	2.0	68.0
Hungary[o]	50.2	24.9	25.3	50.4	49.3	24.8	24.6	49.8
Latvia	10.6	5.1	5.5	52.1	9.2	4.6	4.6	50.3
Lithuania	17.8	8.5	9.2	51.9	12.5	6.3	6.1	49.3
Poland[o]	139.2	71.8	67.4	48.4	113.6	57.5	56.2	49.4
Republic of Moldova	...	...	...	...	...	...	...	...
Romania	52.9	25.0	27.9	52.7	79.2	39.1	40.1	50.6
Russian Federation[w]	...	...	...	...	...	...	...	...
Slovakia	...	...	...	...	...	...	...	...
Slovenia	...	...	...	...	...	...	...	...
The former Yugoslav Rep. of Macedonia	6.9	2.9	4.0	58.5	8.1	3.9	4.2	51.9
Turkey[o]	...	...	...	...	...	...	...	...
Ukraine	...	...	...	...	...	...	...	...
Yugoslavia[1]	...	...	...	...	...	...	...	...
Central Asia								
Armenia	...	...	...	...	...	...	...	...
Azerbaijan	...	...	...	...	...	...	...	...
Georgia	...	...	...	...	...	...	...	...
Kazakhstan	...	...	...	...	...	...	...	...
Kyrgyzstan	78.2	38.3	39.9	51.0	82.3	40.6	41.7	50.7
Mongolia	30.1	17.3	12.7	42.3	26.9	15.7	11.2	41.6
Tajikistan	97.9	41.6	56.3	57.5	89.0	34.2	54.8	61.5
Turkmenistan	...	...	...	...	...	...	...	...
Uzbekistan	...	...	...	...	...	...	...	...
East Asia and the Pacific								
Australia[o]	94.1	52.0	42.1	44.8	94.5	52.7	41.8	44.3
Cambodia	362.3	116.3	245.9	67.9	250.9	67.4	183.5	73.1
China[w]	7 063.6	4 752.7	2 310.9	32.7	9 080.9	5 728.3	3 352.5	36.9

1. Numbers of out-of-school children have not been estimated for this country due to inconsistencies between enrolment and the United Nations population data.
2. Numbers of out-of-school children have not been estimated for this country due to lack of United Nations population data by age.

Table 13 (continued)

Country or territory	ESTIMATED OUT-OF-SCHOOL CHILDREN (IN THOUSANDS) 1998/99				1999/2000			
	Total	Male	Female	% Female	Total	Male	Female	% Female
Cook Islands[2]	...	...	...	...	...	...	...	...
Democratic People's Rep. of Korea	...	...	...	...	...	...	...	...
Fiji	...	...	...	...	...	...	...	...
Indonesia[w]	2 328.7	973.0	1 355.7	58.2	2 267.9	947.2	1 320.8	58.2
Japan[o]	...	...	...	...	...	...	...	...
Kiribati	...	...	...	...	...	...	...	...
Lao People's Democratic Republic	140.6	59.0	81.6	58.0	131.6	54.3	77.3	58.8
Malaysia[w]	...	...	...	...	...	...	...	...
Marshall Islands	...	...	...	...	...	...	...	...
Myanmar	953.1	464.9	488.2	51.2	895.9	443.8	452.1	50.5
Nauru	...	...	...	...	...	...	...	...
New Zealand[o]	...	...	...	...	...	...	...	...
Niue	...	...	...	...	...	...	...	...
Papua New Guinea	...	...	...	...	...	...	...	...
Philippines[w]	...	...	...	...	...	...	...	...
Republic of Korea[o]	109.4	64.8	44.6	40.8	109.2	69.9	39.3	36.0
Samoa	...	...	...	...	...	...	...	...
Solomon Islands	...	...	...	...	...	...	...	...
Thailand[w]	1 541.6	724.0	817.6	53.0	1 214.2	555.8	658.4	54.2
Tonga	...	...	...	...	...	...	...	...
Tuvalu	...	...	...	...	...	...	...	...
Vanuatu	...	...	...	...	...	...	...	...
Viet Nam	309.3	...	336.5	108.8	342.6	37.9	304.7	88.9
Latin America and the Caribbean								
Anguilla[2]	...	...	...	...	...	...	...	...
Antigua and Barbuda[2]	...	...	...	...	...	...	...	...
Argentina[w]	...	...	...	...	...	...	...	...
Aruba[2]	...	...	...	...	...	...	...	...
Bahamas	...	...	...	...	...	...	...	...
Barbados	3.7	1.9	1.8	48.0	2.3	1.2	1.1	47.7
Belize	...	...	...	...	...	...	...	...
Bermuda	...	...	...	...	...	...	...	...
Bolivia	35.7	16.2	19.5	54.7	11.2	6.2	5.0	44.3
Brazil[w]	277.9	...	383.2	137.9	457.4	14.6	442.8	96.8
British Virgin Islands[2]	...	...	...	...	...	...	...	...
Cayman Islands[2]	...	...	...	...	...	...	...	...
Chile[w]	210.0	102.5	107.5	51.2	193.3	94.3	99.1	51.2
Colombia	600.2	306.6	293.5	48.9	543.9	275.9	268.1	49.3
Costa Rica	42.1	21.3	20.9	49.5	44.8	22.6	22.2	49.5
Cuba	30.8	18.2	12.6	40.8	7.7	0.5	7.1	93.0
Dominica[2]	...	...	...	...	...	...	...	...
Dominican Republic	133.2	72.7	60.5	45.4	105.7	58.2	47.5	44.9
Ecuador	55.4	32.5	23.0	41.4	38.3	22.0	16.3	42.7
El Salvador	...	...	...	...	...	...	...	...
Grenada	...	...	...	...	...	...	...	...
Guatemala	340.3	151.8	188.5	55.4	348.4	155.9	192.5	55.2
Guyana	...	...	...	...	...	...	...	...
Haiti	...	...	...	...	...	...	...	...
Honduras	...	...	...	...	...	...	...	...
Jamaica[w]	32.4	16.6	15.8	48.9	19.2	9.6	9.6	50.2
Mexico[o]	...	...	...	...	...	...	...	...
Montserrat	...	...	...	...	...	...	...	...
Netherlands Antilles	0.8	0.5	0.4	42.6	1.1	0.6	0.5	44.6
Nicaragua	161.5	83.6	77.9	48.3	163.8	84.9	78.9	48.2
Panama	7.1	3.5	3.7	51.4	7.2	3.5	3.6	50.5
Paraguay[w]	69.3	36.8	32.5	46.9	71.7	37.3	34.4	48.0
Peru[w]	...	...	...	...	...	...	...	...

1. Numbers of out-of-school children have not been estimated for this country due to inconsistencies between enrolment and the United Nations population data.
2. Numbers of out-of-school children have not been estimated for this country due to lack of United Nations population data by age.

Table 13 (continued)

Country or territory	ESTIMATED OUT-OF-SCHOOL CHILDREN (IN THOUSANDS)							
	1998/99				1999/2000			
	Total	Male	Female	% Female	Total	Male	Female	% Female
Saint Kitts and Nevis[2]	...	...	...	...	...	...	...	...
Saint Lucia	0.7	0.4	0.4	50.8	1.0	0.6	0.4	40.1
Saint Vincent and the Grenadines[2]	...	...	...	...	...	...	...	...
Suriname	...	...	...	...	...	...	...	...
Trinidad and Tobago	12.1	6.2	6.0	49.3	11.5	5.7	5.8	50.4
Turks and Caicos Islands[2]	...	...	...	...	...	...	...	...
Uruguay[w]	24.7	13.1	11.6	46.9	20.9	11.6	9.3	44.7
Venezuela	451.2	237.7	213.5	47.3	392.5	267.7	124.8	31.8
North America and Western Europe								
Andorra	...	...	...	...	...	...	...	...
Austria[o]	...	...	...	...	...	...	...	...
Belgium[o]	...	...	...	...	...	...	...	...
Canada[o]	...	...	...	...	...	...	...	...
Cyprus[1]	...	...	...	...	...	...	...	...
Denmark[o]	...	...	...	...	...	...	...	...
Finland[o]	...	...	...	...	...	...	...	...
France[o]	...	...	...	...	...	...	...	...
Germany[o]	...	...	...	...	...	...	...	...
Greece[o]	...	...	...	...	...	...	...	...
Iceland[o]	...	...	...	...	...	...	...	...
Ireland[o]	...	...	...	...	...	...	...	...
Israel[o]	...	...	...	...	...	...	...	...
Italy[o]	...	...	...	...	...	...	...	...
Luxembourg[o]	...	...	...		...	...	...	...
Malta	...	...	...	...	...	...	...	...
Monaco	...	...	...	...	...	...	...	...
Netherlands[o]	...	...	...	...	...	...	...	...
Norway[o]	...	...	...	...	...	...	...	...
Portugal[o]	...	...	...	...	...	...	...	...
San Marino	...	...	...	...	...	...	...	...
Spain[o]	...	...	...	...	...	...	...	...
Sweden[o]	...	...	...	...	...	...	...	...
Switzerland[o]	...	...	...	...	...	...	...	...
United Kingdom[o]	...	...	...	...	...	...	...	...
United States[o]	...	...	...	...	...	...	...	...
South and West Asia								
Afghanistan	...	...	...	...	...	...	...	...
Bangladesh	...	...	...	...	...	...	...	...
Bhutan[1]	...	...	...	...	...	...	...	...
India[w]	...	...	...	...	...	...	...	...
Iran, Islamic Republic of	2 444.3	1 223.5	1 220.8	49.9	2 398.9	1 201.1	1 197.8	49.9
Maldives	...	...	...	...	...	...	...	...
Nepal	...	...	...	...	...	...	...	...
Pakistan	...	...	...	...	...	...	...	...
Sri Lanka[w]	...	...	...	...	...	...	...	...
Sub-Saharan Africa								
Angola	662.2	301.8	360.4	54.4	1 130.1	550.5	579.6	51.3
Benin	353.9	104.5	249.4	70.5	322.8	91.1	231.7	71.8
Botswana	49.0	27.0	22.0	44.8	48.7	27.0	21.6	44.5
Burkina Faso	1 284.7	583.0	701.7	54.6	1 298.2	590.0	708.2	54.6
Burundi	700.4	331.4	369.0	52.7	631.7	288.0	343.7	54.4
Cameroon	...	...	...	...	...	...	...	...
Cape Verde	...	...	...	...	...	...	...	...
Central African Republic	...	...	...	...	...	...	...	...
Chad	570.6	204.5	366.1	64.2	564.1	203.9	360.2	63.9
Comoros	55.7	26.0	29.8	53.4	50.4	22.8	27.6	54.7
Congo	...	...	...	...	...	...	...	...

1. Numbers of out-of-school children have not been estimated for this country due to inconsistencies between enrolment and the United Nations population data.
2. Numbers of out-of-school children have not been estimated for this country due to lack of United Nations population data by age.

Table 13 (continued)

Country or territory	ESTIMATED OUT-OF-SCHOOL CHILDREN (IN THOUSANDS) 1998/99				1999/2000			
	Total	Male	Female	% Female	Total	Male	Female	% Female
Côte d'Ivoire	1 149.2	474.3	674.9	58.7	1 081.0	435.7	645.3	59.7
Democratic Rep. of the Congo	...	...	...	...	...	...	...	...
Equatorial Guinea	9.6	2.0	7.6	78.8	12.3	3.7	8.7	70.3
Eritrea	299.4	143.8	155.6	52.0	288.4	137.3	151.1	52.4
Ethiopia	...	...	...	...	...	...	...	...
Gabon	...	...	...	...	...	...	...	...
Gambia	73.2	33.2	40.0	54.7	56.0	23.5	32.5	58.0
Ghana	...	...	...	...	...	...	...	...
Guinea	683.9	294.3	389.6	57.0	642.3	278.6	363.8	56.6
Guinea-Bissau	82.3	32.9	49.4	60.0	84.3	33.8	50.5	59.9
Kenya	...	...	...	...	...	...	...	...
Lesotho	129.1	73.1	56.0	43.4	146.4	80.7	65.7	44.9
Liberia	...	...	...	...	...	...	...	...
Madagascar	745.9	375.4	370.5	49.7	729.3	367.9	361.3	49.5
Malawi	...	...	...	...	...	...	...	...
Mali	...	...	...	...	...	...	...	...
Mauritius	7.7	4.0	3.8	48.7	7.2	3.7	3.5	48.3
Mozambique	1 310.4	598.0	712.4	54.4	1 232.2	559.0	673.2	54.6
Namibia	64.1	36.8	27.3	42.6	68.9	39.4	29.5	42.8
Niger	1 280.1	605.5	674.6	52.7	1 408.4	721.6	686.9	48.8
Nigeria	...	...	...	...	...	...	...	...
Rwanda	48.0	28.7	19.3	40.3	31.6	16.8	14.7	46.7
Sao Tome and Principe[2]	...	...	...	...	...	...	...	...
Senegal	603.1	265.7	337.4	55.9	579.0	262.5	316.4	54.7
Seychelles[2]	...	...	...	...	...	...	...	...
Sierra Leone	231.5	106.5	124.9	54.0	236.2	108.7	127.5	54.0
Somalia	...	...	...	...	...	...	...	...
South Africa	...	...	...	...	...	...	...	...
Swaziland	28.4	15.0	13.4	47.3	12.3	6.8	5.5	44.7
Togo	36.4	...	...	...	63.7	...	...	...
Uganda	...	...	...	...	...	...	...	...
United Republic of Tanzania	3 501.8	1 784.8	1 717.0	49.0	3 542.6	1 807.8	1 734.7	49.0
Zambia	602.9	298.9	304.0	50.4	663.9	327.8	336.1	50.6
Zimbabwe[w]	495.3	251.3	244.0	49.3	505.1	256.3	248.7	49.2

	sum	sum	sum	% Female	sum	sum	sum	% Female
World[3]	113 605	49 922	63 683	56.1	115 414	50 447	64 967	56.3
Countries in transition	6 297	3 056	3 241	51.5	5 374	2 727	2 647	49.3
Developed countries	1 866	953	913	48.9	1 861	957	904	48.6
Developing countries	105 442	45 914	59 528	56.5	108 179	46 763	61 416	56.8
Arab States and North Africa	8 147	3 350	4 797	58.9	8 107	3 340	4 767	58.8
Central and Eastern Europe	4 405	1 951	2 454	55.7	3 585	1 672	1 914	53.4
Central Asia	2 224	1 124	1 100	49.5	2 126	1 073	1 053	49.5
East Asia and the Pacific	13 842	7 653	6 189	44.7	15 248	8 366	6 882	45.1
Latin America and the Caribbean	2 357	1 021	1 336	56.7	2 198	1 026	1 172	53.3
North America and Western Europe	1 903	969	934	49.1	1 875	962	913	48.7
South and West Asia	39 007	14 023	24 984	64.0	39 859	13 749	26 110	65.5
Sub-Saharan Africa	41 720	19 831	21 889	52.5	42 416	20 259	22 157	52.2

3. World and regional figures include estimates for countries without data.

1. Numbers of out-of-school children have not been estimated for this country due to inconsistencies between enrolment and the United Nations population data.
2. Numbers of out-of-school children have not been estimated for this country due to lack of United Nations population data by age.

References

Abdelkader, G. K. 2001. La Scolarisation des filles dans un pays sahelien: le cas du Niger [Schooling for girls in a Sahel country: the case of Niger]. *Cahiers du GRETAF*.

ABT Associates. 2001. Impacts of HIV/AIDS on the South African Departments of Education, Technical Report submitted to the Department of Education. Johannesburg, ABT Associates.

ActionAid. 2002. Education Mapping of Poverty Reduction Strategy Papers. Nos. 32, 41.

ADEA (Association for the Development of Education in Africa). 2001. HIV/AIDS and education: lessons from Arusha. *ADEA Newsletter*, Vol. 13, No. 4, October–December.

Aguilar, P.; Retamal, G. 1998. Rapid educational response in complex emergencies: a discussion document. Hamburg, UNESCO International Institute of Education (see also www.ginie.org).

Ainsworth, M.; Filmer, D. 2002. Poverty, AIDS and Children's Schooling, A Targeting Dilemma, Evidence from 28 Developing Countries. World Bank, Washington, D.C., January 8 (Power-point presentation, publication forthcoming).

Alkire, S. 2002*a*. Human Capabilities and Basic Education. Background note for *EFA Global Monitoring Report 2002.* (Processed.)

—. 2002*b*. *Valuing Freedoms*. Oxford, Oxford University Press.

Alliance of Mayors and Municipal Leaders on HIV/AIDS in Africa's Website. 2002. HIV/AIDS and Poverty Reduction Strategies. UNAIDS Policy Notes. http://www.amicaall.org (accessed 10 October 2002).

Al-Samarrai, S. 2002. Bilateral and Multilateral Support for Education and The EFA Goals. Commissioned Paper for the 2002 EFA Monitoring Report. (Processed.)

Appleton, S. 1999. Education and Health at the Household Level in Sub-Saharan Africa. Cambridge, Mass., Harvard University Center for International Development. (Working Paper No. 33.)

Asian Development Bank and Afghan Assistance Coordination Authority. 2002. *Afghanistan: Comprehensive Needs Assessment in Education*. [n.p.] (Final draft report.)

Badcock-Walters, P.; Heard, W.; Wilson, D. 2002. Developing District-Level Early Warning and Decision Support Systems to Assist in Managing and Mitigating the Impact of HIV/AIDS on Education. Barcelona, July 7–12 (presentation at 14th International AIDS Conference.

Bagai, D. 2002. *Education for All and Poverty Reduction Strategy Papers.* Paris, UNESCO. (Background papere for the *EFA Global Monitoring Report 2002*. (Processed.)

Bangura, Y. 1999. New Directions in State Reform: Implications for Civil Society in Africa. UNRISD Discussion Paper No. 113. October. New York, UNRISD.

Barnett, T.; Whiteside, A. 2002. *AIDS in the Twenty-first Century*. Basingstoke: Palgrave MacMillan.

Barro, R. 1999. Human Capital and Growth in Cross-Country regressions. *Swedish Economic Policy Review,* Vol. 6, No. 2, pp. 237–77.

Baxter, P. 2001. The UNHCR peace education programme: skills for life. *Forced Migration Review*, Vol. 11 (see also www.fmreview.org).

Beaton, A. E. et al. 1999. The Benefits and Limitations of International Educational Achievement Studies. Paris, UNESCO International Institute for Educational Planning and International Academy of Education.

Behrman, J. 1990. Human Resource-Led Development? *Review of Issues and Evidence.* New Delhi, ILO-ARTEP.

Benavot, A. 2002. Educational Globalization and the Expansion of Instructional Time in National Education Systems. Paris, UNESCO. (Background Paper for *EFA Global Monitoring Report 2002*, processed).

Bennell, P. 1996. Rates of Return to Education: Does the Conventional Pattern Prevail in Sub-Saharan Africa? *World Development,* Vol. 24 No. 1, pp. 183-99.

—. 2002 Estimating the cost of achieving education for all: a review of UPE resource requirement studies. Paris, UNESCO. (background paper for *EFA Global Monitoring Report 2002*; processed).

Bennell, P.; Furlong, D. 1998. Has Jomtien Made and Difference? Trends in Donor Funding for Education and Basic Education Since the Late 1980s. *World Development,* Vol. 26, No. 1, pp. 45–59.

Bennell, P.; Chilisa, B.; Hyde, K.; Makgothi, A.; Molobe, E.; Mpotokwane, L. 2001. *The Impact of HIV/AIDS on Primary and Secondary Education in Botswana: Developing a Comprehensive Strategic Response.* Report prepared for the Ministry of Education, Botswana and the Education Department, United Kingdom Department for International Development (DFID). March.

Bennell, P.; Hyde, K.; Swainson, N. 2002. *The Impact of the HIV/AIDS Epidemic on the Education Sector in Sub-Saharan Africa: A Synthesis of the Findings and Recommendations of Three Country Studies*. Brighton, University of Sussex. Institute of Education. Centre for International Education.

Bennett, J. (forthcoming). *Starting Strong: Education and Care Systems in an International Perspective*. Munich, Staatsinstitut für Frühpädagogik.

Bentall, C. Peart, E. Car-Hill, R. and Cox, A. 2001. Funding Agency Contributions to Education For All. Education for All 2000 Assessment. Thematic studies. Paris, UNESCO. Downloadable text, unesdoc.unesco.org/images/0012/001234/123485e.pdf

Bird, L. 1999. The Tanzanian Experience. Dar es Salaam, UNICEF (see also www.ginie.org).

Bonnel, R. 2000. HIV/AIDS: Does it Increase or Decrease Growth in Africa? Washington, D.C., ACTafrica/World Bank.(Processed).

Brock.; Cornwall.; Gaventa. 2001. *Power Knowledge and Political Spaces in the Framing of Poverty Policy*. Brighton, University of Sussex, Institute of Development Studies. (Working paper No. 143, p. 65.)

Brossard, M.; Gacougnolle, L.-C. 2000. *Financing Primary Education for All: Yesterday, Today and Tomorrow.* Paris, UNESCO.

Brown, T. 2001. Improving quality and attainment in refugee schools: the case of the Bhutanese refugees in Nepal. In: J. Crisp et al., Learning for a Future: Refugee Education in Developing Countries. Geneva, UNHCR (see also www.unhcr.ch)

Bruer, J. T. 1999. *The Myth of the First Three Years. A New Understanding of Early Brain Development and Lifelong Learning*. New York, Free Press.

Buddha Dharma Education Association website. Sangha Metta Project, Mahamakut Buddhist University, Lanna Campus, Thailand, http://www.buddhanet.net/sangha-metta/project.html

Canada, Government of. 2002*a*. G8 Africa Action Plan. http://www.g8.gc.ca/kan_docs/afraction-e.asp

—. 2002*b*. Promoting universal primary education. http://www.g8.gc.ca/summiteduc-e.asp

—. 2002*c*. The Kananaskis summit Chairs summary. (http://www.g8.gc.ca/kan_docs/chairsummary-e.asp).

—. 2002*d*. A new focus on Education for All. (http://www.g8.gc.ca/kan_docs/etfr-e.asp).

—. 2002*e*. Moderators final report. (http://www.g8.gc.ca/taskforce/moderatorreport-e.asp).

Castro-Leal, F. 1996. Who benefits from public education spending in Malawi? Results from the recent education reform. Washington, D.C., World Bank. (Discussion Paper No.350.)

Centre for International Development (CID). 2001. Supporting AIDS-affected Children in Africa (statement developed at workshop held on 9th April). Cambridge, Mass., Centre for International Development, Harvard University. 25 June.

CIDA (Canadian International Development Agency). 2002. *Action Plan on Basic Education.* Ottawa, CIDA. http://www.acdi-cida.gc.ca/education-e/plan (14 October 2002) (En, Fr).

Cochrane, S. 1988. The Effects of Education, Health and Social Security on Fertility in Developing Countries. Washington, D.C., World Bank. (Working Paper WPS 93, Population and Human Resource Development.)

Colclough, C.; Lewin, K. 1993. *Educating All the Children: Strategies for Primary Schooling in the South*. Oxford, Clarendon Press.

Colclough, C.; Al-Samarrai S. 2000. Achieving Schooling For All: Budgetary Expenditures on Education in sub-Saharan ub-Saharan Africa and South Asia. *World Development*, Vol. 28, No. 11, pp. 1927–44.

Colclough, C.; Al-Samarrai, S.; Rose, P.; Tembon, M. Forthcoming. Achieving Schooling for All in Africa: Costs, Commitment and Gender. Brighton, University of Sussex. (Processed.)

Coombe, C. 2000. *Mitigating the Impact of HIV/AIDS on Education Supply, Demand and Quality: A Global Review*. Pretoria, University of Pretoria Faculty of Education. (Report prepared for the UNICEF Innocenti Research Centre, Florence, November.)

—. 2001*a*. *The Challenge of Universal Primary Education*. London, DFID.

—. 2001*b*. *Children Out of School*. London, DFID.

De la Fuente, A.; Domenech, R. 2000. Human Capital in Growth Regressions: How Much Difference Does Data quality Make? London, Centre for Economic Policy Research. (Discussion Paper No. 2466.)

Delamonica, E.; Mehrotra, S.; Vandemoortele, J. 2001. *Education for all is affordable: a minimum cost estimate.* New York, UNICEF.

Donnelly-Roark, P.; Ouedraogo, K.; Ye, X. 2001. *Can local institutions reduce poverty?: rural decentralization in Burkina Faso*. Washington, D.C., World Bank. (Africa Region, Environment and Social Development Unit Policy Research Working Paper No. 2677.)

Dreze, J.; Sen, A. 1995. *India: Economic Development and Social Opportunity*. Delhi, Oxford University Press.

East Timor. 2002. Ministry of Education Culture Youth and Sports. Reported by GINIE. 2002.

Education Watch. 2001. *Renewed Hope, Daunting Challenges: State of Primary Education in Bangladesh.* [n.p.]

European Commission, Development. 2001. The European Community's Development Policy – Statement by the Council and the Commission. (http://europa.eu.int/comm/development/lex/en/council20001110_en.htm)

European Commission, Development. 2002*a*. Note on International Initiatives on Education. (DEV/B-3 D (2002). http://europa.eu.int/comm/development/sector/social/docs/education_note_en.pdf

—. 2002*b*. Seminar Action Aid Alliance, Oxfam, Save the Children on: EU role in delivering international Education Goals. Brussels, 29 May. (Speaking notes for Koos Richelle.) http://europa.eu.int/comm/development/speeches/en/richelle_20020529.htm

European Council. General Secretariat. 2002. Draft resolution on education and training in the context of poverty reduction in developing countries. Brussels. (Doc no 12/1/02 REV 1 (DEV GEN)).

European Parliament. 2001. Basic education in developing countries. European Parliament resolution on basic education in developing countries in the context of the United Nations General Assembly Special Session on Children in September 2001 (2001/2030 (INI). (A5-0278/2001). http://europa.eu.int/eur-lex/pri/en/oj/dat/2002/ce072/ce07220020321en03600364.pdf

Fassa, M. 2000. HIV/AIDS and Education: Sharing experiences, views and ideas from the Cote d'Ivoire and Central African Republic [on] HIV/AIDS impact assessment, measure and response. Paris, International Institute for Educational Planning. (Paper presented at workshop, 'Impact of HIV/AIDS on Education', 27–29 September.)

Fiske, E. B.; Ladd, H. F. 2002. Paper commissioned for the *EFA Global Monitoring Report 2002*. (Processed.)

Foster, G.; Williamson, J. 2000. A review of current literature of the impact of HIV/AIDS on children in sub-Saharan Africa. *AIDS*, Vol. 14, Suppl. 3, pp. S275–84.

Fountain, S. 1999. Peace education in UNICEF. New York, UNICEF (see also www.unicef.org).

G8 Education Task Force. 2002. *A New Focus on Education for All.* Report of the Education Task Force to the G8 Summit Meeting, Kananaskis, Canada, 25–27 June (http://www.g8.gc.ca/kan_docs/etfr-e.asp, 15 October 2002). (En, Fr)

Gillespie, A. 2002. Skills-based health education to prevent HIV/AIDS: the case against integration. www.unicef.org/programme/lifeskills/priorities/placement.html and www.unicef.org/programme/lifeskills/sitemap.html [n.d.].

Global Campaign for Education. 2002*a*. *An Action Plan to Achieve the MDGs in Education.* Amsterdam EFA Conference, April. (Briefing paper.)

—. 2002*a*. Education now to build a better future. Global Campaign for Education Briefing Paper for the Johannesburg World Summit. (August). http://www.campaignforeducation.org/_html/2002-docs/08-brief-joburg/frameset.shtml

—. 2002*c*. Every child in school. Are the G8 serious? June. (Global Campaign for Education Briefing Paper.) http://www.campaignforeducation.org/_html/2002-docs/06-everychild_en/gce-everychild.doc

Global Campaign for Education e-news. 2002. October 17.

Global March website http://globalmarch.org/index.html. (26 September 2002).

Global Mobilization for HIV Prevention. 2002. A Blueprint for Action, Global HIV Prevention Working Group. 2002. http://www.gatesfoundation.org/nr/downloads/globalhealth/aids/hivprevreport_final.pdf (26 September 2002).

Govinda, R. (ed.) 2001. *India Education Report: A Profile of Basic Education*. Delhi, National Institute of Education Planning and Administration/Oxford University Press.

Govinda, R. 2002. Planning for EFA in India. Communication to UNESCO, based on an unpublished paper.

Grassly, N.; Desai, K.; Pegurri, E.; Sikazwe, A.; Malambo, I.; Siamatowe, C.; Bundy, D. 2002. The economic impact of HIV/AIDS on the education sector in Zambia. August. (Final draft paper for submission to *AIDS*.)

GREFCO (Groupe de Recherches de Formation et de Conseils). 2001. *Status Review in Burkina Faso For a National Strategy for Sustainable Development*. [n.p.] (www.nssd.net/country/burkina/bf02.htm, 10 October 2002).

Guimaraes de Castro, M. E. 2002. *The National Education Plan Brazil.* Amsterdam. (Paper presented at the conference on 'Accelerating Action Towards Education for All', 10–11 April).

Gustafsson, I. 2002. Education for All Fast-track Initiative – Some problems and tensions. Paper commissioned for the Monitoring Report 2002. (Processed.)

Hansen, H.; Loaizia E. 2002. Early Childhood and Care: the Experience from the Multiple Indicator Cluster Survey in 48 Countries. New York, UNICEF. (Processed.)

Hartwell, A. 2001. *The End of Planning: Notes on Policy and Education Plans*. www.riseinstitute.org/detail.htm (9 September 2002).

Heneveld. W.; Craig, H. 1995. Schools Count: World Bank Project Designs and the Quality of Primary Education in Sub-Saharan Africa. Washington, D.C., World Bank. (Technical Paper No. 303.)

Huebler, F.; Loaizia. 2002. The Current State of Primary Education in Africa: Empirical Evidence from Recent Household Surveys. [New York,] UNICEF.

Hunter, S.; Williamson, J. 2000. *Children on the Brink. Updated Estimates and Recommendations for Interventions*. Washington, D.C., USAID.

Hunter, S.; Williamson, J. 2000. Updated Estimates and Recommendations for Intervention. Executive Summary of *Children on the Brink*. Washington, D.C., USAID.

Hyde, K. A. L.; Ekatan, A.; Kiage, P.; Barasa, C. 2002. *HIV/AIDS Education Uganda: Window of Opportunity?* Washington, D.C., World Bank.

ID21. 2002. *The Impact of HIV/AIDS on Primary and Secondary Education in Botswana: Developing a Comprehensive Strategic Response*. www.id21.org, 8 October.

ILO/UNCTAD. 2001. The Minimum Income for School attendance (MISA) Initiative. Geneva, ILO/UNCTAD Advisory Group. May.

India, Planning Commission. 2002. *Tenth Five-year Plan, 2002–2007.* May.

Interagency Network for Education in Emergencies website: www.ineesite.org (26 September 2002).

International Literacy Institute. 2002. Towards Guidelines for the Improvement of Literacy Assessment in Developing Countries: Conceptual Dimensions Based on the LAP Project. Philadelphia, University of Pennsylvania. (Working Document.)

International Monetary fund. 2002. Heavily Indebted Poor Countries (HIPC) Initiative: Status of Implementation. Paper prepared by the staffs of the IMF and World Bank, September. Downloadable text, http://www.imf.org/external/np/hipc/2002/status/092302.pdf

Isaacs, A. 2002. *Education, conflict and peacebuilding: a diagnostic tool*. Ottawa, CIDA.

Italy, Government of. 2001. G8. Genoa Summit 2001. Communiqué. (http://www.g8italia.it/_en/docs/XGKPT170.htm)

Japan, Government of. 1999*a*. Archives. Cologne Charter – Aims and Ambitions for Lifelong Learning. (http://www.yomiuri.co.jp/summit2000/archives/99cologne/g8_charter-e.htm)

—. 1999*b*. Archives. G8 Communiqué Cologne. (http://www.yomiuri.co.jp/summit2000/archives/99cologne/g8_communique-e.htm).

Japan, Ministry of Foreign Affairs. 2000. G8 Communiqué, Okinawa 2000. Downloadable text, http://www.mofa.go.jp/policy/economy/summit/2000/documents/communique.html.

Johannessen, E. 2000. *Evaluation of human rights education in southern Caucasus*. Oslo, Norwegian Refugee Council.

Jones, S. 2001. Presentation. Paper presented at the Association of Commonwealth (ACU) Workshop 'HIV/AIDS: Towards a Strategy for Commonwealth Universities'. Lusaka, 8 November.

Kadzamira, E. 2000. The experience of gender reforms in Malawi. Brighton, IDS. (Processed.)

—. 2002. *Achievement of UPE in Malawi.* Paris, UNESCO. (Background paper commissioned for *EFA Global Monitoring Report 2002*.

Kadzamira, E.; Chibwana, M. P. 2000. Gender and Primary Schooling in Malawi. Research Report No. 40. Brighton, IDS.

Kathmandu Post. 2002. Government Urged to Revamp Poor Planning Process. *The Kathmandu Post*, 22 September.

Kelly, M. J. 2000. *Planning for Education in the Context of HIV/ AIDS*. 2000. Paris, UNESCO-IIEP.

—. 2002. The Cost Impacts of HIV/AIDS in Attaining the EFA Goal of Primary Schooling for All. Paris, UNESCO. (Background paper for *EFA Global Monitoring Report 2002*.)

Kingdom of Cambodia, Ministry of Education, Youth and Sports – Department of Non-Formal Education; UNDP Office in Cambodia; UNESCO PROAP. 2000. Report on the Assessment of the Functional Literacy Levels of the Adult Population in Cambodia. Phnom Penh.

—. 2002. *Education For All: A Commitment and an Opportunity*, The Progress of Education for All Planning in the Kingdom of Cambodia.

Knight, J.; Sabot, R. 1989. *Education, Productivity and Inequality. The East African Natural Experiment*. Oxford, Oxford University Press.

Kyereme, S.; Thorbecke, E. 1991. Factors Affecting Food Poverty in Ghana. *Journal of Development Studies*. Vol. 28, No.1 (October), pp. 39–52.

Lange, E. 1998. *The IRC education programme for refugees in Guinea, 1991–1998: A best practice study.* Geneva, UNHCR.

Lavinas, L. 2001. The Appeal of Minimum Income Programmes in Latin America. Geneva, ILO.

Little, A. Forthcoming. *EFA Policy and Planning: Lessons from Sri Lanka.* London, Department for International Development. (DFID Education Research Serial, No. 46.)

Little, A.; Miller, E. 2000. *The International Consultative Forum on Education for All 1990–2000: An Evaluation: A Report to the EFA Forum Steering Committee.* Paris, UNESCO. (Report to the EFA Forum Steering Committee, International Consultative Forum on Education for All, Dakar, 26–28 April). [En, Fr].

Lockheed, M.; Jamison, D.; Lau, L. 1980. Farmer Education and Farm Efficiency: A Survey. *Economic Development and Cultural Change*, 29 October, pp. 37–76.

Lucas, R. E. 1988. On the Mechanics of Economic Development. *Journal of Monetary Economics,* Vol. 22, p. 3–42.

Machel, G. 1996. *The impact of armed conflict on children.* New York, United Nations (see also www.unicef.org).

—. 2001. *The impact of war on children: A review of progress since the 1996 United Nations Report on the impact of armed conflict on children.* London, Hurst.

Macro International. 1998–2001. Demographic and Health Surveys (DHS). http://www.measuredhs.com/

Malinga, F. 2000. Uganda: Designing Communication and Education Programs to Combat HIV/AIDS. *ADEA Newsletter*, Vol. 12, No. 4, p. 94.

Mahshi, K. 2002. Afghanistan: So Much to Do with Almost Nothing. *IIEP Newsletter,* Vol. 20, No. 3, July-September.

Mason, A. D., Khandker, S. R. 1996. Measuring the opportunity costs of children's time in a developing country: Implications for education sector analysis and interventions. Washington, D.C., World Bank. (Human Capital Development Working Papers, No.72.)

Mbilinyi, D.A.S.; Mduda, A.G. 1995. Girls' Secondary Education Support Pilot. Dar-es-Salaam, Ministry of Education and Culture, United Republic of Tanzania.

McBride, R. 2002. *Down and Out in Zomba: The Situation and Education of Orphans in Malawi.* Norwich, University of East Anglia, Overseas Development Group. Reported in ID21, www.id21.org (August 2002).

McGee, R. 2001. *Participation in Poverty Reduction Strategies: a Synthesis of Experience with Participatory Approaches to Policy Design, Implementation and Monitoring.* Brighton, University of Sussex Institute of Development Studies. (Working paper, No. 109, pp. 64, 70.)

McMahon, W. W. 1999. *Education and Development: Measuring the Social Benefits.* Oxford, Oxford University Press.

Mensch, B.; Lentzner, H.; Preston, S. 1986. *Socioeconomic Differentials in Child Mortality in Developing Countries.* New York, United Nations.

Midttun, E. 1998. Brief history and main features of the TEP for Angola 1995–8, as developed and extended by the Norwegian Refugee Council, by arrangement with UNESCO-PEER. Oslo, Norwegian Refugee Council.

—. 2000. *Education in emergencies and transition phases: still a right and more of a need.* Oslo: Norwegian Refugee Council.

Mingat, A. 1998. Assessing Priorities for Education Policy in the Sahel from a Comparative Perspective. Dijon, IREDU. (Processed.)

—. 2002, Primary School Teacher Salaries in African Countries. Paris, UNESCO. (Working paper for *EFA Global Monitoring Report 2002.*)

Motivans, A. 2002. Primary Teachers Count: Ensuring Quality Education for All. Montreal, UNESCO Institute for Statistics. (Policy Research Note No.1, processed.)

Murphy, L. and Mundy, K. 2002. A review of International Nongovernmental EFA Campaigns, 1998–2002. (Background paper for *EFA Global Monitoring Report 2002.*)

Myers, R. 1992. *The Twelve Who Survive: Strengthening Programmes of Early Childhood Development in the Third World*. London, Routledge.

NEPAD. New Partnership for Africa's Development. http://www.nepad.org/

Netherlands, Ministry of Foreign Affairs. 2000. *Education: A Basic Human Right.* The Hague, Ministry of Foreign Affairs. Downloadable text: http://www.right-to-education.org/content/strategy/netherlands.html

Nicolai, S. 2000. Emergency Education in East Timor: Lessons Learned. New York, International Rescue Committee.

NSSD. Burkina Faso: Planning Framework. http://www.nssd.net/country/burkina/bfo2.htm

O'Hara, D. 1979. Mutivariate Analysis of Mortality. Washington, D.C., World Bank. (Processed.)

OECD. 2002. *Understanding the Brain. Towards a New Learning Science*. Paris.

OECD DAC. Online database, http://www.oecd.org/dac/stats

OECD/INES. 2001. Education at a Glance. Paris, OECD.

Opolot, J. 1994. Study on Costs and Cost-effective Approaches to Primary Education in Uganda. Kampala, UNICEF. (Processed.)

Oxenham, J. 2000. Literacy for Development. London, Department for International Development. (Paper prepared for meeting in Nepal, 4–6 December 2000.)

Oxenham, J. et al. 2001. Strengthening Livelihoods with Literacy. [n.p.] Institute for International Cooperation of the German Adult Education Association.

Oxfam. 2002. G8 disappoints again. (http://www.oxfam.org.uk/campaign/africa/g8response.html)

Pakistan, Ministry of Education. 2001*a*. *Draft National Plan of Action on Education For All (2000–2015).* Islamabad, Ministry of Education. 21 August.

—. 2001*b*. *Education Sector Reforms Action Plan 2001–2004.* 1 January.

Penrose, P. 1998. Cost Sharing in Education: Public Finance, School and Household Perspectives. *DFID Education Research Report,* No.27. London, DFID.

Pigozzi, M. 1997. *Implications of the Convention of the Rights of the Child for Education Activities Supported by UNICEF.* New York, UNICEF. (Processed.)

—. 1999. Education in emergencies and for reconstruction: a developmental approach. New York, UNICEF (see also www.unicef.org).

Postlethwaite, T. N.; Schleicher, A.; Sinalsco, M. 1998. The Conditions of Primary Schools: A Pilot Study in the Least Developed Countries. Paris, UNESCO/UNICEF. (Report.)

Programme d'Analyse des Systems Educatifs de la CONFEMEN (PASEC). 2002. L'arbitrage entre extension de la scolarisation et qualité de l'éducation [The tension between the expansion of schooling and the quality of education]. (Working Paper.)

Psacharopoulos, G.; Patrinos, H. 2002. Returns to Investment in Education: A Further Update. World Bank, Washington, D.C. (Policy Research Working Paper No. 2881).

Pyakunyal, B. 2002. Tenth Plan and Challenge Ahead. *The Kathmandu Post.* August 23.

Quattek, K. 2000. The Economic Impact of AIDS in South Africa: A Dark Cloud on the Horizon. *Konrad Adenauer Stiftung Occasional Papers*. Johannesburg, June.

Retamal, G.; Devadoss, M. 1998. Education in a nation with chronic crisis: the case of Somalia. In: G. Retamal; R. Aedo-Richmond. (eds.)., *Education as a Humanitarian Response*. London, Cassell.

Retamal, G; Aedo-Richmond, R. (eds.). 1998. *Education as a Humanitarian Response*. London, Cassell.

Romer, P. 1990. Endogenous Technical Change. *Journal of Political Economy*, Vol. 98, pp. 571–93.

—. 1994. The Origins of Endogenous Growth. *Journal of Economic Perspectives*, Vol. 8, pp. 1–23.

Rose, P. 2001. Cost-sharing in Malawian Primary Schooling: From the Washington to the post-Washington Consensus. Sussex, University of Sussex. (Draft of unpublished PhD thesis.)

Rose, P.; Yoseph, G.; Berihun, A.; Nuresu, T. 1997. Gender and Primary Schooling in Ethiopia. Brighton, IDS. (Research Report No. 31.)

SADC. 2001. Report on Country Preparedness in Dealing with HIV/AIDS in the Education and Training Sector among SADC Member States. Manzini, Swaziland, SADC HRD SCU.

Sangha Metta Project, Mahamakut Buddhist University, Lanna Campus, Thailand (www.buddhanet.net/sangha-metta/project.html, 20 September 2002).

Santiago, P. (forthcoming). Teacher Demand and Supply: Improving Teacher Quality and Addressing Teacher Shortages. Paris, OECD. (Working paper.)

Save the Children. 2001. *Education: Care and Protection of Children in Emergencies.* London, Department for International Development.

Scheerens, J. 2000. Improving School Effectivness. *Fundamentals in Educational Planning*, No. 68. Paris, UNESCO-IIEP.

—. 2002. To what extent can school surveys open the black box of schooling? Montreal, UNESCO Institute for Statistics. (Processed.)

Schonwalder, G. 1997. New Democratic Spaces at Grassroots? Popular Participation and Latin American Local Governments. *Development and Change,* Vol. 28, p. 66.

Schultz, T. P. 1995. Investments in the Schooling and Health of Women and Men – Quantities and Returns. *Investment in Womens Human Capital*. Chicago, University of Chicago Press, pp. 15–50.

Seers, D. 1969. The Meaning of Development. *International Development Review* (December) pp. 2–6.

Sen, A. 1990. Gender and Cooperative Conflicts. In: I. Tinker (ed.), *Persistent Inequalities*. Oxford, Oxford University Press.

—. 1992. Missing Women. *British Medical Journal*, Vol. 304, March.

—. 1996. On the Foundations of Welfare Economics: Utility, Capability and Practical Reason. In: F. Farina, F. Hahn, and S. Vannucci (eds.), *Ethics, Rationality and Economic Behaviour*. Oxford: Clarendon Press.

—. 1999. *Development as Freedom*. New York, Knopf Press.

—. 2002. Basic Education and Human Security. Calcutta. 2–4 January.

Shrestha, C. 2002. Sustainable and Transferable Learning Abilities: Building Experience from the Field. Hyderabad. (Paper presented at policy dialogue on 'Adult and Lifelong Learning'.)

Sida (Swedish International Development Co-operation Agency). 2000. Sida's policy for sector programme support and provisional guidelines. Gotemburg, Novum Grafiska AB. http://www.sida.se/Sida/articles/12400-12499/12439/SidaPolicySectEng.pdf

—. 2001. *Education for All: A Human Right and Basic Need. Policy for Sida's Development Co-operation in the Education Sector.* Stockholm, SIDA.

Sinclair, M. 2001. Education in emergencies. In: J. Crisp et al., *Learning for a Future: Refugee Education in Developing Countries.* Geneva, UNHCR (see also www.unhcr.ch).

—. Forthcoming. *Planning Education in and after Emergencies.* Paris, UNESCO-IIEP. (Background paper for *EFA Global Monitoring Report 2002*, processed.)

Siniscalco, M. 2002. A Statistical Profile of the Teaching Profession, International Labour Organization and United Nations Educational, Scientific and Cultural Organization. ILO/UNESCO: Paris. http://www.ilo.org/public/english/dialogue/sector/papers/education/stat_profile02.pdf

Smith, A.; Vaux, T. 2002. *Education, Conflict and international Development*. London, Department for International Development.

Sommers, M. 1999. *Emergency Education for Children*. Cambridge, Mass., Mellon Foundation/MIT.

—. 2002*a*. *Agency Support for Education in Countries in Conflict and Emergency*. (Unpublished paper.)

—. 2002*b*. Children, education and war: reaching education for all (EFA) objectives in countries affected by conflict. Washington, D.C., World Bank (Conflict Prevention and Reconstruction Unit).

Southern Africa Consortium for Monitoring Educational Quality (SACMEQ). 1998. The Quality of Education: Some Policy Suggestions Based on a Survey of Schools. Paris, UNESCO International Institute for Educational Planning. (Policy Reports Nos. 1–5.)

Spain. 2002. EU's commitments: looking beyond the Monterrey consensus. (Note to be distributed to Delegations, NGOs and Media by the Spanish Presidency of the European Union). http://europa-eu-un.org/article.asp?id=1239

Stanecki, K. A. 2000. The AIDS Pandemic in the 21st Century. The Demographic Impact in Developing Countries. Durban, South Africa, 9–14 July. (Paper presented at the 13th International AIDS Conference, processed.)

Sumra. 1998. Interim review and evaluation of the girls secondary Education Support (GSES) Programme. Dar es Salaam, University of Dar es Salaam Faculty of Education.

Swainson, N.; Bendera, S.; Gordon, R.; Kadzamira, E. 1998. Promoting Girls' Education in Africa: The Design and Implementation of Policy Interventions. *Education Research Serial*, No. 25. London, Department for International Development.

Swaziland, Ministry of Education. 1999. Impact Assessment of HIV/AIDS on the Education Sector. Mbabane, Ministry of Education.

Talbot, C. 2002*a*. Education in Emergencies: The Challenge of Reconstruction. *IIEP Newsletter*, Vol. 20, No. 3, July–September, p. 106. [En, Fr].

—. 2002*b*. Kosovo: Dilemmas of Post-Conflict Reconstruction. *IIEP Newsletter*, Vol. 20, No. 3, July–September, p. 114.

Talbot, C.; Muigai, K. 1998. Environmental education for refugees: guidelines, implementation and lessons learned. In: G. Retamal; R. Aedo-Richmond (eds.), *Education as a Humanitarian Response*. London, Cassell.

Tawil, S. (ed.) 1997. *Final report on case studies of the workshop on educational destruction and reconstruction in disrupted societies*. Geneva, UNESCO-International Bureau of Education.

Tembon, M.; Diallo, I. S.; Barry, D.; Barry, A. A. 1997. Gender and Primary Schooling in Guinea. Brighton, IDS. (Research Report No. 32.)

The Kathmandu Post. 2002. Government Urged to Revamp Poor Planning Process. *The Kathmandu Post*, 22 September.

Tomasevski, K. 2002. *Our Unpaid Debt to the World's Children: The Universal Right to Education.* (Background note for *EFA Global Monitoring Report 2002.*)

Torres, R. M. 1999. *One Decade of Education For All: The Response to the Proposal*. UNESCO-IIEP.

U.S. Department of State. 2002. U.S. offers 'Compact for Development' for Monterrey Conference. http://usinfo.state.gov/topical/global/develop/02031601.htm.

UNAIDS. 1998. *AIDS Epidemic Update: December 1998*. Geneva, UNAIDS.

—. 2000*a*. *Costing Guidelines for HIV Prevention Strategies*. Geneva, UNAIDS.

—. 2000*b*. *Report on the Global HIV/AIDS Epidemic, June 2000*. Geneva, UNAIDS.

—. 2002*a*. HIV/AIDS and Education: A Strategic Approach Draft prepared by the UNAIDS Task Team.

—. 2002*b*. *HIV/AIDS and Poverty Reduction Strategies.* NewUNAIDS Policy Notes.

—. 2002*c*. Kosovo: Dilemmas of Post-Conflict Reconstruction. *IIEP Newsletter*, Vol. 20, No. 3, July–September, p. 114.

—. 2002*d*. *Report on the Global HIV/AIDS Epidemic*. Geneva, UNAIDS. http://www.unaids.org/barcelona/presskit/report.html (9 September 2002). (Fr, Sp, Rus)

UNDP. 2000. *Botswana Human Development Report 2000*. New York UNDP (see also http://www.undp.org/hiv/index.html).

—. 2001. *HIV/AIDS, Responding to the world's most serious development crisis, Uganda partnership*. New York, UNDP (http://www.undp.org/hiv/uganda.pdf, 20 October 2002).

—. 2002. *Palestinian Human Development Report*. New York, UNDP.

UNESCO-Bangkok and Asia and Pacific Regional Bureau for Education. 2002. *Lao National Literacy Survey Experience*. Bangkok. (Processed.)

UNESCO. 1997. *International Standard Classification of Education (ISCED).* Paris, UNESCO.

—. 1999. *The Right to Education: An Emergency Strategy*. Paris: UNESCO.

—. 2000*a*. *The Dakar Framework for Action, Education for All: Meeting our Collective Commitments. World Education Forum Dakar, Senegal. 26–28 April 2000*. Paris, UNESCO. http://unesdoc.unesco.org/images/0012/001211/121147e.pdf

—. 2000*b*. A Decade of Education: Education for All Assessment. Paris, UNESCO. (CD ROM.)

—. 2000*c*. Education for all 2000 Evaluation for Benin (Processed.)

—. 2000*d*. Education for all 2000 Assessment for Mauritania (Processed.)

—. 2000*e*. Education for all 2000 Assessment for Pakistan (Processed.)

—. 2000*f*. Education for All 2000 Assessment. Paris, UNESCO. (CD-ROM.)

—. 2000*g*. Education for All: initiatives, issues and strategies. Report of the meeting of the Working Group on Education for all held at UNESCO Headquarters, 22–24 November. Paris, UNESCO. http://unesdoc.unesco.org/images/0012/001228/122850e.pdf

—. 2000*h*. *World Education Forum, Final Report*. Paris, UNESCO.

—. 2000*i*. *The World Education Report 2000, The Right to Education: Towards Education for All throughout Life.* Paris, UNESCO Publishing. http://www.unesco.org/education/information/wer/PDFeng/wholewer.PDF

—. 2001*a*. *Applying New Technologies and Cost-Effective Delivery Systems in Basic Education*. Paris, UNESCO. (Thematic study.)

—. 2001*b*. Communiqué from High-Level Group On Education for All First Meeting, Paris, UNESCO, 29–30 October. http://www.unesco.org/education/efa/bulletin/en/communique.shtml

—. 2001*c*. *Community Partnerships in Education: Dimensions, Variations and Implications*. Paris, UNESCO. (Thematic study.)

—. 2001*d*. *Early Childhood Care and Development*. Paris, UNESCO. (Thematic study.)

—. 2001*e*. *Education for All and Children Who are Excluded*. Paris, UNESCO. (Thematic study.)

—. 2001*f*. *Education in Situations of Emergency and Crisis: Challenge for the New Century*. Paris, UNESCO. (Thematic study.)

—. 2001*g*. Final report of the second meeting of the Working Group on Education for All. Paris, UNESCO,

10–12 September. http://www.unesco.org/education/efa/global_co/working_group/final_report_en.pdf

—. 2001*h*. *Girls' Education*. Paris, UNESCO. (Thematic study.)

—. 2001*i*. The Global Initiative towards Education for All. A framework for mutual understanding. Office of ADG/ED. An Education Sector Working Document.

—. 2001*j*. *Inclusion in Education: The Participation of Disabled Learners*. Paris, UNESCO. (Thematic study.)

—. 2001*k*. Information Kit on Education for All, *National EFA Action Plans.* Paris, UNESCO.

—. 2001*l*. *Literacy and Adult Education*. Paris, UNESCO. (Thematic study.)

—. 2001*m*. *Monitoring Report on Education for All*. Paris, UNESCO. (En, Fr) http://www.unesco.org/education/efa/fr/monitoring/rapport_de_suivi_sommaire.shtml

—. 2001*n*. *Preparation of national plans of action: Country guidelines*. En, Fr, Sp) http://www2.unesco.org/wef/en-docs/angguid.pdf 135.

—. 2001*o*. *Reason for Hope: The Support of NGOs to Education for All*. Paris, UNESCO. (Thematic study.)

—. 2001*p*. *School Health and Nutrition*. Paris, UNESCO. (Thematic study.)

—. 2001*q*. *Textbooks and Learning Materials 1990–99*. Paris, UNESCO.UNESCO. (Thematic study.)

—. 2002*a*. Asian South Pacific Bureau of Adult Education (ASPBAE). *Tracking Civil Society Participation in the Development of EFA National Action Plans in the Philippines*.

—. 2002*b*. Education for All. An international strategy to put the Dakar Framework for Action on Education for All into operation. Paris, UNESCO. http://unesdoc.unesco.org/images/0012/001266/126631eo.pdf

—. 2002*c*. *The Constitutional Provisions on the Right to Education and Modernizing/Developing National Legislation in Keeping with State Obligations/Government Responsibility under the Dakar Framework for Action*. Prepared for the 28th Session of the Committee on Economic, Social and Cultural Rights (CESCR), Geneva 29 April–17 May.

—. 2002*d*. Early childhood Care? Development? Education? *Policy Briefs on Early Childhood*, No. 1, March.

—. 2002*e*. Information from UNESCO's Regional Bureaux. Personal telephone and e-mail communications. July, September.

—. 2002*f*. International Literacy Prize Submission (Cuba). [Manuscript.]

—. 2002*g*. International Literacy Prize Submission (Pakistan).[Manuscript.]

—. 2002*h*. An International Strategy to Put the Dakar Framework for Action on Education for All into Operation. (En, Fr, Sp)

—. 2002*i*. Planning for Access: Develop a Data System First. *Policy Briefs on Early Childhood*, No. 2, April.

—. 2002*j*. Provisional Briefing on EFA Planning.

UNESCO/International Labor Organization. 2002. *Statistical Profile of the Teaching Profession.* Paris/Geneva.

UNESCO-BREDA. 2002. State of Progress of the EFA process in Sub-Saharan Africa.

UNESCO-IBE. 2001. Synthesis report: Involvement of Civil Society in EFA. 46th Session of the International Conference on Education IBE, Collective Consultation of NGOs for EFA (CCNGO/EFA), 5 to 8 September 2001, Geneva, 2001, UNESCO. http://www.unesco.org/education/efa/partnership/special_session_8.9.2001.pdf 26 September 2002. Available in French.

UNESCO Institute for Statistics (UIS). 2001. Education Counts: Key Statistics of National Education Systems. (CD-ROM)

UNESCO-PROAP. 2001. *EFA Planning Guide Southeast and East Asia*. Principal Regional office for Asia and the Pacific. Keen Publishing.

UNFPA, United Nations Population Fund. 2001. Proposed project and programmes. http://www.unfpa.org/regions/africa/countries/uganda/1uga0105.pdf (10 October 2002)

UNGEI website. 2002. (United Nation Girls' Education Initiative). www.undg.org. (26 September).

UNHCR. 1995. Revised guidelines for educational assistance to refugees. Geneva, UNHCR.

—. 2001. *Learning For a Future: Refugee Education in Developing Countries*. Switzerland, Presses Centrales Lausanne.

—. 2002. *Refugees and others of concern to UNHCR: 2001 statistical overview* (UNHCR, Geneva; www.unhcr.ch).

UNICEF. 1999*a*. *Honduras report: lessons learned after the impact of Hurricane Mitch in the education sector.* Geneva, UNICEF.

—. 1999*b*. *The State of the World's Children 1999: Education*. New York, UNICEF.

—. 1999–2000. *Multiple Indicator Cluster Survey(MICSII).* New York, UNICEF.

—. 2001*a*. *Humanitarian Action: East Timor Donor Update.* 15 Jan 2001. Ministry of Education Culture Youth and Sports. Reported by GINIE 2002.

—. 2001*b*. *Technical notes: special considerations for programming in unstable situations.* New York, UNICEF.

—. 2002*a*. *Finance Development Invest in Children.* New York, UNICEF.

—. 2002*c*. *Quality Education for all: From a Girl's point of View.* New York, UNICEF. (En, Fr, Sp)

—. 2002*d*. *Young People and HIV/AIDS: Opportunity in Crisis*. New York, UNICEF. Available in French and Spanish.

UNICEF/UNAIDS/USAID. 2002. *Children on the Brink 2002: A Joint Report on Orphans and Programme Strategies.* New York.

United Nation Relief and Works Agency for Palestine Refugees UNRWA website: www.un.org/unrwa (26 September 2002).

United Nations. 1948. *Universal Declaration of Human Rights. Adopted and Proclaimed by the General Assembly of the United Nations on the Tenth Day of December, 1948.*

—. 1950. *Universal Declaration of Human Rights.* Final Authorized Text. New York.

—. 1979. *The International Covenants on Human Rights and Optional Protocol, 1966.* New York, United Nations Office of Public Information.

—. 1987. Fertility Behaviour in the Context of Development. *Population Studies*, No. 100. New York, United Nations.

—. 2002*a*. Follow-up efforts to the International Conference on Financing for Development. Report of the Secretary-General. (A/57/319). http://www.un.org/esa/ffd/a57-319-ffd-followup.pdf

—. 2002*b*. Outcome of the International Conference on Financing for Development. Report of the Secretary-General. (A/57/).http://www.un.org/esa/ffd/a57-344-ffd-outcome.pdf

UNRWA United Nation Relief and Works Agency for Palestine Refugees website

USAID. 2002*a*. *Helping Children Outgrow War*. Technical paper No. 116. Africa Bureau Information Center.

—. 2002*b*. Millenium challenge account update. Fact Sheet. June 3. (http://www.usaid.gov/press/releases/2002/fs_mca.html).

Vargas Baron, E. 2001. *The Challenge of Education in Emergencies – Policy and Practice*. Institute for Reconstruction and International Security Through Education for the third preparatory Committee for the 2001 UH Special Session on Children. June 12, 2001. 125.

Vargas-Baron, E.; McClure, M. 1998. The new heroics of generational commitment: education in nations with chronic crises. In: G. Retamal; R. Aedo-Richmond. (eds.)., *Education as a Humanitarian Response*. London, Cassell.

Virtosu, L. 2002. Republican Seminar on Results-based Planning and Management for Education For All. United Nations, Republic of Moldova press release. 4 September.

Weir, S. 1998. *The Determinants of School Enrolment in Rural Ethiopia: Attitudes, Returns and Resources*. Oxford, Saint Johns College (PhD thesis).

Weir, S.; Knight, J. 1996. Demand for Schooling in Rural Ethiopia. Washington, D.C., World Bank. (PHRD Study, No.1a.)

Whiteside, A.; Sunter, C. 2000. *AIDS: The Challenge for South Africa.* Cape Town: Human, Rousseau and Tafelberg.

Winter, C.; Burnett, N. 2002. *Working Together to Achieve Education For All.* Washington, D.C., World Bank presentation. (Processed.)

Wolf, J. 1995. An analysis of USAID programs to improve equity in Malawi and Ghana's education systems. Washington, D.C., USAID. (Sustainable Development Publication Series. Technical Paper No.10.)

World Bank. 1991. *World Development Report 1991*. New York, Oxford University Press.

—. 1996. Republic of Zambia Education and Training Sector Expenditure Review. Washington, D.C., World Bank.

—. 2000*a*. A Chance to Learn: Knowledge and Finance for Education in Sub-Saharan Africa, p. 56. Washington, D.C., World Bank. (Paper presented at World Education Forum, Dakar, 2000.)

—. 2000*b*. Exploring the Implications of the HIV/AIDS Epidemic for Educational Planning in Selected African Countries: The Demographic Question. Washington, D.C., World Bank AIDS Campaign Team for Africa (ACTafrica).

—. 2001*a*. *Annual Reports* 1990–2001. Washington, D.C., World Bank.

—. 2001*b*. Costs of Scaling HIV Program Activities to a National Level in SSub-Saharan sub-Saharan Africa: Methods and Estimates. March 31. Washington, D.C., World Bank AIDS Campaign Team for Africa (ACTafrica).

—. 2002*a*. *Achieving Education for All by 2015: Simulation Results for 47 Low-Income Countries*. 2002. Human Development Network. Africa Region Department.

—. 2002*b*. *Education and HIV/AIDS: A Window for Hope*. Washington, D.C., World Bank.

—. 2002*c*. Financial Impact of the HIPC Initiative, first 26 country cases, produced by the HIPC Unit. Washington, D.C., World Bank. http://www.worldbank.org/hipc/Financial_Impact_July02.pdf

—. 2002*d*. Project Appraisal Document on a Proposed Trust Funded Credit in the amount of US $20 Million to the West Bank and Gaza For a Emergency Services Support Project. Human Development Sector middle East and North Africa Region.

—. 2002*e*. Skills and Literacy Training for Better Livelihoods. *Findings*, Vol. 209, June.

World Bank Development Committee. 2002*a*. Education for dynamic economies: Action plan to accelerate progress towards Education for All (EFA). (DC2000-0005/Rev1). Washington, D.C., World Bank.

—. 2002*b*. Note from the President of the World Bank. (DC2002-0007/Rev1). Washington, D.C., World Bank.

World Bank/IMF. 2002. *Review of the Poverty Reduction Strategy Paper (PRSP) Approach: Early Experiences with Interim PRSPs and Full PRSPs*. Downloadable text, http://www.worldbank.org/poverty/strategies/review/earlyexp.pdf

World Trade Organization. 2001. Doha WTO Ministerial 2001: Ministerial Declaration WT/MIN(01)/DEC/1 http://www.wto.org/english/thewto_e/minist_e/min01_e/mindecl_e.htm

www.worldbank.org/education

Young, M. E. (ed.). 2002. From Early Childhood Development to Human Development. Washington, D.C., World Bank.

Glossary

adult literacy/illiteracy rate (estimated). Number of literate/illiterate adults expressed as a percentage of the total adult population aged 15 years and above. A person is considered literate/illiterate if he/she can/cannot read and write with understanding a simple statement related to his/her life.

early childhood care and education (ECCE). Programmes that, in addition to providing children with care, offer a structured and purposeful set of learning activities either in a formal institution (pre-primary) or as part of a non-formal child development programme. Early childhood care and education programmes are normally designed for children aged 3 years and above and include organized learning activities that constitutean average equivalent of at least 2 hours per day and 100 days per year.

enrolment. Number of pupils or students enrolled in a given level of education, regardless of age. See also gross enrolment ratio and net enrolment ratio.

entrance age (official). Age at which pupils or students would enter a given programme or level of education assuming they had started at the official entrance age for the lowest level of education, had studied full-time throughout and had progressed through the system without repeating or skipping a grade. Note that the theoretical entrance age to a given programme or level may be very different from the actual or even the typical or most common entrance age.

gender parity index (GPI). Ratio of female-to-male value of a given indicator. A GPI of 1 indicates parity between sexes; a GPI that varies between 0 and 1 means a disparity in favour of boys; a GPI greater than 1 indicates a disparity in favour of girls.

grade. Stage of instruction usually covered in one school year.

gross enrolment ratio (GER). Number of pupils enrolled in a given level of education, regardless of age, expressed as a percentage of the population in the relevant official age group. Note that GER can be higher than 100% as a result of grade repetition and entry at younger and older ages than the typical grade-level age.

gross intake rate (GIR). Number of new entrants into first grade of primary education, regardless of age, expressed as a percentage of the population of official entrance age to primary education.

gross domestic product (GDP). Sum of gross value added by all residents producers in the economy, including distributive trades and transport, plus any product taxes and minus any subsidies not included in the value of the products

gross national product (GNP). Sum of gross value added by all resident producers in the economy, including distributive trades and transport, plus any product taxes, minus any subsidies not included in the value of the products plus net receipts of income from abroad. Since net receipts from abroad may be positive or negative, it is possible for the GNP to be greater or smaller than the GDP.

gross national product per capita. Gross national product in current US dollars ($) divided by the total population.

International Standard Classification of Education (ISCED). A classification system designed as an instrument suitable for assembling, compiling and presenting comparable indicators and statistics of education both within individual countries and internationally. This system was introduced in 1976, and revised in 1997.

life expectancy at birth. Theoretical number of years a newborn will live if the age-specific mortality rates in the year of birth are taken as constant, i.e. the sum of the mortality rates by age.

lower secondary education (ISCED Level 2). Generally designed to continue the basic programmes of the primary level. Teaching at lower secondary level is typically more subject-focused, requiring more specialized teachers for each subject area. The end of this level often coincides with the end of compulsory education.

net enrolment ratio (NER). Number of pupils in the official age group for a given level of education enrolled in that level expressed as a percentage of the total population in that age group.

net intake rate in primary education (NIR). Number of pupils at the official school entrance age who are new entrants into the first grade of primary education, expressed as a percentage of the population of official admission age to primary education.

new entrants. Pupils entering primary education for the first time.

out-of-school children. Children in the official school age group who are not enrolled in school.

percentage of new entrants to primary education with ECCE experience. Number of new entrants to primary education who have attended some form of organized early childhood care and education programmes equivalent at least 200 hours, expressed as percentage of total number of new entrants to primary education.

pre-primary education (ISCED Level 0). Refers to programmes at the initial stage of organized instruction, which are primarily designed to introduce very young children, usually from age 3 or so, to a school-type environment, i.e. to provide a bridge between home and school. Such programmes are variously referred to as infant education, nursery education, pre-school education, kindergarten, or early childhood education. See also early childhood care and education programmes.

primary education (ISCED Level 1). Sometimes called *elementary education*, refers to educational programmes that are normally designed on a unit or project basis to give pupils a sound basic education in reading, writing and mathematics along with an elementary understanding of other subjects such as history, geography, natural science, social science, art and music. In some cases religious instruction is also featured. These subjects serve to develop pupils' ability to obtain and use information the children need about their home, community, country, etc. Synonym: primary schooling.

private enrolment. Number of children enrolled in an institution (school or college) that is not operated by a public authority, but is rather controlled and managed on either a profit or non-profit basis by a private body such as a non-governmental organization or association, a religious body, a special interest group, a foundation or a business enterprise.

public expenditure on education. Total public finance devoted to education by local, regional and national governments, including municipalities. Household contributions are normally excluded. Public expenditure on education includes both capital and current expenditure. **Capital (public) expenditure** includes expenditure for construction, renovation and major repairs of buildings and the purchase of heavy equipment or vehicles. **Current (public) expenditure** includes expenditure for goods and services consumed within the current year and which would need to be renewed if there were a need for prolongation the following year. It includes expenditure on: staff salaries and benefits; contracted or purchased services; other resources including books and teaching materials; welfare services; and other current expenditure such as furniture and equipment, minors repairs, fuel, telecommunications, travel, insurance and rents.

public current expenditure on primary education as percentage of total public current expenditure on education. This indicator shows the relative share of public current expenditure on primary education within overall public current expenditure on education.

public current expenditure per pupil on primary education as percentage of GNP per capita. Measures the average cost of a pupil in primary education in relation to the country's GNP per capita. In other words, this is the share of primary education unit cost in the GNP per capita.

public expenditure on education as a percentage of GNP. Total public expenditure on education at every level of administration according to the constitution of the country, i.e. central, regional and local authorities, expressed as a percentage of the gross national product.

public expenditure on education as a percentage of total government expenditure. Total public expenditure on education at every level of administration according to the constitution of the country, i.e. central, regional and local authorities, expressed as a percentage of total government expenditure on all sectors (including health, education, social services etc).

pupil. Refers to a young person who is enrolled in an educational programme. For the purposes of this Monitoring Report, 'pupil' refers to a child enrolled in primary school, whereas children or adults enrolled at more advanced levels are students.

pupil/teacher ratio (PTR). Average number of pupils per teacher at the level of education specified in a given school year. When data are available the calculation of the pupil/teacher ratio is based on teachers and pupils expressed in full-time equivalent.

purchasing power parity (PPP). The rate of currency conversion into US$ that eliminates the differences in price levels among countries. Thus, when expenditure on GNP for different countries is converted into a common currency by means of the PPP, it is, in effect, expressed at the same set of international prices so that comparisons between countries reflect only differences in the volume of goods and services purchased. In other words, this means that a given sum of money, when converted into US$ at the PPP rate (PPP$), will buy the same basket of goods and services in all countries.

repetition rate by grade. Proportion of pupils enrolled in a given grade in a given school-year who study in the same grade the following school-year.

school life expectancy. Number of years a child is expected to remain at school, or university, including years spent on repetition. It is the sum of the age-specific enrolment ratios for primary, secondary, post-secondary non-tertiary and tertiary education.

school-age population. Population of the age group which officially corresponds to the relevant level of education, whether enrolled in school or not.

survival rate. Percentage of a cohort of pupils who enrolled in the first grade of an education cycle in a given school year and who reach a given grade either with or without repeating a grade.

teacher or teaching staff. Number of persons employed full-time or part-time in an official capacity for the purpose of guiding and directing the learning experience of pupils and students, irrespective of his/her qualification or the delivery mechanism, i.e. whether face-to-face and/or at a distance. This definition excludes educational personnel who have no active teaching duties (e.g. headmasters, headmistresses or principals who do not teach) or who work occasionally or in a voluntary capacity in educational institutions (e.g. parents).

total debt service. Sum of principal repayments and interest actually paid in foreign currency, goods, or services on long-term debt, or interest paid in short-term debt, as well as repayments (repurchases and charges) to the International Monetary Fund (IMF).

trained teacher. Teacher who has received the minimum organized teacher training (pre-service or in service) required for teaching at the relevant level in a given country.

transition rate to secondary education. Number of pupils admitted to the first grade of secondary education in a given year, expressed as a percentage of the number of pupils enrolled in the final grade of primary of education in the previous year.

youth literacy/illiteracy rate (estimated). The number of literate/illiterate young adults aged 15–24 years expressed as a percentage of the total youth population aged 15–24 years. A person is considered literate/illiterate if he/she can/cannot read and write with understanding a simple statement related to his/her life.

Acronyms

ABD Asian Development Bank
ACTafrica AIDS Campaign Team for Africa
ADEA Association for the Development of Education in Africa
ALLs Adult Literacy and Life Skills Study
AMICAALL Alliance of Mayors Initiative for Community Action on AIDS at the Local Level
ARV anti-retro viral
BLCC Bunyad Literacy Community Council
BPRM Bureau for Population, Refugees and Migration
BREDA Bureau Regional de l'UNESCO pour l'Education en Afrique (*UNESCO Regional Office for Education in Africa*)
CCA common country assessment
CCNGOs Collective Consultation of Non-governmental Organzations
CID Center for International Development at Harvard University
CIDA Canadian International Development Agency
CGIAR Consultative Group on International Agricultural Research
CRS creditor reporting system
CSO civil society organization
CONFEMEN Conférence des Ministres de l'Education des Pays Ayant le Français en Partage [Conference of Ministers of Education having French as a common language])
DAC see OECD
DAW/DESA/UN Division for the Advancement of Women, Department of Economic and Social Affairs of the United Nations
DeSeCo definition and selection of competencies
DFID Department for International Development, United Kingdom
DHS demography and health survey
E9 nine high-population countries (Bangladesh, Brazil, China, Egypt, India, Indonesia, Mexico, Nigeria, Pakistan)
EC European Commission
ECCE early childhood care and education
ECD early childhood development
Ed-SIDA/AIDS Education and HIV/AIDS initiative
EENET Enabling Education Network
EFA education for all
ESIP Education Sector Investment Plan
ESP Education Strategic Plan
ESSP Education Sector Support Programme
ETTA East Timor Transitional Administration
FAO Food and Agriculture Organization of the United Nations
FRESH Focusing Resources on Effective School Health
FTI Fast-Track Initiative
FYPPE Five-year Plan for Primary Education
G8 Group of eight countries (Canada, France, Germany, Italy, Japan, Russia, United Kingdom and United States) and representatives from the European Union who meet to discuss economic and foreign policies
GABLE Girl's Attainment of Basic Literacy and Education
GCE Global Campaign for Education
GDP gross domestic product
GINIE Global Information Networks in Education
GNP gross national product
GREFCO Groupe de Recherche,de Formation et de Conseils [Research, training and consulting Group]

GRETAF	Groupe d'Étude sur l'Éducation en Afrique [Study Group on Education in Africa]
HIV/AIDS	human immuno-deficiency (or immunodeficiency) virus/acquired iImmune deficiency syndrome
IADB	Inter-American Development Bank
IALS	International Adult Literacy Study
IBE	UNESCO Bureau of Education
IBRD	International Bank for Reconstruction and Development
ICRAF	International Centre for Research in Agroforestry
IDA	International Development Association
IDP	internally displaced population
IEA	International Association for the Evaluation of Educational Achievement
IFAD	International Fund for Agricultural Development
IIEP	International Institute for Educational Planning
ILO	International Labour Organization
ILO	International Labour Organization
IMF	International Monetary Fund
INEE	Inter-Agency Network on Education in Emergencies
INES	International Indicators of Education Systems
INGO	international non-governmental organization
ISCED	International Standard Classification of Education
LAP	literacy assessment practices
LDC	least developed country
LNLS	Lao National Literacy Survey
MEBA	Ministry of Basic Education
MICS	Multiple Indicator Cluster Survey
MinEd	Ministry of Education
MINEDAF	Conferences of the Ministers of Education of African Member States organized by UNESCO
MTT	Southern African Mobile Task Team on HIV/AIDS in Education
MLA	monitoring learning achievement
MoE	ministry of education
NACA	National AIDS Coordination Agency
NAFFRE	National Alliance for Fundamental Right to Education
NEC	National Education Commission
NEPAD	New Partnership for Africa's Development
NFE	non-formal education
NFE-MIS	non-formal education management information systems
NGO	non-governmental organization
NORAD	Norwegian Agency for Development Cooperation
OCHA	Office for the Coordination of Humanitarian Affairs
OECD	Organisation for Economic Cooperation and Development
OECD/DAC	OECD's Development Assistance Committee
PASEC	Programme d'Analyse des Systemes Educatifs des Pays de la [Programme for the Analysis of the Educational Systems of Member Countries of CONFEMEN]
PDDEB	Plan Décennal de Développement de l'Education de Base [Ten-year plan for the Development of Basic Education]
PEPP	Primary Education Planning Project
PIRLS	Progress in Reading Literacy Study
PISA	Programme for International Student Achievement
PPP	purchasing power parity

PROAP	UNESCO's Principal Regional Office in Asia and the Pacific
PROAPE	Programa de Alimentacao de Pre-Escolar [Pre-school Nutrition Project]
PRSP	Poverty Reduction Strategy Paper
SACMEQ	Southern Africa Consortium for Monitoring Educational Quality
SADC	South African Development Community
Sida	Swedish International Development Agency
SRH	sexual and reproductive health
SSA	sub-Saharan Africa
TIMSS	Third International Mathematics and Science Study
TT	teacher training
UEE	universal elementary education
UIS	UNESCO Institute for Statistics
UN	United Nations
UNAIDS	Joint United Nations Programme on HIV/AIDS
UNCTAD	United Nations Committee/Conference on Trade and Development
UNDAF	United Nations Development Assistance Framework
UNDCP	United Nations International Drug Control Programme
UNDG	United Nations Development Group UNDP- United Nations Development Fund
UNDP	United Nations Development Fund
UNESCO	United Nations Educational, Scientific (and) Cultural Organization
UNESCO PEER	UNESCO's Programme for Education for Emergency and Reconstruction
UNFPA	United Nations Population Fund
UNGASS	United Nations General Assembly Special Session
UNGEI	United Nations Girls' Education Initiative
UNHCR	United Nations High Commission for Refugees
UNICEF	United Nations Children's Fund
UNIFEM	United Nations Development Fund for Women
UNRISD	United Nations Research Institute for Social Development
UNRWA	United Nations Relief and Works Agency for Palestine Refugees in the Near East
UPE	universal primary education
USAID	United States Agency for International Development
WFP	World Food Programme
WHO	World Health Organization